a history of financial intermediaries

RANDOM HOUSE, NEW YORK

a history of financial intermediaries

herman e. krooss
Graduate School of Business Administration
New York University

martin r. blyn
California State College, Dominguez Hills

ISBN: 0-394-31001-2

Library of Congress Catalog Card Number: 78-127552

Manufactured in the United States of America
by H. Wolff Book Mfg. Co., Inc., New York, N.Y.

Typographic design by Pedro A. Noa
Cover photo by George Gardener
Cover design by Hermann Strohbach

First Edition
9 8 7 6 5 4 3 2 1

preface

This book differs from other histories in the field of money and banking in two ways. First, it is concerned with financial intermediaries, not simply banks. So far as we know there is no other published history of financial intermediaries. Most of the historical works on money and banking and the historical sections of money and banking texts deal with commercial banks and coin and currency, ignoring the other intermediaries altogether. The excellent pioneering works of Margaret Myers and George Edwards in the 1930s covered a wider field by embracing the security exchanges and some of the subdivisions of the money market such as call money. Fritz Redlich's classic *The Moulding of American Banking* explored investment banking and savings banking as well as commercial banking. But these works were unusual and did not considerably alter the traditional preoccupation with commercial and central banking. The objective of this book is to summarize the history of insurance companies, investment banking, credit unions, investment companies, trust companies, and savings and loan associations in addition to commercial banks, central banking, and savings banks.

The second way in which this book is different is in its general approach. Standard money and banking histories are concerned with institutions, laws, and policy. They do not treat the subject from the point of view of the participants in the market—the banks and the borrowing public—but stress such things as the First and Second Bank, the National Banking System, the "silver crusade," the Federal Reserve System, and so on. They are, in the economist's language, concerned more with the macro than the micro economy and more with policy than with practice. There is, we hasten to add, nothing wrong with this approach. If there were, so much would not have been written along these lines. We, however, are interested in a different approach. Our principal concern is with the borrowers and the lenders and the processes by which these two were brought together. There are two main reasons for this point of view. The macro part of money and banking history—the First and Second Bank, the National Banking System, the coinage, the Federal Reserve, and so on— has been treated exhaustively in texts and monographs. Our second reason is that the behavior and the activities of the financial intermediaries have been just as important as, if not more important than, the development of institutions and monetary policy. Undoubtedly, the Bank of the United States, the National Bank Act, and the silver controversy had an enormous impact. But we believe that what the individual financial intermediaries did in bridging the gap between the saver and the investor had an even greater effect on everyday life and on the aggregate growth of the

v

American economy. How businessmen, governments, and homeowners got the funds for their investments and purchases is far more important than the weaknesses of the National Banking System.

Our point can best be illustrated by an example expressed in personalities. Take the case of Nicholas Biddle, one of the most brilliant bankers history has produced. Biddle's fame in the history books rests almost exclusively on his unsuccessful fight with President Andrew Jackson over the rechartering of the Second Bank of the United States. But Biddle's importance in American history should rest not so much on that celebrated and much publicized war as on his role as a central banker and an investment banker. His innovations and activities in these fields made a deeper impression on American life and on the future course of American economic development than his activities in the more famous bank war. Biddle was a great banker and a poor politician. The most significant point about him was that he was more than a match for Europe's merchant bankers, but he was no match at all for Andrew Jackson.

In keeping with our objective, the original draft of this book went so far as to ignore almost completely the institutional framework of commercial banking on the ground that the major subject had already been more than adequately covered in the literature. Needless to say, we ignored the history of coin and currency altogether, for our concern was with financial intermediaries. The reaction on the part of the readers of the manuscript gave us pause to reconsider. One reader was "appalled," another "frustrated." Apoplectic strokes were avoided by one last gasp of pain. Although we did not share these traumas, we recognized that there was a point to the readers' protests and, therefore, reincorporated the traditional material on banking. But we did not choose to omit the other financial intermediaries—the mysterious private bankers, the unglamorous and heretofore ignored savings banks, the mundane insurance companies, the building and loan associations, and so forth. All this is by way of an apology for a book that is longer than a book of this size should be.

Although the endeavor has been a joint one, there has been a division of labor. The senior member of the duet is mainly responsible for the history up to 1900, whereas the junior member wrote the history of the twentieth century.

Each of us is heavily indebted to Miss Lee Silman, who, with her usual good nature, managed the well-nigh impossible task of transforming our unreadable handscript to a neat and orderly typescript.

contents

4 Accelerated Growth, 1836–1860   67

5 Finance Comes of Age, 1860–1890   91

6 The Age of High Finance, 1890–1920   117

list of tables and figures

a history of financial intermediaries

1 · introduction

A standard way of beginning a book of this kind is to define what is being talked about. This step is especially important in a study that deals with such a relatively new concept as "financial intermediaries," for although there is agreement on all sides on the specific definition of financial intermediaries, at present no complete agreement exists on precisely which institutions should be included in the term.

DEFINITION OF FINANCIAL INTERMEDIARY · A financial intermediary is defined as an enterprise whose assets and liabilities consist almost exclusively of financial instruments. Such instruments would include loans and mortgages, stocks and bonds, bank deposits, savings and loan shares, insurance and pension contracts, commercial paper, shares in investment companies, and so forth. The ıunction of financial intermediaries is to act as middlemen between savers and investors. They gather savings from individuals and businesses that make more than they spend and lend these savings to individuals, entrepreneurs, and government agencies that spend more than they make. Thus the liabilities of financial intermediaries are associated with "savers," and their assets tend to define "investors." From the social point of view, the chief problem associated with financial intermediation has always been how to bring in touch with one another the man who has capital funds and no enterprise and the man who has enterprise but no capital.

The number of different institutions that one may include in the concept of financial intermediaries varies from as few as six to as many as twenty, depending on who is doing the counting. In this book we choose to consider only private institutions, and of these only the following ten: commercial banks, investment banks, trust companies, mutual savings banks, savings and loan associations, life insurance companies, general insurance companies, noninsured pension funds, investment companies, and credit unions.[1]

Those who operate financial intermediaries do not produce or exchange goods. They are not farmers, manufacturers, or tradesmen. They deal in paper—in evidences of debt and shares in equity. Consequently, it is easy for analysts to skip over them in their models of economic growth. Eco-

---

[1] The more inclusive list would also include government agencies (the Federal Reserve Banks, the postal savings system, Federal Land Banks, Federal lending agencies, social security funds, government pension funds), security brokers and dealers, mortgage companies, finance companies, and small business investment companies. See Raymond W. Goldsmith, *Financial Institutions* (New York: Random House, 1968), pp. 13 ff.

nomic growth is ordinarily pictured as a process in which business entrepreneurs combine various amounts of labor and capital on a fixed piece of land to produce as many goods and services as they are able to. Financial intermediaries do not fit easily into this picture; yet few would deny that their role is important. Nevertheless, most writers seem to suggest that the financial system somehow adjusts passively to the needs of the real sectors. The common view, in other words, gives one the impression that the evolution of the financial system, embracing as it does instruments, institutions, and markets, is dependent on the pace and character of growth in the commodity sectors.

Whether active or passive, however, the more than 50,000 financial intermediaries in the United States today do perform a set of distinctive services in economic life. They lead to increased saving and to the creation of capital by improving the opportunities and rewards for saving. It was the financial institutions that were mainly responsible for the creation and growth of such saving-facilitating financial instruments as the bill of exchange, bonds, stocks, bank notes, bank deposits, and checks. The intermediaries performed a further service by giving liquidity to these financial instruments, or financial assets, which in themselves ran the gamut from the illiquid to the liquid.

By increasing the liquidity of the economy, financial intermediaries also make it possible to use assets more productively. They do so in two ways. They make available liquid assets (currency and demand deposits) to those who own illiquid assets (real estate and inventories). Secondly, they transfer assets from savers who would not otherwise use them to investors (entrepreneurs) who will utilize them in acquiring plant and equipment. In short, financial intermediaries bring savers and investors together. By supplying the means of exchange and purchasing power, and by adding mobility and liquidity to capital funds, they oil the wheels of commerce and keep the economic machine rolling.

THE THEORETICAL BACKGROUND · This book is concerned with how financial intermediaries came to be what they are today and the problems that they faced in becoming what they are today. The emphasis centers on the process of innovation. Innovation in the world of the financial intermediaries, as in all worlds, is the art of doing new things or of doing old things differently. It is a gradual process, resembling the weaving of a patchwork quilt. The whole creation is spectacular, but there is very little that is spectacular about each piece.

In broad terms there are three types of financial innovation: those that encourage saving, those that make it easier to borrow funds, and those that narrow the gap between the saver and the investor by improving liquidity and by adding to geographic mobility. But all three types have the common characteristic of increasing the volume and improving the mechanics of capital formation.

The accumulation of capital—that is, the increase in the stock of goods in the hands of business and government, plus residential housing and inventories[2]—is a prerequisite for the increase in output per person that spells economic progress. To be sure, there is no precise one-to-one relationship between capital accumulation and economic growth, but net capital formation *is* essential to the growth process.

Capital formation does not, of course, require a financial system. Even in the earliest and most primitive economy some men devoted part of their labor to making goods to be used in round-about production, that is, in the production of other goods. Bows and arrows, fishing nets, canoes, and the baskets of Robinson Crusoe are traditional examples of round-about production undertaken by primitive peoples. All this activity takes place without the use of money or the existence of financial institutions and financial instruments.

Among advanced economies, too, the act of saving and the act of investing may and sometimes do go hand in hand, with both performed simultaneously by the same person or business. The farmer who builds fences to enclose his fields and the business firm that finances its capital accumulation out of current income are typical examples. Yet everywhere that national economies have developed, saving and investing have tended to become separate and distinct activities. Thus, with both savers and investors relying more and more on specialized financial intermediaries, the proportion that the assets of financial intermediaries bear to total wealth has become larger and larger with the passage of time. In early American history, this proportion was about one-tenth; by 1900 it had increased to one-seventh; by 1920 to one-quarter; and by the middle sixties to one-half. Just as specialization has bestowed bountiful material blessings in commodity production, so specialization in the saving-investment calculus has sped the pace of economic advance.

In the simple world of primitive economies, where there are no financial assets and no financial liabilities, each spending unit must keep its spending in balance with its income. What is not consumed out of income, or, in other words, what is saved, may be used to acquire additional capital goods or else hoarded. The significant point, however, is that each unit's current income, plus what it has saved in the past, sets an upper limit on current expenditure, for there is neither debt nor credit in such an uncomplicated and unreal world. In such a regime, no unit can invest beyond its savings. It does not require much thought to see that in such a world of balanced budgets, optimum levels of capital accumulation cannot be obtained. Many valuable investment projects never come to fruition because the financing they require exceeds the personal resources of possible promoters. Something very close to this kind of world existed in the early years of American colonial history, when the vast majority of capital projects were self-financed.

The appearance of debt and credit even in their most rudimentary forms pushes an economy up several rungs on the ladder of sophistication and

[2] This is Kuznets' definition. Goldsmith includes consumer durables in his definition. Which is best seems to us a matter of what the definition is to be used for; the Kuznets definition is more useful in the analysis of economic growth; the Goldsmith definition gives a clearer picture of national wealth at any given moment of time.

economic progress. This result follows because the ability to borrow makes possible greater specialization, and greater specialization, in turn, makes it possible to produce more income out of scarce resources. Imaginative and daring entrepreneurs can borrow the savings of those who are less adventurous or of those who have less business ability, and with their superior talents these borrowing entrepreneurs can push the economy ahead faster than it otherwise would have traveled. In early stages of economic development—for example, America in the late colonial period and in the early nineteenth century—borrowing and lending take place mostly among deficit and surplus units themselves. Naturally, such direct transfers bring into being financial assets and liabilities of equal value. Every borrower issues financial claims—promissory notes, mortgages, bonds, and shares of stock—in evidence of his debt. These primary securities (the obligations of nonfinancial units) become, in turn, the financial assets of lenders, and the balance sheet is balanced.

Enterprising units, then, can hope to acquire command over potential resources in excess of what their personal accumulations allow by bidding for the financial savings of other units. As a consequence, the level of savings should rise, for high returns on favored projects (returns in excess of what these units could earn on projects undertaken by themselves) can now be shared by those choosing to participate in their financing. Allocation of savings, therefore, improves as marginal undertakings are replaced by more productive ones.

Intuition points to the central role of money in this process, but the relationship is complicated and paradoxical. Money preceded debt and credit in the development of economic institutions. Yet money is itself a primary security; it is a claim to wealth rather than wealth per se. In early America, notes of indebtedness were frequently issued by businesses and individuals and circulated as money in payment for goods and services received. At the same time, governments issued interest- and noninterest-bearing debt, which circulated as money for want of other tender. In the modern world, most money is checkbook money. Checkbook money is, in the economic sense but not in the legal sense, the promissory notes of commercial banks. The smaller part of the money supply—pocketbook or folding money as it is known colloquially—is nothing more than the promissory notes of the central bank.

The system of direct finance that enabled savings units to extend credit to and thereby obtain claims on deficit units constituted a solid advance over earlier institutional arrangements. But it also had limitations that, with the passing of time and under the pressure of rising capital requirements, resulted in the emergence of financial intermediation and thus indirect finance.

Economic efficiency demands that savings be placed at the disposal of those most capable of putting them to use and that transactions costs to lenders and borrowers be kept as low as possible. Neither condition is adequately met by direct finance. Although individuals can undertake capital formation requiring more resources than their income would give them command of, there are practical limitations on the size of the borrowings they can make. Entrepreneurs must, themselves, seek out potential lenders, convince them of the merits of their scheme and the solidarity of their characters, and issue to them financial claims to their liking. Limited amounts of external funds can be obtained from relatives and friends, but once entrepreneurs attempt to acquire large amounts of capital, problems arise in searching out potential lenders and in devising financial claims attractive to both issuer and holder. Lenders, unless they have a high preference for risk, will generally want to loan their savings for short periods of time, thereby keeping themselves liquid. Borrowers, on the other hand, especially if they are acquiring fixed capital, prefer loans with longer maturities. Furthermore, lenders may wish to protect themselves by demanding conditions that entrepreneurs may be reluctant to agree to. Thus transactions costs (for example, those incurred in the search for lenders) tend to be high, interest charges (including risk premiums) tend to be high, especially on long-term funds, and many capital-intensive undertakings are abandoned for want of financing.

Savers have their problems, too. How, for example, can they allocate their financial savings in the most rational manner when their knowledge about investment alternatives, the character of potential borrowers, and pertinent facts concerning the risks of alternative uses of funds is circumscribed?

Under direct finance, therefore, total capital formation is less than it might be, because of the difficulty of accumulating large amounts of capital, because of the high-risk premiums asked by savers, and the compromises borrowers and lenders must make with respect to the duration and terms of the loan. In addition, limited channels of communication between borrowers and lenders do not result in efficient allocation of savings. Each lender may direct his funds to the best use he knows, but this action does not ensure that optimum allocation occurs for the community at large.

WHAT FINANCIAL INTERMEDIARIES DO · In time innovators came to see that financial intermediation could perform a useful and profitable function by standing, so to speak, midway between borrower and lender. But first let us reconsider what it is that financial institutions do. Financial institutions issue claims on themselves known as secondary or indirect securities (for example, demand deposits, saving certificates, saving and loan shares, and insurance policies) that are exchanged for the financial savings of surplus units; then they loan these funds to borrowers, taking in return primary securities (promissory notes, mortgages, stocks) issued by these units. Debt is the stock-in-trade of financial institutions; in contrast to the real assets that characterize the commercial or industrial firm's balance sheet, the assets of intermediaries are mainly composed of paper claims issued by nonfinancial borrowers. And the margin between interest rates paid for loanable funds and interest rates earned on extensions of credit constitutes the profits of financial institutions.

Compared with direct finance, indirect finance based on financial intermediation possesses several advantages for the borrower and for society.

First, potential borrowers and lenders are spared much of the burden of seeking out their opposites, for attracting savings and finding suitable uses to which these savings can be put are now the job of the financial entrepreneur. Second, specialization, particularly when financial institutions come to be run by professional management, makes the intermediary a better judge of the risks attached to any loan. Numerous loans further lessen risks, for although any one loan may turn bad, it is most unlikely that sizable losses on the whole portfolio will occur. And the knowledge that comes from specialization makes the allocation of savings a more rational process if for no other reason than that large aggregates of loanable funds come to be concentrated, enabling financial institutions to rank and pass upon the applications of numerous potential borrowers in order of expected net returns.

But perhaps most important are the incentives to saving and investment that derive from substitution of financial claims issued by intermediaries for primary securities issued by nonfinancial borrowers. One major limitation of direct finance, pointed out earlier, focuses on the conflict between borrowers and lenders over loan terms and maturities, with lenders preferring short-term extensions to keep their control close and borrowers preferring long-time loans more in accord with the nature of the real investments they intend to make. The results of this conflict are that saving and investment levels are constrained and that interest rates tend to be high, particularly on long-term loans.

Intermediation resolves this conflict; financial institutions issue short-term liquid financial claims to lenders while themselves acquiring less liquid claims on borrowers. Stated another way, intermediaries permit the substitution of indirect for primary securities in the asset portfolios of savers. Thus commercial banks issue liabilities to lenders (demand deposits and time and saving deposits) payable on demand while acquiring financial assets that often, as in the case of term loans and mortgages, have distant maturities.

Several results follow. First, savings may be expected to rise as savers are able to acquire financial assets to their liking. Moreover, as risks diminish, so do the risk premiums asked by savers. Thus the volume of savings increases. Entrepreneurs benefit because intermediaries are more willing takers of primary securities. Furthermore, the cost of long-term financing falls from the levels prevailing under direct finance.

THE HISTORICAL GROWTH OF
FINANCIAL INTERMEDIARIES · With such clear advantages, it was only natural that financial intermediaries grew faster than the economy in general. It is estimated that over the course of American history, the assets of financial institutions (in constant prices and on a per capita basis) grew at a rate of about 2¾ percent a year, more than half again as much as the 1⅚ percent growth in per capita production. As late as 1800 the assets of the existing banks and insurance companies amounted to less than $50 million, or about $10 per capita. Today the assets of the

ten financial intermediaries with which we are concerned are equal to about $5,000 for every man, woman, and child in the United States.

This rapid rate of increase becomes more impressive when it is related to the rate of saving, for saving, the fuel that feeds finance, has been declining in proportion to net production. In the late nineteenth century, for example, net capital formation ran at a rate of about 15 percent of net national product, but in recent years the rate has fallen to 6 percent of net product.[3]

Even though financial intermediation had distinct advantages for borrowers and lenders, for investors and savers, and for the financial institutions themselves, spectacular growth was not inevitable and axiomatic. Human beings do not necessarily maximize their well-being as portrayed in models based on a careful and thoughtful balancing of costs against income. They must be persuaded and prodded, cajoled and convinced. Americans always regarded banking and finance with uneasy suspicion. Yet the culture also placed a high premium on money making, thrift, and saving, which more than compensated for the hostility to Wall Street in encouraging the growth of financial intermediaries. The growth was further aided by changes in how Americans made their living, where they lived, how long they lived, how they managed their businesses, how they spent their incomes, and how the government regulated the money and capital markets.

Financial intermediaries thrive best in an urban society, directed by innovative and imaginative entrepreneurs and characterized by rapid technological development, rising national income, complicated industrial processes, a highly specialized labor force, widespread home ownership, and a continuous lengthening span of life. All these factors the United States had in profusion. They were part of the warp and woof of American economic history, and over time they could be expected to encourage the enhancement of the financial intermediaries.

---

[3] These rates are based on the Kuznets definition of capital formation. If the Goldsmith definition were used, the conclusion would show a much smaller, perhaps no, decline in the rate of capital formation.

2 · financial intermediaries in early american history

Financial intermediaries did not come into being until late in the colonial period. The first fire insurance company, the Philadelphia Contributionship, began operations in 1752. Thomas Willing in 1757 organized the first marine underwriting association. The first commercial bank, by the modern definition of the word, was the Bank of North America, established in 1781. The first life insurance company, the Pennsylvania Company for Insurances on Lives and Granting Annuities, opened in 1812.[1] Three institutions that were founded from 1816 to 1819, the Philadelphia Saving Fund Society, the Provident Institution for Savings in the Town of Boston, and the New York Bank for Savings, vie for the honor of being the first savings bank in the country. The first trust company, or perhaps it might be better to call it the first investment trust, the Massachusetts Hospital Life Insurance Company, was chartered in 1818. The first building and loan association—the forerunner of the modern savings and loan association—the Oxford Provident Building Association, was established in Philadelphia in 1831.

Each of the various institutions in the money and capital markets appeared as the need for its services developed. They came into existence as a result of two basic forces: the changes in the economic and social environment and the innovations accomplished by human beings. Population growth and other forces produced a need and entrepreneurs were quick to fill the gap. But this statement does not mean that the process was neat and logical or that it occurred automatically and smoothly according to a flawless model. Lags are the essence of life and the institutional wheels of economics grind very slowly. Financial institutions started slowly and gathered momentum as they adjusted to the needs of their environment. However, all of them had their ups and downs. They rose or faltered in response to what was taking place in the external economic, social, and political environment and because of the ingenuity, imagination, and aggressiveness of the entrepreneurs who made the decisions that guided them. In order to grow, these entrepreneurs had to overcome a series of obstacles and, much more important, they also had to take advantage of every encouraging shift in the economic, social, and political milieu.

---

[1] The Presbyterian Ministers' Fund was really the first to insure lives, beginning in 1759, but its underwriting was restricted to members of the profession.

THE COLONIAL PERIOD · Of the financial intermediaries that we recognize today, only two, general insurance and private banking, existed in the colonial period, and neither one appeared before 1750. Actually, the colonists had no pressing need for financial institutions although they were in great need of capital. The economy was in an early stage of development, and until late in the period it was progressing through various stages of poverty. The population was small and dispersed over the entire Eastern coastal plain. Nine-tenths of the working population was engaged in farming, and most of the remaining tenth consisted of independent, small-scale artisans. There were a few professionals and a scattering of merchants. Understandably, it was only the latter who needed and wanted financial intermediaries. Most of the farmers operated on a noncommercial basis, and although they admittedly needed capital and wanted to increase their wealth and raise their standard of living, they did not think they were in need of outside money institutions. They cleared their land, built their own barns and fences, and increased their herds without recourse to financial middlemen. The artisans were equally independent. They borrowed little but expanded their businesses by plowing back earnings.

Since the colonists were just entering the road to economic wealth, there was a chronic shortage of capital. Although attempts were made to create a money system, they were not completely successful, and most transactions were handled on a barter basis. Nationalism and sentimentalism to the contrary, the colonies were nothing more or less than a frontier outpost of the British Empire. Foreign trade was of immense importance, and the colonial merchants who imported goods relied on Britain with its already well-established financial network and liberal credit terms. Every merchant of importance depended for credit on his English agent, usually a merchant banking house. The smaller merchants, who had no contact with England, depended on a larger firm to act as a go-between.

Already in colonial days the big merchants were following a practice that would become increasingly common in the first quarter of the nineteenth century. They were drawing sterling bills of exchange against goods shipped. The links in the credit chain were somewhat as follows: an American merchant advanced credit to his customers and, in turn, received credit from another merchant, or from a private banker, or, if he were sufficiently well known, he could draw a bill of exchange on an English merchant banker and cover the acceptance by sending goods. But in all these choices, the English banker held the last link.

Colonial dependence on English finance could not possibly be exaggerated. The most persistent problem in the colonial merchant's life was to stay abreast of his accounts with English merchants, and, in turn, the most persistent problem of colonial farmers and workers was to maintain a satisfactory credit arrangement with the colonial merchant. It should be emphasized that the reliance on the English bankers would continue long after political independence had been achieved—that is, well into the nineteenth century. Indeed, as late as the twentieth century, European merchant bankers would still be financing a large part of American foreign trade.

THE AGRARIAN HOSTILITY TOWARD

FINANCIAL INSTITUTIONS · There was another reason, in addition to dependence on England, why financial intermediaries were late in appearing: most Americans had a deep antipathy toward financial institutions. Agrarians had no sympathy for finance and regarded banks and, to a lesser extent, other financial houses with suspicious hostility. Thomas Jefferson thought that banks were "monarchial inventions of ruinous tendencies." His political opponent, John Adams, believed that "every bank of discount, every bank by which interest is to be paid or profit made is downright corruption." This sentiment was so deeply ingrained in the rugged individualism of the American culture that it would continue in great popularity with different shadings and overtones for the next century. In 1833 President Thomas Cooper, of the University of South Carolina, although not the first to denounce banking, was one of the first to denounce it because it "made the rich richer and the poor poorer." At around the same time, the Locofoco Party denounced bankers as "the greatest knaves, imposters and paupers of the age who swear they have promised to pay their creditors 30 or 35 millions of dollars on demand, at the same time that they have only 3 or 4 millions to do it with. We are opposed to all bank charters because we believe them at war with good morals . . . and calculated to build up and strengthen . . . the odious destruction of wealth and power against wants and equal rights."

Although widespread, antibank sentiment was not unanimous. The probank group, in the minority to be sure, had its eloquent spokesmen. In the early history of the United States, banking was not a matter to be regarded with indifference. The quotations given earlier show that the members of the antibank group expressed themselves forcefully and sometimes vehemently; the probank group was equally talented. Mathew Carey, the publisher and economist, was one of the most articulate. He believed that banks, if operated correctly, advanced the public interest. They could be counted on to foster industry, extend trade and commerce, and widen competition by assisting those who had no other assets but ambition, a strong back, a reasonable amount of intelligence, and a willingness to work. If operated foolishly, banks could "blast the happiness of a community with the force and fury of a diabolic curse."

Carey came close to having a precise insight into the relation between money and prices. He knew that prices rose when too-liberal bank accommodations fostered a spirit of speculation until "there was a loud clamour against the cheapness of bank notes, and the rise in price of almost everything else." It occurred to Carey that it might even be possible to calculate how much banking capital would be proper by studying comparative data on population, houses, building, import duties, and other indicators of trade conditions, and he made a couple of ingenious attempts to solve the problem.

Carey recognized that the need for credit was not unaffected by arbitrary manipulation of the supply. He knew that sudden, immoderate, and unusual liberality could fan a speculative flame that would result in unhealthy business expansion. Sharp curtailment, on the other hand, was just as pernicious, for it brought wretchedness, ruin, and bankruptcy.

Carey therefore maintained that the "grand and leading feature of the good management of a Bank" in fitting its aid to the real needs of the community, was "to preserve an even tenor in the business of loaning money." He went so far as to approve "a resisting pressure on the part of the banks whenever a speculative spirit sprang up." But he also contended that the appearance of economic distress cried so loudly for liberal credit extension that no intelligent alternative was possible. Thus he had an early nineteenth-century "lean against the wind" philosophy.

COLONIAL MARINE AND FIRE INSURANCE · Despite the ubiquitous hostility to financial institutions, some did appear in the colonies. Because foreign trade was so important and, at least theoretically, threatened so much danger, merchants needed marine insurance. Their first thought was to obtain such insurance in England, but doing so was difficult because communication and transportation facilities were primitive. Under the circumstances, the best that the merchants could do was to spread the risk among themselves by an extensive method of self-insurance. When a merchant was about to embark on a venture, he went to a broker who wrote a policy and set a premium. The policy was then signed by various of his colleagues, each of whom stipulated the share he would take. Thus practically all merchants were insurance underwriters. Eventually a group of these merchant underwriters formed a formal association. The innovator in this action was Thomas Willing, a member of a well-known merchant family, who established Thomas Willing & Co. in 1757 in Philadelphia. His example was soon followed by other merchants, and by 1783 when the Treaty of Paris officially ended the Revolutionary War, there were enough brokers and underwriters to warrant a semimonthly paper concerned mostly with insurance news. By then, too, underwriters had acquired a permanent capital and had thereby achieved the basic prerequisite for financial intermediation.

As can be imagined, fire was also a great hazard in colonial America, but fire insurance seems to have been almost as hazardous. Between 1720 and 1750 at least three unsuccessful attempts were made to start a company. But then in 1752 a group led by Benjamin Franklin formed the Philadelphia Contributionship for the Insurance of Houses from Loss by Fire. The company, which is still in existence today, wrote a single-payment, seven-year contract and invested the unearned premiums. Thus the Contributionship, which was a mutual organization rather than an incorporated stock company, fulfilled the function of a financial intermediary in that it acted as a middleman between savers and investors.

COLONIAL LAND BANKS · Just as there were some insurance organizations in the colonial period that only dimly resembled those of today, there were also some banks that in function as well as in appearance bore only a faint resemblance to the modern commercial or investment bank. In fact, the only resemblance between the two lay in the fact that both used the name "bank." Colonial banks did not accept deposits, nor did they discount commercial paper. They made loans in the form of paper money against real and, occasionally, personal property. A colonial farmer mortgaged his farm for a bank loan and in return received paper money issued by the bank. In short, the banks that existed in colonial times were land banks, not money banks, and have been considered by most monetary historians pseudo rather than genuine financial intermediaries, particularly as no prior act of saving was required. Yet because they were the pioneers in banking and because they performed a valuable and useful function, they deserve more than a word of description.

Establishment of a bank was apparently attempted in Massachusetts in 1652 and again in 1671. In 1686 a bank was actually chartered to issue bills on personal and real property, but it lasted only a couple of years. In the eighteenth century, however, land banks thrived, especially in the middle colonies. It has been said that they were nothing more or less than batches of paper money. This description is true in the sense that they did not do a deposit and discount business, but it is not true in the sense that they did not perform a useful function, or that they were simply pawns in the age-old struggle by debtors to obtain higher prices by raising the quantity of money. The colonists wanted banks, not to help debtors but to help the economy. The dominant theory among the colonists was not that an increase in the quantity of money was, in itself, an addition to wealth or that it need always lead to such but that in the absence of an adequate supply of money, paper-money issues would greatly stimulate industry and trade. The argument between the easy- and hard-money forces was not an argument between debtors and creditors. It was an argument between those who, like Benjamin Franklin, believed that a larger money supply in the form of paper money could advance the economy and those who thought that more money would merely increase prices and who, therefore, regarded paper money as nothing more than an inflationary heresy. The argument, suffice it to say, is still going on today.

HOW BORROWERS OBTAINED FUNDS · When all is said and done, the colonists possessed nothing more than a handful of pseudofinancial intermediaries. There were no money or capital markets in the true sense of the word. In their absence, how did borrowers obtain the credit and capital funds without which economic progress could hardly occur? There was, of course, much direct financing through private loans and through arrangements by which sellers retained a mortgage or lien on that which they sold. Advertisements soliciting borrowers appeared frequently in the early newspapers. Commercial paper[2] was already in existence in the form of bills of exchange and promissory notes with or without collateral but was usually endorsed so as to make it two-name rather than single-name paper.

---

[2] In the broad sense and in its legal interpretation, the term "commercial paper" includes all classes of short-term negotiable instruments: promissory notes, bills of exchange, or acceptances in negotiable form. To a banker, however, commercial paper today refers to his investments in short-term promissory notes, not to his loans and discounts.

In the absence of banks and checks, the bill of exchange[3] was the prevalent means of payment. As early as 1704 colonial merchants were selling domestic bills of exchange, but the dealings were between merchants directly rather than through middlemen. Thus in 1708 Benjamin Faneuil advertised in a Boston newspaper that he could supply bills to merchants and others who had money in New York and wished to remit to Boston.

THE LOTTERY DEALER · Another pseudofinancial intermediary was the lottery dealer, who was very popular until about the third decade of the nineteenth century. In the colonial period, lotteries were authorized by law and conducted by volunteers. The proceeds were used to finance churches, colleges, hospitals, internal improvements, and so forth. Practically everyone "played the numbers." George Washington, for example, was an inveterate participant, and, according to Scoville's *The Old Merchants of New York City,* "In the old time, there was hardly a merchant of note, unless he belonged to the church, who did not speculate in lottery tickets."

Although it is ahead of our story, it would be convenient here to describe the later history of the lottery. By 1820 lotteries had been reorganized on a business basis and their management was taken over by syndicates. Their business then soared. "In the year 1824," the New York grand jury reported, "there were but eight or ten lottery ticket sellers in the city, while at this time [1833] there are one hundred and forty-seven and some of our principal streets are literally disfigured by their advertisements." At the height of their frenzied career, there were about 200 lottery offices in Philadelphia alone. On any typical day in the 1820s one could find a half-dozen advertisements in the metropolitan press, urging the readers to pick a number and win a fortune before opportunity vanished. Many of these lottery businesses were operated by men who would later make contributions to brokerage and banking. But one at 139 Broadway, New York City, was owned by P. Canfield, whose son Richard came to own and operate the most famous gambling establishment in the country and whose name has been given to a particular form of solitaire.

In time the easy riches associated with lotteries offended the sensibilities of a large and articulate block of Americans, and as opposition crystallized, more and more states banned what Scoville called "the curse of lotteries." By the 1840s lotteries were prohibited in most states, but some continued to be conducted illegally and, according to Scoville, "cleared annually a few hundred thousand dollars, ruining thousands of virtuous but poor families."[4]

Savers could put their money into lotteries, invest in mortgages, buy a share in a shipping venture, make loans to other individuals, invest in

---

[3] A bill of exchange is the reverse of check. It is a written order issued by the drawer calling on a second party (the drawee) to pay a certain sum of money on a certain date in the future.

[4] Joseph A. Scoville (Walter Barrett, pseud.), *The Old Merchants of New York City* (New York, 1899), p. 257.

some closely held company, or buy British government securities through a London merchant or a private banker. Borrowers—individuals, businesses, and governments—also had a number of choices, not very attractive choices to be sure but nevertheless choices. Householders who wished to borrow to buy a home ordinarily did not find it difficult to find a mortgagor. Governments bypassed the nonexistent capital markets and printed paper money to cover their budgetary deficits. Businesses could rely on the more enterprising merchants for credit, for merchants were in the banking business from the beginning, offering long- and short-term credit to their customers. In fact, it was a member of a Philadelphia merchant family, John Biddle, who established the country's oldest bank in 1764.[5] But, more commonly, leading merchants interposed their credit for the weaker credit of their customers in the European money markets. Better known than their fellow townsmen, these merchants could get credit in England and sometimes on the Continent. The practice would, of course, continue all through the first half of the nineteenth century but along different lines and involving more goods and shorter credit terms. In the colonial period, however, merchants like Thomas Hancock extended credit payable in six months or one year with 6 percent interest on the unpaid balance.

FINANCIAL INSTITUTIONS IN THE
POST-REVOLUTIONARY GENERATION · In the years from 1783 to 1815, American financial organization continued to be very simple, only a step more complicated than in colonial times. Capital was primarily invested in local business ventures, and it was more immobile than mobile. Certainly no Eastern capital went West through the usual channels. Only a few corporations existed, and they were in public utilities, canals, and banking. But then the economy was also very simple. As late as 1824, a decade after the close of this period, the Secretary of State estimated the combined manufacturing capital of New York, Pennsylvania, Maryland, and Massachusetts at less than $24 million.

Yet this was a period of some significance in the history of financial innovation. The Revolution had had its effects. Like all wars, it had broken the cake of custom by disturbing the customary ways of doing business. One brief statistic is perhaps the best way of illustrating the change that was taking place: the entire colonial period saw only a half-dozen incorporations. By contrast, there were eleven between 1781 and 1785 and 136 more by 1795.

New business groups had risen during the war, and both older and newer merchants were about to embark on new ventures that would make them much wealthier. Old investment habits had been disrupted as the country amassed what was then considered a vast national debt. The

---

[5] John and Clement Biddle were originally merchants, with banking as a sideline. It became a full-fledged banking house in the 1820s under Thomas A. Biddle, Nicholas' cousin. Today it survives as Yarnall, Biddle & Co., the country's oldest private banking house.

volume of trade with England had been sharply curtailed, although it had continued through what was really a civil war. More important from our point of view, however, was the interruption of the flow of credit from England. In the years from the Revolution to about 1815, there was less foreign investment in the United States than at any other time. It has been estimated that foreign holdings of American government bonds totaled about $32 million in 1803 and about $25 million in 1818.[6] But this is not to say that foreign influence had become unimportant—far from it. In the opening years of the nineteenth century, it was said that the Marquis of Carmathen owned the Manhattan Company "body and breeches." The English financial community continued to wield an enormous influence over American finance through Anglo-American bankers, especially the Baring Brothers. The Barings owned 2,200 shares of the Bank of the United States in 1802. The Dutch also had extensive holdings in United States government bonds, canal stock, and a piece of the New Jersey Manufacturing Company.

The interruption of foreign credit flows meant that the American merchant had to create his own independent financial institutions. These were, therefore, years of pioneering, the years that saw the beginnings of commercial and central banking, the stock exchange and investment banking, and an incorporated insurance business.

**THE IMPORTANCE OF COMMERCIAL BANKING
AS A FINANCIAL INTERMEDIARY** · In the pages that follow, we shall devote much more space to the commercial banks than to any of the other financial intermediaries. The reason for doing so calls for some explanation. Why, for example, do we give so much more attention to incorporated commercial banking than to private banking?[7] After all, private banks performed the same functions as the commercial banks. They made loans and investments, issued paper money, and accepted deposits. At one time, because they were first on the scene, they were larger than the commercial banks. Why, then, the concentration on commercial banks?

To begin with, the affairs of commercial banking were much more open to the public. This situation, to be sure, was not a matter of choice but of necessity. Commercial bankers, during most of American history, preferred to operate behind a financial curtain, but they were publicly chartered institutions. Private bankers, on the other hand, did not have to explain their behavior to anyone, and therefore they were able to maintain the mystery they so much relished. A second reason why private banking received so little attention is that they were not as aggressive as commercial banks in seeking accounts. Then, too, commercial banks quickly became the largest of all financial intermediaries, whereas the private banks grew much more slowly. It has been estimated that by 1850 the

---

[6] Margaret G. Myers, *The New York Money Market* (New York: Columbia University Press, 1931), I, 19.

[7] The essential and legal difference between commercial banks and private banks is that commercial banks operate and always have operated under charters from the national or state governments. Private banks need no charter.

commercial banks, with $500 million of assets, accounted for approximately four-fifths of the assets of all financial intermediaries. Admittedly, their relative position began to slip after the middle of the century as life insurance companies, savings banks, and other nonbank intermediaries assumed a larger role, but in 1900 their $10 billion of assets still represented 50 percent of the aggregate.

Aside from size, we must focus most of our attention on the commercial banks because they have been the most diversified of intermediaries. To be sure, all early financial institutions were diversified, but the trend by midcentury was in the direction of specialization. Commercial banks, however, moved against the tide, in the direction of becoming "department stores of finance," in contrast to other institutions that continued to specialize along relatively narrow lines in their financing activities and in the sources from which they sought their funds.

Finally, we concentrate on the commercial banks because of the intimate link they have had with monetary history. Rightly or wrongly, money ordinarily is defined as currency and demand deposits and is accorded a very special place in economic theorizing. Commercial banks alone can create checkbook money—that is, demand deposits—and commercial banks are the only institutions that do not have to rely on prior savings to create credit. All other financial intermediaries create credit but not money, and in their creation of credit, they use previous savings to advance loans to their customers.

THE BEGINNING OF COMMERCIAL BANKING · In the United States, unlike the Old World, commercial banks rose from a lack of capital funds, not from an oversupply of capital funds. Once having started, progress was rapid. To be sure, it is impossible to ascertain precisely how many banks there were at any specific moment in the early history of the United States. Bankers were recognized by their contemporaries as the most close-mouthed and secretive of human beings. "I have found," wrote a "Friendly Monitor" in 1819, "considerable embarrassment in obtaining the most simple information. . . . If I ask a director, the seal of his finger is significantly impressed on his lips. There is a species of masonry in banking which to a certain extent is highly proper and necessary. It implies a mutual pledge that nothing shall be divulged which may be prejudicial to the interests of the bank." And Mathew Carey, in his own distinctive fashion, lamented that he had "labored under a most discouraging destitution of materials." Under the circumstances, the best that even contemporaries could do was to make a rough guess as to the number of banks, their capital, circulation, and deposits.

One thing about which we are fairly certain is that the Bank of North America, founded in Philadelphia in 1781, was the first commercial bank—that is, a money bank rather than a land bank. By 1790 each of the four major cities—Philadelphia, New York, Boston, and Baltimore—had a bank. The combined capital of these institutions was $2.5 million. The banking business expanded rather rapidly in the next ten years, and by 1800 every state except Vermont, Georgia, North Carolina, and New

Jersey had chartered a bank. There were at that time at least twenty-nine, including one in Maine and one in the District of Columbia. The banks in the four large Atlantic port cities, with almost $10 million, controlled about half the country's total banking capital.

THE FIRST BANK OF THE UNITED STATES · The banks mentioned in the preceding paragraph were all chartered by state governments, hence the name "state banks."[8] But, in addition, there was a federally chartered bank, the first Bank of the United States. This institution had all the attributes and powers of a central bank. It issued bank notes, held much of the United States government's deposits, and assisted other banks in times of crisis.

Secretary of the Treasury Alexander Hamilton was primarily responsible for creating the Bank, which he visualized as one of the pillars of the financial system he was forming. He was well versed in banking, for he had written the charter of the Bank of New York and subsequently would write the charter of the Merchants' Bank in New York. The agrarian opposition to his financial proposals was equally well versed. The ensuing debate, therefore, revealed the depths of the disagreement that existed over the question of banking.

In his *Report on a National Bank* in December 1790, Hamilton argued that a national bank would make a threefold contribution to the economy: it would increase the country's active or productive capital, because under the principle of a fractional reserve, a bank could issue two or three dollars in paper money for every dollar it had in specie; it would help the government in borrowing; and it would facilitate the payment and collection of taxes. "It is evident," he wrote, "that whatever enhances the quantity of circulating money, adds to the ease with which every industrious member of the community may acquire that portion of it of which he stands in need," and by having more money, every "industrious member" would find it easier to pay taxes.

The Jeffersonian party opposed the Bank as unconstitutional, for the power to create a bank was not specifically stated in the Constitution. It also thought the Bank would dangerously extend federal powers. In answering the constitutional objections, Hamilton advanced the theory of "implied powers," holding that the Constitution gave Congress the power to establish any instrument that would aid the national government in performing its constitutionally designated functions. The Bank was such an instrument, for it would help the government to regulate coinage, collect taxes, borrow money, and disburse funds.

The opponents of the Bank did not confine themselves to political arguments but insisted that banks increased usury, diverted funds from agriculture, increased speculation, and drove specie out of the country. Since the Bank would be so large and since it would have the blessing of the federal government, it would be even more dangerous than most banks. Although conceding that these charges were true in certain cases,

8 The Bank of North America was originally chartered by the Continental Congress, but it later acquired a Pennsylvania charter.

Hamilton argued that it would be to the Bank's interest to "succor the wary and industrious; to discredit the rash and unthrifty; to discountenance both usurious lenders and usurious borrowers." In addition, he insisted that a national bank would promote lower interest rates by increasing the supply of money. Nor would it diminish the supply of funds for agricultural loans, since there would always be lenders who, "from a spirit of caution, will incline to vest their funds in mortgages on real estate, rather than in the stock of a bank, which they are apt to consider as a more precarious security." Anticipating by over one hundred years the future debate over the effect of security loans on the availability of commercial loans, Hamilton declared, "Stock may indeed change hands, but the money which the buyer takes out of the common mass to purchase the stock, the seller receives and restores to it." In answering Adam Smith's criticism that paper money would drive specie out of circulation, Hamilton pointed out that the abundance of a country's precious metals was not so important as the "quantity of the productions of its labor and industry" and that "in the early periods of new settlements, the settlers not only furnish no surplus for exploitation, but they consume a part of that which is produced by the labors of others." Therefore "precious metals will not abound in any country which has not mines, or variety of manufactures." To the charge that banks encouraged speculation—a charge that was to be made for many years in the future and was eventually to become an important part of business-cycle theory—Hamilton merely questioned whether it would be wise to root out the advantages of credit because it now and then ran to excess.

Sentiment in Congress favored the Bank by almost two to one, so that in February 1791 the Bank received its charter, which was to be in effect for twenty years. The Bank was capitalized at $10 million, although, in accordance with the common practice of the day, less than $1 million was paid in. The Bank was a private institution, not a public one, even though the government subscribed one-fifth of the capital and appointed 5 of the 25 directors. The Bank was not permitted to buy or sell goods and real estate, to purchase federal government debt, to charge more than 6 percent interest, or to permit its debts (except deposits) to exceed its capital.

The Bank of the United States was the most influential bank of its day because it was the largest bank and because it had an important influence over the other banks and the money market. Because it was so large and because it acted as the government's fiscal agent, it was continually receiving the obligations of the state banks. It was, therefore, a creditor of these institutions, and as a creditor it could be lenient or stern. It chose to exert its influence in the direction of conservatism, and thus it had a dampening influence on state bank expansion. The result did not make for popularity, and as hostility built up, the Bank lost much of its political power. When its charter came up for renewal in 1811, it was defeated by one vote.

THE GROWTH OF COMMERCIAL BANKING · The state banks immediately took advantage of the demise of the watchdog and embarked on a new career of expansion. In doing so, they were abetted by the policies followed by the federal government in financing the War of 1812. Although not one of the major conflicts in history, the war did cost in excess of $75 million, most of which was borrowed from the state banks, which expanded very rapidly with such encouragement. In 1811 there were 88 banks with a capital of $53 million. By 1816 there were 260 banks with $82 million in capital and $200 million in "bank notes, credits, and bank paper in one shape or other."

Conservatives were aghast at the rapidity of financial expansion. They continually expressed the opinion that banks were being created in much greater numbers than the welfare of the country called for. Yet bank formation was not a steady thing; it occurred in short and intense waves. In 1792, during the first wave, which the newspapers called a bancomania, eight banks were formed. The second wave came twenty years later and again filled the merchants with apprehension. Henry Remsen, president of the Manhattan Company, wrote Governor Clinton that there was more banking than was needed and that the "big banks would swallow up the smaller banks." "The increased population, trade, and manufacturing and agriculture has no doubt rendered additional banks necessary," he observed, "but the increase has exceeded the necessity." What was happening shocked even those who were more sanguine about bank expansion. For example, Mathew Carey, more a spokesman for easy than for tight money, criticized the action of the Pennsylvania Legislature in incorporating 41 new banks, 37 of which went into operation. Said Carey, "There are in various parts of the country three or four times more banks than are necessary."[9]

The "epidemics" of bank formation were due to something more than economic growth. They also reflected a great change in the nature of bank entrepreneurship. In the days immediately after the Revolution and until 1805 or so, banks were mercantile institutions—that is, the very early banks were formed and controlled by the merchants just as they were in England. According to Fritz Redlich, the three great innovators in the banking history of this period were Robert Morris, Jeremiah Wadsworth, and Alexander Hamilton. Of these three, Hamilton was a lawyer, but the other two were prominent merchants. In every city, merchants were in the forefront. The founders of the Philadelphia banks, Thomas Willing, John Nixon, and George Clymer, were prominent merchants. William Phillips in Massachusetts and John Brown in Providence were outstanding New England merchants. In New York all the founders, directors, and officers of the first banks except Alexander Hamilton, Peter Jay Monroe, and Aaron Burr were merchants. There was a very simple reason why the merchants were the first to form banks; they needed them as they needed all financial institutions once political independence from Britain had become a reality.

Because they were vitally interested in every type of financial intermediary, it was only natural that a great deal of interlocking existed

---

[9] Remsen Papers in the Manuscript Collection, New York Public Library. Mathew Carey, *Essays on Political Economy* (Philadelphia, 1822), p. 231.

between the directors and officers of the different intermediaries in the different cities as well as within the cities themselves. Of the six petitioners for the Massachusetts Bank, at least four were involved in Massachusetts insurance. Seven of the twenty-five who organized the Bank of North America were later charter stockholders of the Insurance Company of North America. Jeremiah Wadsworth, once the largest stockholder in the Bank of North America and a director of the Bank of the United States, was the first president of the Bank of New York and a founder of the Hartford Bank. Oliver Wolcott was the first president of the Merchants' Bank and later the first president of the Bank of America. The Coster brothers included a president of the Manhattan Company, a large stockholder in the Merchants' Bank, and directors in two insurance companies.

THE MERCHANTS AS COMMERCIAL BANKERS · The philosophy that governed the actions of the merchants in their banking behavior was the same philosophy that governed all their economic and social actions. They had been reared in the traditions of England. Their overriding objective seemed to be to establish a replica of the English social system. For themselves, they desired to achieve the status of a landed gentry. Their outlook was paternalistic and there seems to have been much concern with rights and duties. As would be expected, their economic philosophy was derived second hand from England, and as is usually the case, the English notions of political economy were just beginning to be adopted here at about the same time that they were being cast off at home. At the end of this period—that is, about 1815—it would not be too much of an exaggeration to say that American political economy was entering the stage of England at the time of Adam Smith.

The older merchant-founded banks, as Albert Gallatin said, financed the merchants, whereas the later bankers financed the retail shopkeepers. The older bankers emphasized safety. According to Isaac Bronson, an astute New York and Connecticut banker, "No paper was issued unless the directors felt an almost perfect certainty that it would be punctually redeemed." Although they were very conservative with the public at large, the older bankers made numerous and often questionable loans to their friends. A. C. Bryan, the historian of Maryland banking tells us, "There can be no doubt that the directors enjoyed special favors, both in respect to rates and amounts." And in Philadelphia, the Bank of North America found itself in considerable difficulty because its directors were overly lenient in making loans to the friends of the Bank and were not sufficiently agile in adjusting to changing times. "By 1804," wrote Lawrence Lewis, the historian of the Bank, "the methods of doing business were rapidly and materially altered. The Bank was under a management too conservative to keep pace with these innovations, and, as a consequence, its profits were sensibly decreased."[10]

---

[10] *An Appeal to the Public on the Conduct of the Banks in the City of New York* (New York, 1815), p. 2; A. C. Bryan, *History of State Banking in Maryland* (Baltimore: Johns Hopkins University, 1899), p. 360; Lawrence Lewis, Jr., *A History of the Bank of North America* (Philadelphia, 1882), p. 84.

The merchants viewed banking as a monopoly that was to be directed for the advantage of themselves and their colleagues. They wished, naturally enough, to maintain their monopolistic position, and they rationalized their view by insisting that several banks in one community would "eat each other up" by exhausting each other's specie reserves. "Three great banks in one city," warned Alexander Hamilton, "must raise such a mass of artificial credit as must endanger every one of them, and do harm in every view."

Those who were outside the pale refused to accept the mercantile view. Instead of resigning themselves to the existing situation, they determined to break the monopoly, an action that the merchants immediately and vigorously opposed. When a group of influential Pennsylvanians appealed for a charter for the Bank of Pennsylvania, Thomas Willing, president of the Bank of North America and later president of the Bank of the United States, mobilized his influence to stop them. In 1803 the directors of New York's Manhattan Company tried desperately and unsuccessfully to prevent the chartering of the Merchants' Bank, arguing that (1) there were already three banks in the city and another would "jeopardize the interest of the community . . . thereby to increase the influx of bills of credit, altogether too great, and to further banish from circulation the precious metals," (2) the formation of the bank was "obviously to promote the cupidity of a few individuals at the expense and manifest prejudice of those banks already established," and (3) should the said bill become law, "the public opinion will attribute it to means the most foul and unwarrantable."

Most foul or not, new banks were chartered. Even before the end of the eighteenth century, there were signs that the older merchants were being shunted aside. By 1810 it was clear that they had lost their dominant position. This point was well illustrated by the fact that the board of the Farmers and Mechanics Bank, formed in 1810 in Philadelphia, contained only three merchants. The other ten were a saddler, a farmer, a paper manufacturer, a currier, a bookseller, a watchmaker, an ironmonger, a brewer, a hatter, and a lawyer.

COMMERCIAL BANK CREDIT POLICY · The new group of bankers took a much different view of the world than did the merchants. They were more aggressive and much less tradition-minded. Oliver Wolcott later wrote of this period: "A great number of new banks were also established by men who possessed neither capital nor experience, the credit of which rested solely on the breath of public opinion."[11] Most of the old-timers regarded the upstarts as ruthless and inhumane. To all of this, the new bankers replied in kind. What they lacked in tact, they made up in *hubris.* They accused their predecessors of being a set of old fogeys who were deficient in enterprise but who had made enormous profits out of a monopoly position.

---

[11] Oliver Wolcott, *Remarks on the Present State of the Currency* (New York, 1820), p. 12.

After the older merchants ceased to dominate the banks, lending policies did become somewhat less conservative. Indeed, they were regarded by some as regrettably radical. Hezekiah Niles, the distinguished editor, mourned the passing of the bank that used to be "the institution bottomed on solid capital." Critics charged that bankers were accommodating "mere speculators." But these charges were exaggerated. The intense antagonism between the older and the younger generation was more a matter of words, attitudes, and philosophy than of behavior. Neither the older merchant banks nor the upstart business banks followed a consistent easy-money policy. On the contrary, both groups were far from impetuous in rushing into loans and investments. Long after the newer banks had taken over, it was still commonly complained that banks were not offering as much credit as the economy needed, especially for fixed capital. To solve this problem, promoters of enterprises that needed large amounts of capital created banks—so-called improvement banks—for the specific objective of providing that capital. For example, the New York Manufacturing Company, which later became the Phoenix Bank, petitioned in 1812 for a charter with banking privileges, among other reasons because of "the difficulty of inducing persons to invest in untried enterprises."

The charges and countercharges were really not as contradictory as they seemed. The truth was that the flow of credit was extremely uneven and reflected the movement of the business cycle. The business cycle, in turn, was primarily influenced not by the banks but by fluctuations in foreign trade and the flow of specie. The banks were, therefore, more the playthings than the manipulators of external economic forces, for specie reserves were then, as well as throughout the period and much later too, the dominant factor in determining bank policy.

But the behavior of the banks did aggravate and accentuate the ups and downs in business activity that occurred intermittently and dramatically in the roller-coaster, boom-and-bust type of economy that prevailed in the United States. Even at this early date the bankers behaved as they would continue to behave for the next century. They watched their reserves closely and expanded or contracted as specie flowed in or flowed out. They offered credit liberally in recovery and boom when their specie reserves seemed high. Then as specie flowed out because of a fall in export prices or because of a flood of imports and an unfavorable balance of trade, they tried desperately to maintain their reserves by stringent contraction. This was recognized as the best and most sensible policy for banks to follow. "All banks, if prudently and ably managed," wrote James Cheetham, a financial journalist, in 1804, "find it necessary to curtail their discounts when their specie gets low."[12] In other words, the banks were the slaves of foreign trade and a specie standard, and the only difference among them was the degree to which they felt themselves bound in the vise. The more aggressive would be much slower in curtailing their loans as reserves ran down and much quicker to expand them on the way up.

[12] Quoted in Bray Hammond, *Banks and Politics in America* (Princeton, N.J.: Princeton University Press, 1956), p. 161.

THE BANKS AND THE MONEY SUPPLY · One way of judging how the banking system was meeting credit needs is by examining what happened to the money supply and the total volume of credit these years. In the spring of 1792 capital markets went through their first convulsion. When specie reserves began to fall, the banks reacted with a "total stop of discounts." Almost five years later, another storm hit the economy, but it was relatively short-lived. With recovery, credit again eased. The Olivers, the prominent Baltimore merchants who had previously complained about tight money, said in 1801 that they could get all the credit they required.[13] By 1803 notes and deposits in the Boston banks were close to $2 million, where with minor variations they remained for a few years. Then, beginning in 1810, investments, note circulation, and deposits soared upward. By 1814 the Boston banks owed noteholders and depositors over $9 million. The same events were taking place in the other large cities. Pennsylvania incorporated forty banks in 1814, four of them in Philadelphia, or as many as had been previously incorporated. The banks discounted freely. Country merchants prospered and more money came into the city than ever before. "This was the golden age of Philadelphia," wrote Mathew Carey. "The rapid circulation of property—the immensity of business done—and the profits made produced a degree of prosperity which she had perhaps never before witnessed." In 1811 three of the incorporated Philadelphia banks were circulating $1.9 million in notes and held deposits of $3.3 million, or a combined total of $5.2 million. At the height of the boom in mid-1815, deposits and circulation of seven Philadelphia banks were well over $10 million, or twice as much as four years before. In Baltimore combined notes and deposits in 1815 must have been close to $10 million. There are no figures for New York, but "a well-informed Citizen" thought that the active capital of the New York City banks was $13.5 million. He also thought that their combined "notes, deposits, and circulation" totaled about $23 million. If this figure was accurate, it meant that the capital-to-debt ratio was about 60 percent, which, in turn, meant that New York banking practices were as aggressive as those of any other city and much more aggressive than most, for the ratio in Philadelphia was about 70 percent and in Boston about 100 percent.

Some statistics are available on the state of two individual banks, the Bank of North America and the Bank of Massachusetts. From these data, which admittedly suffer from accounting idiosyncrasies, we can see how the ebb and flow of reserves (specie plus other bank notes) determined what discounts were offered and what money was created. In both banks, reserves dropped sharply and steadily from 1803 to 1806, and as a defense measure both banks curtailed their loans and investments. Then, beginning in 1808 and continuing to 1814, reserves shot upward and the banks expanded with enthusiasm. The Massachusetts Bank, whose reserve increase was especially large, quadrupled its loans and investments, whereas the Bank of North America did not quite double its commitments. Deposits and circulation followed the course of loans and investments. In the Massachusetts Bank, reserves against deposits and notes ran between

---

[13] Stuart W. Bruchey, *Robert Oliver, Merchant of Baltimore, 1783–1819* (Baltimore: Johns Hopkins University Press, 1956).

20 and 30 percent through most of these years. In the Bank of North America, which was not quite as conservative as the Bank of Massachusetts but much more conservative than the other Philadelphia banks, typical reserve ratios ranged from 15 to 25 percent.

Many of the newer bankers believed that banks could increase the country's money supply and capital. This doctrine was fiercely contested by the conservatives, mostly agrarians, who argued that bank money was not an addition to the money supply but a displacement of specie—that is, gold and silver. The contemporary writer Condy Raguet described the new view with the statement that "A bank, by many, was no longer regarded as an instrument by which the surplus wealth of capitalists could be conveniently loaned, but as a mint in which money could be coined at pleasure." The faith of "the many" in this doctrine was to be badly shaken by the effects of the War of 1812, but its fascination was never completely shattered.

It is not difficult to understand why bankers thought that banks increased the money supply. As almost everyone knows, the mechanics of making bank loans in the pre-1850 era differed significantly from today's mechanics even though the economic effects were the same. In early banking, most banks—that is, those outside the financial centers of the very big cities—issued their own bank notes, and when customers borrowed, they received bank notes in exchange for their promissory notes, mortgages, or other evidences of debt. Today, by contrast, no bank issues bank notes. Instead, banks give their borrowers bank deposits against which they may write checks. In other words, most banks in pre-1850 America issued pocketbook money, whereas today they issue checkbook money. But the important point is that the early bankers were sure that they were increasing the money supply because they were actually issuing money. As a matter of fact, they were more right than wrong, for bank loans, then as now and whether in the form of pocketbook money or checkbook money, *did* increase the money supply and *did* increase the supply of loanable funds, but they did not increase capital (produced instruments of production) except indirectly. However, the operation of an increasingly complex economy was just as much a puzzle to most nineteenth-century Americans as it is to most twentieth-century Americans; and when some economists explained that it was an error to think that banks increased the money supply, many people felt themselves compelled to question what had previously seemed to them so obviously true.

To put it harshly, very few bankers understood the complicated set of operations known as banking, particularly the principle known as fractional reserves. Economic sophisticates understood that commercial banks could create more money than they had in specie, simply because they knew that not all the creditors of the bank would decide to cash their credits at the same time. These sophisticates thought that banks should maintain a reserve equal to about 20 percent of their liabilities to take care of the claims that could be expected to be presented. But there was nothing magical about 20 percent. At best, the requirement was based on experience; at worst, it was merely an arbitrary figure. And bankers who were not awed by authority wondered just why 20 percent? Why not 50, or

15, or 5? In time many pushed their reserves to absurdly low amounts, so that when claims were greater than expected, the bank was put in the embarrassing position of not being able to meet its claims, and the result was failure.

Of course, no reserve, no matter how large a fraction of liabilities, could guarantee solvency. If a run took place, only time and good fortune could save the bank. So it came to be that a bank's ability to survive depended ultimately on the public's respect for and faith in the management. And this situation, in the last analysis, depended on the bank's ability to meet its obligations promptly—in other words, its liquidity.

For most banks in this period, liabilities consisted primarily of note issues, or "circulation." Every bank note that was issued circulated at a discount equal at least to the cost of bringing it back to the place of issue for redemption in hard money. When an individual received a note, he could pass it on, or hold it until he could get to the place of issue, or sell it to a note broker, who would eventually accumulate a volume to take back for redemption. In any event, any recipient of a note understood that it would not be worth par. The best notes (those that were issued by solidly situated banks) circulated at a minimum discount. The notes of less-respected banks circulated at higher discounts, depending on the public's judgment of the chances of ultimate redemption.

ACCOMMODATION LOANS · As the cliché would have it, new brooms sweep clean, and both the pioneers and the later innovators entered banking with the ambitious intention of hewing absolutely to the line established by custom and theory. The first banks, influenced by a doctrine that had attained great vogue in England, resolved that they would make no long-term loans but would confine their lending to short-term, nonrenewable discounts. In its early days, the Bank of Massachusetts granted credit for only 30 to 60 days and never renewed a note. At its opening, the Bank of New York announced that no discount would be made for longer than 30 days, and no note or bill would be discounted to pay a former one. Banks quickly learned, however, that short-term credit was impractical even in the big cities. The economy did not move that rapidly. Most borrowers needed long-term credit and could make little use of short-term funds. Before long the Bank of New York was granting loans for forty-five days and up to two years in unusual cases. By 1807 the Philadelphia Bank was making four-month loans, and somewhat later the Bank of the United States was doing the same. At the same time, renewals became easier for a borrower to obtain.

What banks were doing was shifting to so-called accommodation loans —loans that produced business in contrast to trade paper that was pro-duced by business. Or to define the term in another way, accommodation loans were used to finance fixed-capital expenditures, whereas trade paper financed working capital. Such loans clearly violated what had become traditional practice in England. Accommodation loans were se-cured by anything from real property to nothing more than the borrower's promise to pay. Being based on promissory notes ("accommodation paper"), they were rare in England largely because they were not backed by actual goods. But a young and developing economy found the accommodation loan and accommodation paper very helpful, for it seemed an easy way to meet the seemingly insatiable need for fixed-capital financing. In the absence of enough other financial intermediaries, the commercial banks tried to fill this need by making extensive accommodation loans. Even in such an eminent an institution as the first Bank of the United States, these loans made up 75 percent of total loans.

INTEREST RATES ON BANK BORROWING · Banks discounted promissory notes, double-name paper, and bills of exchange. The interest rate was usually stated at 6 percent, but this figure was the legal ceiling rather than the market rate and was a legend to a great extent, for banks found ways and means of procuring a higher return. The most important was for banks to turn more and more to bills of exchange, which had the added attraction of being in greater supply than local paper. Then, too, they were more certain of being paid at maturity. Payment of a bill of exchange at a distant point eliminated the personal touch; thus banks could insist on prompt payment much more easily than they could or would on a local note where personal acquaintance or friendship required whatever indulgence the bank could give.

The use of fictitious bills of exchange to extort usurious interest was illustrated by a specific case in a Missouri legislative committee report in the late 1830s. A businessman attempted to borrow $10,000 from a bank on his personal note. He was refused, whereupon he drew a bill of exchange on a person in a distant city who agreed to pay it four months after date. After the bill was endorsed by two or three others, the bank advanced the $10,000 less a premium of $500 and interest of $233.33, or $733.33 for the use of $10,000 for four months. At the end of the four months, the maker of the bill paid it off by drawing another bill. By the end of the year, when the whole transaction was cleared, the borrower had paid 15 percent in premiums and 7 percent in discounts. In addition, he had to pay 5 percent every four months for the expense of transmitting the money to pay the bills. Thus he paid a total of 37 percent for the use of $10,000 for one year.

In other ways, too, banks got around the law's ceiling on interest rates. One way was to require a borrower to maintain a balance in the bank, a practice that is still in existence under the name "compensating balances." Banks also made a little extra by sometimes giving postdated notes instead of cash to a borrower. Moreover, occasionally they were able to make an arrangement with a borrower under which they gave him bank notes and he agreed not to circulate them within a given area or within a given period of time. Banks that came into possession of notes drawn on other banks were often able to make an additional fraction by giving these notes instead of their own to borrowers.

BANK DEPOSITS · Bankers, circa 1810, also viewed other aspects of their business much differently than present bankers do. In the early days, most bankers did not recognize any difference between time and demand deposits. It was believed that all deposits were time, or "lodged" as they were sometimes called. In other words, most bankers believed that bank money (paper money issued by banks) was created by loans, but deposits were the result of a depositor actually depositing money for safekeeping. Despite the efforts on the part of the initiated and sophisticated to correct this error by explaining that deposits as well as note issues arose out of loans, most bankers continued to believe that deposits were unprofitable, whereas note issues, which created money, were profitable. After all, deposits were liabilities, not assets. Consequently, most bankers, at least in the beginning, discouraged deposits. Indeed, the Bank of Massachusetts actually charged a fee for holding them. There were, of course, many exceptions to this generalization. Some banks, especially in New York, seem to have cultivated a deposit business from the day they opened, and some banks made an effort to attract deposits by offering interest. The Farmers' Bank of Annapolis, Maryland, was the first to do so in 1804. The practice became somewhat more common after 1810 and very common after 1820, by which time many of the less-sophisticated bankers had begun to understand that deposits were almost as profitable as note issues because both were the result of loans and discounts.

SCALE OF OPERATIONS AND PROFITABILITY

OF THE EARLY BANKS · What with loans, discounts, bills of exchange, and deposits, banks were considered extremely busy by their contemporaries, but judged by today's huge volume of activities, even the biggest were very small scale. In 1803 the Merchants' Bank, a substantial New York institution, employed just 13 persons. Thomas Willing said that the Bank of North America had 600 accounts in the early days of his presidency. Its daily entries were between 300 and 400, and total cash transactions were about $26.5 million a year. The bank discounted $150,000 a week. In January 1809 the Boston Bank, with a capital of $1.8 million, had deposits of a little over $400,000, a note circulation of a little over $150,000, and discounts of $1.7 million. The Massachusetts Bank, capitalized at $800,-000, owed depositors $340,000 and noteholders $110,000, whereas it had outstanding discounts of a little over $1 million.

Banking in the very early days was a profitable business. Banks before 1802 paid dividends of 9 to 12 percent a year, but then dividends dropped sharply. According to Mathew Carey, dividends paid by the Philadelphia banks fell from 10 to 15 percent in the early years to 8 to 9 percent after about 1804. An index of bank stock prices dropped from 104 in 1802 to 86 in 1805, 95 in 1809, and then to 75 in 1814, where it remained until about 1825.[14]

The performance of the banks could also be measured by the failure rate. According to Albert Gallatin, 208 banks had failed by 1815. Since the first bank failure of which we have any record occurred in 1809, this meant an average of almost 30 banks a year, and the Gallatin estimate was probably an understatement.

[14] Walter B. Smith and Arthur H. Cole, *Fluctuations in American Business, 1790–1860* (Cambridge, Mass.: Harvard University Press, 1935).

Competition certainly contributed to the deteriorating performance of the banks, but more emphasis was put on competition than it deserved. Very often those who had feared the worst from competition found that the results were not nearly as bad as they had expected, which was perhaps a disappointment to those who had resignedly anticipated total disaster. The directors of the Bank of North America, who had strenuously opposed both the Bank of the United States and the Bank of Pennsylvania, confessed that their establishment "hath not upon the whole lessened the business; but hath increased it in several departments." Then, too, competition did not explain the disparate performance of the individual banks. The simple fact seems to have been that the newer banks did better than their predecessors because they were more efficient.

A bank's management also had something to do with its profitability. Once the banking system began to operate in full gear, the decisions on their loan, discount, and deposit policies were made as in other businesses by those entrepreneurs in the individual concerns who took it upon themselves to exert their leadership. At first, the seat of power was in the board of directors by tradition, but as banking expanded and the power of the early merchants began to be diluted, more and more of the significant decision making concentrated in the hands of the cashier, the bank's administrative officer. The president tended to become a figurehead, and the board became a passive consenting body rather than an active policy maker. Toward the end of the period under discussion, however, this procedure was subject to some penetrating criticism, and things changed once again. Power began to shift toward the bank presidents, but the change did not become a reality until the 1820s. Nicholas Biddle, president of the second Bank of the United States, about whom we shall have more to say later, was mainly responsible for this innovation in management.

GOVERNMENT REGULATION OF

COMMERCIAL BANKING · Until the late 1830s banks were chartered by special act of the state legislature or, in rare cases, by the federal government. Because of the deeply ingrained antipathy toward banks, charters were obtained by subterfuge in many cases. Thus Robert Morris applied for a charter for the Bank of North America, stressing that its function would be to "furnish a supply for the armies of the United States" and de-emphasizing the fact that its charter as a bank would run far beyond the end of the Revolution. Aaron Burr obtained a charter for the Manhattan Company ostensibly to provide a water supply for New York, but the charter also permitted the company to use its surplus "in anything not inconsistent with the laws and constitutions of the United States and the State of New York."

Most of the early bank charters required the organization to make substantial loans or pay subsidies to the state from which the charter was obtained. In addition, governments required banks to invest in internal improvement projects. Not infrequently, governments bought stock in new banking ventures. Pennsylvania, for example, invested $2 million in three

Philadelphia banks. The federal government bought one-fifth of the stock of the Bank of the United States, but it should be noted that none of this purchase represented cash, the stock being paid for by a loan from the bank. This arrangement of paying for bank stock in notes rather than cash was universal among the early banks. Nominal capital was one thing; paid-in capital was something else. Even as late as the 1830s, the paid-in capital of the exemplary New York system was estimated to be just about half the nominal capital.

There was nothing terribly dangerous about issuing stock against stockholders' notes, but it was evidence of a tendency to establish and operate banks on a thin financial thread. In time, as the old conservative merchant families began to be replaced by entrepreneurs who had more imagination than capital, the standards of banking ran down. As a historian of New York banking expressed it, "After the close of the War of 1812, a very loose system prevailed; it was provided in many of the charters that on payment of 12 to 50 percent of the capital in specie, a bank might commence. . . . In some cases, individuals would make arrangements to procure 12 percent . . . and after retaining the specie for a few weeks would return it to the real owners."[15] This particular strategy was symptomatic of early banking in the country's underdeveloped areas. It appeared in New York in the period after 1812; it would appear again in the Middle West in the 1830s and again in the Great Plains at a later date. Americans wanted banks. To be sure, they preferred safe banks, but if this condition were impossible because the economy would not warrant it, banks would appear anyway.

As has always been the case with financial intermediaries, government regulation had much to do with bank operation. In the early years, state governments made little attempt to regulate banking aside from insisting on the payment of bonuses when the charter was granted and requiring banks to make loans to certain privileged groups, such as farmers or internal improvement companies. Massachusetts, which in this era was far ahead of the rest of the country in industry and capital accumulation, was the only significant exception. In 1799 its legislature passed a law prohibiting note issues in denominations of less than $5. This restriction was to become a common provision of government regulation, for it was believed that specie had the "inherent value" that paper money lacked. Specie was, therefore, considered superior, and anything that encouraged the use of specie and discouraged the use of paper was considered clearly beneficial. Since most transactions involved amounts less than $5, the prohibition of small-denomination notes would force the community to use specie.

Not only was specie viewed as superior, but small-denomination notes tended to circulate longer and thus worked in favor of those banks that had inadequate specie reserves. Yet though the prohibition of small-denomination notes fitted well with the current notions of what constituted good banking, it was largely disregarded in early Massachusetts as well as in other states.

[15] Azariah C. Flagg, *Banks and Banking in the State of New York, 1777–1864* (Brooklyn, N.Y., 1868), p. 123.

In 1803 Massachusetts went further and began to require semiannual statements on the condition of the banks. Seven years later the legislature imposed a penalty of 2 percent a month to be paid to noteholders for failure to redeem notes on demand, and in 1811 bankers were required to swear that paid-in capital would not be removed after a charter had been granted. Banks were also prohibited from issuing notes in excess of 150 percent of capital. In time other states would join Massachusetts in passing extensive regulatory legislation, and most of these pioneering attempts would meet with varying success, depending on the degree of economic development that had been attained. In Massachusetts and New York regulation was effective and workable, whereas regulation in the Southwest and the Middle West failed to achieve its aims and appeared to be an absurdity when first introduced.

THE EMERGENCE OF NEW YORK
AS A FINANCIAL CENTER · One of the most significant developments during the period under consideration was the emergence of New York City as the country's leading financial center.

When the Constitution was signed, Philadelphia was clearly first in the economic life of the United States. The city's supremacy in finance can be seen in the fact that six of the first seven financial intermediaries were born in Philadelphia. In addition, the city was the home of the first central bank and the first private bank. Only the trust company had its origin in another city.

By the close of the period under discussion, New York had overtaken Philadelphia. The former had many natural advantages; moreover, it had a more favorable political climate and a collection of more aggressive and more innovative entrepreneurs. Its government had a more lenient tax system, and it protected its bankers better than did rival cities. Until 1826 the only restriction of any consequence on New York banks was that debt could not exceed three times the paid-up capital. At the same time, however, the government protected existing banks by holding down the number of new entries.

New York was also more tolerant of institutions and actions that most people disapproved. An outstanding example was the attitude toward call money.[16] New York created and developed a call-money market, which Philadelphia did not have and Boston could not cultivate. But we leave New York, its call-money market and its stock exchange for the next chapter.

PRIVATE BANKS · The private banking firms of early America were, as has already been suggested, as important as, if not more important than, the commercial banks. They had their origins either in brokerage, shipping, or merchandising. Those that began in commerce resembled the British merchant-banking houses. They financed mercantile transactions, followed a conservative policy, and became, where possible, family institutions. Two examples of this different type of private banker were Alexander Brown and Stephen Girard.

[16] Money borrowed for the purpose of purchasing securities.

Brown came to the United States in 1801 to start a dry goods business specializing in linens. Since he had some connections in England, several of his fellow Baltimore merchants depended on him for foreign exchange, and eventually this department of his business displaced the dry goods department altogether. By 1818 Alexander Brown & Sons was operating branches in Baltimore, Philadelphia, New York, and Liverpool. Although they were great innovators in merchant banking, they were regarded by the disrespectful as a branch of the Liverpool firm. They avoided industrial investments and viewed the stock exchange with suspicion and distrust.[17] When approached to invest in an English cotton mill, Alexander Brown wrote: "However profitable the business may be now, we know of none subject to more reverses . . . and becoming once interested . . . your capital, credit, and resources would be called into action for the use of that establishment whenever it would be required."

Stephen Girard's bank, which took over the premises and some of the business of the Bank of the United States when that institution lost its charter in 1811, provides an excellent example of just how important private banking was in the country's early history. The bank was capitalized at $1.5 million from the fortune that Girard had accumulated in shipping and foreign trade. As the twelfth largest bank in the country, it wielded a wide influence. It had correspondent relations with the Barings, the Bank of South Carolina, the City Bank, and the Bank of America in New York, among others. Girard was a member, along with John Jacob Astor and David Parish, of the first syndicate in American financial history, a syndicate that picked up most of a $16 million loan that the Treasury floated during the financing of the War of 1812. Later Girard was also instrumental in negotiating the charter of the second Bank of the United States. In these negotiations he had the support of Astor, Parish, and Jacob Barker, all of whom were involved in private banking. Yet despite Girard's far-flung activities, he did not seem much concerned with industry, and the same could be said for his allies, Astor and Parish.

Other private banking houses began as money brokers or "note shavers." Their chief function was to buy paper money at a discount for eventual redemption at par, but they soon branched out. They did some business on the stock exchange but much more factoring (buying accounts receivable), insuring, lottery selling, and banking than security dealing.

These brokerage firms were the forerunners of the later investment bankers, and like all pioneers, they led a precarious life. Diversified though they were, they found it impossible to stay above water. There were three reasons for this situation. First, there was not enough business for investment banking in the hazardous financial environment of a developing economy. Second, and more important, no investment house in early America could survive unless it had iron-bound relations with an

---

[17] In so doing, they shared a prominent characteristic of all merchant bankers all over the world. Merchant bankers were less interested in the production of goods than in their marketing. The early manufactures of England and the United States were financed by commercial banks, by friends and relatives, and by plowed-back earnings.

English house. Third, and perhaps most important, the managerial arrangement of investment banking, with its emphasis on family succession, made failure almost inevitable.

THE FIRST INSURANCE COMPANIES · In contrast to banking, about which we know a great deal although certainly not as much as we would like to know, insurance in these early years is a mystery, about which we know only a few facts. We know that general insurance, especially marine, was the most active of all the financial intermediaries. We also know that most people regarded insurance companies as sellers of services rather than middlemen in the saving-investment process. Their function was primarily to cover financial losses resulting from disasters. In the process, they accumulated saving, but this aspect of their business, which was to become increasingly important, was almost completely disregarded by the public. We also know that although many attempts were made to create a thriving life insurance business, none of them achieved any considerable success. Indeed, the whole life insurance business was the ugly duckling of early nineteenth-century financial intermediation. Noah Webster, the noted lexicographer and authority on matters of financial intermediation, expressed the prevalent view succinctly and frankly. Speaking of the Manhattan Company, Webster said, "To these operations [banking] has been added the business of insuring lives, and granting annuities on lives—a business which is novel in this country and of small value to the insurers."

Despite the fact that life insurance did not make any impressive progress until a generation later, early entrepreneurs were fascinated by the business. In the last decade of the eighteenth century, at least five of the many all-purpose insurance companies that were formed had the right to write life insurance, but only one actually did insure lives and then only on a short-term basis similar to today's air-flight policies. Specialized life insurance began in 1807 when Israel Whelen started an agency for the Pelican Life of London, but he did very little business. Then in 1812 came the first corporate company offering to insure lives without regard to occupation, but this company, the Pennsylvania Company for Insurances on Lives and Granting Annuities, was really an investment trust. It did a small amount of advertising, had no agency system, and insured few lives; its main business was to invest its $100,000 capital in sound securities. By 1814 ten life companies had been chartered, six of which were quickly discontinued.

The reasons for the lack of energy on the part of the life insurance business seem clear once the problem is given some thought. There was not enough discretionary income to persuade income earners that they needed what they considered to be a luxury. Then, too, life was cheap in a country in which population was growing rapidly, even though labor was extremely scarce. The economy was 90 percent agrarian, and this fact had its effect on all aspects of life. Insurance was unheard of on the farm. The young entered the labor force very quickly. There was no need for even the small amount of education that seemed necessary in the city. And like the young, the women did not need any unusual protection, for more frequently than now, they died before men as a consequence of the rigors of frontier living and childbirth. But most important of all, life insurance companies did not make any serious efforts to market what they had to sell, and since life insurance has ordinarily been considered something to be purchased with spare income, the business did not thrive.

General insurance was a different matter, for there was no denying the great risks presented by fire, shipwreck, and other acts of God. By 1800 there were 32 general insurance companies in the United States; in addition, almost all the great merchants did some underwriting on the side. So far as we know, there is no comprehensive list of insurance companies for the United States in this period, but scattered data show that in 1824 there were at least 34 general insurance companies in New York, 20 in Boston, 11 in Philadelphia, and 9 in Baltimore. Their combined capital exceeded $25 million.

The Insurance Company of North America, founded in Philadelphia in 1792, was one of the first and most successful general insurance companies. It owed its origins to Samuel Blodget, Jr., an innovator of many diverse talents. Blodget was a statistician whose national wealth estimates are still cited by economists. He was also an architect and a military figure, but his chief claim to fame should be as a promoter of lotteries and as an expert in tontines, an arrangement whereby a group of people deposited a sum of money to be divided among the survivors at some specific date in the future. The tontine was the brain child of Lorenzo Tonti, an Italian physician-banker living in France at the time of Louis XIV. The original tontine stipulated that the sums deposited, plus interest, would be paid to the last surviving member of the group. This extreme form was never popular in the United States, for it was believed that it encouraged homicide and was against public morals. But at some time or other, various modified forms of tontines aroused much excitement among Americans. Thus the famous Old Tontine Coffee House, the City Hotel, and the Park Theatre in lower Manhattan were financed by an arrangement whereby the property would revert after a specific number of years to those investors who were still surviving. A tontine also preceded the Union Bank in Boston. The financing of the Old Tontine Coffee House was an excellent example of how a tontine worked. It was erected in 1794 by the contributions of 203 subscribers. The agreement was that the last seven survivors would share the property, an event that finally occurred in 1876.

In 1792 Blodget formed the Universal Tontine Association. He issued 100,000 shares priced according to a crude life-expectancy table. Thus a 5-year-old paid $22.85 a share, while a person aged 85 paid $3.20. The plan called for a distribution at the end of 20 years. Blodget attempted to sell half the shares in Philadelphia and half in Boston, but he was unsuccessful. When this became evident, the tontine company was abandoned and in its place, Blodget, with the help of Ebenezea Howard, formed the Insurance Company of North America. Shares then sold very rapidly among various occupational groups, and the company began business with

$600,000 of paid-in capital. Although it had the right to write all kinds of insurance, it confined itself at first to marine at premiums ranging from 2¼ percent up, depending on the length of the voyage.

Although they did advertise, which is something the banks did not do, the managers of the insurance companies were even more secretive than the bankers. There are very few financial statements for the years before 1840. But by stretching the sparse information that is available, we can conclude that insurance companies were strong suppliers of social capital and heavy purchasers of government stock and bank stocks. In 1794 the Insurance Company of North America had over $600,000 invested in bottomry loans (loans secured by the ship and the cargo), the Lancaster Turnpike, and stock in the Bank of Pennsylvania. In 1807 it had half its assets of $750,000 in governments, another $300,000 in cash and notes, and the remainder invested in bridges, toll roads, banks, other insurance companies, and mortgages. It can be readily seen that there was little left over for the latter investments.

Even though they were conservatively managed, insurance companies in the big cities had a much higher mortality than the banks. Theirs was a boom and bust business in the literal meaning of the words. In its second six months, the North American took in $151,350 in premiums and paid out only $19,474 in losses. But when American shipping became involved in the crossfire between the French and the English, losses mounted. In 1798 the company took in $1.3 million and paid out $1.2 million, and most other companies were doing far worse. Losses mounted much higher when the Napoleonic wars burst forth in their full fury. During these years, only one bank of all those in the four largest cities failed, but at least six insurance companies failed in Philadelphia and New York.

The Napoleonic wars had other effects on the insurance business. They pushed the more adaptive companies out of marine and into fire insurance. In the ten years ending in 1802, the North American's fire premiums were $81,000, while losses were $31,000. When the Embargo Act was passed in 1807, John Inskeep, the resourceful president of the North American, turned definitely toward fire protection and expanded the company's territory to what was then the Far West. Using the agency system, the company's fire business began to increase much faster than marine, although it would not be until about 1850 that fire finally became more important than marine.

THE ECONOMIC IMPACT OF THE
EARLY INTERMEDIARIES · It would be an exaggeration to assume that the financial intermediaries of the very early nineteenth century made a substantial contribution to the total economy, and it would be unreasonable to criticize them effusively for their failure to do so. They were in the early stages of experiment, and if this point is kept in mind, their contribution becomes much more impressive.

Certainly the general insurance companies and the commercial banks encouraged the saving that was so essential to economic progress. The insurance companies accomplished this step as a complement to their primary function. The commercial banks encouraged saving by granting loans, which eventually had to be liquidated through saving, by paying interest on deposits, and by issuing stocks, which were a popular form of investment.

It is debatable, however, whether the financial community made as much of a contribution to the investment side of the saving-investment calculus. The question is, however, a difficult one to answer inasmuch as the data available are so limited. We do know that the banks in the large cities closely followed the rules of what used to be called the gold standard game. In other words, when the reserves began to fall, they curtailed their outstanding loans. The banks, therefore, rather than the borrowers, triggered economic downturns. Recessions were due not to a lack of borrowers but to a lack of lenders.

Contractions must have reduced the total money supply, but there are no precise figures on the aggregate money supply. The data that we have show that bank capital multiplied almost four times between 1800 and 1815, but bank capital was a nebulous sort of thing in these years, often existing more in the imagination of the ambitious than in hard cash. There would, of course, be nothing on such modern yardsticks as "excess" or "free reserves."

The one remaining yardstick by which students of the money market conclude that credit expansion is taking place at a reasonable or unreasonable pace is the movement of interest rates, and we do have some data on this point even for the early years. In general, market interest rates, as contrasted to those restricted by state usury laws, fluctuated between 9 and 12 percent, but in times of great pressure, such as the last months of 1810, rates climbed to as high as 18 percent.[18] Thus the price of funds, judged by modern experience, was high in the early 1800s, but this fact may have been due to a large demand for funds rather than a short supply of them.

Even though financial intermediaries were not important in terms of size, they were certainly important in the transfer of funds between surplus and deficit units, and to that extent they were a persuasive force in the creation of social overhead capital and other investment projects yielding high returns where direct finance might not have operated effectively.

If the adequacy of the contribution to investment is debatable, the same cannot be said for the contribution to mobility. In these early years, the United States was still a frontier outpost of the British economy. As such, its money market was provincial rather than cosmopolitan. Capital was concentrated in the large cities—Boston, Philadelphia, and New York. Of the 2,176 shares of the Bank of North America in 1786, 1,235 were owned in Philadelphia, 285 were owned by foreigners, and 606 shares were in the hands of people living in the United States outside of Pennsylvania. The ownership of the stock of the first Bank of the United States showed the same kind of distribution: $4.7 million of the shares were owned in Philadelphia and $1.8 million were owned in New York. To be sure, the large

18 Mathew Carey, *Nine Letters to Dr. Adam Seybert* (Philadelphia, 1811), p. 68.

banks had correspondent relations with each other, and many banks operated branches. The wide use of bills of exchange also enhanced mobility, but there were, nevertheless, constant complaints about the difficulties of getting funds into the pioneer regions. Certainly there was much substance to these complaints, for during these opening years of the century, the banks and insurance companies did not engage actively in financing the westward movement, a condition that would gradually change in the next generation.

3 · accelerated innovation, 1816–1836

The twenty years after 1816 were some of the most significant in financial history, for they were distinguished for a dozen or more innovations in financial intermediation. Savings banks, trust companies, investment trusts, building and loan companies, and mutual life insurance companies first appeared in these years. In commercial banking, there were two major milestones—the New York Safety Fund and the Suffolk System. Central banking reappeared in a much stronger form with the second Bank of the United States in 1816, and investment banking first emerged as a vital force in the 1820s. The innovator most responsible for these developments was Nicholas Biddle, the third president of the Bank of the United States. In addition to creating new concepts and new policies as a bankers' banker, Biddle also led investment banking out of its infancy into the stage of adolescence.

THE FACTORS RESPONSIBLE FOR INNOVATION · The age was ripe for innovations of all sorts, for the country was undergoing a fundamental transformation economically, politically, and philosophically as it began to emerge into a more advanced stage of development. These were the years of the beginning of the westward movement, of nascent industrialism, and commercial farming. The population grew steadily, and with it the level of living also advanced. This progress is not so apparent from the estimates of gross national product that we have for these early years, but it is attested to by the high rate at which large fortunes were being accumulated. It was said that in the first years of the century there were only fifteen or seventeen persons in New York who owned a carriage, an accomplishment considered to be the mark of great affluence. The largest and most expensive house in the city, that of Alexander McComb on lower Broadway, was valued at only $25,000. William Jauncey's house at 55 Wall Street was worth only $8,000 and Edward Livingston's at 45 Wall Street, $9,000. A few years later, there were a dozen or more "comfortably fixed" merchants in each of the great seaports. Scoville, thinking back on the financing of the War of 1812, recalled that 89 New Yorkers had subscribed $10,000 or more to the government's bond drives. In 1832 a House committee added further evidence that fortunes were being accumulated when it reported that $2 million of the stock of the Bank of the United States was owned by people "holding upward of $100,000 each." Not much later, in the middle forties, it was said that there were fourteen New Yorkers with fortunes of $1 million or more, two of whom possessed over $10 million each. Boston was reported to have sixteen millionaires, one of whom was said to be worth $6 million. Such fortunes established a launching base for the expansion of financial intermediaries, providing capital funds for commercial banks, insurance companies, and trust companies as well as reserves for savings banks.

But this increasing evidence of wealth would not have set in motion the rapid growth of finance that actually occurred. Something more was needed, and this something consisted of a set of aggressive entrepreneurs who were constantly searching for ways and means to augment the supply of capital. The country also had an adequate supply of influential politicians who thought that government should play an active role in promoting economic growth. This belief was in keeping with public opinion, for in the early nineteenth century the public at large undoubtedly favored government expenditures for internal improvements even though such expenditures meant that governments, especially on a state and local level, would have to go into debt to finance these projects. According to a contemporary commentator, "The public are now firmly convinced that, in the United States, where the fortunes of private individuals are limited in amounts, great public works can only be accomplished by the expenditure of the public treasury." Between 1820 and 1838 the states borrowed $60 million for canal construction, $53 million to capitalize state banks, $43 million for railroads, $7 million for turnpikes, and lesser amounts for schools, hospitals, statehouses, and jails. On the municipal level, debt, which had hardly existed in 1800, exceeded $20 million in the 1830s. The District of Columbia placed a loan in Amsterdam in 1830. Philadelphia and Boston borrowed in England in 1833. But New York City was by far the largest municipal borrower, accounting for half of the total city debt.

THE DEMAND FOR AND SUPPLY OF FUNDS · One blade of the demand-supply scissors—the demand for funds—was similar then to what it is today. The difference was in degree rather than in kind. Householders needed funds for mortgages against the purchase of homes. Merchants needed working capital to finance imports and exports. Retailers borrowed from wholesalers, who, in turn, needed credit to keep going. Manufacturers needed both fixed and working capital to set up and carry on business. Governments needed funds to pay for internal improvements.

On the other hand, the sources that provided the supply of funds were much more limited then than they are today. Much of the needed capital came from plowing back earnings. Another block came without going through intermediaries: individuals provided funds through mortgage money, personal loans, lotteries, and the purchase of securities. But lest this point be misunderstood, it is important to note that the infant manufacturers of the time seem to have avoided loans from individuals wherever possible. Here intermediaries stepped in and provided much of what was needed. Commercial banks made loans of every type—long and short and for fixed and working capital—as did trusts, savings banks, and insurance companies.

The demand being great and the supply limited, suppliers of funds had all they could do to satisfy existing demand. It would not be until much later, a whole century in fact, that banks would try to persuade consumers to borrow to cover the purchase of consumer durable goods. It would then take another generation for banks to engage in persuading consumers to borrow to cover the purchase of services and nondurable goods.

Although only meager and scattered data exist for the first third of the 1800s as well as later, it would be well to summarize whatever evidence we have that gives any hint of financial growth in quantitative terms.

A contemporary student of finance painstakingly counted all the banks, insurance companies, savings banks, and miscellaneous institutions in the eastern United States in 1830. As would be expected at a time when financial data were not considered necessary for civilization's progress, he missed a number of institutions, such as savings banks, trust companies, and life insurance companies, and he underestimated the capital of the commercial banks. Still, his estimates do reveal something. He counted 98 insurance companies with $30 million in paid-in capital in 25 cities in 15 states. There was also $90 million in paid-in bank capital.[1]

Other estimates put bank capital at $145 million in 1830 and $250 million in 1836. Bank assets in the latter year were $538 million. The Boston and New York banks alone had $35 million in capital in 1830 and $50 million in 1835. Savings bank assets were at least $10 million in 1835, and the Massachusetts Hospital Life Insurance Company (MHLI), the largest private financial institution in the country, had resources of $5.5 million in 1830 and $6.2 million in 1836. Putting all these figures together, without allowing for understatement, we get at least $585 million as the combined assets of banks, general insurance companies, and MHLI. To this amount should be added the minute amount in life insurance companies, the one building and loan, the nonreporting commercial banks, and the somewhat larger holdings of the miscellaneous trust companies. The total would be at least $585 million and more likely $600 million.

To put this picture in perspective, national income estimates for 1839 (a depression year) range from about $1.5 billion to $2 billion, with most contemporary estimates running higher than those made more recently. On the basis of conservative estimates, the financial intermediaries already held assets equal to one-third the national income. But large as this figure was for its time, it was small when compared to today, when the assets of intermediaries are well over twice as much as the national income.

THE SECOND BANK OF THE UNITED STATES · By 1815 commercial banks were the most important financial intermediaries in the country. They had emerged from the War of 1812 in what could best be called an overrobust state. In helping to finance the war, they had flooded the country with a massive collection of heterogeneous paper money issues. To bring the banks back to what was considered a saner position, the Madison administration reluctantly proposed to establish a second Bank

---

[1] Thomas S. Goddard, *A General History of the Most Prominent Banks in Europe and the United States* (New York, 1831).

of the United States. The result was a triumph of pragmatism, for President Madison had often expressed the twofold conviction that it was unconstitutional for the federal government to charter a bank and that banking and paper money were inherently evil. Yet there was general agreement among national leaders that a central bank was the only means by which the state banks could be forced to contract the outstanding note issues that they had issued with such abandon during the war.

In April 1816 Congress issued a twenty-year charter to the second Bank of the United States. The Bank's organization and its powers were similar to those of the first Bank but were on a much grander and more influential scale. Its capital was $35 million, of which the government, again as in the first Bank, subscribed one-fifth and had the right to appoint five of the twenty-five directors. The Bank was to act as the government's fiscal agent. It was to hold the Treasury's funds and to transfer government funds without charge. In keeping with the real bills doctrine, the Bank was enjoined to deal only in bills of exchange, specie (gold and silver), and the sale of goods truly pledged as security for money loans.

The second Bank of the United States was a central bank in every respect but name. It was the government's fiscal agent, it issued money and dealt in foreign exchange, it had close relations with foreign bankers, and it was in a position to influence if not to control credit and money. This last power, the most important in its possession, deserves further description. Control over its own circulation, which amounted to about 25 percent of all the paper money in the banks, gave the Bank one method of regulating the money supply; but its indirect control over the state banks provided a much more potent method. Through many important channels, the Bank was brought into daily contact with the state banks and continuously collected a stream of state bank notes. First of all, it was the government's fiscal agent. Second, it was the leading dealer in foreign exchange, and third, it was constantly transferring an extensive volume of funds through its branch system. It was, therefore, a creditor of the state banks with all the powers of a creditor. As the government's fiscal agent, it would not accept in payment of government dues any notes that were not redeemable in specie on demand. Furthermore, whenever it chose, it could send the state bank notes that it had collected back to the issuing bank for redemption in specie. Thus it could control the amount of loans that state banks could make and the amount of money they could issue. A decision to redeem state bank notes put exaggerated pressure on the whole system, for in order to redeem $1 million of notes in specie, it was necessary for a state bank to contract its loans by $4 million to $5 million.

All these powers gave the Bank's officers an immense amount of influence—too much influence, its critics argued and still argue today—but how the influence was exerted was up to the discretion of those who made the decisions. The Bank's first president, William Jones, chose to play a passive role. The administration instructed him to put pressure on the state banks so that they would contract their note issues. But at the same time, the Treasury asked Jones to make sure that no one was hurt by the application of pressure. Both the Treasury and Jones were the victims of inconsistent objectives. They wished to bring inflation to a halt, but doing so would mean deflation, and deflation would produce some suffering for which no one wished to be responsible. The dilemma thus produced has been repeated time and time again ever since.

Jones' behavior when confronted by the unattractive choice between inflation and deflation was to do precisely nothing. The Bank made no special effort to force the state banks to contract their business. Consequently, the state banks, after some initial hesitation, continued to extend their commitments, and the country experienced what has since become known as "a riot of speculation." We do not have any comprehensive figures on total commercial banking, but data are available for Massachusetts, and although Massachusetts was hardly typical of the whole country, its experience sheds light on the general trend. Total deposits in 1814 were over $9 million. They dropped to $2.1 million in 1816, then climbed to $5.4 million in 1821.

The Bank's failure to keep the state banks in line placed it in a precarious position. It continued to redeem notes, but it did not press the state banks for redemption. Its gold reserve evaporated, and it found itself unable to meet its obligations. Jones resigned after he and his directors had belatedly begun to put pressure on the Bank's debtors. Langdon Cheves, who took over as president in 1819, continued the deflationary policy with an even firmer hand. In the one hundred days after June 30, 1818, the Bank chopped off $4.5 million of discounts. This step, according to William Gouge, a prolific financial writer of the 1830s, "had a very disastrous effect on the merchants." It also had a most disastrous effect on the banks. Nearly half of those formed between 1810 and 1820 failed by 1825. Biddle, in 1828, said that of 544 banks in the United States, 144 had gone bankrupt and another 50 had suspended operations. Between 1816 and 1820, estimated note circulation fell from $68 million to $45 million in a steep and severe deflation. Once again the Massachusetts banks illustrated the trend. Combined deposits and note issue fell from $6 million in 1817 to $5.1 million in 1819, and it was said that the Massachusetts banks bore up under the strain better than the banks of any other state. Deflation had saved the Bank, but it had done so at enormous expense to debtors all over the United States. As Gouge later put it, "the Bank was saved and the people ruined."

COMMERCIAL BANK OPERATIONS · Early nineteenth-century banking was well described by a visitor from England in 1822:

> The number of banking companies in America surprises a stranger. In the city of New York there are ten or a dozen, all issuing their own notes, besides a multitude of others in the immediate neighborhood. A list of the banks in the United States has been recently published, containing between three and four hundred, although there is every reason to believe that it is not complete. Some of the memoranda in this catalogue are not a little inexplicable to a stranger. Under the name of one of the banks you will find; "The notes of this bank signed with red ink, at a discount of 25 per cent those signed with black 5 per cent discount;" after the name of another;

"Not in good credit." The paper of one town is not received by the banks of another, unless when specially payable there, and the consequence is that it requires not a little circumspection, in a stranger who is travelling about, to avoid losing by the discount upon notes, which increases regularly as he recedes from the place where they are issued. This in the paper of private companies is less remarkable, but the United States' Bank, which has eight or ten branches scattered over the country, issues notes dated at each of these places, none of which will be received by any of the other branches except for government duties and taxes; so that a merchant with his pocket full of the notes of the United States' Bank at Philadelphia, cannot pay his bill in the office of the same bank at New York, till he has gone to a broker and paid him a premium for exchanging them. This discount upon bank notes has given rise to a regular trade of buying and selling them. . . . The brokers, or shavers, as they are familiarly designated, are numerous in all the towns.[2]

The commercial banking situation was aggravated by the fact that the morals of the country bankers were often notoriously low. Some were milking their banks for their own gain at the expense of the community at large. An extreme example occurred in Florida, where a group of cunning promoters formed a bank, which granted each of them a loan in the form of bank notes. Rumors were then circulated to the effect that the bank was in imminent danger of collapse. As the bank notes depreciated, the promoters bought them up at discounts and used them to pay off their loans.

Banking was also an avocation that attracted those who had no special qualifications for any specific job. As one successful Middle Western banker later explained when asked how he happened to enter banking, "Well, I didn't have much to do and so I rented an empty store and painted bank on the window. The first day a man came in and deposited $100, and a couple of days later, another man deposited another $250 and so along about the fourth day I got confidence enough in the bank to put in $1.00 myself."

Despite their failure rate and despite a mode of operation that conservatives denounced as villainously antisocial, the state commercial banks performed an important economic service. Both Mathew Carey, a bank sympathizer, and Condy Raguet, a critic, agreed that the West got capital cheaper than if it had been loaned by Eastern institutions through the regular and more orthodox channels.

Every little clique seemed to know the cause of the inordinate number of bank failures. One group insisted that as long as there were banks, disastrous failures would be sandwiched between bursts of speculative inflation and dollar-destroying deflations. Their solution to the problem was simple: they would merely prohibit banks and paper money. But this action was completely unacceptable, especially to businessmen. "The President," wrote Henry Remsen, "and those who advocate certain opinions of the practicality of making the currency purely metallic are wonderfully ignorant, for without paper based on specie capital, our country would be obliged to go back more than 100 years."

2 Henry Wysham Lanier, *A Century of Banking in New York, 1822–1922* (New York: George H. Doran Company, 1922), p. 24.

Other commentators on the business cycle explained that disaster was the result of incorrect lending policies on the part of the banks. However, there was less agreement on what constituted a poor loan. One group singled out for condemnation the call-money market that was just beginning to appear in New York City and that was withering away in Philadelphia. As in every subsequent period of banking travail, it was argued that money loaned out on call for the purpose of purchasing securities took credit away from more legitimate economic activities. It, so to speak, starved the economy, while at the same time encouraging speculation that had to end in disaster according to the escalator theory—that is, what goes up must come down and the farther up it goes the farther down it must come.

ACCOMMODATION LOANS AS A CAUSE
OF BANK FAILURES · Another group denounced the accommodation loan as the culprit that was causing all the difficulty. To be sure, the volume of such loans was smaller than it had been. City banks, even those that contained the word "farmers" in their title, had ceased making loans to farmers about 1820, and at about the same time participants in the money market like Henry Remsen were reporting that the banks were reducing their accommodation loans. Nevertheless, such loans were still important. It was estimated that security loans averaged about 10 percent of bank assets during this period. Lance Davis has estimated that commercial banks provided about half of the capital for the early textile industry. Albert Gallatin in 1831 wrote that "a large portion of their (bank) loans consist of what the merchants consider as permanent accommodation."

Accounts receivable, the principal type of commercial paper in pre-1870 America, was considered the worst form of accommodation. Since the retail buyer had no general credit, he established relations with one or two wholesalers. The goods that he bought were mostly staple, accumulated by the wholesaler in anticipation of his busy season. The goods were billed, and the bill was approved by the buyer and settled immediately either by a promissory note or draft for acceptance at eight months' sight. So far as the sale was concerned, the transaction was closed; the seller knew exactly the amount and terms of the credit extended, and the buyer often pledged himself to seek no further credit until the note was paid. To obtain money with which to pay the manufacturer or importer for his stock in trade, the wholesaler discounted the notes of the country merchant, endorsing them and thus making them double-name paper.

The retail merchant performed the function of a country bank. He traded on an elaborate system of accounts receivable and payable, which needed very little cash. A country store frequently went through a week's business without seeing so much as $5 in real money. At the harvest season, the consumer settled by turning over his crop to the retail merchant; the latter, in turn, shipped it to a market, where it was sold and the note was paid with the proceeds. The farmer, who was the chief customer of the country merchant, was so dependent on credit that the seller practically charged whatever price he pleased for his merchandise. Profits were several times what they would have been under a cash system, and people who never did a business of over $300,000 to $400,000 a year retired with fortunes.

The extent of long-term lending, security ownership, and accommodation varied widely from section to section and from bank to bank. A big city bank like the Philadelphia Bank had a little over 2 percent of its assets in stocks, but the Bank of Pennsylvania had almost 40 percent of its assets in Pennsylvania state securities and canal loans. In commercial centers, accommodation paper was much less common than in the country and frontier regions. New Orleans banks, for example, always kept to short-term credit. In agricultural states, on the other hand, accommodation loans were accepted as part of the facts of life. In Georgia the Banking Act of 1828 explicitly provided for long-term renewable accommodation loans but tried to prevent any ill effects by restricting any one loan to $2,500. Just how important accommodation loans were can be seen from a breakdown of the 1,968 customers who were indebted to the State Bank of Indiana in 1835: 722 were farmers; 366 were merchants and storekeepers; 272, mechanics; 134, produce and cattle dealers; 87, manufacturers; 121, professionals; and the rest, unknown. Thus, for over 50 percent of the borrowers, short-term credit was impractical.

The critics of accommodation had a point. Commercial banks were issuing short-term obligations in the form of bank notes that were ostensibly redeemable in specie on demand. If much of their assets was invested in long-term loans and investments, they might not be and often were not in a position to meet the demands of their noteholders and depositors. The modern bank is, of course, faced by the same problem, but the modern bank has a solution. It can rely on the central bank to provide it with liquid funds. In the early nineteenth century, banks could rely on the central bank so long as a central bank was in existence and so long as it was in a position to provide liquidity. But in the absence of a central bank or on those occasions when the central bank itself was in dire straits, the ordinary commercial bank had no haven to which to flee when a storm of liquidation broke loose. In such circumstances they failed. Consequently, the pursuit of safety became a search for liquidity.[3]

THE "REAL BILLS DOCTRINE,"
A CORNERSTONE OF NINETEENTH-
CENTURY BANKING THEORY · Concern over the liquidity of commercial banks has occupied the thoughts of bankers and, in no small measure, the thoughts of economists and government authorities for more than two centuries. Traditional thinking on the subject came to be summarized as the "real bills" or "commercial loan" doctrine. Commercial banks, so went the thinking, "should make only *short-term, self-liquidating, productive* loans." In England, where it originated, the doctrine predates Adam Smith and was accepted by a decided majority of bankers and economists until well into the present century. Much later (after 1820) the doctrine received almost as much homage in this country. Isaac Bronson, the

---

3 The use of the word "liquidity" did not become common until the 1840s.

brilliant New York and Connecticut banker, was an early proponent of real bills. He thought that a "real commercial bank should furnish a medium of trade and not capital." What he was saying was that deposits should arise from short-term loans, but he did compromise by using the bank's capital for long-term loans.

Those who defended the real bills doctrine held that if only real bills were discounted, the expansion and contraction of bank money would always be in proportion to the needs of trade. Closely associated with this thinking was the doctrine that if nothing but commercial loans were made, the currency would have a desirable elasticity and the banks would at all times be in a position to meet their liabilities.

The rationale for real bills was well expressed by Condy Raguet in 1839:

> It is absolutely essential . . . for the interest of the public that banks of circulation [commercial banks] should retain unimpaired their control over their loans. So soon, therefore, as they exchange their promissory notes payable on demand in gold and silver, not for the promissory notes of individuals given for property (goods) sold, and payable at short periods, but for notes payable at distant periods, or for notes understood expressly or implicitly, to be renewable in whole or in part, they annihilate their power, and place themselves at the mercy of the public. They are liable to be called upon for payment of their notes faster than their debtors are bound or are able to pay *them;* and instead of fulfilling their engagements promptly and in good faith, they are obliged to resort to discreditable expedients, to deter the holders of their notes from demanding payment.

The commercial loan theory, observed its better-taught champions, not only would solve the problem of commercial bank liquidity but would also serve as an appropriate and automatic regulator of the supply of money and credit. Raguet, again, presented the argument with clarity:

> In order to render legitimate the operations of a bank of circulation its loans should not only be for short periods, but should be confined solely to the discounting of what is called *business paper,* that is, promissory notes and acceptances received by the holders for merchandise and property sold. If none others were discounted, the expansion of the paper system [bank-created money] would only be in proportion to the expansion of business. When this was extended, so as to call for more currency, as at particular seasons of the year, more currency would be created; and when business was diminished as at other seasons, so as to require less currency, the excess would be absorbed by the payments made back to the banks. In these operations, the level of the currency would not be disturbed to produce a depreciation, for although at times there would be a greater quantity of bank notes in existence than at other times, yet this quantity would be in exact proportion to the increased demand, arising from an increase of transactions. Thus would the *elasticity* of the banking principle accommodate itself to the state of commercial wants. Money would always be procurable when it was really wanted, and it would never be so plenty as to depreciate the currency.[4]

4 Condy Raguet, *A Treatise on Currency and Banking* (New York: Augustus M. Kelley, 1967), p. 92. The work was originally published in 1839.

Legislators also thought that real bills were overwhelmingly superior to accommodation paper. "While the bank deals in real bills," reported a committee of the Kentucky Legislature, "it is not so likely to run into excessive issues as when it deals in notes and discounts. The bill business is limited by the actual operations of commerce, the accommodation business is as limitless as the want of money, the rage of speculation, or the spirit of gambling."

Thus the requirements of both liquidity *and* monetary management seemingly dictated that commercial banks limit their acquisitions of primary claims to those of short duration based on the sale of goods. From the point of view of liquidity, the self-liquidating loan proved to be an illusion. Made to finance a commercial transaction involving the purchase of goods for resale, it seemed natural that once the goods had been sold the borrower would be in a position to repay the loan. So he would, *if* the transaction *was* completed and *if* the net revenue at least equaled the amount of the loan. Adverse economic conditions, characterized by falling prices and declines in demand for goods, made no loan self-liquidating. In such a case, the borrower would have to borrow elsewhere to repay his original debt; that is, credit would have to be extended by *another* commercial bank.

Nor was the act of limiting commercial bank credit to the "real" needs of business the self-regulating device with respect to the appropriate level of credit and money that Raguet and others thought it to be. This fact should have been obvious from the quantity theory of money, to which, in one or the other of its variants, most economists of the time adhered. Suppose that demand for current output exceeded available output. Prices would rise. The result would be an increase in the cost of acquiring inventories for resale and in the cost of raw materials for fabrication. The financing requirements of business therefore increase, leading, under the commercial loan theory, to an increase in both commercial bank credit and money supply. But this increase, as quantity theorists and "practical" men both knew, would lead only to another round of price inflation. An initial decline in prices would cause, by the same logic, a contraction in the "real" needs of business, a contraction in both bank credit and money supply, and, via the quantity theory, a further reduction in prices.

More than any other doctrine, the commercial loan theory was adopted in principle by the banking fraternity. Nor is its intellectual hold entirely absent today, for many bankers still consider the short-term business loan the only *appropriate* extension of bank credit. For the nineteenth century it was very much "in." Nevertheless, although honored in word, the commercial loan doctrine was more often than not ignored in practice. Raguet was well aware of this inconsistency, for in his plea for real bills he admonished American bankers to follow the example of "England and France . . . where discounts of paper having more than sixty or a hundred days to run are wholly discountenanced."

It was probably of little consequence to the typical banker that banking fact and banking theory differed over much of American history. In fact, the American banker has always violated "sound" banking doctrine. Because he lived his economic life like most Americans, pragmatism was certainly the first of his rules.

ATTEMPTS TO REFORM BANKING · Pleas to put their houses in order not being enough for the maverick bankers, the more conservative took matters in their own hands; through their own efforts and through government regulation, they tried to force the banking system into a mold of safety and solvency. The first step was an action by the city banks to bring the country banks into line.

In the nineteenth century, city bankers wasted little love on their country cousins. The so-called foreign banks issued notes in a rather indiscriminate fashion, circulated them where they could, including the cities, redeemed them only after long delays or not at all, pushed city bank notes out of circulation, and prevented the city banks from getting their share of the potential business. As soon as the first country bank appeared in New England, the problem of country bank notes presented itself. City people who received the country notes could cash them in one of two ways, neither of which was particularly attractive. They could take them back to the place of redemption and exchange them for goods or specie, but this practice was expensive and inconvenient. Much more frequently, city holders of out-of-town bank notes sold them at a discount to a note broker, a step that was also expensive.

The Boston banks reacted to what they considered "funny money" by refusing to accept country bank notes for deposit. The result, of course, · was a severe blow to Boston merchants who had customers outside of Boston. In 1804 a group of merchants formed the Boston Exchange Office, which proposed to accept country bank notes and loan them to each other. Clearly this operation could not work, for in the long run, the choices remained as before. Then in 1808 Nathan Appleton, a New England manufacturer and banker, attacked the country banks' "evasion and delay" by threatening to sue on every failure to redeem. Appleton carried his threat one step further when, with the help of his fellow Boston associates, he founded the New England Bank, which agreed to collect country notes at 1 percent discount while the note brokers were charging what the traffic would bear. Again, this tactic did not work as well as had been hoped.

The next step in the attack on the country banks came when the Suffolk Bank of Boston also undertook to redeem out-of-town bank notes. Eventually it persuaded other Boston banks to join it and thus the Suffolk System came into existence in 1824. Essentially it was a collection clearing house for the New England banks. Each country bank agreed, after much arm twisting by the city banks, to keep a deposit with the system in return for which the system agreed to redeem notes for not more than the cost of collection.

The Suffolk System's success meant that all New England bank notes circulated at par throughout New England, but it also meant that the New England area experienced a mild deflation that was not experienced in the other regions. Yet the other sections of the United States also desired the safety and solvency that appeared in New England. In New York the city banks chafed under the same country bank irritants that had bothered Boston, but in the city the problem was solved by the use of correspondent banks, notably the Isaac Bronson banks and the Mechanics' Bank. And later, in 1851, the Metropolitan Bank copied the Suffolk System; at the same time, Pennsylvania instituted a similar collection system but it was not all-embracing.

New York also introduced a separate innovation in the interest of protecting the bank customer. In 1827, in a reaction to the depression of the early 1820s, the state passed a set of regulations limiting bank loans to three times the paid-in capital, imposing double liability on stockholders, and requiring annual reports to the comptroller. These regulations were soon deemed too stringent, but some action was necessary to protect the bank customer. Joshua Forman, a prominent businessman and lawyer, proposed a safety fund, an idea patterned after an arrangement originated by the merchants of China under which the stronger merchants supported the weak. The idea was supported by Governor Van Buren and became law under the Safety Fund Act of 1829. Banks had to contribute ½ of 1 percent of their capital annually for six years to a fund that was to be used to pay off the creditors of insolvent banks. The Safety Fund was, therefore, the forerunner of the present Federal Deposit Insurance Corporation (FDIC).

NICHOLAS BIDDLE, CENTRAL BANKER · The Safety Fund and the Suffolk System were confined to a few states.[5] A more extensive way of ensuring safety and solvency came when Nicholas Biddle became president of the Bank of the United States.

The Bank, as we have seen, was always in a position to influence significantly the activities of the state banks and therefore of the entire money market. Its powers over the money market were limited only by international factors and by the ambition and self-confidence of its managers. Given the existence of a specie standard, the Bank was subject to the limitations imposed by foreign trade. When gold flowed out in response to the demands of foreign creditors, the Bank would logically have to pull in its horns; and if the Bank's decision makers were timid about their own powers, they would not be inclined to exert their controls over the banks or the money market.

Under William Jones and Langdon Cheves, the Bank had operated in a hobbled fashion. Biddle, however, was an entirely different personality and he was in an entirely different position. He knew and understood banking. He was, as Fritz Redlich has pointed out, the world's first conscious central banker. He was, moreover, a brilliant innovator with the imagination and the willingness to utilize his powers.

Biddle explained his objectives as a regulator of the state banks. "The great object," he said, "is to keep the State banks within proper limits, to make them shape their business according to their means. For this pur-

5 Vermont and Michigan copied the Safety Fund.

pose they are called upon to settle, never forced to pay specie, if it can be avoided, but payment is taken in their bills of exchange or suffered to lie occasionally until the bank can turn around; no amount of debt is fixed because the principle we wish to establish is that every bank shall always be ready to provide for its notes."

Biddle did not think that a central bank should strive to achieve maximum profit. Instead its goal should be to regulate the economy. His views were far ahead of his time, for not even the Bank of England held such advanced ideas and was not to do so until many years later.

An optimist by nature, Biddle favored the policy of keeping the boom alive. Yet he favored "steady" dividends and he set aside reserves to take care of possible crises. He preferred bills of exchange to local paper and he avoided, although not entirely, accommodation loans. He followed the theory first made popular in England that foreign exchange and the movement of specie should regulate the expansion or contraction of note issue. He therefore kept a close watch on the movement of specie. When gold was in heavy demand, he did not expand his note issues, and thus he cut off the means by which gold could be acquired.

Although his talents in the domestic money market were most impressive, he was even more of a master in the international market. At a time when the United States was still dependent on the London money market, he was well able to hold his own with such experts in international finance as the Baring Brothers and the House of Rothschild. The Barings, in fact, regarded him as an impudent upstart who was too smart for his own good. Their agent, T. W. Ward, said, "The Bank shows a power that should be dreaded." Ward thought it should be saved from its friends, and it is possible that he was right. Similarly, Joshua Bates, the American-born Baring partner, thought that Biddle had a penchant for getting into all sorts of scrapes and that "a straightforward man would be more suitable for that institution." The basis of the Barings' complaint was actually that Biddle took advantage of them in the money market. He overwhelmed them with money when money was easy, and he borrowed heavily through overdrafts when money was tight.

A word of caution is necessary here. We may have given the false impression that as a central banker Biddle was omnipotent. But the Bank was also in a vulnerable position. It also issued notes, some of which came into the hands of the state banks, who would then present them for redemption and put pressure on Biddle's Bank. "Tsar Nicholas," as he was frequently called, recognized this fact and always took it into account.

Biddle's policies increased the Bank's circulation, deposits, loans, and ownership of real estate and stocks. But these policies also increased the specie reserve and kept the amounts due from the state banks at a low figure. Restricted by the Bank's maneuvers, state banks did not quite make the progress they had made before. Yet their combined note issue and deposits did rise from $80 million in 1820 to $117 million in 1830. Biddle made enemies by the score, and many powerful groups regarded him and his bank as dangerous to the economy and to a democratic society. Champions of uncompromising democracy denounced the Bank as an antidemocratic monopoly. The workers, who were beginning to appear in some numbers, disliked all banks and all paper money because their wages were often paid in depreciated currency. Moreover, many farmers were still loyal to the agrarian, hard-money opposition to banks. State bankers, like all debtors, regarded the Bank as an oppressive creditor.[6] When Biddle applied for a new charter in 1832, the antagonism and opposition of the antibank forces led by President Jackson were too strong for him to overcome. The Bank's charter was not renewed, and it ceased to be a central bank, playing out the rest of its days gloriously, ingloriously, and dramatically under a charter from the state of Pennsylvania. With its demise, the state banks experienced a new burst of growth. There were 506 banks in 1834 and 634 in 1837. In the former year, their combined circulation and deposits were $170 million. In three years these liabilities increased by over $100 million, so that in 1837 they totaled over $276 million.

Biddle was a complete banker—a commercial banker, a central banker, and an investment banker. If investment banking is defined to mean providing long-term capital, then all financial intermediaries, especially in early American history, were investment bankers. The stockholder lists of the early textile companies, for example, include the names of 35 commercial banks, 7 savings banks, 5 general insurance companies, 5 brokers, 2 private banks, one life insurance company, and one investment trust (the Massachusetts Hospital Life Insurance Company). But if the term is defined to mean underwriting, refinancing, reorganizing, and protecting the market, then Biddle, as an investment banker, was far ahead of his time. He underwrote an enormous volume of securities for that day and age. He operated as an adviser on financial matters to governments at every level, and he had close contacts in Europe. After the Bank of the United States lost its federal charter, Biddle placed greater emphasis on investment banking. His Bank of the United States of Pennsylvania came to resemble the European institutions that combined commercial banking with large-scale investment banking.

**THE CONTINUED IMPORTANCE OF ENGLAND
IN THE AMERICAN MONEY MARKET** · Biddle's career was all the more remarkable in that the investment banking business in the United States was still nothing more than an adjunct of the London money market. A number of American firms, it is true, were in the picture—Brown Brothers & Co.; Prime, Ward & King; Nevins Townsend & Co.; Astor & Sons; J. L. & S. Josephs. Moreover, Grinnell, Minturn & Co., The Manhattan Co., the Phoenix Bank, and the Morris Canal & Banking Co. also did some investment banking. But all these houses were insignificant in comparison with the Anglo-American firms in England. According to Scoville, "the greatest firm ever known in New York was LeRoy, Bayard & Co.," but the size of their operations could be seen from their holdings of Erie Canal stock in 1821—$50,000.

[6] It has been argued that far from being implacable enemies of the Bank, state bankers came to favor its rechartering. Jean Alexander Wilburn, *Biddle's Bank: The Crucial Years* (New York: Columbia University Press, 1967).

Americans were still accustomed to looking toward England on matters of finance and economics, although this orientation was diminishing toward the end of the period. In 1815 Remsen wrote an analysis of the economy based almost wholly on international factors. "Bills on England," he reported, "have been 12 percent above par, but now 6. This fall may have been from the quantity of cotton shipped and a reduction of discounts made by our banks preparatory to the resumption of specie payments. The amount of specie shipped to England has been immense. . . ." By 1822 it was estimated that the United States owed Europe approximately $50 million: $24 million of the federal debt, $20 million in commercial debt, $3 million of the stock of the Bank of the United States, $2 million in state debt, and another $2 million in state banks and insurance companies.

European houses were interested in the United States for very logical reasons. The United States was the most rapidly advancing underdeveloped country in the world. Europe was still in a state of turmoil, although the end of the Napoleonic wars made it possible for the great merchant banking houses like the Rothschilds and Barings to look for new investment outlets. Then, too, interest rates were double what they were in Europe.

The House of Baring was by far the most important in Anglo-American relations. The Barings first became active in 1815 when they underbid the Dutch firm of Willinck & Van Staphorst on an American issue. Despite their increasing influence, they confined their lending to the federal government and the Bank of the United States until the early 1820s, when they began some small lending to state governments and "quietly" made a loan of £200,000 to the Bank of New York. The Barings' American agent, T. W. Ward, was a man of great ability who kept the partners informed in detail of what was going on in the United States. The house also made it a practice to have an American among the partners.

In the United States, the Barings dealt with the houses of Donnell, Oliver, and Gilmor in Baltimore; Willing and Girard in Philadelphia; Ropes and Perkins in Boston; Goodhue and Grinnell in New York. New England firms counted for over half of Barings' active correspondents, but the Bank of the United States and the firm of Prime, Ward & King in New York were by far the most important in terms of the volume of business. Eventually Prime, Ward & King could draw up to £50,000 before sending specie or securities to cover.

Like most bankers of long reputation, the Barings were conservative in their operations. They thought in terms of "overheating" and "unsustainable economic activity." Consequently, they were in a constant state of trepidation about the status of the American economy, and they contracted their operations severely at the slightest hint of trouble. These contractions, of course, had much influence on the course of the American economy.

THE INFANT SECURITIES MARKET · Conservative European merchant bankers and conservative American private bankers were primarily interested in financing merchandise transactions. But they did deal in federal debt with occasional flurries in state bonds and bank stocks. Whether they liked it or not, exchanges quickly appeared to deal in these securities as well as in others of less dignity. Of course, security dealings went back to colonial times when merchants had bought and sold British issues, but no organized markets existed until after the ratification of the Constitution.

The financing of the Revolution gave an impetus to a domestic securities market. Secretary of the Treasury Hamilton proposed that the debt of $85 million produced by the Revolution be funded into long-term securities. When Congress adopted the Hamilton plan, certain brokers created a market to deal in government securities. In July 1791, for example, McEvers & Barclay sold $180,000 worth of government bonds at auction. Soon thereafter bank stocks began to be bought and sold.

In March 1792 the newspapers announced that A. L. Bleeker, John Pintard, McEvers & Barclay, Cortlandt & Ferrers, and Jay & Sutton had opened a "stock exchange office" at 22 Wall Street and would hold public sales at noon. Two months later, on May 17, 1792, seventeen subscribers agreed to deal in shares for ¼ of 1 percent of the selling price. In 1800 Philadelphia organized a stock exchange, and in 1817 the New York Stock Exchange began its history under the name the New York Stock Exchange Board. Ten years later its list included 19 insurance companies, 12 banks, one canal company, one utility, and assorted government bonds. By then the Boston Stock Exchange listed some manufacturing companies, but it would be another 10 years before an industrial security appeared on the New York Exchange.

When the exchanges were new, stocks were sold by auction. The auctioneer called the name of each "stock" for bids. This procedure would continue until 1875, by which time the invention of the stock ticker had made speedier trading imperative. In the early days, payment for purchases had to be made in 30 days. There was no call-money market as we know it today. Loans were made on securities but, as in Europe, they were time, not demand. One of the reasons why New York surpassed Philadelphia as the country's financial headquarters was that the former created and encouraged a call-money market. Philadelphia did not do so and Boston could not. New York had the advantage that from the beginning its banks were used as depositories by out-of-town banks. The federal government also maintained substantial deposits. These were demand deposits, and their liquidity had to be maintained. Recipients of the government's business, like the Mechanics' Bank and the Manhattan Company, put part of their funds out on demand in the call-money market, from which funds could be liquidated quickly and painlessly. Two words of caution are necessary. First, it should not be inferred that financial specialization appeared suddenly. It would be decades before specialization achieved full stature and before its existence became well recognized. It was not until the middle 1840s that the term "call-money market" would be used to describe demand loans against securities, and the concept would not become common until the late 1850s. Secondly, it is not altogether clear which was cause and which was effect, whether the call-money market acted as a magnet for bankers' balances or whether bankers' balances acted as a stimulus to the creation of a call-money market.

Despite the laborious mechanics of stock dealing, active speculation in government and bank stocks existed as early as the 1790s. Rights to shares in the Bank of the United States rose to $312 and then broke to $150. However, the volume of trading was absurdly low by modern standards. Daily turnover was 100 shares in 1827 and 1,000 in 1830. Then, with "speculative prosperity," average sales in 1835 climbed to 6,000 shares, although volume reached 7,875 shares on one tremendous day. The dullest day in stock market history occurred on March 16, 1830, when 31 shares changed hands: 26 shares in the Bank of the United States were sold at 119 and 5 shares of the Morris Canal & Banking Co. were sold at 74¼. Yet this minute volume of activity is somewhat misleading because far more shares were bought and sold outside than within the exchange. Private bankers like Prime, Ward & King would buy an entire issue or take it on consignment and sell it on the street rather than through the exchanges. Nevertheless, regardless of how they are measured, security transactions were light. Most firms were not large enough or sufficiently well known to go to the stock exchanges. For these people, impromptu arrangements and personal contacts were temporarily satisfactory mechanisms so long as business relations could be conducted in the face-to-face manner that prevailed in a small-town atmosphere. But that day, it was evident, was rapidly coming to an end; by 1830 New York's population was over 200,000, Philadelphia's was over 80,000, and Boston's was over 60,000.

NEW INTERMEDIARIES:
BUILDING AND LOAN, TRUST COMPANIES,

INVESTMENT TRUSTS, SAVINGS BANKS · Somewhat greater activity in the securities market demonstrated the continuous progress of the financial intermediaries, both absolutely and in proportion to national assets and national savings. Even more convincing evidence was given by the appearance of several new financial intermediaries: building and loan associations, trust companies, the investment trust, and savings banks. The first building and loan association was the Oxford Provident Building Association, formed in a suburb of Philadelphia in early 1831. Its object was to furnish a safe method of saving and a means of securing mortgage money at a reasonable rate of interest. The Oxford Association was apparently a decade ahead of its time, for building associations were not to show any significant growth until the 1840s. The other three intermediaries, however, quickly achieved substantial importance in the financial community.

In February 1822 the New York State Legislature granted a charter to the Farmers' Fire Insurance and Loan Company with a capital of $1,500,-000, of which $500,000 was actually paid in. The person chiefly responsible for this new company was John T. Champlin, a member of the merchant and shipping house of Minturn and Champlin. The company was authorized to make loans on real estate, to grant annuities, to hold stock, and to write fire insurance, but it was not permitted to do any deposit or discount business. All these powers were being commonly granted to insurance companies at that time. What made the company distinctive was that in April the Legislature gave it the power "to assume and execute any trust which has been, or may be, created by any deed as aforesaid."

The trust idea goes far back in history. In England, for example, Richard III held so many trusts that the whole law on fiefs had to be rewritten when he came to the throne. The device was also well known in the East, for in 1829 a group of Philadelphia financiers proposed to add trusteeship to their activities, their attention being drawn to the "remarkable success of what are called in India agency houses—concerns organized to transact business for trustees." What was unusual about the Farmers' Loan and Trust Company, as it was renamed in 1836, was that it was the first corporation in the United States, and probably the world, to have trust powers.[7] As the Farmers' Loan argued:

> The public will readily perceive, that the advantages of this Company to protect property for the benefit of infants or others, or to answer any special purposes, either of a public or private nature, are far greater than those of individual executors or other trustees, who are always liable to casualties, which no foresight can guard against or prevent; as the numerous and frequent applications to the court of chancery for filling up of vacancies occasioned by death, insolvencies or other causes, most incontestibly show: and the expenses of such proceedings often swallow up a great part of the Trust Estate.

But it would be a long time before the company used its trust powers to any great extent. In its early years, it operated with utmost conservatism. One of its original objectives was the making of agricultural loans. As a general rule, it made no loan of over $10,000 on country security and never for more than one-half the appraised value, not including buildings. Some loans were for as little as $400. Up until 1835 the largest loan was for $30,000.

THE MASSACHUSETTS HOSPITAL
LIFE INSURANCE COMPANY · The most unusual financial institution to appear in the early nineteenth century was the Massachusetts Hospital Life Insurance Company (MHLI), which was chartered in 1818 but began to conduct business in 1823. The company was somewhat similar to a trust company, but the funds deposited were commingled rather than kept as separate trusts, and it was, therefore, more like a modern investment trust. Like all other pioneer financial institutions, it exhibited the influence of the early merchants and capitalists. Ebenezer Francis, the moving spirit in the company's formation, was a director of the Boston Bank and later the first president of the Suffolk Bank. William Phillips, first president of MHLI, was also president of the Massachusetts Bank and the Provident Institution for

---

7 The first company to have the word "trust" in its title was the New York Life Insurance and Trust Company (1830). The first company organized to act as an executor and trustee was the United States Trust Company (1854).

Savings. In its first one hundred years, one-third of its officers and directors came from eighteen proper Bostonian families. As its biographer said, the institution performed a service function for Massachusetts merchant families.

The trust, for that is what it was, charged a fee of ½ of 1 percent on the principal. It never advertised and it was never an aggressive marketeer. Nathaniel Bowditch, its first actuary and the man most responsible for its early phenomenal success, called it "a species of savings bank for the rich and middle class." It did not take deposits of less than $500 or for less than five years, and it discouraged the business of anyone who had the talent to take care of his own estate.

Although ostensibly in the life insurance business, MHLI insured few lives. Between 1823 and 1831, it insured 22 students, 16 merchants, 12 teachers, 9 clerks, 7 lawyers, 6 clergymen, 4 brokers, 4 cashiers, and 14 others, including blacksmiths, auctioneers, physicians, manufacturers, and bookbinders. All 94 people were insured for small sums. Yet despite the sparsity of its insurance business, the company was the largest financial institution of its day. In 1838 it was one-sixth as large as all thirty-two Boston commercial banks combined. Its resources were half again as large as those of the twenty-eight savings banks in Massachusetts. But then its growth atrophied. By the 1860s, a point in time a little later than this chapter, it was only one-eleventh as large as the commercial banks and one-sixth the size of the savings banks. Yet it had been so big that as late as 1900 it was still the fifth largest financial firm in the country. It managed to achieve its unique position by providing funds in volume to the infant Massachusetts manufactures and by astute investment decisions.

By its charter, it agreed to contribute one-third of its net earnings to maintain the Massachusetts General Hospital. However, New England families poured so much of their accumulated savings into the institution that it managed to maintain the hospital as well as much of the textile industry. It was the most important single source of intermediate-term credit for New England manufactures. In the thirty-seven years between 1823 and 1860, it loaned $40 million to 42 firms. In 1825, 65 percent of its assets were invested in real estate, and another 32 percent in personal security. By 1835 only 50 percent was in real estate and almost 40 percent was loaned on the personal security of businessmen.

The record of the Massachusetts Hospital Life Insurance Company was extremely impressive. The best example of its great success was the Franklin Fund. By his will, Benjamin Franklin left a share of his estate to be accumulated for one hundred years. Then after a distribution of part of the proceeds, the remainder was to be accumulated for another hundred years. Part of the Franklin Fund—$10,000 in 1827 and $5,950 more between 1827 and 1865—was deposited in the MHLI. In 1894 the City of Boston received $329,300. In December 1931 it got another $423,661, and in 1937 it received $50,000. This situation was a testimonial to astute investment as well as a demonstration of the miracle of compound interest.

The MHLI also acted as a model for other trust companies, including the New York Life Insurance and Trust (1830), the Ohio Life Insurance and Trust (1834), the Girard Life Insurance and Trust (1836), and the Rhode Island Hospital Trust Company (1867). The New York Life[8] was also the creature of prominent New York men who were active in other financial institutions, including John Jacob Astor, Nathan Prime, Philip Hone, Peter Lorillard, and Gulian Verplanck.

If it was so successful, why did it decline so drastically? The answer is that it was not interested in growth. It made no investments and took no deposits from outside of Massachusetts, nor would it take deposits from other than financial incompetents. In addition, as competition increased, the 6 percent return allowed by Massachusetts seemed too meager to enterprising investors.

THE ORIGIN OF SAVINGS BANKS · In the early nineteenth century, investment banking and the securities markets were definitely for the rich—that is, for those who could afford to take risks and to speculate. Middle-income groups were not supposed to engage in buying and selling securities, and the poor certainly could not. Similarly, the Massachusetts Hospital Life Insurance Company, known as "the Great Savings Bank," was designed for the rich and the well-born, not for the poor, nor even for the middle class, despite Bowditch's statement.

Nevertheless, the sanctity of thrift was deeply ingrained in the American character. Everything, it was held, should be done to encourage habits of saving among all income classes, the poor as well as the affluent. And the financial entrepreneurs of the day, with their urge for comprehensiveness, were eager to do what they could to persuade lower-income groups to save. It was thought that the best way for the poor to rise from poverty was by saving part of their income. But the motives of philanthropy were not wholly eleemosynary. Those who wished to encourage saving among the "indigent poor" were not unmindful of the possibility that ways and means of assisting the poor to rise above their station would reduce the burden of poor relief for the most affluent.

Using the European and English experiments in providing a depository for the savings of the poor as a model, groups of benevolent citizens who were active in each of the financial communities of the four Atlantic ports banded together to establish savings banks.

New York, Philadelphia, and Boston each has a claim to innovation in savings banking. The first proposal to establish a savings bank in the United States seems to have been made by Thomas Eddy, a New York insurance broker. In April 1816 he received a letter from a friend in London calling attention to the formation there of a "provident institution or savings bank." Under Eddy's leadership, a group of leading New York citizens drew up a constitution and elected a set of officers and directors, of whom at least five were intimately connected with commercial banks. The directors appointed De Witt Clinton chairman of a committee to obtain

8 Now part of the Bank of New York.

a charter from the New York State Legislature, but despite the prestige and influence of the committee, the Legislature in 1817 rejected the application "in consequence of the principles not being distinctly comprehended and the preponderating objection against the incorporation of any more banks, with which, not only this, but almost every state in the Union were inundated, whereby serious consequences were apprehended." It was suggested that instead of establishing a new bank, the business of savings banking be handled as a sideline of an existing commercial bank.

In short, the petition had been rejected because it had aroused the opposition of the antibank group. But in the next year, the "Society for the Prevention of Pauperism in the City of New York" applied for a charter, which was granted in 1819 to the Bank for Savings in the City of New York "to ameliorate the condition of the poorer classes."

In Philadelphia, in 1816, another group of financiers led by Condy Raguet, president of the Pennsylvania Company for Insurances on Lives, each contributed $10 to a fund of $250 to start a savings institution. Taking a lesson from New York, they deliberately avoided the use of the word "bank." Instead they petitioned for and received a charter for the Philadelphia Saving Fund Society, a "benevolent institution . . . to aid and assist the poor and middling classes of society in putting their money out to advantage."

The third claimant to being the first savings bank, the Provident Institution for Savings in the Town of Boston, was founded by a group of merchants, including William Phillips of the Massachusetts Bank, Josiah Quincy, and John Lowell.

At first savings banks conducted themselves according to their originally expressed objective of providing a depository for the savings of the poor. Some banks restricted the size of deposits and some paid graduated interest rates. In Philadelphia the size of individual deposits was restricted by law. Indeed, in 1823, some depositors were asked to withdraw part of their balances because they had come to exceed the legal maximum. The Baltimore Savings Bank limited deposits to $10 a week. In its first years the Provident Institution limited deposits to $100. The Bowery Savings Bank paid 5 percent on accounts of less than $500 and 4 percent on larger ones.

Actually, the savings bank business in its first years was regarded as a sideline of more important finance. All the pioneer institutions were founded by men who were active entrepreneurs in insurance and commercial banking. Investment policies also clearly demonstrated the ancillary nature of savings banking, for they emphasized what was considered to be safe, secure, and solvent. New York State did not permit real estate loans until 1830. In the first few years, therefore, funds were concentrated in government obligations and in commercial bank deposits. The Bank for Savings held 30 percent of Erie Canal stock, really a government enterprise, in 1821. Eventually it was to own $1 million of the stock. The Philadelphia Saving Fund also invested mostly in governments. But all savings banks relied on commercial banks. The Bowery Savings Bank deposited all of its first accounts in the Butchers and Drovers Bank, the directors of which had created the Bowery. In Massachusetts, where government restrictions were much more liberal and permitted funds to be invested at "best advantage," the savings banks, nevertheless, depended so much on the commercial banks that they came to be regarded as nothing more than adjuncts of the latter.

The financiers who founded the first savings banks continued to manage them for a few years, but gradually their decision-making functions were turned over to professional managers. Since mutual savings banks could not make profits, these new managers tended to view growth as their prime business objective. However, it soon appeared that savings banking offered little prospect for growth so long as it concentrated on the poor, for although some of the poor, especially domestic servants, did save, their skimpy incomes did not permit them to save very much. Consequently, the original goal of helping "to ameliorate the condition of the indigent poor" was more and more de-emphasized, and savings banks became a financial intermediary catering to anyone in any income group who was more concerned with safety than with growth. How quickly this transformation away from the poor took place was evidenced by one of the items of intelligence in Henry Remsen's letters to his son. "Gardner Andrew," wrote the merchant and banker in 1828, "has more than $250 in the savings bank and is therefore comparatively wealthy."

Gradually the restrictions on investments and on deposits were broken down, and although all banks did not participate with equal alacrity in the change, it could be said that savings banking in the late twenties was much different from what it had been before 1820. In 1824 Pennsylvania repealed the restriction on the size of deposits, and by 1828 the Philadelphia Saving Fund Society had 206 accounts of over $500 and 29 with accrued interest of $1,000 or more. In 1830 New York permitted real estate investments.

One manifestation of the departure from the objective of providing service for the "indigent poor" was an extension of business hours. In the early years, banks were open only a few hours a week, for example, on Monday and Thursday from 9 A.M. to 11 A.M. By 1835 hours had been extended to 9–1 and 3–7 on Mondays and Thursdays.

Bank managers also began to move out of government obligations and more and more into loans based on "securities" and loans based on "personal security."[9] The Philadelphia Saving Fund began to make three-month loans on a restricted list of securities. The Baltimore Bank had almost three-quarters of its assets in security and personal security loans in 1825. These loans were concentrated among a small group of merchants, including Alexander Brown, John S. Gettings, and Johns Hopkins. Similarly, in Massachusetts, loans on personal security took about one-quarter of assets in 1835.

Under the impetus of changed objectives and the more aggressive policy thereby permitted, savings banks experienced a significant growth after 1825. In 1820 ten savings banks with 8,635 depositors held somewhat

---

9 "Security" loans were made against securities as collateral; loans on "personal security" had no *special* collateral. In early banking statistics, it is not easy to segregate one from the other.

over $1.1 million in deposits, an average of $130 per depositor. By 1825 the number of depositors had increased to 16,931 in 15 banks. By 1835 there were 52 banks with 60,058 depositors holding $10.6 million in deposits, an average of $175 each. But the business was very unevenly distributed; New York had over half the total deposits and one bank held about three-quarters of the New York total.

INSURANCE IN THE EARLY NINETEENTH CENTURY · The insurance business continued to rival commercial banking and savings banking in importance among financial intermediaries. As late as 1820 it was said that the capital of New York State insurance companies exceeded by a small amount the state's total commercial bank capital.

As had been the case in the early period, life insurance lagged far behind general insurance. In fact, the business really did not exist as such. It was a minor sideline of trust companies that wrote life insurance on a nonrenewable term basis. Up to 1836 the various states had chartered 25 companies that had the power to insure lives. Eight had gone out of business, leaving a net of 17 with a reported total of $2.8 million in force. The total amount was undoubtedly larger, for no figures are available for such venerable institutions as the Presbyterian Ministers' Fund and the Episcopal Corporation. Nevertheless, it is still true that life insurance would be a sideline of the more lucrative and the more attractive trust business for another decade. Indicative of this situation is that one company, the New York Life and Trust Company, wrote $1.9 million of the $2.8 million total life insurance. The Pennsylvania Company had only $700,000 in force and MHLI only $300,000.

General insurance, marine and fire, continued to occupy the center of the stage up to about 1860. In 1830 there were 8 marine insurance companies in New York City with $3 million in capital and 20 fire insurance companies (16 of which had been founded after 1815), capitalized at $7.8 million. At around the same time, there were 48 insurance companies in Massachusetts (29 of which were in Boston), capitalized at $9.4 million.

The fire insurance companies, especially in New York City, were dealt a severe blow by the city's great fire of 1835. Most of the companies in New York went into bankruptcy, and it would be many years before the industry fully recovered. By then, however, the marine insurance companies would be experiencing really "hard times," but that is a story for another chapter.

FINANCIAL INSTITUTIONS AND THE ECONOMY · Discussions involving the interrelationship of financial intermediaries and the economy in the twenty years between the end of the War of 1812 and the panic of 1836 have always concentrated on two things: the rise and fall in economic activity and the rise and fall of the Bank of the United States. It is only natural that this should be the case, for booms and busts in this period were particularly evident, and, among the intermediaries, the Bank of the United States clearly monopolized the limelight.

A jolting recession followed the inflation of the War of 1812. Then came alternating periods of prosperity and recession, culminating in the great boom of the early 1830s and the devastating panic of 1837. It has been traditional to assign the Bank of the United States the midwife's role in these economic ups and downs. Its sheer size, its strategic position in the money market, the personality of its last president, and its battle with the Jackson administration inevitably made it the center of attention in one of the most dramatic and melodramatic periods in financial history. Just as today's students of the money market concentrate on the behavior of the Federal Reserve, so historians have concentrated on the Bank of the United States.

The analysis runs somewhat as follows. At the end of the War of 1812, the economy was overloaded with state bank notes, and the price level was twice as high as it had been before the war. The Bank of the United States was created to bring this inflation to an end. At first it did nothing, thereby allowing an overstimulated economy to become further stimulated. Then in 1819 it overacted. It cut off the flow of credit, precipitating a severe depression. When the economy recovered, the Bank, under Biddle's leadership, kept it from overheating by imposing a tight rein on the expansion of the state banks. This ideal state of affairs could have continued indefinitely, so the argument runs, but the Jackson administration ended it by vetoing the bill to recharter the Bank. When the Bank ceased to be the fiscal agent of the government, it also ceased to be a central bank, and it could no longer control the state banks. Freed to do as they pleased, the state banks indulged their paper money mania, and the economy embarked on a "speculative orgy" of "unsustainable growth."

So goes the oft-repeated story of the 1830s, but traditional though it is, it is not the whole truth. The influence of the first and even the second Bank of the United States, although important, can nevertheless be exaggerated. Neither the Bank nor Biddle was omnipotent. Their powers were limited by the restraints imposed by the international money and capital markets. Then, too, the Bank's powers over the private banks and other intermediaries were exerted only indirectly and thus with weakened force. Finally, the Bank's powers were somewhat vitiated by the fact that it also issued bank notes and thereby became a debtor of the state banks, just as the state banks were its debtors. Any number could play the game of note redemption, and the state banks were not averse to applying embarrassing pressures to the central bank.

All this discussion adds up to the conclusion that the Bank's powers as a central banker were more limited than those of the modern central bank. However, aside from the question of how much power the Bank had, the Bank and Biddle did not wield what powers they did have in the way that has been described in the conventional analysis. The usual description implies that Biddle and the Bank held the money supply in check, but this allegation is not true. The money supply fluctuated widely, for it was not the *money supply* on which the banks focused their attention, but the *reserve ratio*.[10] The whole commercial banking system in the United

---

[10] In the contemporary difference of opinion over monetary policy, the critics of the Federal Reserve System make the same charge—that the System concentrates its attention on "free reserves" instead of on the money supply.

States and in England tried to adjust its policies to the yardstick of bank reserves. Commercial banks paid more attention to their reserves than to their customers' clamor for loans. The Bank of England watched the inflow and outflow of gold and lowered or raised its discount rate accordingly. Biddle was equally sensitive to the reserve ratio. His objective in regulating the state banks was not to control the stock of money but to keep "every bank" in a position where it would "always be ready to provide for its notes."

Nothing in Biddle's program prevented the money supply from increasing or decreasing sharply. If reserves went up, the money supply could also go up without becoming a cause of alarm. In the 1830s, a series of events resulted in a substantial inflow of gold and silver.[11] The balance of trade was, of course, against the United States, as it is against all young and developing countries. But in the balance of payments, the adverse balance of trade was more than compensated for by shipping and by an outflow of securities. This favorable balance of payments brought in a steady flow of specie, which was helped not insignificantly when President Jackson's administration devalued the gold dollar in 1834.

As specie flowed in, reserves rose, and the banks, including Biddle's Bank, took advantage of what seemed so favorable a turn of events by greatly expanding the money supply. This expansion of the money supply produced the fuel that stoked the furnace of increased spending, and the economy embarked on a major boom. Viewed from the point of view of today's monetary theory and today's notions of correct monetary policy, the Bank of the United States was more a passive than an active central bank.

If what has been said in the preceding paragraph is true, Jackson's veto of the Bank was not as disastrous as has often been thought. The boom, which many have assumed led to the bust, would have occurred whether the Bank of the United States had or had not survived.

Does this mean that Jackson's veto of the recharter was a good thing? Not at all. There is no simple answer to that complicated question. The Bank was undoubtedly a large and powerful institution with considerable influence, whether that influence has been exaggerated or not. The fight against the Bank was, therefore, an early example of trust busting, of small business against big business, and of the masses against the few. In another sense, however, it represented states rights versus federalism, free local banking against the restraints of central banking, and laissez faire against monopoly. Whether one supports Jackson or the Bank depends primarily on the relative importance one places on social values as against economic values. It also depends on one's attitude toward "rule by men" as opposed to "rule by the marketplace," and whether or not one believes that economic growth is best advanced by giving enterprise as much encouragement as possible. Those who believe that big business is bad regardless of any possible economic justification would support

---

[11] Cotton exports and British investment brought specie from England, silver came in from Mexico, and the outflow of silver to China ceased. All this has been explained in Peter Temin, *The Jacksonian Economy* (New York: Norton, 1969).

Jackson's side in the Bank war. So, too, would those who believe that because man is essentially a fallible animal, it is better not to give great power to any individual, even so talented an individual as Biddle. In Jackson's camp would also be those who believe that the Bank restricted the flow of credit and thus hobbled enterprise.

But the consensus would still support the Bank. The majority believe that the economy, if left to itself, will inevitably produce overheating and unsustainable growth, which must by equal inevitability produce recession and depression. Consequently, those who believe in stability and "leaning against the wind" must support the Bank in the interest of consistency; and most people, for good or ill, support the notion of stability and "leaning against the wind."

4 · accelerated growth, 1836–1860

The nature of the forces that shaped, encouraged, and discouraged the formation and growth of financial intermediaries changed very little over the course of the nineteenth century. They did vary in magnitude. At times they acted as a lodestone and at other times as an accelerator, but they were still the same forces. With the entrepreneur acting as protagonist to make the decisions and to call the turns, such factors as population growth, the pace of the national income, the progress of technology, urbanization, the westward movement, the trend toward increasing specialization, and the ever more widespread division of labor were the forces that influenced the rise of financial intermediaries and the speed at which they traveled.

THE ECONOMY, 1836–1860 · During the years 1836 to 1860, the population of the United States more than doubled from approximately 15 million to over 30 million. Much of this growth took place in the West. In 1830 approximately 2 million people lived in New England, half a million more than lived in the East North Central states. Thirty years later, by contrast, the East North Central area contained almost 7 million compared with 3 million living in New England. More people, more widely dispersed over the country was a fundamental cause of the continuous erosion of the face-to-face direct financing that had been reasonably satisfactory when the country was new and the economy was comparatively primitive.

Although more widely dispersed, the total population was also becoming more concentrated within urban pockets. From 1820 to 1850, city population grew at the fastest rate in American history. In 1800 only six cities had populations of more than 10,000 and only 3 percent of the total population lived in them. By 1860 one out of eight Americans lived in the 93 cities with over 10,000 population. Spreading urbanization encouraged intermediation just as did the growth in population.

That financial intermediaries would grow was a foregone conclusion. The real question was, how fast would they grow? The answer depended on the pace at which the economy grew. The faster the rate of economic growth, the more accelerated would be the pace of institutional growth.

Estimates of how much the economy grew in the first half of the nineteenth century vary widely. A Massachusetts statistician writing in *Hunt's* magazine calculated that taxable property rose from $45 million in 1790 to $300 million in 1840. Per capita wealth climbed from about $100 to approximately $400; a figure that "seems to be small, but in reality is larger than the average in almost any other state in the Union." More recent estimates, such as those made by Professor Robert Gallman, imply that national output increased approximately 2½ times between 1839 and 1859. But, as always, the path was not smooth; at times it was very rocky indeed. The period opened with a severe depression that lasted until 1843. As late as 1846, high-grade securities were selling at 79 to 90 percent less than their price in 1836. Bankruptcy was one of the most common forms of activity. Nine out of eleven Philadelphia insurance firms failed; almost all the investment banking houses collapsed; and 160 commercial banks were liquidated. At the same time, the depression slowed the rate of population growth, the westward movement, and the pace of urbanization.

Contemporaries, attempting to explain what had happened, relied mostly on the escalator theory, stressing speculation and overheating and condemning banks and paper money as the chief culprits. A writer in *Hunt's Merchants' Magazine* in May 1850 recalled that the thirties were a decade of "extraordinary speculation," when growth rested more on credit than on saving. The resulting depression was "inevitable." By contrast, he found the forties a decade in which the pace of economic growth did not outrun the rate of saving. "The exertions of enterprise," he said, "have been directed to production. . . . Lending concerns have not been increased, but mines and factories have drawn largely upon available capital." Henry Remsen, whose correspondence always touched on the important matters of the day, blamed the depression chiefly on "the general extravagance of the inhabitants . . . the overissue of bank bills . . . the multiplication of banks."

After a period of some progress in the forties and fifties, the United States again dropped into a depression in 1857. Once more "overheating," to use a modern word, was blamed. A lengthy article in *Hunt's* held that the causes of this new economic calamity were

> first, excessive imports . . . the accumulation of large foreign debts, and the exportation of large amounts of specie. . . . Secondly, the immense amount invested in railroads—much more than our country was able to afford. . . . Thirdly, extensive speculations in stocks. . . . Fourthly, the large amount of loans made upon the pledge of stocks and bonds. . . . Holders of railroad stocks and bonds probably number more than 200,000. . . . Thousands of holders purchased them on speculation, with borrowed means and pledged them as security in many instances for moneys payable on demand. . . . Fifthly, the more immediate cause of the panic is the operation of the electro telegraph.[1]

THE ROLE OF TECHNOLOGY:
THE TELEGRAPH AND THE RAILROAD

Technological progress was a vital factor in the economic growth of the period, and it also starred in the building of financial intermediaries. A writer in *Hunt's* in January 1843 remarked on the "increasing tendency to reside in towns and cities . . . growing out of the combined agency of steam power and machinery." Two innovations were especially important—the railroad and the telegraph.

[1] *Hunt's Merchants' Magazine*, December 1857, p. 660.

The telegraph was considered so important that some people, as we have noted, ascribed to it a vital role in the business cycle. As a demander of capital funds, it was undoubtedly important, for by 1860 its invested capital had passed $100 million. However, its importance in facilitating communication was even greater. It was the first mechanism, aside from smoke signals, that separated communication from transportation.

The railroad industry, especially after 1850, had an even more voracious appetite for capital. Professor Albert Fishlow has estimated that railroad investment in dollars of constant purchasing power averaged $12.4 million a year in the decade 1834–1843 and $40.7 million in 1844–1853. It then boomed to an average of $70.3 million in the years 1849–1858. Second only to agriculture as a consumer of capital funds, the railroad accounted for 10 percent of gross capital formation in the 1830s and 1840s and 15 percent in the 1850s.[2]

There is another way of expressing how important the railroads were in the financial community. Before 1850 only 2 roads were capitalized at over $10 million, but 10 had a greater capital in 1855, and half of these had issued approximately $20 million in stocks and bonds. By contrast, in 1850 only 41 textile mills had a capital of $250,000 or more.

Together with the multiplying population and the flow West and to the urban centers, technology made possible constantly greater division of labor. This spreading specialization could be seen in the occupation statistics, poor as they are for these years.

The census of 1820 contained little data on what people did for a living, but three comprehensive classifications were discernible: agriculture, manufacturing, and commerce. By 1840 the breakdown had added navigation and the professions, and in 1850 a few more were included. In 1860, 60 percent of the labor force was still in agriculture and another 20 percent built and manned the factories; but 8 percent was in trade, and the rest provided the services—education, the professions, government, and domestics. An intricate financial structure accompanied the increasingly intricate occupational structure, for specialization in one meant and required specialization in the other.

A contemporary writer in the May 1847 issue of *Hunt's* summed up what an advancing level of living and a more complicated way of working meant to commercial banks. He estimated that paper money circulation per capita had multiplied five times. Asked what this increase meant, he answered, "The people have come into the habit of buying more than they used to and they have become more dependent upon others than they formerly were."

A PERIOD OF CONSOLIDATION IN
FINANCIAL INTERMEDIATION · Unlike the previous era, the years between the depression of 1836 and the Civil War did not produce any new financial intermediaries. It was a period of integration, when the institutions that had been formed in the previous two generations succeeded in

[2] Albert Fishlow, *American Railroads and the Transformation of the Ante-Bellum Economy* (Cambridge, Mass.: Harvard University Press, 1965), pp. 303–310.

establishing themselves more firmly in the economic environment. Direct financing, however, continued to be immensely important in the capital and money markets. By the 1840s the country could boast or bemoan a large number of great fortunes, some of which were old and some new. There are some private records that reveal how these wealthy families managed their savings. One family that had inherited extensive real estate made bank deposits of $22,267 in 1849. Of this amount, $16,308 apparently was income and the remainder was the proceeds from land sales. About 9 percent of the income came from securities, another small fraction came from rents on buildings, and the bulk resulted from rents on unimproved land and from mortgages. During the fifties, the family gradually shifted its investments away from unimproved land into houses, buildings, and, to a smaller extent, securities. By 1857 total deposits were $68,415, of which $63,787 was income. Approximately 10 percent of the total income was derived from insurance, bank, and railroad securities.

TABLE 1
Growth of Intermediaries, 1836–1860 (Millions of Dollars)

Year	Commercial Banks			Savings Bank Deposits	Life Insurance Assets	General Insurance Assets	Building and Loan Shares
	No.	Assets	Deposits				
1836	713	$ 622.0	$166	$ 10.6	negligible	n.a.	n.a.
1860	1,562	1,000.0	310	149.3	24.1	80.6	n.a.

Source: U.S. Department of Commerce, *Historical Statistics of the United States: Colonial Times to 1957;* general insurance assets calculated from annual year-end reports by property insurance companies to insurance commissioners of seven states.

As illustrated in Table 1, the assets of all institutions soared upward in the years after the depression of 1837. The number of banks doubled and their assets rose by one-third. Savings bank deposits multiplied almost fifteen times. Life insurance in force did even better, expanding almost one hundred times. Marine insurance was the only financial business that had fallen on evil days, but its decline was more than offset among the general insurance companies by the growth of fire insurance. Investment banking also demonstrated an erratic career. Severely damaged by the panic of 1836, it recovered strongly in subsequent years.

As the national income billowed upward, the dollar volume of saving also grew, even though the rate of saving remained fairly stable. Savers were, moreover, participating much more actively in financial institutions simply because the institutions were there and were more convenient. Very few people had checking accounts, but over 270,000 people in New York and over 200,000 in Massachusetts had a savings account in 1860, which meant that one in 18 of the whole population in these states had a savings account. The stock of the Merrimac Company, a textile firm, was owned by 390 holders, including 68 females, 52 retired businessmen, 40 clerks, students and "unspecified," 18 physicians, and 15 farmers.

THE DEMAND FOR CAPITAL FUNDS FOR
FINANCING INTERNAL IMPROVEMENTS · The growth of population and the march to the cities forced the municipalities and the state governments to provide such services as street paving and lighting, water supply, sewerage, and garbage removal, that were unneeded and unknown in rural areas. These undertakings, in turn, required capital funds, most of which were raised by selling bonds through investment bankers. Excellent examples abound. In the late 1830s and early 1840s, New York City built the Croton reservoir and aqueduct. The project raised the city's debt from $5 million to $9 million. At the same time, Boston spent $5 million to construct municipal works, and Baltimore loaned $4 million to railroads, all of which was typical of the purposes for which cities were borrowing money. By 1860 municipal debt, which had been about $25 million in 1843, had climbed to $200 million.[3]

States borrowed to help build canals, railroads, and banks; to construct universities, hospitals, and statehouses; and to control riots. State debt, $170 million in 1838, was over $250 million by 1860, or four times as much as the federal debt. Pennsylvania was far ahead of all the others with a debt of over $40 million. New York, Ohio, Illinois, Louisiana, Maryland, and Virginia each owed $11 million or more. There was much opposition to the expenditures that gave rise to these debts, and it was widely recognized that increased spending was adding significantly to the business of the intermediaries. A contemporary commentator struck a popular theme when he said, "Partisan leaders have sought to strengthen their constituency by advocating local expenditures, nominally for public purposes, but really for the private advantage of hosts of contractors, bankers, stock-jobbers, brokers, and petty office-holders."

THE RISING IMPORTANCE OF THE
COMMERCIAL PAPER MARKET · The commercial paper business, which had always occupied an important position in American trade, underwent a series of significant changes in the decades surrounding the Civil War. These changes could be grouped under two headings: those that were associated with the general growth of the economy and the country's continuous geographical expansion and those that were induced by the transformation of the prevalent methods of distributing goods.

Early in the century, a middleman had appeared to create a market in commercial paper. He came with the first banks and the first note brokers. Then, as the country's trade and territory expanded and the scale of operations broadened, middlemen became specialized and began to buy and sell commercial paper instead of acting as brokers. Private bankers bought and sold paper far away from home. The house of S. & M. Allen and its successor, E. W. Clark & Co., for example, roamed far to the West and South to pick up commercial paper. To a more limited extent, commercial bankers also went beyond their borders to pick up attractive investments. This geographic expansion and functional specialization

---

[3] The leaders were Philadelphia, New Orleans, Baltimore, New York, and Boston.

meant that the commercial paper business was becoming organized and established. As the *Bankers' Magazine* described it in 1850,

> Formerly no person went into the street for loans, except he was pressed for funds, or wished to rid himself of doubtful assets, and the notes thus offered were hawked around privately, until some capitalist was tempted to make the purchase. Now at some of the principal brokers every name has its price, and the holder may dispose of his bill at once, or limit it and leave it for the inspection of purchasers.

Two other changes of equal importance came in the 1850s, when the great advancement of transportation, the use of the credit agency, and the spread of country banking encouraged longer-sighted wholesalers and jobbers to send salesmen out to the retailer rather than to wait for the retailer to come to them, as had been the custom in earlier periods. Among other things, this step made it possible to buy in smaller lots. The whole evolution brought two profound innovations in commercial paper. The terms of credit were shortened because faster transportation speeded the whole process of distribution. At the same time, because of the credit agency, trade bills declined, giving place to single-name promissory notes rather than the two-name acceptances that had previously been the chief document in short-term credit.

The Civil War gave an impetus to the trend toward shortening credit terms and replacing two-name paper with single-name notes. Two of the by-products of the war—political uncertainty and rapid currency depreciation—made long-term credit an extremely hazardous adventure. In order to avoid it, wholesalers offered their customers attractive discounts for rapid payment. To take advantage of these discounts, retailers borrowed on their own name in the open market and were encouraged to do so by their bankers.

THE CONTINUED IMPORTANCE OF ENGLISH

MERCHANT BANKERS Foreign bankers continued to occupy a primary position in American finance, although by the end of the period their relative importance was showing some signs of decline. As shown in Table 2, it was estimated in 1853 that they owned almost 20 percent of American debts and equities. Britain was far and away the most important creditor, accounting for at least three-quarters of the total. In addition, it had a substantial amount invested in short-term credit to finance American international trade. Cautious as ever, foreign bankers continued to concentrate in government bonds, but they were beginning to deal in a few private issues, especially railroad bonds.

The most important of all foreign bankers in the American market were the seven English merchant banking firms[4] known as the Anglo-American houses. Of these, Baring Brothers was especially important.[5] Indeed, it is

---

[4] Baring Brothers Co., Timothy Wiggin & Co., George Wildes & Co., Thomas Wilson & Co., Morrison, Cryder & Co., William & James Brown & Co., and F. de Lizardi & Co.

[5] "There are six powers in Europe," said a phrase-coining diplomat, "Great Britain, France, Russia, Austria, Prussia, and the Baring Brothers."

TABLE 2
Foreign Holdings of American Debts and Equities, 1853
(Millions of Dollars)

Type of Holding	Total	Foreign Owned	Percent Foreign Owned
U.S. governments	$ 58.2	$ 27.0	46
State governments	190.7	111.0*	58
Local governments	93.3	21.5	23
Railroad bonds	170.1	43.9	26
Bank and insurance stocks	279.6†	7.1	3
Railroad stocks	309.9	8.0	3
Canals and navigation	58.0	2.5	4
Miscellaneous	18.8	1.1	6
Total	$1,178.6	$222.1	18

Source: Report of the Secretary of the Treasury, 33rd Cong., 1st Sess., Executive Document No. 42, March 2, 1854.
* *State officials reported $72.9 million; Winslow Lanier & Co. reported $111.0.*
† *$266.7 million in bank stock; $12.9 million in insurance.*

not too much to say that in this era the Bank of England and the Barings had a more potent influence on the American economy than did any American house, including the Bank of the United States. In fact, the behavior of the Bank of the United States itself depended largely on the actions of the English bankers. The decade of the thirties with its boom, panic, abortive recovery, and sustained depression impressively demonstrated this dependence.

Fed by an unusual amount of investment spending and a substantial growth in the money supply, the American economy quickened in the early 1830s. As the boom developed, the English merchant bankers occupied a strategic role in bringing investors and savers together. They bought bonds for their British clients, and even more important, they financed the import and export trade.

The Barings, by far the largest firm in the trade, were also the most conservative. As early as 1832 they became convinced that business "was not likely to be profitable for the coming few years and the utmost caution was in order." Therefore, they began to restrict their commitments and contracted very stringently in the last quarter of 1835. What they refused to take, however, the other houses snapped up. For most of the Anglo-American bankers, it was a day of great optimism, and they expanded their credits to the United States with enthusiasm concerning the present and complacence about the future. In the three years beginning in January 1834, the acceptances of just three of the houses rose from £2.4 million to £5.6 million. When the boom reached its peak in 1836, United States mercantile debt to England was estimated at £20 million.

In July and August 1836, the Bank of England, alarmed by the decline of its reserves, raised the discount rate to 5 percent. What was more important, it refused to discount American paper or to make loans against American securities any longer. Of course, the money market tightened perceptibly both in England and in the United States. Interest rates jumped sharply. The discount rate for first-class paper in Boston and New

York was 5 percent in January 1835, 10 percent in December, and 36 percent in October 1836. Commodity prices at first held fast but then deteriorated rapidly. Cotton, by far the most important American export, fell 25 percent in late 1836 and early 1837.

By December 1836 the American and British economies were clearly rushing toward disaster, but the Bank of England and the Barings kept a tight rein on the money market. In December 1836 Wiggin & Co. admitted that it was in severe trouble. Its six competitors came to its rescue with cash and a prescription for uncompromising deflation. As a consequence, all seven Anglo-American bankers, as well as the joint-stock commercial banks, ruthlessly pruned their outstanding debts. By June 1837 the three "W's" had cut their outstanding acceptances in half. But the cure did not work, for all three were forced to suspend in the spring of 1837. Baring Brothers remained in good health, and the other three were successfully supported by the Bank of England, although it was a tight squeeze in each case.

The British contraction, whether necessary or not, had a deplorable effect on the American economy and was a major factor in pushing the American economy into a panic and depression. In May 1837 the American banks suspended specie payments. Unemployment was severe and failures among merchants were high. As early as April 1837, Horace Greeley said that "one-fourth of all connected with the mercantile and manufacturing interests are out of business."

Yet this phase did not last very long. By the spring of 1838, British bank rate had dropped to 3 percent, and the English were back in the business of supplying credit to the United States, although much more uneasily than before. Specie payments were resumed in some of the states in May 1838. Biddle, who was convinced that American prosperity depended on high prices for cotton and continued advances of European credit, formed a pool to raise the price of cotton with the help of credit obtained from foreign bankers. Assisted by a short crop in 1838, Biddle was initially successful.

Meanwhile, however, events abroad had again frightened English bankers. The British wheat harvest was abnormally low, giving rise to abnormally high imports, which, in turn, reduced the Bank of England's reserves. The Bank responded by raising the discount rate to 5 percent in May 1838 and to 6 percent in August. At the same time, the Barings, now quite clearly the dominant house in Anglo-American relations, also began to curtail their activities severely.

Cut off from European credit, the American economy sank into depression. The money supply fell drastically, perhaps by as much as 25 percent from its peak in 1836. The wholesale price level was cut almost in half. Biddle's pool failed, bringing eventual ruin in 1841 to the Bank that he had done so much to build. Most of the American states defaulted on their debts, the bulk of which were held abroad. Until the end of the depression in the early 1840s, Americans could borrow nothing in Europe. Baron Rothschild, approached for a loan, informed an American emissary that he could return to the United States with the news that the most powerful banker in Europe had told him that he could not borrow a dollar. The

Barings added a postscript to this doleful news by refusing to buy any of the federal securities that were issued by Washington to cover the depression deficit.

COMMERCIAL BANKING GROWTH, 1830–1860 · The ups and downs in economic activity meant a bumpy road for all financial intermediaries but especially for commercial banks. Commercial bank deposits raced beyond $100 million during the boom of the early 1830s. Note circulation passed $130 million. During the next six years of the depression, valiant promoters, believing that one of the reasons for the sad state of affairs was that there were not enough banks, and encouraged by state governments, formed new banks with patient determination. The new banks failed with even greater regularity, so that by 1843, when the total number was about 700, there were about 100 fewer banks than there had been at the outset of the depression. Over the whole period to 1860, it is estimated that two-fifths of all the banks that had been chartered ended in failure. New Jersey statisticians calculated that 45 charters had been granted in that state from 1804 to 1853. Some of the charters never operated, but in any case 24 banks were still in operation in 1853. The broken banks eventually paid 20 percent of their liabilities. The total loss was at least $1.5 million, but *Hunt's* thought it was "probably $3 million."

Commercial bank deposits in 1843 were down to little more than $55 million and bank note circulation was about the same. Total bank loans and investments had diminished to less than $300 million from over $500 million in 1837. Then, as the economy recovered, commercial banking experienced an even more impressive resurgence. By 1860 there were over 1,500 banks and branches, circulating about $200 million in bank notes and holding over $250 million in deposits. Total loans and investments had climbed to over $750 million.

Note that the volume of deposits had finally bypassed bank notes. The nation's economy was continuously using more checkbook and less pocketbook money. Checks had become more important than bank notes in the big cities about 1830; they became more important for the United States as a whole about 1860; but they would not take care of the major part of rural transactions until 1890. The ratio of deposits to circulation in New York was $1.00 to $1.05 in 1836, $1.00 to $.75 in 1847, and $1.00 to $.30 in 1857. The national ratio was $1.00 to $1.30 in 1837 and $1.00 to $1.00 in 1860.

The growth of banking was decidedly different from one section of the country to another, as can be seen from the figures in Tables 3 and 4. The figures are incomplete because they represent reporting banks, and in some sections of the United States not all banks bothered to report. Nevertheless, the figures do show a rapid countrywide growth. In the late 1840s there were 28 cities with $1 million or more in bank capital; in 1855 there were 42 such cities with 30 percent more capital than they had had 8 years before. In the middle 1850s circulation was still more important than deposits in every section except the Middle Atlantic states, but in all the large cities deposits were far more important.

Most of the gain by the commercial banks came as a result of the country's expansion in population and in income. Some of it came because of the discovery of gold in California, which poured $320 million into the economic stream in the six years after 1848. Part of this amount, as much as one-half, went to increase bank reserves and thus formed a more substantial base for the growth of the money supply as well as for commercial bank operations.

Another large block of commercial bank growth came at the expense of or with the help of other financial institutions. As lotteries lost their respectability, their shrewder promoters shifted to brokerage and banking. The career of Solomon Allen was especially illustrative. Allen, an Albany printer, began to sell lottery tickets in 1808. He opened Allen's Truly Lucky Office in New York City in 1815 and by 1820 he had offices in ten different cities. Then with the swing of public opinion, he turned more and more to money brokerage. He also did a thriving business in commercial paper, buying and selling bills of exchange and "notes of hand" over a wide territory as early as 1823. One of Allen's relatives and associates, E. W. Clark, founded an exchange business that became the immediate ancestor of Jay Cooke & Co. and the remote ancestor of the present house of Smith, Barney & Co. An even better example of a switch from lotteries to commercial banking was the career of John Thompson, who founded both the First National Bank and the Chase Bank.

TABLE 3
Six Leading Cities in Terms of Bank Capital, 1848 and 1855
(Millions of Dollars)

City	1848		1855	
	No. of Banks	Capital	No. of Banks	Capital
New York	25	$24.0	52	$48.5
Boston	26	18.9	37	32.5
Providence	23	8.0	37	12.9
Philadelphia	14	9.2	15	10.6
Charleston	7	9.2	9	10.8
New Orleans	6	17.7	8	14.7

Source: *Hunt's Merchants' Magazine*, 1848, 1855, quoting Homans' *Bankers Almanac* and the *Bankers' Magazine*.

The financial institutions that contributed the most to the growth of commercial banks were the savings banks and the insurance companies. Both kept substantial balances with various commercial banks. Therefore, as they grew, the commercial banks also had to grow, for part of the assets of the one became the liabilities and, through lending, the assets of the other.

THE PHILOSOPHY OF COMMERCIAL
BANKING IN 1860 · The philosophy that guided the theory of bank operation was not too different from the one that had prevailed in the previous generation. The difference, as in most of economic history, was one of degree rather than kind. More people now understood that bank deposits

TABLE 4
Bank Capital, Deposits, and Circulation in the Early 1850s
(Millions of Dollars)

Area	Capital	Deposits	Circulation
Illinois (1854)	$ 2.5	$ 1.3	$ 2.3
Tennessee (1857)	9.1	4.4	6.3
Ohio (1851)	7.5	5.4*	11.2
Rhode Island (1852)	14.0	2.1†	3.3
Pennsylvania (1852)	18.9	15.6	11.9
Baltimore (1852)	7.1	3.9	2.2
New York (1851)	33.1	41.1	7.1
Detroit (1852)	0.8	0.7	0.6
New England (1854)	84.6	24.9	49.4
Middle states (1854)	114.8	116.9	61.1
Southern states (1854)	46.7	14.6	40.9
Southwestern states (1854)	38.4	20.1	33.3
Western states (1854)	17.0	11.7	20.1
Total	$301.4	$188.2	$204.7

Source: *Hunt's Merchants' Magazine*, 1851–1858.
* *Individual deposits only.*
† *$.4 at interest; $1.7 noninterest-bearing.*

were very much the same in their economic effects as bank notes. More people also understood that both deposits and note issues came into existence chiefly as a result of an expansion of bank loans and investments. Among the experts, it was also increasingly understood that bank influence had ramifications on the whole economy, not just on lenders and borrowers. However, most writers on the subject still believed that banks were more passive than active and that their notes and deposits were an effect rather than a cause of economic change. The orthodox point of view was expressed in an article in *Hunt's Merchants' Magazine* in 1859:

> Banks are the aggregation or association of previously acquired individual wealth. They do not create wealth of themselves any more than does a plow or a hoe. They aid and facilitate business as a steam engine aids and promotes mechanical production. Business exists and banks are required; they are not the forerunners but the followers of business. Business is made or created in a community, and a bank is required as a place of deposit to collect and to facilitate the transmission of funds between different points and to provide a currency. In these and other ways, they aid in creating wealth; they are a labor-saving machine, one of the most important of modern times.

Some eminent economists, like Amasa Walker, continued to argue that banks caused the money supply to fluctuate widely and that they consequently disrupted and damaged the whole economy. But others regarded fluctuation as perfectly natural. Professor George Tucker wrote in *Hunt's* January 1859, in reply to Walker:

This fluctuation we regard as perfectly normal, forming no argument against a paper currency. If paper money of itself made the corn grow, built and equipped the factory, pegged the boots and shoes, constructed the railroad, it might be. Its office is of a very different character. After the corn is grown and ready for market it comes into aid in selling it and in distributing it to consumers over the country. It lends its aid in the same way in scattering over the country all kinds of merchandise. . . . As this corn, these goods, and boots and shoes are chiefly sold during five or six months of the year, it is very natural that more money should be required at one time than at another, causing a fluctuation in business and a corresponding fluctuation in the amount of paper money in circulation.

In their operations, the commercial banks continued to veer away from accommodation loans, thus providing grist for the mill of the real bills doctrinaires. Tucker, writing in *Hunt's* in February 1858, found it possible to be tolerant of accommodation loans, a sure sign that they were fading from the picture:

It would not be wise to proscribe accommodation notes altogether, but the preference due to paper representing *bona fide* commercial transactions should be formally recognized and habitually acted on. There should be a limit to the time for which an accommodation loan should be continued. The more the discounts of a bank are confined to business paper, the more is the institution a handmaiden to commerce, the more is its capital within its reach and consequently the more safe it is from the adverse fluctuatons of trade.

As accommodation loans receded, call loans made for the purpose of financing security purchases increased. The orthodox found this situation almost as unsatisfactory as they had found accommodation paper. What bothered the critics was their conviction that every dollar loaned on call was a dollar taken away from manufacturing, agriculture, or trade. A Massachusetts writer said that it was a common practice of loan officers "to appear on exchange or on the curbstone for the purpose of negotiating with other banks or bankers, at the same time refusing their own customers money for good paper for the proper transaction of business in their own locations."

FURTHER ATTEMPTS TO REFORM BANKING · The public and the lawmakers who represented them regarded banks with mixed feelings. They wanted a continuous expansion of the money supply to feed the country's credit needs, but they did not want inflation. They wanted banks to be liquid, but they frowned at the most liquid bank loan of all—the call loan. They wanted laissez faire, but they thought that government regulation was necessary to keep banks from failing. The latter belief appeared in bold relief with each recession or depression. It was then that public clamor and legislative indignation produced more stringent bank regulation.

The panic and depression in the years following 1836 were no exception to the general rule. As soon as the economy turned down and the Bank of the United States lost its charter (which meant that all of its 19 branches closed down), the states began to move to reorganize and reform their banking systems. It was commonly believed by the public and, of course, by the legislators, that government regulation could accomplish anything, and one of the things that its omnipotence could accomplish was the safety and solvency of the banks. This belief was more than naïve, for no amount of regulation could make a commercial banking system safe and solvent unless the underlying economic factors were favorably disposed toward commercial banking. Sparsely populated territories that had no manufacturing, trade, or commerce but only fishing, farming, and forestry were incompatible with solvent commercial banking.

In order for a bank to meet its obligations to noteholders or depositors who wanted cash, it had to be able to do one of two things: liquidate its assets quickly or sell them to or borrow against them from some other agency. Neither action was possible in the small agricultural communities of the post-1836 world. Country banks could not liquidate their assets quickly because their loans to bank borrowers were long-term commitments and consequently were not liquid. They could not shift their assets because no agency existed to which illiquid bank assets could be sold or borrowed against. Under the circumstances, any attempt to make banking safe by simple government fiat was bound to fail.

One of the immediate reactions to widespread bank failure was prohibition of banking. By the 1850s banking was prohibited by law or constitution in seven states, two territories, and the District of Columbia. However, these prohibitions did not solve the problem. Paper money was still being issued but by private banks or by institutions that did not use the word "bank." What took place in Iowa clearly illustrates this point. The depression caused a general revulsion against banks. Consequently, the state constitution of 1846 prohibited all *banks of issue,* but the people of Iowa soon found that life on hard money was much more difficult than life on bank credit. Private bankers stepped in to fill the breach. At first they confined their activities to land, buying parcels from the federal government and selling them on time to settlers at as much as 40 percent interest. By the mid-1850s, however, the bankers were making loans on securities and accepting time and demand deposits. Residents in other parts of the United States, as far away as central Pennsylvania, bought the certificates of deposit of these private bankers.

Another method of dealing with loose banking was to have the states own and operate banks. Thus banking became a state monopoly in Indiana and Mississippi, but government ownership was no panacea. In one case, banking was conducted conservatively, much to the irritation of the general public. In the other case, banking was conducted loosely, and the result was the same rate of failure as had been experienced with similarly conducted private institutions.

The third method of dealing with the bank problem became the most popular in the long run. This method was the institution of so-called free banking. In the days before free banking, every bank charter required a special act of the legislature. Free banking meant that bank promoters could obtain a charter without a special legislative act. They could now do so by applying to the state official in charge of banking and by conforming to a set of specific rules and regulations. Free banking laws also required a minimum reserve against note issue and against deposits. The law also instituted a system of bank examination under a constituted authority, such as a department of banking and insurance.

The first free banking law in the United States was adopted in Michigan in 1837. It was a fiasco simply because Michigan was not ready for commercial banking at that time. The law required every bank to deposit securities up to the full amount of its note circulation, but the securities could be the personal bonds of the stockholders or bonds and mortgages on real estate. The first very often turned out to be nothing more than promises to pay, and the second were often issued on property that was grossly overvalued. Many so-called bankers disappeared, leaving their bank notes without a redeemer. A provision in the law requiring that at least 30 percent of the bank's capital had to be paid in specie was a similar farce. Specie was shipped from bank to bank, always a step or two ahead of the bank examiner, and kegs of nails or broken glass were given a thin coat of gold icing to deceive the public and the examiners. Failures were common under such a system. In the first year, 1837, more than 40 banks were formed in a state having a population of only 200,000. Two years later, more than 40 banks had failed. In the last analysis, the unsoundness of Michigan's system was caused by the area's lack of capital and was characteristic of frontier conditions. Had the law been enforced, Michigan would have had no banks. This situation would have meant a low rate of failure, but it probably also would have meant a lower rate of economic growth.

The experience in New York was decidedly different from that of Michigan. During the panic of 1837, the safety fund system broke down. Eleven banks suspended operations. Of these, 2 recovered, but the other 9 drew $2.6 million from the fund, draining it of most of its resources. Consequently, in 1838, under pressure from labor and the radical wing of the Democratic party, the state adopted a free banking law under which every new bank had to deposit with the comptroller a package of government bonds, real estate bonds, or mortgages equivalent to the amount of notes it had in circulation. Failure to redeem bank notes in specie entailed a 14 percent fine, and if the failure continued, the comptroller was authorized to sell the securities and use the proceeds to redeem the notes. The New York law was widely copied. By 1860 15 states had adopted free banking, and during the Civil War, the United States government would adopt the system under the National Bank Act.

Free banking, however, did not ensure soundness and efficiency. It was only as safe as the securities deposited against the notes. In the beginning, New York banks bought Southern and Western state bonds that were selling far below par. Thus, in the early years, the banks deposited a total of $5 million of bonds, and all but $480,000 of these were out-of-state obligations. When banks failed, the comptroller could not realize enough from the sale of securities to satisfy the noteholders. Up to 1843, 29 banks with a circulation of $1.2 million failed; their securities covered only $1 million. In time the loophole was closed by restricting eligible securities to United States and New York State bonds. The system then produced safe banking as far as notes were concerned, but it did not protect the depositor, and it did not permit the money supply to expand beyond the point set by the existing reserves of the New York State banks.

SAVINGS BANKS, THE FASTEST-GROWING INTERMEDIARY, 1830–1860

· Savings banks were the fastest-growing financial institutions in mid-ninteenth century United States. As is true of all banks, the data are not complete, but savings bank deposits swelled from $10 million in 1836 to at least $150 million in 1860. Then, as now, savings banking was not a universal institution but was confined to a few states, with New York and Massachusetts accounting for 75 percent of deposits. Within the states themselves, most of the business was done by relatively few banks. In New York City, for example, one-third of the banks held over 80 percent of the deposits.

The whole nature of savings banking underwent a fundamental transformation during the cycle of the 1830s. By the 1840s career executives had definitely taken over the management and control of the institutions from their founders, who had been part-time executives at best. The professionals rapidly altered the whole concept of savings banking. It was no longer considered an institution primarily for the benefit of the poorer classes. To be sure, the less-wealthy members of the community continued to use savings banks, and in surprisingly large volume. A report in the Cincinnati Railroad Record in 1857 concluded: "These institutions have few depositors from the wealthy class. They are almost exclusively made up from the working people: not merely laborers, but small mechanics, traders, clerks, and salary men." In the middle 1840s the Bank for Savings had among its depositors 1,287 domestic servants, 517 laborers, 226 seamstresses, and 223 clerks. But beside the domestics, laborers, and seamstresses, it had 172 shopkeepers, 91 merchants, 27 engineers, and 18 attorneys.

By the 1840s and 1850s many of the savings banks were doing a quite diversified business. They were buying corporate stocks and making business loans as well as investing in mortgages. In the middle 1850s 50 percent of New York savings bank assets was in bonds and mortgages and 40 percent was in stock. The largest bank in New York City owned more than $4.5 million of stock and held $2.9 million in bonds and mortgages; the second largest owned $2.8 million worth of stock and $3.4 million of bonds and mortgages. In Massachusetts, where the savings banks had wide discretion in their investments, loans on mortgages and personal security soared from $871,000 in 1835 to $23,520,000 in 1860, or from a little more than 20 percent of deposits to almost 60 percent. The loans on personal security were really business loans. Textile firms borrowed heavily. The Amoskeag Mills owed the Provident Institution $150,-000 all through the 1850s, and the Massachusetts Mills maintained a debt of $100,000 to $200,000.

The story was much the same in other cities. In 1860 the Savings Bank of Baltimore had 42 percent of its assets in governments, 23 percent in real estate, and 21 percent in loans against personal security. This rate was somewhat less than had been the case in 1855, when 32 percent was in loans against personal security.

Once embarked on a program of aggressive expansion, savings banks tended to pay little or no attention to liquidity. However, a few unfortunate experiences induced greater caution. Along with other financial institutions, the savings banks were badly mauled by the 1837 depression. In his diary, Phillip Hone described what happened on May 10, 1837:

> The Savings Bank also sustained a most grievous run yesterday. They paid to 375 depositors $81,000. The press was awful. The hour for closing the bank is six o'clock, but they did not get through the paying of those who were in at that time till nine. I was there with the other trustees and witnessed the madness of the people. Women were nearly pushed to death, and the stoutest men could scarcely sustain themselves, but they held on as with a death's grip, upon the evidences of their claims, and exhausted as they were with the pressure, they had strength to cry "Pay! Pay!"

It took more than one experience to bring the lesson home. In time, however, savings bankers found that their deposits were very sensitive to the movement of the business cycle. They were "cycle-elastic," expanding with great alacrity in times of recovery and falling off in periods of slack business. As a result of the recession of 1854, when "many work people were thrown out of employment," deposits in New York grew by only $900,000. In 1856, when the economy strengthened, deposits advanced by $4 million. As the banks weathered runs and weathered the economic breakdown in 1857, they built up their liquid assets, became more specialized, shifted more to government bonds, and no longer were so sharply competitive with the other intermediaries.

PIONEERING IN MARKETING LIFE INSURANCE · Although they did not grow as quickly as the savings banks, the life insurance companies had a much more spectacular set of years than any of the other intermediaries. Certainly more innovations were introduced in life insurance at this time than in any of the other intermediaries.

In 1841 only 1,211 policies were written and only $4 million was in force. Total premiums were only a little over $250,000. At that time, fourteen companies were in operation. Then came two developments that propelled the industry forward. The first was the inauguration of mutual companies that catered to all members of society and the other was the creation of the agency system and the beginning of aggressive selling. Life insurance took on the distinction of being the financial industry that was most anxious to sell its services, and the results were spectacular.

Willard Phillips of the Boston merchant family formed the first modern mutual company, the New England Mutual Life Insurance Company, in 1835. It was modeled after the Massachusetts Hospital Life Insurance Company, and because of a fear that it might have to emulate MHLI's contribution to charity, it did not begin operations until 1842. By then, as with all innovations, the idea was being picked up by other ambitious and energetic men: Morris Robinson of the Mutual Life Insurance Company of New York, Benjamin Balch of the State Mutual Life Insurance Company of Worcester and the National Life Insurance Company of Vermont, and Robert L. Patterson of the Mutual Benefit Life Insurance Company. Of all these, Balch probably had the most fertile imagination and the largest stroke of genius, but he did not have the personality for business success. He drove people hard and got them to do things, but he was an unpopular, restless, unhappy person. Robinson made a more permanent contribution to the business. He was the first to separate life insurance from the trust business. He advertised and he started personal solicitation. He was, in other words, the trailblazer in marketing life insurance; as a result, he was paid the princely salary of $1,500 in 1843 when he launched the Mutual of New York.

Carrying Robinson's ideas a step further, the Connecticut Mutual Life Insurance Company established an agency system in 1846. It was not, however, until 1853 that the first sales manager or general agent appeared in the person of Henry H. Hyde of the Mutual of New York. Hyde was very successful, but it was his son, Henry Baldwin Hyde, who really launched the aggressive selling that gave rise to the rhyme: "No one has as much endurance as the man who sells insurance." As the representative of the Mutual of New York and later of the Equitable Life Assurance Society, Baldwin Hyde was the stereotype life insurance man; his career, which began in 1859, is dealt with in the next chapter.

By 1850 there were 48 life insurance companies with combined assets of about $10 million. In any new business that is embarking on a period of spectacular growth, there will paradoxically be a great deal of shaking out of competitors; the number of firms will narrow, but the total business will soar. So it was with the life insurance business in the 1850s. During the decade, 21 companies were formed, and 26 went out of business, so that in 1860 there were only 43 companies, but their combined assets were almost $25 million. The companies that were doing the business were the recently founded mutuals. Of the $205 million of life insurance in force, $125 million had been written by five mutual companies: Mutual of New York ($40 million), Connecticut Mutual ($26 million), Mutual Benefit ($25 million), the New York Life Insurance Company and the New England Mutual ($16 million each).

As the business grew, new policies and new ideas were introduced voluntarily or by request of government agencies. The nonrenewable term policy that had been the only one written by the trust companies faded into insignificance. Its place was taken by the whole life policy, which appeared in the 1840s, and the endowment, a product of the 1850s. Non-forfeiture provisions, such as cash values and paid-up insurance, were instituted by the New York Life in 1860.

Life insurance companies were conservative investors. The New England Mutual in 1860 had one-eighth of its assets in railroad, manufacturing, and bank stocks, one-third in real estate loans, one-tenth in government bonds, and about one-twentieth in loans on personal security. Much of this conservative investing was due to the influence of government regulatory agencies, which were constantly being expanded. In 1837 Massachusetts passed a law restricting life insurance investments in stocks to a specific list of local companies. In 1849 Wisconsin and New York adopted similar laws. In 1859 New York also established an insurance department. Meanwhile, states all over the country were trying to protect their own insurance companies by imposing discriminatory taxes on out-of-state companies. But it was not only insurance that was subject to government regulation. Banks were even more heavily controlled in their operations, their reserves, and their investments. New York State, for example, passed a law providing that incorporated banks could "not directly or indirectly deal or trade in . . . buying and selling any stock created under an Act of the United States or any particular state unless in selling the same when truly pledged by way of security for debts due."

Just as the savings banks added to the country's stock of capital funds, so did the life insurance companies, for there is hardly any doubt that each picked up savings that would otherwise not have come into existence. The savings banks did not do any aggressive marketing, but their message received enough publicity to induce some extra sacrifice, thereby leading to a larger volume of saving. The life insurance business, on the other hand, suddenly broke loose from its lackadaisical ways and launched a most aggressive marketing campaign that unquestionably caused many people who would otherwise never consider it to buy insurance. At the same time, both intermediaries were supplying funds to borrowers who otherwise might not have been able to buy a home or expand a business. They were not in the business of supplying venture capital so much as they were in the business of supplying credit to solid risks.

THE RELATIVE DECLINE IN
PROPERTY INSURANCE · Property insurance did not fare nearly as well as life insurance. Marine insurance fell on especially bad days as American shipping steadily deteriorated from the advantageous position it had previously occupied. Fire insurance continued to make slow progress, growing only in line with the rising population. Thus no spectacular growth could occur. It was merely a matter of taking in unearned premium income and investing it. By 1860 general insurance company assets were estimated at $80 million, a relatively small amount compared with the assets of other intermediaries.

Many general insurance companies were ultraconservative. The Philadelphia Contributionship was an extreme example; it had no desire to grow, and its investment policies were most solid. It invested almost all its assets in real estate and mortgages. In 1846 it owned 481 shares in 4 companies, $460,000 in real estate and mortgages, and $30,000 in other assets. In 1856 the Merchants' and Mechanics' Mutual Insurance Company had $179,000 of its $209,000 assets in bonds and mortgages. However, more adventurous companies were wandering afield. The Union Insurance Co. in 1860 had $400,000 in assets, of which $270,000 was in stocks and bonds. The Phoenix Mutual Insurance Company held $94,000 in governments, $44,000 in stock, $28,000 in real estate, $20,000 in railroad bonds, and $6,000 in mortgages.

INVESTMENT BANKING AND THE SECURITIES MARKET For the most part, as can be seen, the financial intermediaries—commercial banks, savings banks, and insurance companies—concentrated on business loans, bonds, and mortgages. They did not participate very actively in the equity side of the securities markets. That field of activity was left to the investment bankers, most of whom did not appreciate the concession. Buying stocks was still not considered altogether respectable. Government bodies spent much time thinking of ways and means of curtailing what was commonly referred to as "stock jobbing." Short selling and the call-money market were especially criticized, the first because it was considered immoral to sell what one did not possess and the second because it was considered immoral to borrow money in order to "gamble" in the stock market. New York at first prohibited short selling, but it repealed this prohibition in 1858.

The press was equally critical. During the depression of the late 1830s, *The New York Times* announced, "The New York Stock Exchange as at present managed is little more than an enormous gambling establishment." To be sure, the market's prestige did improve, but progress was slow and was continuously interrupted by recession or depression. As late as 1853 *Hunt's* editorialized:

> We do not say that the business of the stock broker is not honorable; there is a large amount of money seeking a regular investment in stocks, which is legitimately passed through the hands of those who have a seat in the board, and the capitalist, in business or out, who has surplus means, may certainly purchase such securities as he shall fancy. But the large array of forces in this department is chiefly supported from the losses of outside speculators. The sumptuous living, and the elegant establishments, are most generally paid for out of the money of those who ought never to have touched the traffic, and for whose permanent prosperity the excitement is as dangerous as the chances of the gaming table. It is needless to theorize upon the causes which leave the whole burden of loss upon the casual dealer in stocks, or to except the few who have made a fortunate "turn" and escaped unscathed. It is notorious that the whole system is chiefly supported from the capital of those who have not a dollar to invest, and who ought never to have attempted the speculation.

Most of the pioneer investment houses that had dabbled in securities failed in the panic and depression following 1837. Nicholas Biddle's bank failed. So did the Morris Canal & Banking Co., J. L. & S. Josephs, and the North American Trust & Banking Co. The only survivors of any account were Prime, Ward, & King and Thomas Biddle & Co.

The private banking houses that emerged from the depression were mainly merchant bankers rather than investment bankers. Many had their roots in Europe, where their firms had been accustomed to financing merchandise transactions rather than to dealing in securities. For example, Philip Speyer, scion of a German-Jewish house that went back to the 1400s, opened a private bank in 1837 to engage in the financing of exports and imports. Francis Martin Drexel, an Austrian portrait painter, came to Philadelphia in 1838 and founded a foreign exchange business. Both houses, as well as other merchant bankers, would eventually shift to securities and investment, but that step would come much later, after the railroads had entered their period of great growth.

Despite all the obstacles, however, stock dealing did make slow progress. In the early 1830s thousand-share days were not altogether rare; yet after the federal debt had been entirely paid off in 1835, many commentators thought that the stock exchange had lost the only logical reason for its existence. The early railroads, however, gave the stock exchanges a new and more important reason for existing. In the boom of the 1850s, transactions over one 4-week period aggregated almost 1 million shares. By then the stock exchanges were dealing in securities valued at $1.5 billion.[6] The New York Central Railroad counted 2,500 stockholders and the Massachusetts Western Railroad, over 2,300.

Many forces moved from all directions to break the dam in the way of security dealings. First, there were always many promoters and entrepreneurs who were actively seeking capital. This was especially the case with the railroads, for they needed immense funds for their day and age. Indeed, they needed so much and needed it so badly that railroad promoters went from house to house peddling stock for pennies. Sometimes the shoe was on the other foot. When the money market slackened and money became plentiful, as in periods of depression, funds gravitated to the securities markets. In its comments on general business in the recovery that finally seemed definitely under way in January 1844, *Hunt's* noted:

> Unemployed capital continues to accumulate. . . . The amount of business paper is . . . small, so small that during the next quarter, probably greater difficulty will be found in investing the proceeds. . . . This latter circumstance has been the cause of the increased amount loaned to brokers, who, for the most part, employ the means thus obtained in stock operations.

The stock market had already created the structure that was required for handling the flow of funds. The call-money market, which as we have seen antedated this period, was by 1857 well recognized as an important and long-established institution. By then, it was estimated, out-of-town banks had deposits of over $25 million in New York City banks and most of this amount was in the call-money market.

Other inventions and innovations also helped to add to the activity in securities. The invention of the telegraph and the creation of the railway express company and the credit agency made it much easier for people

---

6 The list included 360 railroad stocks, 360 railroad bonds, 985 bank stocks, 31 state bonds, 113 local bonds, U.S. bonds, 16 canal stocks, 16 canal bonds, 75 insurance companies, and 377 county bonds and miscellaneous stocks. Not all stocks were traded every day. On one day in 1853, for example, the following were traded: 11 railroads, 3 banks, 3 coal companies, 2 insurance companies, 1 canal, and 4 miscellaneous.

who were distant from the exchanges to buy and sell stocks. The telegraph speeded communication, the express agency speeded transportation, and the credit agency, which was a product of the 1837 "revulsion," speeded the financial reputation of buyers and sellers.[7]

Finally, there was the indispensable entrepreneur acting as the *deus ex machina* in the expanding market. Many of the newer houses in banking and brokerage that appeared on the ash heap left by the panic were as adventurous and imaginative as only the young can be. Clark and Co. came out of lotteries in 1837. In the same year, August Belmont arrived as the agent of the Rothschilds and soon acquired a reputation as a gambler in stocks.

The most spectacular personality of the era, Jacob Little, opened a brokerage office in 1835. A man who made and lost a few fortunes, Little was an innovator who dealt in "fancy stocks." He probably invented the convertible bond, and with John Ward and Daniel Drew he accomplished the first real corner in Wall Street when he gained control of the Morris Canal & Banking Co. in 1835. Although he had the charisma that surrounded all the fabulous Wall Street plungers from Little to Livermore, his contribution was more in gadgetry than in fundamental innovation. A far more important innovator was the almost anonymous house of Winslow, Lanier & Co., which in the late 1850s was doing a business of as much as $1 million a day.

Winslow, Lanier were pioneers in dealing in railroad securities. In 1849 James F. D. Lanier, who had been a bank manager in Indiana, came to New York and formed a partnership with Richard H. Winslow. Following is his description of what happened:

> At that time there were in operation in the West (Ohio, Indiana, Michigan and Illinois) only about six hundred miles of line. These roads were chiefly the remains of the old State systems which had been sold out to private companies, and were almost without exception badly located and imperfectly built. . . . They had, consequently, involved in heavy loss all who had been engaged in their construction. I felt, however, their want of success to be no argument against lines properly constructed upon good routes. I undertook to demonstrate this in every way in my power, particularly in newspaper articles and pamphlets, of which I published great numbers in connection with the negotiation of the securities of various companies which we undertook. The results of our efforts soon far exceeded our expectations. Although we began in a very small way, every step we took gave us increased business and strength, and we soon had all the business we could attend to. . . . We not infrequently negotiated a million of bonds daily. The aggregate for the year was enormous. We were without competitors for a business we had created, and consequently made money very rapidly. The commissions for the negotiations of bonds averaged at first five percent. With their negotiation we often coupled contracts for the purchase, at a large commission, of rails. Our business soon became so great that it was a question with us, not so much what we would undertake, as what we would reject. We not

---

[7] Lewis Tappan, merchant and editor of the *Journal of Commerce,* founded the first credit agency in 1841. Bradstreet's financial credit rating came in 1849.

infrequently took, on our own account, an entire issue of bonds of important lines.

The negotiation of the securities of companies was followed by arrangements that made our house the agent for the payment of interest accruing on them, as well as transfer agents. Such arrangements naturally led the way to the banking business to which we afterward chiefly confined ourselves.[8]

THE EARLY BUILDING AND LOAN ASSOCIATIONS · A word remains to be said about building and loan associations, which, although still very small, made relatively great progress from 1840 on. Indeed, the first permanent building and loan association appeared in Charleston, South Carolina, in 1843. It was distinguished for another reason: it was interested in savers as well as home owners.

Like the other financial intermediaries, the building and loan association was not indigenous to the United States, but it was in the United States that it would eventually have its greatest growth. When it first appeared, the institution was an exact replica of those in Europe. Variously known as mutual loan associations, homestead aid associations, and savings and loan associations, building and loan offices were first organized to enable small home owners to acquire homes. Upon joining the association, the stockholder or member agreed to pay a minimum sum, for example $1, each month until the combined payments plus interest and profits equaled the maturity value of the stock, usually $200. At that time, the stockholder would surrender his stock and cease to be a member. Should he desire to sell his stock before maturity, the by-laws of the association would stipulate the cash value.

Ordinarily the members of a building and loan association were would-be house owners. Ordinarily, too, the association's funds were used to make mortgage loans to members. A member who wished to borrow would have to hold shares whose maturity value would equal what he proposed to borrow. If he met this requirement, he was eligible to participate at the association's regularly held fund auctions. At these auctions, the borrower who bid the highest premium over and above the regular rate of interest was awarded the loan. In short, the building and loan association offered a way of obtaining a mortgage and of amortizing it by regular payments over a stipulated period of time.

THE ECONOMIC IMPACT, 1836–1860 · What can be said about the economic contribution of American financial intermediaries in the twenty-five years between 1835 and 1860? What of their contribution to total saving, total investment, and capital mobility? Or, to express this question in another way, what of their safety and what of their ability to act as middlemen between those who wanted to save and those who wanted to spend for capital investment in plant, equipment, tools, machinery, barns, and so forth?

---

8 J. F. D. Lanier, *Sketch Life of J. F. D. Lanier* (New York, 1870). This quotation is reproduced more extensively in Alfred D. Chandler, Jr., *The Railroads* (New York: Harcourt, Brace & World, 1965), pp. 65 ff.

Taken as a whole, the years between 1835 and 1860 saw the country's financial intermediaries as unsafe as they would be at any other time in their history. No one really knows how much loss was involved in the high rate of commercial bank mortality during this period, but there are impressions. John Jay Knox, later Comptroller of the Currency, made the most conservative estimate—5 percent of total circulation per year. A writer in *Hunt's* in 1862 thought that losses amounted to at least $100 million since banking first began. But Jay Cooke, the most famous banker of his day, put the figure much higher. His description of the safety of banking as it existed before 1860 was anything but complimentary:

> Confusion worse confounded was the order of the day. Exchanges upon Philadelphia, New York and Boston, when procurable, rated all the way from 1 to 15 percent premium, according to locality. Notes were printed upon every variety of paper and no two banks issued bills of similar appearance. It was generally the case that bank notes current in one state could not be circulated in the other states, and it was impossible for any one but those most skilled in handling money in vast quantities to detect the innumerable counterfeits and altered notes which were in circulation. The banks were breaking constantly and in many cases circulating notes became almost worthless. Fifty millions of dollars per annum, it is safe to say, would not cover the loss to the people of this country growing out of broken banks, counterfeits, altered notes and cost of exchange between different points.[9]

Other intermediaries also suffered heavy losses, although they were never as sensational or as shocking as those that occurred in the commercial banks. General insurance company losses were very large, chiefly because of history-making fires and unusual disasters on the high seas. But even among those solidly entrenched institutions, the savings banks and the life insurance companies, losses were unusually high. At least 12 savings banks failed during this period and 28 life insurance companies went out of business.

Turning to the question of their performance as middlemen, it is difficult to measure the intermediaries' contribution to economic development through the financing of spending for plant, equipment, and other producer-durable goods. It is evident that all the institutions were supplying venture capital through the purchase of every type of security—mortgages, equities, bonds, and promissory notes—and they were at least holding their own in the contest between the demand for and the supply of capital funds, for interest rates showed a tendency to decline over this period. To be sure, the decline was not very significant but it at least existed. Interest rates on New England municipal bonds averaged 5.33 percent at the beginning of the century, 4.95 percent in the decade 1830–1839, and 5.06 percent in 1850–1859. But the impression of stability that one gathers from these figures is deceiving. In reality, interest rates varied widely throughout the period. This situation was, of course, typical of all monetary phenomena, especially, and probably most importantly, the

---

[9] Ellis Paxon Oberholtzer, *Jay Cooke: Financier of the Civil War* (Philadelphia: George W. Jacobs & Co., 1907), I, 327.

money supply. There were two reasons. First, the banks were, as they had been, much concerned about their reserve ratios, and, second, bank reserves continued to be subject to the decisions made in the English money market and thus they fluctuated widely. When the Bank of England tightened the money supply, the American money market contracted sharply, with disastrous results for both the banks and the mercantile community.

In hindsight, the alternate expansions and contractions in the money market probably had a net effect of slowing economic progress. They were, therefore, deplorable, but at the time they seemed an inevitable part of human existence. It was generally believed that a period of "overtrading" had to be compensated for by a later period of "undertrading." The precept that what goes up must come down was among the initiated just as much a part of the eternal verities as Newtonian physics.

There were, of course, many other ways by which the intermediaries affected economic and social life. Among other things, they provided enough venture capital to give an upward thrust to social mobility. Thus the records of the Baltimore Savings Bank and the Institution for Savings in the Town of Boston reveal that loans were made to a "laborer," who appeared in the next directory as an "umbrella manufacturer," to an expressman, who then became an owner of a company, and to a carpenter, who advanced to a packing box manufacturer.

But it would be an error to jump to the conclusion that mobility was being impelled forward at breakneck speed—especially geographic mobility. Although competition between institutions was spirited, most of the intermediaries tended to stay in their own backyards. Commercial banks continued to open branches and to use correspondents but as a matter of necessity rather than from a desire to spread loans and investments. Commercial and private bankers who dealt in commercial paper went much farther from home than was considered expedient and proper. By the 1830s brokers like S. & M. Allen in New York were dealing in Western and Southern paper, and banks in New England were buying New York paper. Older and allegedly clearer heads warned, however, that such investments were not safe, and the more provincial thought it disgraceful that loanable funds created in one area should be exported to another, a prejudice that, incidentally, is still alive today.

Insurance companies also wandered fairly far afield despite the efforts of the various states to keep the trespassers out. But savings banks remained provincial. Because of rigidities in the movement of capital funds, interest rates varied widely in different sections of the country. In Baltimore, for example, the rate on prime paper was 6 percent in contrast to Boston's 3.5 percent.

5 · finance comes of age, 1860–1890

The last decades of the nineteenth century, like the opening decades, were characterized by outstanding innovation in the cycle of innovation and integration that has characterized the history of financial intermediation. Just as the thirty years before 1860 was a time of solidification, so the thirty years after 1860 was again a time of new developments in finance. One of the chief forces in this new burst of innovation was the Civil War. Whether the war advanced or retarded industrial progress and the national income is a moot question, but there is no doubt at all that it had a profound effect on the evolution of the financial intermediaries.

In proportion to the size of the population and the national wealth, the Civil War was the bloodiest and the most costly in the nation's history. Thus it was bound to have an important effect on the financial structure. Among its direct effects, it created the National Banking System and gave an immense impetus to the insurance and investment banking businesses. The war may also have had an indirect effect on the intermediaries. It may, as many students have argued, have given a mighty push to heavy industry and to the national income. But whether the war was or was not responsible, the late nineteenth century was the time when industry and the economy did come of age. It was the time of heavy industry. It was the age of steel, and toward its end it was beginning to be the age of electricity and the internal combustion engine.

The last half of the century was also a time of rapid progress in the standard of living. The amount of goods and services available to the average man, woman, and child almost doubled between 1860 and 1900. Industrial production multiplied more than six times. All of this was grist for the financial intermediation mill. With saving averaging about 20 percent of national income, expanding income provided an ever greater supply of capital funds. Heavy industry required immense amounts of these capital funds, but it could hardly raise what capital was needed by tapping individual savers directly; and it became less and less practical for savers to loan their funds directly to business, as had been the case when the population was small and face-to-face relations prevailed. However, it was practical for both the suppliers and the demanders of capital funds to deal with each other through the middlemen of finance; and the more complicated the economy became, the greater the reliance on these middlemen.

THE DEMAND FOR AND THE SUPPLY OF FUNDS · The participants on both the demand and the supply side of finance were much the same as they had been before and as they have been since. Households, businesses, and governments continued to bid for funds, and individuals and institutions continued to supply them. Between 1860 and 1866 the federal government's debt, under the pressure of war, soared from $65 million to $2.3 billion. Then as revenue continuously expanded in the postwar years, the Treasury chopped the debt down to $725 million in 1890.

The performance of municipal debt was much the opposite. It had been just a little over $100 million in 1860; by 1890 it was approaching $1 billion. As early as 1870 eight cities each owed a net debt of over $10 million.[1] State debt performed still differently, varying little over the whole three decades. There was, to be sure, a rise from $250 million to $350 million during the reconstruction era, but by 1890 debt was down to a little over $200 million.[2]

By 1890 it was estimated that total private debt in the United States was on the order of $30 billion, including $11.5 billion in mortgage and consumer debt, $6.3 billion of railroad and other bonds and stocks, and $10.3 billion of insurance debt. In addition, there was another $5 billion in bank deposits, making a total of $35 billion in the financial markets.

Whatever may have been the reasons, the last half of the nineteenth century witnessed an economic and financial revolution that was just as significant to the everyday life of the people as the industrial revolution of mid-eighteenth-century England and the political revolution of late eighteenth-century France. Just as the industrial revolution had transformed technological rarities like the machine and the factory into commonplaces, so the financial revolution transformed such rarities as the corporation, large-scale commercial banking, and investment banking into economic and financial commonplaces.

THE GROWTH OF THE INTERMEDIARIES · The growth of the financial intermediaries can best be measured by relating it to the growth of the national income and of national wealth. Although not precisely accurate, the figures do give evidence of the trends and of the volumes of magnitude. During the period under discussion, the assets of the financial intermediaries increased at twice the rate achieved by the national income.[3] Finance was, therefore, growing at a much faster rate than national wealth. As can be seen from the estimates in Table 5, the total assets of banks, insurance companies, and building and loan associations advanced from approximately $1.1 billion in 1860 to $7.8 billion in 1890. In

1 Philadelphia ($25 million), Baltimore ($21 million), New York ($18 million), Brooklyn and St. Louis ($13 million each), Chicago and New Orleans ($11 million), and Boston ($10 million).

2 Pennsylvania still owed the most, $40 million, followed closely by New York and Virginia. Missouri owed more than $20 million, and Ohio, Tennessee, Illinois, Indiana, and Louisiana each owed more than $10 million.

3 The best estimates available for national income during this period show a threefold increase. The assets of the intermediaries multiplied six times.

the same years national wealth increased from about $12 billion to $46 billion. These conservative estimates reveal that the assets of the intermediaries represented about 10 percent of the national wealth in 1860 and some 17 percent in 1890.

In the general process of economic growth that highlighted late nineteenth-century America, the domestic intermediaries were gradually pushing the foreign institutions into the shadows. According to the director of the Bureau of Statistics, foreigners owned approximately $600 million of the debt and equities of American business and government in 1866. A more liberal estimate made by *Hunt's Merchants' Magazine* put the figure at $938 million. By 1869 it was said that foreign holdings had jumped to $1.5 billion and to $3.4 billion by 1897.[4] Thus foreign holdings by the most liberal estimate showed a fivefold increase, but since total institutional assets had multiplied more than six times, the relative position of the foreign merchant bankers was declining. Another evidence of this fact was that American investment bankers were, at the end of the era, becoming much more active in exporting capital funds. The first important international loan made by Americans came in 1879 with a $3 million advance to Quebec. From then on loans floated by American bankers in international markets would show a continuous and impressive expansion.

TABLE 5
Assets of Financial Intermediaries, 1860–1890
(Millions of Dollars)

Year	All Banks	State Commercial Banks	National Banks	Savings Banks	Building and Loan	Life Insurance	General Insurance	Total Assets
1860	$1,000	$ 851	$ *	$ 149†		$ 24	$ 81	$1,105
1870	2,331	215	1,566	550†		270	182	2,783
1880	3,399	482	2,036	882		418	239	4,056
1890	6,344	1,539	3,062	1,743	300	771	352	7,767

Source: Data derived from *Historical Statistics of the United States; All Bank Statistics; Annual Report of the Superintendent of Insurance, State of New York,* 1961; Institute of Life Insurance, Division of Statistics and Research; year-end reports made by property insurance companies to insurance commissioners of various states.
* *Not in existence.*
† *Deposits; assets included in "all banks."*

There is a simple explanation for the relative decline of foreign investment. The unusual growth of the national income produced a supply of saving sufficiently large to enable the domestic market gradually to slough off the dependence on the older world of banking and finance. Yet the position of the foreign investors had been built up over such a long period and had become so solidly entrenched that years of erosion would wear only a small seam in their status. As late as the early 1900s, long after the

4 In 1866, $760 million in governments, $158 million in railroads, and $20 million miscellaneous. In 1869, $1.1 billion in governments, $233 million in rails, $100 million in real estate, and an assortment of miscellany.

process of erosion had begun, Henry Clews, the garrulous banker, could still bemoan the eminence of the Europeans in the financing of the export-import trade. "In the present stage of our national development," he said, "it is becoming a grave reflection upon our men of capital that we should remain almost entirely dependent on foreign bankers for transacting our immense foreign commerce."

The growth that was taking place among the financial institutions was not being shared equally. Figure 1 shows a decided relative growth in commercial banking. Savings bank deposits grew steadily in the postwar years but then flattened out in the depression years of the 1870s. Life insurance performed in much the same fashion, but general insurance moved along a straight line. The securities business pursued a most erratic course—that is, if one uses the price of a stock exchange seat as a proxy for activity on the exchange. After some ups and downs in the sixties and seventies, the price skyrocketed in the early eighties and then fell off once again.

"SOUND MONEY" VERSUS "EASY MONEY" · Much of the erratic performance of the financial institutions was due to the boom-and-bust performance of the economy and to the pressures and pulls exerted on the money supply by the continuous debate between advocates of sound and easy money.

Even though the whole period was one of remarkable economic advance, the progress was not linear. The thirty years between 1860 and 1890 were marred by the longest depression in history (1873–1878) and by two severe but shorter-lived recessions. Whether these downturns were the fault of the money system or whether the money system reacted to the downturns is a debatable question that has not as yet been resolved. In any case, the money supply fell off in the depression, thereby aggravating the exasperations of many who were already frustrated by a general decline in prices and by the money system's general failure to expand.

When the Civil War ended, the price level was more than double the prewar average. Then as industrial and agricultural production increased, prices began to drop. Debtor classes complained that they had to pay their debts in scarcer and dearer dollars. Believing in a crude quantity theory of money, farmers and impecunious seekers of capital blamed their difficulties on an insufficient supply of money and demanded that the government take steps to increase it.

The advocates of "sound money"—the creditors and financiers—contended that the secular price decline was caused by expanding production. They denied that increasing the money supply would help debtors by causing a rise in prices. Some exponents of sound money frankly favored a contraction of the money supply and a deliberate deflation of prices in order to make possible a quick return to the specie standard that had been abandoned during the war.[5]

---

[5] "Specie payments"—that is, the redemption of paper money for gold or silver—had been abandoned in every prior depression and major war. In the Civil War period, resumption did not occur until 1879, so that the United States was "off the gold standard" for approximately seventeen years.

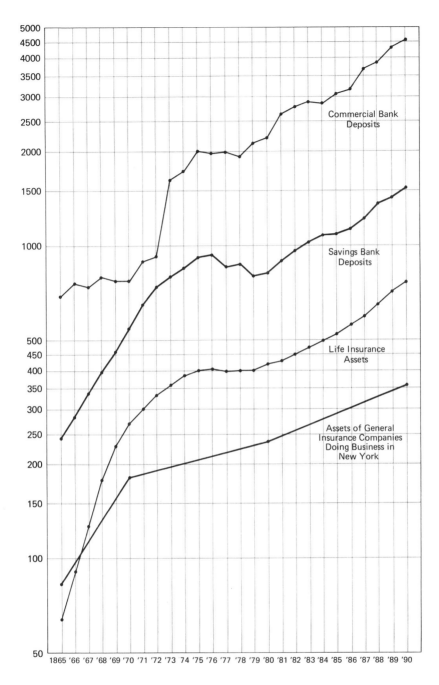

Figure 1
Deposits and Assets of Intermediaries, 1865–1890 **(Millions of Dollars)**

Source: Data derived from *Historical Statistics of the United States; All Bank Statistics; Annual Report of the Superintendent of Insurance, State of New York,* 1961; Institute of Life Insurance, Division of Statistics and Research; year-end reports made by property insurance companies to insurance commissioners of various states.

In the monetary controversy that raged for thirty years after the war, the sound-money people prevailed. The supporters of easy money pressed their claims only when prices fell. When prices rose and relative prosperity came to the farm, agitation for monetary panaceas declined. The creditor classes then breathed more easily and mistakenly thought that the so-called monetary heresies had passed away.

THE NATIONAL BANKING SYSTEM · In the banking world, the controversy between the easy- and the sound-money groups centered around the national banking system established by the National Bank Act of 1863.

The act had its roots deep in the past. For many years, critics of the state banks had expressed continuous disapproval of the existing state of commercial banking and had called for fundamental reforms. Some of the states, as we have noted, instituted sweeping reforms, the chief of which was the establishment of free banking, but difficulties continued. The rate of bank failures was high, and the many different bank notes of highly diverse quality seemed even more annoying. At the outbreak of the Civil War, there were 1,600 state banks, each going its own merry way; 7,000 different kinds of bank notes circulated. Over half of them were spurious and many of the others circulated at a discount.

No one argued that the existing system was perfect, but not until late in the war were the monetary conservatives finally able to accomplish one of their goals: the reestablishment of a dual banking system, that is, a system under which both the state and the federal governments issued bank charters.

Secretary of the Treasury Salmon P. Chase was the foremost champion of national banking, and as early as 1861 he strongly recommended it on the ground that it would (1) create a uniform currency, (2) provide a market for government bonds, and (3) prevent overexpansion and depreciation of the currency. Over a year passed before Congress acted, for there was considerable opposition to any move to nationalize bank charters. It is hardly likely that the bill would have passed had the South, with its easy-money, antifederal outlook, still been represented in Congress.

The act as amended in 1864 gave the federal government the power to grant charters to national banks through a newly established office of Comptroller of the Currency. National banks were required to have a minimum capital ranging from $200,000 in cities of 50,000 or more to $50,000 in cities with a population of 6,000 or less. Each national bank was required to deposit with the Comptroller United States bonds equal to one-third of its capital, but not less than $30,000. In exchange, the bank received national bank notes equal to 90 percent of the par or market value (whichever was lower) of the deposited bonds. The total issue of national bank notes was limited to $300 million, one-half distributed among the states on the basis of population and the remainder on the basis of existing banking facilities. National banks in so-called reserve cities were required to maintain in their own vaults a 25 percent reserve in lawful money against deposits. Those in other cities were also required to maintain a 25 percent reserve, but one-half of this amount could be deposited in banks in New York City. Country banks had to maintain a 15 percent reserve, three-fifths of which could be deposited in a city bank. All banks had to maintain a 25 percent reserve against their note circulation and were taxed semiannually ½ of 1 percent on the average amount in circulation.

THE DECLINE AND RECOVERY OF
STATE BANKING Bankers did not greet the national banking system with enthusiasm. By October 1864 the number of national banks had grown to only 508. Many of the largest were new banks founded by private bankers. Most of the bankers who had converted from state charters had been persuaded to do so against their initial inclination. The combined note circulation of the 508 banks was only $45.3 million. Nor had Chase's hopes of securing a captive market for government bonds been realized, for total national bank holdings of government securities amounted to only a little over $100 million. It was apparent that bankers preferred to operate under state charters if for no other reason than that state regulation was less stringent than national regulation. Most state laws required less capital and lower reserves, and they permitted branch banking and loans on real estate, whereas the National Bank Act prohibited the latter and permitted the former only in exceptional cases. Congress was not unaware of this situation, and it proceeded to make national bank charters more popular by making state banking less attractive. In 1864 it imposed a 2 percent tax on state bank notes. In 1865, when this step failed to have the desired effect, Congress raised the tax to 10 percent, making it unprofitable for state banks to issue notes. Since the banks outside the big cities did most of their business in bank notes, the tax exerted pressure on them to convert to national charters. By October 1865 there were 1,513 national banks with $171.3 million circulation, and by October 1866 there were 1,644 with $280.3 million circulation.

Up to 1874 changes in the National Bank Act and the declining importance of state banks caused a relative as well as an absolute increase in national bank note circulation. In the decade after 1874 the quantity of national bank notes remained about the same, but other forms of money increased. After 1884 the volume of national bank notes declined. The main reason for this decline was that the price of government bonds rose markedly as interest rates went into a secular decline. It was not profitable for banks to issue bank notes when government bonds were selling at a premium and yielding only 1.4 to 2.7 percent, or less than enough to cover taxes on circulation and other costs.

Checkbook money also helped to stop the expansion of national banking at the expense of state banking. In the early postwar years, the 10 percent federal tax on state bank notes "persuaded" more and more state banks to take out national charters, and during the next decade the number of state banks declined almost 60 percent, and their loans declined about 70 percent. However, with the increased use of checkbook money and the declining importance of bank notes, state banking began to regain its importance, for state regulation of banking continued to be less rigid than national regulation.

Inflationists used the decline of national bank currency as ammunition in fighting for expansion of currency. But while they threw brickbats at Wall Street, their argument was vitiated by the continuous increase in the use of checks. Sound-money men were quick to point out that this growth in checkbook money more than offset the decline in the circulation of currency and coin. However, in the West and the South, where the quantity theory had its largest following, farmers were unimpressed, for unlike city dwellers, they still transacted their business in currency.

THE DEFECTS OF NATIONAL BANKING · In one sense the increased use of checkbook money illustrated the pervasiveness of industrial capitalism in post–Civil War America. Equally illustrative was the fact that commercial banks were able to put more of their assets into commercial loans in contrast to the earlier period of heavy real estate loans and the later period of large investments, especially in government bonds. The orthodox therefore viewed this period as the golden age of banking. It was the period when lip service to the "real bills" doctrine and the gold standard was at its peak and when bank assets were most distinguished for liquidity. To be sure, the system was still not perfect from the orthodox view. There were too many time deposits, too many security loans, and banks attracted deposits by paying interest on them. George Coe, the articulate president of the American Exchange National Bank and a power in the New York Clearing House, expressed the prevailing conservative opinion when he denounced interest payments because the funds on which such payments were made were ordinarily loaned on property or on stocks and bonds and were therefore the same as the accommodation paper that had always been considered outside the acceptable realm of commercial bank operation.

The national banking system was superior to the old state banking system. It replaced a heterogeneous mass of paper issues with a more uniform currency and tended to strengthen the banking system against failures and overissue. But it was not completely satisfactory. The volume of its bank notes was inelastic; reserves were pyramided and immobile; the geographic distribution of circulation was arbitrary; and without a central bank, central bank functions could not be performed efficiently.

In the long run, national bank currency was inelastic and could not conform to the needs of business, for it was secured by United States bonds and depended not on the requirements of business but on the current market rate of interest, the state of the government bond market, and the fiscal policy of the United States Treasury. During the thirty-five years following the Civil War, market interest rates were declining. Since the interest on government bonds was fixed, the bonds naturally went to a premium, prompting the banks, as already described, to sell them and to contract their circulation.

But even over short periods, national bank currency did not expand and contract with the needs of business. In periods of prosperity, when the business community wanted more money, national bank circulation declined because the banks had outlets for their funds that were more attractive than government bonds. The situation was reversed in periods of recession, and currency expanded even though the demand for it was lacking. At the same time, the system hampered government fiscal operations, because the Treasury was reluctant to pay off the debt on which the national bank notes depended.

Nor was national bank currency well adapted to the needs of commercial agriculture. Rigidly restricted as it was by government securities and the possibilities of profit on bond sales, it could not satisfy the farmer's need for extra funds in the spring for planting and in the fall for moving crops.

Perhaps the greatest weakness of the system lay in the fact that it encouraged the tendency for bank reserves to concentrate in New York City. For many years out-of-town bankers had deposited their excess funds in New York City because (1) it had a thriving call-loan market in which funds could be invested without sacrificing liquidity, (2) many New York banks offered interest on out-of-town deposits, and (3) New York banks were well known, for the city was the chief center for export and import trade.

The National Bank Act encouraged this flow of funds by allowing out-of-town banks to deposit part of their reserves in New York banks. Thus reserves were pyramided, for both the depositing bank and the depository bank counted the same funds as reserves. In addition, the practice made reserves immobile and continued to subject the commercial banking system to the peculiar demands of the farming communities. In order to take care of the increased demand for farm loans during spring planting and fall harvesting, country banks drew extensively on their deposits in New York.[6] Consequently, twice a year credit in the New York money market tightened and interest rates rose, thus creating a mild crisis. But as soon as the seasonal burst of activity in agriculture spent itself, the financial community returned to normal. Unfortunately, there were times, such as 1873, 1893, and 1907, when the demand for funds was larger than anticipated or loans could not be easily liquidated. Then credit would be unobtainable at any price, cash would go into hoarding, and panic conditions would prevail.

Under the national banking system, there was no central organization or institution that could act as a stabilizing influence in the money market during periods of rapid inflation or deflation. The Treasury, operating through the subtreasuries, and a few national banks, such as the First National Bank of New York, did exert some central banking influence, but it was weak and ineffective. Local clearing houses also assumed some leadership; however, most of their activities were undertaken after a crisis had begun, not before. The other advantages of central banking were also completely lacking. There was no agency to act as a link between the banks and the Treasury, the government lacked a centralized fiscal agent, there was no central control over the nation's gold supply or discount rate, and there was no bankers' bank that could rediscount paper for individual banks.

[6] A different explanation for this flow of bank deposits is given in C. A. E. Goodhart, *The New York Money Market and the Finance of Trade, 1900–1913* (Cambridge, Mass.: Harvard University Press, 1969).

The most annoying weakness of the national banking system was that clearing of checks between different geographic areas was carried on through correspondent banks in an antiquated and costly manner. The classic example was the clearance of a check drawn on Sag Harbor, Long Island, and deposited in Hoboken, New Jersey. Before it made the return trip of 93 miles to Sag Harbor, the check traveled for ten days, covered 1,223 miles, and passed through ten banks. The mobility of capital funds, under the circumstances, was not at its optimum efficiency.

OTHER CRITICISMS OF NATIONAL BANKING · From its outset, the national banking system failed to gain public favor. The ever-popular charge of monopoly was levied against it, even though it was based on the New York free banking system, which had been expressly passed as an antimonopoly measure. The government's practice of favoring certain national banks with deposits was also criticized as inimical to the American tradition of equal opportunity. Finally, it was commonly believed that the national banks made a double profit: one from interest on the securities deposited with the Comptroller of the Currency, another from interest on the bank notes issued against the bonds. Despite its wide acceptance and superficial logic, the charge was not true, for the constant decline in national bank note circulation offered conclusive evidence that the expenses and restrictions involved in issuing notes were so great that it actually did not pay banks to take advantage of the privilege. The national banks had to pay the cost of redeeming national bank notes. In addition, they had to pay ½ of 1 percent semiannual tax on circulation. Note issues also restricted a bank's lending power, for neither national bank notes nor government bonds could be counted as reserves, and until 1874 a 25 percent reserve had to be maintained against note issues. Furthermore, notes could be issued only up to 90 percent of the par value of bonds. Since bonds always sold at a premium, banks had to tie up large amounts of their funds, against which nothing could be issued.

The public was on more solid ground in contending that the limit imposed on total note circulation and the method of its distribution among the states were neither fair nor economically wise. Originally the limit was $300 million. Half was distributed according to population and half according to the existing banking capital, resources, and business of the states and territories. Thus the older states, having the largest populations and banking capital, received the lion's share of the national bank note circulation. The state of Connecticut had more circulation than Michigan, Iowa, Minnesota, Kansas, Missouri, Kentucky, and Tennessee combined, and the per capita circulation of Rhode Island was $77.16, whereas that of Arkansas was $ .13.

THE BANKING SYSTEM AND THE PANICS OF 1873 AND 1884 · The severe depression of 1873 and its preceding circumstances illustrated how the banking system accentuated economic difficulties. During the first eight months of 1872, bank loans increased slowly but continually. In the latter part of August, large amounts of cash were withdrawn from the New York banks and the money market tightened. The Treasury gave some assistance by buying some $5 million of bonds to increase bank reserves, but the pressure on the banking system was not relieved until the movement of farm crops had been completed. Another similar seasonal difficulty developed in the spring of 1873, but this time liquidation of loans and securities was difficult because of weaknesses in railroad securities. Three brokerage houses suspended operations in May, but by June the situation was so much improved that businessmen decided that a new spurt of prosperity was about to begin. Unfortunately, this optimistic view was ill-founded. Railroads could not continue to meet their fixed charges, capital imports declined from their high level, and the stock market began to fall. Banks began to contract credit, country banks clamored for funds, and hoarding by individuals increased. In September seven New York banks, holding 72 percent of total interbank deposits, could not liquidate their loans fast enough to meet the increasing demand for funds, and in a short time they were operating with a reserve deficiency. Businessmen and banks had nowhere to turn, and with progressively accelerated speed, the New York money market headed for inevitable disaster. Then on September 18 came the shock of the decade, when the great banking house of Jay Cooke failed.

The events of 1873 were repeated on a smaller scale in the spring of 1884. The usual seasonal demand for funds combined with difficulties in railroad financing sent the banking system into convulsions. Loans and discounts were called, thereby wiping out secondary deposits. Primary deposits were withdrawn into hoards and rapid deflation took place. Fortunately, the repercussion of 1884 was comparatively short. By the latter part of 1885 business activity was recovering, and the demand for funds again caused an expansion of bank deposits.

THE RISE OF THE TRUST COMPANY · Bankers, being pragmatic Americans, sought ways and means of circumventing the presumably overrigid requirements of the national banking system. One way was to convert to a state charter as the use of checkbook money spread and gradually overcame the need to issue bank notes. Another and even more attractive method for city bankers was to establish a trust company. Not that trust companies were new. As previously mentioned, trusts go back into medieval times, and trust companies first appeared in the United States in the early 1820s. But by 1890, having passed through both infancy and adolescence, they were mature institutions.

In the first period of their history—that is, from the 1820s until the early 1850s—trust company functions were closely related to personal asset administration, especially estate administration. In the next era, through the 1880s, trust companies became closely connected to the security exchanges. Their activities expanded to include trusteeship under bond indentures. In addition, they became registrars and agents for stock transfer and dividend payment. Some simple reasons explained this situation. In the 1870s and 1880s bond issues became larger and maturities longer. Then, too, the Stock Exchange, in 1869, required all listed stocks and bonds to have a paying agent located in New York. Since trust powers were not included in the scope of commercial banks, the trust companies automatically obtained this windfall.

At the end of the Civil War, there were seven trust companies.[7] By 1890 there were 255 companies with deposits of at least $336 million and assets of at least $450 million. New York held about half of this total. The career of one of the New York companies, the United States Trust Company, illustrates the phenomenal prosperity enjoyed by the trusts in the last part of the century, especially in the eighties and nineties. As can be seen in Table 6, the firm's total assets more than doubled in its first ten years of business, more than tripled in the next six years, rose by 50 percent in the 1870s, and then almost doubled again in the 1880s. Deposits increased almost ten times in the years between 1865 and 1894.[8] At the same time, the composition of the assets also changed. Mortgages, once the foundation of the trust, increased hardly at all; but loans on personal security swelled continuously, and security holdings expanded impressively from the eighties onward. At first the security investments were confined to federal, state, and municipal obligations, but by the 1890s the portfolio contained a variety of gilt-edge railroad bonds.

TABLE 6
Selected Balance Sheet Items, United States Trust Company, 1855–1894

Item	1855	1865	1871	1880	1894*
Mortgages	$ 827,530	$1,151,400	$ 1,708,000	$ 2,403,500	$ 2,895,500
Loans on personal security	694,168	1,506,850	9,828,414	17,802,750	18,124,865
Securities	281,913	1,857,647	2,656,076	2,178,704	16,163,522
Total assets	2,076,005	5,804,891	18,019,003	27,708,477	50,429,744
Capital	1,000,000	1,000,000	1,500,000	2,000,000	2,000,000
Deposits in trust	914,361	4,005,399	14,890,541	22,130,692	38,389,468†

Source: Annual Reports provided by courtesy of the United States Trust Company.
* *June 1, 1894.*
† *"Deposits as per ledger."*

But the United States Trust Company did not represent all trust companies, for trusts were a decidedly heterogeneous group of institutions. The Title Guaranty Trust Company, for example, operated like a savings bank, and the New York Life Insurance and Trust operated like an investment trust.

There were many reasons for the rise of the trust companies. They could

---

[7] Farmers' Loan & Trust, New York Life Insurance and Trust, United States Trust, Ohio Life Insurance & Trust in New York, the Pennsylvania Company for Insurances on Lives and Granting Annuities, Girard Life Insurance Annuity and Trust in Philadelphia, and Merchants Loan and Trust of Chicago.

[8] Trust company assets in 1890 were $450 million; commercial bank assets were $4.6 billion.

not issue notes, but the increased emphasis on deposits and the gradual fading of note issue eliminated this disadvantage. And from this point on, it seemed that all the advantages lay with the trust company as contrasted to the standard commercial bank. The trust could hold mortgages and securities, its deposits were more stable, it held a lower reserve (10 percent usually) against deposits, and it paid interest on deposits, whereas most city banks did not. The percent paid declined as market rates fell. At first the standard rate was 5 percent on time deposits and 4 percent on demand, but by the late eighties 1½ percent prevailed.

Although their growth was quite extraordinary, little attention was paid to the trust companies. It was said that in 1890 the attorney general of one state returned a questionnaire on trust companies with the notation that the only trust company doing business in that state was Standard Oil of New Jersey. The story is probably apocryphal, but like all apocryphal stories it reveals a truth. Trust companies were so unknown that state governments did not get around to putting them under regulation until 1872, when Connecticut placed them under the jurisdiction of the banking department. Two years later, New York State did the same.

BUSTLING ACTIVITY IN THE
SECURITIES MARKET · Still another reason for the surge of the trust companies was that they were intimately associated with investment banks and with life insurance companies, both of which also experienced a robust growth in the last of the century. Indeed, the years after 1850, with their booming national income, their high rate of saving, and their demand for capital funds to finance such major undertakings as the building of the railroads, were the beginning of the halcyon days of investment banking and so-called security capitalism.

On all sides, commentators of the day, from the English political scientist and traveler Lord Bryce to the broker James K. Medbery, remarked on the ubiquity of security speculation. "Today," wrote Medbery in 1870, "the wires of our telegraph companies are constantly burdened with orders to brokers from gold[9] or stock operators. . . . Many of these persons are large capitalists; the majority are salaried men, small merchants, individuals who deem it an averagely safe business to divert their surplus to the chances of the market."[10]

Admittedly, these commentators spoke from a biased sample. After all, Medbery was a broker, and Bryce, as one wit expressed it, "looked at America over a champagne glass." But activity in the securities markets did spring from peak to peak in the seventies and eighties. The volume of shares traded averaged 51.2 million a year in the last years of the 1870s, 104.4 million in the early 1880s, and 83.1 million between 1885 and 1889. As early as 1865, Hallgarten & Hartzefelt and Gentil & Phillipps, two active brokerage houses, each did a volume of business in excess of $160 million. And it was not simply the volume of business that attested to the fact

[9] An allusion to those who bought and sold gold in the free gold market that operated during the suspension of the gold standard, 1862 to 1878.
[10] James K. Medbery, *Men and Mysteries of Wall Street* (New York, 1870).

that the securities business was thriving. The Dow-Jones average appeared in the 1890s, and in 1890 F. W. Hopkins, a partner in S. V. White & Co., delivered a lecture on industrial securities at Yale University.

As usual, there were a multitude of reasons for the awakening of investment banking and the securities market. The booming economy was the main cause of what became known in some circles as "finance capitalism." The expansion of the national income, the much greater supply of dollar saving, and the larger number of wealthy individuals provided the fuel to stoke the furnace. Investment bankers appeared in much larger numbers to tend the furnace, and an eager public prepared to consume what the furnace produced.

As the volume of transactions grew, improvements in the market's technical and business organization removed some of the more obvious bottlenecks and rigidities that might have interfered with expansion. In 1866 the Atlantic Cable began to operate. The stock ticker appeared the following year, and in 1878 telephones were installed on the floor of the Stock Exchange. In 1863 a group of the impatient rebelled against the Old Guard, who, it was said, were preserving a monopoly. The young Turks established a second board in William Street in 1864, and soon this "coal hole" was handling half the business. In the same year, the exchange established a Government Bond Department. By the end of the decade, differences between the original and the rump exchanges had been patched up, and the separate pieces were consolidated into a reorganized exchange.

Not all who played the market emerged with their wallets bulging. Indeed, most of those who were most familiar with Wall Street regarded the pastime with exaggerated pessimism. Listen to "Advice to People about How to Speculate in Wall Street" in *Hunt's Merchants' Magazine* in 1870:

> It is a common saying among bankers and brokers, when a "new man" brings his theories and his money into the stock market, that he is come to be fleeced. Every house in Wall Street that keeps active speculating accounts, knows well that nine out of ten of its customers lose more than they win, and that more than half of them in the end lose all they have. Most bankers will candidly tell new customers so; and we have heard one experienced broker and speculator urge his clients strongly if they had money to throw away in gambling to take it to a faro bank at once and "fight the tiger," as on the whole a pleasanter and less dangerous way than depositing it with him. . . . There is no other business so thickly strewn as stock-jobbing with impressive illustrations of the old Spanish proverb, "many come for wool who go home shorn."
>
> But these gloomy generalities do not affect the hopeful mind of the confident youth. . . . The whole secret of speculating is to buy cheap and sell dear. . . . Only when a few bitter experiences have taught them the impossibility of applying any general test of "cheapness" or "dearness" to prices, do they begin to understand that the market price at the moment is always the result of the combined judgments of many hundreds of men, applied to the subject with an intensity which only personal interest excites, and with a shrewdness which nothing but long experience can produce. He who would

predict the course of prices for a day must needs be wiser than "a multitude of counsellors. . . ."

Admittedly, the stock market did burst into new highs and plummet downward with some frequency in the post-1870 era. During the panic of 1873 and the early months of what was to be the longest depression in financial history, stock prices fluctuated in a most exciting fashion. New York Central, 105½ on August 11, dropped to 77⅞ in November, then climbed back to 96½ in December. Union Pacific dropped from 28⅜ to 15⅜, then soared to 32¼. Wabash went from 71¾ to 34⅜ and then back to 54.

What added to the excitement of the game were the well-publicized activities of a group of plungers who seemed constantly engaged in cornering stocks, selling short, and thinking of new ways of beating the odds. One of the most spectacular corners was engineered in the late 1860s, when William H. Marston and Henry Keep got a corner in Michigan and Prairie du Chien Railroad, better known as the "Prairie Dog Road." The stock went from 57 to 275 in two weeks. These were the days of Jay Gould and Jim Fisk, of the great bears, Daniel Drew and Charles F. Woerishoffer, and of Russell Sage, who made much, spent little, and introduced puts and calls into the American market.[11]

THE GOLDEN DAYS OF

INVESTMENT BANKING · In back of these spectacular brokers and professional stock market players were the conservative, mysterious investment bankers. In the late 1800s they could be divided into four separate groups, not necessarily allies but groups each having its own distinct geographical background. First of all, there was the group that surrounded the house of Jay Cooke—the firm itself and its allies, mostly brokers, Vermilye Co., Henry Clews, and John Cisco & Co. Cooke was unquestionably an innovator of more than ordinary importance, for as agent for the federal Treasury during the Civil War, he was the one who introduced modern methods of distributing securities. Unlike his contemporaries, who dealt with persons of large fortune, Cooke placed loans with small banks and local capitalists. This practice stood him in good stead in selling Civil War securities. With a staff of 2,500 salesmen and with liberal use of throwaways and advertising that appealed to patriotism, he was phenomenally successful in selling the five-twenties[12] and the 7.30 notes[13] that raised most of the money the Union needed to finance the war. After the war, Cooke undertook to finance the Northern Pacific Railroad. Somewhat of a lone wolf and not having strong enough ties with European bankers, Cooke did not have the resources required for

---

[11] Like many other financial gimmicks, puts and calls were well known in Europe before they were dealt in in the United States. Puts and calls can be defined as contracts that give the owner of the contract the power to buy or sell securities at some time in the future at a specified price.

[12] So called because they matured in twenty years and were callable in five years.

[13] Notes that paid 7.3 percent, or a penny a day on $50.

this mammoth undertaking. He failed in 1873, probably the most surprising failure in American financial history. Just as Cooke had emerged from the failure of Clark & Co., so the house of Charles D. Barney emerged from Cooke's failure.[14]

The members of the second group—the German-Jewish group—sprang from quite different backgrounds. The founders of many of the firms were originally peddlers. Thus the Seligmans of J. & W. Seligman & Co., the Lehman brothers, Abraham Kuhn and Solomon Loeb, Philip Heidelbach of Heidelbach, Ickelheimer, and Marcus Goldman of Goldman, Sachs progressed from peddling to banking via cotton brokerage, clothing stores, and dealing in commercial paper. Most of these houses climbed the ladder without any direct help. The eight Seligman brothers built their peddling business into a chain of small stores, then opened an importing business in New York, began to sell the federal government's obligations in the early years of the Civil War, and, finally, in 1864, opened a bank that by 1870 was advertised as "fiscal agent of the United States State Department." Goldman, Sachs & Co. began when Marcus Goldman left peddling to become a dealer in commercial paper; that is, he bought the promissory notes of small businessmen and resold them to banks both in the United States and abroad. In 1882 Goldman formed a partnership with his son-in-law, Samuel Sachs, and the present firm emerged in 1885, primarily as a commercial-paper house.

Some German-Jewish houses grew and prospered with the help of talent and capital imported from the long-established banking houses of Frankfurt and Hamburg. The leading example was Kuhn, Loeb & Co., which benefited immensely through the infusion of Schiffs and Warburgs. Jacob H. Schiff, who came to the United States in 1865 and shortly became senior partner in the firm, married Theresa Loeb, and Paul Warburg married Nina Loeb.

A third group of bankers of some considerable importance consisted of the non-Boston New Englanders: Levi Morton of Morton, Rose & Co. and Morton, Bliss & Co., Harvey Fisk, and, above all, J. Pierpont Morgan. Morgan's father was a partner in Peabody & Co. in London and later senior partner in J. S. Morgan & Co. J. P., therefore, had valuable connections with the leading British houses—the Rothschilds, the Barings, and naturally J. S. Morgan. By 1863 the younger Morgan formed a merchant banking partnership, Dabney, Morgan & Co. The firm dealt in securities, bills of exchange, acceptances, foreign exchange, gold, and other commodities. In 1871 Morgan and Anthony Drexel of Philadelphia created Drexel, Morgan & Co. with headquarters at 23 Wall Street.[15] The firm specialized in underwriting securities, and with the help of Morton, Bliss & Co. took over much of the government bond business from Jay Cooke. In 1879, when the Treasury had accomplished the refunding of the Civil War debt, Morgan turned his attention to railroad finance. For the remainder of the nineteenth century and well into the twentieth, the House of Morgan

---

14 The present firm of Smith, Barney & Co. represents an amalgamation of Charles D. Barney and Edward B. Smith & Co., formed in Philadelphia in 1892.

15 Drexel died in 1894 and the firm was reorganized as J. P. Morgan & Co.

was preeminent in railroad finance. In the 1890s the firm began to become seriously involved in industrial consolidation and reorganization. The formation of the General Electric Co. in 1892 was a pioneering venture, but most of this history will be kept for a later chapter.

J. P. Morgan's personality was a cardinal factor in the House of Morgan's success, but it was by no means the only one. The firm was the best organized of any in the investment banking business. Moreover, Morgan had the supreme gift of the outstandingly successful entrepreneur —the ability to select men of great talent, weld them into the organization, and get the best out of their talents. Morgan was the conductor, and his partners, Burns, Fabri, Coster, Stetson, and others, were superb specialists, much more expert than Morgan in their particular sphere.

The House of Morgan had another advantage in addition to capital, talent, and connections. It had the ability to enlist other houses as allies in its ventures. At one time or another, most of the major financial houses participated in Morgan underwriting, but some relations were much more intimate than others. The alliance with George F. Baker of New York's First National Bank was the essence of an entente cordiale. In addition, there were close associations with Morton, Bliss; the National Bank of Commerce; Lee, Higginson & Co.; Kidder, Peabody & Co.; James Stillman's National City Bank; and later an added number of insurance companies and trust companies.

The fourth group of bankers of unusual power in the world of finance were the Boston firms, chiefly Lee, Higginson & Co. and Kidder, Peabody & Co. Just as mysterious as most investment bankers, these houses, whose ancestry antedated all the others, played a quiet hand in almost every major financing that took place in the nineteenth century. But inbreeding, financial conservatism, and an imperfect managerial structure eventually had their effect; by the end of the nineteenth century, the Boston firms had become satellites of the more efficiently managed House of Morgan.

In addition to the better-known alliances and ententes, there were many smaller firms of private bankers, firms that have been virtually ignored in the preoccupation with commercial banking. As mentioned earlier, private bankers were much more important than can be gathered from the literature on banking and finance. The main reason for this oversight is that there are practically no data on how they conducted their business activities. All that exists are scraps of tantalizing information.[16]

From the available information, we know that there were at least 617 private banks in the United States in 1855, 830 in 1865, 2,578 in 1880, and 4,365 in 1890. In the latter year, there were more private banks than state or national commercial banks, although their assets were much less. After 1890 and until World War I, the number of private banks remained about the same; then it dropped drastically.

The growth of private banking from the 1840s on was attributable more

---

[16] In 1887 the Comptroller of the Currency began to publish figures on the number and the assets of private banks in 18 states. *The Banker's Almanac and Register* annually published a list of private bankers.

to geography than to finance. Private bankers needed little capital, and they could supply personalized banking services to communities that were too small to permit incorporated banks. As the rural areas spread across the United States, private banking thrived, but its advantages disappeared with the end of the frontier.

Private banking could afford to be mysterious, and its practitioners did not feel any compulsion to report their activities to the Comptroller of the Currency. In 1890, for example, only 30 percent of the private bankers submitted reports. Their assets were equal to slightly more than 10 percent of state bank assets and 5 percent of those of national banks.

THE ESTABLISHMENT OF THE
COMMERCIAL-PAPER HOUSE · As has been noted, dealing in commercial paper was one of the private banker's most important activities. Commercial paper was also one of the most important media in the money market, and it deserves much more attention than it has thus far received.

The modern commercial-paper house,[17] unlike other economic institutions, is an American product. Indeed, it is the only financial mechanism that is indigenous to the United States. But like all other institutions, it is the product of a long process of pioneering and innovating. The pioneers, the first houses that bought and sold paper, appeared early in the nineteenth century. The innovators, the specialists whose example would be generally copied, came on the scene just before the Civil War. One of the first specialists in commercial paper was Henry Clews & Co., founded in 1857. As Clews wrote, in a not overly modest fashion,

> My firm became the largest dealer in mercantile paper, which business had formerly been controlled by two other firms for at least a quarter of a century, and whose old fogy methods were by my innovation easily eclipsed. The merchants at that time would go to these discount firms and leave their receivables, bearing their endorsement, on sale there, and only when sold by piecemeal could they obtain the avails thereof. I had inaugurated the system of buying acceptances and receivables out and out.

But firms like Henry Clews were small indeed compared with the giants that appeared at the end of the century. Then the business became truly cosmopolitan as houses were established in Chicago, Kansas City, and other Western centers, and as the home offices of the large Eastern commercial-paper houses hired traveling representatives to tour the country. It is easy to deduce what effect this activity had on capital mobility.

The total volume of commercial paper for the country as a whole is hard to estimate for the early years, but it certainly became a thriving business as soon as it started. One estimate of outstanding paper in 1862 puts the total at about $700 million. Volume presumably expanded after the panic of 1873. In 1882 a bank president said that New York banks were buying $1 million a day. In the same year, a prominent note broker handled $42

---

[17] A commercial-paper house is one that does a sizable business in buying and selling paper. It seldom, if ever, acts as a broker between buyer and seller.

million of paper. As early as 1883 one New York bank, the Importers and Traders, had established a credit department, but it was far ahead of its time, for in 1890 only one or two banks had such a department. Systematic credit investigation became common only in the next decade.

One of the reasons for the popularity of commercial paper was that it was a cheaper way of borrowing for Southern and Western businessmen, because bank rates in their vicinity were much higher than rates in the East. Yet at times rates soared fantastically. In November 1873, for example, paper was bought at a discount of 18 to 24 percent.

LIFE INSURANCE: THE FASTEST-GROWING FINANCIAL INTERMEDIARY OF THE LATE

NINETEENTH CENTURY · Of all the financial intermediaries, life insurance experienced the most phenomenal growth. Between 1860 and 1890, life insurance companies watched their assets multiply 32 times, from an insignificant $24 million to $771 million, an amount more than twice as large as the assets in the hands of general insurance companies although still considerably less than the assets of the savings banks.

The amount of life insurance written in 1868 was greater than the national debt. The industry had become, in the words of the New York insurance commissioner, "one of the great business interests." By the end of the century, Americans owned more life insurance than the rest of the world combined. But as had been the trend ever since 1845, the sale of life insurance continued to be unevenly distributed among the various companies. Three companies, New York Life, Mutual of New York, and the Equitable Life Assurance Society, had $2 billion in force in 1890, more than the next 22 companies combined.

There were five reasons for the extraordinary rise of life insurance. The first and most important was the revival of that hardy perennial of the insurance business—the tontine. As has been said, the tontine, which originated in seventeenth-century France, was the seed for the birth of the Insurance Company of North America in the eighteenth century. It fell out of favor in the early 1800s but the idea itself never died. In 1847 an article in *Hunt's* treated the advantages of endowments, annuities, and tontines. Then in 1867 Henry Hyde of Equitable, an extraordinary person in every way, resurrected the idea. It was then quickly adopted by his competitors in Mutual of New York and New York Life.

The traditional role of life companies had always been thought to be, in the words of Colonel Jacob Greene of Connecticut Mutual, "providing family protection at its mathematically ascertained cost." To ascertain the "mathematically ascertained cost" has always been a logical but complicated procedure. There is a cost involved in the writing of insurance—agents' commissions, medical fees, and so on. This "loading," as it is called in the trade, has always been generously overestimated, but the rationale is that all excess loading in a mutual company is returned to the policyholder in the form of dividends, which are, therefore, not really dividends but a return of an overcharge. The net premium (the gross premium minus loading) is used to pay for the cost of the actual insurance. In order to maintain a level premium, it is necessary to overcharge the policyholder in the early years when mortality is low and to undercharge him in later years when mortality is high. The excess premiums in the early years are deposited in a reserve fund to take care of the insufficient premiums in the later years.

From 1846 on, the policyholder who ceased to meet his premiums was guaranteed a set of nonforfeiture values—that is, he could take the reserve against his policy in cash, or he could use it to buy paid-up life insurance, or he could use it to buy limited-term insurance equal to the face of the policy.[18] It is plain that under the orthodox concept of life insurance held by Colonel Greene, the capital funds available in life insurance companies were limited to the total amount of reserves—that is, the unearned premiums plus the small year-by-year excess loading. This policy hardly satisfied the more ambitious entrepreneurs like Hyde, and it was all but swept aside by the introduction of the tontine policy.

Under the tontine plan that was conceived in the Equitable, the beneficiaries of policyholders who died received the face value of the policy; those who let their policies lapse received nothing; those who kept their policy in force until the end of a stipulated period (10, 15, or 20 years) were paid the face value of the policy, plus their own accumulated dividends for the whole period, plus a share of the dividends of those who died, plus a share of the accumulation of those who let their policies lapse. The policyholder could now view his insurance not just as family protection in the event he died, or as a way of saving small amounts, but as a speculation in which he was betting on outliving the majority of participants—in short, as yielding a substantial personal return.

The tontine feature, coupled with aggressive salesmanship, enabled a few companies to take over the business and build up large reserves that enabled them to become important forces in the capital markets. Companies like Connecticut Mutual that refused to offer the tontine policy sank rapidly. Second largest in 1878, it had dropped to fourteenth by the end of the century.

Tontines benefited the capital markets and, at least in the short run, the companies that wrote them, but these benefits came at the expense of the policyholders, who voluntarily participated in what was essentially a swindle.[19] When the plan was at its height, Equitable was writing $300 million a year. In the ten years from 1885 to 1894, the company wrote a total of $1.4 billion. Of this amount, $463 million lapsed, two-thirds in tontines.

A second innovation accounting for the growth of life insurance companies as financial intermediaries was the introduction of industrial life insurance. The regular life companies sold their policies primarily to the higher- and middle-income classes. Generally policies were not available with a face value of less than $500, which for the 1870s was no small amount. Moreover, the annual or semiannual premium was a sum much in excess of what the average wage earner could afford. Not only were

---

18 Values that are, of course, still available to the policyholder today.

19 The word "swindle" may seem excessively harsh, but it was a swindle because most of those who participated really did not understand what they were participating in.

persons of limited means unable to acquire protection, but the life companies themselves were failing to provide a means of gathering the petty savings of these millions of individuals. It was to remedy these defects that the Prudential Insurance Company of America, under the leadership of its founder, John F. Dryden, in 1877 brought industrial insurance into the United States from England, where it had originated in 1854.

Industrial insurance was distinguishable from regular life insurance by its unique marketing characteristics. Industrial policies had a small face value—the Metropolitan Life Insurance Company offered policies of as little as $25. Then, too, industrial insurance was sold on a door-to-door basis by a task force of salesmen. Payments were collected weekly, again door to door. Finally, for the same features industrial insurance was far more costly than regular life insurance. But it did contain, on a much smaller scale to be sure, the same features as regular life policies, particularly the element of saving.

Companies like Prudential, Metropolitan, and John Hancock, which specialized in industrial insurance while also writing regular life coverage, grew rapidly to huge size. Metropolitan, which had been eighteenth in size among life insurance companies in 1875 with $25 million in force, became the largest company in 1910 with over $2 billion on the books. Prudential, which in 1876 had but $250,000 in insurance in force, expanded to $139 million in 1890.

Both the tontine and industrial insurance showed that life insurance had become a very imaginative business in which the emphasis was on growth through marketing and aggressive salesmanship. This stress that the life insurance business placed on marketing was another major reason for the pace at which the industry did expand.

Still a fourth reason for the industry's emergence was the liberalization of government restriction in the seventies and eighties. In 1869 New York, like many other states, had passed a law limiting investments to government securities and New York mortgages. In the seventies investment power was somewhat broadened geographically, and in the eighties New York companies were permitted to lend on mortgages anywhere in the United States. New England had long since made the same concessions to a national market.

The insurance companies were in a position to do something about capital mobility. They had the funds, and rates of return were higher in the West than in the East. All of them kept some of their deposits in banks far from the home office. According to a plan decided on at the time of its formation, Connecticut Mutual was the first to make substantial investments in Western securities. In 1861 it began to lend on farm mortgages. President Greene said in 1896 that in its fifty years, the company had loaned $146 million to 60,000 Westerners. Other companies also advanced money on agricultural loans. The Aetna, in alliance with the Illinois Central Railroad, made many loans to small farmers in Illinois at 10 percent interest. The Northwestern had $30 million in Illinois mortgages, the Union Central was active in Indiana, and the Mutual Benefit spread all through the Middle West.

In the process of spreading their investments, the life insurance companies changed their investment portfolio drastically. The percentage of assets invested in mortgages, policy loans, cash, deferred premiums, and premium notes fell off impressively; the percentage in stocks and bonds rose (see Table 7).

TABLE 7
Distribution of Life Insurance Company Assets, 1860–1890 (Percent)

Year	Mortgages	Stocks & Bonds	Real Estate	Other
1860	59.2	9.1	2.7	29.0
1870	40.1	17.8	3.4	38.7
1880	39.6	29.9	12.3	18.3
1890	40.2	35.2	10.4	14.1

Source: Division of Statistics and Research, Institute of Life Insurance.

The motivating powers putting all of these forces together were the ambitious, aggressive entrepreneurs who emerged at the heads of the fastest-growing companies: Hyde of Equitable, Frederick S. Winston and Richard McCurdy of Mutual, William H. Beers and John McCall of New York Life, Dryden of Prudential, and Joseph F. Knapp and John R. Hegeman of Metropolitan. Certainly these men had much to do with the astonishing growth of the industry. They all shared an insatiable enthusiasm for growth at almost any cost. Profits and rates of return faded into the background, and the motive became not profit maximization but, as one competitor put it, "more, perhaps, for the pride in doing it than otherwise."

As the life insurance business grew to become a great fount of capital, it also took on the barnacles, the decay, and the stultification associated with growth. The structure became honeycombed with bureaucracy; the leading firms became intermeshed with other financial intermediaries in the banking world; the aggressive entrepreneurs tired; and the business became a tool rather than an entity of its own. Home office staffs grew to awesome size. Prudential's staff rose from 89 in 1883 to 250 in 1890; Metropolitan's grew to 1,081 in 1897. The president of the latter company was referred to as "a business machine," and its home office proudly proclaimed that it had more typewriters than any other office building in the world.

Boards of directors deteriorated to mere rubber stamps and committee minutes became a mass of clichés. Elaborate home office buildings were erected to house the trappings of bureaucracy. Inevitably, the leaders of yesterday could echo the words of John Hegeman: "The business some time ago outgrew me." As they tired, they gave way to the bright salesmen and the financial wizards. George Perkins took over New York Life, and Gage Tarbell of Equitable and Haley Fiske of Metropolitan Life played similar roles.

Relationships with banks and trust companies reached the point where insurance companies were described as "the financial annexes to Wall Street interests." Mutual of New York in the 1890s depended on the finance committee headed by George F. Baker of the First National Bank of New York; New York Life on George Perkins, a Morgan partner; Equitable on General Louis Fitzgerald of the Mercantile Trust Company. Prudential relied on the brokerage house of Robert Winthrop & Co., Metropolitan on Vermilye & Co. But insurance companies also had a controlling interest in banks and trust companies even if they did not exercise it: Equitable in the Mercantile and Equitable Trust Companies in New York, the Commercial Trust Company in Philadelphia, and the Franklin National Bank in New York; Mutual in the Guaranty Trust, the United States Mortgage and Trust Company, and the Morton Trust Company; Metropolitan in the Hamilton Trust Company in Brooklyn and the National Shoe and Leather Bank; the New York in the New York Security & Trust Company; Prudential in the Fidelity Trust Company.

Decay in the business structure, as well as excessive salaries, nepotism, and a general ignorance of what was going on, resulted in a continuous decline in the net rate of return. From 6.90 in 1871 the rate dropped to 5.10 in 1890, all of which foreordained that the industry was in for severe trouble.

STABILITY IN GENERAL INSURANCE · In contrast to the life insurance business, general insurance produced no significant innovations or changes. But its growth performance was better than that of the national income and the population. The capital of joint stock, property insurance companies almost tripled in the thirty years after 1860. Total insurance in force in both stock and mutual companies grew astonishingly from $1.6 billion to $19.6 billion. Premiums rose from $30.8 million to $156.8 million. Despite some heavy losses, the surplus of general insurance companies rose from $8.8 million to $31.5 million.

As in the past, fire companies could not come through one generation without meeting a major disaster, in this case, the Chicago fire of 1871. Of 202 companies involved, 68 went bankrupt, 83 settled in part, and 51 settled in full.

THE RELATIVE DECLINE OF SAVINGS BANKS AND RISE OF BUILDING AND LOAN · The last of our financial intermediaries are the savings banks and the building and loan associations. Up to the panic of 1873, savings banks continued to enjoy a high rate of growth. A number of them had deposits of over $10 million each. The idea of savings banking was spreading, for there were such institutions in 18 states and the District of Columbia. Had the rate of growth experienced up to 1873 continued, savings bank deposits would have been over $5 billion by 1890. In actuality, they were only about $1.5 billion. Apparently they had run into a stone wall. The first difficulty was the panic of 1873. Savings bank failures in the aftermath of this economic disaster were higher than at any other time in history. There were 123 suspensions between 1875 and 1879, 13 in the next five years, and 11 between 1885 and 1889. The chilling effects of this catastrophe, even though total dollar losses were minute, resulted in a sharp swing to conservatism. Savings

bank officials surrendered their illusions of grandeur, and state governments moved to put the savings banks into a position of impregnable
safety. In 1875 New York passed a law restricting deposits to $5,000 and
investments to United States and New York State and municipal bonds,
plus those state bonds that had not been in default for ten years. Mortgage
loans were restricted to 50 percent of the assessed value of improved
property and 40 percent of unimproved.

In other states savings banks were stymied not so much by state regulation as by the activities of competing institutions. Savings banks continued
to thrive in New York and New England, but they quickly deteriorated in
other areas. In the West commercial banks caught most of the savings
accounts in their interest-bearing, time-deposit net. In Pennsylvania the
savings banks ran into the competition of building and loan associations.

Conservatism, regulation, and competition dampened savings bank
growth despite the robust rise in the national income. Table 8 shows that
the number of depositors continued to multiply. However, the average size
of deposits dropped after the depression of 1873 from $390 in 1875 to $350
in 1880, where it remained for the rest of the century.

TABLE 8
The Growth of Savings Banks, 1860–1890

Year	No. of Depositors	Total Deposits (Millions of Dollars)	Percentage Growth in Depositors	Percentage Growth in Deposits
1860	693,870	$ 149.3	—	—
1865	980,844	242.6	41	63
1870	1,630,846	549.9	66	127
1875	2,359,864	924.0	44	69
1880	2,335,582	819.1	—	—
1885	3,071,495	1,095.2	32	34
1890	4,258,893	1,524.8	39	39

Source: U.S. Bureau of the Census, *Historical Statistics of the United States.*

Like most financial institutions, building and loan associations did not
receive any particular notice until long after they had sprung into full
growth. According to Seymour Dexter, who wrote the first full treatment of
the associations in 1891, they did not "attract general attention" until
1888. Yet by then they were in thriving condition, for it was estimated in
1893 that there were 5,838 associations with $450 million in assets.

Pennsylvania had many more associations than any other state in the
Union. In the 1860s, 148 such institutions were chartered. In the early
1870s, 317 more came into existence. By 1891 the state had 900, half of
them in Philadelphia. Ohio was second with about 600, Illinois third with
550, and New York fourth with about 300.

It is impossible to say how much building and loan assets amounted to
in the 1870s and 1880s. In most states, there were no associations before
the late 1870s, but once begun, they increased rapidly. New Jersey offers

a typical example. In 1880 there were approximately 100 with assets of $5.8 million, and in 1882, 128 with $6.7 million in assets. It appears from what data are available that there were no more than 2,000 associations in the United States in 1888, but by 1893 there were over 5,000, a rather astonishing rate of growth.

More important, however, is that by the late nineteenth century, indeed by the 1870s, building and loan associations had changed their main objective. Before the Civil War, they had been small, temporary, and designed primarily to help would-be home owners; by the end of the century, they were more involved in gathering up savings. Encouraging home owners had become a secondary objective. Yet the process of change had been pushed ahead chiefly by real estate promoters, many of whom were financed by these same associations.

THE INTERMEDIARIES AND THE ECONOMY · How well were the financial intermediaries performing during the last decades of the 1800s? We have three general yardsticks by which to measure safety and solvency, mobility, and the contribution to the supply of investment funds: the number of bank failures, comparative interest rates, and the money supply.

Commercial bank suspensions averaged approximately 28 a year between 1863 and 1890, ranging from 2 in 1870 to 80 in 1878. The losses could not have been very great, for most of the suspensions were among smaller banks where deposits and capital were not high. Altogether 168 savings banks failed in the 30 years after 1860, 60 of them in 1878. Again the losses were not very large. Three Massachusetts bank failures, for example, involved losses of less than $75,000. It seems safe to conclude that banks were more solvent in this period than in any other up to 1933.

Insurance companies were another matter. Life companies found themselves in a precarious position in the depression of 1873 and many of them failed. Property insurance companies were badly damaged by the great Chicago fire, but at other times life was placid and serene.

How satisfactorily the financial system met the country's investment needs can best be shown by what happened to the money supply and interest rates. Between 1867 and 1890 the money supply, conventionally defined as commercial bank deposits in the hands of the public and currency outside the banks, tripled.[20] The trend was by no means an uninterrupted one. As could be expected, the money supply fell in the recessions of 1867 and 1883 and in the depression years 1873–1878. But for the whole period, the growth of the money stock exceeded the growth of population and the growth of gross national product.

Interest rates dropped secularly during the late 1800s. The rate on commercial paper was over 8 percent in 1866 and about 5.5 percent in 1890. Yields on railroad bonds fell even more, from about 8 percent in 1866 to 4.5 percent in 1890. But interest rates in the different sections of the country still tended to vary from one another although not as much as

---

[20] The bank component rose much faster, from $729 million to $3.0 billion, or more than four times. Mutual savings bank deposits rose even more, from $276 million to $1.4 billion, or five times.

had been the case at an earlier period. In the 1890s discount rates averaged a little under 5 percent in the East and over 8.5 percent in the West.

If any date deserves to be distinguished as a watershed in American history, it is 1890. By then the country had moved to the top rung of the economic ladder. Its steel mills were producing as much as England and Germany combined; its gross national product was larger than that of any other country; and its financial institutions were emerging from adolescence to maturity.

Of all the intermediaries, seven were already robust by 1890, and their overall growth rate was much higher than the growth rate of the economy in general. Each of the seven had at some point or other experienced an accelerated burst of activity. In the early years it was general insurance that attracted attention. Soon thereafter, commercial banking took over the stage. In the sixties and seventies, savings banking had its day in the sun. At about the same time, life insurance flourished. Toward the end of the period, the trust companies were making spectacular gains, investment banking was approaching the peak of its career, and building and loan associations were finally being noticed.

Each of the seven also had its moments of travail. Acts of God in the form of fire or storm at sea intermittently drained the general insurance companies. Commercial banking seemed wedded to a high mortality rate. Savings banks and life insurance companies had a series of embarrassing moments when they forgot the objectives for which they were formed. The early investment bankers were almost all wiped out, and it was a piece of conventional wisdom that most people who bought securities on the stock exchange lost money.

Regardless of the losses they brought to depositors and policyholders, however, the intermediaries did a good job in fulfilling their functions. They encouraged saving, provided investment capital, and reduced the immobility of capital funds.

6 · the age of high finance, 1890–1920

The years between 1890 and the end of World War I saw the continuation of America's growth as a first-ranking industrial power. The end of the frontier, announced by the Census Bureau in 1890, did not, as some had feared, signal an end to economic expansion. To be sure, the slowdown in population growth did cause the economy to advance at a more moderate gait, while the railroad was no longer the expansive force it had once been. Yet in terms of per capita income growth no slowdown occurred. Per capital GNP (in 1929 dollars) increased from $415 in 1890 to $689 in 1920, or by an average rate of 1.7 percent a year, a little better than the long-term historical trend.

THE TRIUMPH OF INDUSTRIALIZATION · In an important sense, the years around 1890 represented the close of one chapter in American economic and social history and the beginning of another—industrialization's coming of age. Agriculture, which had been so important in the early stages of development, continued, as it had for over a century, to lose in relative importance, first to commerce and later to manufacturing. In 1870 agricultural workers still made up over half the labor force; by 1890 their share had declined to slightly over two-fifths and fell steadily thereafter until in 1920 only about one worker in four labored in agriculture. By 1889 the value of farm products was for the first time exceeded by the value of manufactured products. A few years later, almost simultaneously with the official closing of the frontier, the United States became the world's leading manufacturing nation.

The constantly increasing importance of manufacturing, which had come to characterize the nation's economy, also necessitated wide-sweeping changes in business organization. At the end of the nineteenth century, "big business" was rapidly replacing the local manufactory as the vital economic unit. In 1904 the less than 1 percent of manufacturing establishment with sales of $1 million or more employed over 25 percent of manufacturing workers and produced almost 40 percent of total manufacturing output. A decade later, manufacturing firms with sales exceeding $1 million (1.4 percent of total manufacturing enterprises) employed 35 percent of manufacturing workers and produced nearly 50 percent of manufacturing output.

**FINANCIAL INTERMEDIARIES IN THE
GROWTH OF BIG BUSINESS** ·⎡The formation of "big business" would
have been almost impossible without the assistance of financial intermediaries, who through their control over the sources of investment capital
provided the financing for these new and consolidated enterprises. Indeed,
some have characterized the period between 1890 and 1929 as the era of
"financial capitalism."⎤In a certain sense it was that, for the leaders of
high finance, men such as Morgan, Schiff, and Stillman, carried great
influence in the world of business. But in a more significant sense this was
the beginning of an environment of "giant" enterprise in which financial
capitalism played on important but temporary role.

On the average, between 1890 and the start of World War I, financial
intermediaries absorbed more than two-fifths of the financial savings of
the household sector. The share of financial intermediaries in gross
financing (external financing, plus internal saving, plus depreciation) of
all sectors of the economy was quite a bit lower. In the years 1901 to 1912,
intermediaries provided only 16 percent of the financing of nonfinancial
corporations, 7 percent of the financing of the federal government, and 6
percent of the financing of nonfarm households. However, when we consider external financing only, financial intermediaries played a much more
substantial role, providing 36 percent of the external financing of nonfinancial corporations, 70 percent of the external funds used by nonfarm
households, and 43 percent of the external funds used by state and local
governments. The importance of financial institutions, especially investment banks, was additionally enhanced by the influence they carried with
the sources of money capital, on the one hand, and with corporate users
of credit on the other. To a great extent, therefore, the flow of credit
directly into the securities markets took place under the watchful eye, if
not the actual control, of the leaders of high finance.

**CREATION OF THE FEDERAL
RESERVE SYSTEM** · ⎣Certainly the most significant change between 1890
and World War I was the creation of the Federal Reserve System in
December 1913. For eighty years the United States had operated without a
central bank. Most people believed that the existing national banking
system was immeasurably superior to the old state banking system, for it
had been a move in the direction of a more uniform currency and it had
strengthened the banking system against failures and overissue. Nevertheless, it possessed several glaring defects. As we have already noted, the
supply of bank notes was inherently inelastic because of its linkage with
the public debt. An even greater defect was that the national banking
system encouraged the pyramiding of reserves in money market centers,
especially New York. In the spring and again in the fall, country banks
would withdraw some of their New York deposits. As New York City bank
reserves dropped, credit became tight and interest rates increased.
Generally the result was only a mild crisis. Occasionally, however, the
situation would deteriorate to panic proportions.

These defects were aggravated by the absence of a central bank that could stabilize the financial markets during crises and provide continuing surveillance over the economy. To some extent, especially after 1900, the Treasury did perform certain central banking functions. Secretary of the Treasury Shaw explicitly recognized that it was the government's duty to protect the people against financial panics and tried to use his powers to maintain stability. To offset the country banks' seasonal demand for funds in the spring and in the fall, he withdrew government deposits from the national banks in the winter and summer, held them as a cash reserve, and redeposited them as stringency developed in the money market. In 1902 he contributed, probably beyond his legal authority, to an expansion of bank note currency. Under the terms of the National Banking Act, the government could deposit funds in any national bank, but the Secretary was directed to require security "by deposit of United States bonds *and* otherwise." Sensing an imminent shortage of bank reserves, Shaw informed the banks that he would accept selected state and municipal obligations as security against government deposits provided the released United States bonds were used as a base for the issue of additional bank note circulation. Although these were welcome actions, the Treasury was a long way from acting as a central bank.

Because of its tendency to encourage bank expansion and contraction, the national banking system aggravated money market disturbances. The panic of 1907 exhausted the patience of the bankers, the public, and the politicians. As currency disappeared, as interest rates skyrocketed, and as the securities markets collapsed, the belief spread that the weaknesses of the banking system were too serious to be ignored any longer. As a stopgap measure, Congress enacted the Aldrich-Vreeland Bill, which had among its provisions the establishment of a National Monetary Commission to make a comprehensive study of the monetary and banking system and to make recommendations concerning desirable reforms. The published output of the commission built the groundwork for the Federal Reserve Act. The act was drafted largely by Carter Glass, Chairman of the House Banking and Currency Committee, with the technical assistance of Dr. H. Parker Willis. But although the Glass Bill formed its backbone, the final measure was, as is inevitably the case, the work of more than a score of individuals, including academic experts, political leaders, and bankers.

Although ready agreement that reform was needed existed within banking circles, the American Bankers Association (ABA) was convinced that the act was inherently bad. "For those who do not believe in socialism," it stated, "it is very hard to accept and ratify this proposed action on the part of the government." For its own part, the ABA would clearly have preferred something like the plan submitted in 1910 by Paul M. Warburg of Kuhn, Loeb & Co., which put control squarely in the hands of the bankers. At the other extreme was the overly enthusiastic response of the Comptroller of the Currency, who believed that the act would make financial panics "mathematically impossible."

The major provisions of the Federal Reserve Act, or more technically, "An act to provide for the establishment of Federal Reserve banks, to furnish an elastic currency, to afford means of rediscounting commercial paper, to establish a more effective supervision of banking, and for other purposes, were as follows:

1. The country was divided into not less than eight or more than twelve districts, with the actual number to be determined by a special committee.
2. A Federal Reserve Bank was to be established in each district.
3. A Federal Reserve Board, with headquarters in Washington, was set up to supervise the entire system. It was to consist of seven members, including the Secretary of the Treasury, the Comptroller of the Currency, and five members appointed by the President for a term of ten years.
4. National banks were compelled and state banks were allowed to become members.
5. Every district bank was permitted to issue Federal Reserve notes secured by 100 percent commercial paper and a reserve of 40 percent in gold or gold certificates.
6. Each district bank was required to maintain a 35 percent reserve in "lawful" money against deposits.
7. Each district bank was permitted to rediscount commercial paper for member banks, such paper to be for a term of ninety days or, in the case of agricultural obligations, six months.
8. District banks were permitted to buy and sell government obligations under rules and regulations of the Federal Reserve Board.
9. District banks were permitted to deal in gold coin or bullion, to maintain foreign bank accounts, to establish branches, and to act as fiscal agents for the government.
10. Legal reserve requirements against demand and time deposits were set for member banks: in reserve cities, 18 percent; in cities, 15 percent; and for country banks, 12 percent.
11. A Federal Advisory Council of one member from each of the twelve districts was formed to make recommendations on banking and credit policies and to discuss business conditions.
12. A system for clearing checks without cost to the payee or the payor was set up, and any bank could become a member of this par collection system without being a member of the Federal Reserve System itself.
13. National banks were permitted to make five-year loans on farm real estate mortgages.

EARLY OPERATIONS OF THE
FEDERAL RESERVE SYSTEM

The Federal Reserve Act was weak in that it did not create a central bank such as that existing in Europe or operating in the United States eighty years before. The System did not have power, despite the fond hopes of its most optimistic founders, to prevent financial crises or bank failures. On the other hand, it was a better system than had existed, for it corrected at least partially the more glaring weaknesses of the national banking system, including inelasticity of currency, pyramiding of reserves, and expensive and inefficient check clearing. In addition, it supplied what was lacking under the national banking and independent Treasury systems: centralized control over the discount rate and the gold stock, a reservoir of credit to which the banks could turn in emergencies, and a fiscal agent to link the Treasury with the banking system.

The major limitations of the act, apart from the lack of firm central control, followed from the fact that its creators believed strongly in the "real bills" doctrine and the gold standard. Both principles, of course, were inherently incompatible with internal stabilization policy. To be sure, the provision allowing national banks to lend on farm mortgages was a departure from the commercial loan doctrine, but it only made legal for national banks what was already possible for state banks. On the other hand, adherence to "real bills" and the gold standard was clearly evident in the provisions dealing with rediscounting and the issuance of Federal Reserve notes. Consequently, the inelasticity of the currency was not altogether eliminated, nor were the rediscounting powers of the district banks sufficiently broad, given the realities of banking practice.

The act also placed entirely too much reliance on the discount rate as the chief instrument of control over the money market. For in time it was learned that raising the rate was without effect in periods of speculative boom and that lowering the rate was ineffective if nobody wished to borrow. Moreover, the management of the discount rate was diffused among twelve district banks without the exercise of control by the Federal Reserve Board.

Other instruments of credit control were at first either ignored or regarded with indifference. Reserve requirements were rigid and could not be altered as part of any attempt to control credit expansion or contraction. More significantly, open-market operations (the purchase and sale of earning assets by the district banks) were not regarded as of major importance. The System was further weakened by a lack of enthusiasm on the part of the commercial banks, who feared that their earnings would be diminished by the clearing facilities offered by the Federal Reserve Banks. By the end of 1914 only 43 percent of the country's commercial banking resources were controlled by member banks, and at the end of 1916 only 37 state banks had joined the System. As a result, the effectiveness of "moral suasion" by the System was greatly limited.

It was also unfortunate for the new central banking system that World War I broke out shortly after its birth. When the United States became involved, the Treasury realized it would have to borrow large sums to finance war expenditures. It was determined to hold down the cost of this borrowing by keeping interest rates low. At times like these, the first reaction is to turn to the central bank, and the Federal Reserve could not very well refuse to cooperate. It became the main instrument in carrying out an easy-money policy. The rediscount rate was kept at 3 percent, and advances on promissory notes secured by government obligations were made at rates below the coupon rate of the security. Reserve requirements for member bank demand deposits were reduced to 7, 10, and 13 percent. In addition, all member bank reserves were required to be deposited in the district banks.

By these three maneuvers, bank reserves were not only greatly increased but the lending potential of the district banks was greatly strengthened as well. Discerning students of the money system came to understand that the Federal Reserve System was capable of creating an infinite amount of paper money.

Spurred on by the easy-money policy made possible by the preceding amendments to the Federal Reserve Act, the Reserve Banks created a pool of credit that enabled the commercial banks both to buy government obligations and to make loans to individuals. The banks responded with alacrity, acquiring about $3.6 billion of government debt between June 1916 and June 1919 and thus increasing their holdings from $1.5 billion to $5.1 billion. This action, of course, added greatly to the expansion of the money supply, which increased over the same period from $13.8 billion to $21.2 billion.

NEW TYPES OF INTERMEDIARIES:

CREDIT UNIONS · In addition to the creation of the Federal Reserve System, several new forms of intermediaries—credit unions, pension funds, and investment companies[1]—made their debut in the first part of the century. Although none was to have any real significance in this period, each did reflect some of the very basic changes that were taking place in the American economy. Meanwhile, too, the assets of the classic intermediaries continued to expand. (See Table 9.)

TABLE 9
Assets of Selected Financial Intermediaries, 1890–1922
(Millions of Dollars)

Institution	1890	1900	1912	1922
Commercial banks	$4,601	$10,011	$21,822	$47,467
Mutual savings banks	1,743	2,430	4,015	6,597
Savings and loan associations	300	490	952	2,802
Life insurance companies	771	1,742	4,409	8,652
General insurance companies	352	484	1,001	2,358
Credit unions	—	—	—	11
Private noninsured pension plans	—	—	—	90
Investment companies	—	—	—	110
Total	$7,767	$15,157	$32,199	$68,087

Source: U.S. Bureau of the Census, *Historical Statistics of the United States;* Raymond Goldsmith, *Financial Intermediaries in the American Economy since 1900* (New York: National Bureau of Economic Research, 1958).

Because consumer loans were scarcely available through the established financial intermediaries, a number of experiments took place during the last years of the nineteenth century and early years of the twentieth century in providing consumer credit, especially for the city worker.

The prevailing philosophy was that virtue was best upheld by denying to the poor and the middle classes the means of spending beyond their incomes. Bankers would have nothing to do with the making of $5 and $25 loans, which is what consumer loans amounted to in those days, just as many commercial bankers saw little advantage in doing any kind of busi-

[1] Pension funds and investment companies will be discussed in the next chapter, for they first attained importance in the 1920s.

ness, including savings banking, with this segment of society. At times, of course, people did have to borrow. Their only sources were the loan sharks and, what were little better, the local small-loan companies that were found in almost every town. Once involved with these lenders, it was hard to get out of debt, for the exorbitant interest charges made it very difficult to pay off the principal.

Toward the end of the century, a number of philanthropic institutions were established in several of the nation's cities to provide the working classes with consumer-loan facilities. Among the first of these was the Provident Loan Society in New York, which was founded in 1893 for the purpose of making pawnbroker loans. The rate of interest charged on these loans was set at 12 percent per annum, which was quite a bit lower than rates (18 to 36 percent) authorized under the pawnbroking law of New York State. The Provident was especially fortunate to count among its staunch supporters such New York notables as James Speyer, George F. Baker, and Cornelius Vanderbilt (the Commodore's son). Speyer seems to have been the propelling force behind the new institution, having been much impressed by the municipal pawnshops of European cities, whose existence, like the House of Speyer, dated back several centuries.

Loan institutions similar to the Provident Loan Society were organized in Baltimore, Boston, Cincinnati, Cleveland, Chicago, and elsewhere. By 1909 there were 15 and by 1920 there were 32, with a total capital of $14 million. On the average, the loans tended to be quite small, ranging from $32 in San Francisco to $150 in Sioux City, Iowa.

Just as professional executives had taken over the operation of savings banks from the merchant philanthropists in mid-nineteenth century, so organized promoters stepped into the small-loan business in the early twentieth century. In 1910 the first of the so-called Morris Plan banks, sometimes referred to as "industrial banks," was started in Norfolk, Virginia, by a young attorney named Arthur J. Morris. Operating as the Fidelity Savings and Trust Company, the bank made consumer loans at the comparatively low rate of 18 percent per annum, drawing its financing for the most part by selling its investment certificates to the public. By 1929 industrial banks (not all of which received Morris Plan licenses) were granting loans of more than $400 million a year. Morris was a great promoter, and as soon as his Norfolk venture proved successful, he proceeded to recruit paid organizers to establish additional industrial banks in Atlanta, Baltimore, Memphis, and other cities.

None of these philanthropic or quasi-philanthropic ventures was cooperative in nature, depending as they did on externally raised capital. Indeed, a number of promoters who followed Morris' example in setting up industrial banks were not entirely without the profit motive; and over the years many of these institutions took on a wide variety of operations, including the making of mercantile loans. On the other hand, the credit union movement, which paralleled the rise of the Morris Plan banks, was entirely based on the cooperative principle (since the membership through periodic saving was to provide the money capital to be used for making loans), with a heavy dose of the self-help philosophy thrown in.

Like all previous intermediaries, credit unions were imported from abroad. They had their origin in the latter part of the nineteenth century in Germany, a decade or so before the first such institution appeared in the United States in 1909. It was then that Alphonse Desjardins, a Canadian, who had done much to promote credit unions in his home province of Quebec as well as throughout the other provinces, organized one in New Hampshire.

Although credit unions were to spread across the United States in the next two decades and although they were promoted with a zeal common only to religious, political, and social reformers, it would be many years before they became important financial intermediaries. Assets of credit unions in 1930 totaled less than $50 million, and this amount was parceled out among some 1,300 units with a membership of about 300,000.

It was not possible for credit unions to become large organizations, for they were local associations serving more or less homogeneous memberships. Credit unions in the United States have been organized mainly by and for employee groups, although groups with other common bonds (for example, church memberships and local ethnic communities) have participated in their establishment. But this is not to say that credit unions were not successful. For the purposes they were intended to serve—to provide their membership with small loans at reasonable rates of interest and to encourage thrift and self-reliance—they were highly successful.

The spread of the credit union idea was due almost wholly to the promotional efforts of a small group of faithful pioneers, of whom the most important, at least in a financial sense, was Edward A. Filene. Part owner of a leading department store in Boston, Filene was a remarkable entrepreneur and innovator. As a department store merchant, he was one of the pioneers in establishing the "bargain basement." Filene was convinced that, with the economy built up as much as it was, the key to economic prosperity depended on maintaining high levels of consumption rather than encouraging thrift. The danger, according to Filene, was that more goods could be produced than the people could buy. Therefore he argued vigorously for high wages and low prices, beliefs that were to make him appear to other businessmen as "radical or mad." If Filene and his sympathizers were correct in their assumption that consumption had to replace the frontier and investment as the dynamic element in America's economic growth, the country would simply have to get rid of its archaic attitude toward the use of credit. Finally, he had a strange commitment to the idea of cooperation, to worker cooperatives in particular. Indeed, he took the matter so seriously that for a long time he tried to persuade his employees to take over the business and run it as a cooperative.

Filene had many other interesting and sometimes quaint ideas, but for our immediate purposes he possessed all the ingredients for a fervent belief in the credit union movement. Once it was brought to his attention, he, almost alone, undertook its underwriting and promotion. Over more than a quarter of a century, until his death in 1937, he spent perhaps $1 million supporting the work of the Credit Union National Extension Bureau, which was set up under the direction of Roy Bergengren to promote the formation of credit unions and the passage of credit union legislation.

No doubt the credit union movement benefited greatly from all the promotional activities undertaken by such men as Bergengren and Desjardins, as well as the activities of the Russell Sage Foundation, which lent financial aid. Bergengren alone crisscrossed the country on innumerable trips, trying to activate local credit unions. In a sense he was the Johnny Appleseed of the credit union movement. However, credit unions also benefited from the attractive dividends they paid to their members. During the twenties, when almost all credit union assets consisted of high-yielding consumer and mortgage loans, dividends as high as 8 percent served as an important means of acquiring the sizable savings accumulated by some members.

EXPANSION OF SAVINGS AND LOAN ASSOCIATIONS

Older than credit unions, pension funds, and investment companies, savings and loan associations gained their first prominence as financial intermediaries in the early part of this century. To be sure, their growth in the post-Civil War decades had been rapid, but they were still quite small, both individually and in the aggregate. In 1893 it was estimated that there were some 5,600 associations, with 1,350,000 shareholders and assets of $475 million. Even by 1900 savings and loan association assets of $490 million amounted to less than one-third of the assets of life insurance companies and to but one-twentieth of the assets of commercial banks.

Despite the comparatively small size of savings and loan associations, their highly specialized nature as mortgage lenders made them important suppliers of money to the housing market. Although building and loan assets comprised less than 3 percent of the combined assets of the major intermediaries supplying mortgage credit in 1900, they held nearly 13 percent (about $400 million) of the outstanding volume of nonfarm residential mortgages. The explanation, of course, is that virtually all their assets, after deducting tangible assets and cash reserves, consisted of home mortgages, whereas most other intermediaries had more diversified investments. In 1912 fully 93 percent of all assets of savings and loan associations was supplied to nonfarm households in the form of mortgage loans.

The most important innovations affecting the growth of savings and loan associations concerned matters of internal organization and the types of accounts available to savers. The "terminating" plan, which expired when the members completed their payments, was soon supplanted by the "serial" form, which allowed for the continuous operation of the association. A serial association was little more than a grouping under one roof and under one name of a series of "terminating" plan associations, following one another at three-month intervals. As under the older plan, members joined solely to obtain home financing. Building and loan associations were still not generalized saving institutions.

Subject to some modifications, the serial type of association remained the prevalent type of association in such major states as Illinois, New Jersey, Pennsylvania, Massachusetts, and Wisconsin throughout the twenties. Because the serial form was particularly suited to small associations having assets of several hundred thousand dollars, the structure of the industry in these states tended to be one of large numbers of small institutions. Indeed, even at the end of the twenties, 90 percent or more of all associations had less than $1 million in assets, whereas not more than a few dozen had resources of more than $10 million.

The enforcement of systematic saving remained a central feature of the industry. A variety of devices, including fines and withdrawal fees, were used to promote regularity of payments. And although the number of associations quickly multiplied, asset growth was no doubt slowed by the relative illiquidity of savings shares as well as by the very limited purpose for which savings and loan associations were organized.

As a result of these limitations, a new form of organization, known as the "permanent" plan, evolved. It originated in Charleston, South Carolina, in the 1840s, and like all innovations it took a long while to catch on. It seems probable that a few Iowa associations used certain of its features in the 1870s, but the plan did not become popular until the 1880s. Under the permanent plan, the accounts of all members were kept separately, making it possible for members to add to their savings at any time. Furthermore, individuals could retain their shares even after these shares matured. Finally, under the "Dayton" plan variant of the permanent plan, shares plus dividends were withdrawable without penalty. The permanent plan thus made building and loan associations thrift institutions, and their shares emerged as an attractive medium for persons who wanted to save for diverse purposes and to whom liquidity was an important consideration.

A still later innovation was the development of the "permanent capital" plan, which had become quite common in a number of Western states, particularly California and Oregon, by the end of the twenties. The essential characteristic of this plan was the issuance of a nonwithdrawable class of stock, subscribed and paid for by the organizers, possessing features similar to the capital stock of other private corporations. Unlike the mutuals that hitherto dominated the scene, permanent capital associations were organized to earn a profit for the organizers. The plan had been tried out as early as 1837 in Brooklyn, but the next time it appeared was in Minneapolis in 1884 and from there it spread in the nineties to Kansas, California, and other states.

Despite the innovations of savings and loan associations, their growth was restrained in the 1890s by economic depression and by the rise and subsequent collapse of the "nationals." The latter were similar to local building and loan associations except that they sought to attract funds through very aggressive selling techniques and through the establishment of numerous branches throughout the United States. They also differed from the local associations in that many of them were outright frauds. The sale of shares on a commission basis, the deduction of a substantial portion of each month's payment for expenses, very high withdrawal fees, and in some cases the total loss of savings in the event the purchaser failed to maintain his payments, made the "national" form a very attractive promotion. By 1893 there were 240 national associations. Local building and loan associations were hurt by the aggressive competition of the nationals with their teams of door-to-door salesmen and sometimes misleading advertisements. But they were affected much more seriously by the collapse of the nationals in the late 1890s. This collapse was brought on by the unwise accumulation of risky mortgage loans, but specifically by the fall of the largest of their number, the Southern Building and Loan Association of Knoxville, Tennessee. It was a disaster that severely shook public confidence in building and loans. However, the associations recovered, and in the first two decades of the 1900s their growth rate was better than any of the other old-line intermediaries. Assets multiplied threefold from $950 million to $2.8 billion.

DECLINING RELATIVE IMPORTANCE OF
MUTUAL SAVINGS BANKS · In contrast to the rapid gains made by savings and loan associations, mutual savings banks continued to grow slowly but steadily. Between 1890 and 1922 their assets grew by about 4.5 percent a year, from $1.7 billion to over $6.6 billion. Yet as the economy of the West grew, the *relative* importance of savings banks as financial intermediaries diminished. As the data in Table 9 illustrate, in 1900 mutual savings banks owned 16 percent of financial intermediary assets, whereas their share in 1922 had dwindled to less than 10 percent.

TABLE 10
Savings Deposits and Share Accounts, by Type of
Financial Institution, 1900–1930
(Percent of Total)

Year	Mutual Savings Banks	Commercial Banks	Savings and Loan Associations	Postal Savings	Credit Unions
1900	62.7	25.4	11.9	—	—
1910	45.8	45.1	9.1	—	—
1920	27.8	61.1	10.1	1.0	—

Source: National Association of Mutual Savings Banks, *Mutual Savings Banks: Basic Characteristics and Role in the National Economy* (Englewood Cliffs, N.J.: Prentice-Hall, 1962), p. 54.

To a large extent, the relative decline in the importance of mutual savings banks, particularly among deposit-type intermediaries, was attributable to a failure on their part to take root in the more recently settled and faster-growing regions of the United States. Then as now, savings banks were located almost exclusively in the New England and Middle Atlantic states. During the period under consideration, mutual savings banks operated in 16 states, but it was only in the 11 New England and Middle Atlantic states that they made up an important part of the financial structure.

At the same time, and to some extent correlated with the geographical factor, there was a marked absence of growth in the number of mutual savings banks. Indeed, as Table 11 shows, between 1896 and 1920 the number declined from 638 to 618. Most of those in existence could look back on many years of successful operation, for very few new banks were formed after the 1870s.[2]

TABLE 11
Number of Mutual Savings Banks and
Commercial Banks, 1896–1920

Year	Mutual Savings Banks	Commercial Banks
1896	638	11,474
1900	626	12,427
1910	637	24,514
1920	618	30,291

Source: Federal Reserve Board, *All-Bank Statistics, 1896–1955,* pp. 37, 49.

Several factors combine to explain why mutual savings banks remained more or less confined to the Northeast. First, the frontier did not offer a favorable environment in which the growth of savings banks could take place. Mutual savings banks flourished where there already was, as in New England, a large wage-earning class seeking a safe outlet for their small savings. Such a class existed neither on the frontier nor in the small towns that soon dotted the countryside. Secondly, the community's need for a commercial bank to finance trade and agriculture generally predated its need for a savings bank. And, often, by the time the environment would otherwise have been ripe for the creation of a savings bank, its function had been preempted by the commercial bank, which not infrequently assumed the role of an ersatz thrift institution. Thirdly, the demand for *liberal* mortgage credit favored the organization of building and loan associations. Also, the charters of these associations required much less funds than did mutual savings bank charters. Finally, the proliferation of mutual savings banks was restricted by the limited opportunities for private gain on the part of those who undertook their organization and management. Mutual in form, and with a long tradition of providing public service, such institutions were unlikely to take root in the newer and rapidly expanding regions, where second- and third-generation "money" was not likely to be found and where opportunities to get rich seemed to be ubiquitous.

Yet even in New England and the Middle Atlantic states, the mutual savings banks were losing ground to other financial intermediaries. In 1900 savings bank deposits made up more than half of the combined resources of commercial banks, mutual savings banks, savings and loan associations, and life insurance companies in New England and more than

---

[2] Of the 514 savings banks in the United States at the end of 1960, about two-fifths were established prior to 1860 and about four-fifths were established prior to 1875.

one-fifth of the total in the Middle Atlantic region. By 1929 these shares had diminished to one-third and one-sixth, respectively. Undoubtedly, many factors explained the decline, but an underlying element was the conservative management practices that dominated the industry. Steeped in a tradition of public service, viewing themselves as custodians over the small savings of the lower and middle classes, and not motivated by thoughts of private gain, savings bankers were not as aggressive and innovative as the entrepreneurs of other kinds of intermediaries. Yet this same caution and conservatism was to stand them and their depositors in good stead in the dark days of the thirties as it had in other periods of economic adversity.

FINANCE CAPITALISM · Of all the financial institutions in the decades after 1890, the leading investment banking houses were unparalleled in terms of power and influence. Indeed, their leaders were the archetypes of finance capitalists, so much so that some economic historians use the terms "Morgan era" and "finance capitalism" interchangeably in describing the three decades preceding World War I.

In this period the investment banking industry consisted of a relatively small number of single-office firms. In 1912 the Investment Bankers Association had a total membership of 257 firms, which, in turn, operated less than 280 offices located mainly in New York City but also in Boston, Chicago, and Philadelphia. The most prominent of these houses was J. P. Morgan & Co. Only one other firm, Kuhn, Loeb & Co., possessed comparable prestige and authority. A step lower in the hierarchy were such less well-known but highly respected and influential houses as Speyer & Co., J. & R. Seligman, August Belmont & Co., the Boston firms of Kidder, Peabody and Lee, Higginson, and in Philadelphia, Drexel & Co. As the economist would say, the business of investment banking was a highly concentrated oligopoly, entry into which was made difficult by the shortage of money capital and by the very nature of the business, which demanded reputation and the "right business connections" as essential assets.

Before 1890 "big business" was limited almost exclusively to the railroads. In the 1880s industrial firms with a net worth in excess of $5 million were rare, whereas firms with a net worth of over $10 million amounted to no more than a handful. The typical form of ownership was the partnership, and even where the corporate form was used, ownership usually rested in the hands of a small group of persons. Even such "very large" businesses as Carnegie Steel, Singer Manufacturing, and McCormick Harvester were more or less family affairs. Indeed, the Pullman Palace Car Company was the only manufacturing company regularly traded on the New York Stock Exchange, and that company could be classified as engaged in railroading rather than manufacturing. Only among the leading New England textile firms was there a wide dispersion of ownership. Among the country's distributive enterprises, the very largest, H. B. Claflin & Co. and Marshall Field & Co., were partnerships. Other companies, such as Atlantic & Pacific Tea Company, F. W. Woolworth, and Sears, Roebuck, although growing rapidly, were still quite small, possessing net worth of less than $2 million.

Toward the end of the century, the picture was beginning to change. Large-scale enterprises were becoming increasingly common in manufacturing as a result of internal growth and the merger wave that began in the 1890s. As they became more common, they began to offer their shares for public purchase. "Going public" was not only a natural way of life for large business—it also had decided advantages for the various groups that had a stake in business enterprise: the owners, the managers, the financiers, and the public. For the owner, the sale of equity shares provided an opportunity both to liquidate capital tied up in the business and to diversify his investments. It also meant an enhancement of wealth, for by experience the financial community had arrived at a rule of thumb that said that a family-owned company was worth three times earnings but a publicly owned company, due to the greater market for its shares, was worth ten times earnings. It was also true that public ownership could limit the owner's decision-making power, but this factor was regarded as an advantage by the nonowner managers who were appearing with greater frequency in the large firms. To the latter, one-man control was an obstacle to progress and a barrier to growth. Their view was shared by the bankers, who were beginning to participate more frequently in industrial enterprises and who were more at home in the stock exchanges than in the factories. The last group, the investing public, also welcomed public ownership, for they could now put their savings into securities as well as into real estate loans, savings banks, and commercial bank time deposits.

These changes helped to create the atmosphere and lay the groundwork on which enterprising promoters, such as John R. Dos Passos, Charles R. Flint, and the Moore Brothers, as well as investment bankers, like the House of Morgan, financed the huge aggregations of capital that made possible the development of "big business." Between 1898 and 1902 such industrial giants as American Can, International Harvester, United States Steel, and United Fruit appeared on the New York Stock Exchange. By 1903 the stocks of 136 large industrial companies were listed. It is estimated that in 1900 there were some 1 million stockholders out of an adult population of 42 million. In 1901 over 3 million shares were sold in one day, a record that would stand until 1916.

As previously suggested, the growth of big business, of which "going public" was a necessary consequence, could not have progressed as quickly as it did without the help of the promoter and the investment banker. The promoter—distinct from the investment banker in that he was more an organizer of industrial mergers and distributor of securities than a financier possessing or having ready access to large sums of money— initially led the way in introducing the public to industrial securities. Indeed, until near the turn of the century such conservative investment banking houses as Morgan and Kuhn, Loeb stayed clear of what was still considered a speculative and untested market. Most of the leading houses therefore limited themselves to the familiar business of underwriting railroad bonds and dealing in governments. Gradually some of these firms, such as Kidder, Peabody and Lee, Higginson, turned to the underwriting of industrial bonds and, more important still, to the underwriting of preferred stocks. But the heyday of the promoter was fast drawing to a close. Successful as he was in bringing about the mergers and reorganizations that led to the creation of large-scale enterprise, he possessed neither the resources necessary to underwrite the stock issues that he floated on behalf of his clients nor the funds to provide expansion capital. It was one thing to arrange an exchange of securities or to handle, for private parties, the distribution of a block of stock and quite something else to provide the increasing amounts of cash that were necessary to effect mergers. It was not a trivial operation to raise option money, to obtain fixed-price options on the properties to be merged and the cash to clean up miscellaneous indebtedness, and to provide the long-term working capital that the new enterprise would require. It was to the investment banker, then, that industry increasingly turned.

Although the growth of the investment banking industry was to be especially rapid in the decade after World War I, it was in the Morgan era that the investment banker wielded his greatest influence. Indeed, some economic historians, such as Werner Sombart and the late Professor N. S. B. Gras, saw the finance capitalist replacing the industrial capitalist as the dominant entrepreneurial type in the latter years of this period.

It is easy to exaggerate the influence of the investment banking community and the House of Morgan in particular over American business, but there is no doubt that a close control over the supply of investment capital placed the investment banker in a strategic position. The resources at the beck and call of the House of Morgan were especially awesome. In an age when foreign capital was still an important source of credit, the House of Morgan maintained excellent British and Continental ties. The Morgan partners could also call on the resources of their close allies: in Boston, Kidder, Peabody; in Philadelphia, Drexel & Co.; in New York, George Baker of the First National and James Stillman of the National City Bank of New York. One member or another in this "entente cordiale," in turn, had a controlling voice in a number of other commercial banks, trust companies, and life insurance companies, including the Bank of Commerce, the Chase and Hanover National banks, the Bankers Trust, the Guaranty Trust, the New York Life, the Mutual Life, and the Equitable Life. These various institutions also acted as channels for the distribution of the securities underwritten by the House of Morgan. In addition, Morgan distributed securities through some stockbrokerage firms, such as White, Weld & Co. and Kissell, Kinnicut & Co., which were security jobbers.

Other investment bankers, not being as brilliantly organized and having no battery of retail outlets, had to devise other ways of distributing what they underwrote. As security ownership spread and as more and more companies went public, ambitious and aggressive houses were no longer satisfied to rely on a handful of wealthy investors. They wished to profit from the broadening circle of security buyers. In order to do so, they had to develop a marketing organization of their own. The innovators along these lines were N. W. Harris, N. W. Halsey, and James Jackson Storrow.

Harris, who founded Harris, Forbes & Co., and Halsey, of Halsey, Stuart & Co., were the first to hire house-to-house bond salesmen. Storrow went a step further. Soon after becoming a partner in Lee, Higginson in 1900, he began to put together a trained selling team to distribute the firm's security underwriting. He was also the first to create a statistical service for evaluating securities.

Regardless of the methods they used to underwrite and distribute securities, a few men came to control a significant portion of the supply of investment capital. Within limits, these men could grant or deny financing as they saw fit. So substantial was the prestige and influence of the House of Morgan, and the person of J. P. Morgan in particular, that in a moment of financial crisis in 1895 President Cleveland and his Secretary of the Treasury, John Carlisle, came to him for a loan to assist the Treasury in maintaining the gold standard. Control over the supply of investment funds also gave the investment banking community a voice in the affairs of the industrial and railroad enterprises whose reorganizations they arranged and to which they and their clients extended credit.

As the leading underwriter of railroad securities, the House of Morgan exerted, through representation on the boards of directors, influence over a substantial number of the most important roads. Substantial as it was, such control as Morgan exerted was far from absolute. Like the "money trust" itself, it was part of an entente involving reciprocity between the investment bankers and some of the more "responsible" railroad leaders. Among other things, Morgan and his allies promised to do all in their power to prevent the financing of competing railroads. Thus when Archibald McLeod tried to extend the Reading Railroad into New Haven territory, Morgan simply "cut off McLeod's money supply. The Reading's New England plans collapsed."

The participation of the investment banker in the affairs of business evolved out of a need to represent the interests of security holders. According to the banker, he had a continuing obligation to see that the borrower lived up to the terms of the loan. The banker's participation began with the railroads. Railroad bondholders, many of whom were European, had long suffered from the mischievous maneuverings of unscrupulous promoters and the internecine warfare among the big barons. Through sad experience, Morgan had learned in his attempts to bridle "destructive" competition that not all the parties to "gentlemen's agreements" were gentlemen and that only through direct participation, which usually meant placing one or another of his partners or other allies on the board of directors, could he adequately protect the interests of his clients. As Morgan bluntly put it to one protesting railroad president, "They are not your roads. They belong to my clients." Later, when Andrew Carnegie's vigorous competitive instincts seemed likely to bring havoc to the steel industry, Morgan again responded by buying Carnegie out and setting up the huge United States Steel Company with Elbert H. Gary as its president. As financiers, the bankers were not interested in running the day-to-day affairs of the enterprises they had financed or even making many of the top-level decisions. They were representatives only of "capital." In this capacity they feared nothing so much as the effect of unbridled

competition, particularly as it jeopardized the earning power of the enterprises financed by themselves and their clients. It is not surprising, therefore, that Morgan, the financier, was quite content to leave Gary in charge
of United States Steel, once assured that there would be no price wars or
other forms of industry competition that might prevent capital from earning its "fair return."

Just as conservatism and caution had delayed the entry of the investment banker into the field of industrial financing, so these factors once
again caused him to shrink from the risks involved in financing the new
industries and enterprises that were rising in importance in the opening
years of the new century. As Clarence Dillon, head of the Wall Street
house of Dillon, Read & Co., was to put it years later: "If you had relied on
houses like ourselves you probably would not have had the automobile
industry in this country. We would not have risked it, and we would have
taken it upon ourselves as a virtue." In time this cautious attitude on the
part of the investment banking "establishment" was to be one of the
factors responsible for the relative decline in importance of the older
houses, such as Morgan & Co., and the rise of newer and much more
aggressive houses. The firm of Goldman, Sachs, for example, got its start
in the underwriting business in the early 1900s by specializing in the
underwriting of retail store securities, which the leading houses then
thought an undignified business. By 1917 when it had already taken over
the financing of Sears, Roebuck, May Department Stores, F. W. Woolworth, and others, Goldman, Sachs was the leading underwriter of retail
store securities.

THE HEYDAY OF COMMERCIAL BANKING The thirty odd years preceding World War I were not only the golden days of investment banking
but of commercial banking as well. To be sure, commercial banking
innovations were to be more pronounced in the twenties, but then they
would be mostly limited to a small segment of the banking system—the
big city banks—for in an important sense these innovations were already
an integral part of the country banking scene. Consequently, it is appropriate to examine the commercial banking picture, particularly as it
existed in the countryside, in the several decades before the war.

As shown in Table 12, the number of commercial banks increased from
11,500 to more than 30,000 in the years between 1896 and 1920. Although
they were far from rare in the earlier year, they were plentiful by the latter.
Even as early as 1900, commercial banks were just about everywhere.
Iowa alone had more than 1,000 spread out among nearly 700 separate
communities. Almost half of these were unincorporated—that is, private
banks. By 1915, when there were more than 27,000 commercial banks
operating throughout the United States, the town of Exchange, Pennsylvania, with a population of 80 had a bank. Along with the rise in numbers
came a rapid growth in assets. Between 1896 and 1920 commercial banks
assets grew more than sevenfold, from a little under $6.2 billion to a little
over $47 billion. Nevertheless, the great majority of commercial banks
were small banks in small towns. In 1915 the typical commercial bank had
total assets of less than $1 million. Of the country's more than 27,000

commercial banks, fully 75 percent were state chartered or private institutions with assets averaging less than $650,000. National banks, numbering around 7,500, had assets averaging over $1.5 million. Nevertheless, as late as 1912 only a handful of big city banks (perhaps a dozen or so) could loan $1 million or more to any one borrower.

TABLE 12
Commercial Banks, 1896–1929 (Millions of Dollars)

| Year | | Number | | | Assets | |
	Total	National	State and Private	Total	National	State and Private
1896	11,474	3,689	7,784	$ 6,167	$ 3,354	$ 2,813
1900	12,427	3,731	8,686	9,059	4,944	4,115
1905	18,152	5,664	12,488	14,542	7,325	7,217
1910	24,514	7,138	17,376	19,324	9,892	9,432
1915	27,390	7,597	19,793	24,106	11,790	12,316
1920	30,291	8,024	22,267	47,509	23,267	24,242
1925	28,442	8,066	20,376	54,401	24,252	30,150
1929	24,970	7,530	17,440	62,442	27,260	35,181

Source: U.S. Bureau of the Census, *Historical Statistics of the United States.*

No doubt the spread of banking, particularly in the smaller communities, was affected by the prosperous condition of agriculture in the period preceding 1920, the expansion of the railroad in the late years of the nineteenth century, and the general growth, actual and projected, of towns and cities that perhaps a decade or so before had been frontier settlements. Indeed, it was probably faith in the future more than any other single factor that accounted for the rise in the number of banks. As Professor Paul Trescott has said, "Nothing but great expectations can account for the formation of eight separate banks in Meade, Kansas, in 1886–1887—a town which mustered a population of 457 in the census of 1890."

If commercial banks did not become true "department stores" of finance until the 1920s, they at least achieved the status of "general stores" of finance in the preceding period. Adherence to the commercial loan or real bills doctrine with its emphasis on short-term, self-liquidating business loans would indeed have severely circumscribed the intermediation activities of the commercial banking system. Although the commercial loan doctrine had its adherents among bankers and the regulatory agencies, it was largely ignored in the actual business of banking. As far back as 1893 A. Barton Hepburn, Chairman of the Chase National Bank, properly stated that "the purely commercial function as formulated in textbooks and laid down by the courts as the business of the bank, fails fully to describe the banking of today."

In violation of the prevailing orthodoxy, commercial banks were important suppliers of credit to the securities markets. This process occurred partly through direct purchases of securities for inclusion in the banks' own asset portfolios, partly through the granting of call loans, and, in the case of country banks, not infrequently through channeling funds to their New York correspondents for investment in the money market. Furthermore, commercial bank credit was, to a large extent, secured by stocks and bonds as collateral. By 1892 security loans constituted 30 percent of total loans; by 1910 the share had grown to 37 percent. To be sure, not all of these loans were used to acquire securities, yet the share must have been substantial. At the same time, state-chartered commercial banks, particularly in the Western states, loaned heavily on real estate. In 1914, for example, real estate loans accounted for almost 25 percent of the total loans of state banks and for about 15 percent of total state bank assets.

Also, a significant part of commercial bank credit was used to provide longer-term capital to industry and agriculture, a step that was generally accomplished by automatically renewing short-term loans. Increasingly, however, the larger New York City banks entered into alliances with such leading investment banking houses as J. P. Morgan & Co. and Kuhn, Loeb & Co., becoming in effect something of investment banks themselves. In 1908 the First National Bank of New York, already closely affiliated with investment banking, took a gigantic step forward and organized its own investment banking subsidiary, the First Securities Company, as a holding company to acquire shares that the parent company was barred from holding. The National City Bank followed suit three years later by forming the National City Company.

The larger city banks were not alone in plying the investment banking trade. As has been said, the state banks of the West, favored by liberal banking laws, also invested much of their resources in farm mortgages and sent other funds East for placement in the New York money market. The extent of this investment was suggested in testimony given by Samuel Untermyer, New York attorney and former counsel for the Pujo Committee, before the Senate Committee on Banking and Currency in 1913. According to Untermyer,

> On the 1st of November 1912 . . . the country banks had in 30 of the New York City banks $240,000,000, which the city banks were lending for them on the New York Stock Exchange. . . . This was independently of moneys that formed a part of these country banks reserves with the New York City banks; it was just money sent right on to be put into Wall Street, because of the high rates being paid for money then.

The extent of the relationship between the commercial banking function and the investment banking function was perhaps best defined by an Iowa banker who stated before the same Senate committee, "I know the complaint is made you do not wish to confuse investment banking with commercial banking, but there is not a state bank in the State of Iowa, with 1300 state banks and 300 national banks—there is not a bank in that entire State which is not doing investment banking and commercial banking all through one window, and it is done safely."[3]

Considering all the uses to which commercial bank credit was put, it is

[3] Senate Banking and Currency Committee, *Hearings on the Federal Reserve System,* 1913.

quite clear that the *true* commercial loan made up but a modest fraction of bank assets. How large a share of bank credit was in fact allocated to investment purposes is not known, but contemporary authorities estimate it to be very high. Benjamin Anderson thought that, exclusive of real estate loans, one-half of commercial bank credit in 1909 went for loans or purchase of securities. Clarence W. Barron in 1914 guessed that about two-thirds of all commercial bank credit went for investment purposes and one-third for financing purely commercial transactions.

THE IMPORTANCE OF TIME DEPOSITS · Before World War I, commercial bank deposits were mostly demand deposits. Nevertheless, as Table 13 shows, time deposits were becoming increasingly important. Amounting to only one-fourth of demand deposits in 1896, time deposits increased to about two-fifths in 1910 and to just under 50 percent in 1915.

TABLE 13
Liabilities and Capital of All Commercial Banks, 1896–1929
(Millions of Dollars)

Year	(1) Total Liabilities and Capital	(2) U.S. Government Deposits	(3) Other Demand Deposits	(4) Other Time Deposits	(5) Other	(6) (4) as a percent of (3)
1896	$ 6,167	$ 15	$ 2,844	$ 712	$ 2,596	25
1900	9,059	99	4,345	1,087	3,528	25
1905	14,542	75	6,898	2,146	5,423	31
1910	19,324	54	8,566	3,720	6,984	43
1915	24,106	48	10,703	5,050	8,305	47
1920	47,509	261	21,571	11,121	14,556	52
1925	54,401	182	24,325	16,393	13,501	67
1929	62,442	375	25,160	19,875	17,032	79

Source: U.S. Bureau of the Census, *Historical Statistics of the United States.*

As far as the larger city banks were concerned, savings or time deposits were of no real consequence. In testimony before the Senate committee considering the Federal Reserve Act in 1913, Frank A. Vanderlip, president of the National City Bank of New York, stated, "I have paid no great attention to that [savings deposits], because in any event it probably would not interest the large city banks." On the other hand, country banks, especially state banks in the West and South, were practically doing a savings bank business. Witness after witness at the Senate hearings just referred to confirmed the importance of savings and time deposits to country banks. Typical was the following:

> Senator Nelson [Minnesota]: I call the attention of the committee to the fact that the telegrams received from the country banks in South West Pennsylvania are doing what our Minnesota banks are doing—a saving bank business.

Mr. Shields [Pennsylvania Bankers' Association]: I recently took a trip in Western Pennsylvania and observed the banking conditions very carefully, and I find that in nearly all the banks and trust companies they have saving accounts. . . .

Frequently, savings deposits accounted for between one-half and two-thirds of total deposits. One Minnesota banker, responding to a question put to him, answered: "Our deposits consist of $600,000 in time deposits, upon which we pay interest, and $500,000 in individual demand deposits." Another banker, from Davenport, Iowa, with deposits of $1 million, stated that, "At present 70 percent of our deposits are in time certificates and savings accounts. . . ." The importance of time deposits to country banks, particularly in the West and South, reflected the absence of mutual savings banks in these regions as well as the ability and readiness of country banks, with large portfolios of long-term mortgage and farm loans, to pay attractive interest rates on time deposits. Also, with the passage of the Federal Reserve Act, national banks were empowered to operate savings departments.

Actually, the data shown in Table 13 do not accurately reflect the importance of time deposits in the aggregate deposit structure. Because of both loose reporting standards and the questionable legality of the operation of savings departments by national banks (before 1914), there was a tendency not to differentiate between time and demand deposits on the books of the bank. Thus there is a downward bias in the reported figures. In some cases, city banks issued "demand certificates of deposit," which, although classified as demand deposits, were in effect time deposits. Such deposits, said one Baltimore banker, innocent of the contradiction contained in his statement, were accepted "in the case of a man who comes in with, say, $10,000 or $20,000, for which he has no particular use for 60 or 90 days or four months . . . and feels that he ought not let that lie in a bank earning nothing; we will then give him a demand deposit, at say 2 or 2½ per cent. I have known us to pay as much as 3 per cent, but not habitually."

COMPETITION FROM THE TRUST COMPANIES The years 1890 to 1920 were particularly eventful for trust companies, which were virtually eliminated as a distinctive type of financial intermediary. By the start of World War I, they had so immersed themselves in the banking business that a great many of them were in fact, if not in name, commercial banks possessing the added privilege of doing a fiduciary business. In an article in *Bankers' Magazine* in 1910, Clay Herrick, a noted authority on trust companies, commented on how

the lines of demarcation between the trust company and other classes of financial institutions have been rapidly disappearing. Already in many communities the differences between trust companies and other banks are so slight as to escape the observation of the uninitiated, while even experts must find the differences in the theories upon which the various institutions are founded than in the functions they actually exercise.

The business activities that trust companies, as state-chartered institutions, were permitted to engage in varied widely. In most states, trust companies were allowed to do a general banking business, including the acceptance of demand and time deposits and the making of collateral loans. All these activities were, of course, in addition to their "primary" business of managing personal and corporate trust accounts.

The trust companies' competitive threat to commercial banks was made all the more severe because trust companies operated under fewer regulatory constraints. Not until 1906, for example, were New York trust companies required to keep reserves against their deposits. Trust companies had other advantages, which have already been described. Suffice it to say that it was more favorable to operate as a trust company than as a commercial bank. Indeed, a number of legally chartered trust companies did not even do a fiduciary business but merely used their charters to engage in a general banking business.

Given their substantial advantages over commercial banks, together with the fact that the number of personal fortunes was constantly growing, it was inevitable that trust companies would mushroom. Growth was especially rapid after 1890, for that was a period of industrial mergers and rapid expansion of big business, and, consequently, a huge increase in the number of personal fortunes.

Estimates of the number of trust companies vary widely, but their story is much the same—an enormous increase from 149 in 1890 to 842 in 1908 according to one estimate, and from 255 to 1,470 according to another. Just how fast trust companies grew in terms of the resources over which they had control is not known, for no aggregate data exist on the personal trusts they controlled. Nevertheless, all the indications point to rapid advances. In New York State, the assets of trust companies increased from only $266 million in 1890 to $672 million in 1900 and to $1.6 billion in 1910. For the United States as a whole, trust company deposits rose from less than $150 million in 1882 to more than $400 million ten years later. By 1910 these deposits had swelled to almost $1.7 billion and to $4.2 billion by the end of the decade.

Scattered data tell us something about the growth of personal trusts administered by trust companies. Between 1905 and 1915 personal trust *deposits* (representing the *uninvested* portion of personal trusts) in New York State increased from $35 million to $128 million. More directly, Professor Raymond Goldsmith has estimated that personal trust funds administered by trust companies and the personal trust departments of commercial banks grew from about $3 billion in 1900 to $7 billion in 1912.

Commercial bankers were naturally very much disturbed by the challenge of the trust companies. Indeed, the "trust company problem" was one of the most talked about issues in banking circles in the early 1900s, especially in New York City, where, by 1902, trust company deposits substantially exceeded deposits in the city's national banks. In response to this incursion of trust companies into the commercial banking business, banker interests in New York, led by Morgan partner Henry P. Davison, organized in 1903 the powerful Bankers Trust Company "to which bankers all over the country could give their fiduciary business without fear that the enterprise would compete for their active accounts as the regular trust companies did."

Relief to beleaguered commercial banks also came from another quarter. As trust companies increasingly began to do a general banking business, their banking activities sooner or later were made subject to the same regulations as state-chartered commercial banks. Moreover, as they became less and less distinguishable from commercial banks, it was only natural that the state-regulatory agencies should eventually permit commercial banks to do a fiduciary business. The California Bank Act of 1909 permitted any state-chartered bank, including savings banks, to do a fiduciary business so long as that institution adhered to the regulations prescribed for such a business.

The Comptroller of the Currency, who administered the regulation of national banks, was considerably slower in granting permission to operate trust departments. This line of business did not open to national banks until the passage of the Federal Reserve Act in 1913, and the barriers did not completely drop until 1918. Enterprising bankers, of course, did not wait for the Comptroller to act, for by 1911 there were no less than 300 trust affiliates of national banks in existence. The usual practice was to form "a community of interest" between a national bank and a trust company. This step was accomplished through an arrangement by which the two institutions came under the same control and ownership. One of the earliest of these arrangements was the consolidation of the First Savings and Trust Company with the First National Bank of Chicago. In St. Louis the Mercantile Trust Company and the Mercantile National Bank had such a community of interest, as did the Commonwealth Trust Company of Boston and the New England National Bank.

While national banks were either establishing their own trust company affiliates or taking over the control of established trust companies, the latter were themselves in the midst of a consolidation movement, which started around the turn of the century and continued through the twenties. In New York City, where the number of trust companies reached perhaps 100 in the early 1900s, the consolidation movement was especially active. In 1905 the City Trust Company of New York and the Trust Company of America merged with the North American Trust Company. Several years later this amalgamation, already enlarged by the acquisition of the Colonial Trust Company in 1907, was in turn absorbed by the Equitable Trust Company, which in turn became part of the Chase National Bank in 1929. In 1910 began the great merger of the Morgan trust companies when the Guaranty Trust Company absorbed the Morton Trust Company and the Fifth Avenue Trust Company. In the same year, the Baltimore Trust and Guarantee Company merged with the International Trust Company of Baltimore, and the Old Colony Trust Company merged with the City Trust Company.

We have no way of knowing precisely how the fiduciary resources of trust companies were put to work. No doubt there were significant variations from one institution to another and even between separate trusts at the same institution. The lion's share, however, was distributed between corporate bonds (in the early part of the period, mostly in railroad bonds) and mortgages. As late as the mid-twenties, one of the largest corporate fiduciaries reported that bonds comprised 39 percent of its trust portfolio, whereas mortgages and real estate accounted for 44 percent. Stocks made up only 17 percent of the portfolio. Railroad and utility bonds together made up almost 65 percent of total bond holdings. Government bonds of all kinds, which were to become very important in later years, made up only 4 percent of the bond total. From other data, especially some estimates prepared by Raymond Goldsmith, it appears likely that in the aggregate the share of mortgages and real estate in personal trusts administered by corporate fiduciaries declined sharply, from about one-third in 1900 to less than one-fifth in 1912. And although these figures seem much too low, there is no reason to doubt that the share did decline substantially. For decline was almost inevitable as alternative investment opportunities appeared in great numbers and as industrial securities proved themselves to be solid investments.

LIFE INSURANCE COMPANIES JOIN
THE RANKS OF HIGH FINANCE · The life insurance companies were a fourth role player in finance capitalism. Through their marketing innovations, they were able to join the investment banking houses, the big city commercial banks, and the trust companies as leading suppliers of investment funds. The growth of life insurance in this era was something more than phenomenal.

At the beginning of the period, life insurance in force with American companies totaled only $3.5 billion; 30 years later Americans held life insurance policies amounting to $40.5 billion, and in 1930 the total was $106.5 billion. Over the same period, life companies became among the most important conduits through which the savings of millions of persons became available on the capital markets. Between 1890 and 1929 total assets of life insurance companies increased from $770 million to almost $17.5 billion, or by almost 10 percent annually. So substantial did the role of the great life companies become in the financial markets that by 1923 the industry was hailed as "the great stabilizer." But the financial might of the "big five" (New York Life, Equitable, Mutual, Prudential, and Metropolitan) in the investment markets had already been acknowledged much earlier.

Even before the turn of the century, the leaders of the great companies, whose predecessors had innovated in the marketing of life insurance, were directing their interest and attention to the investment of the enormous resources under their control. In earlier years investments consisted chiefly of mortgage loans and premium notes, items that accounted for nearly 80 percent of insurance company assets in 1860. Contacts with the securities markets were infrequent and uncomplicated. By 1900, however, mortgage loans made up less than 30 percent of total assets, whereas premium notes had all but faded out of sight, for the life companies no longer had to resort to such inducements to make sales. Instead, bonds, stocks, and collateral loans made up fully half the life company assets. These investments, together with the immense resources at the disposal of the life companies, could not help but make them important forces in the capital markets. The three largest held over $600 million of railroad securities in 1905, and all the life insurance companies owned not less than 10 percent of total railroad securities outstanding.

Industrial securities were not, as mentioned before, considered suitable for inclusion in the investment portfolios of conservative investors. Safety had to be the primary objective of institutions devoted to the protection of widows and orphans. Occasionally life companies did make direct investments in industrial and utility securities, but the sums were not large. Equitable, for instance, invested in George Westinghouse's ventures and took part in the creation of the Consolidated Edison Company. In later years, as the tide of investment opinion turned, the life companies were to become important suppliers of long-term capital to public utilities, first to street railway lines, and later, in the twenties, to the telephone and electric utilities. From only $29 million in 1900 and $249 million in 1922, life insurance company holdings of utility bonds surged to $1.5 billion in 1929.

In an important sense, the real financial power of the great life companies did not manifest itself so much in their enormous direct investments as in their relationships and ententes with high finance. The life companies, with their immense capacity to absorb securities and to put out funds to other intermediaries, were well represented in the entente cordiale that dominated the financial community up to World War I. George Perkins of the New York Life was a Morgan partner. J. P. Morgan and George F. Baker were on the finance committee of Mutual. Metropolitan placed William A. Read, of the investment banking firm of Vermilye & Co., on its board of directors and maintained through Read a very close relationship with that firm. Equitable's investment banking connections were far more extensive. Ownership control was vested in the House of Morgan, which was thoughtful enough to make a place for Kidder, Peabody and Kuhn, Loeb. The latter's senior partner, Jacob Schiff, sat on Equitable's finance committee.

The life companies were only one strand in the web of finance capitalism that emanated from the investment banking houses to include commercial banks and trust companies. For the "big three," these relationships became very extensive indeed. Through stock investments, Equitable controlled or had influence with a number of trust companies and banks, including the Mercantile Trust, the Mercantile Safe Deposit Company, the Western National Bank of New York, the Commercial Trust Company of Philadelphia, the Equitable Trust Company, and the National Bank of Commerce. As members of the alliance, each worked to help out the other, not forgetting that only in this way could each one's own interests be better served. Equitable and the Mercantile Trust guaranteed to "back the Western in difficult times," and Equitable took an interest in building up the correspondent and deposit business of Western by inducing "its out-of-town depository banks and large securities sellers to use the Western for their New York City banking needs." Mutual's interests were no less varied and extended to the Guaranty Trust, the Morton Trust, the United States Mortgage and Trust, and the Bank of Commerce. Through the latter, Mutual created a tangential alliance with Equitable, which also had an interest in the bank. New York Life, too, was no laggard in cultivating bank and trust company relationships, concluding alliances with the Central National Bank of New York, the Commercial and Manhattan Trust companies, and the New York Security and Trust.

These alliances proved beneficial to all participants. For the investment banking houses and the commercial banks and the trust companies, with their flexible investment powers, the advantages of alliances with the great life companies centered in the enormous investment funds that the latter could channel into the capital markets. As we noted, it was through their close control over the sources of investment capital that the leaders of finance, especially investment bankers like Morgan and Schiff, were able to rule. Between 1900 and 1905 Equitable alone bought $197 million worth of securities. Equally important was the ability of the large life companies to act as veritable financial reservoirs for their banking and trust affiliates. The president of the Fidelity Trust testified in the course of the Armstrong Investigation of 1905 that when his company needed funds, he asked Prudential to increase its deposits temporarily, and the insurance company usually did so. Similarly, Mutual would add to the deposits of its trust affiliates whenever they had particularly promising investment opportunities.

The benefits accruing to the great life companies were no less important but were somewhat more indirect. Their marketing innovations having proved successful beyond all expectations, the major problem facing these enterprises became that of finding profitable outlets for the plethora of investment funds that were made available to them. The very nature of life insurance companies as quasi-public institutions, along with the legal constraints on their investments, greatly limited the range of their investment opportunities.

Of course, the urge for corporate profits did not drive the large life companies to join the ranks of haute finance; most of these companies were mutual and the rest may as well have been, for in the case of stock institutions there were rigid limits on the dividends that could be paid on outstanding stock. James Hazen Hyde's holdings of Equitable stock, which gave him control of assets totaling more than $400 million, yielded a paltry $3,500 in dividends. The stock, of course, had great value, conveying as it did control over such enormous assets. Hyde finally sold his controlling interest for $2,500,000 to Thomas Fortune Ryan, the finance capitalist and utility tycoon. Undoubtedly he could have done several times better had he acted less impetuously. In a later transaction, much publicized in the Pujo investigation, Ryan sold his holdings to J. P. Morgan for $3 million. After Morgan's death, the stock was sold to T. Coleman Du Pont at a small profit.

Life company executives may have been indifferent to maximizing corporate profits, but the same eleemosynary inhibitions did not prevent them from reaping substantial private gains in the form of high salaries and, more important, through access to credit and "insider" knowledge that came with membership in the inner circles of high finance. As vice-president of Equitable, Hyde drew a salary of $100,000 a year for doing nothing, while Mutual's McCurdy drew $150,000 a year. Few leaders of the great companies were above cutting themselves in for pieces of the action. John Hegeman of Metropolitan participated in many of his company's syndicates and, as a result, made some $65,000 for himself. Hyde saw no impropriety in asking Kuhn, Loeb & Co. to send syndicate allotments not only to Equitable and its affiliated banks, but to "such personalities as I and my associates may designate."

However, the potential for private gain probably was not the sole force that made the life companies participate so fully in the high finance of the 1890s and early 1900s. The emphasis that management put on corporate size, growth, and prestige was equally if not more important. Some insurance leaders, like numerous other entrepreneurs, regarded business as something of a sport. The size of sales force, the volume of sales, the massive home office structures replete with enormous numbers of paper shufflers, and, not least of all, financial power—these were the things that had come to be identified with management success. Equitable's James Alexander did not speak of profits when he said, "we *must* perform some coup and increase the Equitable Trust Company's . . . size and importance. Also in the case of the Mercantile Trust, I would like to buy up a couple of trust companies and double up that concern." The committee that was set up to clean house in Equitable after the Armstrong investigation described this obsession with corporate power and expansion, relating it especially to the financial entanglements:

> The ambition for bigness naturally extends to investment of funds. There is chafing under the laws which govern the investments of a life insurance company. Alliances are made with other institutions with the idea of yielding the Society results which are not possible under the operations permitted to insurance companies. Systematic but uninteresting plodding is neglected, while energies are directed towards "coups."

The world of the great life companies seemed to collapse as the Armstrong investigation (prompted by the struggle for control over Equitable) proceeded to show just how far life insurance companies had departed from their original benevolent function and how much they had become a part of the "money trust." Public indignation, together with effective governmental regulation, led the life insurance companies to disassociate themselves from the world of high finance and to modify substantially their aggressive and often unconscionable marketing practices, particularly the sale of deferred dividend policies.

The weight of the post-Armstrong reforms fell particularly heavily on the "big three." Among other things, it meant a sharp pause in their expansion. Between 1903 and 1910 these companies experienced virtually no growth in the amount of insurance in force. Non-New York companies, on the other hand, benefited from the blunted competitiveness of the New York companies. Northwestern of Milwaukee wrote, by 1908, more insurance than either Equitable or Mutual. With the great monoliths of the industry on the defensive, the number of life companies also took a leap forward—from 112 in 1905 to 250 in 1912.

The changes were no less profound in the area of finance. The great life companies could not, of course, fail to continue carrying weight in the financial markets. However, they no longer sat on the inner councils. With their involvement with high finance severed, the large life insurance companies returned to more conservative investment policies. The purchase of railroad bonds, municipals, real estate mortgages, premium notes, and policy loans became the norm. Securities investments declined, from 51 percent of assets in 1905 to 42 percent in 1915. Mortgage lending took on a renewed importance as some attempt was made to loosen the ties to Wall Street.

In a sense the retrenchment had gone too far. So cautious and conservative had the great life companies become that in the late 1930s the Temporary National Economic Committee's report on life insurance companies raised "the fundamental question . . . whether or not the present investment practices of the life companies are not sterilizing the capital markets. . . ." Despairing over the failure of the life companies, with their huge resources, to provide venture capital, the committee no longer was bothered about "institutionalized power" but about "institutionalized flaccidity."

NEW FORMS OF NONLIFE INSURANCE · Although not able to match the success of life companies, general insurance companies (fire, marine, and casualty), along with other financial intermediaries, experienced considerable growth in the years between 1890 and 1929. The growth of casualty and other miscellaneous insurance companies was especially pronounced. From small beginnings, they benefited enormously from the popularity of the automobile and the resulting demand for liability and collision insurance. Their assets, a minuscule $7.1 million in 1900, had risen to over $1.6 billion in 1929.

Although fire and ocean marine insurance companies remained the mainstays of general insurance, with assets of $413 million in 1900 and $3.1 billion in 1929, these companies did not expand as much as those specializing in casualty and liability insurance. On the contrary, marine insurance actually was draining the resources of those companies writing such risks until near the turn of the century when Benjamin Rush of the Insurance Company of North America effected a set of innovations that restored marine profitability. Fire insurance, too, presented problems. In the early days of electricity, fires due to defective wiring were quite common and resulted in heavy losses. Moreover, disastrous citywide fires continued to plague fire companies. The Baltimore fire of 1904 and, above all, the San Francisco disaster of 1906 brought about the collapse and near collapse of numerous fire insurance companies. Most of the failures were among the local companies whose risks were highly concentrated, but even the solid Insurance Company of North America, with losses in San Francisco of more than $3 million, barely managed to survive, while the Alliance Insurance Company, closely affiliated with the North America, imposed a $15 assessment on each share of stock outstanding.

The failure of marine and fire insurance to grow made it increasingly clear that if overall growth were to be sustained and present and future resources effectively utilized, the general insurance companies would have to expand into new fields. This need to diversify became especially apparent after World War I. And it was not, of course, limited to the fire and marine insurance business. We have already seen how it applied with equal if not greater force to commercial banking. Indeed, the postwar years saw a decided trend toward diversification in any number of different industries. At the Insurance Company of North America, hitherto a strictly fire and marine insurance underwriter, Benjamin Rush sought to expand the company's operations to "include virtually every known form of insurance except life." Other companies embarked on similar strategies.

The two most rapidly expanding fields in which the North America and other old-time fire and marine companies sought to gain a foothold were the inland marine and casualty businesses. The inland marine business had, as the name suggests, originally dealt with the insurance of river or canal boat cargoes. As such, it had not been a profitable line for a variety of reasons. It was hard to make a profit when boat owners had the disturbing habit of wrecking their insured vessels in order to liquidate an increasingly unprofitable business.

By the turn of the century, inland marine had so dwindled as the railroad replaced water and river traffic that some of the inland marine divisions of the larger fire and marine companies took to writing salesmen's floaters, horse and wagon floaters, transportation policies covering merchandise on common carriers, and so on. In 1904 the Insurance Company of North America introduced a tourist floater policy covering travelers' baggage. Several years later the company began insuring registered mail and parcels. Despite the diversity of the business, revenue was very small and insignificant compared with other lines. As late as 1914, the inland marine account of the North America netted premiums of only $250,000.

The motor truck, which was becoming a major means of transporting goods, considerably enlarged the scope of the inland marine business, as did the introduction of the "comprehensive" transportation policy. At the same time, inland marine insurance was extended to cover such diverse items as bridges, trophies, wedding presents, jewelry, and, in addition, virtually anything that might be moved. By 1920 the net premiums of the inland division of the North America increased to $1,743,000 and to $3,500,000 in 1928.

The casualty insurance line also grew very quickly, especially with the rise in automobile coverage. At the beginning of the century, the casualty business, what little there was, was handled by a few life companies and a small number of strictly casualty companies, who were generally regarded by the other companies as "poor relations." In 1903 the casualty business did not exceed $20 million a year. The largest purely casualty company was the Fidelity and Casualty Insurance Company of New York, with assets of $5.7 million. With the emergence of the automobile, however, the older and more affluent fire and marine companies faced the alternative of either writing casualty or seeing a fertile and expanding field pass wholly into the hands of these no longer so poor relations.

The charter provisions of most fire and marine companies prohibited the writing of casualty insurance, which necessitated the incorporation of casualty affiliates. At the end of the war the Hartford Insurance Company set up its own casualty affiliate, and in 1920 the Insurance Company of North America followed by establishing the Indemnity Insurance Company of North America. Other companies, including the Home Insurance Company, followed over the next several years. The casualty business, if not immediately profitable (the North America sustained yearly losses on its affiliate until the early thirties), certainly brought in a lot of business. The Indemnity collected more than $7 million in 1923 in casualty premiums, surpassing those paid on marine insurance.

Conservative as most of the general insurance companies were in their investment activities, the heady atmosphere of the twenties got the best of some. One executive reported, "We don't have to figure as closely as we used to. There are some days when I'd insure a burning building to get the premium to put in the stock market." This was no doubt an extreme utterance, and some companies, like the North America, began to prepare for an eventual collapse of the security markets as early as 1926.

CREATION OF A NATIONAL CREDIT MARKET · Along with the rapid growth of financial intermediaries in the years between the late 1800s and World War I, significant progress was made in improving the mobility of loanable funds between regions, thereby further facilitating the rational allocation of savings. Just how imperfect the credit markets were with respect to capital mobility is suggested by the very wide interregional interest differentials that persisted well into the 1890s. Short-term bank loan rates in the years 1893–1897 ranged from less than 5 percent in New England cities to a high of 9 percent in the Western states. Denver's 10 percent was more than two-and-a-half times that of Boston. Similar interregional interest differentials existed in the long-term credit markets. For the 1880s, mortgage rates averaged slightly less than 6 percent in the New England and Middle Atlantic states, between 7 and 8 percent in the South and Middle West, and between 10 and 11 percent in the Western states. By the early 1900s, however, these interregional variations had been greatly reduced (though certainly not eliminated), especially in the short-term market.

The growth of financial intermediaries and their aggressive involvement in the transformation of the economy had much to do with this development. Commercial banks in high-interest rate regions contributed to interregional mobility by the active solicitation of funds from lower-interest rate regions. The Comptroller of the Currency was particularly upset by the Western banks' practice of issuing certificates of deposits to surplus savings units in the East. The practice did not rise to significant proportions, but it might have if the Comptroller had not moved to stop it. Banks in high-interest regions also sought to increase their excess reserves by rediscounting commercial paper in banks located in lower-interest areas. Given the sentiment among lawmakers and bankers that local banks should serve the local communities, these efforts had only a moderate effect in reducing regional interest rate differentials. The growth of a national commercial-paper market through the creation and expansion of commercial-paper houses with branches in most of the larger cities was much more important. Western bankers complained bitterly on seeing their one-time monopoly broken up. As one Iowa banker explained it to the Senate:

> Until recently, western bankers were able to maintain their loaning regardless of the depression of the eastern markets, but now there has arisen an element that wages constant war on the established rates. It is the festive note broker, who with his eastern capital, steps in to disturb the harmonious relationship between banker and borrower. Just at the time there seems to be an opportunity to dispose of idle funds at a profitable rate, the banker is confronted with the alternative of cutting his rates or seeing his loans going to outside dealers.

Financial institutions also lent their aid in creating a regionally integrated long-term market. Life insurance companies, and trust companies especially, came to conduct their operations on a national scale. This result was partly in response to legislation allowing insurance companies a wider range of legal investments and greater freedom to invest in out-of-state mortgages. In New York the original law prohibited such investments. An 1868 amendment permitted insurance companies to invest in mortgages anywhere within 50 miles of New York; in 1875 the legal boundaries were extended to include adjacent states; and in the 1880s New York mutuals gained the right to invest in mortgages anywhere. But in addition to aggressive professional management and an absence of legal restrictions, the expanding role of life companies in the interregional flow of mortgage credit depended on the parallel development of brokerage institutions designed to service their mortgage portfolios locally.

The creation of a national credit market and the widespread participation of the main types of intermediaries in finance capitalism reflected the coming of age of the United States as a mature industrial nation. If the spirit displayed by financial institutions in their daily actions seemed bold and insensitive to a higher ethic, this was simply in keeping with the spirit that prevailed in other segments of the business community. To some extent, business life was a free-for-all in which the highest stakes went to those who were most audacious and capable of the ruthless use of power. However, it is questionable whether the achievements of the period could have been won by lesser men. Whatever the personality flaws of the so-called robber barons, the economic consequences of their behavior were by no means all bad. They contributed immensely to the development of large-scale industry and to the rationalization of production. In these efforts the captains of industry were either joined or supplanted by the captains of finance, who helped to channel the nation's savings into the cause of economic expansion. Although there was ample justification for some of the public outcry against the "money trust," the economic consequences were largely beneficial. The life insurance industry, for example, was a more vigorous promoter of economic change in its pre-1905 phase than in its later phase, despite abundant evidence of improprieties in the earlier period.

7 · intensified competition: the 1920s

The twenties constitute a brief but most remarkable period in American economic and social history. It was the era of prohibition, isolationism, Harding normalcy, and Coolidge prosperity. More important, in its economic consequences, it was the heyday of security speculation—the Great Bull Market when the trading of securities became a national pastime. Along with a spirit of boundless optimism and the collapse of tradition, the security craze of the twenties was to exert profound, if not wholly salutary, effects on most financial intermediaries.

RAPID ECONOMIC ADVANCES · The twenties were prosperous years for most Americans. Gross national product (in 1929 dollars) increased impressively, from $74 billion in 1919 to $104 billion in 1929. A better indication of economic advance was the gain in per capita income (again in 1929 dollars) from $710 to $857. Inflation, surprisingly, was practically nonexistent, with the price level more or less steady after 1922 and remaining considerably below the previous wartime level.

The fruits of previous industrial achievements ripened in the twenties, making possible America's first fling as a mass consumption society. An essential ingredient, as well as a manifestation, was the changing makeup of the labor force. Between 1920 and 1930 the size of the labor force grew by 15 percent. However, the number of farm workers declined by nearly 10 percent, whereas the number of white-collar workers multiplied by over 40 percent. During the twenties, farmers fell from almost 30 percent of the labor force to a little over 20 percent, a drop that was almost exactly compensated by expansion in the white-collar ranks.

Also related to this upgrading was a continuation of the population shift from the farm to the city. While the population as a whole increased by 16 percent in the twenties, that of the cities increased by 22 percent. At the same time the movement to the suburbs, where population increased by 44 percent, added still another dimension to the shift in the place of living—a shift that had extraordinary meaning for the financial intermediaries.

In the course of the twenties, durable goods, such as the refrigerator, the radio, and most notably the automobile, became a part of American households. Automobile sales rose from less than 2 million in 1919 to 3.7 million in 1929. By the end of the decade more than 23 million automobiles, averaging 4 for every 5 households, were registered. Much of this new spending was on the installment plan, thereby giving a further impetus to the business of intermediation.

TABLE 14
Assets of Selected Financial Intermediaries, 1922–1939

Intermediary	Millions of Dollars				Percent of Total			
	1922	1929	1933	1939	1922	1929	1933	1939
Commercial banks	47,467	66,235	47,127	66,306	55.1	47.6	40.3	42.6
Personal trust funds administered by banks and trust companies	18,000	30,000	25,000	35,000	20.9	21.5	21.8	22.5
Mutual savings banks	6,597	9,873	10,758	11,852	7.7	7.1	9.4	7.6
Savings and loan associations	2,802	7,411	6,231	5,377	3.3	5.3	5.4	3.5
Credit unions	11	42	37	193	*	*	*	0.1
Private life insurance companies	8,652	17,482	20,896	29,243	10.1	12.6	18.2	18.8
General insurance companies	2,358	4,716	3,534	4,871	2.7	3.4	3.1	3.1
Private noninsured pension funds	90	500	700	1,050	0.1	0.4	0.6	0.7
Investment companies	110	2,988	1,283	1,584	0.1	2.1	1.1	1.0
Total†	86,087	139,247	115,566	155,476	100.0	100.0	100.0	100.0

Source: Raymond Goldsmith, *Financial Intermediaries in the American Economy since 1900* (New York: National Bureau of Economic Research, 1958).
* *Less than 0.05 percent.*
† *Percentage totals may not precisely add to 100.0 because of rounding.*

A decade of abundance, in a way perhaps not very different from our own experience in the last several years, convinced most Americans that the country had indeed entered a new era of prosperity and unparalleled social advance. President Hoover typified the spirit of the times when, in his inaugural address on March 4, 1929, he declared that "we shall soon . . . be in sight of the day when poverty will be banished from this nation." John J. Raskob, the millionaire chairman of the Democratic National Committee, carried his optimism even further, claiming that not only need no one be poor but that everyone "ought to be rich." Economists of high repute encouraged the belief that the business cycle could be eliminated through the operations of the Federal Reserve and the new art of economic forecasting.

THE RISE OF NEW YORK AS AN
INTERNATIONAL MONEY MARKET · Less striking but a far more accurate harbinger of America's future was the development of New York as a world financial center. Before World War I the United States was still a debtor nation in the amount of $3.7 billion, despite persistent trade surpluses and the extension, on a modest scale, of foreign loans.

Some very small loans to the Mexican and Peruvian governments had been made as early as the 1860s. In 1879 the Province of Quebec floated a $3 million loan in New York. However, foreign financing first became important near the turn of the century. In 1899 the Chinese government sold $2.2 million of bonds in the United States in connection with the construction of the Hankow-to-Canton Railway. In the next year New York took $12 million of a 10-year loan and $28 million of a 3-year loan floated by the British government and $20 million of German government treasury notes. Other loans were made to Sweden ($10 million), to the city of Cologne ($1 million), and to the Free City of Hamburg ($2 million). A flurry of foreign financing occurred in the years 1901–1905 when the foreign securities floated by American bankers aggregated about $460 million, the largest amount for any half-decade prior to 1915. But these were small figures compared to those of the war years.

The net debtor position of the United States was, like so much else, reversed by the war. By 1919 private United States investments abroad (long- and short-term) totaled $7 billion compared to $3.5 billion in 1914, while foreign investments in the United States dwindled to $4 billion compared with the earlier level of $7.3 billion.

The twenties saw a further enormous expansion of America's role as a world banker. From 1919 to 1930 the net creditor position of the United States almost tripled—from $3 billion to $8.8 billion. Between 1920 and 1930, over 1,700 foreign issues, totaling nearly $11.5 billion, were offered publicly in the United States. Of these issues, more than $9.5 billion represented new loans. By the late 1920s Canadian firms were said to be "beginning to use New York's financial facilities much as businesses do which are located in Michigan and Ohio." Indeed, some American financial institutions, particularly certain large city banks, began during the war and in later years to build an international network by the creation of overseas branches.

CONSOLIDATION AND DIVERSIFICATION
IN INDUSTRY · Another pertinent trend was a revival of the consolidation movement that had occurred so sensationally in the late 1890s. By 1929 the 200 largest corporations controlled almost half of all corporate assets. The three largest automobile producers manufactured nearly 90 percent of all cars and trucks, while 1 percent of the country's public utility companies accounted for more than 80 percent of production. Giantism flourished even in retailing, traditionally a field of small enterprise. The Atlantic & Pacific food chain expanded from 400 stores in 1900 to 5,000 in 1922 and 17,500 in 1928; Drug, Incorporated, a holding company, controlled over 10,000 drugstores and several drug producers by the end of the decade.

A trend toward product diversification by large-scale producers coincided with the merger movement. In some instances companies like Du Pont found product diversification necessary if they were to utilize fully the enormous resources they had put together during the war. For other companies with large research facilities, such as General Electric and Westinghouse, diversification was the result of new technological discoveries and applications. Still others, like General Motors, diversified not out of design but simply through the aggressive acquisition policies of their leaders.

Financial intermediaries, especially commercial banks in the nation's urban centers, participated most importantly in both developments, consolidation and diversification. As a result, intermediaries that had performed more or less distinctive functions in the past now found themselves vigorously competing in the same markets.

COMMERCIAL BANKS REACH FOR

TIME DEPOSITS · No financial institutions underwent more profound changes in the twenties than commercial banks, particularly the big city banks. In a sense, the business of these institutions became as fully diversified as that of their country cousins.

Innovations occurred on both sides of the balance sheet. On the liability side, the most dramatic change was the sharp growth of time deposits. To be sure, this phenomenon was not unique to the twenties, for a trend in this direction was evident as far back as we have data. But the trend underwent a pronounced acceleration in the twenties. Between 1920 and 1929 time deposits rose by almost 7 percent a year, from just over $11 billion to a little less than $20 billion. Demand deposits, in comparison, grew very slowly—from $21.5 billion to $25 billion—a rate of less than 2 percent a year.

Whereas time deposits were important only in the country banks in earlier years, the growth during the twenties took place mostly in the city banks. For commercial banks having federal charters (an admittedly imperfect proxy for the larger commercial banks), time deposits increased from less than $3.5 billion to more than $8 billion between 1920 and 1929, or by an average of 10 percent a year. In contrast, demand deposits were virtually stagnant, increasing by only $200 million over the decade. To make another comparison, in 1920 time deposits in national banks were about one-third the level of demand deposits; by 1929 time deposits had become three-fourths as large as demand deposits.

In a small way, the rapid growth of time deposits is attributable to misclassification of deposits. The distinction under the Federal Reserve Act between time and demand deposits discriminated against the latter by subjecting them to higher reserve requirements; and since the discrimination was partly arbitrary, member banks no doubt classified some demand deposits as time deposits. On the other hand, the rather arbitrary distinction between the two types of deposits probably induced many city bankers to revise favorably their earlier attitude toward time deposits. Nevertheless, during the twenties, as more recently, the growth of time deposits received its stimulus more from necessity than from choice on the part of bankers. Often it was only by actively promoting time and savings deposits that the large commercial banks in urban centers could hope to retain deposits. Wooing time deposits had become especially important because corporations had become more efficient in their cash management practices, and more aware of the cost of holding low-interest-bearing demand balances. Alfred P. Sloan, Jr., tells what happened at General Motors in 1922: "We began calculating a month ahead what our cash would be each day of the month. . . . Against this projected curve we compared each day the corporation's actual cash balances. . . . By reducing our cash balances in banks, this system enabled us to invest the excess cash, principally in short-term government securities."[1] In response, the city banks that handled large corporate accounts actively encouraged their corporate customers to hold excess liquid balances in interest-bearing certificates of deposit or in open time deposit accounts. By 1928 such deposits accounted for about 10 percent of total time and savings deposits of all commercial banks.

Personal savings deposits were much more important than business time deposits in total dollars. The number of savings depositors in commercial banks increased more than threefold, from 13 million in 1920 to 41 million in 1930. Particularly among the larger city banks, the cultivation of the saver, as we shall see, was but a part of a broad return of commercial banks toward a retail business.

CHANGING COMPOSITION OF
COMMERCIAL BANK ASSETS · Changes also occurred in the uses to which commercial banks, notably the large urban banks, put their loanable funds. For these banks, the traditional, although by no means exclusive, form of bank credit was still the "commercial loan." In 1920 loans to business and agriculture, most of which were short term and more or less conformed to the "real bill," still accounted for almost half of total earning assets. Between 1921 and 1929, however, although total bank credit increased by nearly 45 percent, short-term loans to business and agriculture showed practically no growth. By the end of the decade these loans comprised only one-third of total earning assets.

The decline in agricultural loans (from $4 billion to $2 billion) reflected the depressed farm economy. The relative decline of the commercial loan was largely due to changes in the policies and behavior of the treasurers of the large corporations. They came to rely more and more on retained earnings to finance their working capital needs. They also placed more emphasis on efficiencies in inventory control and speeding turnover. Not least of all, they took advantage of the growing public mania for equities by issuing additional stock. Of course, large corporations obtained additional credits from the banking system in roundabout ways, but nevertheless, total short-term loans to corporate customers shrank substantially in the twenties.

The great bulk of what commercial loans remained went to small or medium-sized firms in manufacturing, wholesaling, retailing, and the service trades. With few alternative sources of external financing, these enterprises still required bank financing for much of their working capital needs. Yet according to one observer, "The figures seem to show that . . . they, too, have become somewhat less dependent on bank credit."

Confronted with the loss of demand for their traditional type of credit extension, the large urban banks, where the problem was most acute,

[1] Alfred P. Sloan, *My Years with General Motors* (Garden City, N.Y.: Doubleday, 1963), p. 123.

turned increasingly to real estate loans on urban properties, security loans, and, at the very end of the decade, consumer loans. Between 1920 and 1929 commercial-bank real estate loans increased from $3.2 billion to $6.3 billion. For national banks, however, the gain was proportionately much greater, from only $230 million in 1920 to $1.4 billion in 1929. And although real estate loans usually took the form of farm mortgages in earlier years, the real estate loans of the twenties were almost exclusively limited to urban mortgages.

In addition to having surplus funds that could not be profitably employed in short-term loans to trade and industry, the main force attracting commercial banks into mortgage lending was the active demand for mortgage funds. Indeed, the years 1922–1926 formed a period of unequaled activity in the real estate market. The shift into urban mortgages was also facilitated by the very rapid growth of time deposits, which, in addition to providing loanable funds, provided the banks with a "plausible excuse" for investing in this way.

Commercial-bank security loans, as we have seen, existed long before the twenties, but it was in that decade that they increased significantly. They more than doubled over the decade, while their share in total bank credit jumped from 15.5 percent in 1922 to 24 percent in 1929. For central reserve city banks (those in Chicago and New York), where security loans naturally absorbed much larger portions of bank credit, the increase was from 29 percent to 45 percent. Much of this increase went to finance purchases of stock in the securities markets. Between June 1928 and June 1929, in response to the public's rush for securities, the share of security loans to total loans and investments of reserves city banks increased from 36 to 45 percent.

A third type of commercial bank activity—the consumer loan business—was an innovation of the 1920s, but as with most innovations, years would have to pass before it would attain any real importance. Motivated, no doubt, by the need to find alternative uses of funds, a few commercial banks, led by the National City Bank of New York in 1928, established "Personal Loan Departments," which made loans of between $50 and $1,000 without collateral, but with two co-signers, at 6 percent (9 percent actual) payable in installments. But city bankers continued to regard consumer loans as an inappropriate form of lending, and it is doubtful if as much as $100 million was loaned out in consumer credit before World War II.

Before World War I, American commercial banks had limited their business almost exclusively to domestic banking activities. The large American banks did have correspondent relationships with foreign institutions, but American foreign trade, and certainly that of third nations, was still financed much more in London than in New York. During and following the war, foreign business was given an impetus by the Federal Reserve System. Starting about 1917, the System began to rediscount bankers acceptances. In effect, the central bank was underwriting the new international trade financing of the large city banks. From virtually nothing in 1917, bankers acceptances increased to about $1 billion in 1920 and then to about $1.5 billion at the end of 1929. These sums greatly exceeded the amount of acceptance credit actually extended by the banking system; what was lent more often than not was only the *guarantee* of the big commercial banks and the Federal Reserve Bank of New York, for the acceptances were generally sold to third parties. Commercial banks usually held in their own portfolios no more than 10 percent of the acceptances they issued.

At the same time that American banks were beginning to play a role of some importance in financing America's international trade, several of the largest banks were invading the banking business in foreign countries. In 1913 only four American commercial banks (all in New York City) had branches abroad—in London and Paris. During World War I, with the disruption of traditional banking connections, American banks opened over 200 additional foreign branches in Central and Latin America, the Far and Near East, India, and Western Europe. With Europe's recovery and the reestablishment of traditional financial ties, many of these branches disappeared. By 1926 foreign branches had been reduced to 106, all of which were affiliated with eight large New York and Boston banks.

COMMERCIAL BANKS ASSUME
FIDUCIARY FUNCTIONS · In addition to changing their deposit and loan activities and invading foreign money centers, commercial banks moved in two other significant directions in the 1920s. They became involved in fiduciary activities and investment banking on a much wider scale. Prior to 1913, as noted earlier, national banks were precluded from operating trust departments. In some instances, they got around this limitation by creating subsidiaries. But the decisive growth of fiduciary business by commercial banks came in the twenties, especially in the last few years of that decade when the larger commercial banks sought to take on a full line of investment banking activities. The assets of trust departments (the trust departments of commercial banks, including, of course, those institutions having the word "trust" in their name, and a small number of more or less specialized fiduciary institutions) grew more than four times between 1912 and 1929, from $7 billion to $30 billion. Their growth rate substantially exceeded that of the commercial bank assets, which in the same period rose from $21.8 billion to $66.2 billion. In 1926 over 1,100 national banks were engaged in fiduciary activities; the number had risen to 1,900 by 1930. In dollar terms, trust funds in national banks more than quadrupled, from less than $1 billion in mid-1928 to $4.5 billion in 1930. Despite these gains, the greater part of the trust business was still carried on by the old-line trust companies, which also conducted general commercial banking business.

As in the preceding period, the expansion of corporate fiduciaries reflected the growing wealth of the United States, particularly the enlarged number and size of personal fortunes derived from a rapidly expanding and fluid economy. However, other factors also contributed to the growth of corporate fiduciary assets. New kinds of taxes, especially the federal income tax, made it increasingly necessary for the affluent to receive professional advice. In addition, the enormous variety of financial claims made it more important than in earlier times to place wealth in the control of professional managers. For these and related reasons it became less and less the fashion to leave estate management, especially where large fortunes were involved, in the hands of attorneys or trusted friends and more common to place such wealth under the administration of corporate fiduciary institutions. Thus between 1912 and 1928 the proportion of wealth held by corporate trustees in the state of Massachusetts increased from 1.15 percent to 5.26 percent, with almost all the gain coming after 1920.

The composition of personal trust assets also underwent a significant transformation. The share channeled into mortgages and real estate continued to decline, as it had before the war, from less than one-fifth in 1912 to one-eighth in 1922 and to less than one-tenth in 1929. The extent of this decline, in the case of Massachusetts, is shown in Table 15. What

TABLE 15
Composition of Principal Assets of Trust Departments of All Trust Companies
in Massachusetts, 1915–1930 (Percent)

Year	Bonds	Stocks	Loans on Real Estate	Real Estate Owned
1915	15.9	43.0	25.1	10.4
1920	37.6	38.6	13.0	5.7
1925	40.0	39.6	11.0	5.1
1930	38.5	46.0	7.0	5.6

Source: John W. Harriman, *The Investment Management of Trust Funds by Corporate Trustees in Massachusetts* (unpublished dissertation submitted to the Harvard University Graduate School of Business Administration in 1932), p. 52.

the mortgage market lost, government securities gained. Prior to the war, trusts held few state, local, and federal securities. By the early twenties, however, government bonds made up about 15 percent of total trust department assets. The growth in government security holdings was encouraged by the fact that income earned on these securities was exempt from the federal income tax until 1941. The latter part of the twenties, on the other hand, saw large increases in stock acquisitions as trust departments, like everyone else, sought to participate in the profits of the bull market.

MERGING COMMERCIAL AND

INVESTMENT BANKING · As already indicated, commercial banks were active in investment banking long before the 1920s. It was only in that decade, however, that commercial banks, through their wholly owned security affiliates, assumed *all* the functions of investment banking businesses. As with many other innovations of the twenties, this one, too, was partly the result of the shrinking demand for short-term business credits. As corporations increasingly looked to the equity markets for their financing, the big city banks naturally sought to capture a piece of the business as well as to retain their corporate connections. Furthermore, the machinery of the old private investment banking firms was inadequate for coping with the surge in new offerings of securities. Finally, commercial banks would in any event have been called upon to finance the sale of the new security issues. For all these reasons, the city banks inevitably became directly involved in the investment banking business.

The first two security affiliates—set up by the First National Bank of New York in 1908 and the National City Bank of New York in 1911—remained isolated cases until World War I. These affiliates, moreover, did not really perform a complete range of investment banking activities. Indeed, they were little more than holding companies set up to hold the securities that the parent banks themselves were prohibited from holding. The war brought the majority of commercial banks into extensive contact with security distribution and brought into sharp relief the inadequacies of the existing machinery. Thus in 1917 the Chase National Bank created a security affiliate. A year later the First National Bank of Boston organized a similar institution, and in 1920 three other large banks in New York, Boston, and New Orleans joined the trend. Up to 1927, however, the majority of urban banks maintained only an indirect interest in investment banking. The following year, no doubt in response to the flood of new stock issues coming on the market, the idea of separate investment banking affiliates took on the proportions of a craze. In order to acquire the required sales organization without delay, it was usual to take over one of the already-established investment banking houses. So rapid and pervasive was the trend that by 1929 nearly all the largest commercial banks had one or more investment affiliates.

These subsidiaries performed a complete range of investment banking functions. They originated new security issues, formed and took part in underwriting syndicates, sold new issues to retail banks and to institutional investors, and participated at the retail level in the distribution of securities to individual investors through a network of branch offices. So important were these affiliates that it is estimated that commercial banks and their securities affiliates were handling about half the total distribution of securities in the late twenties. The National City Company, the largest security distribution organization in the United States, alone distributed close to $6 billion between 1927 and 1931.

To round out their investment banking business, some, although not many, of the largest banks began their own mutual funds, or investment trusts as they were then called. As Goldsmith has stated,

> The investment trust affiliate could carry out transactions for which not even the security affiliate was thought fit. It could . . . be used to attract long-term funds, which might provide steady and lasting outlet for issues sponsored by the bank, whereas the security affiliate worked with the banks' own funds. . . . Last, but not least, the control of an investment trust offered the additional incentive of reaping profits made with other people's money, in so far as a large part of the capital was provided by fixed interest securities or by loans.

Nevertheless, commercial-bank-sponsored investment trusts were not numerous. In 1930 national banks had only seventeen directly affiliated investment trusts.

CHANGES IN COMMERCIAL
BANKING STRUCTURE · No discussion of commercial banking during the twenties would be complete without reference to some of the structural changes that occurred within the industry. These changes revealed themselves in two ways: first, in the sizable reduction in the number of commercial banks, from over 30,000 in 1920 to less than 25,000 in 1929, and second, in the concentration of banking resources, particularly in the urban centers.

The outstanding factor accounting for the diminution of commercial banks was the high rate of bank failure. Between 1921 and 1929 close to 20 percent of all commercial banks in existence in 1920 failed. Although fewer than 1,200 commercial banks failed between 1904 and 1920, more than 5,000 failed in the years 1921 to 1929. Most of the banks that failed were small, country, state-chartered institutions in the South and Middle West. The overwhelming majority were capitalized at less than $100,000 and almost 40 percent at $25,000 or less.

The formation of new banks, especially in the South and West, in the first decade of the century had been excessive by nearly all standards. Between 1900 and 1909 the number of banks in the South shot up from 3,500 to 7,100 and in the West increased from 2,100 to 5,600. Such increases in numbers far exceeded population growth in these regions, particularly in the rural areas, and they were also well in excess of increases in production and per capita income. As long as agriculture was prospering, which was the case until about the end of World War I, the overexpansion of country banking did not become apparent. It took the agricultural depression of the twenties to reveal the extent to which overbanking had gone. Indeed, the rate of bank failures was highest in those states most dependent on agricultural activities and least in the industrial states of the East. From 1920 to 1929, 51 percent of the banks in South Dakota, 50 percent in New Mexico, 43 percent in Georgia, and 47 percent in Montana failed, compared with 6 percent in Rhode Island and only 2.5 percent in New York and in Pennsylvania.

Still other factors contributed to the distressingly high rate of bank failures. The tendency of small banks to be less profitable, as evidenced by their higher net expense to gross earning ratios, added to the problem by leaving them particularly susceptible to periods of general adversity. The automobile, too, by bringing the farm and city in close proximity, must have also undermined the position of the rural bank, for with the automobile it was easy and tempting to bypass the town and travel to the big city.

Second to bank failures in accounting for the decline in the number of banks was a sharp increase in bank mergers. Taking place mostly in the cities, the merger movement was also an important factor explaining the increase in banking concentration in urban markets. From less than 150 a year between 1910 and 1920, the number of bank mergers increased to 300–400 a year between 1921 and 1925 and to more than 500 a year from 1926 to 1929.

Mergers among urban banks were no doubt motivated partly by the increase in concentration taking place in other sectors of the economy and, consequently, by the increasing size of the banks' customers. This factor was particularly significant in view of the statutory provisions limiting the amount that a bank might lend to any single customer to 10 percent of the bank's capital and surplus. The quest for the much sought-after million-dollar account and for accounts of ten times that amount (of which there were some) was also a factor, for the balance a customer could safely keep with any one bank was, and still is, thought to be directly related to that bank's total capital and deposit resources. Mergers were also prompted by the desire to provide a complete line of banking and financial services, which only large banking institutions could afford to offer. Other mergers resulted from the desire to spread risks and to effect diversification. Very often this was the motivation behind mergers between banks engaged in different lines of business or catering to different clienteles. Real or imagined economies of scale provided another inducement to merge. Finally, some mergers were effected, especially among banks that were already giants (like the largest New York City banks) for no comprehensible reason other than to grow even larger.

As we have observed, one result of the increase in the number of bank mergers was a growing concentration of banking resources in urban markets. In New York City, the ten largest institutions in 1929 held over two-thirds of total commercial bank resources, compared with two-fifths at the beginning of the century. Boston provided another example: in 1913 the three largest banks controlled almost 50 percent of the banking resources of that city. By 1924 the share increased to about 60 percent. By the end of the decade, as a result of mergers with its leading competitors, one bank, the Massachusetts First National, controlled more than half of Boston's banking business.

Along with the decline in the number of banks and the increase in banking concentration came an upsurge in branch banking. In 1919, 464 banks operated 1,082 branches. A decade later the number of banks having more than one banking office totaled 816, while the number of branches multiplied to 3,603. More striking than the increase in the number of branch systems was the increase in the share of banking resources controlled by multiunit banks, from 16 percent in 1919 to 46 percent in 1929.

Branching, of course, did not occur everywhere; a number of states continued to prohibit any form of branching. Other states allowed branching on a limited basis (for example, within the city or county of the bank's home office), and a few states, notably California, permitted statewide branch banking.

Under the National Bank Act, nationally chartered banks were not allowed to form branches. This restriction was relaxed a little in 1918 when national banks absorbing state banks were given permission to retain any branches of the acquired bank. Further slight relaxation of the "no branching" rule came in 1922 when the Comptroller allowed national banks to establish "teller windows" in the same city as the bank's home office for the purpose of receiving deposits and cashing checks but not for making loans. More significant still was the McFadden Act (1927), which allowed national banks to operate branches within the city of the bank's primary facility, provided state banking laws permitted such branches. However, not until 1933, as part of the Glass-Steagall Act, were national banks accorded the same branching privileges as state-chartered banks and trust companies. National banks responded enthusiastically to the branching legislation. In 1919, of the 464 banks having branches, 446 were state banks and trust companies and only 18 were national banks. Ten years later the number of national banks operating branch systems increased to 160.

Although the average size of branch systems remained small, the branch systems of some of the largest urban banks, in New York City, Detroit, Cleveland, and Philadelphia, grew to include between 50 and 150 separate banking facilities in the city and its suburbs. Where permitted, especially in California, great statewide branch systems developed. The most spectacular of these was the giant Bank of America, which, by absorbing local banks and establishing *de novo* branches, built up a state-wide branch system of almost 300 offices by 1929.

Especially where branching was prohibited or severely limited, "chain" or "group" banking became a common expedient. The distinction between the two terms is minor: a banking chain is a number of separate banks controlled by one or more individuals, whereas group banking refers to control by a holding company whose stock is, in turn, held by one or more individuals. Although widespread, chain and group banking was most concentrated in the Northwest and Southeast. Group or chain banking was also practiced in a number of metropolitan areas, where the growth of population and increasing congestion of traffic made for rapid development of banking in the outlying districts. The downtown banks looked with envy at the lucrative bank business that thus developed. With branch banking prohibited, the only solution was to buy into established banks in the new territory or to establish new ones.

Chain banking, dating at least as far back as 1890, reached its peak in the mid-twenties, after which group banking became the more popular form. Near the end of the decade, there were some 273 banking chains or groups involving 1,858 banks and over $13 billion in aggregate resources. Most chains were small but a few were very large. The Witham chain, which failed in 1926, was the biggest and, at its peak in 1922, controlled approximately 175 banks, mostly in Georgia and Florida.

INNOVATIONS IN INVESTMENT BANKING · The investment banking business, like the commercial banking business, also underwent enormous changes in the years following World War I. The most important elements in the transformation were (1) the increased size and strength of business units, which lessened their dependence on, although certainly not their use of, the investment banker's services; (2) a relative increase in direct investment by individuals in stocks and bonds, which further weakened the authority of the investment banker by loosening his control over the supply of investment capital and, simultaneously, encouraging the rise of retail-oriented investment banking houses; and (3) the emergence of new and very aggressive banking houses to fill the financing needs overlooked by the older and more conservative firms.

The growing reliance on internal financing affected investment banking in one respect at least the same way it had affected commercial banking. It made corporations less dependent on and therefore less subject to control by the investment banker. In another respect, however, the effects were completely different, for to the extent that corporations reduced the use of commercial credit, they increased their activities in the securities markets. As the public's mania for securities—any securities—rose to a high point in the late 1920s, it became advantageous for corporations to obtain their financing through bond, and especially equity, issues. New security issues, which totaled less than $3 billion in 1919, surged to about $10 billion in 1929, with an increasing portion taking the form of stock issues. *The New York Times* allocated less than a page (220 square inches) to a summary of stock transactions for the year 1920. It took more than twice as much (525 square inches) to cover the transactions for 1929. Bond dealings, which required more than double the space given to stocks in 1920, took only a trifle more space than stocks in 1929.

Among the factors contributing to the growth of internal financing was the adoption by industry of a regular dividend policy in the immediate prewar years. The general practice of corporations before the war was to pay generous dividends to stockholders, leaving little to put into retained earnings. A few firms, such as American Telephone & Telegraph and other public utilities, paid regular dividends—that is, a relatively constant dollar amount, independent of current earnings. With much of current earnings paid to stockholders, corporations were often dependent on the sale of additional stock or bonded debt to finance expansion. The adoption of a regular dividend policy enabled the corporation to retain some of its profits for later expansion and thus freed it to some extent from dependence on the investment banker's services and good will.

The change in dividend policy had the additional effect of drawing many small investors into the equities market. Before the war the small investor would usually buy bonds if he needed regular income and stocks if he intended to speculate. The adoption of a regular dividend policy, however, gave the stockholder some assurance of income, thereby making stock ownership more attractive. The growth of direct security ownership by the general public was further encouraged by the several war loan drives between 1917 and 1919, which brought the average American into closer contact with the securities markets.

The war loan drives, carried out largely without the help of the investment banking community, also pointed up the need for the expansion of security-distributing facilities. Indeed, it was in the war years and immediately thereafter that the Chase, the Guaranty Trust, and the First National of Boston organized the investment affiliates and the retail facilities that, together with the older National City Co. and First Securities Co., were to become leaders in the distribution of securities in the 1920s.

In sharp contrast, the leading old-line investment banking houses continued to ignore the little fellow. To do business, any kind of business, with the House of Morgan, for example, required a suitable letter of introduction and a substantial balance. Morgan & Co. did a strictly "wholesale" business. It had no selling outlets, except for the office maintained by Drexel & Co., which was regarded as the "Philadelphia end of J. P. Morgan & Co.," but it did use a network of commercial banks, insurance companies, and trust companies as outlets for its security underwritings. Lee, Higginson in Boston had a sizable sales force, but most old-line firms were like Kuhn, Loeb, which had a single office in New York City with no more than a couple of dozen employees.

The facilities of these houses were limited, and some of their selling practices were quaint. A number of conservative houses objected to sending out typewritten notices, preferring to notify their clients by handwritten letters telling of new issues and inviting the client to drop around to talk over the matter. Such practices were reasonably successful in the prewar era when security issues of $1 million were considered large. In the far more hectic twenties, when one issue followed another in rapid succession and issues of $20 million to $25 million were not unusual, the limited distribution facilities of the older houses were wholly inadequate. The gap was filled by relatively new houses and especially by the investment banking affiliates of the larger city commercial banks, all of which were more than ready to do a retail business.

The up-and-coming retail-oriented banking houses that got their start in the years around World War I further benefited from the emergence of new industries and the growth of industry in formerly agricultural regions. Thus the new California-based house of Blyth, Witter & Co. (later Blyth & Co.) got its start in the developing electric power and light industry of the West Coast. Like Goldman, Sachs and Lehman Brothers of a decade or more before, companies such as Blyth, Witter grew in part because of the reluctance of the older houses to move into new areas. Kuhn, Loeb & Co., for example, decided at an early date not to get into the financing of public utilities but to confine itself to railroad and industrial financing. Not until the late twenties did the House of Morgan react vigorously to the ambitious plans of Halsey, Stuart & Co., a Chicago investment banking house, to dominate the underwriting of public utility securities in which it was already a leader through its close relationship with Samuel Insull's public utility empire.

The leading houses of the Morgan era were further undercut by their reluctance to go after new business in the aggressive manner of their upstart competitors. The House of Morgan made no public offering of common stocks before 1929, but the newer banking houses scrambled madly for new business. By 1929 the more conservative, prestige-minded houses were far from the top in the number of issues handled, whereas the leaders—Eastman, Dillon; Halsey, Stuart; the National City Co.; E. H.

Rollins & Sons; and Harris, Forbes—were firms whose names had been practically unknown a decade or two before.

Conservative investment bankers abhorred the aggressive ways of competition. Otto Kahn of Kuhn, Loeb & Co. later recalled with a shudder "the kind of competition which we had between 1926 and 1929, when, to my knowledge fifteen American bankers sat in Belgrade, Jugoslavia, making bids, and a dozen American bankers sat in half a dozen South and Central American States, or in the Balkan States . . . one outbidding the other, foolishly, recklessly. . . ." Others might go after new business, but not Kuhn, Loeb. As Kahn proudly testified later, "It is not we that go to the corporations and ask them to do business with us. We hope that we have a reputation which is our show window, which attracts customers. . . . We do not go after them. That may be conceited, but we do not. We would rather do less business. We do not go after them." Indeed, Kuhn, Loeb would not accept new business, on any terms, if the corporation was already a client of another banking house and had not clearly severed that relationship. To do so, thought Kahn, would be ungentlemanly. But Kahn was then an old man of a day when a different ethic prevailed. There were few investment bankers and promoters in the twenties who held such quaint ideas.

It was an era of tremendous innovation, but not all innovation is altogether salutary. Whatever the merits of competition in the abstract, it could scarcely be said that all the consequences of intensified competition in the investment banking industry were desirable. The twenties saw the breakdown of the traditionally close relationship between the investment banker and his client firm. This relationship had had decided advantages, for it permitted the investment banker to offer continuing financial advice to the issuer and, on behalf of his other clients, the creditors, to see that the terms of the loan agreement were lived up to. This personal attention, however, became increasingly tenuous in the twenties as a result of the scramble for business between investment banking houses.

No longer was there any regard for staying within one's own field; banking houses now went to almost any lengths to win new business, including commission cutting and, in some instances, outright bribery. In its successful bid to replace J. P. Morgan & Co. as the financial adviser to the Cuban government, the Chase Securities Corporation, the investment affiliate of the Chase Bank, saw fit to "loan" one of President Machado's closest friends over $700,000, the President another $200,000, his influential Secretary of the Public Works still another $200,000, and to place the President's "perfectly useless" son-in-law on the parent bank's books as the joint manager of the Havana office. The height of madness probably came with the bitter struggle, ultimately ending up in the courts, between half a dozen leading houses for the privilege of serving as banker to William Fox's motion picture companies. Under such hectic conditions, with client corporations and governments shifting their business from one banking house to another, many investment banking firms made no effort to see that the corporations or governments whose securities they floated continued in a sound financial condition. Indeed, often they did not even bother to keep a current file on the financial position of these units. Like Otto Kahn, J. P. Morgan, Jr., spoke the sentiment of only a few investment bankers when he stated that, "If he [the investment banker], makes a public sale and puts his own name at the foot of the prospectus he has a continuing responsibility of the strongest kind to see, insofar as he can, that nothing is done that will interfere with the full carrying out by the obligor of the contract with the holder of the security."

A related and even more serious consequence, in its ultimate human tragedy, of the excessive competition of the twenties was the general decline in the quality of newly issued securities. This deterioration was to be expected as corporations and governments found themselves besieged by investment bankers and promoters champing at the bit for new business. The insatiable hunger for new business led the huge National City Co. to underwrite more than $16 million of bonds issued by the Brazilian state of Minas Geraes, despite the advice of its South American expert that "the laxness of the state authorities borders on the fantastic" and that "it would be hard to find anywhere a sadder confession of inefficiency and ineptitude." But with the public more than eager to buy virtually any piece of paper, the National City Co. readily took on the business of this Brazilian state.

Primarily as a result of the lower standards set by investment bankers, a large proportion of the bonds floated in the late twenties went into default in the ensuing depression. Over 30 percent of all bonds issued between 1927 and 1929 were in default by the end of 1931, compared with 19 percent of those issued between 1920 and 1924 and less than 15 percent of bonds issued before 1920. The record of some of the old-line conservative banking houses was, of course, much better. Of more than 150 bond issues underwritten by the House of Morgan in the twenties, only 7 later went into default.

As investment houses turned to underwriting issues for just about any client they could find, it was only natural that they would have to unload these securities on the public. On the whole, doing so was not difficult, for by the late twenties the public seemed willing to buy anything that Wall Street dangled before it. Otto Kahn summed up the public psychology nicely: "The public . . . were determined that every piece of paper should be worth tomorrow twice what it was today." In response to the public clamor for securities, the number of businesses engaged in selling securities increased from 433 in 1919 to 665 in 1929, while the number of branch offices expanded from 186 to 1,237. With one office for every 64,000 people, every whistle-stop in the nation had its brokerage office, complete with stock ticker and stock board. One brokerage house went so far as to place branch offices aboard ocean liners.

In the mad rush to sell securities, it was inevitable that some banking houses and brokerage houses would employ questionable and sometimes even fraudulent selling practices. For ready as the public was to buy securities, it was still important for the brokerage houses and security affiliates of the commercial banks to keep the public trading, to urge even faster turnovers. The National City Co., for example, ran "sales contests," in which prizes were awarded to salesmen who sold the most securities. Many firms recruited, en masse, ivy-league graduates, who, after a brief training period, were turned loose on the investing public. As one of these brokers candidly put it: "What counted for us was the business of keeping our customers trading in and out of securities, so that win or lose we gathered our brokers fees at fifteen dollars for each hundred shares." And the public certainly traded. From approximately 100 million shares of stock traded on the New York Stock Exchange in 1900, volume rose to about 474 million shares during the twenties and to a phenomenal one billion shares in 1929.

PENSION FUNDS AND
INVESTMENT COMPANIES · Industrialism not only brought investment
banking to the fore, it also underscored the need for private pension plans and other devices to compensate for the insecurity associated with industrial employment. The beginnings of private pension plans in the United States can be traced back to the 1870s. The earliest-known industrial pension plans were set up, not surprisingly, by the railroads, which were the first business organizations to attain great size and which, because of the inherent work hazards, found it especially necessary to provide pension relief to the disabled and the superannuated.

The first pension plan was established in 1875 by the American Express Company, which, though not a railroad, was closely associated with railroading. Five years later the Baltimore & Ohio Railroad initiated a second pension plan. Then the number of pension plans grew slowly over the next two decades, so that by 1900 only a dozen pension plans had been established. Even in railroading just over 10 percent of all employees were covered under plans of one kind or another in 1900.

In other industrial sectors, pension schemes were still in the experimental stage. The Consolidated Gas Co. of New York began an informal pension plan in 1892, but by 1911 only eleven public utilities had followed the innovation. In manufacturing only two companies had made attempts at setting up pension plans for their employees prior to 1900. Both were short-lived, the first because the company failed and the other because "The president believes that the class of workmen employed at Solray are not yet ready to appreciate a scheme of this character." Finally, at least two pension plans were initiated by commercial banks, one in Chicago and another in St. Louis.

The pension movement picked up speed in the progressive era. Between 1900 and 1910, some 54 plans were initiated. In the next decade, the growth became very rapid: 221 pension funds were established. By 1929 there were 397 plans of all kinds in operation, covering an estimated 3.7 million employees, or a bit over one-eighth of the labor force in industries where private pension plans existed. In addition to these plans, a sprinkling of union pension plans existed, the earliest of which was adopted by the Pattern Makers' League of North America in 1900. This plan was followed over the next decade by plans initiated by the International Jewelry Workers Union of America, the National Association of Letter Carriers, the International Typographical Union, and the Granite Cutters International. By 1930 at least thirteen internationals and several large union locals had instituted pension plans for retired members.

These plans varied widely. Certain companies, for instance, guaranteed the pension once granted; others did not. The plan of the American Express Company, like a number of others, continued to be informal for many years, granting pensions more or less at the option of the employer. The most common type of plan in the United States was noncontributory— that is, the employer carried the entire cost. This practice was not done so much out of largesse as from a recognition that such a system gave management greater flexibility and control. Other plans, however, called for contributions by both management and labor, whereas under still others (such as the labor union pension plans), employees alone contributed.

Judged by today's standards and even by the cost of living in "the good old days," pension payments were not overly extravagant. The International Harvester plan, of which the company was very proud, paid, at its institution in 1908, a minimum of $18 a month to retired employees over 70 who had 20 years service. The maximum was $100 a month. But the average pension in 1919 was only $32.25 a month.

Until 1916 private pension plans were noninsured. From then on, however, a growing number of insured plans were established through the purchase of deferred annuities from insurance companies or, in the case of partially insured plans, through the purchase of annuities on the retirement of pensionable employees. In all, over 40 insured plans were started between 1916 and 1929, with the majority established between 1926 and 1929. The number of employees covered by insured plans, however, was quite small—only 55,000 out of the 3.7 million covered by all pension plans in 1929. In any event, insured pension plans are not covered in this book except for the role they played in the growth of insurance companies; for employees, in effect, became holders of annuities issued by insurance companies, while the latter controlled the management of the pension's assets.

There are no estimates of the asset size of private (noninsured) pension funds before 1922. In that year they amounted to only $90 million, with about 60 percent in the form of corporate bonds, another 20 percent in stocks, and 10 percent in government securities. Over the next several years, however, pension funds grew at an extremely rapid pace, with assets totaling $500 million by the end of 1929, and with yearly employers' contributions for pension purposes in excess of $125 million. But despite this growth, private pension plans did not become really important financial intermediaries until after World War II.

Industrialization and, even more important, the widespread anxiety to invest in stocks, together with the movement of many closely held companies to public ownership, also gave rise to the investment company. These institutions, holding numerous different securities, offered investors an opportunity to participate as owners and on a diversified basis in the growth of industry. Although the first appeared in the 1890s, the story of investment companies, or mutual funds as they are now called, really begins in the 1920s. In the course of that decade, especially after 1925, investment company assets grew from almost nothing to at least $3 billion. To be sure, the first modern investment companies in the United States had been formed many years before—the long defunct New York State Trust in 1889 and the still-operating Boston Personal Property Trust in 1893. One can go back even further and find historical antecedents in the operation of the Massachusetts Hospital Life Insurance Company (1818) and the United States Mortgage Company (1871). As late as 1923, however, there were only 15 operating investment trusts, with an estimated capital of some $15 million.

From such modest beginnings, investment companies were soon to become one of the rages of the late twenties. At the end of 1929 some 675 investment companies of all types were in operation, with combined assets exceeding $7 billion. Not all of these were investment companies as the term is generally used (pools of personal funds invested in a wide variety of securities in which income or capital gains, in contrast to management, is the specific objective). A small number, but in control of very large assets, were more properly classified as holding companies. Certainly these holding companies would include such "investment trusts" as Christiana Securities Co., with assets of $361 million, and Insull Utility Investments, Inc., with assets of more than $150 million. Perhaps another 200 so-called investment trusts, including some private affairs that were organized to manage the fortunes of individual families, ought to be excluded for one reason or another. But even after these deductions, there were over 400 operating companies by the end of the twenties.

One sign of this robust expansion was the emergence, all in the span of a couple of years, of independent advisory services formed solely to furnish statistical and investment advice to investment companies. A second sign was the fantasies in which some people indulged. One optimist forecast 10,000 investment trusts in another five years, while another, just before the market break in 1929, reported that $2 billion would be raised by investment trusts over the next six months.

A number of factors accounted for the phenomenal growth of the investment company idea in the late twenties. The prosperity of the times was no doubt fundamental. Prosperity gave many individuals higher incomes than they had ever had before. And as Americans began to buy all kinds of goods, it is not surprising that they also bought securities as never before. Before the war investors in stocks and bonds numbered perhaps 500,000; by the late twenties the number multiplied to somewhere between 10 and 20 million. The increase was helped in no small measure by the exposure of many hundreds of thousands of persons to the Liberty Bond and Victory Loan issues of the war. Prior to this period, these savers had been content to limit their investments to deposits in savings banks or to hoarded cash. Many other fledgling investors were drawn, as if by a magnet, into the market by the fantastic gains in stock prices. Before World War I, common stocks were considered highly speculative. They were not for persons of moderate means, who were advised to confine their investments to mortgages, real estate, savings accounts, life insurance, annuities, bonds, and preferred stocks. But with equity prices more than doubling between 1925 and 1929, extraordinary will power or extraordinary indifference were required to resist taking the "plunge." And with so many novices thinking about entering the equity markets, it was not difficult to convince many of them that the safest way to do so was through the purchase of managed investment company shares.

The rise of investment companies was often further helped by the ties of such companies to the leading investment banking houses, commercial banks, or trust companies. About 60 percent of all investment trusts was under the control of investment banking or brokerage houses, and another 10 percent was affiliated with banks or trust companies. Among the best-known investment companies of the early 1920s was the United States and Foreign Securities Corp., organized by Dillon, Read & Co. in 1924. Many investors thought that "this was an opportunity to let the public in on Clarence Dillon's investment brains." Several years later the Goldman, Sachs Trading Corp. was established and syndicated by the investment banking house of Goldman, Sachs & Co. Almost immediately the 900,000 shares made available to the public were selling at substantial premiums. In January 1929 another prominent banking house, J. & W. Seligman & Co., organized the Tri-Continental Corp. Later in the same year Lehman Brothers formed the Lehman Corp. with a capital of $100 million.

Other investment trusts were formed by the security affiliates of commercial banks and trust companies. The $50-million Chatham Phoenix Allied Corporation, organized in September 1929, was established by the security affiliate of the Chatham Phoenix National Bank and Trust Co. of New York. Others included the Old Colony Investment Trust, organized in 1928 by the investment affiliate of the Old Colony Trust Company (Boston), and the Shawmut Bank Investment Trust, set up a year earlier by the National Shawmut Bank (Boston).

Most of the larger trusts had their headquarters in New York, Boston, and Philadelphia and attracted funds from all over the United States, but several were purely local affairs. According to one contemporary, virtually every state had one or more local trusts, "some of them rapidly becoming the pride of their respective communities." Shares of the Wisconsin Investment Co., for example, were almost exclusively held by Milwaukee investors. Boise, Denver, Seattle, St. Louis, Atlantic Beach on Long Island, Los Angeles, and Columbus were among the many cities throughout the country where investment companies were formed in the late 1920s.

During this period, a small but important group of professional trust promoters who participated in the organization and management of a variety of individual trusts emerged. By sponsoring a number of distinct investment companies, it was possible to attract investors with varying objectives, as well as to maintain greater investment flexibility by limiting the size of each trust, and, finally, to take full advantage of the economies of scale associated with investment management. By the end of 1929, some 13 companies made up the United Founders' group, in whose affairs

Harris, Forbes & Co. and Louis Seagrave, who had been sales manager of the investment affiliate of one of the Boston banks, played key roles. The group had a paid-in capital of over $686 million, of which $503 million was contributed by the public. United States Shares Corp. ran 7 investment trusts from its offices at 50 Broadway. One of the most active and conservative promoters of the period, and even more so in later years, was Calvin Bullock, whose securities firm of the same name organized and managed three investment trusts.

Given the times and the unparalleled pace at which new investment companies were being organized, structural weaknesses and abuses were bound to develop. However, these factors did not become apparent until the bull market broke in September 1929. Share prices, which had increased at a heady pace in the late twenties, fell with at least equal speed in the months and years after the market collapse. With the Dow-Jones industrial stock price average plummeting from 386 on September 3, 1929, to a low of 41 in July 1932, investment company shareholders could be expected to sustain large losses. Yet it became all too apparent that a great many trusts had been badly managed and that still others had intentionally violated the trust of the public.

In general, the whole structure of the investment trust was an invitation to disaster in the event the market turned down. In contrast to today's mutual funds, almost all the investment companies of the twenties were closed-end types, which meant that they issued a fixed number of shares that were not subject to repurchase but were traded in the marketplace much the same as other equities. The problem, of course, did not lie so much in the closed-end feature of these trusts as in the fact that many were very highly leveraged. Thus about 40 percent of the capitalization of closed-end trusts consisted of senior securities (preferred shares and bonds), while common stocks made up the remainder. In a fast-rising market, holders of common did very well; but in a declining market, the fixed charges on the senior securities caused common share values to fall much faster than in the case of nonleveraged trusts. According to a Securities and Exchange Commission (SEC) report, "by the end of 1937, the average dollar which had been invested in July 1929 in the index of leverage investment company stock was worth 5 cents while the non-leverage dollar was worth 48 cents." The price decline was made still worse by the fact that most closed-end type investment company common shares were selling at substantial premiums at the time of the market break, in expectation of additional capital gains. By the mid-thirties, however, the SEC reported, "The aggregate market value of shares in investment companies was approximately 35 percent less than the actual value of the assets of these companies."

Shareholders also suffered because the lure of big, quick profits caused many managements to stray quite far from conservative principles. One trust company carried the following provision: "For the protection of the directors and officers they are to be given broad powers of voting and dealing without liability to account, with concerns and with respect to matters in which they may have a personal interest." Another inserted a provision stating that "no investment or reinvestment shall be deemed improper because of its speculative character or . . . by reason of any interest, direct or indirect, which any trustee . . . may have therein, or by reason of any profit they or any of them make. . . ." These provisions were all available for the interested investor to see, but all too few cared, especially when the prospect of stratospheric profits glittered so attractively.

Some of the worst practices involved the use of captive investment companies as depositories for securities that were otherwise unmarketable. This practice was most common in the case of investment trusts controlled by banks, brokers, and investment banking houses. Furthermore, many investment trusts did not limit themselves to stocks and bonds but engaged in a wide range of financial activities, including dealing in puts and calls, foreign exchange, short selling, commodities, and broker loans, some of which were highly speculative.

CENTRAL BANKING IN THE TWENTIES · Considering all this innovation, it was unfortunate that no significant attempt was made to strengthen the banking system in the twenties, to control the credit structure more effectively, and to give the public better protection. The government's failure to keep pace with the frantic and often unreasoned experimentation in the private sector followed from the Harding and Coolidge administrations' sincere belief in minimum government interference with business. The twenties were years of interregnum when "normalcy" was one of the watchwords and "taking the government out of business" one of the most important goals. It would take the tragedy of the Great Depression to bring about a basic and then overdone reform of the nation's financial structure.

Nevertheless, important changes in the concept of central banking were being worked out within the Federal Reserve System. These changes included (1) a gradual shift from the original theories on which the System was based, (2) the development of new instruments of credit control, (3) emancipation of the System from Treasury domination, and (4) the establishment of a set of principles to guide the System in regulating the money market. Probably no other period in the history of the System witnessed a more far-reaching change in both Federal Reserve thinking and policy than the years between 1921 and 1925. On the other hand, it is doubtful that many of these innovations in thought were widely accepted or even understood, either within the System or in academic and banking circles. Furthermore, few significant changes were made in the formal structure of the Federal Reserve System, with the result that it remained a decentralized central bank with no real locus of authority. Throughout most of the twenties, the New York Federal Reserve Bank, under the forceful and creative leadership of Benjamin Strong, assumed an authority that, in principle, should have resided in the Federal Reserve Board. The death of Strong in 1928, along with some divisiveness within the Board and reluctance on the part of the district banks to submit to the Board's authority, produced a dangerous vacuum, which in the view of some economists was a major cause of the later depression.

Although no firm consensus was ever reached in this period concerning the objectives and priorities of central bank policy, events were to demonstrate that the System could not, as originally planned, follow the rules of orthodox central banking. Those rules had been formulated to fit the gold standard. It was still believed that under the gold standard the world economy was driven automatically to equilibrium. The primary objective of central bank policy was, therefore, to protect the gold standard. The policy called for raising the rediscount rate when gold flowed out, and the gold reserve against Federal Reserve Bank liabilities (the reserve ratio) declined. The rationale for this action was based on the premise that the central bank discount rate was an important determinant of market interest rates. Consequently, an increase in the discount rate would cause a general increase in interest rates; and since capital flows to the place where it can get the highest price, the gold outflow would reverse itself. Conversely, the rediscount rate was supposed to be lowered when gold was flowing in. The rationale in this case was that lower interest rates would discourage capital flows and encourage investors to send gold to other countries where the rate of return was higher.

The orthodox analysis may have been replete with logic but it was all academic, for the United States was the only power maintaining gold payments. It should have been clear, therefore, that the rules of the gold standard game were no longer in effect.

In the immediate postwar years, when the reserve ratio was running down, the rediscount rate was raised in order to bring gold in and replenish the central bank's reserves. Either because of this discount rate increase or for other reasons, gold did flow in and it continued to flow in until mid-1924. The play was going beyond the script. It was feared that the heavy gold inflow, amounting to about $1.7 billion, would lead to renewed price inflation. Moreover, in the event that international conditions stabilized, this gold would flow back to where it came from, with the result that inflation might quickly turn to deflation. The new circumstances and the new threats to stability convinced some officials within the System, including Strong, that the traditional precepts of central banking were no longer applicable. Strong believed in the gold standard, but he was also a realist and recognized that its collapse, as a result of the war, called for new guidelines. Orthodox central bank policy was coming into conflict with the quantity theory of money.

At the same time, Strong and others within the System were becoming increasingly aware of the weaknesses in the commercial loan theory. In a talk to the Graduate Economics Club at Harvard on November 28, 1922, he summed up some of the conclusions that he had arrived at: (1) the rules relating to the types of paper that the district banks might discount had no necessary relationship to the uses to which the borrowed funds would be put; (2) there was no reason to believe that the volume of credit would fluctuate with the needs of business; and (3) practically all borrowing by member banks from the district Reserve Banks was ex post facto.

With the gold standard and the commercial loan theory no longer acceptable guides to policy, System officials were forced to look elsewhere. Other automatic guides to action (for example, price level stability) were available, but they were all rejected in favor of a discretionary policy, a decision to which the System would continue to adhere. In its *Annual Report for 1923,* the Board concluded that policy "is and must be a matter of judgment," based on the fullest possible range of evidence about changes in production, trade, employment, prices, and commodity stocks. "The ideal objective," according to the Board, was "the constant exercise of a steadying influence on credit conditions." Although it was a significant departure from traditional concept, this eclectic approach was sufficiently ambiguous to give the System a great amount of latitude in its policy formulation. The first of many problems to arise as a result of this approach occurred in the late 1920s when the System had to decide between the conflicting goals of encouraging business expansion and ending the speculation in the securities markets.

The early twenties also saw the emergence of open-market operations as a tool of monetary policy, if not to its present position of dominance at least to a par with the discount rate. During the depression of 1920, the Federal Reserve Banks began to purchase Treasury obligations. At the time, this strategy was not intended as a stabilization device but rather as a means of replenishing the earning assets of the district banks, which had fallen off due to the decline in member bank borrowings. Between 1920 and 1922 rediscounts declined from $2.7 billion to $618 million.

At first each Reserve Bank carried on its open-market transactions as it deemed fit, but this arrangement was disorderly and ineffective. Strong, seeing that open-market operations could influence money and credit as well as it could maintain district bank earnings, used his influence to establish a Governors Committee in 1922 to coordinate, but not to control, open-market transactions. In April 1923, at the Board's urging and apparently in a move to enhance its own influence, this committee was replaced by an Open Market Investment Committee, to operate under the general supervision of the Board.

Meanwhile, Federal Reserve officials were beginning to understand the importance of open-market operations and the role they could play in changing money market conditions. Strong, in particular, urged that such operations be carried out to stabilize the money market regardless of whether they resulted in a money loss or a money gain for the System. Discount rate policy was still acknowledged as the most important tool, but open-market operations were increasingly thought of as an independent tool as well as one to be used in conjunction with changes in the discount rate. A few, including Strong, were even beginning to realize that the effectiveness of discount rate policy depended on open-market operations, which, depending on the situation, could either force the banks to borrow at the discount window or facilitate the repayment of outstanding loans.

Between 1922 and 1927 the System gained valuable experience in the art of open-market operations. In early 1923, with business recovering from the postwar slump, the discount rate was raised and an attempt was made to neutralize the effects of gold imports by selling government obligations to the member banks. As a result of this early sterilization operation, Reserve Bank holdings of government securities declined by over $500 million between May 1922 and June 1923, or more than total gold imports. When a slight business recession developed in 1924, the System reversed its policy, beginning as early as December 1923 to buy government securities in the open market. It continued to buy until November 1924, increasing its holdings from $84 million to $582 million. No longer were these purchases being undertaken for earnings but rather for broad policy purposes, which may have included helping Great Britain and Germany to return to the gold standard as well as stabilizing the domestic economy. Again in 1927, largely at Strong's urging, the System adopted a policy of ease in the face of a slight recession and at a time when it was thought advisable to do something to alleviate interest rate pressures abroad. Between May and November the System's holdings increased by $336 million, while the discount rate was lowered from 4 percent to 3.5 percent. Despite the loss of $154 million of gold, money market conditions were eased significantly.

But for all its successes, the failure of the System to reach agreement on policy objectives and priorities, as well as the failure of the federal government to introduce effective regulation over the securities markets, was about to plunge the System into a conflict for which it was wholly unprepared. The conflict concerned the System's response to the sharp rise in security speculation. Both the Board and the New York Reserve Bank agreed that action had to be taken to bring speculation under control. The Board's approach called for direct pressure ("moral suasion") to prevent overborrowing by the banks to finance securities speculation. In particular, the Board wished the district banks to deny loan accommodations to banks that continued to make security loans. By using moral suasion, the Board evidently hoped to avoid restricting the availability of credit for productive purposes. The New York Bank, on the other hand, argued that direct pressure would be ineffective and that qualitative controls on the use of member bank borrowings could not be policed. Its solution was to raise the discount rate. Harrison, who became Governor of the New York Bank upon Strong's death in October 1928, believed that "sharp, incisive action" involving a rise in discount rates would quickly put an end to the speculation.

In retrospect, it is doubtful whether either approach would have limited speculation. The securities craze was too far gone to be stymied by admonitions. Similarly, it is unlikely that a rise in the rediscount rate would have worked. What was needed was some means of placing a legal ceiling on the use of credit to buy securities. Authority enabling the Board to regulate margin requirements was, however, lacking and was not to be granted until 1934. In the meantime the System found itself confronted with an insoluble problem that doomed it to criticism no matter which way it moved.

In the late summer of 1929, the Board abandoned its policy of moral suasion, which quite clearly was not working, and attempted to bring speculation under control by allowing the discount rate to be raised to 6 percent. But by this time the wisdom of raising the discount rate was certainly questionable, for the economy was already showing signs of weakness. Indeed, Harrison believed that the time to raise the discount rate had already passed. To offset the effect of the rise in the New York Bank's discount rate, the buying rate on acceptances was lowered from 5⅓ percent to 5⅛ percent. By this inconsistent policy, one action nullified the other, for member banks immediately shifted to the sale of acceptances instead of rediscounting commercial paper.

The usual experimentation that characterized the financial community in the twenties very clearly exceeded the limits of good judgment. Too much changed in too short a period of time. Neither the financial community nor the government had enough experience with the new developments to control the mistakes and excesses that are the inevitable by-products of widespread innovation.

Later, during the thirties, the innovations that had helped to produce prosperity were to be heavily criticized as contributing to the Depression. But it was not innovation in itself that was wrong, for much the same innovations have been resurrected in more recent times without being condemned as harbingers of disaster. Like most innovations, those of the twenties occurred largely in response to environmental pressures. Put another way, financial institutions did what they were supposed to do in responding creatively to the demands made of them. Under the best of circumstances, some of their experiments would have proved unsuccessful, for human experiment is a profit-and-loss affair. Unfortunately, the spirit of the times did not give rise to the wisdom and the sense of caution and public trust that many people naïvely expected of those who sat in high places. The benefits of innovation were further reduced and the potential dangers were additionally raised by misguided public policy and the absence of effective public regulation. Indeed, public policy by omission and commission not only failed to strengthen the financial system but also actually weakened it. Two glaring examples were the refusal to adopt an often-proposed plan for deposit guarantee and the passage of the MacFadden Act, which, by liberalizing the requirements for national bank charters, added another defect to an already defective banking system.

8 · depression years, 1929–1940

Although the National Bureau of Economic Research dates the Great Depression from June 1929 to March 1933, the economic, social, and political reverberations of that debacle completely dominated the remaining years of the thirties and exerted a strong influence on the thinking of at least two generations. Americans had experienced depressions before. Still, the idea of prolonged depression, and especially the idea of permanent stagnation, remained alien to most Americans and certainly to most of the nation's leading economists of the time, who were far more impressed by the economy's expansionary capabilities. In a very real sense, despite some errors in their logic, they were right, for the economy had indeed made enormous strides over the previous half-century and would, of course, continue to do so again. But hindsight is always 20–20. To many millions of Americans who lived and struggled through the Great Depression, it must surely have seemed as if the American dream had failed the test.

THE ECONOMIC BACKGROUND The economic consequences of the Depression were truly awesome. Unemployment soared to the very real, if unimaginable, rate of nearly 25 percent of the labor force in 1933. And although recovery did bring about some decline, the rate never fell below 14 percent during the 1930s. The rise in unemployment, in turn, was a reflection of the decline in current output. Gross national product (measured in 1929 dollars) plummeted from $104.4 billion in 1929 to a Depression low of $74.2 billion in 1933. Not until 1937 was the 1929 level to be regained, only to fall once more in the recession of 1938.

The fall-off in aggregate demand led not only to declines in production but also to widespread price deflation. Wholesale prices dropped to nearly one-half of what they had been in 1929. Retail prices fell less sharply, but nevertheless by almost one-fourth between 1929 and 1933. And despite subsequent recovery, not until World War II did most prices return to their 1929 levels. For the typical American, disposable personal income declined from $683 in 1929 to $362 in 1933. Recovery raised the figure to $573 in 1940. In real terms (1959 dollars), of course, the decline was more moderate, though still enormous: $1,236 in 1929, to $893 in 1933, and a subsequent rise to $1,259 in 1940.

The Great Depression brought more than just a sharp decline in economic well-being; it also became one of those few occasions when a whole people paused to rethink their values and beliefs. This was especially the case with those values and beliefs governing the public's attitude toward the business community, the financial community, and the role of government in the economy. The New Deal was the most visible sign of the public's disenchantment with the ways and values of the past. No longer were Americans going to put so much of their faith and trust in an unregulated economic system. If most people were not ready to discard the system, they were at least prepared to see a growth in the countervailing influence of the federal government and of labor, in addition to a substantial revision of the rules by which the economy operated.

THE DEPRESSION'S EFFECT ON FINANCE · No set of rules received closer scrutiny and, as a result, were more substantially changed than those governing the financial system. All through the thirties the financial community was to be under steady attack. Yet despite a popular belief to the contrary, the depression was only indirectly attributable to the financial excesses of the twenties. Still, the optimism of that decade did result in some unsound financial practices, which, in turn, had much to do with the crash that came in late 1929. Also, the enormous losses suffered by the public as a result of this collapse undoubtedly had a severe contractionary effect on consumer spending.

In the past, financial panics affected mainly the wealthy few. The collapse of the securities markets in 1929, however, was to bring ruin to other Americans, many of whom had taken to playing the market for the first time. The public, with all its buying and selling of securities in the hope of getting rich, was hardly blameless. Nevertheless, a majority were more than ready to place the blame on the men of Wall Street, a reaction that was encouraged not only by the strong element of truth it reflected but also by a series of dramatic disclosures relating to improper conduct by financial leaders. Everywhere there was a cry for reform, if not for actual retribution. Adding force to this clamor was the wholly sympathetic response it evoked in Washington. Indeed, among the multitude of reforms the New Deal sponsored, some of the most far-reaching related to the operation of the securities markets and financial intermediaries.

THE DECLINE IN PRIVATE DEBT AND THE
INCREASE IN FEDERAL DEBT · The depression meant a sharp decline in the amount of business done by financial intermediaries, as well as huge losses on their outstanding loans and investments. Particularly significant was the contraction in the range of investment opportunities facing financial intermediaries. Net private debt declined from $161.2 billion in 1929 to $123.1 billion in 1938. As seen from Table 16, the declines in net private debt were not limited to any one category but were fully reflected in the totals for each component. It is also apparent from the data that the process of recovery did not require much additional debt. Indeed, the 1940 level was not significantly different from the levels in 1932–1933, the depression's bottom year.

In contrast to private debt, federal government debt grew from less than $17 billion in 1929 to nearly $45 billion in 1940. Deficits averaging $2.7

TABLE 16
Net Private and Public Debt, 1929–1940
(Billions of Dollars)

Year	Total	Total Private	Corporate			Individual and Noncorporate Nonfarm				Farm	Total Government	Federal	State & Local
			Total	Short-Term	Long-Term	Total	Mortgage	Commercial & Financial*	Consumer				
1929	$190.9	$161.2	88.9	$41.6	$47.3	60.0	$31.2	$22.4	$6.4	$12.2	$29.7	$16.5	$13.2
1930	191.0	160.4	89.3	38.2	51.1	59.4	32.0	21.6	5.8	11.8	30.6	16.5	14.1
1931	181.9	147.9	83.5	33.2	50.3	53.3	30.9	17.6	4.8	11.1	34.0	18.5	15.5
1932	174.6	136.7	80.0	30.8	49.2	46.6	29.0	14.0	3.6	10.1	37.9	21.3	16.6
1933	168.5	127.5	76.9	29.1	47.9	41.5	26.3	11.7	3.5	9.1	41.0	24.3	16.7
1934	171.4	125.1	75.5	30.9	44.6	40.6	25.5	11.2	3.9	8.9	46.3	30.4	15.9
1935	174.7	124.2	74.8	31.2	43.6	40.5	24.8	10.8	4.9	8.9	50.4	34.4	16.0
1936	180.3	126.4	76.1	33.5	42.5	41.7	24.4	11.2	6.1	8.6	53.9	37.7	16.2
1937	182.0	126.7	75.8	32.3	43.5	42.3	24.3	11.3	6.7	8.6	55.3	39.2	16.1
1938	179.6	123.1	73.3	28.4	44.8	40.9	24.5	10.1	6.3	9.0	56.5	40.5	16.0
1939	183.2	124.3	73.5	29.2	44.4	42.0	25.0	9.8	7.2	8.8	58.9	42.6	16.3
1940	189.9	128.6	75.6	31.9	43.7	43.9	26.1	9.5	8.3	9.1	61.3	44.8	16.5

Source: Economic Report of the President, 1968.

* Financial debt is debt owed to banks for purchasing or carrying securities, customers' debt to brokers, and debt owed to life insurance companies by policyholders.

billion were incurred in every year between 1931 and 1939. Until the business recession of 1937–1938, federal deficits were unplanned, arising from the decline in tax revenues and, after 1933, from large-scale increases in pump priming and public relief expenditures. The recession, however, inspired a new turn in the administration's fiscal thinking. As Secretary of the Treasury Henry Morgenthau explained it, "The early New Dealers from Roosevelt down, were looking forward to a balanced budget. . . . But in the course of time new theories, based in part on the reasoning of John Maynard Keynes . . . had come into vogue." Marriner Eccles, Governor of the Federal Reserve Board and an early proponent of the "New Economics," stated the new view as clearly as anyone:

> One of three alternatives faces this country, either an unforeseen and unforeseeable very large outlet for investment must develop . . . , a very considerable increase must be brought about in the proportion of the national income that goes into consumption, or the government must provide an outlet for idle funds through deficit financing. . . . Unless some or all of these developments take place, we cannot escape continuous depression. . . . It is only as adequate outlays are provided for our savings that the national income can rise to a satisfactory level, and it is only as the national income increases that tax revenue adequate to balance the budget can be achieved.

The overall decline in the private demand for credit, offset only in part by the surge in federal government debt, made it difficult for certain financial intermediaries, such as life insurance companies and mutual savings banks, to find suitable investment outlets for the savings they received. The contraction of traditional investment outlets, along with the drastic rise in liquidity preference, led financial institutions quickly to build up their holdings of federal government securities. With the decline in gross private domestic investment (from $16.2 billion in 1929 to $1 billion in 1932 and to $9.3 billion in 1939) and the consequent decline in the need for credit by the private sector, financial intermediaries became the primary suppliers of credit to finance public investment. For some intermediaries, indeed, the United States government became the largest and best-preferred borrower of funds.

The flow of new funds coming into financial institutions naturally tapered off as a result of the decline in income. The declines, however, varied in magnitude, depending on the kind of institution and the extent of the public's loss of confidence. Although the absolute amount of business done by financial intermediaries declined because of the depression, the relative role of these institutions in the credit markets expanded enormously. The reason was that the ratio of indirect to direct finance increased greatly, for the depression had enhanced the public's preference for the liquidity and solvency usually associated with indirect finance. The ratio of indirect claims to total financial assets increased from an average of 45 percent between 1922 and 1929 to 86 percent between 1934 and 1938. If we were to include government insurance reserves among our intermediary claims, the increase would be even more striking: 47 percent to 105 percent.

Judging from the behavior of interest rates over the period, as well as from the kinds of problems some intermediaries encountered, it is clear that the supply of loanable funds declined much more slowly than the demand. Interest rates fell to very low levels over the thirties. Three-month Treasury bill rates declined from 1.4 percent in 1931 to almost nothing in 1940. Rates on 3–5 year United States government notes showed almost as sharp a drop: from 2.66 percent in 1933 to 0.5 percent in 1940. Commercial-paper rates plunged from 5.85 percent in 1929 to 0.56 percent in 1940.

Corporate and municipal bond rates, in contrast, fell more slowly. Indeed, the large number of defaults on such issues, as well as the frantic quest by savers for liquidity and solvency, succeeded in initially raising the interest rates on these claims. The yield on Baa corporates, for example, climbed from 5.9 percent in 1929 to 9.3 percent in 1932. Bond rates fell thereafter, but the structure of rates still continued to reveal the extraordinary, but understandable, emphasis that savers were placing on safety and liquidity. To illustrate: Aaa corporate rates declined from 4.73 percent in 1929 to 3.01 percent in 1940, while Baa rates fell to only 4.96 over the same period, with the result that the yield spread between Aaa and Baa bonds widened from 117 basis points to 195 basis points.

All the developments that we have mentioned had a great impact on financial intermediaries. The changes were at least as important as those in the twenties. Yet for the most part, they were imposed from the outside and reflected not so much the thinking of the financial community itself as the attitudes and perceptions of government officials and the public. Innovations occurring internally were chiefly of a conservative nature, reflecting a strong reaction to the excesses of the twenties and an almost compulsive urge for solvency and liquidity. Indeed, not until we take up the development of financial institutions in the post-World War II decades will we again see the resurgence of aggressive entrepreneurial innovation.

THE COLLAPSE OF THE BANKING SYSTEM No prior episode in American history so completely shattered the nation's banking system as the 1929–1933 depression. To be sure, bank suspensions had occurred in the past but never to the degree that they occurred in the early thirties. Past money market panics had forced banks to suspend deposit (or note) convertibility into specie; but they remained open and carried on all other normal banking functions. By early 1933, however, the ills of the nation's banks had reached such a critical point that banks were forced to suspend *all* operations in a large number of states. On the eve of Roosevelt's inauguration, bank "holidays" had been declared in about half the states. In the early hours of March 6, 1933, a Presidential proclamation closed all banks except a scattered few until March 9.

Commercial banks had, as we noted earlier, experienced difficulties, even in the prosperous 1920s. The large city banks had managed, through seemingly successful innovation, to get around their problems, but for the country banks, as for the farmers they mostly served, the twenties were a disaster and a prelude to the even greater disaster that all banks were to face in the thirties. For with the coming of general depression, city banks, like their country cousins, were faced with a rapid decline in the income of their customers and the consequent fall in the underlying values of their loans and investments.

Some city banks were forced to suspend operations, following what had become common practice in the rural areas during the twenties. These failures, in turn, weakened other commercial banks and set in motion the wholesale failure of thousands of other institutions, not so much because of their insolvency, as that term is usually understood, but because of their inability to meet the panic-induced withdrawals of a frightened populace. Any sign of trouble, however remote or unrelated, was enough to cause the public to demand currency. This scramble for liquidity had a disastrous twofold effect on the banks. In order to meet their depositors' demands, they were forced to sell off securities at sacrifice prices, thus undermining the whole securities market. In addition, the withdrawal and hoarding of deposits resulted in the loss of reserves to commercial banks and the consequent contraction of bank credit and money supply. A spurt of bank failures—for example, in late 1930 in several agricultural states—caused a contagion of fear that knew no geographical limits. It spread rapidly, resulting in the failure of over 600 commercial banks with some $500 million of deposits in November and December. The collapse of the Bank of the United States, with over $200 million of deposits (the largest American bank ever to fail), in mid-December was of particular significance, for many people both at home and abroad mistakenly assumed that the bank was an official institution. Moreover, the failure or the refusal of the clearing house banks and the Federal Reserve to save the institution caused much additional alarm. All told, somewhere around 9,000 commercial banks closed their doors between 1930 and 1933.

In the past, banking panics had been regular occurrences, and in the absence of deposit insurance, the thirties would have proved no exception. Yet between the panic of 1907 and the collapse in the thirties, a decentralized central bank—the Federal Reserve System—had been established for the express reason of preventing a repetition of the 1907 experience. Under the leadership of Benjamin Strong, Governor of the Federal Reserve Bank of New York, whose capabilities rivaled those of Nicholas Biddle, the System had gained considerable prestige in the twenties. Indeed, some had come to believe that the Federal Reserve had made depressions obsolete. Strong's death in 1928 was most unfortunate, coming at a time when the banking system and the economy were to be in the most urgent need of the central bank's help.

**FEDERAL RESERVE POLICY DURING
THE DEPRESSION** · It is not our intent to examine in detail the Federal Reserve's policy in the thirties. Despite the temptation to speculate over the wisdom of that monetary policy, the task is beyond the scope of this volume. On the other hand, we must consider the effects of central bank actions on the commercial banking system itself, for one of its primary responsibilities was, and is, the preservation and efficient operation of the

nation's commercial banks. Few would now disagree that, from a domestic point of view, these actions (or inactions) had largely negative effects.

During the Depression the money stock declined severely (see Table 17). This unparalleled decline, brought about by the massive withdrawal of

TABLE 17
Commercial Bank Loans and Investments
and the Money Supply, 1929–1939 (as of June 30)
(Billions of Dollars)

Year	Number of Banks	Loans	Invest- ments	Demand Deposits Adjusted	Time Deposits Adjusted	Currency	Money Supply
1929	24,970	$36.1	$13.7	$22.5	$19.6	$3.6	$26.2
1930	23,679	35.0	14.4	21.7	19.7	3.4	25.1
1931	21,654	29.3	15.7	19.8	18.7	3.7	23.5
1932	18,734	22.0	14.3	15.6	14.0	4.6	20.2
1933	14,207	16.5	14.1	14.4	10.8	4.8	19.2
1934	15,348	15.7	17.1	16.7	12.0	4.7	21.4
1935	15,488	15.0	19.7	20.4	12.8	4.8	25.2
1936	15,329	15.6	23.1	23.8	13.7	5.2	29.0
1937	15,094	17.5	22.1	25.2	14.5	5.5	30.7
1938	14,867	16.1	21.1	24.3	14.8	5.4	29.7
1939	14,667	16.4	23.0	27.4	15.1	6.0	33.4

Source: U.S. Bureau of the Census, *Historical Statistics of the United States.*

currency from the banks and the loss of additional reserves through gold outflows, required that the Federal Reserve undertake large-scale open-market purchases and put into effect a more lenient discount policy. Whether such action would have pushed the economy into the road to recovery is still a moot question.[1]

Most people at the time were convinced that it would not. In a letter dated May 1931, one of the most respected American economists expressed his skepticism to an English colleague:

> You may be interested in the enclosed review of Keynes' book. As you perhaps know, it has not made quite so much of an impression on this side as you think it deserves. There was a rather longish review a short time ago in *The New York Times,* and another one in the scientific journals. . . . One of the chief objections that has been made is that the six or seven hundred million dollars of securities bought in the open market operations recently by the Federal Reserve Bank in the endeavor to pump money into circulation all seems to have been in vain. I am afraid that the disease is a little deeper seated than Keynes seems to realize.

At about the same time, an eminent American banker wrote to a French central banker: "I fully share your view that central banks ought to be

[1] Most economists think not. Their reasoning is based on the belief that monetary policy cannot force or persuade businessmen to borrow when demand is weak. This is the "you can't push a string" syndrome. For a contrary view, see George Morrison, *Liquidity Preferences of Commercial Banks* (Chicago: University of Chicago Press, 1966).

careful not to overdo their purchases of government securities in order to create an artificial ease of money. . . . It is easy to inflate, but the road to deflate is always a hard and unpleasant one."

Still later, in 1933, a monetary commission thought that "open market purchases had been on an immense scale." The commission nevertheless urged a "fairly vigorous program of open market purchases" even though monetary action could not, by itself, bring recovery.

But whether it would have worked or not, a policy of extremely easy money should have been tried. It might have triggered recovery, and it would have provided the commercial banks with the liquidity they so badly needed. In the mad rush for liquidity, the banks were compelled to sell off securities and to call in loans, actions that, in the absence of new injections of reserves by the central bank, served only to further depress security prices and to further contract the supply of money and credit. In the words of Professor Jacob Viner, the only banks that could survive were those that turned themselves into safe deposit institutions. But despite some urging by the Federal Reserve Bank of New York that the System follow a policy of positive ease, the majority within the System, and among academic economists and bankers as well, favored a more cautious policy. Between December 1929 and December 1930, Federal Reserve holdings of government obligations increased from $446 million to $644 million. By then some people thought that conditions were already too "easy." In the next six months, Reserve holdings of governments actually declined to $604 million, but then they rose to $777 million in December 1931 and to $1.9 billion by December 1932. Thus the System purchased $1.4 billion in three years, but in the first six months of 1931, it sold on balance.

Failure to act more vigorously in the open market would not have been so disastrous had the commercial banks had freer access to the discount window. To be sure, the discount rate had been lowered, in a series of steps, from a high of 6 percent in 1929 to 1.5 percent by mid-1931. Here again, however, the figures tell only a small part of the story. The monetary authorities and the bankers found it impossible to follow a straightforward policy. They were torn by conflicting objectives. The most glaring example of this conflict occurred in the fall of 1931 when the administration and the monetary authorities became concerned about hoarding and the decline of reserve holdings of gold. Fearing that the gold standard was in jeopardy, they raised the rediscount rate to 3.5 percent, an action that had less economic logic than loyalty to tradition.

Although overall cuts in the rediscount rate were large on the whole, member banks were both reluctant to borrow and were frequently unable to do so. Reluctance to borrow was partly a carry-over from the late twenties when borrowing was discouraged by the System as, indeed, it continued to be in succeeding years. Furthermore, commercial banks were reluctant to borrow so long as depositors, fearful over the safety of their funds, were scrutinizing every bank's balance sheet to see which would be the next to go.

Most important, however, was the general attachment to the commercial

loan theory. The Federal Reserve Act stipulated that only eligible paper—
that is, short-term, self-liquidating, commercial paper—was subject to
rediscount. Yet as we have seen, commercial loans became far less important during the twenties than they had been in earlier years as commercial
banks branched out into numerous diverse activities. To make matters
worse, the McFadden Act of 1927 increased this departure from tradition
by liberalizing the restrictions on national bank lending in order to put the
national banks on a competitive par with state banks. It was no doubt
desirable that banks should have gained additional flexibility to maintain
their competitive position. But, unfortunately, although legislation enabled
the banking system to move further and further away from adherence to
the commercial loan doctrine, Federal Reserve regulations were still
bound to it. Consequently, by the early thirties many banks did not have
sufficient "eligible" paper to discount. Aggravating the problem was the
fact that member bank borrowings in the late twenties were substantial,
with the result that much of their eligible paper was already pledged. Not
until passage of the Emergency Act of 1933 were Federal Reserve Banks
enabled to lend to commercial banks on the security of United States
government securities and, at a penalty rate, on other forms of security.

LEGISLATION TO REFORM BANKING · The federal government made
many efforts to reform the banking system during the Depression. The
objectives of these efforts were manifold and included (1) improving the
solvency, safety, and stability of commercial banks, (2) protecting depositors, (3) increasing commercial bank liquidity, (4) broadening the powers
of the Federal Reserve System, and (5) centralizing these powers in the
Federal Reserve Board.

Direct governmental aid did not come until February 1932 with the
establishment of the Reconstruction Finance Corporation (RFC). The
government provided the initial capital of $500 million and gave the RFC
extensive borrowing powers. The RFC was to extend emergency assistance to financial institutions and to the railroads. Although the RFC could
have done much good, it was much too limited in scope, for it could make
loans only against good assets. Its help also became something of a mixed
blessing, for it was compelled to publish the names of those institutions
that received aid. Borrowing from the RFC was interpreted, quite rightly,
as a sign of weakness, thereby making borrowing institutions the next
likely "panic" victims.

The Glass-Steagall Act of February 1932 was another ambitious piece of
legislation; it represented the first real departure from the commercial
loan doctrine that had hamstrung the effectiveness of the discount window
in meeting the banking system's liquidity needs. Specifically, the act
authorized each District Reserve Bank to make advances, at a penalty
rate, to member banks on the basis of promissory notes "secured to the
satisfaction of such Federal Reserve Bank." It also permitted the use of
government bonds as security against Federal Reserve notes.

These steps could not stop the banking panic that resulted in the
"Banking Holiday" of March 6, 1933. To get the banks open, Congress

passed the Emergency Banking Act on March 9. In addition to giving the President broad emergency powers to control foreign exchange transactions and gold and currency movements, the act authorized the RFC to come to the help of embarrassed banks by investing directly in the preferred stock and debentures of national banks. Also, the Reserve Banks were directed to issue to member banks Federal Reserve Bank notes against direct obligations of the United States and, at a 10 percent discount, of any notes, drafts, or bills the banks might offer.

THE BANKING ACTS OF 1933 AND 1935 · Far more important were the Banking Acts of 1933 and 1935. The most significant provision of the 1933 act was the establishment of Federal deposit insurance, against determined opposition from most of the nation's bankers and in spite of a lack of enthusiasm on the part of the monetary authorities and President Roosevelt. Under the administration of the Federal Deposit Insurance Corporation (FDIC), the deposits of any one depositor in a participating bank (all Federal Reserve member banks were required to join) were to be insured up to a maximum of $2,500 ($5,000 in 1934). This act was the most outstanding piece of banking legislation since the Federal Reserve Act, and it was long overdue, for it did much to remove the possibility of banking panics such as had occurred whenever the solvency of the banking system came into question. As one writer put it, "The ultimate safety of depositors' funds was no longer dependent solely on the value of banking assets and sound management."

Other important provisions of the acts of 1933 and 1935 were aimed at promoting the solvency of banks and lessening the possibility of failure. Thus the Board of Governors was given authority to set limits on the interest rates that commercial banks could pay on time and saving deposits (Regulation Q), and more importantly, member and FDIC-insured nonmember banks were prohibited from paying interest on demand deposits. It was widely believed at the time that banking standards had been badly compromised by the practice of paying interest. Those who shared this belief argued that interest rate competition for deposits, especially for correspondent balances and other large deposits, had forced banks into overly aggressive lending and investment practices that had jeopardized their safety and solvency.

The 1933 and 1935 acts also made permanent all the broadened discounting powers temporarily granted by the Emergency Banking Act of 1933 to the Federal Reserve Banks. Most important, the Federal Reserve's commitment to the commercial loan theory was relaxed by allowing the district banks to make advances on government securities at the discount rate. Nevertheless, attachment to the theory was still strong, as evidenced by the fact that advances based on government securities were limited to 15 days, whereas advances on "eligible" paper had a 90-day limit. Moreover, any advances the district banks might make against other collateral were to be at a penalty rate.

Legislation also narrowly limited the investment banking activities that many of the large city banks had plied so vigorously in the twenties. Banks that had combined commercial and investment banking were directed to choose one or the other. Most chose to remain in commercial banking and therefore had to divest themselves of their banking affiliates. Also, the Reserve Banks were required to keep informed on the lending and investment practices of member banks to ascertain whether undue use was being made of bank credit for the speculative carrying of, or trading in, securities, real estate, or commodities, or for any other purpose inconsistent with the maintenance of sound credit conditions. In addition, limits were placed on the amount of investment securities (other than United States government obligations) that national banks could purchase and on the amount of security loans banks might make. The Banking Act of 1933 also created an Open Market Committee consisting of one member from each district bank to replace the loosely knit Open Market Policy Conference.

The Banking Act of 1935, which in large part expressed the views of Marriner Eccles, Governor of the Federal Reserve Board, was even more important in centralizing and extending the powers of the Federal Reserve System. Eccles was a pre-Keynesian proponent of the "New Economics" —cyclical budgets, centralized credit and monetary controls, and close cooperation between the Treasury and the central bank. Never backward in expressing his views, he took an active part in framing legislation to give the Reserve Board more power. The original Eccles bill frankly stated that its objective was to facilitate monetary management. Although this bill was substantially modified, in its final form, it unquestionably constituted the longest step in the direction of central banking taken by the United States since the passage of the Federal Reserve Act. Thus it (1) dissolved the old Federal Reserve Board and replaced it with a Board of Governors composed of seven members appointed by the President for a period of fourteen years, (2) gave the Board of Governors approval power over the appointments of heads of district banks, (3) enabled the Board to vary reserve requirements within limits set by Congress, (4) gave the Board the final say over the discount rate, and (5) created an Open Market Committee composed of the Board of Governors and five representatives of the Reserve banks. This last provision, together with the use of open-market operations as the System's major policy tool, gave the Board a commanding role in setting monetary policy.

COMMERCIAL BANK OPERATIONS · Up to this point we have stressed the effects of Federal Reserve policy and New Deal banking legislation on the nation's commercial banks. However, the depression exerted other effects on the banking system, primarily on the kinds of business the banks turned to doing. As with other intermediaries, the banks experienced a severe decline in loans. This decline was partially offset by a sharp rise in securities, especially United States government issues. Between 1929 and 1933, the assets of operating commercial banks declined by nearly 40 percent, from $65.6 billion to $40.6 billion. By 1939, however, assets totaled $65 billion, approaching the 1929 level. In 1929 loans made up 55 percent of total assets, while investments accounted for a little over 20 percent. In 1939 loans accounted for just over 25 percent of total assets. Investments, in contrast, soared to $23 billion and made up 36 percent of assets. The growth of commercial bank investment portfolios, and government bonds in particular, reflected the low level of demand for bank credit, but also the very high liquidity preference of the banks themselves; that is, customers did not seem to be eager to borrow, but neither were banks eager to lend.

The decline in short-term lending, which began in the twenties, continued unabated into the thirties. Long-term lending, as noted earlier, was nothing new for commercial banks, for many short-term business loans were regularly renewed. Beginning in the early thirties, however, commercial banks became more explicit about their long-term lending with the introduction of the "term loan." By 1939 term loans accounted for 25 percent of the dollar volume of business loans made by commercial banks.

The increase in term loans derived from structural factors as well as from temporary conditions prevailing in the thirties. The growth of industries with high capital-output ratios, such as automobiles, chemicals. and electrical machinery, generated a demand for long-term funds. This demand, of course, dated back to the turn of the century. It had been met in part by the commercial banks through short-term renewable loans and, in the twenties, through the assumption of investment banking activities. Special conditions in the thirties accelerated, at least relatively, the demand for long-term bank credit. With the equity markets in the doldrums and the passage of the Securities Act of 1933, which imposed many unfamiliar burdens on issuers, demand for long-term financing shifted to the banking system. Moreover, the development of the term loan reflected the wariness of borrowers concerning the use of short-term credits to finance long-run needs. In the early 1930s the tacit understanding regarding renewability of short-term loans often broke down when the banks refused to renew, thereby adding to business difficulties. On the supply side, too, there were pressures leading the banks to make "term loans." The increase in excess reserves brought about by gold inflows after 1933 and the shortage of profitable loan and investment outlets led the banks to seek new means of lending. In addition, business firms had developed new means of financing, mainly the private placement of bonds through life insurance companies, which made it even more difficult for the banks to adhere to orthodox lending standards.

MUTUAL SAVINGS BANKS
WEATHER THE STORM · The long record for safety achieved by mutual savings banks over the years, together with their relative conservatism in the twenties, made them, in the public eye, a bastion of strength throughout the depression. The image was maintained despite the heavy losses that savings banks, along with other mortgage-lending institutions, unavoidably suffered. In contrast to the dismal record of commercial banks and savings and loan associations, less than a dozen savings banks failed between 1930 and 1933, and all of these banks were small. Contrary to

what was happening at other deposit-type institutions, excepting credit unions, savings bank deposits showed a modest increase between 1930 and 1932, rising from $9.1 billion to $9.6 billion. Only in 1933 did savings deposits dip, by about $300 million. The esteem in which the public held mutual savings banks was reflected in the fact that between 1930 and 1937 savings bank deposits grew by about 8 percent (no slight achievement in the thirties), whereas time and savings deposits of commercial banks declined by almost one-fourth and deposits at savings and loan companies declined by almost one-third. For the first time in many decades, the share of mutual savings banks in the total savings depository market increased.

But like everything else in these unhappy years, a good showing meant only that disaster struck less heavily. What growth in deposits mutual savings banks achieved did not derive, as in more prosperous times, from new savings but from dividends credited to existing deposit accounts. In both Massachusetts and New York, the two leading savings bank states, new deposits fell short of withdrawals more or less continuously between 1929 and 1940. Indeed, it was their tradition of safety rather than any actual strength that enabled savings banks to come through the depression as unscarred as they did, for if the public did not flock to deposit new monies, neither did they stand in long lines clamoring for their deposits.

Deposit growth was not considered a problem at the time, in part because any growth was an achievement but also because savings bankers saw few opportunities for the profitable and safe investment of new funds. A number of savings banks actually discouraged new deposits, especially in large amounts, fearing that these funds represented "hot money" seeking a temporary haven. These deposits, it was thought, might be withdrawn at any time and thus would require savings banks to modify their investment policies to provide additional liquidity, thereby resulting in a further lowering of the dividend rate on savings.

On the asset side, the problems were more serious, particularly those connected with home mortgages. Like other lenders, mutual savings banks had succumbed to competitive pressures in the 1920s and, influenced by rising costs and real estate prices, they had made loans on optimistic appraisals. But more than optimism was involved, for during the twenties the rate on mortgages averaged 6 percent while rates on bonds and other securities were not only lower but were declining. Everywhere the share of savings bank assets represented by mortgage loans increased sharply: in Connecticut these assets increased from 38 percent in 1920 to 53 percent in 1930; in Massachusetts they increased from 44 percent to 53 percent, and in New York they grew from 47 percent to 64 percent. Real estate loans, on the average, expanded by nearly 150 percent, while total assets failed to double.

Many years of experience had caused financial institutions, including, of course, mutual savings banks, to think of mortgages as a very attractive investment. The relatively high rate of net return was certainly a factor; so was the opportunity to invest locally, a consideration of some special importance to institutions doing a primarily local deposit business. Moreover, experience pointed to mortgage loans as being a safe investment if wisely made. Recessions in the past had usually been short-lived affairs, without much effect on the underlying value of properties or on the ability of borrowers to meet their obligations. Just how safe real estate loans would be in a period of prolonged and severe depression had not been tested in over thirty years.

The Great Depression provided such a test. The mortgage market could hardly avoid feeling the consequences of a whole decade of depressed economic activity. To make matters worse, the usual mortgage loan was made for a period of three to five years, with no provision for systematic amortization. At maturity it was either paid off, converted into a demand loan, or renewed for another short term. This arrangement worked reasonably well in prosperous times, for most mortgages were renewed. However, when loans came due in the depressed thirties, homeowners were often in no position to make payment. On the other hand, lenders, in their desire for liquidity and safety, were frequently reluctant or unable to renew the loan, particularly since underlying real estate values had slumped badly. Foreclosure was all too often the unhappy outcome.

By 1935 almost one out of every four mortgage loans in mutual savings banks in New York, representing more than 40 percent of the total mortgage principal, were delinquent in some regard. In Massachusetts, where outstanding mortgage loans stood at $1.2 billion in 1930, foreclosures totaled $423 million between 1932 and 1940. Professor John Lintner estimates that Massachusetts savings banks, after crediting all profits and recoveries over the years 1931–1945, lost more than 14 percent of their gross mortgage portfolio at the start of the period. For every $4 of loss on assets over this period, the mortgage portfolio contributed more than $3.

Under such circumstances, the enthusiasm that savings banks had formerly shown for mortgage loans all but evaporated. After 1932 the volume of real estate loans on the books of mutual savings banks declined steadily, from $5.9 billion to $4.8 billion in 1939. About the only mortgage loans that savings banks were willing to make in this period were "purchase money" loans to enable the sale of foreclosed properties. Apart from this type, savings banks quite literally dropped out of the mortgage loan business, so that mortgage loans, which made up about 55 percent of total assets in 1930, accounted for just 40 percent of assets 10 years later.

Until the mid-thirties all mortgage-lending institutions, not just savings banks, tended to shun new commitments in this market. Even if they had wanted to make loans, there was very little demand for new mortgage credit, because construction activity had all but ceased. New mortgage loans made by Massachusetts savings banks in 1934 (excluding "purchase money" loans) declined nearly 90 percent from the 1931 level. But even after the demand for mortgage credit started picking up and after other financial intermediaries were again beginning to enter the market, mutual savings banks remained reluctant lenders. Many banks, indeed, went out of their way to deter borrowers from coming to them.

One extremely important innovation resulted from the depression's unhappy experience with mortgages. More or less accidentally, building and loan associations hit on the idea of having mortgages regularly amortized. Despite a growing preference by borrowers for such contractual amortization, savings banks insisted on making their loans on the basis of the old-fashioned form, which limited the borrower to 60 percent of the bank's appraisal, with no contractual amortization, and at most a 3-year term, after which the note would run on demand. Even mortgages insured by the Federal Housing Administration (FHA), which was started in 1935, failed to interest savings bankers. Therefore, it is not surprising that by 1940 the relative share of nonfarm residential mortgages owned by savings banks (compared with the total held by savings banks, savings and loan companies, life insurance companies, and commercial banks) fell from 34 percent to 28 percent.

The failure of savings banks to participate actively in the mortgage market was a reflection of their strong desire for liquidity and solvency. Retrenchment was clearly the order of the day, manifesting itself both in an unwillingness to compete for deposits and in a radical redeployment of resources into low-yielding but safe government securities. For a time, at least, it was questionable whether savings banks were willing to play the part of private financial intermediaries.

Between 1930 and 1940, United States government securities owned by savings banks multiplied more than fivefold, from $499 million to $3.1 billion. State and local and other securities, on the other hand, were sold off. The increase in United States governments not only accounted for the entire growth of the securities portfolio ($1.6 billion) but also more than offset the decline in mortgage loans (about $1 billion). The craving for liquidity was evident in the enormous increase in government securities as well as in the more than threefold increase in cash, from $291 million in 1930 to nearly $1 billion in 1940. By the latter year $1 out of every $12 of assets was in cash compared with $1 out of every $50 in 1930.

It is ironic that the savings banks, having come through the depression so well and with enhanced public admiration, should have casually thrown away the opportunity of assuming the lead among thrift institutions in the savings and investment markets. Yet, consistent with their philosophy, savings bankers chose to have their institutions grow slowly and safely. It is ironic, too, that the chief beneficiary of unwillingness of savings banks to take the lead in the thrift and mortgage markets should have been the savings and loan industry, whose performance over much of the thirties was among the worst. This strong development is grist for the mill of those who argue that success breeds complacency and that it is the "hungry" entrepreneur who is responsible for economic growth.

Much government effort was spent in the thirties, both by the Hoover administration and by the New Deal administration, to encourage the flow of savings into the mortgage market. It was obvious that the government should turn first to the mutual savings banks as the type of institution best equipped to meet the needs of savers and those desiring real estate credit. Indeed, for a time in the early thirties, the government hoped to get the savings banks to sponsor the development of a system of federal mutual savings and mortgage institutions. The savings banks declined, partly because they feared federal regulation but also because they disliked becoming the vehicle for massive injections of new money into the mortgage market, which was more or less what the government had in mind and which was wholly contrary to the conservative nature of savings banks. Spurned by the savings banks, the New Deal turned next to the savings and loan institutions, which, although not overenthusiastic, were in such desperate need of assistance that they were willing to accept federal rehabilitation.

SAVINGS AND LOANS SUFFER
THROUGH THE DEPRESSION · No other financial intermediary, not even the commercial banking system, was more hard hit by the depression than the savings and loan industry. It had moved into high gear in the 1920s, and between 1922 and 1929 its assets had grown from $2.8 billion to $7.4 billion. At the beginning of the decade there were 8,600 associations; by the time of the crash in 1929 the number had grown to over 12,000. Growth in numbers was most pronounced in several of the major cities of the United States that already had numerous associations and now absorbed hundreds of new entrants as a result of the real estate boom.

Rapid expansion was also revealed in the importance of savings and loan associations as lenders of mortgage money to nonfarm households. Between 1925 and 1930, savings and loan institutions lent more than one-third of the funds being put into nonfarm home mortgages. By 1929 they held 24 percent of all nonfarm residential mortgages outstanding—by far the largest share held by any type of intermediary.

The rapid growth in these several years was largely a response to the real estate and building boom of the post–World War I decade. Total nonfarm construction expenditures rose steadily from less than $2.5 billion between 1915 and 1918 to almost $9.5 billion in 1926, declining thereafter to $7.7 billion in 1929. Residential construction expenditures, with whose financing savings and loan associations were most directly concerned, soared even more, from under $1 billion in 1915–1918 to nearly $5 billion in 1926, falling off to $3.1 billion in 1929. Nonfarm mortgage debt pursued the same course, rising from a total of $11.6 billion in 1919 to $35.8 billion in 1929.

Unfortunately, the depression of the thirties was to bring an abrupt but temporary end to the remarkable growth of the loan associations. It was apparent that much of the gain had been premature. Indeed, not until the late forties and fifties were savings and loans again to experience growth of a magnitude comparable to that of the twenties. By 1935 these institutions had lost one-third of the assets that they had had in 1930. By 1940 there were almost 5,000 fewer associations than there had been in 1929.[2] The industry's troubles were so overwhelming that not until late in World War II did their assets again match pre-Depression levels.

2 From 12,343 in 1929 to 7,521 in 1940.

One need not search very far for an explanation of the sad performance of the savings and loan associations. Every type of intermediary experienced difficulties with mortgage portfolios during the thirties. For savings and loan institutions that specialized almost entirely in mortgage financing, the difficulties were enormous. One measure of the problems is the extent of mortgage foreclosures. During the twenties, real estate owned by savings and loans averaged not more than 3 to 4 percent of total assets; in 1935 and 1936, however, fully one-fifth of their assets consisted of real estate, the bulk of which represented foreclosed properties. Other difficulties also engulfed the industry, one of these being the large number of commercial bank failures. The cash reserves of saving associations were held for the most part with banks as demand deposits, and when the latter failed, these cash reserves were frequently wiped out along with the balances of other depositors. This situation was disastrous for savings and loan institutions, for they kept virtually no secondary reserves of short-term securities. In 1929, for example, these securities amounted to only 0.7 percent of total assets. The loss of cash reserves, therefore, left the affected associations in a very illiquid position. Indeed, it has been noted that "in virtually every area in which a savings association failed or was closed, one or more commercial banks in that area had closed previously," and "where the commercial banks remained open, most if not all, of the savings institutions also remained open."

Withdrawals were an additional source of trouble. Frequently, savings were withdrawn solely to help families carry on during the depression, which, after all, is one of the reasons for saving. And, for the same reason, little in the way of new savings came into savings associations. More dramatic, however, was the rush of panic withdrawals that beset the industry at least up until mid-1933. The combination of frozen assets and heavy withdrawal demands caused many savings associations to be suspended in the unhappy state between that of a going concern and one terminating operations. Such a firm was simply one through which money was no longer flowing. People were not putting new money in, few were getting any out except in dribbles, and no applicant could get a loan because there were no funds to lend.

At first help took the form of state assistance or private ad hoc arrangements. In New York, for example, a small group of savings and loan people known as "flying squadrons" assumed responsibility for rescuing associations at the first hint of trouble. Their strategy was to arrange a loan to tide over the association until confidence could be restored and other problems could be worked out. In Massachusetts, on the other hand, legislation led to the creation of a "central bank" in 1932 and an insurance fund in 1934.

More far-reaching assistance, however, required intervention by the federal government. Such federal assistance was as much directed toward channeling new money into the mortgage market as toward alleviating the problems of distressed mortgage-lending institutions.

The Reconstruction Finance Corporation was the first federal agency to grant loans (totaling $18 million) to ailing savings associations. Financing on a far larger scale was provided by the temporary Home Owners Loan Corporation (HOLC), which extended more than $3 billion of mortgage credit between mid-1933 and mid-1936, with savings and loans receiving nearly $800 million. Lenders, both institutional and private, were able to turn over their distressed mortgage loans, which were then refinanced on more liberal terms. Although the bonds offered by HOLC yielded as little as 2¼ percent and had a face value of 20 percent less than that of the original loan, savings associations and other mortgage lenders rushed to exchange their "frozen" mortgages for the bonds, which could then be sold for cash.

Another significant piece of legislation authorized the establishment of federally chartered savings institutions. The object was to provide additional outlets for personal saving and to encourage the flow of savings into the housing market—a flow that had literally dried up. In order to promote these objectives, Congress authorized the direct investment by the government of up to $1 million in each federally chartered association. But despite this inducement, the number of national associations increased slowly. At the end of 1934, only 639 federally chartered associations had been established, and of this number, 158 were conversions from state charters. With improved economic conditions, however, the number of such associations mushroomed, so that by 1940 there were almost 1,500 out of a total of about 7,500 savings and loans.

More basic was the establishment in 1932 of the Federal Home Loan Bank (FHLB) System to provide a central reserve credit system for savings institutions engaged in home mortgage financing. The structure of the FHLB system followed that of the Federal Reserve System: 12 regional Home Loan Banks and a supervisory Home Loan Bank Board with headquarters in Washington. Membership was open to any savings association, savings bank, or insurance company. The regional banks were to act as wholesalers of funds to member institutions in order to supplement resources available from their own investors and savers. The banks were empowered to make two types of loans: unsecured short-term and collateralized long-term, the latter to be repaid over a period of up to 10 years. The funds for the banks' operations were to come mainly from the sale of their obligations in the financial market, backed by the mortgages that the banks held as collateral. The advantages of membership were readily perceived. By the end of 1933 almost 20 percent of all savings and loan associations, possessing more than one-third of the industry's assets, had taken out membership in the system.

The last and perhaps the most significant piece of Depression legislation relating to the savings and loan industry was the insuring of deposit accounts by the Federal Savings and Loan Insurance Corporation (FSLIC) in 1934. This step helped to restore confidence in the savings and loan business in much the same way in which confidence was restored in the commercial banks through the creation of the FDIC. At the end of the decade, fully 30 percent of all savings associations, controlling over half the industry's $5.7 billion in assets, were insured by FSLIC.

Although the savings and loan industry was much improved with respect to safety and liquidity by the legislation of the thirties, no effort was made to broaden the lending activities of these institutions. This fact is surprising, for much of their problems in this period lay, as we have seen, in their almost exclusive attachment to mortgage finance. Yet the American dream of homeownership remained strong, not least of all among those responsible for legislation and supervision in this field. As we shall see in the next chapter, the specialized nature of savings and loan associations was again to be a source of some concern in the late 1960s.

CREDIT UNIONS CONTINUE TO GROW · In contrast to other intermediaries, credit unions had a field day in the thirties. Of course, they were still insignificant when compared with other types of intermediaries. Their assets grew from $34 million in 1929 to $253 million in 1940; their number from fewer than 1,000 to more than 9,000. Membership grew even faster, from 265,000 to 2.8 million. Most of this growth, naturally, came during the recovery years, but even at the height of the depression credit unions did exceedingly well. Between 1931 and 1933, the number of credit unions increased from approximately 1,500 to more than 2,000, while assets rose from $31 billion to $40 billion.

Insignificant as they were compared with other intermediaries, credit unions were becoming important suppliers of consumer credit. According to one estimate, by the end of the decade credit unions accounted for more than one-fifth of the consumer credit loans outstanding among cash credit lenders. Data compiled by Raymond Goldsmith suggest a more modest role, with credit unions providing under 10 percent of consumer installment loans.

As in earlier years, much of the growth recorded by credit unions was the result of frantic promotion, especially by the federal government. Before 1934, credit unions could be chartered only under state laws. Then, in 1934, the Federal Credit Union established nationally chartered credit unions. Between 1935 and 1940 some 3,700 federally chartered credit unions were started.

The demand for credit unions was pressing, especially in the thirties when many were in desperate want. Moreover, cooperative activities were much in vogue during these years, a factor that was naturally a great help to the credit union cause. The more optimistic adherents expressed the view that credit unions could entirely fulfill the public's need for consumer credit. Perhaps the greatest enthusiasm for credit unions was found in Wisconsin, where in 1931 the state government appointed a credit union organizer to "travel around the state and speak at various plants, parishes, townships or any other places where it was possible to promote a credit union."

Individual credit unions remained small. As late as 1940 the average federally chartered credit union had a membership of barely 300 persons and assets of less than $20,000. Of course, with the number growing, it is not surprising that the average size remained very small, for new credit unions were starting from scratch. In Wisconsin the total resources of all credit unions expanded from $700,000 in 1931 to $2.9 million in 1935, whereas the assets of the average credit union declined from $22,000 to $7,600.

During the twenties, credit unions had diverted some funds into non-consumer loans, especially home mortgages. Of the more than $35 million in outstanding loans of credit unions in 1929, over $12 million were in "other" loans. Credit unions in Massachusetts were making more real estate loans than personal loans. By the end of 1933, mortgage loans accounted for 36 percent of the total assets of Wisconsin credit unions. In fact, in the early thirties the credit unions of Wisconsin more nearly approximated building and loan associations than organizations purporting to care for the consumer credit needs of low income borrowers. Like other intermediaries, a number of credit unions that had invested heavily in mortgages in the twenties found the going rough in the depressed thirties, and some were driven to liquidation as a result. Toward the end of the depression, however, the activities of credit unions centered around the making of consumer loans to members, thus establishing a pattern that has been in effect ever since.

INVESTMENT BANKING REFORM · The securities market crash and the ensuing depression dealt an especially severe blow to finance capitalism. The blow, moreover, was not confined to monetary losses. The wrath of an incensed and insecure public fell in full force on the investment banking community, whose members had been among the heroes of the Roaring Twenties. Part of this reaction was undoubtedly to be expected in view of the enormous security losses taken by investors. However, this indignation was further intensified by numerous disclosures of how investment bankers had deceived the public and reaped huge gains at its expense.

The new administration in Washington completely shared the public's disenchantment with Wall Street. Immediately on taking office, President Roosevelt voiced the common sentiment when he announced that the "practices of the unscrupulous money changers stand indicted in the court of public opinion, rejected by the hearts and minds of men. . . . The money changers have fled from their high seats in the temple of our civilization. We may now restore that temple to the ancient truths." In the weeks and months ahead, the New Deal was to attempt to do just that and, in the process, to remake substantially the environment in which the men of Wall Street carried on their business.

One of the more striking innovations in investment banking during the twenties had been the bold entry of the large commercial banks into the securities business. Indeed, the investment affiliates of these banks assumed, as we have already noted, dominant positions in the underwriting and retailing of security issues. Despite the fact that the initial entry of commercial banks into the investment business had been prompted by the inadequacy of existing underwriting, particularly retailing facilities, the consensus in the early thirties was that this association was improper and out of keeping with banking orthodoxy. On the one hand, deposit funds, payable for the most part on demand, had been used to acquire investment-type securities. More serious, short-term loans that could not be liquidated were frequently refinanced in the form of long-term debt issues through the bank's security affiliate and then passed on to the public. Finally, and very important to the social reformers of the New Deal, there was abundant evidence relating to the unethical practices of these affiliates.

In response (perhaps as an overresponse) to these abuses, the Banking Act of 1933 barred any financial institution from simultaneously engaging in investment banking operations, such as underwriting or dealing in securities, and in commercial banking operations, such as receiving deposits.

The dissolution of security affiliates, called for under the Banking Act, had profound effects on the investment banking industry, just as their inception had had some years before. The action requiring dissolution, like much other New Deal legislation, was too drastic, for the very real abuses referred to could have been remedied through other appropriate legislation. Senator Carter Glass, one of the authors of the act, later conceded as much: "We did it with the avowed hope and expectation that thereafter there would be organized in this country underwriting houses such as exist in Great Britain and continental Europe. . . . That did not take place."

The enforced separation of commercial and investment banking led to the formation of a number of "new" (or "successor") investment banking houses that hoped to take over the business of the liquidated affiliates. The banking house of Morgan Stanley & Co., commencing business in September 1935, had its origins in the decision of the private banking firm of J. P. Morgan & Co. to remain in the commercial banking business. Several Morgan partners and executives, including Harold Stanley and Henry S. Morgan, subsequently resigned to form Morgan Stanley & Co. Another investment house, the First Boston Corporation, began as a result of the impact of the Banking Act on the securities affiliates of the First National Bank of Boston and the Chase National Bank in New York. Similarly, the firm of Brown Harriman & Co. (later Harriman Ripley & Co., Inc.) originated out of the decision of the National City Bank and Brown Brothers Harriman & Co. to remain in the commercial banking business.

In other instances, established investment houses were considerably enlarged by the absorption of added personnel from liquidated security affiliates. The firm of Edward B. Smith & Co. (later Smith, Barney & Co.), for example, took on several partners and several hundred other employees of the Guaranty Company, the investment banking arm of the Guaranty Trust Company of New York.

The formation of these new houses (and the expansion of others) did much to stimulate competition, for a great part of the business was suddenly thrown on the market. Despite an element of "successorship," the frequent dispersion of the former management among a number of old and new banking houses led to a scramble for the business of the liquidated affiliates. More important, whatever ties existed between the issuer and its investment banker were frequently quite loose. Even in the years prior to World War I, investment bankers did not rule supreme in business life. By the thirties their influence was so much diluted that "successorship" meant little. Few corporate managements were in the vest pockets of their bankers to be passed along as chattel property. But, of course, reputation did count for much, as it always has, in the investment banking business and herein lay the significance of "successorship." Yet even the well-connected partners of Morgan Stanley & Co. had to work hard for business. Judge Harold R. Medina explained how:

> When the new organization commenced business, it immediately proceeded to try to obtain business from whatever source it could, and, in this connection, it made every kind of new business effort that its executives could think of. It broadcast announcements of its formation; compiled studies of outstanding securities that might be refunded at a saving; its personnel took turns calling on various people throughout the country; and they called on banks and asked them, if they knew of any business that might be done, to remember that Morgan Stanley was in business.

Competition became a daily way of life even at the regal house of Kuhn, Loeb & Co. Despite Otto Kahn's repeated statements that Kuhn, Loeb never actively sought new business, his "show window" philosophy was in fact a clever competitive instrument, not wholly without meaning to be sure, but one to turn on and off as circumstances dictated. When the business was sufficiently attractive, Kuhn, Loeb was no laggard in competing for it. However, when the firm either did not particularly want the business or saw little chance of getting it, it would then revert to the "show window," announcing that Kuhn, Loeb would take no business away from another banking house, etc., etc. Indeed, Kuhn, Loeb would even engage in price competition when the business was attractive enough. By the forties the "show window" was all but forgotten as Kuhn, Loeb adopted a competitive strategy more in keeping with the times.

Despite vigorous competition among investment bankers, the excesses associated with the twenties were avoided, partly as a result of new legislation protecting investors. The first move in this direction was the Securities Act of 1933, designed to prevent the abuses connected with public sale of securities that had occurred in the twenties. The legislation was "to provide full and fair disclosure of the character of securities sold in interstate and foreign commerce and through the mails and to prevent frauds in the sale thereof." The act was not intended to prevent speculation or, as some feared, to give the government a hand in the allocation of investment funds, but only to ensure that all pertinent facts were put before the public so that investors might know what kinds of risks they were taking. The act aimed at preventing the sort of situation that arose with the National City Company's underwriting of Peruvian bonds in 1927. The prospectus advertising these bonds told of the country's geographic location and population but nothing of its financial abilities, or inabilities, which the underwriter's Peruvian representative described as "positively distressing," and he recommended declining the Peruvian government's business as a "moral risk."

The act required that new security issues be registered with the Federal

Trade Commission, or FTC (after 1934, the Securities and Exchange Commission, or SEC). The registration statement was to include all pertinent financial and other facts relating to the specific issue and to the issuer, as well as the compensation of the underwriters. The FTC and later the SEC was then to decide whether to approve the registration statement and thus allow sale of the issue. To provide muscle, severe civil penalties were authorized in the event the prospectus or registration statement "includes an untrue statement of a material fact or omits to state a material fact necessary in order to make the statements not misleading." Far-reaching as it was, to New Dealers like Adolph A. Berle, Jr., and James M. Landis, the Securities Act of 1933 was to be only the first step in the purge of the "money changers."

The heavy losses sustained by the public after the stock market collapse led to a popular demand for regulation of the security markets as well as security issues. The cry for regulation was, as usual, heightened by disclosures concerning the ways in which security prices had been manipulated by insiders and other speculators. What hurt most were the stories of how investors had often become unwitting participants in the many pools that had manipulated the prices of individual stocks during the boom of the 1920s.

To eliminate such dealings, Congress passed the Securities and Exchange Act of 1934. In order to administer the provisions of the act, a Securities and Exchange Commission was created. In essence, the SEC was to oversee the operations of the various securities exchanges as well as to administer the provisions of the Securities Act of 1933. Each exchange was required to file a registration statement with the SEC, agreeing to comply with the provisions of the act and to require compliance by its members. In particular, the act forbade manipulation of security prices. At the same time, corporations whose securities were listed on registered exchanges were required to submit annual reports on their operations.

Finally, the Securities and Exchange Act provided for margin requirements to be established by the Federal Reserve Board of Governors. It was believed that the market boom of the twenties had derived much of its strength from the excessive availability of brokers' loans and that the high rates paid on brokers' loans (as high as 15 percent) tempted firms to pump funds into the call market instead of financing trade and production. The Standard Oil Company was reported to have made in 1929 over 20,000 short-term brokers' loans, totaling more than $17 billion. In addition, there were the consequences suffered by investors who supposedly had gone over their heads because of the indiscriminate availability of security credit.

ECONOMIC EFFECTS OF THE DEPRESSION
ON INVESTMENT BANKING · No less important than the legislation we have referred to were the economic effects of the depression on the investment banking business. Between 1929 and 1933, the volume of security issues took a nose dive. New capital and refunding issues totaling

approximately $11.6 billion in 1929 (of which domestic corporate issues accounted for about $8 billion) had dwindled to only $1.1 billion by 1933 (with corporate issues down to $161 million). This factor, together with the huge decline in activity on the securities exchanges,[3] had a crushing effect on the investment banking industry, especially on those firms that had built up large sales organizations. As a result, the number of investment banking houses fell from 665 in 1929 to 375 in 1933, while the number of branch offices was reduced by more than half, from 1,237 to 570.

Certain banking houses found themselves particularly hard pressed, having been caught holding large amounts of unsold securities when the market broke in late 1929. Goldman, Sachs, for example, was in the midst of a number of underwritings and lost millions of dollars in having to take up securities at the underwritten price at a time when the market was greatly depressed. Similar problems crippled the old and respected firm of Kidder, Peabody & Co.

With recovery, activity on the security markets picked up somewhat. The number of shares traded on the New York Stock Exchange increased from the 1934 low of 324 million to 496 million shares in 1936. The short recovery on the stock market ended with the market break in the middle of 1937. As gloom once again replaced optimism, the public's interest in stocks waned so that by 1942, volume on the Exchange had sunk to a dismal 26 million shares. Much the same story of recovery and decline applied to the bond market except that there was a flurry of activity due to large-scale refundings, induced, in turn, by the drop in interest rates. The expansion of activity, up through 1936, was reflected in the number of investment banking houses that, rather remarkably, rebounded to 751 in 1936. Branch offices, reflecting the changes since the twenties, increased to only 795.

With the large, retail-oriented, and heavily capitalized security affiliates out of the picture, the investment banking industry was hard pressed to meet the rise in the demand for capital funds. Even as late as 1949, only a handful of investment houses had a capital of as much as $5 million, and not all of this amount was available for underwriting. The problem was dramatized in 1937 by the serious embarrassments suffered by a number of houses in connection with the underwriting of large issues by the Bethlehem Steel Corporation and the Pure Oil Company. Neither of these issues, averaging more than $45 million, found a ready market, with the result that the underwriters suffered heavy losses in addition to having much of their capital frozen in the unsaleable securities of these companies. Repercussions were felt throughout the entire investment banking industry, and thereafter the size of underwriting groups was greatly increased so as to spread risk more widely.[4]

The dominant position of the finance capitalist in the Morgan era rested, as noted previously, in a close control over the supply of investment

[3] Volume on the New York Stock Exchange slumped from the 1.1 billion share peak in 1929 to 324 million shares in 1934.

[4] But the same problem returned during the bear market of the late 1960s.

capital. This control declined during the twenties, although the unparalleled increase in direct investment by the public ensured plenty of business for investment bankers, particularly those who developed strong retailing departments. The thirties saw a new event, which again threatened to diminish sharply the business of the investment banker, already much diminished by the depression and the slackened pace of activity on the securities exchanges. This event was the mushrooming of private placements of security issues directly with other financial intermediaries, especially the large life insurance companies.

Savings coming into financial institutions picked up sharply with the coming of recovery, as the public once again sought the comparative security of indirect investment. On the other hand, the disenchantment of certain intermediaries with traditional investment outlets (particularly residential and farm mortgages), together with the overall decline in the supply of private securities and low-interest rates, prompted a search for new investment media. By default, this medium usually took the form of United States government issues. But with returns on government issues low, various intermediaries sought to finance business directly through the private acquisition of debt securities, thereby openly bidding for the bread and butter business of the investment banker. The life insurance companies and later the pension funds were particularly active in this field.

For the issuer, there were certain advantages to private placement; these included both the avoidance of middleman costs and the sometimes lengthy delays before the proceeds were received. Also important in encouraging private placements were the registration provisions of the Securities Act of 1933 that required the revelation of confidential data, a requirement that seemed onerous to many businessmen. The private placement of a security issue, in contrast to a publicly distributed issue, did not require registration with the SEC and therefore could be done quickly and wthout an airing of the company's affairs. In 1936 approximately 14 percent of new debt issues took the form of private placements, with the share jumping to 73 percent in 1948. In order not to be wholly excluded, some investment banking houses sought to get a piece of the business by acting as agents for issuers. Indeed, such firms as White, Weld & Co. and Goldman, Sachs & Co. became something of specialists in this area.

THE COLLAPSE AND RESTRUCTURING OF
INVESTMENT COMPANIES · Among the financial intermediaries under consideration, none grew up so quickly in the twenties and toppled so badly in the thirties as investment companies. Their growth in the late twenties derived from the stock market boom and the public craze for securities. The subsequent fall in the industry's fortunes was similarly closely linked to the market averages and to the dwindling demand for securities.

The deluge that brought the Dow-Jones average down from a peak of 386 in early September of 1929 to 41 on July 8, 1932, led to a popular revulsion against securities and to a more than 70 percent decline in activity on the nation's largest security exchange. Investment companies, having done amazingly well riding on the wings of fortune, now found themselves not only out of favor but also a source of public rage. The loss of confidence, as well as the increased indignation that in any case would have accompanied a severe market turnaround, was heightened by the wretched performance of many of the leading investment trusts and, even more, by the indiscretions of some of their managements that came to light with disturbing frequency in the depression years.

The effect of the crash on investment company shares was especially severe. Quite apart from the considerable losses taken on the underlying portfolios, investors were to suffer further from the fact that the capital structures of almost all closed-end trusts were highly leveraged (meaning that when underlying stock prices were rising, common share values would rise more than proportionally, but that when the market was sliding, common share values would also drop more than proportionally). The shares bought near the market peak at substantial premiums were now selling at even greater discounts. Indeed, shares of closed-end investment companies traded in the early thirties at about 35 percent below book value.

The loss of interest in investment company shares was compounded by a widespread and not wholly unwarranted reaction against "management" and the so-called experts who had so easily gained, and sometimes abused, the public's confidence. This aversion to management was not, of course, confined to investment companies or even to the financial sphere, but in a generalized way reflected the public's changed attitude toward the nation's business leaders, the men whom the people had previously trusted to make prosperity permanent. In the securities business, particularly, professional management was about the last item investors were ready to buy. After all, they had watched the value of their shares in the Goldman, Sachs Trading Corporation sink from 104 to 1¾. Even more galling, they had heard how Walter E. Sachs and other company officers had reaped huge personal fortunes through devious maneuvering.

So great was the about-face that for a couple of years a considerable flurry of excitement developed over the so-called fixed trust form of investment company, in which the discretionary element was all but eliminated. Such schemes were not unknown in the twenties but did not receive much attention. Sales of certificates in fixed trusts came to less than $50 million in 1928 and to only $88 million in 1929. The essential and most peculiar feature of the fixed trust was its rigidity. And, oddly enough, it was this feature that gave the scheme its appeal. Underwriters would begin by purchasing a variety of stocks (or bonds), to which might be added some cash and/or bonds (stocks). This portfolio was then divided into "units," which were placed with a trustee, and certificates against these units sold to the public at market value, with perhaps a 10 percent charge added to cover costs and profit. The securities underlying the certificates usually could not be changed unless a stock missed a dividend— then it usually had to be sold. As such, the sole, and of course very important, element of discretion was to be found in the initial decision concerning the composition of the portfolio. To prevent the price of certificates from selling below the market value of the underlying securities, holders could elect to redeem their shares either in exchange for the securities making up the unit or to receive the proceeds from their sale.

The fixed trust possessed several fatal weaknesses due to the absence of continuing management. Moreover, a certain element of irony existed, for the buying public, skeptical as it was of "management," was in effect willing to leave to promoters the selection of an optimum portfolio to be carried, with no change, over the long run. Yet for a time, fixed and semifixed trusts somehow managed to work up quite a bit of interest among investors. In 1930, certainly no banner year in the securities markets, several dozen fixed trusts were formed, issuing to the public some $336 million worth of certificates. The boom, of course, did not last long. By 1932 the public had already soured on the scheme, mainly from recognition of its inherent weaknesses but also because the irresponsible sponsorship of some finally gave the fixed-trust field an unsavory reputation.

Of far greater importance to the future of the industry was the emergence of the mutual fund, or open-end, type of managed investment company. Like the fixed trusts, open-end investment companies were a product of the twenties, the first being formed in Boston in 1924 when the Massachusetts Investors Trust gave its shareholders the right to redeem their shares at net asset value, less $2.00 per share. During the twenties, a handful of open-end companies were started, most of them issuing only one class of stock instead of holding to the more complicated capital structures of the closed-end trusts. Nevertheless, the great investment company expansion of the late twenties was almost wholly dominated by the closed-end companies, which, because of their highly leveraged capital structure, seemed to catch the spirit of the times. At the end of 1929 there were less than 20 mutual fund-type companies in operation with combined assets of about $140 million. Of these, the largest (Incorporated Investors) had assets of $41 million, nearly one-third of the industry total.

The market collapse and the subsequent decline in security prices naturally led to losses on open-end company shares. The value of these shares toppled from $140 million in 1929 to a low of $64 million in 1931. But substantial as this drop was, the performance of the mutuals was scintillating compared with the stock market averages, especially when compared with the dismal performance of the closed-end trusts, whose shares were selling at large discounts from market value.

Consequently, as soon as the flirtation with the fixed trusts had run its course and reason took hold, investor interest turned to the mutual fund idea. Between the end of 1932 and the end of 1936, the assets of open-end companies soared from $75 to $506 million. Part of this gain reflected the partial recovery taking place on the securities markets, but a good deal was due to the growth of sales of mutual fund shares, which increased to $237 million between 1933 and 1935, compared with less than $150 million over the preceding three-year interval.

The recession of 1937–1938, coming at a time when the economy was still greatly depressed, proved a rude shock to the millions of investors who were beginning to see a brighter day and who had recovered some of their bullishness over the previous year or so. The slump on the securities exchanges manifested itself in a sharp drop in the sale of investment company shares and losses on outstanding shares. Indeed, the industry, like the securities markets in general, was to stagnate until World War II, when it entered a new phase of expansion that has extended up to the present.

Although the postwar growth of investment companies was to reflect a number of underlying economic influences, the groundwork for this expansion was set with the passage of the Investment Company Act of 1940, which, through a number of major reforms, cleared the air surrounding the debacle of the early thirties.

The act was an outgrowth of the SEC study of the investment company industry authorized under the Public Utility Holding Company Act of 1936. (A number of so-called investment companies were, as we saw earlier, holding companies interested mainly in financial and managerial control.) In general, the spirit of the act had already been accepted by the industry, for the public was certainly in no mood to be sold on further speculation and visions of fantastic riches. Yet the act did serve a purpose. It codified the rules of the game and added greatly to public confidence.

Among the more important provisions of the act was a requirement that investment companies register with the SEC. Each company had to file a registration statement, spelling out its objectives and methods of operation. These objectives and methods could not be changed without a vote of the stockholders. The aim of the provision was to prevent situations such as occurred in the twenties where management would arbitrarily change the company's focus with little concern for investor interests. To prevent conflict of interest—another major problem in the twenties—outside directors were required. Similarly, investment companies could not, as they had in the past, purchase newly issued securities during the underwriting period if anyone associated with the company was also associated with the security underwriter. In order to minimize speculation, investment companies were barred from buying on margin or from selling "short." Finally, with some exceptions in the case of closed-end companies, investment companies were prohibited from issuing any debt (senior securities).

LIFE INSURANCE COMPANIES
DURING THE DEPRESSION · Despite very serious problems, life insurance companies made it through the depression in comparatively good shape. To be sure, the amount of life insurance in force fell from $107 billion in 1931 to $96 billion in 1933, but by 1937 it had already reached a new high of $107.8 billion. Earnings on investments, although considerably reduced by the decline in interest rates, allowed for continuous asset growth. The industry's assets climbed from $17.5 billion in 1929 to $21.8 billion in 1934, and to $29.2 billion by the end of the decade.

Although it survived and grew to much greater stature, the industry had its troubles. Some of its problems were similar to those of other intermediaries, but a few were unique. Thus, between 1929 and 1935, nearly 40 life insurance companies out of more than 350 failed. Most of these were small and inexperienced companies whose volume of business totaled only about 2.5 percent of all life insurance in force. Sales of ordinary life insurance also fell from nearly $13 billion in 1929 to $8.3 billion in 1934 and to $7.3 billion in 1939. Earnings, too, declined, largely because of lower interest rates and losses on investments. The net return on Mutual Life's assets, for example, fell steadily after 1931, from 4.72 percent to 3.04 percent in 1940. The sharp decline in earnings caused Metropolitan to cut its dividend five times between 1931 and 1941. What was happening to these companies was, of course, happening to the rest of the industry as well.

Things would have been worse had the industry not struck off on a more conservative path following the Armstrong hearings of a generation before. Prohibited from investing in stocks or engaging in security underwriting, life companies were able to avoid some of the temptations of the twenties, as well as their unhappy consequences. Thus Metropolitan had only 1 percent of its assets in stocks at the time of the market crash.

The shift away from high finance coincided with a renewed interest in mortgage loans. The share of mortgages in the total assets of life companies increased during the 1920s from less than 30 percent to almost 42 percent. Most of this growth was in city mortgages, which mushroomed from just over $1 billion to $5.2 billion. Like all other mortgage-lending institutions, life insurance companies were caught up in the ebullience of the times. Nevertheless, the growth of the mortgage loan portfolio was viewed as consistent with a conservative and prudent investment policy. For, as in the case of other lenders, the experience of life insurance companies with real estate loans had been favorable, both in income and in safety. In any event, the value of land seemed always to be rising. However, like other investors, life insurance companies were to find to their great dismay that the paper against real estate had no more intrinsic value in a depressed economy than any other security. Indeed, the life companies found their mortgage portfolios not only a source of considerable loss but also a great bother, for they were increasingly drawn into performing the functions of landlord and farm operator.

Farm mortgages presented the most serious problems even though their growth had been much slower than that of city mortgages. The Great Depression, of course, worsened the farmer's plight. At its worst, the specter of a landless peasantry haunted the land. By June 1933 nearly three out of every five of the Metropolitan's farm mortgage loans were delinquent, and in some parts of South Dakota and Nebraska the figure was closer to three out of every four. At the end of 1932 nearly one-fifth of Metropolitan's farm mortgages had been converted to farm real estate, and its plight was not unique. Equitable had, at the end of 1931, $197 million (14 percent of its total investments) in farm mortgages and had foreclosed on only 430 farms with a book value of less than $4 million. Two years later very nearly half of these loans were in "serious default," requiring the society to foreclose on more than 5,000 farms over the next three years. So vast were Equitable's holdings that a small army of fieldmen, trained in agriculture, was assigned to manage the company's properties. Unfortunate as it was in a profit-and-loss sense, the experience with farm mortgages and management was one of the brightest moments in an otherwise dull business. The able way in which the life companies coped with restoring the farms that they had been forced to take over marked one of the few important innovations in late twentieth-century life insurance.

Despite its frequency, foreclosure was a last step and one that sometimes required considerable courage. At Cherokee, Oklahoma, the representative of Equitable was driven out of town. In Le Mars, Iowa, a masked mob kidnapped a judge who would not swear to refuse to sign farm foreclosures, put a rope around his neck, placed a greasy hub-cap over his head, removed his trousers, and then departed. No less awesome were the tight-lipped mobs of local people who gathered at farm auctions, scared away would-be bidders, and bought up properties at ridiculously low prices in order to return them free and clear to the original owners. On one occasion, 12 horses, 10 head of cattle, 7 wagons, and complete farming equipment were "sold" for $5.22.

Experience with city mortgages was only moderately better. Of Equitable's city mortgages, nearly 14,000 or about one out of every four were in default at the end of 1933. A year later 9 percent of the company's outstanding loans were in foreclosure. Metropolitan, in effect, went into the real estate management business, acquiring some 33,000 city properties with a book value of $390 million. Rather than dispose of these properties on depressed markets, most were retained in a quickly growing real estate portfolio. For all life insurance companies taken together, real estate holdings soared from $464 million in 1929 to $2.1 billion in 1936.

Naturally this experience made the life companies reluctant, as it had made other lenders, to make further commitments. Farm mortgage lending slowed to a trickle. Metropolitan loaned only $783,000 in 1933 and a mere $118,000 two years later. In 1928 life companies owned more than one-fifth of all farm mortgages in the United States; by 1939 the figure had slipped to 13 percent and by 1942 to 2.5 percent.

The decline in mortgage lending was primarily offset by the acquisition of bonds, especially of United States government obligations, which multiplied from less than $500 million in 1932 to $5.4 billion by the end of the decade. Equitable's government portfolio soared from $7 million in 1930 to $440 million by 1937. These enormous increases were, of course, due to the declines in demand for credit in most other markets, the heightened emphasis on liquidity and solvency, and the mushrooming of the federal debt.

Less dramatic, but also substantial, was the acquisition by life companies of state and local government bonds, which grew from less than $600 million in 1929 to almost $2 billion in 1940. Corporate bond holdings, on the other hand, did not show a substantial increase until economic recovery was well under way. From 1929 through 1935, they rose from $4.7 billion to $5.7 billion and to $9 billion by 1940.

The growth of public utility bonds was particularly impressive, more than doubling (from $2.1 to $4.3 billion) in the latter half of the decade. A substantial proportion of these bonds was acquired through private placement. Indeed, between 1935 and 1942 private placements accounted for close to half of Equitable's purchases. Private placements were advantageous because they resulted in higher effective yields than could have been obtained on public offerings. The higher yields were due both to the avoidance of the usual banker spread of two or more points and to the fact that borrowers often could not wait until a public issue had been prepared and sold.

The search for new investment outlets also led the life companies to begin investing heavily in "industrial securities," securities not issued by governments, railroad, or public utilities. Holdings of these securities, following the conservative view, had been small in comparison with railroad and public utility holdings. Now with many of the nation's railroads in bankruptcy and other traditional investment channels clogged, interest in the industrials picked up. Equitable's holdings, for example, increased from $37 million at the end of 1934 to $225 million by 1940. Once again the bulk of these holdings was acquired through direct placement. For the industry as a whole, industrials grew to 5 percent of total assets by 1940, up from less than 2 percent in 1930 and 2.5 percent in 1935.

Another item of growth on the asset side, but one wholly undesired, was that of policy loans (loans made to policyholders on the security of the cash value of life policies). Under normal circumstances, most policyholders felt little urge to borrow on their life insurance or to turn in their policies for the cash surrender value. The thirties, however, were not exactly normal years. In 1929 policy loans (already inflated by borrowing to purchase stocks) totaled $2.4 billion, or about 14 percent of life company assets. By 1932, with more than 12 million workers out of work, policy loans reached a peak of $3.8 billion, about 18 percent of total assets. The number of policy loans at Equitable mushroomed from 128,000 in 1928 to 376,000 four years later. With recovery, the number of policy loans declined to 175,000 in 1937 and to only 30,000 by 1945.

One reason for the concern of insurance companies over the rise in policy loans was that frequently they were a first step toward cancellation. In 1932 more than $6.7 billion of life insurance was canceled compared to $2.7 billion in 1929. Metropolitan alone paid out more than $1 billion in surrender values between 1930 and 1935. To meet these demands, insurance companies, which usually did not have to concern themselves very much with liquidity, were forced to liquidate investments in depressed markets.

The "run" on the insurance companies was heightened by the pressure brought to bear on policyholders by the commercial banks and other lending institutions to liquidate their debts by drawing on policy reserves. The result was an enormous drain on the liquidity of life companies, a situation that became serious enough to result in a number of states declaring moratoria on policy loans and surrenders. This step, of course, amounted to a partial suspension of the regular business of life insurance companies.

The depression affected not only the kinds of assets life insurance companies held but also the kinds of insurance they wrote. Sales of ordinary life insurance dropped off sharply. A contributing factor to this decline was the rapid spread of group insurance, which partially substituted for individual insurance. Still another factor, and one also related to the growth of group insurance, was the rising cost of ordinary life insurance, which resulted from the fall in earnings on insurance company investments.

The assumed earnings rate on investments is an important element in calculating insurance premiums—the higher the rate the lower the premium. During the twenties, Metropolitan's assumed earnings rate was 3.5 percent. This figure was conservative, for actual earnings averaged 5.3 percent. By 1934 earnings had declined to 4 percent, at which time the assumed earnings rate was cut to 3 percent. Premium rates on new policies, as a result, were increased by more than 6 percent. Earnings continued to fall, until in 1942 the assumed earnings rate was again lowered to 2.75 percent. The cost of ordinary insurance was additionally raised by the periodic drop in dividends, which also hinged on the earnings rate.

In contrast to ordinary contracts, annuities grew at a somewhat disturbing pace. Until the insurance companies started cutting their assumed earnings rates, annuities and single-payment life policies seemed to be bargains to those who had ready cash. Interest rates on alternative investments were low, and there was, of course, much uncertainty over equity investments. Annuities were so attractive that some policyholders borrowed from banks at 2 percent to buy them. The number of annuity contracts written by Equitable soared from 17,000 in 1929 to 77,000 in 1934, whereas the company's sales of ordinary life policies declined from 216,000 to 139,000 over the same period. Single-payment life and annuity premiums averaged about 1 percent of Mutual Life's total premium income in the 1920s and 21 percent in 1935.

Like other intermediaries, especially the mutual savings banks, life insurance companies faced great problems in putting their resources to work profitably. Consequently, they were often reluctant to attract new funds that might only depress the rate of return on existing savings. This reluctance led to a growing interest in policies that did not have a heavy savings element—that is, term and group insurance. Annuities, at the other extreme, were almost all saving. Starting in 1934 and 1935, therefore, many companies sought to discourage annuity business by raising premiums and by ordering their salespeople to cut down on this type of business. Equitable's sales of annuity contracts slipped to 33,000 in 1937 and to 9,000 in 1940.

Industrial insurance, too, had its problems. The lapse rate on this kind of insurance had always been high, with lower-income families taking it out, often at the urging of high-pressure salesmen, and later discovering that the weekly payments were simply too much of a burden on their meager wages. Buoyed by the general prosperity and optimism of the twenties, the amount of industrial insurance in force more than doubled, from $6.9 billion to $17.3 billion. In the words of one writer, "too much of everything, including insurance, was sold." Indiscriminate purchases of industrial insurance often resulted in too much coverage on children and housewives and too little on the breadwinner. Consequently, the depression found all too many families both overinsured, in relation to their incomes, and underinsured, in terms of the distribution of their coverage. The lapse rate on industrial insurance taken out within the preceding three years rose from an already high 42 percent in 1929 to 54 percent in 1933.

The life companies were themselves partly at fault, having permitted and encouraged a too rapid and unbalanced growth of the business. Some retrenchment was clearly necessary. Aside from general criticism by the public and the state regulatory agencies, the life companies were additionally hounded by growing numbers of so-called insurance counselors. These people made a business of advising financially distressed policyholders how to get the most cash out of their policies and still retain coverage. To drum up business, the "counselors" launched vigorous, sometimes savage, radio campaigns against the life companies, inciting additional policyholder unrest.

But apart from all the static, there was some recognition among the "big three" industrial insurance companies (Metropolitan, Prudential, and John Hancock) that old-style industrial insurance was becoming outmoded by the improved economic status of the workingman, the depression being only a temporary setback to this progress. The future clearly lay in ordinary life insurance or in group insurance, not in small, weekly payment industrial insurance. This recognition, plus the problem of lapses and the resulting public criticism, led the big three to redirect their efforts. As a result, a number of smaller life companies were able to get a foothold in the industrial insurance business and gradually to enlarge their share. In 1929 Metropolitan wrote $1.2 billion of new industrial insurance, about 30 percent of all new business. By 1941 Metropolitan's writings came to only $649 million, with its share of the business dropping to 18 percent.

In comparison to the absence of growth in ordinary and industrial insurance, some newer lines of business experienced rapid expansion. Group insurance increased from $9 billion in 1929 to $15 billion in 1940, a very good rate of growth, given the times. Over the same period, its share of total life insurance in force expanded from 8.8 percent to 13 percent. One of the reasons for the success of group life insurance was that it became increasingly cheap compared to ordinary life insurance, for earnings and dividends are not too important in setting premiums on what is essentially a type of term insurance. Indeed, the premium rates on group insurance actually declined over the thirties.

HARD TIMES FOR THE NONLIFE
INSURANCE COMPANIES · The thirties were not famine years for the nonlife insurance companies, but they certainly were lean years. Largely because of a decline in the value of the common stock portfolio of fire, marine, casualty, and miscellaneous other insurance companies, their assets plummeted from $4.7 billion in 1929 to $3.5 billion in 1933. Recovery restored these losses, but as late as 1939 assets were still only

$200 million ahead of 1929. As in the twenties, casualty business showed considerably greater vigor than fire and marine. Between 1929 and 1939, the assets of casualty companies actually increased from $1.6 billion to $2.0 billion, whereas the assets of fire and marine companies declined from $3.1 billion to $2.8 billion.

Just how hard times were for the industry as a whole can be seen by looking at the experience of one of the more conservative and affluent companies, the Insurance Company of North America. Although North America fared far better than most, its assets, standing at $90.1 million on December 31, 1929, dropped by nearly a third, to $63.3 million three years later. Securities valued at $77.8 million at the end of 1929 had a market value of $52.6 million at the end of 1932. The company's surplus of $28 million in 1929 was slashed to just $18 million in 1932. Disastrous as these losses were, they were not fatal, thanks to conservative investment policies and some remarkable foresight. As early as 1928 Benjamin Rush began to prepare the company for the hard times he was sure would come.

Other companies were not so fortunate. In New York City only stringent first-aid measures kept some sixty fire, marine, and casualty companies alive. To head off a mass collapse, the National Convention of Insurance Commissions authorized insurance companies to value securities above market prices according to what became known as "convention values." A number of companies were kept afloat thanks only to loans from the Reconstruction Finance Company.

General insurance companies sustained current operating losses as well as security losses. Basically it was the old problem of revenues falling faster than costs. At North America, marine premiums tumbled from $9.2 million in 1929 to $4.6 million in 1932, while marine losses fell from $4.2 million to $2.5 million. Operating expenses also proved comparatively insensitive to the volume of underwriting, declining from $4.1 million to only $2.8 million. Consequently, North America's marine branch profits of $956,000 in 1929 were turned into a $592,000 loss in 1932. Much the same story can be told of North America's fire branch, where profits fell from $2.1 million in 1929 to a loss of $1.4 million in 1932.

The loss of premium revenue, of course, reflected the slowdown in general business, with marine insurance hardest hit by the contraction of world trade. The rise in the loss ratio was attributable not to any spectacular losses in these years but to the rapid multiplication of small claims that companies would not have bothered to file in more affluent times. North America, for example, paid one claim for 50 cents to place a patch on a pair of overalls burned when the policyholder sat on a lighted cigarette. It cost the company $7 in postage, stationery, and labor—the same cost as settling a $12,000 loss.

STEPPED-UP GROWTH FOR PENSION FUNDS · The great expansion of private pension plans did not come until World War II, when wage and price controls made the extension of pension benefits one of the few means open to management to recruit and retain scarce labor. The imposition of heavy corporate taxes, especially on excess profits, also acted as an incentive by greatly lowering the cost of establishing and operating retirement plans; for a company in the higher tax brackets, each dollar put into a pension fund cost the firm only 20 cents.

As a consequence, the assets of noninsured pension plans vaulted from $1.1 billion in 1940 to $5.2 billion in 1950. Similarly, the number of pension plans (including insured plans) multiplied sixfold from fewer than 2,000 in 1940 to 12,300 a decade later. At the same time, the number of workers covered under private pension programs, excluding about 1.5 million railroad employees protected by the government-sponsored Railroad Retirement System, increased from 3.7 million to 8.6 million. The fact that the number of pension plans grew much more quickly than the number of workers suggests that the pension idea was becoming diffused among increasing numbers of smaller companies, a sign that the innovation was a success.

By comparison, private pension fund growth was considerably slower in the thirties. The number of plans more than doubled between 1930 and 1940, from 720 to 1,965, while coverage was extended to an additional 1.3 million workers (from 2.4 to 3.7 million). Nevertheless, as late as 1937 fewer than 15 percent of the labor force was covered by some kind of retirement scheme. Moreover, the distribution of this coverage was very uneven: virtually 100 percent in some industries (communications) and virtually none in other sectors (agriculture and retailing).

Various forces interacted to spur the growth of pension plans (and group annuities, in particular) in the thirties, a development that otherwise would surely have slowed in the wake of mass unemployment and sharply diminished profits.

Management could no longer be wholly insensitive to the problems of the unemployed. With millions out of work and with little or nothing for these people to fall back on, it became increasingly evident that the retirement of older workers was preferable to the firing of workers with young families to care for. This situation, in turn, brought the whole problem of the superannuated to the fore and caused many companies to think seriously of establishing some kind of retirement program. Moreover, it was widely believed that progress in this direction was necessary in order to forestall "socialistic" old-age pension legislation.

Ironically, in view of all the fears to the contrary, the passage of the Social Security Act in 1935 was to provide a major stimulus to the growth of private pensions. The long and heated discussion surrounding the act brought the problem of the aged to the public's attention, thereby dramatizing the need for retirement benefits. Individuals who had formerly not considered the subject at all realized that the pensions provided under the Social Security Act would be inadequate to meet the needs of retired workers. Private pension plans, instead of fading away, were seen as fulfilling an essential role in providing for the security of the aged. Indeed, the establishment of social insurance programs by the government seemed to increase the public's appetite for additional protection.

Along with a growing recognition of the importance of pensions came the realization that earlier pension arrangements had been woefully unsatisfactory and that new arrangements would have to be developed.

Up to the thirties, most pension plans were conducted on a more or less informal basis. Almost all were noncontributory (the cost was carried by the firm), mainly to keep control in the hands of management, a fact that led union leaders to oppose vigorously employer-sponsored retirement programs, especially since these programs were often started to inhibit unionization.

In any case, the handling of the program, and even the decision as to who was to receive a pension, was usually left to managerial discretion. But no matter what the sponsorship, nearly all private pension schemes were operated without adequate funding arrangements.

As a matter of fact, it was common practice in the twenties to pay the pensions of retired workers out of current revenues—that is, as a normal operating expense. And even where reserve accounts were set up for future benefit payments, the funds were not segregated but were often plowed back into the firm or invested in the company's stock. In most cases, too, such "reserves" as were set up were not based on sound actuarial principles.

These practices, like many other things, could go unnoticed in the prosperous twenties. Moreover, since most pension plans were relatively new, the number of retiring employees was likely to be small, thus minimizing the cash outflow. The sharp decline in business, however, fully revealed the inadequacy of these financial arrangements. As a result, restrictive adjustments in the pension provisions were found necessary to keep some plans alive. Other plans simply were disbanded, while everywhere there was pressure to make the plans contributory.

The same kinds of problems were faced by union-sponsored pension programs, where the funding provisions were equally unsound. In 1935, for example, the International Typographical Union increased its assessment rate on active-members' pay by 133 percent in order to maintain its $8 a week pension program on a pay-as-you-go basis.

Insured pension plans, by contrast, proved much better able to cope with the depression. Corporations employing a group annuity plan were required not only to set aside funds but also to pay these funds over to the insurance company that underwrote the program. The total of these payments, moreover, was actuarially calculated to be adequate to pay the retirement benefits provided under the plan. Finally, the entire assets of the insurance underwriter were available to guarantee the solvency of the company's plan. As a result of these advantages, almost all the expansion of private pension plans in the late thirties was reflected in the growth of group annuities. Group annuities were first written by Metropolitan in 1921 and later by Equitable in 1924. As late as 1930, however, gross premiums on group annuities amounted to only $25 million. The mushrooming of insured pension programs in the thirties, however, succeeded in raising the premium income on group annuities to $128 million in 1940.

Most important, the growth of insured retirement programs, together with World War II and postwar expansion of fully funded self-administered plans, allowed pension plans to assume positions of importance in the financial markets. As long as pension funds did not set aside reserves (for investment in primary securities) and operated on an informal basis, paying benefits out of current income, they were not performing a true intermediary role but were simply acting to redistribute income. The establishment of a group annuity (or a properly funded self-administered plan), on the other hand, clearly called for the accumulation and investment of savings.

SUMMARY · For most financial intermediaries, the thirties became a period of retrenchment, a time to take in sail and to map out new courses to follow. Except for credit unions and pension funds, which thrived, most intermediaries attempted to weather the storm by retreating under the umbrella of conservatism. Mutual savings banks, to take an extreme example, all but ceased to function in the private credit markets. Most other intermediaries followed in varying degree by placing large portions of their resources in federal government securities and cash. Only gradually, as recovery set in and the shock of failure became dulled, did many financial institutions begin to resume their more traditional activities.

Few institutions could have seriously considered returning to the ways of the twenties. But for any that did have such yearnings, the road back was effectively blocked by government regulations and private sanctions that together substantially altered the business environment. To some extent, what legislation did was to make binding and more permanent the lessons already taught by the depression. In other areas, such as deposit insurance, legislation went far beyond the corrective measures the financial community was prepared to accept. In general, the reforms put into effect in the thirties were beneficial, lessening as they did the chance of a repeat of the kinds of excesses that preceded the collapse and of the responses to it. At the same time, efforts at reform were occasionally overdone. A tendency to confuse institutional practices with behavior sometimes led to corrective legislation that was to circumscribe severely the flexibility of financial institutions in responding to new challenges. Nevertheless, the federal government, aided and encouraged by public opinion, assumed the major innovative role in the thirties, thus setting the stage for the innovations that financial intermediaries were themselves to initiate in the post-World War II decades.

9 · the revival of innovation, 1945–1970

Following the general trend of the economy, financial intermediaries experienced remarkable progress in the quarter-century after World War II. It was a time of striking innovation, leading, in turn, to sharply intensified competition among financial institutions. Whatever advantages relative specialization may once have offered, they were now being heavily discounted, while the advantages of diversification were being widely touted. The result was an unprecedented explosion of multidimensional financial intermediaries capable of providing an increasing variety of financial services, either directly or through affiliates. As in the twenties, innovation was not spontaneous. It was necessitated by changes in the pace and structure of the economy that facilitated a rapid growth of pension funds, investment companies, and savings and loan associations but a much slower growth of such older-type intermediaries as life insurance companies and commercial banks.

ECONOMIC GROWTH IN THE
FIFTIES AND SIXTIES · Although the growth patterns of individual financial institutions varied substantially, all took sustenance from the economy's sustained expansion. Financial institutions fed on the growth of population and income, on stepped-up investment spending and the enhancement of heavy industry, and on migration from the farm to the city and suburbia. All these phenomena appeared with greater intensity in the years after World War II.

What was most remarkable about the era was the absence of serious depression such as had occurred in the past. To be sure, there were occasional setbacks, but these were relatively mild and soon overcome. Consequently, the rate of economic advance outstripped anything in the country's previous history. In the years after 1945, gross national product increased from approximately $200 billion to over $900 billion, or at a rate of over 6 percent a year. Part of this increase, indeed a substantial part, was obliterated by price inflation, and the expansion was further diluted by population increases that considerably exceeded what had happened in the 1920s and 1930s. Nevertheless, for the elusive "average American," postwar prosperity meant a substantial increase in economic well-being as per capita real disposable income rose from about $1,650 to $2,500.

The growth of income, as in the past, derived largely from gains in productivity. Between 1947 and 1970, private output more than doubled although labor input rose only slightly. In turn, more productivity reflected

213

a faster growth of capital inputs, technological progress, and an upgrading of the labor force to more skilled and better-paying jobs.

Accelerated gains in productivity contributed importantly to the structural changes that took place within the economy. Nowhere was this fact better illustrated than in the case of the vanishing farmer. His output per man-hour more than tripled, rising much faster than the output of the other sectors of the economy. It seemed as though the farmer was in a mad rush to produce himself out of existence, for by 1967 fewer than 11 million people—only one out of twenty—lived on farms, compared with 24 million at the end of the war.

Following the trend that began earlier in the century, the exodus from the farm coincided with a sharp increase in white-collar employment. Technological advances greatly reduced the need for labor to attend to machines while enormously increasing the need for supervisory, technical, and office personnel. In 1947 nearly two-thirds of the labor force were employed in the production of "things"; by the midsixties only about two-fifths were so engaged while the rest were employed in white-collar or service occupations. For our purposes, this occupational transformation was of much more than passing importance because every shift from primary production to tertiary production—that is, from processing goods to providing services—adds to the business activity of financial intermediaries.

SAVING, INVESTMENT, AND DEBT · The unprecedented boom in production and income produced an equally unprecedented boom in the dollar volume of saving and the dollar volume of debt. Gross saving in the first years after World War II was approximately $30 billion a year; by 1968 it had increased to approximately $200 billion. Personal saving, ranging from 5 to 7 percent of disposable income, did not vary nearly as much as the saving of other sectors.

The pattern of household saving differed sharply from what had taken place in the 1920s. Then, partly as a result of the stock market craze, somewhat over half of the net increase in household financial assets comprised securities purchased directly in the credit markets. In the midfifties, as can be seen from Table 18, this share fell to below 20 percent, whereas in the midsixties it dwindled to about 3 percent of household financial savings. Virtually all the remainder flowed through financial intermediaries.

One result was the growing institutionalization of the credit markets, particularly the market for corporate securities. Reversing the trend of the twenties, some investment banking houses began withdrawing from the retail market, especially in smaller cities, to concentrate on servicing institutional investors. In 1965 financial institutions accounted for one-third of the total share volume on the New York Stock Exchange, while individuals accounted for less than half the total. Certainly this reversal did not mean that equities had lost their charm—the generous rise in stock prices[1] ensured as much—but that the public increasingly chose to

---

[1] The New York Stock Exchange Index closed at 10.67 in 1945, at 23.71 in 1955, and at 58.90 in 1968.

TABLE 18
Net Acquisitions of Financial Assets by the Household Sector, 1946–1968
(Billions of Dollars)

Acquisition	1946–1950	1951–1955	1956–1960	1961–1965	1966–1968
Indirect Securities					
Demand deposits plus currency	$ 1.6	$ 8.1	$ 2.4	$ 21.3	$ 30.2
Savings accounts					
At commercial banks	5.2	10.8	18.4	45.9	42.6
At savings institutions	11.8	27.6	41.0	68.3	36.6
Life insurance reserves	15.3	13.9	15.1	20.4	14.3
Pension fund reserves	13.6	22.9	36.1	50.2	43.3
Total	$47.5	$83.3	$113.0	$206.1	$167.0
Primary Securities (less net investment in non-incorporated business)					
U.S. government securities	$ 1.6	$ 0.2	$ 3.0	$ 7.6	$ 10.2
State and local obligations	2.0	5.5	8.0	7.1	3.6
Corporate and foreign bonds	—3.3	0.0	2.4	—3.2	6.6
Corporate stock	4.7	6.0	5.5	—5.4	—12.5
Mortgages	2.4	1.5	2.5	—1.6	— 1.0
Total	$ 7.4	$13.2	$ 21.4	$ 4.5	$ 6.9
Net investment in non-incorporated businesses	$12.0	$ 1.0	—$ 13.1	—$ 26.6	—$ 24.6

Source: Board of Governors of the Federal Reserve System, *Flow of funds; Federal Reserve Bulletin.*

make its acquisitions indirectly through pension funds and mutual funds.

As in any boom, debt careened upward at the same dizzy pace set by saving. In 1945 the national debt totaled somewhat less than $500 billion, of which the federal government owed half. By 1968 total debt was over $1.5 trillion, but now the federal government owed less than one-quarter.

SHIFTS IN THE IMPORTANCE OF THE
DIFFERENT INTERMEDIARIES · The increase of over $1 trillion in debt, the accumulation of $200 billion in savings, and the fact that security purchases were increasingly made through institutions more than encouraged the expansion of financial intermediaries. Table 19 shows that their total assets grew from approximately $125 billion in 1940 to over $1 trillion in 1967, outstripping the growth of population, income, and all other economic indexes. By 1965 financial institutions were supplying 85 percent of the horde of funds raised in the credit markets compared to about 75 percent of the much smaller credit pool of the 1950s.

All the intermediaries did not grow at the same pace, however. Pensions, investment companies, and credit unions grew at a seemingly impossible rate. Pensions multiplied 70 times; investment companies, 45 times; and credit unions, 40 times. In 1940 commercial banks, life insurance companies, and mutual savings banks were the giants among the intermediaries. Savings and loan associations and general insurance companies, about equal in size, were far behind the leaders, and the other intermediaries were pygmies. By 1955 this picture had changed. Savings and loan associations had rapidly overtaken the savings banks, and the gap between the giants and the pygmies had diminished considerably.

By 1967 the share of commercial banks and life insurance companies, 55 and 25 percent in 1940, had dropped to 45 and 20 percent. Mutual savings banks, in third place in 1940 with 10 percent of intermediary assets, had fallen to fifth place with only 6 percent of total assets.

TABLE 19
Assets of Selected Financial Intermediaries, 1940–1967
(in Billions of Dollars)

Intermediary	1940	1950	1955	1960	1965	1967
Commercial banks	$ 67.8	$169.9	$211.8	$258.4	$378.9	$ 454.6
Mutual savings banks	11.9	22.4	31.3	40.6	58.2	66.4
Savings and loan associations	5.7	16.9	37.7	71.5	129.6	143.6
Life insurance companies	30.8	64.0	90.4	119.6	158.9	177.8
General insurance companies	5.1	13.2	21.8	29.4	41.8	46.6
Noninsured, private pensions	1.0	6.5	16.1	33.1	58.1	71.8
Investment companies	1.0	3.4	9.0	18.8	35.2	44.7
Credit unions	0.3	1.0	2.7	5.7	11.6	12.9
Total	$123.6	$297.3	$420.8	$577.1	$872.3	$1,018.4

Source: Federal Reserve Board, Social Security Administration, National Association of Investment Companies, Insurance Information Institute, Federal Home Loan Bank, Bureau of Federal Credit Unions.

The most important reason for the growth of intermediation was the diffusion of expanding income, which created a large class of small savers. For this group, the most important considerations were liquidity and safety of principal, needs that traditionally were best satisfied by financial institutions rather than by direct investment. The difficulty of access to primary markets, the relatively large size required for individual transactions, and the comparatively high costs involved in effecting small transactions all contributed to the average investor's preference for institutional savings. Two other factors enhanced the stability of such savings flows: first, much of the saving channeled into financial institutions—pension funds and life insurance companies for example—was contractual and thus relatively unaffected by short-term fluctuations in incomes and interest rates; second, the reforms put into effect during the Great Depression made institutional saving even more desirable to the small saver seeking liquidity and safety.

THE REVIVAL OF MONETARY POLICY · Prosperity not only injected the financial intermediaries with extraordinary vigor, but it also brought money back into the center of the economic stage. In the process of rejuvenation, monetary policy regained most, if not all, the prestige it had lost as a result of the depression and World War II.

The downgrading of monetary policy in the thirties reflected widespread disenchantment with the Federal Reserve's seeming inability to initiate recovery. It was generally conceded that monetary policy was weak as a stimulant to recovery, whatever powers it might have in halting expansion.

The war relegated monetary policy to further obscurity. When the United States became involved and it became clear that large government borrowings would be required, the Treasury determined that the level of interest rates should be kept low in order to minimize the service cost on the debt. The Treasury further determined to keep short-term rates substantially below longer-term rates, for it was realized that short-term issues had special appeal for commercial banks. Although the Federal Reserve System expressed its disagreement with the Treasury's decision to peg interest rates, it was overruled. In April 1942 the Reserve Banks took the enormous step of guaranteeing to buy all Treasury bills at 3/8 of 1 percent and bonds at 2½ percent. By pegging interest rates in this fashion, the System made Treasury securities almost the same as money, thereby giving up control of the money supply as well as of interest rates. Whenever the commercial banks needed additional reserves to support growing deposits and expanding currency, they simply sold bills to the Federal Reserve System. Thus the whole process added enormously to the liquidity of the economy and provided the fuel to feed inflation.

At the end of the war, the Treasury was calling the tune to which the monetary authorities were reluctantly dancing. But once war financing had definitely become a thing of the past, the Fed bent its efforts to throwing off Treasury control and regaining the independence it thought it had once possessed.

Looking back on the experiences of the 1920s, the Treasury read in them a conviction that the high-interest rates permitted to occur in that period had unncessarily raised the cost of government, had depressed the bond market, and had destroyed business confidence, thereby creating the severe depression of 1920–1921. The Treasury had no faith in monetary policy and believed that the only way of preventing a repetition of the economic collapse of the early twenties was to keep interest rates from rising too precipitately.

The monetary authorities had little sympathy for the Treasury's view. They believed that keeping interest rates low required a constant infusion of reserves into the banking system, which meant that the Fed had become "an engine of inflation." The Korean War intensified their belief. Although the war entailed the most ambitious effort ever made to put a military campaign on a pay-as-you-go basis, price inflation did occur, although it was surprisingly short-lived. The Fed argued that it could check the inflationary movement by cutting down on bank reserves but that it was prevented from doing so by the Treasury's intransigence on the interest rate question. The quarrel, however, was not over whether the peg should be pulled out but the speed with which it should be pulled. Once the conflict burst into the open in early 1951, it could no longer be politically tolerated. The Truman administration resolved it by the Accord of March 4, 1951, which was considered a victory for the monetary authorities even though the administration's sympathies were with the Treasury.

By the Accord, the Treasury and the Federal Reserve Board jointly announced that they had reached "full accord with respect to debt management and monetary policies to be pursued in furthering their common purpose to assure the successful financing of the government's requirements and . . . to minimize monetization of the public debt." No matter whose victory it was, the Accord did not mean a complete return to a free market nor the end of the policy of supporting the government bond market, for the Open Market Committee did agree to maintain "an orderly market" for government securities. What the Accord meant was less dominance by the Treasury, more freedom of action for the Fed, especially over the long run, and possibly more power for monetary policy.

THE PHILOSOPHY AND OBJECTIVES OF THE
FEDERAL RESERVE SYSTEM · The philosophy of the monetary authorities in the 1950s did not differ significantly from that of the 1920s. It was undoubtedly more sophisticated and the labels were different, but the philosophy and behavior were much the same. In the 1920s the Federal Reserve System rejected the implications of the quantity theory of money and refused, in its famous 1923 Annual Report, to accept the conclusions of Professor Irving Fisher, the leading quantity theorist of the day. The Fed concluded at that time that no direct relationship existed between the money stock and the price level and that the monetary authorities were, therefore, unable to regulate prices, even assuming that they could control the money supply. They asserted that their objective should be to encourage legitimate business expansion and to discourage speculative expansion.

Much the same philosophy prevailed in the 1950s. The System once again rejected the quantity theory, although this time it came in Professor Milton Friedman's revised version, which placed more emphasis on the relation of the money supply to income than on its relation to prices. Once again, too, there was an undertone of laissez faire. The Reserve Board turned a frigid ear to suggestions that the nonbank intermediaries should also be regulated inasmuch as they were just as important as the commercial banks in the credit-creating process. The Board also seemed intent on establishing "a more self-reliant market," thus giving some people the impression that it wished to be an objective observer rather than an active regulator. As Governor William McChesney Martin, Chairman of the Board, stated it, the System's objective was to "lean against the breezes of inflation and deflation alike."

Before long it appeared that the monetary authorities were more sensitive to the winds of inflation than to the winds of deflation. The belief of many Americans that creeping inflation was an unavoidable and not too tragic condition of modern life was viewed by Martin and many of his colleagues as a pernicious doctrine. On the contention that there is no such thing as a controllable inflation, the System switched its emphasis from "preventing corrections" to "moderating" them. This attitude, of course, did not mean that growth with full employment was to be wholly sacrificed to price stability. Nevertheless, the System seemed constantly haunted by the specter of "unsustainable growth" and an "overheated economy." Consequently, when the requirements of the two objectives of growth and stability seemed in conflict, as was frequently the case, the System's sympathies seemed to lie with first stopping inflation. As Chairman Martin stated early in 1954, "Surely it would be the height of folly to ride the witch's broomstick of inflation to the inevitable crash."

This admittedly oversimplified analysis should not lead the reader to the false assumption that all those who took part in formulating monetary policy agreed completely with the philosophy just described. Almost everyone who expressed an opinion had misgivings about some aspect of Federal Reserve policy. There was no unanimity with regard to either the purpose or the function of the rediscount rate. Nor did everyone see eye to eye on the policy of minimum interference with the market. But the widest disagreement existed over the objectives that were to guide policy. Most of those within the System thought in terms of free reserves and interest rates, but a minority argued that the money supply should be the focal point. These differences of opinion were not totally ineffective. Federal Reserve policy in the 1950s was not altogether rigid and unbending. It did undergo some alteration as a result of the give and take of discussion, the lessons of experience, barbs from outside critics, changes in the domestic and international economic environment, and, to some extent at least, the election returns.

FEDERAL RESERVE OPERATIONS · Federal Reserve operations in money and credit markets varied a great deal during the 1950s and 1960s, which was to be expected of a system whose objective was to lean against the wind and whose powers were more discretionary than objective. For purposes of simplification and generalization, the two decades can be divided into six subperiods, all of which occurred as a reaction to recession and inflation. Figure 2 pictures what happened to the money supply and prices in these six periods, and Figure 3 shows what happened to interest rates.

The Korean episode, of course, dominated the early 1950s. The Fed followed a policy of "credit restraint" that was characterized by rising interest rates and falling reserves. At the same time, however, the money supply expanded rapidly and only began to decline when Korea was almost over.

The second stage opened in the spring of 1953 when the Fed reacted to the mild post-Korean recession. Starting off in low key with a policy designed "to avoid deflationary tendencies without encouraging a renewal of inflationary developments," it soon moved up the scale, and by

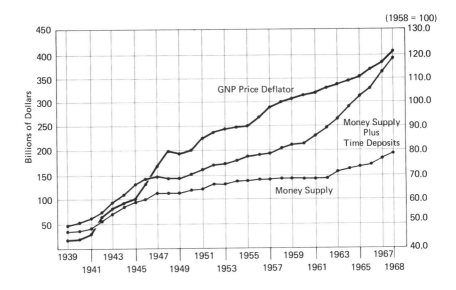

Figure 2
Money Supply and Prices, 1939–1968.

Sources: *Economic Report of the President, 1969*, and U.S. Department of Commerce, *Long Term Economic Growth, 1860–1965.*

the fall when its theme was "active ease," the Board had reduced the rediscount rate slightly and reserve requirements sharply while pouring some $700 million into bank reserves by open-market purchases. The money supply in these 19 months expanded by over 4 percent.

The third period of the 1950s saw the first alarm over inflation and "unsustainable growth." In the first few months of recovery in 1955, the Fed moved slowly under a policy that would "foster growth and stability" while "encouraging recovery and avoiding unsustainable expansion." But by August it had decided that "restraint was clearly appropriate," and it continued in this vein until November 1957, some three months after recovery had passed its peak. Rediscount rates were raised, open-market operations pushed free reserves into a negative position, and the money supply stood still.

The third recession of the post-World War II period occurred in the summer of 1957, and with it came another reversal, albeit belatedly, in Federal Reserve policy. In November 1957 the Fed moved "to foster sustainable growth . . . without inflation, by moderating the pressure on bank reserves." In the following seven months, it again reduced reserve requirements and the rediscount rate and bought some securities in the open market. Free reserves again ran up, long-term interest rates were down slightly, short-term rates were emphatically down, and the money supply was up sharply from its low point in January 1958.

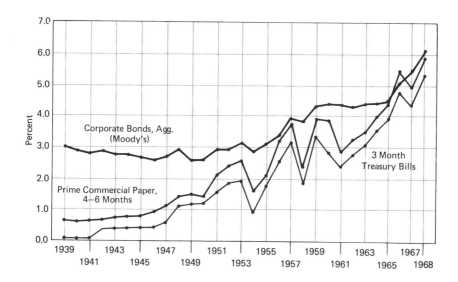

Figure 3
Selected Interest Rates, 1939–1968

Source: *Economic Report of the President, 1969.*

Whether monetary policy or a huge government deficit in fiscal 1958–1959 accomplished the trick or not, the economy recovered in the spring of 1958. The Fed slowly shifted into stage five. Beginning in August 1958 and continuing to May 1960, it acted to keep recovery from becoming overheated. Monetary policy was tight by any yardstick. The rediscount rate was raised from 1¾ to 4 percent. Activities in the open market and Congressional amendments to reserve requirements partially offset each other, but with the help of a steady outflow of gold, free reserves ran down to minus $550 million. Interest rates climbed to over 4 percent, and the money supply declined at an annual rate of almost 3 percent. Yet, it took almost a year to break the boom, but broken it was.

The recession of 1960 accomplished a major shift in monetary policy. Cynics insisted that the Federal Reserve Board, like the Supreme Court, followed the election returns. But whatever the reason, monetary policy in the 1960s veered away from the previous fears of inflation toward a more sympathetic attitude to easy money.

What happened was best illustrated by the behavior of the money supply. Demand deposits adjusted and currency in the hands of the public rose at an annual rate of 3 percent in 1951–1955, 1 percent in 1956–1960, and 2.9 percent between 1960 and 1965. But between mid-1965 and early 1966, it zoomed ahead at a 6 percent rate. Then in 1967 and 1968 it climbed at almost 7 percent.

However, the new policy did not run any more smoothly than the old one. Moreover, the new policy was featured by at least one violent shift from easy to tight to easy money. In 1966 rising interest rates and a new outburst of price inflation caused the Federal Reserve to reverse its easy-money policy radically. The money supply actually declined in late 1966 after having increased at a rate of speed rarely equaled except in time of war. The result in 1966 was a "credit crunch," which made some alarmists fear that there would not be enough money to go around. But these fears were dissipated when the money supply again began to expand at an unusually high rate.

Again in late 1968, in the midst of another extraordinary surge in prices and interest rates, the Fed reverted to a tighter money policy and cut the rate of increase in the money supply in half.

THE CRITICS OF THE FEDERAL RESERVE · In the half-century of its existence, monetary policy has had an excitingly rocky career. The audience has blown hot and cold, heaping at one moment extravagant praise and in the next a barrage of patronizing criticism. In the 1920s it had not been easy to steer a storm-free course through the narrow channel that separated legitimate business expansion from speculation. Yet the prestige of monetary policy reached its zenith in the 1920s. It then sank to an all-time low during the depression, recovered strongly between the end of World War II and the Accord of 1951, and then met a rising tide of skepticism as it became apparent that in navigating by leaning against the winds of inflation and deflation, it was impossible to avoid hitting numerous reefs and floundering on numerous shoals.

One of the little ironies of economics is that criticism of the makers of monetary policy—the Federal Reserve System—varies more or less in inverse proportion to the prestige of the product they are molding. In the 1920s the financial literature abounded in articles and speeches that called attention to the error of the System's ways. But there was little of this attitude in the depression, when the belief prevailed that monetary policy could accomplish very little. As the 1950s and 1960s passed into history, criticism of the Fed became steadily more vehement as the conviction grew that money and monetary policy not only mattered but mattered very much. Champions of easy money criticized the System for too much and too early. Proponents of tight money champed over policies that they thought came too little and too late; and those in the middle criticized the Fed for both faults.

In the 1920s, many people assumed that when Senator Carter Glass *et al.* wrote the Federal Reserve Act, they had put an end to the business cycle. The disenchanting experience of the depression of the 1930s changed that view, but only temporarily. Some innocence returned in the 1950s. Once again, some people believed that if only the monetary magicians would put their minds to it, they could manipulate the economy so as to produce maximum growth without inflation. Those who were responsible for monetary policy did not share this roseate view. Indeed, some of them took pleasure in downgrading the Fed's powers. At the very least, they were well aware that monetary policy could not work miracles, and they took great pains to point out the obstacles in the way. They protested that they could not do the job without the aid of fiscal policy. They also warned that monetary techniques were not overly effective in fighting inflation that was caused by pressure from the cost side. Nor could they deal satisfactorily and successfully with unemployment that was structural in nature. These caveats elicited sympathy, but they did not eliminate doubts as to the effectiveness of monetary policy or answer criticism of how it was being administered.

A more or less ubiquitous conviction that monetary policy offered little or no hope in a period of recession or depression had always existed. But the late fifties gave rise to mounting skepticism as to its effectiveness in periods of prosperity and inflation. Those who were dubious about monetary policy and those who were critical of the Federal Reserve fell into four main groups: the defeatists, the unreconstructed conservatives, those who found fault with the System's technique, and the critics of timing. First of all, there were those who believed that the institutional framework of the modern economy had reduced monetary policy to impotence. According to one line of reasoning, full employment and free collective bargaining inevitably produced rising prices, which the monetary authorities could squelch but only at the cost of recession or depression. Another group in the same school argued that the central bank's ability to neutralize inflationary pressures was fatally weakened by the existence of a large, highly liquid public debt and by the increased importance in the credit market of financial intermediaries and large corporations. When the Federal Reserve tried to tighten money, the commercial banks could increase their reserves simply by letting their short-term governments run out. But even if the banks were restrained, would-be borrowers could obtain funds from the financial intermediaries and from trade credit made available by corporations. The efforts to thwart inflation were consequently stymied before they began. What actually happened during the years after 1953 gave plausibility to this line of reasoning. For tight money or not, prices advanced throughout the period.

The skeptics just mentioned were basically sympathetic to the Federal Reserve System as well as to monetary policy. A second school of critics objected in principle to the whole concept of monetary policy. They believed that the money market should be regulated by the impersonal forces of the marketplace and not by a group who, being human, would certainly make mistakes that would have immense consequences on the whole economy. Those who argued for regulation by rule and not by men proposed that the money supply be advanced in step with the potential growth of the national product, but historians pointed out that something similar to this "neutral money" had been tried and was found wanting in the late twenties.

The monetarists who put their faith in a marketplace philosophy were in the minority in the 1950s, when most economists were still not convinced that money and the money supply were all that important. The fifties was a period of disappointing economic growth, and most economists were still putting most of their faith in fiscal policy—that is, tax reduction, increased government spending, and budgetary deficits—as a means of invigorating the GNP. Remembering the 1930s, when an apparently easy-money monetary policy seemed to have been ineffective in alleviating the depression, they still believed wholeheartedly in the axiom: "You can't push a string."

But the so-called monetarists were not without influence even in the citadel they aimed at destroying. And as the 1960s proceeded, the misgivings about the importance of money and the criticisms that had been so frequently leveled at the administration of monetary policy faded into the background. The foreground was increasingly occupied by skepticism regarding man-guided monetary policy. By the late 1960s, when price inflation had replaced lagging economic growth in the hierarchy of economic problems, the monetarists—those who believed that money, especially the money supply, was immensely important—had achieved a prestige that only a foolhardy optimist would have predicted a decade before.

THE DECLINING FORTUNES OF
COMMERCIAL BANKING · The commercial banking system underwent a more profound change in the post-World War II decades, especially after the late 1950s, than any other financial intermediary. In a sense, the changes marked a continuation and extension of the kinds of innovations begun in the twenties. But as a result of better safeguards, the more recent extensive and far-reaching innovations took place without the unfortunate consequences that followed similar experimentation in the twenties.

Throughout the fifties, the commercial banks continued to lose ground to other and newer types of financial intermediaries. In 1950 the commercial banks held almost 60 percent of all intermediary assets; by 1960 their share had fallen to 45 percent. During the 1960s, this trend toward a declining share for commercial banking slowed down considerably. In 1967 commercial banks still held 45 percent of all assets. As in the 1920s, the pace and character of innovation within the banking system followed in response to the growth of competition in the various financial markets where commercial banks had established roles. As a result of successful innovation, commercial banks were once more experiencing rapid growth by the late 1960s, inhibited only by the restrictive credit policy pursued by the monetary authority in their efforts to stop inflation.

The secular rise in interest rates that characterized the prosperous fifties and, even more, the soaring sixties, along with the spirited competition of savings banks and savings and loan associations, lessened the public's demand for money balances (demand deposits and currency). Much the same thing, of course, had happened in the twenties, but then the trend was in its early stages. In the 1950s and 1960s the urge to economize on cash, partly through the substitution of near-money assets, became widespread. The cash management practices in effect at General Motors in the 1920s were commonplace in American business by the late 1950s, and in the process new techniques had been added. As a result, the demand-deposit liabilities of commercial banks showed very little increase over the postwar years, rising from about $90 billion at the end of 1947 to a little over $150 billion at the end of 1967, a gain of less than 3 percent a year.

The flow-of-funds accounts show even more clearly the public's declining preference for money balances. The rise in demand deposit and currency holdings of nonfinancial corporations, from $23.5 billion to $27.9 billion between 1947 and 1967, was minuscule compared with the nearly fourfold increase in this sector's holdings of total financial assets, which climbed from $83.5 billion to $322.7 billion. Similarly, the money balances of the household sector increased from $57.6 billion to only $96.9 billion, while its total financial assets soared from $371.2 billion to $1,618.2 billion.

The postwar decline in the demand for money coincided with a sharp and sustained rise in the income velocity of money, which more than doubled (from 2.07 to 4.27) between 1947 and 1967. Transactions velocity (which includes financial transactions as well as the purchase of goods and services) increased at a faster rate than income velocity.

For the commercial banks, what was happening produced a great headache, for it entailed an enormous increase in bookkeeping but little growth in their intermediary function. The activization of idle balances and the increased turnover of already active balances did not, to be sure, lead to an outflow of deposits from the banking system. However, it did imply two things: first, that other institutions—for example, savings and loan associations—enhanced their capacity to make new loans and investments; and second, that part of the short-term credits provided by commercial banks would be extended directly by holders of redundant money balances.

In the twenties the banks had met the problem by expanding their time and savings deposit business. But in the new era they did not show a similar willingness to compete aggressively for time deposit funds until the late 1950s. Corporate time deposits continued to be discouraged, partly on the assumption that their expansion would be at the expense of demand deposit balances. Behind this practice, of course, was the feeling that interest-bearing time deposits were less profitable than noninterest-bearing demand deposits. The argument was irrelevant, for the real choice was not between demand deposit growth and time deposit growth but between time deposit growth and no growth. Until the banks began to see the matter in this way, corporation time deposits showed almost no change, rising from $900 million at the end of 1947 to $1.5 billion at the end of 1959. The growth of savings deposits from $31.9 billion to $50.5 billion between 1947 and 1957 was even more disappointing, given the spectacular growth of the savings and loan associations, whose shares multiplied from just under $10 billion to over $40 billion over the same period. Even the mutual savings banks came out better than the commercial banks, managing to increase their deposits from $17.8 billion to $31.7 billion.

Some commercial banks, chiefly those in the large cities, were prevented from acting more aggressively in the savings market by the interest rate ceiling imposed by the Federal Reserve, under Regulation Q on commercial bank time and savings deposits. From 1936 through 1956 the maximum rate was 2.5 percent, which was altogether out of line with money market rates as well as with the rates paid on competing deposit-type claims. Nevertheless, not all banks were feeling the pinch of Regulation Q, for as late as 1956 the average rate paid by member banks on time and savings deposits was only 1.5 percent.

The rise in the Regulation Q ceiling to 3 percent at the beginning of 1957 narrowed the spread between the rates paid by commercial banks and their institutional competitors. Partly as a result, deposit growth at commercial banks accelerated while growth of savings and loans slowed down. Between 1953 and 1956, savings and loan deposits grew four times faster than commercial bank deposits, compared to a rate only twice as fast over the succeeding four-year period.

COMMERCIAL BANK INNOVATION · There was much more to the commercial banking revolution of the 1960s than a willingness on the part of banks to engage in price competition. Although competition was an essential ingredient, the innovations occurring with great rapidity in the sixties were even more important. The banks brought back from the remote past deposit-type claims designed to have appeal to special submarkets. The most significant was the negotiable certificate of deposit (CD), aimed for the most part at halting the outflow of corporate deposits from commercial banks into investment in various money market instruments, such as Treasury bills, commercial paper, and bankers acceptances. As such, the negotiable CD represented a clear break with the traditional practice at many banks of discouraging or refusing corporate time deposits.

Certificates of deposit were known long before 1961, when the leading New York City banks announced that henceforth they would issue such instruments to both corporate and noncorporate customers and a leading government securities dealer indicated that it would maintain a secondary market in CDs. The amount of outstanding CDs at the end of 1960, however, was only slightly in excess of $1 billion. By the end of 1967 they had grown to more than $20 billion. As these figures might imply, negotiable CDs, issued mostly to corporations (in denominations of $100,000 or more), increased much faster than other types of time and savings deposits, rising from only 1.5 percent of the total to more than 11 percent. For the large city banks, CDs have played a much greater role, accounting for 20 percent of time and savings deposits and nearly 10 percent of all deposits. The appeal of negotiable CDs to corporate money managers lay primarily in their attractive yields (set by the banks, within the limits of Regulation Q, to be competitive with alternative money market instruments), as well as in the marketability feature, which enhanced their liquidity.

Certificates of deposit not only aided the banks in retaining corporate balances but also revolutionized the practice of liquidity management. Traditionally, commercial banks had depended on their short-term assets to meet cash outflows and to satisfy additional credit demands. Now they could satisfy their liquidity needs through an inflow of CD funds induced by small changes in the offering rate, rather than by relying exclusively on the sale of short-term assets. But in the late 1960s, CDs lost this advantage. As interest rates soared, depositors liquidated their certificates to take advantage of the unprecedented rates offered in the nonbank money markets. There is every indication that the commercial banks could have retained their deposits by offering a higher rate, but the ceiling set by Regulation Q effectively prevented them from doing so. Regulation Q, therefore, reduced the lending power of the big city banks by limiting their ability to attract funds; at the same time it protected the thrift institutions against the competition of the commercial banks.

A variety of other innovations in the kinds of claims issued by commercial banks followed the introduction of the negotiable certificate of deposit. The most important of these was the consumer-type CD. Although nonnegotiable and issued in fairly small denominations, such deposits carried higher interest rates than regular passbook accounts. On a much smaller scale, some banks sought to expand lendable funds by issuing subordinated debentures, capital notes, and unsecured short-term promissory notes. The last of these has been classified as a form of time deposit since 1966; the others represent nondeposit-type borrowings that potentially offer distinct advantages to issuing banks. For example, no additional reserves or capital have to be kept against outstanding claims, and greater investment flexibility is often possible because of their relatively long-term nature.

These innovations, especially negotiable and consumer CDs, reflected the commercial banks' willingness to accept lower profit margins in return for faster growth. As a result, between the end of 1961 and the end of 1967, commercial bank time deposits increased by $100 billion, from about $80 billion to $180 billion, while savings and loan shares increased from approximately $70 billion to $125 billion. At the end of 1967, commercial bank time deposits accounted for substantially more than one-half of total deposits, compared with only about one-third in 1957 and slightly over one-quarter in 1947.

The new instruments innovated by the commercial banks enabled them to discriminate between depositors in the payment of interest rates. Stated another way, the introduction of CDs and the various other claims allowed the commercial banks to segment the deposit market in a way not possible before. Instead of meeting competition by raising rates across the board, the banks have been able to effectuate selective rate increases on those categories of deposits most likely to be withdrawn. Compared with other deposit-type intermediaries, commercial banks were in a much better position to bid for funds in the tight credit markets that characterized the last half of the sixties.

FEDERAL FUNDS AND EURODOLLARS · Commercial banks proved to be resourceful in other areas as well, especially in learning to circumvent the restrictive credit policies pursued by the Federal Reserve over much of the postwar period. Two developments stood out as particularly significant: the growth of the federal funds market and the more recent recourse to Eurodollar borrowings by the home offices of money market banks having foreign branches.

Federal funds are deposits of member banks with Federal Reserve Banks. They are usually bought by banks that need to supplement their legal reserves on a temporary basis from other banks that have excess reserves. The existence of a federal funds market, therefore, enables the more effective employment of existing reserves by the banking system.

In the early fifties, perhaps 75 to 100 banks were active in the federal funds market; by the early 1960s this number had grown to between 175 and 275. It is estimated that some 300 additional banks, including some very small banks, trade in federal funds from time to time. In addition, about 30 banks make a market in federal funds, as a convenience to their correspondent customers as well as to take advantage of changes in interest rates. Although the market was originally intended to provide reserves on a temporary basis, a number of banks have turned to it as a permanent source of funds. Both for this reason and because many bankers prefer not to borrow at the discount window, the interest rate on federal funds has in recent years gone substantially above the Federal Reserve discount rate, to which it used to be pegged.

Stringent credit conditions have recently led a number of large commercial banks to obtain Eurodollar loans from their overseas branches. Eurodollars are dollar deposits with foreign banks or with foreign branches of American banks. Such deposits have grown very quickly since the late fifties, partly as a result of continuing United States balance-of-payments deficits. A large portion of these deposits are with the foreign branches of American banks and are therefore available to the home offices at their request. An even more recent innovation along these same lines is the issuance of commercial paper by the nonbanking affiliates of some of the "one-bank holding companies," which have become popular over the last few years, for use in participation loans sponsored by the banking affiliate.

Whether these recent experiments in the mobilization of lendable funds will be permitted to become integral parts of the American banking scene is by no means certain, for they all challenge in some way the Federal Reserve's ability to pursue a restrictive credit policy. Nevertheless, along with the issuance of new deposit-type instruments, they reflect the dynamic spirit that has taken over within the banking system.

CHANGES IN COMMERCIAL BANK ASSETS · Although the innovations on the liability side of the banking system's balance sheet were the most publicized, the changes in asset structure were equally important, reflecting as they did the return to normalcy from the Great Depression and World War II years. As Table 20 shows, the biggest change has been the steady decline in commercial bank holdings of United States government securities. As a result of depression and wartime investments, the commercial banks were in Raymond Goldsmith's words "on the way to becoming holding companies for U.S. government securities. . . ." Indeed, at the end of 1945, government securities constituted about three-fifths of total commercial bank assets. By the end of 1955, however, the share of governments had declined to about one-third, and to less than one-fifth by the end of 1967.

TABLE 20
Selected Commercial Bank Assets, June 30, 1940–1967
(Billions of Dollars)

Asset	1940	1945	1947	1955	1967
Investments	23.8	90.9	79.1	80.1	110.9
U.S. government securities	16.6	84.1	70.5	63.3	54.2
State and local government securities	3.6	3.8	5.0	12.8	46.9
Loans	17.4	23.7	33.7	75.2	224.0
Real estate loans	4.4	4.5	8.3	19.8	55.3
Loans to individuals (other than for real estate and for purchasing or carrying securities)	—	2.2	5.0	16.4	49.5
Total assets	$67.8	$146.2	$147.0	$199.2	$412.1

Source: Board of Governors of the Federal Reserve System, *All-Bank Statistics . . . 1896–1955; Federal Reserve Bulletin.*

The relative and absolute decrease in the government portfolio occurred, of course, as part of the renaissance of commercial bank lending to the private sector. At the end of the war, short-term business loans made up less than 10 percent of bank assets. They increased to over 20 percent by the end of 1955, and to over 30 percent by the end of 1965. But substantial as this recovery was, it nevertheless left short-term loans in a very minority position. Ever since the 1920s, the banking system had been departing from its traditional function of supplying short-term credit. One indication of the magnitude of this departure is the high proportion of term loans to total commercial and industrial loans. For large commercial banks, this share amounted to more than two-fifths in 1968.

The asset categories that increased most rapidly were state and local government securities, consumer loans, and mortgages. Together these groups accounted for only 7 percent of commercial bank assets at the end of the war, but rose to 25 percent at the end of 1955, and to over 35 percent at the end of 1965. The rise in the share of state and local government securities was largely a result of the tax exemption privilege. The sharp increase in consumer and mortgage loans, on the other hand, represented a continuation of the trend in this direction begun in the twenties and signified the further growth of retail banking.

CHANGES IN THE COMMERCIAL
BANKING STRUCTURE · Postwar developments in the area of banking structure similarly suggest a strong continuum with the twenties. Compared with the enormous decline in the number of commercial banks between 1921 and 1933, the decline in the postwar period has been slight (from 14,181 at the end of 1947 to 13,721 at the end of 1967). On the other

hand, the trend toward branch banking continued at a much accelerated pace. Between 1945 and 1965, the number of unit banks fell from 12,889 to 10,664, while the number of branch branks grew nearly threefold, from 1,122 to 3,140. In 1965 nearly 1 out of every 4 commercial banks had one or more branches, compared to only 1 out of every 12 in 1945, and 1 out of every 30 in 1929.

In most retail business, technological advance, especially the introduction and wide use of the automobile, cut down the number of units. That had been the trend in banking in the 1920s, when branch banking was extremely limited, but it was no longer the case in the 1950s. The spread of branching increased the number of bank offices from about 18,000 in 1945 to nearly 30,000 in 1965. Although the number of banks had been cut in half since the early twenties, the number of banking offices was almost the same. It seemed to some observers that growth rather than profit had become the overriding objective of the banking business.

As population and businesses shifted to suburbia and exurbia, city banks felt compelled to follow, and at the same time, where permitted by law, growing suburban banks rushed into the cities. Within urban centers, branch offices also proliferated as banks used the creation of new offices as a major competitive weapon in the struggle for growth and diversification. An increasing interest in consumer loans, real estate loans, and savings deposits, for which proximity to customers is an important condition, further spurred the process. Other factors encouraging branching included the greater ease of obtaining permission to open a new branch than to establish a *de novo* bank and the feasibility of establishing branches in places where new banks could not economically survive.

Banking concentration, which increased greatly in the twenties and thirties mainly as a result of the sharp decline in the number of banks, continued to gain but at less than a snail's pace. Between 1949 and 1964, the one hundred largest banks increased their share of commercial bank deposits from 44.5 percent to 46.3 percent. But whether a rise in banking concentration reduces competition is a moot question. A number of researchers have concluded that a rise in branch banking (which, of course, is related to a rise in concentration) stimulates competition. In any case, although increased concentration, apart from that connected with the rise of branching, does imply some increase in borrowing costs and reduction in interest rates paid to depositors, few have found these perverse effects to be important.

THE PHENOMENAL GROWTH OF SAVINGS
AND LOAN ASSOCIATIONS · Thrift institutions, especially savings and loan associations and credit unions, grew at a rapid pace in the postwar years. Between the end of 1940 and the end of 1967, the assets of savings and loan associations multiplied more than 25 times and came to exceed the total assets of the 15 largest industrial corporations. Credit unions, starting from a much smaller base, did even better, boosting their assets from just $300 million to $12.9 billion. Mutual savings banks, by contrast, grew more slowly, increasing their assets only fivefold.

The growth of savings and loans in the fifties and early sixties was all the more remarkable in light of the troubles they experienced in the thirties, when some 1,700 associations closed their doors. Furthermore, much of their competitive success in the postwar period derived, directly and indirectly, from an almost exclusive attachment to the mortgage market. Just as the near demise of savings and loans in the thirties was partly due to their intense specialization in mortgage financing, the industry's spectacular growth in the years after the war depended on the surging demand for housing and the central role of savings associations as suppliers of mortgage credit—a role that grew enormously as the share of outstanding nonfarm mortgage loans on 1–4 family homes made by savings and loans increased from about 30 percent at the end of 1950 to nearly 45 percent at the end of 1967.

Like other intermediaries, savings and loan associations had invested heavily in United States government securities during the war. Indeed, at the end of 1945, United States government issues made up more than one-fourth of total savings and loan assets while mortgage loans accounted for less than two-thirds. By 1950, however, the unique nature of savings and loans as suppliers of mortgage credit was again evident, with mortgage loans comprising over 80 percent of assets. At the end of 1965, mortgages made up fully 85 percent of the industry's assets.

The large share of relatively high-yielding mortgage loans in total savings and loan assets allowed for the payment of comparatively high dividend (interest) rates to savers. Although the interest differential favoring savings and loans with respect to other deposit institutions declined over the period, a substantial margin did exist throughout the fifties. In 1950 savings and loans paid an average dividend rate of 2.5 percent compared with 1.9 percent paid by mutual savings banks and only 0.9 percent paid by commercial banks on their time and savings deposits. By 1960, after a decade of rising interest rates, savings and loans still led; savers received 3.86 percent compared with 3.47 percent received from mutual savings banks and 2.56 percent received from commercial banks.

The reestablishment of the public's confidence after the debacle of the thirties also helped to explain the rapid growth of the savings and loan institutions. Some of this reestablishment of confidence could be attributed to the New Deal legislation that was designed to shore up credit institutions serving the mortgage market. Most important was the establishment of the Federal Savings and Loan Insurance Corporation (FSLIC) in 1934 to insure savings in member associations. Moreover, nearly three-quarters of all savings and loans were insured by the FSLIC in 1967 compared to only two-fifths in 1945, whereas the share of industry assets held by insured associations climbed from 70 percent to 96.4 percent in the same period. Similarly, the establishment in 1932 of the Federal Home Loan Bank System (FHLBS), which stood ready to make loans to affiliated organizations, played a major role in adding to the liquidity of savings and loan associations. At the end of the especially difficult year 1966, outstanding advances of the regional Federal Home Loan Banks amounted to $6.9 billion, spread out among some 2,600 associations. Between 1945 and

1967 membership in the FHLBS rose from 3,658 to 4,919 associations, or from 3 out of every 5 associations to 4 out of every 5. At the same time, the establishment of the FSLIC and the FHLBS did much to improve standards of supervision and regulation of the industry.

Their more favorable geographic location added still another factor to the growth of savings and loans, especially with respect to mutual savings banks. Mutual savings banks were a phenomenon peculiar to the urban centers of the Northeast. As a result, most of them were hampered in the postwar years by the shift of population to the suburbs and by the changing character of the central city, particularly the exodus of the middle classes and the rising proportion of poor people. Savings and loan associations, by contrast, were widely dispersed throughout suburbia and exurbia, where population and per capita incomes had risen more rapidly. In addition, existing state legislation regarding branching and chartering tended to favor savings and loan associations over mutual savings banks. These advantages were buttressed by the industry's success in establishing itself in certain quickly growing states that had no provision for chartering mutual savings banks.

This listing of the factors facilitating the spectacular growth of savings and loan associations up through the early sixties is by no means all-inclusive. One researcher has found the high level of advertising expenditures, including the use of "giveaways," to be a significant variable explaining the industry's growth. Nor should the aggressive approach taken by the industry's entrepreneurs be underestimated. Indeed, all the elements referred to attest to an active entrepreneurial spirit that was less evident among the mutual savings banks.

Savings and loan growth slowed appreciably as commercial banks began competing aggressively for savings and time deposits after 1957, when the interest ceiling set under Regulation Q was increased for the first time since its imposition in 1936. Average annual gains at savings and loan associations declined from 14 percent in the period between 1950 and 1956 to 9.4 percent between 1957 and 1964. As one of the industry's leading spokesmen observed in 1965, "The most important new fact of life in the savings and loan business has been the emergence of commercial banking as a strong, competitive force."

Specialization in the field of mortgage financing was no doubt a leading factor behind the growth of savings and loans in the fifties, but the events of the past few years have demonstrated again the competitive dangers of excessive financial specialization. As the 1960s drew to a close, the question of whether or not specialized intermediaries could survive was being actively debated. Ironically, somewhat the same question had been raised about the commercial banking system only a decade before.

As long as the level of interest rates did not increase sharply over a short period, savings and loan associations enjoyed a favorable position. The violent and sudden rise in interest rates in the late 1960s once again revealed in a dramatic way the basic problems of institutions that specialize in long-term assets (for example, mortgages) while at the same time issuing highly liquid claims payable on demand. When interest rates on all types of claims soared, savings and loan associations found themselves unable to bid successfully for new savings or even to prevent substantial deposit withdrawals. Commercial banks, by contrast, while restricted by tight monetary conditions and by the restraining influence of Regulation Q, were much better able to weather a credit crunch.

To be sure, home mortgage rates rose along with other interest rates, although more slowly. But savings and loan associations could take little solace from this fact. Their assets consisted of mortgage loans made in earlier years when mortgage rates were very much lower. Perhaps 5 percent of savings and loan assets rolled over each year, permitting reinvestment at current market rates. Commercial banks, on the other hand, carried a much more diversified list of assets and a portfolio having a much shorter average maturity. As a result, they were able to relend a much greater proportion of their resources at the currently high interest rates. Furthermore, as is typical in boom periods, short-term rates rose relatively faster than long-term rates, a development that placed commercial banks in a still better competitive position.

On the liability side, too, the commercial banks held an important advantage over the savings and loan institutions. They had successfully segmented the savings market by issuing various kinds of savings and time deposit claims bearing different interest rates. Therefore, they were able, within the limits imposed by Regulation Q, to minimize withdrawals and to attract new deposits through *selective* rate changes on claims issued to those who were most sensitive to interest-rate differentials. Prime examples were the higher-interest rates paid on negotiable certificates of deposit. Meanwhile, savings and loan associations and mutual savings banks continued, for the most part, to issue undifferentiated claims paying a common rate of interest. To meet competition, therefore, any rise in interest rates had to be paid across the board to all savers. As a result, one of the main reasons given for retaining Regulation Q was that it supported the housing market by giving a prop to the nation's specialized thrift institutions.

THE PARTIAL RECOVERY OF
INVESTMENT BANKING · Like the other financial institutions, investment banking in the postwar decades regained a large measure of the vigor that it had lost during the depression. It would have been singularly strange if it had not. The rapid growth of the economy, the absence of extended or severe recession, the resurgence of stock market activity, another great wave of mergers, and a seemingly insatiable desire to go public created a heady atmosphere for the industry. But unlike the other financial institutions, investment banking achieved only a partial recovery. It never succeeded in reestablishing the strategic position in the credit markets that it had held in the so-called Morgan era and to a lesser extent in the 1920s. Professor Irwin Friend, of the University of Pennsylvania, on whose research much of this section is based, concluded in a recent study: ". . . neither capital, personnel, nor volume of new issue business in the postwar period matched the rise since the 1920s in the national income or

in most other forms of economic and financial activity." It was not until the late fifties that the dollar volume of sales on the New York Stock Exchange, the emporium that displayed the wares of the investment banking business, again matched the 1926 level of sales, and it was not until 1967 that trading surpassed the record set in 1929.

THE SLUMP IN NEW SECURITY ISSUES · New security issues, excluding short-term public and private issues, averaged close to 9 percent of GNP through most of the twenties and surpassed 12 percent in 1928–1929. But they averaged only about 5 percent during the fifties and early sixties.

In the twenties, over one-fourth of total corporate financing came from stock and bond issues, but such forms accounted for less than 20 percent in the fifties, less than 15 percent in the early sixties, and less than 10 percent in the middle sixties. Common and preferred stocks slumped especially badly as sources of capital funds. From 1901 to 1929, stock issues provided between one-tenth and one-fifth of all internal and external funds raised by nonfinancial corporations, against only about one-twentieth between 1950 and 1962. Bond issues do not show a similar decline although their share, about 10 percent between 1950 and 1963, is certainly very much smaller than at the start of the century when they accounted for fully one-fourth of total corporate funds raised. Various factors explain these disparate trends, perhaps the most important being the marked increase since the twenties in the rates of personal and corporate income taxes that, in turn, have raised the cost of equity financing.

A number of factors contributed to the diminished importance of the new issues market and its parent, the investment banking business. Compared with earlier periods, business firms were financing a larger proportion of their needs through internal financing—that is, retained earnings and depreciation allowances. A second factor was the stepped-up pace of competition within the financial sector. Here the enormous growth of all types of financial intermediaries was particularly important. Their growth and their enhanced aggressiveness enabled business firms to circumvent the investment bankers and the new issues market through mortgages, term loans, short-term financing, and leasing. At the same time, security issuers were given the opportunity to obtain capital funds from a greatly enlarged number and variety of institutional investors. Because of their great size and sophistication, many of these institutions were able to extend financing directly, thereby reducing the middleman function traditionally performed by investment bankers in the origination and distribution of new security issues. Private placements, mostly with life insurance companies and corporate pension plans, which had played only a modest role in the thirties, assumed more importance in the fifties and sixties. Between 1960 and 1963, for example, over 40 percent of the total value of new stock issues and about 55 percent of new corporate bonds were privately placed, compared with 16 percent and 19 percent, respectively, in the period 1935–1939.

The growth of private placements (primarily of bond issues) reflected a number of real advantages to corporate issuers. Private placement (1) reduced the risks of delay involved in registered public offerings, (2) eliminated underwriting costs, (3) made the proceeds available sooner, and (4) permitted the tailoring of loans to particular situations. In addition, private placement offered a distinct advantage to smaller companies that would normally experience difficulties in floating security issues in the open market.

The sharp rise since the twenties and thirties in "competitive bidding" on new issues has also acted to reduce the investment banker's influence in the securities markets. In the period 1935–1939, for example, investment banking firms acquired only about 2 percent of publicly distributed corporate bonds through formal competitive bidding, compared to between 33 and 50 percent after 1950.

The investment banking community, never having had any stomach for competitive bidding, continued to oppose it as a business-getting technique, accepting it only as an accomplished fact. Some of this hostility could plausibly be explained by the fact that underwriter spreads—the difference between what the underwriter pays and what he receives— were lower than they had been under the old arrangements. But this situation implied a total absence of competition in the earlier period, an implication that was at best a half-truth. We have already noted that competition existed in the 1920s and in the so-called Morgan era as well.

A much more important reason for the bankers' opposition to competitive bidding was the absence of any involved and long-run banker-issuer relationship, such as had frequently existed in the early part of the century. The "traditional banker" relationship had possessed distinct advantages for all parties. The advantages to the banking house were obvious. To the corporate issuer, it offered financial counseling that could best be provided on the basis of an established banker-issuer relationship. The investment banker regarded his position vis-à-vis his client as the same as a doctor to his patient. His commodity was service, and it was understandable that he should have vigorously opposed the extension of competitive bidding, which all but precluded meaningful banker-issuer relationships.

Indeed, although competitive bidding accounted for a large share of the bond issues in the postwar years, its appeal was limited. In 1963, for example, competitive bidding covered almost half of publicly distributed new corporate bonds, but public utility issues accounted for nearly 95 percent of these. For public utilities, of course, the practice was greatly encouraged by SEC Rule U-50 (1941) under the Public Utility Holding Company Act of 1935, which required competitive bidding in the case of all companies subject to the act. As the figures reveal, however, most corporate issuers continue to value the specialized assistance of investment bankers. Outside of the utility industry, the practice has received its greatest acceptance in the distribution of high-grade bonds, where the advance preparation and marketing process are likely to be less difficult, and in the distribution of state and local bonds, where the law requires it. The appeal of competitive bidding is especially limited in the case of stock issues and the more speculative mixed issues, combining the characteristics of senior and junior securities.

Despite the rise of competitive bidding, it is questionable whether its competitive effects have been all that salutary. Certainly, competitive bidding is only one of several forces that have acted to lower gross profit margins in the postwar decades relative to earlier levels. There is, however, other evidence suggesting a rise in competition within the industry since the thirties. Thus the share of negotiated corporate issues acquired by the 10 largest investment banking houses declined from about 70 percent in the mid-thirties to 62 percent in the period 1947–1949 and to 58 percent in 1961–1963. Similar declines in concentration are revealed for both larger and smaller numbers of leading firms.

All the postwar developments to which we have referred (private placements, the growing list of alternative means and sources of financing, competitive bidding, and the associated increase in intraindustry competition), along with the "institutionalization" of the securities markets, interacted to lower the gross underwriting spread taken by investment bankers. Such compensation varies with the type and size of the issue, as well as the rating of the issuer. Underwriting spreads on issues of the same size, for example, are considerably higher on stock issues than on bond issues, varying from less than 1 percent to about 5 percent in the case of bond issues to between 4 percent and 10 percent in the case of equity issues.[2] Compared with the twenties and thirties, however, gross underwriting spreads have been significantly lower in the postwar period. Moreover, the reductions would be even greater if adjustment is made for the fact that an issue of a given dollar amount in the sixties is equivalent in most respects to a much smaller issue in the earlier periods. Whether the fall in gross underwriting spreads coincided with a decline in net income within the industry is not known. At least part of the decline would seem to reflect lower costs (for example, lower distribution costs). Nevertheless, it is likely that the postwar rise in competition in the new issues market, especially in the bond market, has been at least as important an influence as any cost economies that may have been achieved.

THE FALTERING GROWTH OF
LIFE INSURANCE COMPANIES · Although life insurance companies continued to show impressive growth in the postwar decades, they were unable to match the growth of other intermediaries. The amount of life insurance in force continued to climb, increasing from just over $150 billion at the end of 1945 to nearly $1.2 trillion at the end of 1968. Nevertheless, the nearly eightfold increase in life insurance in force resulted in a very much slower gain in life insurance assets, which grew from $55.8 billion to $188.6 billion. Indeed, of all the intermediaries we are considering, with the exception of investment banking, for which asset formation

---

[2] These differences reflect the lower underwriting risks associated with bond issues as well as the greater ease of distributing a bond issue involving large sales to a small number of financial institutions.

was not a significant measure of growth or importance, life insurance companies showed the slowest growth after the mid-fifties.

Much of the reason for this lagging growth lay in the public's diminished preference for combining saving with insurance. The public increasingly sought more attractive outlets for its savings in order to take advantage of rising interest rates and to neutralize the effect of price inflation. Between 1950 and 1965 the flow-of-funds statistics reveal that the household sector's holdings of life insurance reserves—that is, its savings through life insurance companies—failed to double, rising from $55 billion to $106 billion, while its ownership of financial assets ballooned upward from $432 billion to $1.4 trillion.

The shift in the public's preference is even more clearly reflected in the shrinking share of high-savings life insurance (endowment, retirement income, and limited payment life) to total life insurance in force. High-savings insurance made up 45 percent of all ordinary insurance in force and 80 percent of industrial insurance in 1950 and 18 percent of ordinary and 59 percent of industrial in 1966. By contrast, term insurance, which provides no savings, grew from about 10 percent of ordinary in 1950 to 26.5 percent in 1966 and from less than 3 percent to 7.1 percent of industrial.

Industrial insurance, the poor man's insurance, barely grew in the postwar period, rising from $33.4 billion in 1950 to $38.8 billion in 1968. The growth of ordinary insurance was more impressive, rising from $149 billion to $630 billion, but its advance was not nearly as sharp as that of group insurance—from $48 billion to $438 billion—and credit insurance,[3] which grew from $2.5 billion to over $75 billion. The share of voluntary individual life insurance contracts in the reserves of life companies fell to below two-fifths, while more than three-fifths originated in compulsory or quasi-compulsory group contracts. Indeed, the major force stimulating the growth of reserves was the rising number of insured pension plans (nearly 70,000 in 1965), which supplied almost one-third of life insurance funds and accounted for over one-fifth of the industry's total reserves.

The pronounced shift in the product mix of life insurance companies adversely affected not only their role as savings institutions but also their role as suppliers of funds in the credit markets. Between 1950 and 1965, the share of life insurance companies in meeting the financial needs of the economy's nonfinancial sectors declined from about 15 percent to about 11 percent. Nevertheless, the fact that life companies accounted for about one-eighth of all funds supplied by financial institutions indicates their importance in the economy, an importance considerably enhanced by the fact that almost all their investments are long term.

Like many other intermediaries, life insurance companies were quick to redeploy their funds from the uses to which they had been put during the depression and war years. (See Table 21.) By the end of the war, life insurance companies had almost half their assets in United States govern-

---

[3] Credit life insurance refers to term life insurance issued through a lender or lending agency to cover payment of a loan, installment purchase, or other obligation in case of death.

ment securities. In contrast, mortgages, which traditionally accounted for between one-third and two-fifths of assets, had fallen to about 15 percent of assets. By 1968, however, the government portfolio had been reduced to less than 2.5 percent of total assets. By then, too, home mortgages represented nearly 40 percent of assets. Even more spectacular was the increase in holdings of industrial bonds. As in the thirties, a good part of this gain derived from direct placements. Railroad and public utility bonds, on the other hand, continued to decline. Here much of the slack was taken up by common stocks, which the insurance companies had avoided since early in the century. Policy loans also rose, for market interest rates in the sixties went much higher than the rates stipulated in insurance contracts, so that it seemed to pay policyholders to borrow against their insurance in order to take advantage of the high rates in the bond and mortgage market. Both as a result of the rising level of interest rates and the employment of funds in higher-yielding investments, the net rate of interest earned on invested funds rose from 3.1 percent in 1945 to 4.95 percent in 1968.

TABLE 21
Percentage Distribution of Life Insurance Company Assets,
1945, 1950, 1968

Asset	1945	1950	1968
U.S. government bonds	45.9	21.0	2.4
Mortgages	14.8	25.1	37.2
Industrial bonds	4.3	14.9	25.3
State and local government bonds	2.3	2.4	2.7
Railroad and public utility bonds	18.2	21.5	11.2
Policy loans	4.4	3.8	6.0
Real estate	1.9	2.2	3.0
Stocks	2.2	3.3	6.9
Other	6.0	5.8	5.3

Source: Institute of Life Insurance, *Life Insurance Fact Book* (New York, 1969).

The failure of life companies to grow as quickly as their institutional competitors, both as savings repositories and as suppliers of loanable funds, has been an important factor underlying the industry's recent ventures into new fields. Like commercial banks, life insurance companies transformed themselves into holding companies in order to participate in the growth potential of related areas of activity.

In addition to opening lucrative opportunities in related fields, the holding company form of organization made possible increased freedom of action in financing. Insurance companies, barred by regulatory agencies from issuing senior securities in raising new capital and handicapped by the shift to nonsavings-type contracts, became concerned over their ability to provide funds in periods of financial stress. Holding companies, being free of such constraints, offered a way out. The holding company is also a much better means of taking advantage of opportunities to acquire other companies in related businesses, such as a mutual fund or a variable annuity subsidiary to meet the competition of the distributors of equity securities. The holding company route offers the further advantage of more fully utilizing a firm's human resources.

Whatever the reason in individual cases, the diversification of life companies into related financial fields increased the amount of overlap that was one of the most prominent features of financial competition in the 1960s. Indeed, the decision of various other intermediaries to follow much the same course has paved the way for the multiline institutions that seem likely to play an increasingly important role in the financial markets of the future.

THE STEADY GROWTH OF GENERAL
INSURANCE COMPANIES · The consistent prosperity of the 1950s and 1960s turned much of the financial world topsy-turvy. Consider what happened in the insurance industry. For years life insurance had expanded and reexpanded, while general insurance plodded along. In the post-World War II era, however, nonlife insurance companies experienced a better rate of growth, increasing their assets by better than 8 percent a year. Much of this growth, as in the case of most other intermediaries, derived from the stepped-up pace of innovation and competition within the industry.

The introduction of "multiple-line" insurance in the late forties and its subsequent adoption throughout most of the industry suggested the industry's future course of innovation.

Traditionally, American insurance companies have specialized in one or another of three major types of insurance—casualty, property, and life. Up to the mid-1800s the monoline principle was enforced by public opinion and by a desire on the part of the companies to specialize within closely related lines of underwriting. By the late 1800s this voluntary acceptance of the monoline principle had given way to regulations in a number of states, including New York, enforcing the separation of different lines of insurance. Especially important in this regard was the so-called Appleton Rule, which was put into effect in New York State about 1900 and which prohibited companies operating in the state, no matter where they were chartered, from doing any kind of business, anywhere, that was not allowed to companies chartered by the State of New York.

The logic behind the prohibition against insurance companies writing policies in more than one line rested partly on a belief that specialization would make individual insurers more competent and, secondly, on the feeling that different lines of insurance called for different investment policies. In addition, it was felt that specialization would be an advantage from the standpoint of state regulation and supervision.

Although New York State did not permit full multiple-line underwriting within the property and casualty fields (and thus its extension elsewhere in the country) until 1949, much progress had already been made in the twenties and thirties in this direction through the formation of insurance company groups, or "fleets" as they are sometimes called, that often included both property and casualty companies. These fleets, generally composed of individual companies tied together by stock ownership, were often formed for purposes wholly unrelated to multiple-line company goals. A group of several fire companies, for example, without any casualty affiliates, might be formed to enlarge the total number of sales agents in a particular territory, or a casualty company might add another casualty company in order to enter a new casualty line that appeared profitable. Nevertheless, growing numbers of old-line fire and marine companies did organize casualty affiliates during the twenties. By 1929 there were some 90 different stock company groups, a number of which included both property and casualty units. By 1948, after various ups and downs, the number had climbed to 108.

Freed from the prohibitions imposed under the New York law, a number of multiple-line groups, as well as a number of monoline independent companies, were subsequently reorganized into single multiple-line insurance underwriters, writing all kinds of policies except life. In New York State the number of companies with full multiple-line powers increased from 48 in 1949 to 360 in 1957. Indeed, very few large monoline companies were left in the industry by the late fifties.

The creation of multiple-line companies proved mutually beneficial to the buying public as well as to the companies concerned. The buyer had a wider choice of product, as well as the option of purchasing all-risk policies, the only exclusions being perils not amenable to insurance principles. Moreover, multiple-peril contracts that combine a group of coverages formerly written separately and usually by several companies reduced the possibility of gaps between coverages and also of nonconformity of amounts and types of coverage. Also, loss settlement was likely to be simpler and more certain when only one issuer was involved.

From the issuer's point of view, multiple line offered the opportunity of entering more lucrative lines of business. It could also lead to substantial economies, especially where integration occurred through the merger of formerly independent companies. Simpler corporate structures were likely to result in lower tax and license fees, lower administration expenses, smaller gross salaries, and lower underwriting and loss adjustment expenses. In addition, the costs of certain seldom-purchased coverages were especially likely to decline, because of the better spread of risks, when they were automatically made part of a package, or multiple-peril policy. Just how substantial the cost reductions could be was indicated by the fact that the savings passed on to buyers of multiple-peril homeowners' policies have amounted to as much as 40 percent of the separate costs of the included coverages. Partly as a result, the amount of insurance in such separate lines as fire and extended coverage, liability (other than automobile), burglary and theft, and inland marine have remained relatively stable, with buyers showing a decided preference for the all-inclusive and more economical package policies issued by multiple-line companies. Thus while net premiums for all lines of property and liability insurance increased from $12.1 billion in 1957 to $23.8 billion in 1967, premium income on homeowners' multiple-peril insurance soared from

$241 million to $1.8 billion, and on commercial multiple-peril insurance from $28 million to $775 million. Fire insurance premiums, in sharp contrast, remained unchanged at $2.3 billion.

The multiple-line principle was not extended to life insurance, but property and casualty companies moved into the business through the acquisition of life company affiliates, thereby repeating the practice of the twenties and thirties that brought together property and casualty companies in commonly owned groups.

The low level of underwriting profits, more than anything else, explained the accelerated invasion of life insurance by the property-casualty companies. The aggregate underwriting loss sustained by stock companies amounted to about 1 percent of premiums. However, the total profit picture for property-casualty companies has not been so bleak due to the large incomes (nearly 10 percent a year) earned on their investment portfolios. General insurance company stocks traded on the securities market, therefore, greatly resembled mutual funds.

In addition to innovations that took the industry into new fields, intense competition has developed within the industry itself as a result of the relatively spectacular growth of the so-called specialty groups, originally concentrating on automobile insurance but later expanding into other lines of coverage as well. A specialty company is a sort of discount house. It utilizes cost-reducing techniques of every kind, such as continuous policies, direct billing, and payment in advance. Most important, these companies distribute their policies either directly—through salaried employees—or through exclusive agents instead of through independent agents and brokers, which is the traditional practice among stock companies. These savings, plus additional economies gained by careful screening and classification of buyers, permitted the specialty companies to write insurance at rates 20 percent or more below those of their competitors.

The largest specialty groups, including such companies as State Farm, Allstate, and Nationwide, benefiting from these cost advantages, grew very quickly between 1949 and 1959, increasing their net premiums by 463 percent compared to only 175 percent in the largest stock-agency groups. This intraindustry competition cast considerable doubts on the future of the independent agency system, which until recent years characterized the marketing of property-casualty insurance.

CREDIT UNIONS ASSUME A
POSITION OF IMPORTANCE · Of all the thrift-type financial intermediaries, credit unions made the most enormous strides in the postwar period. By the late fifties they were assuming a position of importance as a savings depository and as a lender to households.

During World War II, despite the rise in incomes, the credit union movement, adversely affected by curbs on credit and by purchases of war bonds, lagged badly. Assets rose slightly, but membership remained unchanged and the number of unions actually declined. As late as 1945 the assets of the 8,683 operating credit unions totaled only $435 million.

Installment credit loans of credit unions amounted to barely $100 million, less than 6 percent of the total installment credit extended by financial intermediaries.

By 1966, however, the credit union movement, which bankers and others had long regarded as amateurish, assumed far more significant proportions. The number of credit unions increased to nearly 23,000, and membership increased to 18 million, a more than sixfold gain over the number in 1945. Assets increased some 26 times to over $11.5 billion. Installment credit loans grew still faster, reaching a level of $8.5 billion. The individual credit union, true to its purpose, remained very small as far as financial intermediaries go, although by 1966 the average association could boast of assets in excess of $500,000 and a membership of nearly 800.

The success of credit unions reflected the same combination of elements that had operated in the past: vigorous promotion, their relatively low interest rates on consumer loans, high dividend rates, and various kinds of financial assistance to members on a "shirt-sleeve" basis. Of course, none of these factors would have been effective if it had not been for the yeast provided by the economy's rapid growth, especially the more or less steady rise in per capita incomes.

The phenomenal growth of credit unions had to impinge on other types of savings institutions. Some savings that may have gone into savings banks, commercial banks, and savings and loan associations went into credit unions. Between 1945 and 1965 the share of net personal savings placed in credit unions rose steadily from only .1 of one percent to 3.9 percent. At the same time, credit unions succeeded in enlarging their share of the installment loan business. In 1966 credit unions accounted for 13 percent of total installment loans held by financial intermediaries, more than twice the share they held in 1945. Nor were these loans of the $5 and $25 variety they had once been; in 1966 the average loan exceeded $1,000.

Compared with several other financial intermediaries, credit unions remained highly specialized institutions. Yet the idea of establishing "people's banks" did not die and moves were made periodically to add to the functions performed by credit unions. In 1965, for example, Representative Wright Patman of Texas, a supporter of credit unions and a strong critic of commercial banks, unsuccessfully introduced a bill to permit federal credit unions to provide deposit accounts and checking services for their members. But as credit unions continue to grow, particularly as professional management takes over, they are likely to enlarge their range of operations, as other intermediaries have been doing.

NONINSURED PENSION FUNDS · As we noted in the previous chapter, the years since the end of World War II witnessed a rapid growth of private pension plans. Despite the substantial advances made in the late 1930s, private pension plans covered less than 1 out of every 5 workers employed in commerce and industry in 1940. By the end of 1967, however, 2 out of 5 were protected, whether well or poorly, by some kind of plan.

In 1940 pension funds totaled about $1 billion; by 1967 they ran to over $70 billion. Few other intermediaries in the entire history of the world could boast such remarkable growth in so short a period.

In the savings market, private pension funds were, in 1963, already absorbing nearly 25 percent of personal saving. They played a more stellar role in the corporate securities markets, for they were the largest institutional buyer of corporate stock, buying more than twice as much as open-end investment companies, the next largest purchaser. Indeed, their purchases of common stocks exceeded total new stock issues in the decade ending 1965, signifying the "institutionalization" of the corporate equities market as well as the strategic role of pension funds in this market. In addition to owning over $40 billion in stocks, more than half of all their assets, noninsured pension funds have also become a major factor in the bond market, accounting for almost one-fourth of total purchases by financial intermediaries. By the end of 1966 their holdings approached $25 billion.

The more flexible investment policy of noninsured pension funds was one of the major factors that allowed for their faster growth in comparison with insured pension plans. Between 1945 and 1964, membership in insured pension plans increased more than fourfold, while membership in noninsured plans increased about threefold. Asset (or reserve) growth was, however, much greater for noninsured plans.

The outlook, however, is for more equal growth. One factor likely to make this so is the more flexible investment policies that life insurance companies can utilize in managing corporate pensions. Until recent years, life companies could not invest group annuity reserves differently from other assets; as a result, corporate stocks represented only a small fraction of total portfolios. Recent legislation in most states allows life companies to maintain separate investment accounts, each set up for a given pension plan or group of plans. Considerably more investment latitude is permitted for these separate accounts than in life investments generally. Moreover, the formation of pension plans in the future is likely to be dominated by smaller companies seeking to offer retirement benefits to their employees. Such companies have, for a variety of reasons, always been more willing to turn over administration of the program to life companies.

INVESTMENT COMPANIES:
AN EXAMPLE OF FINANCIAL RECOVERY · Despite the favorable reaction to the Investment Company Act of 1940, there was a natural hiatus in the growth of investment companies during the war. Starting in the late 1940s, however, investment companies grew at a spectacular rate. Assets of open-end companies, or mutual funds as they are more commonly called, amounted to only $1 billion in 1940 but were $45 billion in 1967.

Very little of the growth experienced by open-end companies spilled over to the closed-end companies that had dominated the investment company field in the twenties. Although the stock market crash had dealt a devastating blow to closed-end companies, as late as 1943 they still held more assets than mutual fund-type companies, despite the already substantial strides made by the latter. But succeeding years left the old-line "investment trusts" far behind as mutual funds fired the public imagination. In 1948 mutual fund assets were already twice as large as those of closed-end companies. As of 1968 there were only 14 diversified closed-end companies, compared with about 240 mutual funds.

As a group, diversified closed-end companies are a far cry from the highly speculative investment trusts of the twenties. Senior capital was almost totally eliminated among the older companies, although the flurry of interest shown in "dual-purpose" funds in the 1960s signaled a return to more highly leveraged structures. Dual-purpose funds issue two classes of shares: income shares and capital shares. To the former accrue all net investment income but no capital gains, and they therefore tend to be issued to investors whose primary objective is income. Capital shares, on the other hand, participate in changes in the value of the entire portfolio (that is, in capital gains and losses). As a result, there is income leverage for holders of income shares and capital leverage for holders of capital shares.

With the surge in personal incomes, continued price inflation, higher-corporate profits, reactivated security activity, and rising stock prices, it was only natural that the public's depression-induced fears concerning the stock market gradually yielded to new optimism. For the "little fellow" who wanted to make the plunge, the investment company route seemed the most sensible. From less than .5 million in 1945, the number of shareholder accounts climbed to 7.7 million in 1966. Although many persons held shares in more than one mutual fund, the quickly growing popularity of the mutual fund field cannot be doubted. Not all investors in mutual funds were individuals, as evidenced by the growing numbers of fiduciary, business, and institutional accounts seeking appropriate diversification and continuous supervision. In 1966 there were more than 700,000 of these accounts, valued at about $4 billion compared to about 36,000 accounts valued at less than $300 million in 1954.

In addition to the underlying factors mentioned in the preceding paragraphs, the growth of mutual funds, as opposed to the very much slower growth of closed-end funds, was spurred by several specific factors. Certainly not the least of these factors was the fact that mutual funds did not have to overcome the kind of ill feelings that the closed-end trusts had built up in the thirties. Many people, too, felt more secure in the knowledge that their shares were readily redeemable at or near asset value instead of fluctuating in price like ordinary common stocks. This point has been especially significant since the leverage feature of closed-end funds has become very much less important, thereby reducing the speculative appeal of such shares. As mentioned, however, this situation may be changing with the innovation of the dual-purpose fund. The fact that the shares of most closed-end funds, despite rising stock prices, sold well below their book values naturally discouraged promoters from raising new capital in this way. Finally, mutual funds were merchandized on an unparalleled scale. The sales commission (ranging from 8 to 9 percent for sales of up to about $10,000) was undoubtedly a major factor in stimulating the sales effort behind load funds, with some spill-off to the no-load funds, for they seem to represent bargain investments by comparison.

The attractiveness of mutual funds was also enhanced by the initiation and promotion of voluntary accumulation and withdrawal plans. The former permitted an investor to deposit a modest amount of money periodically for the purchase of shares. The investor was charged only the usual sales premium and could withdraw at any time and demand the cash as well as any securities that belonged to him. This arrangement was different from the much older contractual accumulation plan also in use, whereby an investor contracted to put a certain amount of money into shares over a specified number of years. At the end of the period he took possession of all his property, but if he defaulted on his payments he was penalized by having paid most of the charges involved during the first year or two, even though it might be a 10- or 15-year plan. Formal withdrawal plans whereby shareholders might receive payments from their investment at regular intervals also attracted investors interested in receiving an income, plus preserving principal. Furthermore, dividend reinvestment plans encouraged asset growth by automatically converting dividends into additional shares.

Although their growth lagged far behind that of mutual funds, closed-end companies made real efforts to develop broader investment understanding and interest through limited advertising and expanded shareholder reports. Moreover, many investors recognized the advantage of purchasing shares in closed-end companies selling below asset value, with the result that discounts were sharply reduced.

The main impact of investment company growth was, of course, in the equities market. Throughout most of the postwar period, corporate stocks accounted for close to 90 percent of the assets of open-end investment companies. Investment companies did not purchase significant amounts of newly issued stock, the overwhelming bulk of their purchases being in the secondary markets. But whether or not mutual funds, together with private pension funds, exerted a stabilizing influence on the stock market, as is sometimes claimed, is uncertain, especially in recent years with the introduction of "performance" and "go-go" funds seeking short-term gains.

SUMMARY · Closeness in time to the innovations of the last two decades makes it difficult to evaluate their significance or permanence objectively. Although the view has been expressed here that improved public regulation and such innovations as deposit insurance make it unlikely that the rapid pace of experimentation in the sixties will have consequences similar to those of the twenties, the possibility still remains. Just as many people thought the Federal Reserve System made the business cycle obsolete, so may we also be lulled into believing that our financial structure is so well conceived as to weather any storm. From the point of view of the financial entrepreneur, however, the innovations of the past twenty or so years have, as in the twenties, been in response to the changes taking place in the rest of the economy. And in the competitive business environment, where not growing is usually the first step on the road to failure, successful adaptation to new conditions is a necessary condition to survival. That the innovations of the fifties and sixties bore a more than casual relationship to those of the twenties suggests that financial institutions have been responding to long-run changes, a process only interrupted by the depression and World War II. If this is so, it is not unlikely that financial intermediaries will continue to evolve in the direction they have been—toward a point where the variety of financial functions presently performed by distinctive types of intermediaries will be carried on by comparatively undifferentiated, multifunction institutions.

a note on sources

It is not our intention to give a complete bibliography on the history of financial intermediaries. The following, together with the footnote references, represents a fairly complete list of the sources on which we have relied.

Statistical data were derived from the following sources:

U.S. Bureau of the Census, *Historical Statistics of the United States; Statistical Abstract of the United States*

Comptroller of the Currency, *Annual Reports,* 1876, 1921, 1931

Federal Deposit Insurance Corporation, *Annual Reports*

Board of Governors of the Federal Reserve System, *All-Bank Statistics; Annual Reports*

Hunt's Merchants' Magazine

Banker's Almanac and Register, 1851–1913

Fact Books published annually by:

    National Association of Mutual Savings Banks (New York)

    United States Savings and Loan League (Chicago)

    Investment Company Institute (New York)

    Consumer Finance Association (New York)

    Institute of Life Insurance (New York)

    New York Stock Exchange (New York)

    Credit Union National Association (Madison, Wisc.)

    Property Insurance Fact Book, National Board of Fire Underwriters (New York)

On savings and financial intermediaries in general:

Goldsmith, Raymond W. *Financial Institutions.* New York: Random House, 1968.

————. *Financial Intermediaries in the American Economy since 1900.* New York: National Bureau of Economic Research, 1958.

————. *The Share of Financial Intermediaries in National Wealth.* New York: National Bureau of Economic Research, 1954.

————. *A Study of Saving in the United States.* Princeton, N.J.: Princeton University Press, 1955–1956.

Kuznets, Simon S. *Capital in the American Economy.* Princeton, N.J.: Princeton University Press, 1961.

The literature on commercial banking and central banking is immense. See the bibliographies in Fritz Redlich, *The Molding of American Banking* (New York: Johnson Reprint Corporation, 1968) and Paul Studenski and Herman E. Krooss, *Financial History of the United States* (New York: McGraw-Hill, 1963).

On banking history Redlich, cited above, is an indispensable source. Two other general works that are especially helpful are:

Edwards, George W. *The Evolution of Finance Capitalism.* New York: Augustus M. Kelley, 1967. Reprinted.

Myers, Margaret. *The New York Money Market.* New York: Columbia University Press, 1931–1932.

Documents on banking history can be found in:

Krooss, Herman E. (ed.). *Documentary History of Banking and Currency.* New York: McGraw-Hill, 1969.

The energy and imagination of the reprint houses have made the following interesting and informative contemporary works readily available:

Carey, Mathew. *Essays on Banking.* New York: Augustus M. Kelley, 1970.

Gouge, William M. *A Short History of Paper Money and Banking.* New York: Augustus M. Kelley, 1968.

Raguet, Condy. *A Treatise on Currency and Banking.* New York: Augustus M. Kelley, 1967.

On central banking—the Second Bank:

Hammond, Bray. *Banks and Politics in America: From the Revolution to the Civil War.* Princeton, N.J.: Princeton University Press, 1957.

Smith, Walter Buckingham. *Economic Aspects of the Second United States Bank.* Cambridge, Mass.: Harvard University Press, 1953.

On the Federal Reserve System:

Friedman, Milton, and Anna Jacobson Schwartz. *A Monetary History of the United States, 1867–1960.* Princeton, N.J.: Princeton University Press, 1963.

Harris, Seymour F. *Twenty Years of Federal Reserve Policy.* Cambridge, Mass.: Harvard University Press, 1933.

Wicker, Elmus R. *Federal Reserve Monetary Policy, 1917–1933.* New York: Random House, 1966.

On banking philosophy and policy:

Miller, Harry S. *Banking Theories in the United States before 1860.* Cambridge, Mass.: Harvard University Press, 1927.

Mints, Lloyd W. *A History of Banking Theory in Great Britain and the United States.* Chicago: University of Chicago Press, 1945.

Ritter, Lawrence S. "Official Central Banking Theory in the U.S., 1939–61," *Journal of Political Economy,* Vol. 70 (1962).

On savings banking:

Keyes, Emerson W. *A History of Savings Banks in the United States.* New York: Bradford Rhodes, 1870.

Kniffin, William H. *The Savings Bank.* New York: The Bankers Publishing Co., 1928.

Lintner, John. *Mutual Savings Banks in the Savings and Mortgage Markets.* Cambridge, Mass.: Graduate School of Business Administration, Harvard University, 1948.

Welfling, Weldon. *Mutual Savings Banks.* Cleveland, Ohio: Case Western Reserve University Press, 1968.

On trust companies:

Barnett, George E. *State Banks and Trust Companies since the Passage of the National-Bank Act.* Washington, D.C.: Government Printing Office, 1911.

Herrick, Clay. *Trust Companies.* New York: The Bankers Publishing Co., 1915.

On investment banking:

See Redlich and Edwards cited above.

Friend, Irwin, *et al. Investment Banking and the New Issues Market.* Philadelphia: Wharton School of Finance and Commerce, University of Pennsylvania, 1965.

Navin, T. R., and Marian V. Sears. "The Rise of a Market for Industrial Securities, 1887–1902," *Business History Review,* Vol. 29 (1955).

On insurance, life and property:

Buley, R. Carlyle. *The American Life Convention, 1906–1952.* New York: Appleton-Century-Crofts, 1953.

Clough, Shepard B. *A Century of American Life Insurance.* New York: Columbia University Press, 1946.

Fowler, J. A. *History of Insurance in Philadelphia for Two Centuries, 1683–1883.* Philadelphia: Review Publishing and Printing Company, 1883.

James, Marquis. *Biography of a Business: The Insurance Company of North America.* Indianapolis, Ind.: Bobbs-Merrill, 1942.

Keller, Morton. The *Life Insurance Enterprise, 1885–1910.* Cambridge, Mass.: Harvard University Press, 1963.

O'Donnell, Terrence. *History of Life Insurance in Its Formative Years.* Chicago: American Conservation Company, 1936.

Stalson, J. Owen. *Marketing Life Insurance.* Cambridge, Mass.: Harvard University Press, 1942.

Zartman, Lester. *Investments of Life Insurance Companies.* New York, 1906.

———. *Property Insurance.* New Haven, Conn.: Yale University Press, 1914.

On miscellaneous intermediaries:

Bodfish, Henry Morton. *Savings and Loans: Principles and Practices.* Englewood Cliffs, N.J.: Prentice-Hall, 1938.

Bullock, Hugh. *The Story of Investment Companies.* New York: Columbia University Press, 1959.

Cox, Edwin B. *Trends in the Distribution of Stock Ownership.* Philadelphia: University of Pennsylvania Press, 1963.

Dexter, Seymour. *A Treatise on Cooperative Savings and Loan Associations.* New York: D. Appleton & Co., 1891.

Ezell, John S. *Fortune's Merry Wheel.* Cambridge, Mass.: Harvard University Press, 1960.

Greef, Albert O. *The Commercial Paper House in the United States.* Cambridge, Mass.: Harvard University Press, 1938.

Hammond, Bray. "Long- and Short-Term Credit in Early American Banking," *Quarterly Journal of Economics,* Vol. 49 (1934).

Hidy, Ralph. *The House of Baring in American Trade and Finance.* Cambridge, Mass.: Harvard University Press, 1949.

Jenks, Leland H. *The Migration of British Capital to 1875.* New York: Alfred A. Knopf, 1927.

Ketchum, Marshall D. *The Fixed Investment Trust.* Chicago: University of Chicago Press, 1937.

Latimer, Murray W. *Industrial Pension Systems in the United States and Canada.* New York: Industrial Relations Counselors, 1932.

Lewis, Cleona. *America's Stake in International Investments.* Washington, D.C.: The Brookings Institution, 1938.

Peach, William H. *The Security Affiliates of National Banks.* Baltimore: Johns Hopkins Press, 1941.

index

The Amnesias

THE AMNESIAS

A Clinical Textbook
of Memory Disorders

Andrew C. Papanicolaou

With
Rebecca Billingsley-Marshall • Sonja Blum • Vasilis
P. Bozikas • Pramod K. Dash • Alexandra Economou •
Aikaterini Giazkoulidou • April E. Hebert • Mary H.
Kosmidis • David W. Loring • David Molfese • Barbra
Novak • Sokratis G. Papageorgiou • Jason D. Runyan •
Ioanna Savvidou • Panagiotis G. Simos

OXFORD
UNIVERSITY PRESS

2006

OXFORD
UNIVERSITY PRESS

Oxford University Press, Inc., publishes works that further
Oxford University's objective of excellence
in research, scholarship, and education.

Oxford   New York
Auckland   Cape Town   Dar es Salaam   Hong Kong   Karachi
Kuala Lumpur   Madrid   Melbourne   Mexico City   Nairobi
New Delhi   Shanghai   Taipei   Toronto

With offices in
Argentina   Austria   Brazil   Chile   Czech Republic   France   Greece
Guatemala   Hungary   Italy   Japan   Poland   Portugal   Singapore
South Korea   Switzerland   Thailand   Turkey   Ukraine   Vietnam

Copyright © 2006 by Oxford University Press, Inc.

Published by Oxford University Press, Inc.
198 Madison Avenue, New York, New York 10016

www.oup.com

Oxford is a registered trademark of Oxford University Press

Library of Congress Cataloging-in-Publication Data
Papanicolaou, Andrew C.
The amnesias : a clinical textbook of memory disorders / Andrew C. Papanicolaou ;
with Rebecca Billingsley-Marshall ... [et al.].
p. ; cm.
Includes bibliographical references and index.
ISBN-13: 978-0-19-517245-4
ISBN-10: 0-19-517245-0
1. Memory disorders.
[DNLM: 1. Amnesia—physiopathology. 2. Memory—physiology. WM 173.7 P213a 2006]
I. Billingsley-Marshall, Rebecca. II. Title.
RC394.M46P365   2006
616.85′232—dc22   2005008890

9 8 7 6 5 4 3 2 1

Printed in the United States of America
on acid-free paper

In memory of
Photine Papanicolaou
and
Ioanna Savvidou

Preface

Books on memory and its disorders have never been in short supply. They vary in sophistication from introductory to advanced and in scope from monographs on a particular aspect of memory to the all-encompassing edited volumes such as the *Oxford Handbook of Memory* (Tulving & Craik, 2000), the *Handbook of Memory Disorders* (Baddeley, Wilson, & Watts, 1995), or *Memory and Its Disorders* edited by the late L.S. Cermak (2000).

This book differs from monographs and edited volumes in several ways. Unlike the monographs that treat some aspects of memory or amnesia, this book encompasses the basic features of all amnesic syndromes and includes in an extensive Appendix a comprehensive account of the neuropsychological tests that are used in assessing them.

Also unlike the monographs and the comprehensive edited volumes that are intended for a restricted audience (typically the specialists in the area), this book is meant to address not only specialists but also graduate and advanced undergraduate students in psychology and the neurosciences, and residents in psychiatry and neurology. To ensure accessibility of the material to nonspecialists, all relevant phenomena are described and all constructs defined in the first chapter, the relevant neuroanatomical and neurochemical information is laid out in the second chapter, and the terminology established in these first two chapters is used consistently throughout the book.

Moreover, unlike most monographs and most comprehensive volumes, where theory, fact, and conjecture are intertwined, this book focuses primarily on generally accepted facts. That way, it may serve as a resource of practical and clinically relevant information for the clinically minded reader but also as a foundation of solid data that the aspiring theorist may use as a springboard for speculation. For, if the purpose of speculation is to arrange the empirical facts in an intelligible order, where causal relations may become clear, its fulfillment requires the presence of a body of such facts.

It is true that the nature of any fact is conditioned by prior theory, which informs and guides the procedures used for their collection and which, therefore, determines what will be recognized as a fact. In the present case, the role of the guiding theory has been assigned to clinical commonsense as conditioned, primarily, by the collective experiences of psychologists, neurologists, and psychiatrists with the effects of brain lesions.

It may be objected that in adopting such an approach, we have failed to take advantage of so much already developed theory on one hand and of the masses of data generated by the new methods of functional neuroimaging on the other. But this objection is not really justified: It can be said of no theory today that it commands universal acclaim, whereas it can be said of them all that they are little more than aggregates of conjecture in a constant flux. Also, any serious assessment of the harvest of the neuroimaging methods will convince the fair-minded that it rarely contains reliable data that can support generalizations but that, instead, it consists in an assortment of indications and hints, also in perpetual flux, for the simple reason that these methods are still developing both in their technological and methodological aspects.

Now, the fact that our approach does not rest on and does not promote a particular theory does not mean that there are no working hypotheses guiding it. These, as mentioned previously, derive mainly from the known effects of lesions. They also derive in part from commonly held conceptions, such as the distinction between episodic and semantic memory. Finally, they derive from our own sense of and desire for logical consistency and expositional clarity. That desire has motivated some apparently arbitrary choices on our part as, for instance, the designation of episodic, semantic, and implicit memories as phenomena rather than as functions. Much like all our choices, this one also is anything but arbitrary. It reflects our unwillingness to follow the habit of talking of episodic and semantic memories as "systems," thereby insinuating that for each phenomenally distinct type of mnemonic experience, there exists in the brain a separate set of mechanisms for encoding, consolidating, retrieving, and storing their traces, an idea at odds not only with the ideal of parsimony but also with any reasonable notion of the evolution of the human brain.

For the sake of expositional clarity, but also for the purpose of making this textbook easy to use, a consistent format is maintained throughout the chapters, with the exception of the two introductory chapters and the concluding chapter. This format features an introduction to each syndrome and representative case reports; differential diagnosis; detailed description of the symptoms that constitute the disorder and the neuropsychological tests used in establishing them; demographic, psychological, and physiological predisposing factors; the pathophysiology of the syndrome; its prognosis and treatment, if available; and, finally, a discussion of the implications of the disorder for the function of memory at large and for its cerebral mechanisms in particular. As for the rest of the chapters, we have already mentioned that the first lays out the conventional terminology and the largely conventional classification of mnemonic and amnesic phenomena and the putative cognitive operations that produce them, whereas the second describes the putative cerebral mechanisms of these operations. Finally, the concluding chapter consists of a few comments regarding the import of the reviewed facts on amnesia for any cohesive theory of memory.

Andrew C. Papanicolaou

Acknowledgments

We wish to express our gratitude to Vanessa Fuller for handling all secretarial aspects of this work with exemplary efficiency and Dr. Shirin Sarkari for editing the entire manuscript and definitely improving it. We also wish to thank Dr. Christina Andreou for translating into English parts of the chapter on Psychogenic Amnesia from the Greek original, after the untimely passing away of our dear friend and colleague, Ioanna Savvidou, M.D., the leading author of that chapter. Also, we wish to express our appreciation to the publishers of the following journals: Archives of Neurology, Brain, Brain & Cognition, Clinical Neurology and Neurosurgery, Clinical Pediatrics, Cognitive Neuropsychology, Cortex, Digital Anatomist Project/University of Washington, International Journal of Neuroscience, Journal of Neurology, Neurosurgery, & Psychiatry, Journal of Neuroscience, Journal of the American Academy of Child and Adolescent Psychiatry, Neuropsychologia, Philosophical Transactions of the Royal Society: Biological Sciences, Psychiatry Research, Neuroimaging, Science, Seizure; and John Wiley & Sons publishers of the "Handbook of Memory Disorders", and WB Saunders Company, publishers of "Transient amnesia: Clinical and neuropsychological aspects", for allowing us to quote extensively from their pages. Finally, we wish to thank Fiona Stevens at Oxford University Press for her patience and support.

Contents

Contributors

REBECCA BILLINGSLEY-MARSHALL
Division of Clinical Neurosciences,
    Department of Neurosurgery and
    the Vivian L. Smith Center for
    Neurologic Research
The University of Texas-Houston
    Medical School
Houston, Texas

SONJA BLUM
Department of Neurobiology
    & Anatomy
The University of Texas-Houston
    Medical School
Houston, Texas

VASILIS P. BOZIKAS
2nd Psychiatric Clinic
Aristotle University of
    Thessaloniki
Thessaloniki, Greece

PRAMOD DASH
Department of Neurobiology &
    Anatomy and the Vivian L. Smith
    Center for Neurologic Research
The University of Texas-Houston
    Medical School
Houston, Texas

ALEXANDRA ECONOMOU
Department of Psychology
National University of Athens
Athens, Greece

AIKATERINI GIAZKOULIDOU
Department of Psychology
Aristotle University of Thessaloniki
Thessaloniki, Greece

APRIL E. HEBERT
Department of Neurobiology
    & Anatomy
The University of Texas-Houston
    Medical School
Houston, Texas

MARY H. KOSMIDIS
Department of Psychology
Aristotle University of Thessaloniki
Thessaloniki, Greece

DAVID W. LORING
Department of Neurology
University of Florida, Gainesville
Gainesville, Florida

DAVID MOLFESE
Neuroscience Graduate Program
Baylor College of Medicine, Houston
Houston, Texas

BARBRA NOVAK
Department of Linguistics
Rice University
Houston, Texas

SOKRATIS G. PAPAGEORGIOU
Neurology Clinic, Aeginition
    Hospital
National University of Athens
Athens, Greece

ANDREW C. PAPANICOLAOU
Division of Clinical Neurosciences,
    Department of Neurosurgery and
    the Vivian L. Smith Center for
    Neurologic Research
The University of Texas-Houston
    Medical School
Houston, Texas

JASON D. RUNYAN
Department of Neurobiology &
    Anatomy
The University of Texas-Houston
    Medical School
Houston, Texas

IOANNA SAVVIDOU
1st Psychiatric Clinic
Aristotle University of Thessaloniki
Thessaloniki, Greece

PANAGIOTIS G. SIMOS
Department of Psychology
University of Crete
Rethymnon, Greece

The Amnesias

1

Phenomena and Constructs

ANDREW C. PAPANICOLAOU

AMNESIA VERSUS AGNOSIA, APRAXIA, AND APHASIA

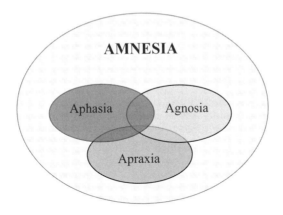

We use the word "memory" to refer, interchangeably, to at least six distinct things, a process that causes a great deal of confusion in ordinary speech and in technical discourse. First, the word refers to a function or operation conceived in the abstract; second, to the brain structures and processes that mediate such operations; third, to the neural codes or traces that, when activated, represent specific memory experiences; fourth, to any such experiences; fifth, to a category label for a particular kind of such experiences; and sixth, to a system consisting of a set of functions and brain structures and a set of mnemonic traces that are also collectively referred to as "contents" of the memory system.

To minimize unnecessary confusion, we will endeavor throughout this book to make clear which of the six is the intended meaning of memory in the different contexts where it may occur. At this point, we will describe briefly the six alternative referents of the term "memory," starting with function.

A function, or its constituent operations, is conceived in the abstract as a set of algorithms, analogous to the computer programs necessary for producing particular concrete tokens of it, in this case particular memories. An example of a function (as the word will be used here) is "working memory"; an example of an operation is "retrieval" or "encoding." For an algorithm to be implemented, it requires specific "hardware." In the case of memory functions, that hardware comprises sets of brain structures and the electrochemical events that occur within them. We will be using the term "brain mechanism of a function" to refer to those structures and processes that are believed to mediate it.

We postulate the existence of two memory systems, each with its own functions and brain mechanisms: primary and secondary memory systems. The first consists of two functions, "short-term (or immediate) memory" and "working memory." Short-term memory consists of the operations of effortless or incidental encoding and of retrieval, as well as the operation of maintaining or "holding" and "rehearsing" encoded experiences. Working memory entails the operations of effortful encoding and retrieval, that is, encoding and retrieval involving deliberate strategies, each of which may entail additional operations, as well as any operations that manipulate the experiences maintained in consciousness. The experiences that form the contents of either operation are said to depend on traces retrieved or newly encoded but in either case "active" ones, consisting of patterns of electrochemical activity.

The secondary memory system is viewed here as consisting of the operation or function of "consolidation," whereby active traces of experiences are gradually turned into permanent ones as soon as they cease to be active. Moreover, secondary memory may involve an additional function or set of operations of "storage," whereby traces are maintained in a nascent form for subsequent retrieval.

We further postulate (and here we part company with many commentators on memory and amnesia) that the same set of operations of encoding, retrieval, consolidation, and storage handle all different types of memory phenomena, although we follow common practice in recognizing that these phenomena form two classes: the class of explicit, or declarative, memories (further subdivided into semantic and episodic) and the class of implicit, or nondeclarative, ones. In other words, we will try to use the terms "semantic," "episodic," "implicit," and "explicit" only to identify distinct types or categories of concrete phenomena: We will try not to use them to refer sometimes to phenomena and sometimes to functions or systems, as is done routinely in the professional literature.

But, whether as a function, a system, or as the name of a collection of kindred phenomena, memory is among the ubiquitous natural occurrences. No wonder then that all psychological and biological phenomena are often thought of as manifestations of it and all biological functions as fundamentally mnemonic. In fact, one may justifiably assert that the performance of a complex motor skill is, simply, a manifestation of a memorized sequence of specific movements; that the recognition or the appropriate use of objects is, similarly, remembrance of their names or their significance and usage; and that all behavioral and all psychological disorders are no more than disorders or failures of memory. That is, one may assert that all apraxias represent, simply, the forgetting of sensorimotor habits; all agnosias the forgetting of the name and use of different kinds or classes of things; all aphasias the forgetting of the value of verbal symbols or the forgetting of how to sequence articulatory acts to produce symbols that convey specific meanings.

Moreover, all concept formation, all learning, all skill acquisition, and all acquisition of language during development can, similarly, be considered as the establishment of new mnemonic traces or representations. All learning may therefore be viewed as the strengthening of the persistence of past experiences into the present and all learning disabilities and all developmental disorders as mere failures of retaining perceptual experiences, thoughts, ideas, and sensorimotor acts.

Although this is so and although it has always been appreciated as such (all Muses, personifying the human skills, were, according to the ancient myth, daughters of Mnemosyne), the term "memory" is reserved for only some categories of behavioral and psychological phenomena, and so is the term "amnesia." As for the segregation and distinction of mnemonic from non-mnemonic (and amnesic from nonamnesic) phenomena, it is by no means based on ontological or epistemological criteria. That is, it does not reflect well-established differences in the defining attributes or in the neurophysiological mechanisms of the mnemonic and the nonmnemonic phenomena, nor does it reflect a formal (i.e., logical) categorical divide between them. Rather, it is a division drawn by convention, along the continuum of their common attributes and, quite possibly, their common cerebral mechanisms. But conventions vary with the prevailing theoretical winds; therefore, the border that separates amnesias from the rest of the disorders shifts accordingly. Thus, some phenomena close to the dividing lines are at times called amnesic and at other times aphasic; some experts identify some phenomena as instances of apraxia or agnosia, whereas others think of them as instances of amnesia instead. The convention followed here for segregating amnesic phenomena may be roughly summarized thus:

Not understanding speech, not being able to automatically and effortlessly connect particular sound aggregates (spoken words) with the particular concepts that each aggregate symbolizes, will be called aphasia. And it is commonly agreed that aphasia is the proper label here, to the degree that all or most words of one's language are involved. On the other hand, if one consistently forgets new words, the meaning of which one has recently learned, then the condition is called amnesia.

More analytically, if words cease to have meaning, in the sense that they are not recognized as words of one's language, then the condition is one of receptive aphasia. If, on the other hand, the words are recognized as such and are not mistaken for nonsense sounds, yet their referent escapes us, then the condition may be classified as amnesic. In amnesia, the words are recognized as words in one's language and are never mistaken for nonsense speech or for tokens of an unknown language.

Moreover, not comprehending speech, especially when it is delivered at high rates or when it involves long sentences with many embedded clauses (even though one may understand isolated words), is not aphasia but amnesia, as is the inability to deliver cohesive speech when one loses the stream of his thought in midsentence. However, the inability either to sequence articulatory acts to produce intelligible words or to sequence words to construct meaningful sentences may not be considered an amnesic but an aphasic disorder.

Notice that we designate as amnesic phenomena those that involve the forgetting of specific tokens or products of the function but not the procedures for producing them, and we designate as aphasic those phenomena that involve the opposite. Specifically, expressive aphasia involves problems with plans of production (articulatory or syntactic), and receptive aphasia involves problems with procedures for recognizing speech sounds as meaningful.

Similar rules of classification apply to agnosia: If one can no longer recognize, describe, name, or use common objects, the condition is classified as agnosia, which is a perceptual disorder. But if an individual cannot recognize, describe, name, or appropriately use a gadget the name and function of which were explained to him on a couple of occasions (say, an hour ago), then the condition is called, once again, amnesia. Instances of amnesia should also be those where forgetting involves particular tokens of kinds or of categories of things, although this convention is not consistently followed, as the case of prosopagnosia demonstrates.

Prosopagnosia is the difficulty or the inability to connect the percept of a face (a visual object) with a name and with other circumstances associated with that face. A prosopagnosic does not confuse faces with houses unlike "the man who mistook his wife for a hat" (Sacks, 1970). He simply cannot identify facts connected to particular faces that establish their individuality and identity. Prosopagnosia, then, could be considered a memory disorder and not a perceptual one, for the same reason that not being able to identify different models of automobiles (that were previously memorized) does not constitute agnosia but amnesia for learned facts. It seems then that the agnosias may be said to differ from the amnesias in two points. First, the former involve difficulties with recognizing particular tokens as instances of kinds (e.g., recognizing this object as a hat and that as a book), which is a difficulty with a fundamental procedure that mediates the process of coming to know the nature of particular objects of perception. Amnesias, on the other hand, involve the inability to retain specific incidental information associated with specific things, the kind of which is nevertheless recognized. Second, agnosia involves difficulties with extremely frequently used processes and with processes that have been used for a long time, whereas amnesia involves difficulties with less frequent, less overlearned items.

The same conventions could apply to the distinction between amnesia and apraxia: Not being able to play-act brushing one's teeth, which is an automated habit, is not called amnesia, but apraxia, whereas not being able to play on the piano a piece of music that one has just learned is amnesia. Here again, apraxia involves, first, difficulties with procedures of sequencing actions automatically. (In fact, expressive aphasia may be viewed as a variety of apraxia involving symbolic actions). Amnesia, on the other hand, involves the forgetting of particular actions (e.g., how to operate your new digital camera rather than how to dress, or how to operate any camera although some time ago you could). Second, as in the case of agnosia and aphasia also, in apraxia what is lost is the ease of production of sequences that are overlearned, automated, and frequently performed, whereas in amnesia what is lost are not specific overlearned or entirely automated action sequences but knowledge of specific experiences or facts.

In general, then, it appears that the continuum on which the dividing line is drawn between amnesias, on one hand, and the aphasias, the apraxias, and the agnosias, on the other hand, is the degree of automaticity that memorized habits, behavioral or experiential units or sequences have attained, as well as the degree to which, and the length of time, these habits have been in existence. Moreover, whereas the aphasias, the agnosias, and the apraxias involve an inability to use procedures and concepts, the amnesias involve difficulties with particular instances or specific tokens of different kinds of procedures or concepts.

MNEMONIC AND AMNESIC PHENOMENA

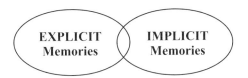

On one side of the above-mentioned conventional divide, the side of memory and the amnesias, there is a great variety of things remembered and forgotten. These fall into two broad classes. In one belong things of which we are, or can be, consciously aware; in the other belong things the presence or absence of which we can only infer. Examples of the first kind may be the recalled events that transpired last Christmas Eve or the recollection of the date Columbus discovered America. An example of the latter may be the fact that my typing speed has improved after 10 days of practice, a fact that justifies the inference that every time I worked on hitting the intended keys, my nervous system did retain something of the experience of the correct sequence of the sensorimotor acts involved. Phenomena of the former type constitute the so-called explicit, or declarative, memory, and those of the latter type the implicit, or nondeclarative, memory. (Notice that here, the meaning of "memory" is shifted and the word is used as a category label.)

The reason why episodic memories (and other kinds of memories that also involve consciousness or awareness) are always "explicit" should be clear: Our being conscious of them makes them so. Moreover, being conscious of anything concrete, such as the image of a past percept, implies that the image always will be both declarative of the type of thing of which it is a token and declarable, that is to say, admitting of articulation or expression through verbal or other symbols. And this is the origin and rationale of the additional (or alternative) label of "declarative" for episodic and other memories that are similarly declarable and declarative.

Explicit Memories and Their Groupings

Explicit memories have been classified into two main categories: one is the category of remembered concrete episodes and is called episodic; the other is the category of remembered information. Because most information is known to us though a variety of symbols that carry meaning, mainly verbal symbols, this category of memories is named "semantic," an adjective derived from the Greek word for "meaning" or "denotation" (Tulving, 1972).

In recent years, the term "autonoetic awareness" or "autonoetic consciousness" was coined, as well as the term "noetic awareness" or "noetic consciousness," to denote awareness of episodic and semantic memories, respectively. Moreover, the distinction between "remembering" and "knowing" was reintroduced to denote the experiencing episodic and semantic memories and also to remind us of the differences in the quality of experience attending the remembering of episodes versus the remembering (or knowing) of facts or concepts. But the phrase "autonoetic awareness or consciousness" is a tautology ("autonoetic" being the adjectival form of "self-awareness"), and all the rest of the newly coined terms do little more than reaffirm the well-known fact that there is such thing as possession of knowledge of facts and concepts that was always called knowledge and knowing, as well as possession of personal memories that was always called memories and remembering, and which feels very different from recalling and using our knowledge of things, a difference that some people may have lost sight of once the terms "semantic" and "episodic" memory were introduced.

So, the issuing of the new terms has at least served to remind those who had forgotten of the distinct realities of remembering and knowing. But because these newer terms express the same abiding realities as the familiar (albeit not necessarily more apt) ones, namely "semantic" and "episodic," and in the interest of containing the already exploding odds of pointlessly confusing the reader, we will retain the latter.

Although most facts are known and conveyed to us through verbal symbols, not all of them are so conveyed and registered, for there are all sorts of symbol systems besides language; for example, geometric or pictorial. Thus, not all semantic memories are verbal. Similarly, though many episodes contain verbal incidents, many, if not most, do not. In fact, our episodic memories, much like our psychological present, that is, our current experiences, are dominated by visual sensations and percepts. Therefore, both categories of explicit memory entail both, verbal and nonverbal (mostly visual) elements. This fact is worth noting because it corresponds to a neurophysiological fact of hemispheric specialization for explicit memories. Namely, it appears that there is a difference between the two cerebral hemispheres with the left specializing, in some, still unclear ways, for verbally encoded memories and the right for nonverbally encoded ones.

Varieties of Episodic Memories

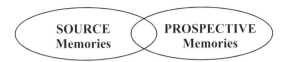

There are two types of phenomena that are deemed, unequivocally, mnemonic: first, the reexperiencing of an event that has transpired in the past along with the realization that it is reexperienced, and second, the carrying out of a decision or a plan, made in the past, at the preappointed time and place. And there are two types of phenomena deemed, as unequivocally, amnesic: first, consistently forgetting events that have transpired, and second, forgetting, also consistently, to carry out plans without also experiencing notable difficulties with other cognitive functions. Remembered episodes and plans constitute episodic memory and consistently forgetting them constitutes amnesia for episodes, or episodic amnesia. There are two types of episodic amnesia. One, which we may call immediate episodic forgetting, refers to the phenomenon of never reexperiencing an episode once it was experienced. The other, which we may call episodic forgetting proper, refers to the phenomenon whereby an episode is forgotten after having been reexperienced at least once. This distinction is necessary if we are to avoid confusing these phenomena with those of anterograde and retrograde amnesia, which, as explained in a subsequent section of this chapter, refer to the forgetting of events and facts acquired before and after the onset of some cerebral pathology, respectively. Clearly, one's anterograde amnesia may include forgetting things experienced after the lesion and never again remembered, as well as forgetting things also experienced after the lesion but which had been remembered at least once. Similarly, someone's retrograde amnesia may include forgetting of events experienced before the lesion but never remembered and events or facts that had been remembered at least once.

However, whereas remembered episodes compose a type of plain episodic memory, remembered plans constitute prospective memory—a rather curious name. Consequently, consistently forgetting concrete episodes is plain episodic amnesia, whereas forgetting to carry out plans, on schedule, must, for the sake of consistency, be given the rather awkward name of "prospective" amnesia, a name that, possibly for reasons of elementary linguistic sensibilities, most of us instinctively avoid using.

Moreover, remembering the particular circumstances, notably the time and place in which an episode has transpired, is an indication of yet another variety of episodic memory, namely "source" memory, which, in view of the fact that the circumstances, especially the particular time and place an episode has occurred, are the defining features of episodic memory at large, is a rather gratuitous subcategory. Convention and convenience, however, has established its use as a shorthand expression for the very detailed memory of, typically, a particular variety of episodes, mostly episodes where verbal information is exchanged, which includes the people and circumstances that constitute the "source" of the information.

Consequently, source amnesia is a variety of episodic amnesia, an embarrassing instance of which is repeating a piece of news, as news, to the very person who first informed us of it. Now, source amnesia need not be amnesia for verbally encoded material only. Episodes dominated by visual or auditory elements may be as easily forgotten as failing to remember people's faces or places just visited or to recall a melody just heard plainly demonstrate.

But we have come a long way without having explicitly commented on the nature of the basic unit of episodic memories; that is, the "episode." An episode, then, is a cohesive and identifiable set of several sensorimotor, and sometimes affective, experiences and thoughts, including the experiences of the time, the place, and the other circumstances that define it as a unique and concrete experiential entity. But no episode would be a mnemonic one if it were not for an ineffable quality that attends it and differentiates it from current percepts, actions, emotions, and thoughts experienced for the first time. In fact, it is rather uncommon to confuse a current experience with a mnemonic one.

Now, percepts and sensations that compose a mnemonic episode are not all experienced in exactly the same manner by all people, a fact that may prove significant for understanding the nature of memory: Most people have no difficulty in recalling, in detail, visual and auditory percepts but are unable to reexperience in the same manner and with the same degree of clarity, gustatory, olfactory, tactile, or somatesthetic sensations. Similarly difficult, or impossible, is for most people to remember emotions. For most people, it appears as if only percepts, that is, representations of the external world, may be readily recalled as such, whereas recall of sensations and emotions as such, that is, recall of states of the body, is either rare or not possible at all. Instead, people recall or recognize the external circumstances or the thoughts that had occasioned or surrounded these sensations, and, in the case of emotions, people may "reexperience" the state, but that experience does not have that ineffable quality, alluded to before, which allows us to know without doubt whether it is a new, current one or a reenactment of a past episode. That is, remembering of an emotion is remembering its source and circumstances, which, in turn, results in a current emotional state, analogous to the original one. Similarly, to recognize a taste or a smell is to associate it with that perceptual object encountered in the past that had that particular taste or smell. That is, once again, the remembering of a sensation is fundamentally the remembering of its external causes; that is, objects and events that belong to the external world.

Another observation worth noting here is that, by and large, each of the sensorimotor experiences and thoughts that may compose a given episode entail knowledge of the world; that is, concepts already developed and motor behavior and perception already learned and automated. For example, both the episode of experiencing a car accident and its recollection presuppose ready recognition of cars, roads, stop signs, possession of driving habits, knowledge of traffic regulations, and so on. They presuppose, in other words, memory of facts, habits, and concepts, which means semantic as well as all sorts of implicit memory (about which more below) in addition to general procedures and functions of knowing, of communicating, and of acting (disturbance of which, as it has been said, results in agnosia, aphasia, and apraxia). Now if, as most people believe, concepts and habits do not predate birth but are formed gradually by repeated exposure to concrete episodes during development, then we are faced with a paradox where being conscious of episodes presupposes semantic and habit memory while formation of such memories presupposes the accumulation of episodic memories. Curiously, current debates regarding the logical and temporal priority of either the episodic or the semantic memory give the impression that the issue is an important discovery of our age. Rarely is it realized that such debates are rather amateurish reenactments of millennia-old philosophic reflection. Setting aside this paradox that has plagued Western thought since it first emerged from the epic clash between the Platonic and the Aristotelian doctrines and passing it over to students of cognitive development, we may simply register the fact that episodic memories of sentient human beings consist of already familiar concepts, habits, and percepts.

Varieties of Semantic Memories

Semantic memories are always born in the form of an episode. At least this is what all empiricists since Aristotle insist, but this does not make their assertion more than a merely reasonable one. They are transformed, or so most experts believe, from remembered episodes to remembered facts when the "source" information, those features of the episode that allow us to recreate the circumstances of its original occurrence, is forgotten. For example, I can no longer see or hear in my mind's eye and ear the teacher who made sure we understood that the sum of the angles of a triangle adds up to 180 degrees, but I still remember this fact about triangles in Euclidian space: An episodic memory of mine has been transformed into a semantic one that is also mine, but mine in an entirely different sense of the word. It no longer has the intimacy of an episodic memory that is in some ways similar to the intimacy of somatic sensations; it is not mine as a pain is mine. It is mine in the same sense that the image of an external object perceived by me is mine. That is, it is incidentally mine while in truth it belongs to itself, again unlike a pain or a pleasure or the recollection of an episode that is exclusively mine. Moreover, the memory of a fact differs dramatically from the memory of an episode in that it is atemporal; it is not experienced of an episode as a sequence of successive phases unfolding in time but it emerges as if it were a single flash of intuition, all at once.

Although the manner in which facts and concepts arise in the first few years of life is not at all clear, once conceptual development is complete, once all basic concepts are formed, one may justifiably claim that semantic memories (i.e., memories for additional facts) derive from episodic ones. Sometimes a fact may emerge out of a single episode. I am sure that I learned the fact that "bella" in Italian means "beautiful" on that particular occasion that I asked someone what the repeated phrase "bella ciao," in the song with the same title, meant.

And my remembering both the episode and the fact does not make the memory of the meaning of the word any less factual. But there are certainly cases were the single episode out of which a fact emerged is forgotten, leaving behind it the plain fact. The knowledge that "fire burns" is a good example of such cases because few people would remember the relevant episode, but also few would doubt the likelihood that they acquired that factual memory in a single trial. Not a single person, though, would deny that typically facts emerge from exposure to several episodes, provided that all of them contain the essence of the facts in question: Learning the meaning of the symbol a^x, for instance, would be a good example of the process. The meaning of the symbol has most likely been acquired through the use of different examples, in the context of different episodes, where a may now represent the number 5 and later the number 10, and x may represent the number 3 or the number 25; where the symbol is now written in chalk on the blackboard and now spoken by Mr. X; and now shouted above the din of a noisy class by Mrs. Y; and where the different feelings of understanding, in each occasion, each associated with slightly different nuances of the meaning of the symbol and with different implications of its use, coalesce into the "knowledge of the symbol." Meanwhile, the voice of Mrs. Y, the face of Mr. X, the gang in the back of the classroom, making all that noise, and all the rest of the experiences, different during each episode of learning a^x, have dropped off by the wayside, leaving the meaning or the "semantic" memory of a^x standing alone, naked and purged of all irrelevant sensorimotor or affective elements.

Needless to say, how many episodes it takes for a semantic memory to emerge is a matter that depends on many factors, two of which are obvious: First, the nature of the fact. Learning the meaning of the statement "the speed of light is constant in all reference frames" may take a few more trials to internalize than the statement "Columbus discovered America"—the ultimate truth of either statement being beside the point. Second, it depends on the intentions and the abilities of the learner.

But no matter how many trials it takes, repetition of episodes that include the kernel of the factual knowledge-in-the-making will eventually result in the emergence of facts. These, like the episodes whence they sprung, will be explicit and declarative. However, with a lot of use, they may acquire automaticity, thus requiring less and less conscious effort in being summoned and used. And, under some circumstances, they may even acquire that feature of habits that enables them to materialize, in the present, without entering at all the field of our consciousness.

This paradoxical feature characterizes some types of semantic memories; because there are, indeed, several types. There are, first, the memories of facts—both verbal and nonverbal—of the type "Columbus discovered America" or "I weighed 9 lb. when I was born" or "this is the smell of cinnamon" or "these are the first notes of Beethoven's Fifth." Then there are the more abstract memories, the concepts: "a^x," "brown," "horse," "car," "face," "justice," "square," and so forth. Then, there are the symbols or symbolic memories, a specific subcategory of which are the memories of the meaning of words. Finally, there are memories of different sorts of explicit and declarative automatisms, like those of tunes that we can hum sometimes forgetting that we are humming them or like the multiplication tables, the days of the week, prayers, poems, and other overused items that sometimes we use being only half-aware of their meaning while using them correctly! These memories are of particular interest in that they point to some fundamental regularities, to some cardinal features of the architecture of memory: The degree of automaticity of memories varies proportionally with the number of repeated episodes in which they have appeared, and the more automated and more effortlessly remembered, the more unconscious but also the more resistant to extinction they become.

Semantic amnesias are phenomena whereby facts, concepts, or symbols are forgotten consistently. Given that concepts and facts can be learned in one trial, immediate semantic forgetting and semantic forgetting proper (analogous to immediate and proper episodic forgetting, with the first referring to forgetting of a fact or concept before having been remembered once after acquisition; the second referring to forgetting of a fact or concept after it has been remembered at least once) are observable phenomena. This distinction is, again, worth retaining as it was in the case of episodic memory (and amnesia), to avoid confusion with the concepts of anterograde and retrograde amnesia.

Implicit Memories and Their Groupings

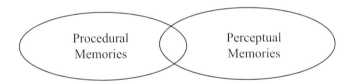

Implicit memories reside in the unconscious. Unlike explicit ones (which, though also residents of the same region, can often emerge into awareness), implicit memories cannot easily be brought into awareness, in spite of the fact that most of them were once explicit. Certainly, most of our habits and mannerisms are learned, and while learning them, we were aware of the individual sensations and movements that were required for their performance. But, as previously mentioned, with learning and automatization, consciousness of the sensorimotor events that constitute these habits receded into the unconscious. Once implicit, these learned habits, much like innate patterns of behavior, such as reflexes, remain implicit.

Implicit memories come in two basic varieties. In one belong the memories of temporally ordered sensorimotor sequences; that is, motor skills, habits, and mannerisms of all kinds. We may follow common practice and call them procedural memories. In the same category, one could include automated and unconsciously performed articulatory sequences that form the basis for speech production as well as the implicit knowledge of the appropriate temporal ordering of words, that is, the rules of syntax, which account for the fact that our speech output is grammatical, were it not for the fact that these habits constitute linguistic knowledge, and their disruption is the essence of aphasia.

In the other category belong memories of spatially extended encounters, which were not focally attended and in all likelihood were never consciously perceived. These memories may be called subliminal in view of their association with subliminal perception. They cannot be brought to consciousness, yet their existence can be inferred from the fact that they influence consequent performance. For example, you may be exposed to a visual scene for short-enough time to be unable to tell what it was about. Yet later on, having to choose between that scene and another, you choose the one to which you were exposed with sufficiently higher probability to ensure that something of the first exposure was registered and saved. The creation of this sort of memories does not require repetition, as the creation of the temporally ordered sequences of sensorimotor experiences that constitute habits do. In that respect, these memories resemble those episodes that entail strong affective components, which are also memorized after a single exposure; a similarity that may be indicative of shared components of their respective cerebral mechanisms.

Implicit memories of both varieties are extremely resistant to extinction, surpassing in that aspect explicit memories. Also, new implicit memories can be formed in individuals unable to form any new episodic memories, as it has been demonstrated in the case of the famous patient H.M. (Scoville & Milner, 1957). That, however, does not imply that people who experience difficulties in acquiring explicit memories can acquire implicit ones with the same ease as people without any memory difficulties: We all know that one "cannot teach an old dog new tricks," or that it is very difficult, at any rate, for aging individuals to learn new things, whether these involve retaining facts and episodes or just temporally ordered sensorimotor activity.

Autobiographical Memories

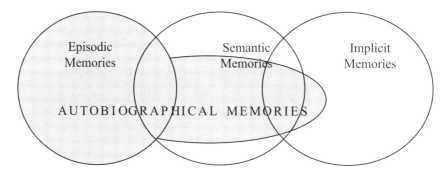

There is a class of explicit memories, both episodic and factual, that along with some implicit ones constitute our private autobiography and contribute to our "sense of self." In fact, the class of autobiographical memories includes all episodic memories, as a cardinal feature of the latter is the feeling of familiarity, commented on previously, and there is no familiarity without a self to whom things appear familiar.

It is interesting to note, in this connection, that in recalling any episode, the self that first experienced it (our former self) figures into the recollected memory as one among the other individuals or objects involved. Try to recall any concrete episode in your life: No matter how you try, you cannot avoid seeing in your mind's eye your former self doing the things you did as if you were one among the other actors of the scene. As for the percepts you remember having experienced, they seem as if they are percepts of the self that is doing the remembering now, not the former self that first experienced them. A personal example, appropriate in a commentary on autobiographical memory, may elucidate this rather opaque narrative: On a particular winter day, soon after having mastered the dangerous art of bicycle riding, I decided to race down a steep hill on a slippery country lane full of puddles of muddy water and with my hands in my coat pockets because it was rather cold. When I recollect the episode, I can't help but "see" very clearly in my mind's eye a child with severely cropped hair (that I had seen in real life on the barber's mirror just before the bicycling adventure) that I know is me, and I see the splashing water of the puddles and I see the child smiling in the exhilaration of the bumpy ride. And I also see the child suddenly falling and I see the world turning upside down just as the child had seen it, but I remain an outsider, a mere observer witnessing what the child of the recollection had witnessed in that distant afternoon.

This phenomenon of objectification of the self indicates, first, that recall of episodes is a constructive process and not a passive replay of the "record" of the original experience, because that record could not have included the self that was experiencing it as if that self was among the objects and events perceived, like them, from another's perspective. Second, it indicates that the reconstructed record is not experienced directly as it was originally but is "viewed" by an agent external to it, who is the current self. Besides these two indications that should be kept in mind if one is to attempt an explanation of the nature of memory, the same phenomenon points to the fact that it is always difficult to separate episodes recalled once versus those that have been recalled several times—as is the case with this and most other autobiographical stories. And, frequent iteration of the same episodes makes it hard to separate them from factual, that is, semantic, memories.

Aside from all episodic memories, a subset of fact memories, like the fact that I was born in a room of my grandfather's house, or that I was given the name of the uncle who was killed in the war before I was born, and other such semantic memories plus another subset of implicit ones, are the elements out of which "autonoesis" as well as our personhood, as others perceive it, are born. Among the latter type of memories, there are the tendencies to behave in particular ways of which we are not directly aware but of which others around us are (that is why they can recognize us, for example, when we approach from a distance before they can make out our features, each of us having our own particular way of walking). The fact that autobiographical memories are so varied and yet they are all connected to a single point of reference, the experiencing self, may explain why self-knowledge, knowing who we are, is the last to be extinguished by any lesion that interferes with the cerebral mechanisms of memory.

THE TWO MEMORY SYSTEMS

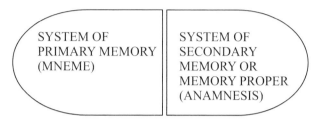

Thus far, I have been describing and classifying mnemonic and amnesic phenomena on the basis of their characteristics. The resulting groupings (implicit or explicit, semantic, episodic, or procedural memories) do not each imply separate functions or distinct cerebral representations. Rather, as it has been mentioned previously, they are meant as names of classes of memory phenomena. We now turn to the description of memory systems defined in terms of their constituent functions or operations such as the operations of "consolidation" or "retrieval." These functions are presumed to be real entities that have both psychological and neurophysiological validity. That is, they are, presumably again, algorithms embedded in the brain circuitry and are necessary for engendering the phenomena of memory.

More analytically, a function and all the subsidiary operations that may compose it may be conceived as sets of algorithms, necessary for the production of specific phenomena (in this case, representations of past experiences). These algorithms, though they are presumed to be real, not being known, are postulated, and their form may, consequently, be conceived either rightly or wrongly, in the following two senses: First, in the sense that they may or may not account satisfactorily for the characteristics of the mnemonic phenomena and the circumstances in which they transpire (psychological validity). Second, in the sense that they entail a neurophysiological mechanism that is correctly or wrongly specified (neurophysiological validity). As for the neurophysiological mechanism of a function, it may be conceived as a set of brain circuits in which the aforementioned algorithms are embodied. In other words, the function and its mechanism may be viewed as analogous to the software and the hardware of computing machines, necessary for the generation of different types of outputs and performances. Therefore, a mnemonic operation, or the memory function more generally, can be said to have psychological and neurological validity if interference with specific circuits of the brain result in predictable types of errors in the production of mnemonic output (i.e., memory deficits or amnesias). This being the case, it is clear how the study of the amnesias is likely to result in better understanding and specification of how the memory function works.

The way the memory function and its component operations will be specified here is, largely, conventional and does not derive from any one particular theory. Moreover, it is not proposed as one with already established validity but as a way of organizing the description of the facts of amnesia; that is, as a set of "working hypotheses" that these facts may vindicate or falsify, raising in the latter case, the need for conceiving them differently and replacing them with a different set.

The operations mentioned thus far and others to be mentioned below cohere into two sets, forming as it were two related yet sufficiently distinct memory systems: The system of "primary memory" and the system of "secondary memory" or "memory proper," to use the terms William James used in his *Principles of Psychology* (James, 1890). The distinction, however, was first articulated by Plato (ca. 360 BC) and the two memory systems were more aptly named the first mneme (holding in mind) and the second anamnesis (holding, again, in mind).

The neurophysiological validity of the distinction or, alternatively speaking, the existence of distinct brain mechanisms corresponding to each system is not a settled matter. Yet, the preponderance of the evidence indicates that the primary memory system entails different functions from that of secondary memory and consequently different brain mechanisms. Specifically, primary memory functions are most likely mediated by frontal lobe structures and secondary memory functions by the temporal, parietal, and occipital lobes. It is also generally believed that whereas activated traces, much like all other neural codes of experiences that constitute the current contents of consciousness, are Hebbian reverberating circuits (Hebb, 1949), that is, recurring patterns of activity in a set of neurons, permanent nascent traces of past experiences that constitute the content of the secondary memory system consist of patterns of structural changes in the synapses of sets of (most likely) the same neurons.

Constituent Functions of the Primary Memory System

The Psychological Present

The operations that constitute primary memory, along with perception, are jointly responsible for the generation of that manifold of experiences and actions that has been called the psychological present. The psychological present, unlike the ideal, abstract, mathematical present, which is that imaginary durationless point that keeps "past" and "future" separate, occupies duration, that is to say it occupies a certain amount of clock time. What is "currently experienced" requires a minimum of duration that cannot extend beyond a certain limit without changing the current experience into the next "current" one. Though this description of the psychological present may sound esoteric, mysterious, and other-worldly, there is nothing more ordinary and more directly experienced than it. To begin with, it is no different than the experience of "episodes" described earlier.

As episodes, the successive psychological presents may consist entirely of new sensorimotor experiences or percepts, but much more frequently they consist of not only new perceptual experiences but memories as well, or of memories alone. An example of a complex episode or a "psychological present" isolated in the perpetual flux of conscious experience, or the "stream of consciousness" to use William James' apt phrase, may remove some of its mystique: You are walking in the country at dawn and your friend tells you, while pointing in the direction of a ravine, "Do you hear that bird over there? It must be a nightingale, don't you think? . . . it said in the tour guide that there are nightingales around here . . . . Remember?" The onset of your companion's question has drawn your attention away from whatever you were thinking of at the time; it has changed the contents of your consciousness and it has initiated the current episode, this particular psychological present. This psychological present, like any other, has a beginning, an end, and a certain duration. It unfolds, approximately, over the amount of time it took your friend to utter the question, to point, and for you to comprehend the meaning, not only of each word, but of all of them together and to comprehend it in light of the following: First, in light of your companion's gesture, that you perceived while you were listening to the words uttered. Second, in light of the significance of the gesture and the common store of knowledge that you, your friend, and a huge sector of humanity share, which constitutes the grounds of the inference as to the type of bird it was that was singing in the ravine. Third, in light of the memory of a previous episode that emerged in your mind's eye, namely your memory of yourself reading over your friend's shoulder, in the lobby of the hotel, the tour guide she was holding open for you to see. But in order for the meaning that merges together the various components of this experience into one cohesive unit to emerge, it was necessary to "hold" in mind the echo of each gesture and word as they were reaching, one after the other, your sensory apparatus. This "holding," then, of percepts and memories may be posited as one of the necessary operations that create the psychological present. Another is the "merging" or "chunking" of them together, in ways we cannot specify, because we are not directly aware of them but can only surmise after the fact that this merging is a prerequisite for the emergence of the overall meaning and significance of the episode. Psychologists postulate a set of operations preceding the "holding," namely encoding, whereby external inputs are coded in some neurophysiologic medium in order to be "held" in sensory registers, whether iconic or echoic. Whether and to what degree encoding differs from perception is not a relevant question. For the present purposes, encoding and perception may be considered as two names for the same set of operations. The echoes now, and the icons thus held in the sensory registers, constitute part of the contents of the primary memory system. Another part of the contents is, in our example, the remembered episode of reading the tour guide; still another the also remembered fact that you knew, since childhood, that nightingales do sing in the coolness of dawn and the other fact that the bird song coming from the ravine resembled what you also have experienced and known from before (and now recognized) as the song of the nightingale. And these facts accounted for the note of confidence in your response ". . . yes it is a nightingale," while the feeling of confidence, along with your verbal response and with all the linguistic operations it required, cohere into a unitary single experiential unit: the episode that constitutes this psychological present.

But let us, for the moment, consider only the "holding" operation, as all the rest are not exclusively or primarily mnemonic. The holding lasts without special effort long enough for events, such as those of the example, to transpire. Its duration has also been called the "span of apprehension." Because its potential duration varies with attentional effort, ability to concentrate, or training, or any of a host of other variables, its estimates have varied widely. Less widely vary the estimates of the number of discreet experiential units, whether chimes of a clock, spoken words, or numbers that can fit within the span of apprehension. In fact, they seem to vary from about five to nine, Miller's (1956) famous number "seven plus or minus two."

One may object that it is inconsistent to claim that the holding capacity of the span of apprehension or of the psychological present or of an episode is only about seven items, when the immediately preceding description of the example of a typical episode certainly implied a much vaster holding capacity, a much more spacious "psychological present." The words heard and spoken alone, considered as separate items, are more than double the magical number seven. But there is no inconsistency here. Simply the words spoken and heard, and the facts and episodes recalled and recognized, are separate events only after the fact, only when described from the outside. While happening, though each had a beginning and an end, they were not individually attended; they were not appreciated as separate experiential units but as one experiential unit, one item. To understand how that may be possible, count the number of different phrases in the example above. You will find there are four. So potentially, your span of apprehension held five items. Only four items, then, made up your psychological present; only four experiential units constitute that episode. Now count the number of words: The same span of apprehension now seems to hold about 26 items. Go once more over the utterances but now count the number of phonemes. Now your span of apprehension suddenly widens to hold around 100 items. "Merging" then or "chunking" performs the miracle of condensing a virtually limitless number of external events into a single experiential, internal unit. Attentional effort or concentration, both operations of the working memory function (see below), may therefore be judged and measured in terms of how many external events or how long a stretch of objective clock time can be incorporated and merged into one experience, because, clearly, more effort is required to merge into a single experience the meaning of a long sentence, with many embedded clauses, read or heard, than a short phrase.

Rehearsal is another operation that contributes to "holding" some of the items that constitute an episode for prolonged time periods, or, to put it differently, that contribute to prolonging the psychological present, or the duration of an episode. Only, there is no expansion and no prolongation in this case (as opposed to the case of intense concentration spoken of above) but an iterative "repetition" of the separate experiential units that constitute the episode.

Rehearsal can be automatic or spontaneous, as when the chime of a clock seems to reverberate in "our head" in the silence that follows it, or when we repeat, reflexively to ourselves, the name of a person to whom we have just been introduced. Rehearsal can also be quite deliberate, as when we try to memorize a passage, where repetition of similar episodes creates, as detailed in a previous section, a semantic memory. In either case, rehearsal does prolong awareness of some items and is one of the most frequently exercised operations of the primary memory system.

The Immediate, or Short-Term, Memory and Working Memory Functions

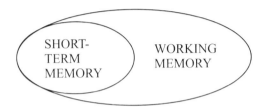

The contents of primary memory or the psychological present, insofar as they are passively held in "iconic" and "echoic" "registers," or are only rehearsed, are said to be handled by the immediate, or short-term, memory, which is one of the two functions of the primary memory system, the other being the so-called working memory. The difference between the two functions is rarely articulated clearly, but it is usually based on either or both of the following factors: the type of constituent operations each entails and the degree of effort each involves. Working memory is said to entail deliberate and strategic encoding and rehearsal, effortful retrieval, and a number of additional operations for manipulating the items that constitute the psychological present. Immediate or short-term memory, on the other hand, entails only the "holding," simple rehearsing, and effortless or incidental encoding and retrieval operations. As for its two alternative appellations (immediate and short-term), they are relics of different conceptual frameworks, but in this book they will be retained and will be used as mere synonyms, because they occur with such high frequency in the literature.

A very basic and clear example of the difference between immediate and working memory is afforded by the two versions of a subtest of the Wechsler Intelligence Scale, through which they may be assessed: The "digits forward" version of the subtest requires repetition of numbers in the order in which they are presented; the "digits backward" version requires repeating equivalent series of numbers but in the opposite order to that in which they were heard. Performance on the former, which requires repeating out loud the numbers as they were just heard, is considered a measure of the efficiency of the immediate or short-term memory function. Performance on the latter, which requires the additional operation of reversing the order (whether through visualization of the number series and "reading them off" in the opposite order or some other operation) is operationally defining the efficiency of the latter. The distinction of the two types of the primary memory functions is not trivial in the sense that each appears to involve different cerebral mechanisms as can be gathered from the fact that specific types of brain pathology (mainly in the frontal lobes) may interfere with the one but not with the other. But even in the absence of the physiological evidence, one would be hard-pressed to equate simple awareness of things with their mental manipulation; that is, with thinking itself. Parenthetically, it should be mentioned at this point that the way the concept of working memory is used in the literature differs little if at all from the concept of "thinking" on the one hand and the concept of "executive functions" on the other. And, inferring working memory whenever manipulation of items constituting the psychological present is in evidence, precludes the possibility of formally distinguishing it from thinking or executive functions for the following simple reasons: All items that constitute every psychological present, including percepts of newly witnessed objects and events, presuppose recognition, that is, classification (however automatic) of sensory input, in particular preexisting semantic categories. Moreover, no executive action—even the simplest decision to move—can be made in the absence of memory. Any decision (as opposed to a completely random action) is, after all, a choice among alternatives, and those cannot be anything but contents of the psychological present.

As mentioned earlier, the operation of rehearsal, whether deliberate or spontaneous, whether part of the immediate or the working memory function, increases the chance that the episode rehearsed will be preserved even after it disappears from awareness and is no longer part of the psychological present. In fact, the mere perception of an event or the mere "having of a thought" may suffice for them to be remembered at some distant time in the future. This transition of the contents of the psychological present into whatever it is that they are transformed into for the purpose of preservation is affected by the function or the operation of "consolidation." This term will be retained to denote the operation whereby the traces corresponding to experiences held in primary memory are transformed into more permanent types of neuronal code and strengthened for safekeeping.

Whatever this transformation and the strengthening may entail, it may transpire effortlessly and spontaneously or it may be aided through voluntary deliberate effort, rehearsal, as well as various other deliberate operations known as "mnemonic techniques," which were in great demand at the time that writing was a luxury and memorization was the only practical means of accumulating and transmitting knowledge.

Primary Memory and the Sense of Self

Given that all awareness, whether of new or past experiences, is present awareness; given that everything that exists, including the relics of the past, exists in the present; and given, finally, that primary memory includes the functions that contribute to the creation of the psychological present, we have no option but to endorse the notion that our "sense of self," or to follow current terminology, our autonoetic awareness, is a creation of primary memory.

What exactly is the sense of self, I do not pretend to know, though I do know that renaming it "autonoetic" does not really do much to advance our understanding. It is safe to say, however, that it is related to awareness of current experience, whether of our environment or our physical bodies, but more so, to awareness of our history or to our autobiographical memory—episodic, factual, and procedural. Most likely, that huge mass of autobiographical memories cannot easily coexist in the psychological present, as they would likely exceed its capacity by far. Nor can they occupy the perpetually renewable present, without rendering the person a useless narcissist, pathologically self-absorbed and entirely cut off from the rest of the world.

This being the case, we must assume that most of our autobiographical history must lay beyond the fringes of our span of apprehension (filled as the latter is with the constantly updated results of monitoring the world and interacting with it) but must be readily accessible in short notice: Percepts, ideas, and plans all have meaning only in reference to and in the light of our personal history. It is therefore necessary for the operations of primary memory to dart into that metaphorical space beyond the fringes of awareness to fetch the needed fragments of memories that are part of our autobiography and in light of which the rest of the contents of current awareness acquires meaning: It would not be possible for somatic sensations to be "our" sensations, fleeting thoughts to be "our" thoughts, and the surrounding objects that constitute the world to be "our" environment, our space and time, unless we possess a prodigious capacity to concentrate all memories that constitute our history and condense that mass into a single experience: the sense of self. But whatever the case might be precisely, it is the primary memory system that creates our sense of identity.

The ready access to an enormous variety and number of memories, on the part of primary memory functions, or its even more prodigious capacity to merge them all into one experience, may explain the fact that to be confused about who we are, to be "disoriented to person," as the expression goes, requires a great deal of interference with the cerebral mechanisms of memory. It is much easier to be disoriented with respect to time. Mild inattention or fatigue could produce such disorientation because, in the absence of a calendar that would provide us with time, day, month, and year, at one glance, the point we occupy in time must be inferred from a recreation, within the psychological present, of a subset of recent episodes that are largely disconnected but contain the relevant clues. Disorientation with respect to place (i.e., where we are) is more difficult to produce possibly because there are more *external cues* that can help us orient ourselves in space even when the brain mechanisms of primary memory are severely compromised by diseases, whereas no such cues are readily available for orienting ourselves in time.

Retrieval

Because retrieval operates on experiences that have passed outside the psychological present and have become part of the long-term, or secondary, memory system, it is often misconstrued as a secondary memory operation. But it is obvious, upon reflection, that retrieval manifests itself in the psychological present. It is "now" that I spontaneously recall an episode, now that I recognize a person, and now that I remember the fact about which I am asked; it is "now," in short, that I access and recreate images of my past.

Accessing the past and retrieving memories is accomplished in various ways, and we postulate different subsidiary operations of retrieval corresponding to each. These operations may be ordered according to the degree of attentional effort each entails. Least effortful is the operation of "recognition," whereby a version of or a part of a past episode is perceived in the present, giving rise to the feeling of recognition, as for example when we perceive a person and recognize her as the one we met yesterday. Equally effortless is the operation of spontaneous recall of episodes or facts that come to mind (that is, in the psychological present) for no apparent reason. One may further consider as manifestations of spontaneous recall such things as an errorless and fluid performance on the piano, of a piece learned last month, or the uttering of a grammatically correct sentence in a newly learned foreign language without having to think through, beforehand, how we should order the words we are about to articulate. Needless to say, the former examples are of the operation of recall involving explicit and the latter implicit memories.

Next in order of difficulty come the various operations of cued recall, whereby a percept or a concept associated in different ways and to different degrees with particular episodes prompt the recall of the latter. A typical example of the implementation of this type of an operation of retrieval is paired-associates learning. Clearly, the strength of the association between the cue and the episodes or facts to be recalled determines the relative ease or the degree of effort the operation entails. At one extreme, cued-recall is as easy as recognition, provided that the cue is almost identical to some aspect of the episode or the fact to be recalled, as for example when the odor of pine reminds us of the park we visited last week. At the other extreme, cued recall can be extremely demanding as in cases where the cue or cues are nonspecific and tenuously connected with the memories to be retrieved, as for instance in the case of the so-called free-recall (which, more often than not, is confused with spontaneous, or unbidden, recall). In free-recall, there is always a cue, namely the suggestion to recall a set of episodes that happened at a specific time and place, as for example when we are told to recount a story we were just told or a list of items, whether words, pictures, or objects, that we were shown.

Considerably more effortful are retrieval operations that involve additional sets of operations of working memory. These sets are virtually unlimited in number in that one can conceive of situations and tasks where retrieval may involve any number of alternative combinations of operations. Some of these sets are used more frequently than others in daily life; some others are used only in the laboratories of creative scientists. Examples of the former are situations where we are asked to remember particular aspects of a past episode, like "what color were the walls of the meeting room" out of which we had just walked. If that aspect of the episodes that constitutes the memory of the meeting were not focally attended or, to use an alternative expression, were not deliberately encoded in anticipation of having to be recalled, its retrieval would require re-creating, in the psychological present, the entire series of episodes that constituted the "meeting" (like entering, looking around, talking to people) in the hope that among them we would discover that episode that includes a glimpse of the color of the room or an episode that includes the hearing of a random comment like "what a bright room this is! I guess it is the yellowish color that makes it so!" that prompted us to look momentarily and encode that particular aspect of our past experience.

Incidentally, the fact that we often surprise ourselves with our ability to retrieve things that we were not aware we had experienced has led some theorists to propose that not only things we are aware of, as we move through time (in other words, not the contents of our ever-renewable psychological present alone) are preserved, but also things at or beyond the fringes of our awareness—a proposal that raises serious difficulties for the very concept of storage of memories or of the preservation of our past, as we will see in the last chapter.

Still more effortful retrieval operations are those of "monitoring," or of keeping within the span of present awareness, episodes or aspects of episodes that one has just retrieved. Monitoring operations are embodied in the frequently used "n-back" tasks used to assess the integrity of working memory or to identify the cerebral mechanisms of its constituent operations through functional imaging studies.

In addition to these operations of retrieval, there is another one, which is inferred from behavioral performances and which indicates reactivation of implicit memories. Properly speaking, it cannot be considered a retrieval operation any more than the operation of consolidation can, in that it consists in the gradual emergence of a fact, like the learning of a poem, through rehearsal, or the gradual formation of a sensorimotor procedure, like the playing of a piece on the piano or the uttering of a sentence in a foreign language, and is inferred from incremental improvements in such performances. Specifically, the inference is that with each iteration of the performance, something is saved or gained, and the experimental method that records these gains in performance has been called the method of "savings."

Akin to it is the experimental procedure of "priming," thought to reveal the occult operation of either retrieval or consolidation that underlies performances indicative of implicit memory, formed in the context of perceptual tasks, in the absence of any awareness of that which has been implicitly memorized. For this occult operation, a neurophysiological mechanism in the posterior region of the brain has been postulated, and verification of its existence is sought indirectly through the study of amnesias and, directly, through neuroimaging.

The Secondary Memory System and its Constituent Functions

Once the current experiences pass outside the moving circle of the light of awareness that illuminates the psychological present, they are either lost forever or they are preserved in some way or another. But as commented on earlier, there are those who, like the once prominent philosopher Henri Bergson (e.g.,

Bergson, 1911), believe that nothing is ever lost but that the entire past is preserved, embedded somehow into the present, albeit into the unconscious regions of the present. Intriguing as these proposals might be, they will not concern us here, though they ought to be kept in mind when alternative solutions to questions regarding the nature of memory are considered.

Whether or not all experiences survive oblivion, the fact is that many of them do, and the question of immediate urgency is how they manage to do so. To answer it, it appears necessary to postulate that they are preserved in the brain in a form suitable not only for preservation but for easy access as well. Specifically, we assume a function or a set of operations that we call "consolidation," the first act of which is to transform the neurophysiological events that correspond to current experiences into traces suitable for preservation.

A subsequent act of consolidation, or a series of acts, is to gradually strengthen these physical traces, rendering them resistant to extinction. In addition to consolidation, sometimes people postulate separate "storage" operations that maintain these traces. Although these operations of secondary memory are largely hypothetical, current research is unveiling gradually the brain mechanisms in which they are embodied and through which they are implemented. One such neurochemical mechanism is the one involving "long-term potentiation," through which the reverberating circuits that Hebb (1949) postulated to represent primary memories are transformed into a pattern of synaptic modifications of sets of neurons, and in that form they are "stored" and preserved. A more detailed account of this process is given in the next chapter.

Here, we will make a few comments on the ways theorists have conceived the general form that traces may assume in the brain. Two basic forms have been proposed. One form may be called the wax-tablet imprint in recognition of Plato's contribution to the issue of how memories are preserved. In his dialogue "Theaitetus" (ca. 360 BC), Plato proposed (and countless generations of scientists reaffirmed the proposal over the centuries) that each experience, each episode or concept or fact, once it appears in consciousness, leaves on the substance of the soul (or, for that matter, the brain) an imprint like a stamp would on a tablet of wax. The theorists who either never noticed or simply forgot that Plato proposed the "wax-tablet" idea—only to demonstrate its utter inadequacy to account for how information is acquired and retained—found similar, more sophisticated analogues of traces in photographs, audio tapes, and digital CDs to bolster its apparent validity, retained its main feature (namely, that there is a strict isomorphism or correspondence of each aspect of the stored experience to an aspect of the imprinted trace), but they added one new idea to the original proposal, thus creating two varieties of imprinted traces. The first variety of traces, the original one, consists of one contiguous imprint that preserves the continuity of the original experience. For example, the visual experience of a horse is etched like a drawing or a picture on a set of contiguous neurons. The second, newer variety of traces consists of a noncontiguous imprint of the original experience. Here, the mnemonic trace of a horse would look like a mosaic, the pebbles of which are spread out over widely separated neurons. That way, it becomes possible to explain why focal lesions have never rendered anyone incapable of remembering a horse's front right leg, let us say, while allowing one to remember the rest of the horse.

Moreover, to address the vexing issue as to how an apparently limitless number of experiences can all be accommodated by a finite set of cell assemblies (whether contiguous or not), some theorists have proposed yet another variety of traces, each of which retains the imprint of one of a finite set of features, various combinations of which may suffice to create an infinite number of episodic memories or of facts and concepts, much like combinations of the 26 letters of the alphabet suffice to create an infinite number of meaningful sentences.

A particular variant of the second form of traces proposed is even more intriguing in that it does away with imprints isomorphic to experience, whether pictures or tracts of audio tape or video, in favor of the hologram. This conception of the mnemonic trace introduced by Pribram (1971) has the advantages of distributed storage and the advantage to store on the same piece of medium, the same neuron or neuronal assembly, a virtually limitless number of different traces, superimposed one on top of the other. The main difficulty with this form of traces is that thus far it has not been shown what electrochemical processes in the brain may play the role of the different components of any hologram.

Whether in the form of holograms or in the form of the more conventional traces, memories undergo definite changes. The most common and familiar of those is ordinary forgetting. Memories, once clear and distinct, may with the passage of time fade and become indistinct or disappear altogether. A less commonly observed change is a gradual one documented by Bartlett (1932/1995) in which the content of the remembered experience is modified, while the transformed experiences, though deviating more and more with each successive recall, feel as authentic clear and veridical as ever.

These changes indicate that the mnemonic traces are far from immutable, and they undergo decay and/or transformation either on their own or through interference by newly formed traces with which they possibly share the storage medium (i.e., the same set of neurons). The fact that we have no direct access to the "stored" traces but only indirect access, conditioned by primary memory functions, especially retrieval, raises a series of hardly answerable questions. First, it raises the question as to how much of what appear to us to be veridical memories are in fact confabulations. That some of them must be is rather certain, as Bartlett's observations suggest. But whether just a few or most of them are confabulations is far from certain, and such uncertainty undermines the validity of all sorts of testimony as in courts of law where the veridicality of memories are of great importance. Second, it raises the even harder question to answer, namely whether all or just some experiences that were part of a bygone psychological present are permanently stored. Although we are inclined to assert the latter, situations like the one in our previous example, where we may recall the color of the carpet of a meeting room never focally attended, give us pause as does the following excerpt from Camus' famous novel *The Stranger*. The hero of Camus' story, in trying to overcome boredom in his jail cell, turned to his memories for solace and, he tells us, once I'd learned the trick of remembering things, I never had a moment's boredom. Sometimes I would exercise my memory on my bedroom and, starting from a corner, make the round, noting every object I saw on the way. At first it was over in a minute or two. But each time I repeated the experience, it took a little longer. I made a point of visualizing every piece of furniture, and each article upon or in it, and then every detail of each article, and finally the details of the details, so to speak: a tiny dent or incrustation, or a chipped edge, and the exact grain and color of the woodwork. At the same time I forced myself to keep my inventory in mind from start to finish, in the right order and omitting no item. With, the result that, after a few weeks, I could spend hours merely in listing the objects in my bedroom. I found that the more I thought, the more details, half-forgotten or malobserved, floated up from my memory. There seemed no end to them.

So I learned that even after a single day's experience of the outside world a man could easily live a hundred years in prison. He'd have laid up enough memories never to be bored. . . . (Camus, 1942, pp. 98–99)

So, once again, are all our experiences stored or are most of our memories mostly confabulations? Whether the study of the amnesias in which we are about to embark will suffice to procure answers to these particular riddles, I very much doubt. But I do believe it will illuminate other, equally vast, tracts of ignorance that remain for us to conquer.

SYNDROMES OF AMNESIA: AN OVERVIEW

In this book, we approach the facts of the amnesias with three fundamental questions in mind: First, what kinds of memories are forgotten: only episodes, both episodes and facts, only autobiographical, only verbal, both verbal and nonverbal, mostly visual or olfactory? Second, the disruption of what memory functions or constituent operations are responsible for such forgetting: only effortful retrieval, all working memory operations, both working memory and consolidation? Third, what neurophysiological mechanisms are implicated?

Our search is guided by certain characteristics of mnemonic and amnesic phenomena, taught to us by experience, common to all workers in the field, which have helped us formulate the above questions. The same common experience has enabled us to draw some broad theoretical categories necessary for identifying and classifying the amnesic phenomena. And, treating those theoretical constructions as mere working hypotheses, we will endeavor to determine whether the clinical evidence justifies or disconfirms them and, if so, what alternative hypotheses they might lead us to adopt.

A set of such hypotheses regarding the putative cerebral mechanisms of different mnemonic operations are offered in Chapter 2. They are intended to provide a convenient means for illustrating the neuroanatomical and neurotransmitter systems, the malfunction of which appears responsible for the various amnesic syndromes. We will begin the description of the latter with the most benign and natural one; that is, normal decline of memory with advancing age. How consistently one must forget things, what and how many things and under what circumstances, before we are justified in replacing the term "forgetting" with the term "amnesia" in describing the condition, is not at all clear. The difficulty in separating normal forgetting from amnesia is compounded when increases in the rate of forgetting are accompanied by decrements in other cognitive functions, as in the case of aging. The reason for this difficulty is obvious, given that performance on every test of cognition or intelligence presupposes and requires memory, and given that working memory, as currently conceived, is almost coextensive with thinking. The issues associated with establishing, with clarity, differences between normal forgetting and generalized decrements in cognition on one hand, and amnesia on the other hand, are discussed in Chapter 3, which deals with decline of the function of memory in all its aspects and manifestations in normal aging.

In Chapter 4, we review accelerated and pathological forgetting associated with neurodegenerative dementing disorders (Alzheimer, frontotemporal dementia, Huntington, and Parkinson diseases), as well as dementias due to vascular diseases.

In Chapters 5 and 6, we describe the "semantic" and "limbic" amnesias, respectively. The former involves selective forgetting of facts and concepts. The latter constitutes what most people consider the prototypical amnesic syndrome, in that it involves inability to accumulate new memories (especially episodic), as well as forgetting of both episodes and facts already learned.

In Chapter 7, we review the constellation of symptoms and signs that characterize the amnesia produced by head injuries, which we have called, following common practice, "traumatic amnesia." The next group of three chapters (Chapters 8, 9, and 10) describe three types of transient amnesias: namely, "transient global amnesia"; the syndrome produced by epileptic seizures, "transient epileptic amnesia"; and the one produced by electroconvulsive therapy (ECT), "ECT-induced amnesia."

The fact that some of these transient amnesias are precipitated by events of precisely known or determinable onset, duration, and intensity (such as the ECT) enables us to identify and distinguish between "retrograde," "anterograde," and "posttraumatic" or "postictal" amnesias; the first referring to the inability of remembering events that transpired before, the second of events that transpired after the precipitating event, and the latter for either type of event (i.e., either retrograde or anterograde amnesia), so long as it is manifested and for as long as it is manifested after the traumatic event.

Chapter 11 will cover the so-called psychogenic amnesias. The cardinal feature of those is "disorientation to person," an apparent failure of the primary memory system to summon autobiographical information to the fore.

Notice that the classification of these as well all other amnesic syndromes presented in this book is not always based on the presenting symptomatology or aspects of it but is also based on precipitating factors, the pathophysiology, or whatever aspect has traditionally appeared most prominent or more expedient for diagnosis or for addressing the usual referral questions. Besides expediency, we are following, in this respect, this common practice, because symptomatology is not always sufficiently clear, and the pathophysiology is often unknown for either of them to be used consistently as the sole basis for classifying the amnesic syndromes.

As mentioned above, in all chapters we have endeavored first to specify the types of memories, the absence of which marks a particular syndrome, and the diagnostic instruments used in assessing and classifying them; second, to identify disruption of which operations may be implicated; and third, to list all credible evidence regarding the pathophysiological mechanisms mediating each syndrome. Each chapter concludes with some generalizations regarding memory that the evidence reviewed allows. Finally, a brief commentary of the implications of all the reviewed evidence will be attempted in Chapter 12, the only speculative part of this volume.

2

Putative Brain Mechanisms of the Various Memory Functions

PRAMOD K. DASH, JASON D. RUNYAN, SONJA BLUM,
APRIL E. HEBERT, PANAGIOTIS G. SIMOS, AND
ANDREW C. PAPANICOLAOU

As was noted in the previous chapter, a distinction may be drawn between memories (mnemonic phenomena) on the one hand and memory functions or operations on the other. The latter may be conceived as sets of procedures or algorithms embodied in and expressed by neuronal activity in different sets of brain structures, referred to as mechanisms of the respective functions. In this chapter, we will review the putative mechanisms of the basic functions of primary and secondary memory. First, the gross anatomical units constituting these mechanisms and their interconnections will be presented. Second, the "microscopic" biochemical events, starting with those constituting neurotransmission and including those that partake in operations like encoding, consolidation, and retrieval of memories will be discussed. Finally, the influence of hormone release and of drugs on these biochemical events will be described in order to facilitate understanding of the effects of drugs on memory and, more generally, understanding of the interaction between autonomic nervous system events, like those implicated in emotional states, and the cerebral mechanisms of memory.

ANATOMY

Mechanisms of the Primary Memory System

Two basic functions constitute the primary memory system: "short-term" and "working" memory. As mentioned in the previous chapter, the difference between the two, according to current convention, is that the former entails the operations of automatic and effortless encoding, holding, and retrieving (as in recognition and spontaneous recall), and the latter entails operations of selective attention, monitoring, and manipulation of memories that render the operations of encoding and retrieval deliberate and effortful and furnish the core ingredients for all thinking and all other "executive" functions (e.g., Belleville, Peretz, & Arguin, 1992). The mechanisms of these operations will be described in the following sections.

Brain Structures Involved in Encoding

The generation of neuronal activity patterns that represent features of sensory input takes place in the primary sensory and the association areas of the brain. "Storage" of the traces representing experiences also require these same association areas; however, the selection, manipulation, and, in part, the temporary maintenance of these representations in consciousness seems to require the participation of the prefrontal cortex (e.g., Petrides, 2000). The approximate location and extent of association areas in the anterior (frontal) and posterior (temporal and parietal) parts of the human cortex is shown in Figure 2–1.

Damage to posterior association areas generally impairs primary memory in that it interferes with initial encoding of the experiences. For instance, brain lesions that encroach upon auditory association cortices cause deficits in verbal short-term memory, such as the ability to hold, or maintain in the psychological present, a short list of words, in addition to impairments in phonological processing and comprehension of spoken language (Heilman, Scholes, & Watson, 1976). Generally, the performance of patients sustaining lesions in these areas, on a variety of short-term memory tasks, is consistent with the view that the brain regions involved in the encoding of complex stimuli overlap, at least partially, with the regions that support the temporary maintenance of the awareness of these stimuli (Martin, Saffran, & Dell, 1996). The performance of patients with acute lesions in posterior temporal and temporoparietal regions suggests impairment in the ability to store verbal information for periods of minutes either passively or effortfully (Vallar, Di Betta, & Silveri, 1997). The role of structures located deep inside the temporal lobe (medial temporal lobe structures such as the hippocampus) in the temporary maintenance of information is a much contested issue. Lesion studies in humans indicate that the hippocampus is not necessary for short-term memory of familiar stimuli (e.g., letters) (Cave & Squire, 1992), but bilateral hippocampal lesions may disrupt the ability to "hold" novel stimuli, such as spatial locations, even over short time periods (i.e., for 12 seconds or more; Owen, Sahakian, Semple et al., 1995).

Multiple prefrontal regions appear to be necessary for the operations of effortful or deliberate encoding. Orbitofrontal Brodmann area 10 (BA 10) and mesial frontal regions (anterior portion of the cingulate gyrus; BA 24) appear to play an important role in directing and maintaining attention toward particular aspects of specific stimuli or internally generated or reactivated representations of past events (Knight, 1984), as in learning a list of words which can be aided significantly by intentionally focusing on specific similarities among the items to be encoded. The processes of monitoring incoming words for common features and

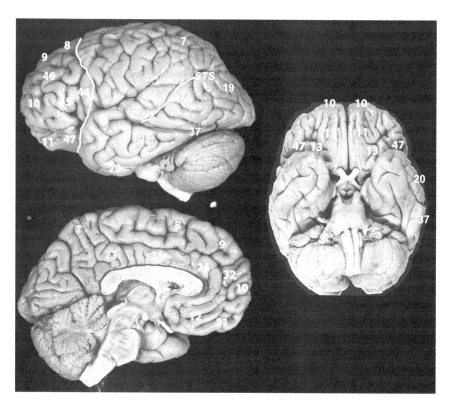

Figure 2–1 Regional subdivision of posterior and anterior association cortices according to the Brodmann cytoarchitectonic map. The posterior association cortex includes temporal, parietal, and occipital regions, whereas the anterior association cortex includes the entire frontal lobe, except for the motor strip. Prefrontal regions are subdivided into dorsolateral Brodmann areas (BA) 8, 9, 10, and 46; ventrolateral, the lateral part of area 11 and area 47; and ventromedial, that is, the medial part of area 11 and area 12. Area 20 covers the anterior portion of the temporal lobe, area 21 is located in the vicinity of the superior temporal sulcus (STS), and both are considered to be multimodal association areas. Area 37 is bordered dorsally by area 21 and caudally by visual association area 19 and is closely linked to visual processes such as recognition of faces and writing. Superior (BA 7) and medial parietal cortex (BA 31) are involved in visuospatial functions but also in the storage of memories. (From the Digital Anatomist Project, University of Washington)

of identifying and isolating those features are supported by neurophysiological mechanisms in dorsolateral prefrontal cortices (D'Esposito & Postle, 1999).

Evidence of the involvement of prefrontal cortex in the operation of "maintaining" information has emerged from electrophysiological studies with animals whereby prefrontal neurons, named "memory" or "delay" cells, remain active while the animal is holding items in memory in order to make an appropriate response at some future time (Fuster & Alexander, 1971; Kojima & Goldman-Rakic, 1982; Fuster, 1990; Cohen, Perlstein, Braver et al., 1997; Ungerleider, Courtney, & Haxby 1998). Further, studies in humans consistently show increased levels of blood flow/metabolism (Braver, Cohen, Nystrom et al., 1997; Owen, Doyon, Dagher et al., 1998) and neurophysiological activity (Campo, Maestu, Ortiz et al., 2005) during brief time periods when participants are mentally rehearsing verbal information. In addition, permanent damage to this area selectively disrupts the ability of monitoring reactivation of memories (for a review, see Petrides, 2000).

Brain Structures Involved in Retrieval

The retrieval of explicit memories entails bringing into current conscious awareness the events experienced in the past. In view of the fact that retrieval operates in the psychological present, it is considered an operation of primary memory although it operates on material belonging to secondary memory, or memory proper. Retrieval is either effortless and automatic or deliberate, effortful, and aided by explicit strategies. In either case, it entails activation of the association areas where mnemonic traces are said to be stored. Possibly always but almost certainly when retrieval is effortful, it entails the activation of prefrontal regions as well. Communication of the posterior and prefrontal cortex is facilitated by two prominent fiber bundles, the "uncinate" and "arcuate" fasciculi (see Figure 2–2).

It is further thought that the infero-lateral prefrontal cortex and temporo-polar regions support the retrieval of stored memories (Markowitsch, 1995b). These two cortical regions are densely interconnected by the ventral branch of the uncinate fasciculus.

The mid-dorsolateral region of the prefrontal cortex appears to be a specialized area in which information can be held online for manipulation. Note that the manipulation of items implies the simultaneous consideration of several of them, thus it requires monitoring of all of them, and this region, which roughly corresponds to Brodmann areas 46 and 9 (BA 46 and BA 9), is thought to be responsible for such tasks. Another part of the prefrontal cortex, the mid-ventrolateral prefrontal region (BA 45, BA 47), may be critical for effortful retrieval; that is, retrieval initiated with conscious effort by the subject and guided by the subject's plans and intentions. The posterior portion of the cingulate gyrus (BA 23) as well as the precuneus in the posterior association cortex (BA 7/31) are also thought to be involved in this operation. There are some further indications that the right prefrontal cortex is more involved than the left prefrontal cortex in retrieval of explicit memories, whereas the opposite is the case for encoding (Tulving, Kapur, Craik et al., 1994; Markowitsch, 1995b; Fuster, 2001), but the status of such lateralization is still uncertain.

Mechanisms of the Secondary Memory System

Once information departs from the psychological present (awareness), it undergoes changes that lead to its long-term preservation. A number of processes have been proposed to explain how long-term memory storage transpires and how mnemonic traces become consolidated. While these proposals vary considerably on the precise role they assign to the various brain structures implicated in

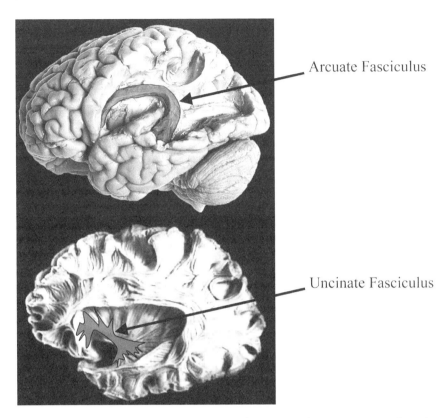

Arcuate Fasciculus

Uncinate Fasciculus

Figure 2–2 The arcuate and uncinate fasciculi. Upper: The cortex surrounding the Sylvian fissure has been cut away to reveal the arcuate fasciculus (shaded arc-like structure), a large fiber bundle connecting the frontal to the occipital and temporal lobes. The fibers pass from the frontal lobe to the lateral sulcus where projections radiate into the occipital lobe and to anterior portions of the temporal lobe. Lower: The cortex of the left hemisphere has been removed to uncover the bundle of fibers (shaded area) that runs between the inferior part of the frontal lobe and the temporal lobe. (From the Digital Anatomist Project, University of Washington)

these operations, they vary less with respect to which structures they consider to be implicated.

Brain Structures Involved in Consolidation

Consolidation refers to the operation of rendering mnemonic traces resistant to decay and available for reactivation hours, days, or years after their initial encoding. The term was coined by Muller and Pilzecker (1900) and was occasioned by the observation that it takes time for new memories to become resistant to interference, a phenomenon first observed by Ribot (1882) and repeatedly confirmed by the presence of the retrograde amnesia gradient after damage to various parts of the limbic system (see below).

The limbic system can be tentatively divided into three main sectors. The medial temporal sector, which consists of the perirhinal, entorhinal, and parahippocampal cortices, the hippocampus, and the amygdala; the diencephalic sector, which comprises anterior and mediodorsal nuclei of the thalamus and the mammillary bodies; and the basal forebrain region, which includes the septal nuclei, the nuclei of the diagonal band, and the nucleus basalis of Meynert. The limbic system also includes neocortex located in the mesial surface of the hemispheres, the cingulate gyrus. The various limbic structures are interconnected via bundles of fibers, chief among which are the fornix, the mammillothalamic tract, and the cingulum (see Figures 2–3, 2–5, and 2–6). The role of each of these structures in consolidation is inferred from the effects of lesions in them and on subsequent ability to retrieve (either through effortful recall or automatic recognition) memories acquired at different time periods preceding the onset of the amnesia. Damage to the hippocampus, with or without damage to the surrounding medial temporal cortex, the anterior thalamus, and the basal forebrain is known to cause temporally graded retrograde amnesia for episodic and semantic memories (von Cramon, Hebel, & Schuri, 1985; Gade & Mortensen, 1990; Zola-Morgan & Squire, 1990; Kim & Fanselow, 1992; Morris, Bowers, Chatterjee, & Heilman, 1992; Rempel-Clower, Zola, Squire, & Amaral, 1996; Manns, Hopkins, & Squire, 2003; Van der Werf, Jolles, Witter, & Uylings, 2003).

The hippocampus is located within the parahippocampal gyrus and is further divided into the dentate gyrus, cornu ammonis, and the subiculum (see Figure 2–3). Input from cortical association areas enters the hippocampus mainly through the entorhinal cortex and proceeds from the dentate gyrus to the CA3 subregion, then to the CA1 subregion, and finally to the subiculum. The white matter tracks that carry signals from the hippocampus consist of the alveus and fornix and contain fibers that terminate mainly in the septal region and the mammilary bodies. The fornix also carries input to the hippocampus, mainly from the septal region and the nucleus basalis of Meynert. Consequently, damage to the fornix (Spiers, Maguire, & Burgess, 2001) and mammillothalamic tract (Tanaka, Miyazawa, Akaoka, & Yamada, 1997) results in memory deficits similar to those observed after hippocampal damage.

Several theories have been proposed to explain the process of consolidation and storage (e.g., Marr, 1971; Teyler & DiScenna, 1985; Nadel & Moscovitch, 1997; Dash, Hebert, & Runyan, 2004), differing in a number of ways but converging in that they recognize the early role of the hippocampus in consolidation (however, see Dash et al., 2004) and the role of neocortex in the storage of mnemonic traces.

Long-Term Storage of Memory Traces

Storage of explicit memory traces is believed to take place in association cortices (see Figure 2–1) (McCarthy & Warrington, 1994), and it is thought to depend on changes in synaptic efficacy within large populations of neurons. The property of neurons in the association cortices to receive input from more than one

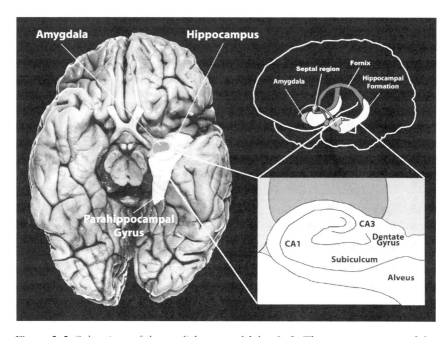

Figure 2–3 Subregions of the medial temporal lobe. Left: The anterior portion of the temporal lobe has been removed to display the anatomical location of the two internal structures: the hippocampus and the amygdala. The extent of the parahippocampal gyrus is also shown on this basal view of the brain. The schematic in the upper right corner of the figure indicates the relative location of the two hippocampi and amygdaloid nuclei in relation to the fornix and septal region. The inset in the lower right-hand corner displays a schematic drawing of a coronal section through the hippocampus showing the spatial layout of hippocampal subregions: the CA1 and CA3 sections of the cornu amonis (or Amon's horn), dentate gyrus, and subiculum. The alveus contains fibers that connect the hippocampus with subcortical structures and with the contralateral hippocampus and gives rise to the fornix. (From the Digital Anatomist Project, University of Washington)

primary sensory area renders them ideal for storing multimodal representations of events. Though it is believed that memory storage takes place in the association cortices, it is not known what anatomical pattern cortical information storage assumes. Moreover, the precise nature of the "units" of information stored remains conjectural as does the degree to which storage is local or diffuse and the degree to which the same neurons participate in storage of more than one distinct trace. Furthermore, it is not known whether cortical areas alone are able to represent an event or if input from the hippocampus, central modulatory areas such as the thalamus, or emotional-encoding regions such as the amygdala and the septal area is also required.

The Role of Thalamic Nuclei in All Memory Functions

The thalamus is composed of several nuclei (Figure 2–4), which can be distinguished on the basis of their cytoarchitectonic features, as well as on the basis

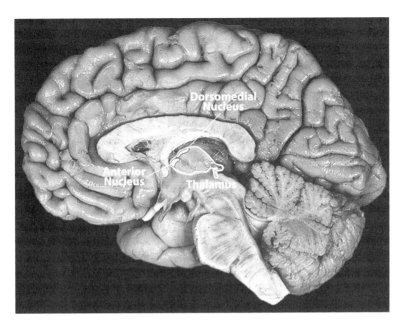

Figure 2–4 Location of thalamic nuclei displayed on a midsagittal section of the brain. (From the Digital Anatomist Project, University of Washington)

of the patterns of connections they form with other cortical and subcortical areas, and the types of afferent connections they receive from the brain stem. Whereas certain nuclei serve as "relay" stations for sensory input to the neocortex (posterior-lateral nucleus, lateral and medial geniculate nuclei), others receive nonspecific regulatory input originating in the brain-stem reticular formation.

Nuclei in the anterior part of the thalamus receive input from the hippocampus, directly through the fornix, and indirectly through the mammilary bodies as shown schematically in Figure 2–5. In addition, they receive signals from posterior association cortices (mainly inferior temporal regions) (Ridley, Baker, Mills et al., 2004). In turn, the anterior and mediodorsal nuclei of the thalamus project back to the hippocampus through the cingulum.

Another key structure of the limbic system, the amygdala, is bidirectionally connected with the mediodorsal thalamic nucleus (see Figure 2–6). The latter forms reciprocal connections with prefrontal and temporal cortices (Tanaka, 1976; Markowitsch, Emmans, Irle et al., 1985).

It appears, therefore, that the thalamic nuclei must be closely connected with structures involved in all mnemonic operations, as the various amnesic phenomena to be reviewed in subsequent chapters, especially Chapter 6, indicate. Damage to the anterior thalamic nuclei is sufficient to cause both anterograde and temporally graded retrograde episodic memory deficits, and its electrical stimulation interferes with learning (Johnson & Ojemann, 2000; Van der Werf et al., 2003). Moreover, damage to the mediodorsal thalamus, which connects to prefrontal structures, results in retrograde (episodic-autobiographic) amnesia,

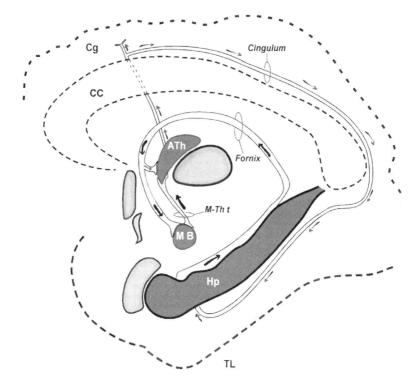

Figure 2–5 The Papez circuit: Schematic drawing of the main structures and pathways composing the Papez circuit (lateral view of the left hemisphere). The hippocampus (Hp) is connected through the fornix to the mamillary bodies (MB), which then project to the anterior nucleus of the thalamus (ATh) through the mamillothalamic tract (M-Th t). Efferent fibers that originate from the anterior nucleus join the cingulum. Some of these fibers form synapses with target neurons in the cingulate gyrus (Cg), while the majority continue caudally above the corpus callosum (CC) and terminate in the hippocampus.

possibly because it mediates strategies used for retrieval (Van der Werf et al., 2003). In addition to its role in episodic memory encoding and retrieval, the role of the thalamus as a relay of information between the prefrontal cortex and other cortical regions appears to be important for certain key components of primary memory such as selective attention (Corbetta, Miezin, Dobmeyer et al., 1991).

Memory and Emotion

A large body of evidence indicates a close relationship between emotional state and memory functions, particularly encoding and consolidation (Papez, 1937; Adolphs, Tranel, Hamann et al., 1999; McGaugh, 2004). The link between memories and emotions is apparently facilitated by the overlap between the structures that mediate both types of phenomena. One such set of closely inter-

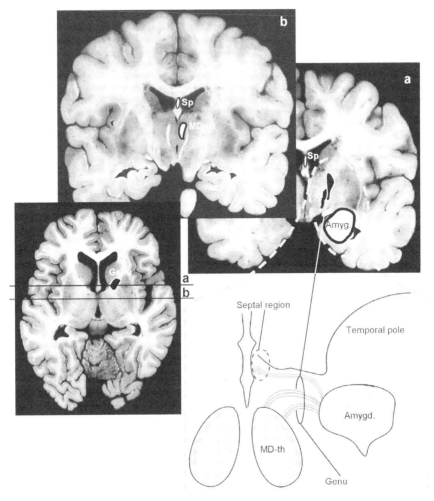

Figure 2–6 Approximate locations of the mediodorsal nucleus of the thalamus (MD-th), the amygdala, and part of the internal capsule. Connections between the amygdala, the mediodorsal nucleus of the thalamus, and the septal region (Sp) are shown schematically in the inset. (Brain sections from the Digital Anatomist Project, University of Washington)

connected structures is known as the Papez circuit and includes the hippocampal formation, fornix, mamillary bodies, mamillothalamic tract, anterior thalamus, cingulate gyrus, and the cingulum (Papez, 1937) shown in Figure 2–5. Two additional structures, the amygdala and the septum, have been independently implicated in memory formation, as well as in emotion, and together with the mediodorsal nucleus of the thalamus (von Cramon, Markowitsch, & Schuri, 1993; Markowitsch, Calabrese, Wurker et al., 1994; Young, Aggleton, Hellawell et al., 1995; McGaugh, Cahill, Roozendaal et al., 1996) form the basolateral limbic circuit, the integrity of which is required for generating proper emotional responses (Sarter & Markowitsch, 1985).

Infarcts of the internal capsule affecting its middle portion interrupt the connections among the structures that form the basolateral limbic circuit and result in memory impairment (see Figure 2–6) (Markowitsch, von Cramon, Hofmann et al., 1990). It is thought that the memory impairments which follow damage to the amygdala or the septum result from an inability to access the emotional valence of events (Bechara, Damasio, & Damasio, 2003). Furthermore, enhanced activity of the amygdala observed during emotional learning conditions correlates with enhanced consolidation efficacy (Kilpatrick & Cahill, 2003).

NEUROTRANSMITTER SYSTEMS IMPLICATED IN MEMORY

Neurotransmission

Chemical synaptic transmission between neurons in the mature nervous system involves the release, in the synaptic cleft, of a variety of biochemical molecules called neurotransmitters. In this section, we provide a brief introduction to the principles of neurotransmission and to the major neurotransmitter systems in the brain that are implicated in various memory functions.

Neurotransmission in the central nervous system can be viewed as a sequence of five steps: (1) synthesis and storage of the neurotransmitter, (2) release of the neurotransmitter, (3) binding to the postsynaptic receptor, (4) receptor action and intracellular signal transduction, and (5), removal of the neurotransmitter. Changes in both presynaptic transmission (the transmitting step) and in postsynaptic response (the receptive step) play a role in the formation of memories (Kandel, 2001).

In order to exert its effect, each neurotransmitter "binds" or attaches itself to specific receptor proteins that are embedded in the membrane of neurons. Neurotransmitter molecules travel the narrow gap between the releasing (presynaptic) and the receiving (postsynaptic) neuron and bind on embedded receptor proteins (see Figure 2–7).

The same neurotransmitter can bind to more than one receptor type, leading to different effects. There are two types of receptors: ionotropic and metabotropic. The binding of a neurotransmitter and the activation of ionotropic receptors results in the opening of ion channels, which allows the movement of electrically charged molecules (ions) into and out of the neuron. A change in ionic flow through the membrane results in graded changes in the neuron's electrical properties. These, in turn, permit the generation of action potentials (very brief electrical pulses) that propagate along the axon, resulting in neurotransmitter release from the axon terminal.

The most common ionotropic receptors in the central nervous system are either excitatory (e.g., glutamate and acetylcholine nicotinic receptors) or inhibitory (e.g., $GABA_A$ and glycine receptors). Excitatory ionotropic receptors are essential for communication between neurons and are consequently required for activity-dependent changes in neuronal morphology, the presumed

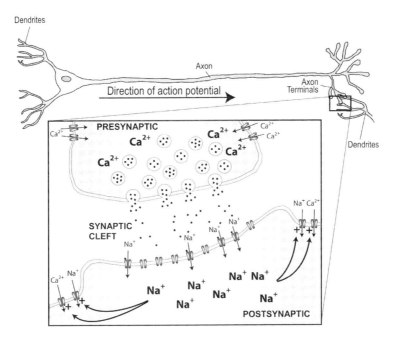

Figure 2–7 Schematic representation of neurotransmitter release and binding. Arrival of an action potential at the presynaptic terminal leads to calcium (Ca^{2+}) entry and release of neurotransmitter molecules into the synaptic cleft. Neurotransmitters diffuse across the synaptic cleft to bind to specialized receptors located on the postsynaptic cell. The end result is the opening of ion channels located in the postsynaptic membrane (in this case, sodium channels).

cellular basis of storage of memories. This supposition has been supported by numerous studies showing that blocking glutamate receptors in structures involved in memory functions results in anterograde amnesia.

The second class of "metabotropic" receptors (also referred to as G-protein–coupled receptors) activate intracellular enzymes, leading to increases in "messenger" molecules such as cyclic adenosine monophosphate (cAMP) and calcium. The activation of metabotropic receptors and the subsequent generation of intracellular second-messenger molecules can (a) change the electrical state of the membrane and help trigger action potentials and (b) change a neuron's response to subsequent neurotransmitter input for a period of seconds, minutes, days, or longer. These processes form the neurochemical basis of memory consolidation and storage. The prominence of metabotropic receptors in the establishment of new memories is only recently being appreciated. G-protein–coupled receptors, important for memory, include α–and β-adrenergic receptors, $GABA_B$ receptors, metabotropic glutamate receptors, serotonin receptors, and dopamine receptors.

Initial characterization and classification of neurotransmitter receptors was carried out using pharmacological agents. A neurotransmitter "agonist" is a molecule that binds to and activates a receptor specific to that neurotransmitter, whereas an "antagonist" is a molecule that binds to and inactivates the receptor. In addition to acting on the receptor, pharmacological agents can interfere with neurotransmitter action at several steps including blocking the flow of ions, altering G-protein activation, or blocking the action of intracellular molecules activated by G-proteins (second-messenger molecules). These agents have been important tools for studying the neurochemical basis of the formation of memories. Recently, molecular and genetic analyses have been performed to classify neurotransmitter receptors further, as well as intracellular processes, and specify their role in learning and memory.

Some drugs can selectively inactivate enzymes that help synthesize a neurotransmitter; some can block or activate postsynaptic receptors and others influence the chemical degradation or reabsorption of transmitter molecules (i.e., "reuptake") back into the presynaptic cell. The latter processes directly affect the amount of neurotransmitter that remains in an active state, capable of binding to postsynaptic receptors. These drugs can result in either enhancement or inhibition in the overall action of neurotransmission. For example, drugs such as tacarine inhibit the acetylcholine degrading enzyme acetylcholinesterase and increase the available amount of acetylcholin in the synapse. Chemicals that inhibit the actions of this enzyme, called acetylcholinesterase inhibitors, are used to improve neuronal signaling through acetylcholine in Alzheimer patients. Other drugs, such as physostigmine, suppress the action of acetylcholine on its receptor (they are known as anticholinergics). These agents have been studied extensively for their negative effects on memory. Yet another class of agents bind to and inhibit the action of proteins that mediate the reuptake of transmitter molecules back into the presynaptic terminal (transporter proteins). For instance, antidepressants such as fluoxetine (Prozac) and imipramine block serotonin transporter proteins, prolonging the action of serotonin by a similar process. These types of drugs are often referred to as "reuptake inhibitors."

Long-Term Potentiation

Several neurotransmitters have been specifically linked to the formation of long-term memory traces. Experimental work on the molecular mechanisms of memory, using animal models, has demonstrated that the basic principles underlying memory storage transcend the evolutionary chain (Kandel, 2001). These studies have isolated two types of neurophysiological phenomena, long-term potentiation (LTP) and long-term depression (LTD), as the functional antecedents of storage of neural representations of external events. LTP refers to an increase in synaptic efficacy; that is, the capacity of one neuron (presynaptic) to cause another (postsynaptic) neuron, with which it is connected synaptically, to fire. LTD is in effect opposite of LTP, consisting of a reduction in synaptic efficacy between two neurons, resulting from repeated failure of the presynaptic neuron to excite the postsynaptic neuron (Ito, 1986).

As part of the LTP phenomenon, this functional change in synaptic efficacy is a direct consequence of the common firing history of both neurons. In other words, the more often two neurons fire in rapid succession, the stronger the synaptic link between the two becomes. The phenomenon evolves in distinct phases. Immediate changes consist of increased synaptic "readiness," or sensitivity in existing synaptic contacts between the two neurons. Over a period of hours or days, structural changes in both the presynaptic and the postsynaptic neurons are known to occur as a result of altered gene expression. This is the process through which the gene's coded information is transcribed inside the cell, triggering the synthesis of intracellular proteins. Protein synthesis is required for changes in cell morphology (such as an increase in the number of postsynaptic contact sites) and the facilitation of transmitter release from the presynaptic neuron (among others).

With an idea of how synaptic connections between neurons can store information, let us proceed to an outline of the neural mechanisms that support storage of memory traces, starting with the signaling mechanisms for the major neurotransmitters: glutamate, GABA, acetylcholine, dopamine, serotonin, and norepinephrine.

Neurotransmitters

Glutamate

Glutamate is the primary excitatory neurotransmitter of the forebrain that binds and activates several types of receptors, including the ionotropic AMPA (a-amino-3-hydroxy-5-methylisoxazole-4-proprionic acid) and NMDA (N-methyl, D-aspartate) receptors and metabotropic glutamate receptors. LTP, which was mentioned above as a possible mechanism for memory formation, requires NMDA- and AMPA-mediated signaling. Activity of NMDA receptors requires (1) postsynaptic neuronal depolarization, or postsynaptic activity, as a result of previous presynaptic neurotransmitter release, and (2) the binding of glutamate as a result of current presynaptic activity. Because of the rapid time course of depolarization, these two events must occur in temporal proximity, a requirement that renders NMDA receptors prime candidates for mediating LTP-type phenomena in the brain.

The activity of the NMDA receptor in structures such as the hippocampus has been shown to be necessary for memory formation (especially consolidation) (Day, Langston, & Morris, 2003), whereas blocking AMPA receptor activity within specific brain structures has been shown to impair retrieval (Barros, Izquierdo, Mello e Souza et al., 2000; Day et al., 2003).

GABA

The action of γ-aminobutyric acid (GABA) is largely inhibitory and is involved in regulating and often in spatially limiting the extent of neuronal activity within populations of neurons. Levels of GABA are highest in the thalamus and hypothalamus but provide essential inhibitory regulation throughout most of the central nervous system. $GABA_A$ receptors are ionotropic and allow the influx of negatively charged ions, which hyperpolarize the neuron and reduce its rate of firing. In contrast, $GABA_B$ receptors are G-protein–coupled receptors, capable of suppressing neuronal signalling via two complementary processes: (a) by opening potassium channels in the postsynaptic neuron and inducing hyperpolarization and (b) by inhibiting the release of another, excitatory neurotransmitter from the presynaptic neuron. In addition to shaping general brain activity, GABAergic inhibitory input is thought to be involved in shaping both acquisition and retrieval by depressing unrelated or irrelevant activity that would interfere with formation of clear and readily accessible mnemonic traces (Durstewitz, Seamans, & Sejnowski, 2000). In addition, GABAergic activity indirectly affects the release of other neurotransmitters such as glutamate and norepinephrine, both of which are involved in mnemonic operations. This action may facilitate selective firing in local neuronal networks, thus promoting maintenance of neuronal activity related to the information to be learned.

The $GABA_A$ receptor consists of three major parts, each displaying preference for different chemical agents: $GABA_A$, to which GABA and alcohol bind; the benzodiazepine receptor; and the barbiturate receptor. Benzodiazepines are used to treat a wide range of disorders including epilepsy, anxiety, and insomnia. Although they have little effect on autonomic function, at high doses they impair acquisition of new episodic memories (anterograde amnesic effect). The recall of word lists and other material learned after their administration is significantly impaired, whereas recall of word lists learned prior to their administration is not impaired (Ghoneim & Mewaldt, 1990). This amnesic effect appears to be independent of sedation as suggested by the fact that tolerance develops for sedation but not for the memory impairment. Finally, there is some controversy on the differential effects of benzodiazepines on explicit and implicit memories. For instance, although diazepam was found to impair recall of explicit memories, but not implicit ones, tested by word-stem completion (Fang, Hinrichs, & Ghoneim, 1987), Brown, Brown, and Bowes (1989) reported opposite findings for another benzodiazepine, lorazepam. Although benzodiazepines disrupt the encoding and consolidation operations, there is no evidence that they disrupt primary memory functions (File & Lister, 1982). Interestingly, recall of distant memories may be enhanced, especially for individuals suffering from anxiety when faced with performance situations, a phenomenon known as "retrograde facilitation" (Hinrichs, Ghoneim, & Mewaldt, 1984).

The memory impairment seen after alcohol intoxication closely resembles the benzodiazepine amnestic syndrome, which is consistent with the common role of benzodiazepines as agonists of the $GABA_A$ receptor. Acute consumption of alcohol impairs acquisition of new information without significantly affecting retrieval of previously learned material. Performance is disrupted on a variety of short-term memory tasks, from verbal list learning to picture recognition (Parker, Alkana, Birnbaum et al., 1974). Conversely, immediate recall of material learned prior to alcohol consumption is unaffected or even enhanced (Parker, Birnbaum, Weingartner et al., 1980). Priming, an experimental paradigm that assesses the capacity to activate implicit memories, remains intact. This pattern of deficits is similar to the pattern produced by damage to the hippocampus and may be related to the fact that the receptor channels affected by alcohol are heavily expressed in the hippocampal formation. There is also mounting evidence from research in humans and rodents that medial temporal structures are particularly sensitive to the effects of even moderate doses of ethanol (Ryback, 1971; Peterson, Rothfleisch, Zelazo, & Pihl, 1990; Ryabinin, 1998).

Alcohol-induced blackouts refer to amnesia for events of any part of a drinking episode, without loss of consciousness, and are distinguished into two types: "en bloc" and "fragmentary." En bloc blackout has a definite starting point, and the drinker has a sense of lost time. The memories for events that happened during the blackout cannot be recalled under any circumstance, and thus the memory loss is considered permanent. Conversely, the characteristic of the fragmentary blackout is that the memories can be retrieved later with the aid of contextual cues.

Acetylcholine

Acetylcholine is synthesized by the enzyme choline acetyl transferase and is broken down chemically at the synaptic terminals by the enzyme acetyl-cholinesterase. Agents that block acetylcholinesterase increase the availability of acetylcholine at the synapse. In the central nervous system, the metabotropic muscarinic receptor is the predominant receptor. Activation of these receptors results in G-protein activity, which modulates intracellular signal transduction. Drugs that inhibit the breakdown of acetylcholine (such as tacarine and physostigmine), as well as cholinergic agonists (such as arecoline), have been shown to improve sentence learning (Sitaram, Weingartner, & Gillin, 1978). Conversely, muscarinic acetylcholine receptor antagonists such as scopolamine block memory formation, specifically acquisition of new episodic memories (Drachman & Leavitt, 1974; Drachman, 1977).

Consistent with a role in the formation of new episodic memories, the major cholinergic projections are to the neocortex and the hippocampus. Local cholin-ergic signaling in these structures appears to be important for all primary memory operations (Hasselmo, 1999; Rogers & Kesner, 2003; Thiel, 2003). In fact, enhanced cholinergic signaling after administration of the acetylcholinesterase inhibitor physostigmine is accompanied by parallel changes in activity in pre-frontal and posterior cortical regions (Furey, Pietrini, & Haxby, 2000).

The major cholinergic projections to the neocortex and the hippocampus arise from the basal forebrain complex, which includes three main neuronal aggregates: the medial septal nucleus, the basal nucleus of Meynert (or nucleus basalis magnocellularis), and the vertical nucleus of the diagonal band. Figure 2–8 illustrates the origin of major acetylcholine projections to limbic and neo-cortical regions.

The bulk of cholinergic projections to the amygdala and the cerebral cortex arise in the basal nucleus of Meynert (Selden, Gitelman, Salamon-Murayama et al., 1998). The hippocampus receives cholinergic innervations mainly from the medial septal nucleus and the vertical nucleus of the diagonal band. The dis-ruption of cholinergic input to medial temporal lobe structures is implicated in the memory deficits observed in Alzheimer disease (Whitehouse, Price, Struble et al., 1982; DeKosky, Harbaugh, Schmitt et al., 1992).

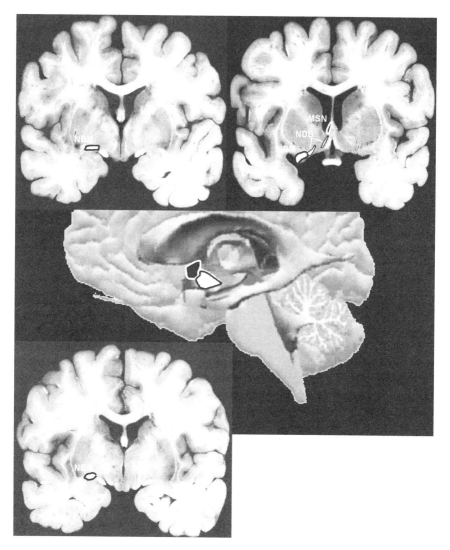

Figure 2–8 Approximate locations of cholinergic neurons within the basal forebrain complex. The medial septal nucleus (MSN), which is part of the septal region, and the basal forebrain complex (nucleus of the diagonal band [NDB] and the basal nucleus of Meynert [NBM]) are shown in black or white on a three-dimensional view of the mesial aspect of the brain (middle panel) and on sequential coronal sections (upper and lower panels). It should be noted that with the possible exception of the septal nuclei, cholinergic neurons do not form well-delineated nuclei. (From the Digital Anatomist Project, University of Washington)

Anticholinergic drugs, such as scopolamine, can impair formation of new episodic memories (Drachman & Leavitt, 1974) but do not seem to interfere with retrieval of semantic ones (Litvan, Sirigu, Toothman, & Grafman, 1995; Vitiello, Martin, Hill et al., 1997). Counteracting the sedating effects of anticholinergics by nicotine or amphetamine does not prevent their impact on episodic memory, which is usually tested by free recall of word lists learned after or prior to drug administration (Drachman, 1977; Ghoneim & Mewaldt, 1977). Recognition ability is also spared for items learned under the influence of anticholinergic drugs, whereas primary memory functions are affected especially when the load of to-be-remembered items is heavy. Procholinergic drugs (cholinergic agonists), such as physostigmine, reverse these cognitive impairments (Fibiger, 1991) and can even improve performance on short-term memory tasks (Furey et al., 2000).

Dopamine

Dopamine exerts either inhibitory or excitatory effects depending on the type of receptor it binds to (D1 or D2, respectively). Dopamine receptors are meta-botropic (i.e., G-protein–coupled) receptors that change postsynaptic activity by activating or inhibiting the action of intracellular enzymes. Dopamine-mediated transmission plays an important role in the normal function of the basal ganglia and the prefrontal cortex. The highest concentration of neurons that produce dopamine is encountered in two neighboring midbrain loci: the substantial nigra and the ventral tegmental area (Figure 2–9).

As shown in Figure 2–9, these neurons send projections to many brain areas via three partially overlapping pathways: the nigrostriatal, mesolimbic, and mesocortical pathways. Nigrostriatal projections originate in the substantia nigra and terminate in the striatum (the caudate and the putamen). The nigrostriatal pathway appears to be implicated in long-term plasticity in the striatum, the section of the basal ganglia involved in certain forms of procedural (implicit) memory functions. Mesolimbic projections originate in the ventral tegmental area and project to limbic structures. Mesocortical fibers also originate in the ventral tegmental area and diffusely project to neocortical regions, including the prefrontal cortex. Drugs affecting the activity of dopaminergic neurons include antipsychotic and anti-Parkinson drugs and CNS stimulants. The action of antipsychotic drugs, which are primarily D2-receptor antagonists, presents an interesting case, because chronic use leads to the increased synaptic action of D2 receptors in the brain, leading to the reduced efficacy of neuronal signaling associated with D1-receptor activation. This effect appears to be associated with working memory deficits in primates: concurrent administration of selective D1 agonists reverses the memory impairment (Castner & Goldman-Rakic, 2004). In animal models, direct, regional regulation of D1-receptor activity in the prefrontal cortex strongly affects performance on primary memory tasks (Sawaguchi & Goldman-Rakic, 1994).

Few psychopharmacological studies have been conducted in healthy volunteers. Generally, D2-receptor antagonists, such as haloperidol (an antipsychotic drug), do not affect episodic memory formation or retrieval, perceptual learning, or retrieval of semantic memories. However, haloperidol selectively impairs the ability to switch cognitive sets (Vitiello et al., 1997), as well as performance on other tasks involving working memory. Conversely, there is some evidence that the administration of dopamine agonists may improve working memory function

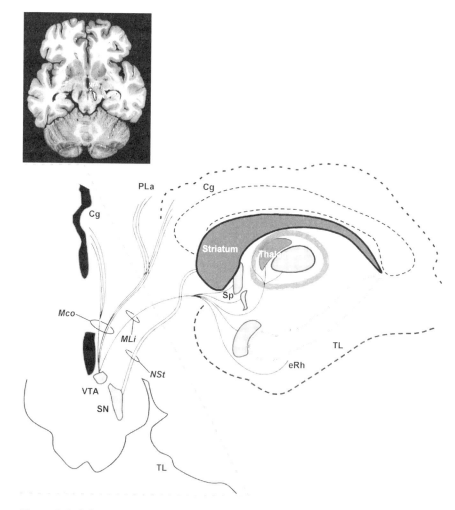

Figure 2–9 Schematic rendering of ascending dopaminergic projections on an axial slice through the pons (lower left drawing and MRI inset) and on a lateral view of the left hemisphere (right drawing). Dopamine-producing neurons in the substantia nigra (SN) send fibers primarily to the striatum (the caudate nucleus that is shown here, and the putamen) via the nigrostriatal pathway (NSt). Dopaminergic neurons in the ventral tegmental area (VTA) project to limbic structures via the mesolimbic pathway (MLi) and to the anterior cingulate gyrus (Cg) and mesial paralimbic frontal areas (PLa) via the mesocortical pathway (Mco). TL, temporal lobe; An, amygdaloid nucleus (amygdala); SP, septal region. (Brain section from the Digital Anatomist Project, University of Washington)

in humans. For instance, the nonspecific dopamine agonists, amphetamine and methylphenidate, may enhance working memory function in healthy individuals by improving both accuracy and speed of recall. This effect is observed in individuals with poor baseline working memory performance, whereas working memory is impaired in those with normal or above-average baseline perform-

ance (Mattay, Callicott, Bertolino et al., 2000). This is consistent with findings
in schizophrenics, who suffer from impaired working memory, presumably due
to excessive activity within the dopamine system (Goldman-Rakic, Castner,
Svensson et al., 2004).

The role of dopamine-mediated synaptic transmission in memory is further
supported by reports of the beneficial effects of L-dopa treatment in Parkinson disease. This treatment, at least initially, improves performance on working memory
tasks, especially those that tap into spatial working memory (Costa, Peppe,
Dell'Agnello et al., 2003). This effect appears to be associated with improved
perfusion of the prefrontal cortex (Cools, Stefanova, Barker et al., 2002).

Serotonin

Serotonin (5-hydroxytryptamine; 5-HT) is derived from the amino acid tryptophan and exerts its action through either metabotropic receptors (5-HT1, 5-HT2;
by modulating neuronal response to other excitatory and inhibitory input) or
ionotropic receptors (5-HT3). In addition to metabotropic serotonin receptors
that mediate the postsynaptic response to serotonin through the regulation of
G-proteins, serotonin autoreceptors maintain a balance of serotonin neurotransmission. Figure 2–10 illustrates the anatomic location of the major sources of
ascending serotonergic projections.

Serotonin-producing neurons are located mostly within the raphe nuclei and
project diffusely to most cortical and subcortical areas. A substantial proportion
of ascending serotonergic fibers travel along the medial forebrain bundle. The
pattern of serotonergic projections is indicative of a modulatory system, lacking
functional specialization. Pharmacologic agents that affect serotonergic pathways include most antidepressants such as tricyclics and selective serotonin reuptake inhibitors (SSRIs). These agents increase the available quantity of serotonin
at the synaptic terminal.

The literature on the cognitive effects of serotonergic agents in humans is
somewhat confusing. Administration of agents that reduce the levels of serotonin
in the brain by depleting its chemical precursor (tryptophan) impairs performance on episodic memory tasks (Riedel, Klaassen, Deutz et al., 1999). Performance
on short-term memory and perceptual tasks and psychomotor speed are not
affected, whereas the speed of retrieval of semantic memories may actually
improve. Administration of these agents after the learning phase does not impair
memory, suggesting a role in encoding and not in consolidation. No evidence
was found for an effect of tryptophan depletion on measures sensitive to frontal
lobe function (Park, Coull, McShane et al., 1994). Conversely, tryptophan loading impairs working and short-term memory (Luciana, Burgund, Berman, &
Hanson, 2001).

Riedel and colleagues (Riedel, Klassen, & Schmitt, 2002) suggest that improved retrieval of semantic memories, concomitant with impaired acquisition of
new episodic memories, suggests a dissociation of the effects of the serotonergic
system on different brain regions subserving these two types of memories (Robbins,
1997). In contrast, studies with healthy volunteers who were administered

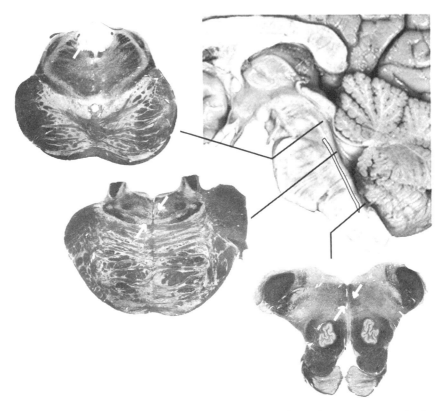

Figure 2–10 The anatomical location of serotonergic and noradrenergic neurons in the brain stem. Serotonin-producing neurons are found in a string of six nuclei (raphe nuclei) that together extend from the upper pons to the lower medulla (outlined region on the midsagittal section through the brain stem; upper right-hand panel). White, upward-pointing arrows indicate the approximate location of raphe nuclei on horizontal sections through the mid-pons (middle left-hand panel) and the medulla (lower right-hand panel). Norepinephrine-producing neurons are predominantly found in the locus ceruleus, located in the upper pons, shown by the white, upward pointing arrow on the horizontal brain-stem section (upper left-hand panel). Downward-pointing arrows indicate the location of the medial forebrain bundle on each horizontal section. (From the Digital Anatomist Project, University of Washington)

selective serotonin reuptake inhibitors either acutely or subchronically (thereby increasing serotonin function) report vigilance decrements but no other systematic effects on cognitive functions including learning and memory (O'Hanlon, Robbe, Vermeeren et al., 1998).

Norepinephrine

Norepinephrine (or noradrenaline) and epinephrine (adrenaline) bind to specific metabotropic receptors, which are found in virtually every tissue of the body including the brain. Both compounds belong to a class of neurotransmitters (along with dopamine) known as catecholamines. There are two main classes of adrenergic receptors: alpha (α) and beta (β). Many drugs including amphetamines, cocaine, and antidepressants block reuptake thereby prolonging the action of these neurotransmitters.

The central location of neurons that synthesize norepinephrine (noradrenergic neurons) and project to the hippocampus and neocortical regions is the locus ceruleus. Figures 2–10 and 2–11 show the location of the locus ceruleus and the medial forebrain bundle that carries the bulk of ascending noradrenergic projections (in addition to serotonergic afferents as described in the previous paragraph). Noradrenergic afferents to the amygdala, the hypothalamus, and the

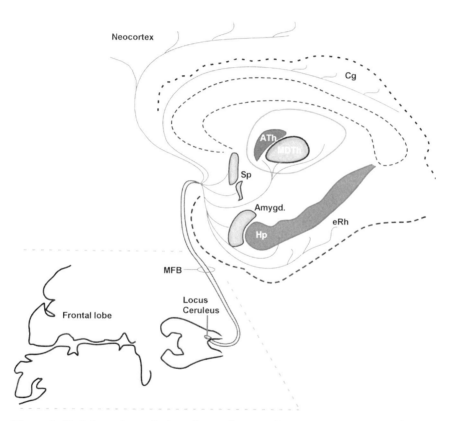

Figure 2–11 Schematic rendering of ascending noradrenergic projections involved in memory function displayed on an axial (lower left) and on a lateral view (upper-right) of the left hemisphere. Neurons producing norepinephrine in the locus ceruleus send fibers that travel along the medial forebrain bundle (MFB) and terminate in virtually all limbic structures, including the hippocampus (Hp), amygdala, septal region (Sp), anterior (ATh) and mediodorsal thalamic nuclei (MDTh). Diffuse noradrenergic terminals are also found in neocortical areas including the frontal lobe and the cingulate gyrus (Cg) and in cortical limbic regions such as entorhinal cortex (eRh).

septal region arise mainly from norepinephrine-producing cell groups in the medulla. The main targets of noradrenergic projections are displayed schematically in Figure 2–11.

Norepinephrine-releasing cells are active during wakefulness, increasing their activity during startle or watchful situations. Norepinephrine is also released by spinal cord and peripheral neurons and acts on peripheral organs mediating autonomic responses including those related to stress. Finally, epinephrine produced by the adrenal medulla and released into the bloodstream as a hormone contributes to the stress response.

It has been suggested that norepinephrine is crucial for certain cognitive functions associated with the frontal lobes, particularly the prevention of distractibility by irrelevant stimuli. The α_2 receptors in the prefrontal cortex appear to be of particular importance in this respect. Profound depletion of norepinephrine in the prefrontal cortex in primates impairs performance on working memory tasks. This effect can be reversed directly by administering α_2-receptor agonists (such as guanfacine), suggesting a direct link between α_2 receptor–mediated synaptic transmission and working memory. It is likely, however, that this action is mediated by the effects of α_2-transmission enhancement on selective attention (Arnsten & Contant, 1992). Beta-adrenergic receptors have been implicated in emotion-laden memories and the stress response. Pharmacological blockade of the β-adrenergic system impairs memory for emotionally arousing events but does not affect memory for closely matched but relatively neutral events (Cahill, Prins, Weber, & McGaugh, 1994; van Stegeren, Everaerd, Cahill et al., 1998).

Effects of Antidepressant Drugs

A note regarding antidepressant medications is in order here. Based on their cognitive side-effect profiles, antidepressant medications can be classified into three general categories: sedative drugs that impair cognitive function, drugs without effects of cognitive function, and those that improve cognitive function.

Antidepressants that impair both short-term and secondary memory show strong anticholinergic action (by antagonizing the muscarinic acetylcholine receptor) or have a high affinity for the H1 histamine and/or adrenergic receptors (such as amitriptyline). Paroxetine is a selective serotonin reuptake inhibitor with mild anticholinergic activity. Paroxetine specifically impairs long-term (verbal) memory. The additional anticholinergic effects of paroxetine could account for its induction of long-term memory impairment (Schmitt, Kruizinga, & Riedel, 2001).

Antidepressants that target the serotonergic system (SSRIs) or affect the dopaminergic or noradrenergic system have negligible or even positive effects on memory. Examples include bupropion, which modulates dopaminergic function; viloxazine, which is a norepinephrine reuptake blocker; and fluoxetine (Prozac), an SSRI. An example of an antidepressant that may have positive cognitive effects is sertraline (Zoloft), which is an SSRI with putative dopamine reuptake activity. Sertraline is said to improve performance on a verbal fluency task (Schmitt, Kruizinga, & Riedel, 2001), an effect likely due to enhancement of dopaminergic transmission.

Interaction of Neurotransmitters and Hormones

The central nervous system (CNS) and the autonomic nervous system (ANS) interact to coordinate central and peripheral changes through the combined action of neurotransmitters and hormones. Hormones are released into the bloodstream and act, often diffusely, on distant targets including peripheral organ systems and the brain. Some of them act as neurotransmitters when they are released from presynaptic terminals in the brain and spinal cord and as hormones when they are released directly into the bloodstream. One example of the joint action of a hormonal and a neurotransmitter system on memory function is afforded by the stress response, which is mediated by the hypothalamic-pituitary-adrenal (HPA) axis.

The stress response is designed to prepare the organism for optimal performance. However, although acute stress can improve memory function, chronic stress is rather detrimental as will be described below.

Acute Stress and Memory

The effects of acute stress on memory depend on the task, the severity of the stressor, the type of material (emotionally relevant or neutral), and the timing of the stressor relative to learning and retrieval phases of the task. Although performance on easy tasks may improve with increasing levels of stress, performance on complex tasks is dependent on the level of stress, demonstrating an inverted U-shaped function, with both high and low levels of stress associated with poor performance and medium levels of stress enhancing performance (Yerkes & Dodson, 1908). Performance on explicit memory tasks is affected by acute stress, whereas the ability to learn and retain implicit (procedural) memories is minimally affected. Moreover, emotional events or details regarding an emotional situation tend to be remembered better than neutral details (Adolphs, Denburg, & Tranel, 2001; Cahill, Gorski, & Le, 2003).

In general, acute stress, induced during a task, affects both performance and retention, whereas acute stress induced after a task mainly affects retention. These effects can coexist; for instance, the stress of a job interview may impair memory retrieval during the interview and enhance retention of the details of the embarrassing interview itself. Animal studies suggest that stress can influence encoding and consolidation of new memories, yet there is no evidence to suggest that stress can cause permanent retrograde amnesia.

The effects of stress on memory are mediated by at least two distinct but interacting mechanisms: (1) modulation of the level of circulating corticosteroid hormones (cortisol in humans and corticosterone in rats) and (2) modulation of synaptic transmission in limbic circuits. The former mechanism is mediated via the HPA axis and can be briefly outlined as follows: Neural input that signals a threatening event (stressor) reaches the amygdala, triggering efferent input to the hypothalamus. The latter releases corticotrophin-releasing hormone (CRH) into capillaries that drain into the pituitary, triggering the synthesis and secretion of adrenocorticotropic hormone (ACTH) into the bloodstream. ACTH travels to the adrenal cortex, causing the synthesis of corticosteroids, which are also released into the bloodstream and travel throughout the body and brain. Corticosteroid receptors are found in almost all brain areas including the neocortex, hippocampus, and amygdala.

There are two main types of corticosteroid receptors: Type I and Type II. Type I receptors are highly concentrated in the hippocampus, whereas Type II receptors have greater density in the prefrontal cortex and other neocortical areas (Lupien & Lepage, 2001). Type I receptors bind corticosteroids with a nearly 10-fold greater affinity than Type II receptors. Type I receptors are activated at basal levels of circulating corticosteroids and Type II receptors at higher levels (Reul & de Kloet, 1985). Slight increases in the level of corticosteroids lead to increased neuronal excitability in the hippocampus (McEwen & Sapolsky, 1995), enhancing hippocampal function. Consistent with this view, administration of a single dose of cortisol prior to exposure to an emotionally arousing situation enhances long-term retention of emotionally loaded details (Buchanan & Lovallo, 2001), whereas administration of drugs that reduce circulating cortisol level blocks this effect (Maheu, Joober, Beaulieu, & Lupien, 2004).

A further increase in corticosteroid levels leads to Type II receptor activation in the prefrontal cortex, decreasing neuronal excitability in this region (Joels & de Kloet, 1989). Given the role of the prefrontal cortex in primary memory operations, even moderate stress would result in performance deficits in related tasks.

The second mechanism mediating the effects of acute stress (including exposure to highly arousing stimuli) on memory apparently involves another key component of the stress response: central effects of norepinephrine triggered by autonomic nervous system activation. In addition to triggering ACTH synthesis in the pituitary in response to emotionally arousing stimuli, the hypothalamus stimulates the adrenal medulla directly through autonomic preganglionic fibers. This triggers the release of norepinephrine and epinephrine into the bloodstream. Circulating norepinephrine crosses the blood-brain barrier and, in addition to increasing glucose use in the brain, induces long-term changes on neuronal excitability. The role of catecholamines on memory is supported by evidence that injection of high doses of propranolol, which inhibits β-adrenergic receptors, blocks the memory-enhancing effects of stress but does not affect memory for the neutral details (Cahill, Prins, Weber, & McGaugh, 1994; Maheu, Joober, Beaulieu, & Lupien, 2004). One of the key loci of the central effects of norepinephrine is the amygdala, which facilitates hippocampal function, leading to enhanced encoding of aversive explicit memories. Bilateral lesions of the amygdala abolish the enhancing effects of arousal on the ability to recall emotionally charged details (Strange, Hurlemann, & Dolan, 2003).

Due to their different modes of action, epinephrine and cortisol have qualitatively different effects on memory. The effects of norepinephrine evolve rapidly, modulating activity in the amygdala and hippocampus in response to emotional events. Corticosteroids act by binding to intracellular receptors, triggering changes in gene expression that, in turn, are necessary for secondary memory but not for primary memory. This prediction is generally supported by empirical evidence. Transient increases in the level of circulating catecholamines either during or after the learning phase enhance both immediate and delayed memory performance. Also, pretraining blockade of central adrenergic transmission during the learning phase can impair long-term declarative memory (Maheu et al., 2004). Conversely, blockage of the effects of corticosteroids on neuronal signaling primarily affects performance on secondary memory tasks.

It should be noted that the receptors affected by a specific neurotransmitter or pharmacological inhibitor are often present in both the brain and in the periphery, especially within the autonomic nervous system. Thus, in addition to directly influencing the specific brain mechanisms involved with memory, a drug can influence memory indirectly by affecting the state of the autonomic nervous system outside the blood-brain barrier or by indirectly influencing regulatory mechanisms. These types of drugs may also influence memory through a primary action on arousal.

In summary, there is evidence that low levels of acute stress affects declarative memory positively, whereas high levels of stress affect it negatively.

Effects of Chronic Stress on Memory Systems

Chronic stress can cause systemic diseases (Brindley & Rolland, 1989) and various cognitive deficits. It is believed that these effects are mediated primarily by chronically elevated levels of cortisol. Elevation of cortisol levels can be caused by damage or dysfunction of the adrenal medulla (as in Cushing disease) but is also observed independently in the elderly and in patients who suffer from depression. Chronic elevations in corticosteroid levels result in fatigue, depression, apathy, and impaired concentration (Erickson, Drevets, & Schulkin, 2003) and can lead to deficits in spatial, contextual, and episodic memories, largely sparing implicit ones (McEwen, 1999). According to one hypothesis, supported by several lines of evidence, these deficits reflect, primarily, hippocampal atrophy caused by chronically elevated cortisol levels (Sapolsky, Krey, & McEwen, 1986), which also result in inhibition of neurogenesis (Lowy, Gault, & Yamamoto, 1993; Magarinos, McEwen, Flugge, & Fuchs, 1996; McKittrick & McEwen, 1996; Gould, Tanapat, McEwen et al., 1998), as is the case in Cushing syndrome (Starkman, Gebarski, Berent, & Schteingart, 1992), in recurrent depressive illness (Sheline, Wang, Gado et al., 1996), in posttraumatic stress disorder (Bremner, Randall, Scott et al., 1995; Gurvits, Shenton, Hokama et al., 1996), in schizophrenia (Bogerts, Lieberman, Ashtari et al., 1993; Fukuzako, Fukazako, Hashiguchi et al., 1996), and in aging (Golomb, Kluger, de Leon et al., 1994; Convit, de Leon, Tarshish et al., 1995). Moreover, atrophy of the frontal lobes may be seen in patients with depression (Coffey, Wilkinson, Weiner et al., 1993; Rajkowska, Miguel-Hidalgo, Wei et al., 1999; Lupien & Lepage,

2001), and chronic stress can mimic prefrontal dysfunction (Arnsten, 1998a; Koenen, Driver, Oscar-Berman et al., 2001).

Hippocampal dysfunction may further impair the regulation of the stress response, triggering an additional increase of circulating cortisol levels (Brown, Rush, & McEwen 1999). The hippocampus can regulate the HPA axis, acting in an inhibitory manner to shut off the stress response (Herman & Cullinan 1997). Therefore, impaired hippocampal function reduces the capacity of the hippocampus to regulate the stress response, resulting in an increase in the set point for basal ACTH levels that determines basal blood cortisol levels. Importantly, in some chronic stress cases, atrophy appears to be reversible when cortisol levels return to baseline levels, followed by at least partial recovery of memory function.

In summary, memory functions constitute two systems: The primary (working and short-term memory) and secondary (long-term memory) memory systems. The operations or functions of encoding and retrieval fall within the primary memory system, and consolidation, the process underlying the long-term storage of memories, falls within the secondary memory system. The prefrontal cortex appears to be involved in information processing and manipulations necessary for working memory, encoding, and retrieval. Limbic structures, such as the medial temporal lobe, the thalamus, mammillary bodies, and septal areas, seem to be involved in the consolidation process leading to memory storage within cortical association areas. The functions ascribed to these brain regions are mediated by neurochemical signaling between neurons that results in excitatory (glutamate, glycine), inhibitory (GABA), or modulatory (dopamine, serotonin, norepinephrine) actions. These neurotransmitters act on cell-surface receptors, leading to the molecular changes within neurons that constitute the mechanisms of the various memory functions. Drugs or environmental events, such as anticholinergics, stress, or emotional states, can influence memory functions by interacting with this neurochemical signaling and thus the functioning of these brain mechanisms.

3

Age-Related Memory Decline

ALEXANDRA ECONOMOU, PANAGIOTIS G. SIMOS,
AND ANDREW C. PAPANICOLAOU

Recognition among psychologists that memory declines with age is credited to
Kral (1958), although as early as the seventh century BC, Pythagoras had commented on it (Berchtold & Cotman, 1998), registering thus a valid, albeit mundane, observation about a ubiquitous phenomenon. Memory problems of the
elderly have received much attention lately as the population of many regions of
the world ages. Memory decline attributed to aging is estimated to occur in 40%
of individuals older than 60 years (Hanninen, Koivisto, Reinikainen et al., 1996).
The rest (60%) remain cognitively intact (Weintraub, Powell, & Whitla, 1994;
Rosen, Prull, O'Hara et al., 2002a; Snowdon, 2003; Perls, 2004), suggesting that
"successful" cognitive aging is also a biological possibility. For those who experience deficits, the central problem becomes one of separating memory decline
(and cognitive decline, more generally) caused by recognizable diseases from
decline due to "normal" wearing down of the brain.

Although we currently lack a universal definition of normal or successful
aging, we define it as the absence of specific diagnostic or medical conditions,
like cardiovascular disease, chronic obstructive pulmonary disease, or cancer,
with intact physical and cognitive functioning (Newman, Arnold, Naydeck et al.,
2003). Given such an ambivalent definition, it comes as no surprise that clinicians struggle when asked to inform elderly patients whether their memory complaints are justifiable; that is, whether they are to be expected for their age, or
whether they constitute an early sign of dementia. The attempts of clinicians
to address this situation have resulted in constructs like "age-associated memory
impairment" (Crook, Bartus, Ferris et al., 1986) or the more recent "age-associated
cognitive decline" (AACD), referring to mild impairments in multiple cognitive
areas that are, nevertheless, insufficient for the diagnosis of dementia (Petersen,

Stevens, Ganguli et al., 2001). But it is painfully obvious that thus defined, AACD may represent either cognitive decline as a consequence of normal aging or decline indicative of pathology and hardy addresses the clinician's problem.

The even more recent concept of "mild cognitive impairment" (MCI), which emerged in the mid-1990s (Petersen, 1995; Petersen, Smith, Waring et al., 1997), denotes a transitional stage in the cognitive continuum, from memory decline due to normal aging to memory decline due to dementia. The criteria of "amnesic" MCI, according to Petersen and colleagues (Petersen, Smith, Waring et al., 1999), include subjective memory complaints confirmed through formal neuropsychological testing, lower scores on memory tasks than those of age-matched normal control subjects, preserved level and quality of activities, and absence of a dementing disease.

The prevalence of MCI, thus defined, in persons over 65 years of age is estimated to be about 19% and can go up to 29% in those older than 85 years (Lopez, Jagust, DeKosky et al., 2003a). But such estimates may be of questionable accuracy because large-scale studies on aging often do not exclude other common medical conditions, besides neurodegenerative diseases, that are known to affect cognitive processes, such as untreated high blood pressure and subclinical vascular disease (Tzourio, Dufouil, Ducimetiere, & Alperovich, 1999; Meyer, Rauch, Rauch, & Haque, 2000; Sliwinski, Hofer, Hall et al., 2003), diabetes (Fontbonne, Berr, Ducimetiere, & Alperovich, 2001), or even sensory impairments (Anstey, Hofer, & Luszcz, 2003).

Community-based studies of elderly persons that control for the effects of such disorders are few. It is nevertheless possible to separate MCI from normal aging on the basis of results from longitudinal studies showing that being a cognitively and physically intact elderly person is a biological possibility (Rapp & Amaral, 1992; Seeman, Lusignolo, Albert, & Berkman, 2001; Davis, Small, Stern et al., 2003; Snowdon, 2003). In fact, Davis and colleagues (2003) showed that a subset, of more than 25%, of a group of elderly subjects in their sample performed better in word recall than a group of younger participants, as did 10% of the very old subjects (76–90 years of age). Therefore, healthy centenarians do exist who have escaped the major age-associated diseases and are living examples of successful aging (Gonos, 2000; Perls, 2004).

ESTABLISHMENT OF THE SYMPTOMS

Although preservation of a vigorous memory in the elderly is possible, the fact remains that a significant proportion of them experience and report diminished capacity for remembering things as easily as they used to remember. They frequently report difficulty in acquiring new cognitive and motor skills, which implies an anterograde memory deficit, as well as problems with retaining the names of people they meet or the names of people encountered a long time ago, indicative of an anterograde and, possibly, a retrograde episodic memory deficit. They also frequently complain about forgetting newly learned facts, like telephone numbers, about being able to keep up with planned activities (prospective memory deficit), and about forgetting the circumstances surrounding recent actions, resulting in embarrassing situations like telling the same story repeatedly to the same people as if for the first time, indicative of the so-called source memory deficit. Often, these complaints cannot be confirmed by the results of formal neuropsychological testing. But in some cases, at least, failure to confirm subjective reports may be attributed to inadequate norms of standardized tests rather than to groundless complaints on the part of the elderly. For example, an older person of formerly superior memory capacity may well score within or above the normal range despite considerable deterioration of his exceptional capacity. More often, however, subjective reports do accord with, and are substantiated by, the results of formal testing.

Objective neuropsychological data suggest that age-associated memory decline does not equally affect all types of memory phenomena: Explicit memories are affected more than implicit ones, and of those, episodic memories are affected more than memories of facts and concepts. Aging is not associated with an equal degree of decline in all memory functions either, presumably because the underlying biological mechanisms of these functions are not compromised to the same extent. Working memory, for example, appears to decline more rapidly than effortless encoding, or effortless retrieval, as will be discussed in some detail below.

Explicit Memory Difficulties

As mentioned in Chapter 1, primary memory operations vary along a continuum of relative complexity and difficulty. On one end of the continuum is simply "holding" things in mind as exemplified by the operation of remembering a phone number long enough to dial it. On the other end of the continuum are operations of complicated "manipulation" of items retrieved from long-term "storage" like those that occur in problem-solving situations. Between the two poles of the continuum range tasks that make demands of an intermediate level of difficulty and complexity like the "digits backward" task or the task of performing an intended action at some designated time in the future ("prospective memory").

It appears that the severity of primary memory decline in the elderly ranges along the same continuum: Short-term (or immediate) memory for location (Olson, Zhang, Mitchell et al., 2004) remains intact, but immediate memory for unrelated lists of single-digit numbers shows a slight decline (Wechsler, 1997; Park, Lautenschlager, Hedden et al., 2002) as does performance on "digits backward" (Park et al., 2002; Hester, Kinsella, & Ong, 2004), and "spatial span" is more impaired than digit span (Park et al., 2002; Hester, Kinsella, & Ong, 2004). Working memory operations, on the other hand, are significantly more affected (e.g., Anderson, Craik, & Naveh-Benjamin, 1998; Park et al., 2002).

Acquisition of new information becomes harder with advancing age even among "successfully aging" individuals (Small, Stern, Tang, & Mayeux, 1999; Daselaar, Veltman, Rombouts et al., 2003). Young people learn verbal material faster than the old and require fewer repetitions to recall the same amount of information (Stuss, Craik, Sayer et al., 1996; Davis et al., 2003). Yet, "success-fully aging" people, after having acquired the information, albeit with greater effort, retain it as well as the young (Rybarczyk, Hart, & Harkins, 1987). In con-trast, individuals with MCI, or those in the early stages of dementia, may display relatively intact immediate memory but are unable to retain the information acquired even after a short delay of a few minutes.

Difficulties in sustaining focused attention appear to play a role in the mem-ory problems of the elderly (Anderson et al., 1998). Such difficulties become more obvious in tasks of divided attention, known as dual-task conditions. The ability to organize information and use contextual cues in retrieving it is another factor that differentiates young and old people on tasks that require retention over short delays. Retrieval, as we have commented before, ranges from the automatic and effortless (as in the case of recognition) to the laborious and deliberate process of recalling episodes out of context and on demand. Situations where retrieval is aided by a "cue" may be considered of intermediate difficulty. Here, too, the degree of age-related memory decline appears to vary with the degree or complexity of the retrieval task and the effort required to do it. Retrieval errors or intrusions are common, reflecting the reduced ability of the aged to reject infor-mation irrelevant to the task. Moreover, intrusion errors, no less than omission errors, increase with increasing task demands (Oberauer, 2001).

Prospective memory impairments are also prevalent in population studies of the elderly and increase with each successive decade after the age of 60 (Huppert, Johnson, & Nickson, 2000). These failures in carrying out intended actions point to a difficulty with retrieval and not with loss or eradication of the memory for the planned actions, as the intended action was eventually remem-bered but only after the appropriate time had passed. Nonetheless, the precise nature and causes of this deficit remain conjectural. Aging may have a negative effect on the efficiency of encoding or registering of intentions to carry out a par-ticular plan at a specific point in time or contingent on certain circumstances, or it may reflect a reduced ability on the part of the elderly to use different types of environmental cues that would automatically remind younger people that the time for the planned action has come (West, Herndon, & Covell, 2003). Most likely, these and many other factors may conspire to render prospective memory problematic among the elderly. But the lapses in prospective memory have much to do with inadequate attention and not with eradication of the memory of the planned action; that is, with primary and not secondary memory func-tions. This has been demonstrated in the laboratory and is not just inferred from incidental real-life observations (West & Craik, 1999): Shifting of attention away from a recalled action plan, even for short time intervals, and even when noth-ing significant happens during those intervals, is often sufficient to block con-sciousness of that intention (Einstein, McDaniel, Manzi et al., 2000).

Deficits in primary memory functions, whether related to retrieval or to effi-cient encoding through utilization-deliberate strategies appear to underlie source amnesia as well (Schacter, Osowiecki, Kaszniak et al., 1994; Norman & Schacter, 1997; Bayen, Phelps, & Spaniol, 2000; Naveh-Benjamin, 2000; Glisky, Rubin, &

Davidson, 2001; Dehon & Brédart, 2004). However, it is far from clear that difficulties with primary memory function alone are responsible for the forgetting of episodic information among the elderly. To begin with, no one can ever be certain if any particular deficit, be it of prospective memory or of source memory, is due to a retrieval or due to a consolidation failure, because the possibility of at least a partial retrieval failure in all cases of forgetting cannot be formally excluded. However, it is always possible to hazard an educated guess on the basis of the preponderance of the evidence. For example, when it is clear that a plan of action fails to materialize at the preappointed time, but the failure is later on realized, it appears reasonable to claim, as we have in fact claimed in the previous section, that the failure is of the primary memory system, specifically of the retrieval operation and not of the secondary memory system. In other situations, however, such guesses may be less readily justifiable. Examples of such situations are furnished by studies reporting on failures on the part of the elderly to retain "source" or "context" information while they are better able to retain the content of episodes they experience (Schacter, Kaszniak, Kihlstrom, & Valdiserri, 1991; Ferguson, Hashtroudi, & Johnson, 1992; Brown, Jones, & Davis, 1995; Spencer & Raz, 1995; Wegesin, Jacobs, Zubin et al., 2000; Glisky, Rubin, & Davidson, 2001; Wegesin, Friedman, Varughese, & Stern, 2002; Dumas & Hartman, 2003). The context can be spatial, such as the location of a particular encounter; temporal, such as the placing of the encounter within a sequence of events; or source, such as who said what during an encounter, or even the emotional valence of the encounter.

It is not clear which types of context are more vulnerable, but it is quite certain that context memory difficulties increase susceptibility to errors of commission, that is distortions, in addition to those of omission. In the laboratory, the elderly are clearly more prone to experimentally induced false memories than young adults are (see review by Schacter, Koutstaal, & Norman, 1997). Difficulties with context memory can give rise to diminished reality monitoring and impair the social functioning and general adaptation of the elderly.

Diminished ability to form episodic memories is expected to affect semantic memory as well, given that all semantic memories are initially encoded as episodes. Word-finding difficulties and, particularly, difficulty learning new proper names are very common in the elderly. The elderly report difficulty remembering the names of people they know well but see infrequently or even the names of very famous people. Word-finding difficulties need not be limited to names of people, or of places, or of other elements of episodes but may include the concepts, especially infrequently used ones, that were formerly accessed without special effort. These difficulties, however, are mild and difficult to explain, especially in view of the fact that verbal knowledge appears to increase rather than decrease with age (Park et al., 2002). No definitive evidence exists concerning the characteristics of the words that the elderly may have difficulty retrieving, beyond frequency of use.

Word-finding difficulties aside, semantic memories are better preserved than episodic ones among the elderly. When older persons recount episodes from different periods in their lives, they report fewer details but more context-free (that is, nonepisodic) information than younger persons (Levine, Svoboda, Hay et al., 2002).

There is only equivocal evidence regarding material-specific (verbal vs. visuospatial) differences in the degree of the episodic memory impairment in the elderly (Park et al., 2002; Haaland, Price, & LaRue, 2003). Organization of verbal material plays an important role in word-list recall and is used less by the elderly than by young persons (Davis et al., 2003). When older people do employ a strategy, it tends to be a low-level one, such as mere rehearsal. Younger people, on the other hand, use elaborate strategies such as integrating items into meaningful contexts (Naveh-Benjamin, 2000).

Longer delay times (e.g., a day or longer) between acquisition and testing result in more rapid forgetting in the elderly than the 20-minute delay, typically used in memory testing, which does not show a large effect of age. Indeed, when young and elderly persons are matched for level and rate of acquisition, the elderly show greater forgetting at a long delay (1 day) but not at a short delay (20 minutes) in free-recall performance. Moreover, the elderly show only a marginal decline in recognition performance in the long delay as compared with younger persons (Davis et al., 2003), although on measures of free-recall for the same information they do worse than younger subjects, reinforcing the notion that the more effortful the task, the more obvious the age-dependent memory decline becomes. Also supportive of this view is the fact that recognition errors tend to occur more frequently when the person is exposed to more than one category of information, such as more than one list of items, and is later asked to respond only to items from a particular list (Benjamin, 2001).

Implicit Memory Difficulties

As specified in Chapter 1, implicit memory involves the unconscious possession of information and the possession of automated and unconsciously performed procedures that may have been initially learned through conscious effort. Experimental paradigms of implicit memory phenomena fall into two main categories, those that are purely perceptual and those involving visuomotor learning.

A well-studied perceptual memory phenomenon is repetition priming. In this paradigm, stimuli are presented during a study phase, and the same or related stimuli are presented during the test phase, along with novel stimuli. A reduced difference in performance between recently presented and novel items is viewed as evidence of an anterograde implicit memory deficit, implying a relative failure to form persistent traces of the studied items. Although most studies show no age-related decline in most priming tasks, making any generalizations is difficult due to the existence of only a few studies for each of the priming tasks (see review by Fleischman & Gabrieli, 1998). Word completion is another paradigm used to study perceptual memory and involves presentation of a list of words followed by presentation of part of a word, such as the word stem. The person is asked to respond with the first word that comes to mind. Effects of aging are relatively weak and are restricted to the very old and institutionalised elderly (Winocur, Moscovitch, & Stuss, 1996; Fleischman & Gabrieli, 1998).

In contrast to perceptual memory that is relatively spared in the elderly, procedural memory shows considerable age-related decrements. As people age, it becomes increasingly more difficult for them to acquire new motor skills, such as driving a car with manual transmission, typing, or using new technologies (implying an anterograde implicit memory deficit). This deficit is likely to involve deterioration of many such skills or generalized slowing that manifests itself in all tasks that require timing (Salthouse, 2000). Skill acquisition is a process of transition from the conscious control of actions to their effortless and automatic implementation.

Deficits in acquiring new procedural memories among the elderly, though commonly observed in daily life, have proven difficult to demonstrate in the laboratory. Even more difficult is the demonstration of deterioration of already acquired skills, that is of retrograde implicit memory deficits, which are evident when tasks that used to be automatic become less automatic with age and require additional cognitive resources. In the laboratory, the elderly are particularly impaired when the to-be-learned visuomotor sequences are repeated at longer intervals and mixed with "distracting" sequences but not when no distracting elements intervene (Howard et al., 2004). They also show a reduction in the acquisition of classically conditioned responses, another type of procedural implicit learning, which is typically assessed through the eyeblink response. Age differences in classical conditioning tasks are large, and persons even in their forties show a progressive decline in both speed of acquisition and the magnitude of conditioned responses (Woodruff-Pak & Thompson, 1988; Woodruff-Pak & Jaeger, 1998).

DIFFERENTIAL DIAGNOSIS

As mentioned at the opening of this chapter, the major challenge facing the clinician is to differentiate between memory decline in older people that is to be "expected" and decline that is a sign of impending dementia. The difficulty in making a differential diagnosis is due to the overlap of scores of elderly individuals in the prodromal stages of dementia or MCI and those aging normally and due to the wide variation in test scores and their dependence on demographic factors, such as educational level. To partially overcome these difficulties, clinicians rely on using age and education-level corrected norms and often take into account the degree of deterioration in performance across successive examinations over time (faster decline in memory test scores is a likely sign of pathology). Also important for differential diagnosis is to rule out other cognitive, affective, and motivational factors that may indirectly affect memory performance. The following two case reports illustrate the process of differentiating between age-appropriate and defective memory performance in elderly clients likely to seek a neuropsychological evaluation.

Case 1

Mr. N, a 73-year-old retired university professor of engineering, complained of poor memory and difficulty performing mental computations, which he first noticed about 9 years prior to seeking help but which got much worse in the past 2 years. He forgets people's names, has poor recall of what he reads, and has difficulty paying attention when watching a movie. Mr. N also complains of getting lost, even in familiar places, and forgetting where he has parked his car. He is very functional in all aspects of his daily life. Neuropsychological testing revealed average to superior performance in all domains: immediate and delayed recall (auditory and visual) and recognition were above average, and working memory was superior (Wechsler Memory Scale, Third Edition; WMS-III). Performance on a list-learning task (California Verbal Learning Test; CVLT) was very good overall: he showed good immediate recall, improvement with the repetition of the items, the ability to organize the material semantically, no loss of the information over time, and excellent recognition without a significant number of false positive responses. His Digit Symbol, Matrix Reasoning, and Arithmetic performance were superior (Wechsler Adult Intelligence Scale, Third Edition; WAIS-III). His Stroop performance was very high. Performance on a visual perception task that requires no construction (Judgment of Line Orientation) was perfect. Verbal fluency, phonemic and semantic, was superior. Mr. N acknowledged very few symptoms of depression on the Beck Depression Inventory-II. He was evaluated two more times over the course of the next 3 years. His memory complaints persisted. He mentioned particular difficulty recalling phone numbers, something that he could always do effortlessly, and the tendency to dial the wrong number. He attributed his difficulties to a sense of "laziness" with tasks requiring effort. His performance remained virtually unchanged in all domains with the exception of an increase in errors of repetition in his CVLT performance, indicating poor monitoring of the information. (Courtesy of Alexandra Economou)

Case 2

Mrs. L, a 70-year-old retired university professor of business administration, complained of memory difficulties, which she first became aware of 6 months prior to seeking help. She is functional in her daily life but has started forgetting things. She gets confused with appointments and has to keep an appointment book, although in the past she kept mental track of all her family's activities and appointments. She used to have an excellent memory for numbers but can no longer remember telephone numbers. Despite her memory complaints, she rated her recall of what she reads or watches on TV as very good and judged her attentional skills and prospective memory to be even better than before. She also judged her orientation in space to be good. Neuropsychological testing revealed very impaired memory performance: immediate and delayed recall (auditory and visual) were deficient, as was recognition, but working memory was in the average range. Mrs. L recalled a very reduced amount of verbal information after a delay (WMS-III). Performance on a list-learning task (CVLT) was also very poor: she showed very limited immediate recall and minimal improvement with the repetition of the items. Most of the items she recalled came from the end of the list. Recall after a short and a long delay was very reduced. She showed some improvement when semantic cues were provided but with an increase in intrusion errors. She was able to recognize all the items on the list, but her numerous false positive responses resulted in chance level ability to discriminate the information. Her Digit Symbol performance was deficient, though her copy of the symbols was fast. Her Matrix Reasoning performance was superior, but the task was performed very slowly, laboriously, and with scatter (WAIS-III). Her Stroop performance was mildly impaired, with some errors. Performance on a visual perception task that requires no construction (Judgment of Line Orientation) was deficient. Verbal fluency, phonemic and semantic, was mildly impaired. Mrs. L acknowledged very few symptoms of depression on the Beck Depression Inventory-II but expressed anxiety over the possibility of having Alzheimer disease. (Courtesy of Alexandra Economou)

A direct comparison of the memory performance of the two clients is possible given their similar ages, levels of education, and professional attainment. Mr. N showed very good performance on all memory measures. Although his subjective complaints may conceivably correspond to an actual decline from even higher former levels of memory functioning, the lack of decline in his performance over the course of the 3 years from his first evaluation makes such a possibility less likely. Furthermore, his near-ceiling performance on tests of attention, speed, and manipulation of numbers makes the evaluation of his subjective complaint concerning the performance of mental computations difficult; he may be very sensitive to even slight age-associated decline because of superior earlier functioning and resulting expectations. Most importantly, for excluding a possible diagnosis of MCI, his ability to learn new information out-of-context is excellent, as indicated by a normal learning curve on a test of verbal learning (CVLT), and his ability to retrieve this information over a rather long retention interval is also excellent.

Mrs. L, on the other hand, shows significant memory impairment, making possible the diagnosis of amnesic MCI. Her performance indicates reduced ability to encode information when it exceeds her memory span and significant loss of information over a delay of only a few minutes as indicated by her CVLT scores. She shows less severe deficits on tests of primary memory and executive functions. Her working memory is much higher than her secondary memory test scores though possibly below her premorbid level. Both patients obtained very high scores on a test of fluid intelligence, which is sensitive to age, consistent with their high level of education. Both persons showed no significant depressive symptoms, but both were worried enough about their memory to seek an evaluation.

The clinical significance of memory complaints is a much-debated issue. In cognitively normal elderly individuals, the presence of memory complaints shows mild correlation with deficits on tests of memory and speed in some studies (e.g., Dik, Jonker, Comijs et al., 2001; Comijs, Dik, Deeg, & Jonker, 2004) and may even be predictive of conversion to dementia (Geerlings, Jonker, Bouter et al., 1999; Palmer, Backman, Winblad, & Fratiglioni, 2003). The presence of memory complaints, on the other hand, depends on certain personality characteristics (Pearman & Storandt, 2004) and is precipitated by depression (Zimprich, Martin, & Kliegel, 2003). Therefore, memory complaints in the elderly should be evaluated in the context of a comprehensive clinical and neuropsychological evaluation.

To determine whether the memory decline shown by an elderly person is significant, most clinicians use the following convention: Abnormal memory for a given age is defined as performance falling 1.5 standard deviations below that of individuals of similar age and education (Petersen, 1995; Petersen et al., 1997). Although arbitrary, this convention could be clinically useful, assuming that the performance of an individual who presents for evaluation is measured longitudinally and compared with the longitudinal performance of the appropriate reference group. But longitudinal memory performance data are often lacking. Neuropsychological studies typically examine age-related memory decline using cross-sectional designs; that is, by comparing the performance of persons of different age groups. There is agreement among these studies that there is a substantial decline in memory in older relative to younger persons. Although some proportion of the differences may indeed be attributed to aging, inferring age-related changes from cross-sectional studies is problematic. People of different generations or cohorts may have had considerable differences in life experiences and opportunities, which are much more complex than differences in mere level of education, and these variables cannot be easily controlled. Consequently, cross-sectional studies may overestimate cognitive decline attributed to aging (Williams & Klug, 1996; Small, 2001; Li and Schmiedek, 2002). Prospective follow-up of a group of individuals, on the other hand, may underestimate cognitive decline due to practice effects if alternate forms of a test are not used and to selective attrition of the most impaired individuals (Small, 2001). One such study suggested that age-related memory decline may be restricted to the acquisition and immediate retrieval of new information and not to problems with retention (Small, Stern, Tang, & Mayeaux, 1999).

Problems with accurate diagnosis based almost entirely on neuropsychological evaluations, with their inherent problems, have led to the use of different diagnostic categories. Some investigators (Morris, Storandt, Miller et al., 2001) have employed the terms "questionable dementia" or "very mild Alzheimer disease (AD)" as related terms. According to the investigators, the detection of "very mild AD" can be achieved with a high degree of confidence using only clinical criteria that pertain to cognitive functions, as evaluated by relatives and the affected person. According to Morris and colleagues (2001), many patients with MCI actually suffer from "very mild AD." People with MCI appear more like patients with AD than normal elderly individuals in terms of memory function but resemble the normal elderly more in terms of general cognitive function and daily functioning (Petersen, Smith, Waring et al., 1999). This profile is evident in the second case study. MCI is associated with a greater rate of decline in selected memory functions, most notably episodic memory, with relatively pre-

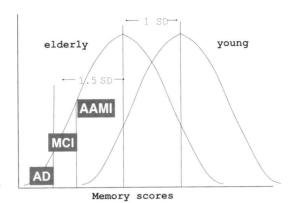

Figure 3–1 Relation between memory scores of individuals who are aging, have age-associated memory impairment (AAMI), mild cognitive impairment (MCI), and Alzheimer disease (AD).

served short-term memory. In early dementia, including MCI, both the encoding of information and its retention are significantly impaired, whereas in aging the encoding of information declines gradually, but the consolidation and retention of information are relatively preserved (Moulin, James, Freeman, & Jones, 2004).

Nevertheless, a small number of elderly people who meet the MCI criteria may never progress to AD. The specific tests and cutoff scores (see, e.g., Figure 3–1) employed in an assessment can result in very different prevalence rates for age-related memory decline as well as for MCI.

There is a substantial heterogeneity in the cognitive decline of the elderly that we have observed in many studies. As we have seen, many processes contribute to this cognitive heterogeneity, some of which are frequently observed with increasing age but are not an intrinsic part of the aging process, such as vascular risk factors (hypertension, diabetes, transient ischemic attacks, etc.) or the presence of a dementia at a preclinical stage, and so forth. Ideally, what we ought to establish are the neural correlates of the intrinsic changes that occur with aging.

AGE-RELATED CHANGES IN THE BRAIN

Macroscopic Anatomical Findings

The few quantitative, volumetric magnetic resonance imaging (MRI) studies that have been conducted longitudinally show a decrease in global brain volume over time, with conflicting findings concerning whether atrophy rates accelerate or remain stable with increasing age (Mueller, Moore, Kerr et al., 1998; Resnick, Pham, Kraut et al., 2003; Scahill, Frost, Jenkins et al., 2003). The reduction is observed in both gray and white matter volumes, with the greatest decline observed in the frontal and parietal lobes. Gray matter loss is especially evident in orbital, inferior frontal, cingulate, insular, and inferior parietal regions and is even observed in a subgroup of healthy elderly persons (Resnick et al., 2003). Gray and white matter reductions are also correlated with age in cross-sectional studies of healthy adults (Murphy, DeCarli, Schapiro et al., 1992; Mueller et al., 1998; Raz, Gunning-Dixon, Head et al., 1998; Ge, Grossman, Babb et al.,

2002b), but whereas gray matter volume decreases linearly with age, white matter volume decreases only after middle age (Jernigan, Archibald, Fennema-Notestine et al., 2001; Ge, Grossman, Babb et al., 2002a).

The frontal lobes appear to be selectively affected by nonpathological aging, measured cross-sectionally, and their integrity is related to working memory performance (Head, Raz, Gunning-Dixon et al., 2002). Studies comparing MRI scans of young and elderly persons reveal age-related changes within the prefrontal cortex in both gray and white matter (Tisserand, Van Boxtel, Gronenschild, & Jolles, 2001; Tisserand, Pruessner, Sanz Arigita et al., 2002b; Tisserand & Jolles, 2003; Salat, Buckner, Snyder et al., 2004; DeCarli, Massaro, Harvey et al., 2005), and also in the thalamus (Van der Werf, Tisserand, Visser et al., 2001), insula, the superior parietal gyri, the central sulci, and the cingulate sulci (Good, Johnsrude, Ashburner et al., 2001).

Age-associated reductions in white matter follow an anterior-to-posterior gradient: they are greater in the anterior section of the corpus callosum (connecting the frontal lobes) as opposed to posterior sections and are greater in frontal lobe white matter than in white matter in the temporal, parietal, and occipital lobes (Head, Buckner, Shimony et al., 2004; see review by Buckner, 2004). Compared with healthy elderly persons, on the other hand, patients with Alzheimer disease show generalized reductions in the size of the corpus callosum (Bartzokis, Sultzer, Lu et al., 2004) and a decrease of white matter predominantly in posterior brain regions (Head et al., 2004).

The significance of medial temporal lobe atrophy for memory performance in nonpathological aging is still debated, but there are indications that it plays a relatively lesser role in age-related memory decline than frontal lobe dysfunction. Hippocampal and parahippocampal volume reductions are not consistently observed in cross-sectional studies of nonpathological aging (e.g., Sullivan, Marsh, Mathalon et al., 1995; Murphy, DeCarli, McIntosh et al., 1996; Bigler, Blatter, Anderson et al., 1997; Pruessner, Collins, Pruessner, & Evans, 2001; Van Petten, 2004) or in the few longitudinal studies that have been conducted (Jack, Petersen, Xu et al., 1998; Mueller, Moore, Kerr et al., 1998; Resnick, Goldszar, Davatzikos et al., 2000). When hippocampal volume reduction is adjusted for shape differences and global tissue volume loss, then hippocampal atrophy is not observed in cross-sectional studies of nondemented elderly (Raz, Gunning, Head et al., 1997; Good et al., 2001; Tisserand, Visser, Van Boxtel, & Jolles, 2002a).

Longitudinal evidence concerning the relation of hippocampal atrophy to memory performance in healthy elderly is sparse. Mild hippocampal atrophy was unrelated to memory decline in nondemented elderly in one longitudinal study (Ylikoski, Salonen, Mantyla et al., 2000), but hippocampal atrophy has been related to memory performance in cross-sectional studies of nondemented elderly (Golomb, Kluger, de Leon et al., 1994; Convit, de Leon, Tarshish et al., 1997; de Leon, George, Golomb et al., 1997; Petersen, Jack, Xu et al., 2000; Hackert, den Heijer, Oudkerk et al., 2002; Small, Tsai, DeLaPaz et al., 2002) and separates normal elderly from persons with MCI after adjusting for generalized atrophy, age, and gender (Convit et al., 1997).

The rate of atrophy increase is the most significant predictor of future memory decline in nondemented elderly persons (Rusinek, De Santi, Frid et al., 2003). The pattern of brain atrophy is very different in the nondemented elderly who later develop dementia, showing reduced volume in the temporal cortex and hippocampal or anterior cingulate cortex atrophy (see review by Chetelat & Baron, 2003), and medial temporal lobe atrophy rate is the most significant predictor of future memory decline in nondemented elderly (Rusinek et al., 2003). Consequently, when significant hippocampal volume reduction is observed in nondemented elderly persons, it is unclear whether it can be attributed to the aging process itself or to the inclusion, in the sample, of people who will later develop dementia.

Atrophy of the hippocampus and entorhinal cortex can distinguish normal elderly persons from patients with MCI and AD. Elderly persons with age-associated cognitive decline have significantly smaller parahippocampal volumes that are intermediate between those of AD patients and cognitively intact elderly persons (Pantel, Kratz, Essig, & Schroder, 2003). Both entorhinal cortex and hippocampal volumes are lower in persons with MCI than in healthy elderly persons. However, entorhinal cortex volume loss is significantly greater than hippocampal volume loss in persons with MCI than in healthy elderly persons, and discrimination between the two groups is best achieved using entorhinal cortex volume than hippocampal volume (Dickerson, Goncharova, Sullivan et al., 2001; Pennanen, Kivipelto, Tuomainen et al., 2004). Nondemented patients with cognitive complaints do not differ in mean normalized (i.e., adjusted for intracranial volume) entorhinal cortex volume from patients with very mild AD. However, these patients have significantly smaller mean normalized hippocampal volume than normal controls and significantly greater hippocampal volume than patients with very mild AD (Dickerson et al., 2001). Patients with AD show an annual rate of entorhinal cortex atrophy approximately three times greater than the rate shown by cognitively normal elderly persons (Du, Schuff, Zhu et al., 2003).

Moderate cerebellar atrophy with age has also been documented in a number of studies (e.g., Sjobeck, Dahlen, & Englund, 1999; Raz, Gunning-Dixon, Head et al., 2001; Andersen, Gundersen, & Pakkenberg, 2003) and is consistent with observed reductions in motor control.

Despite the above observations, the relationship between brain atrophy and cognitive performance in nonpathological aging is indirect. First, brain atrophy or neuronal loss associated with nonpathological aging is relatively small and topographically selective (Gómez-Isla, Price, McKeel, & Morris, 1996; Gómez-Isla, Hollister, West et al., 1997; Morrison & Hof, 1997; Pakkenberg & Gundersen, 1997; Uylings & de Brabander, 2002; Resnick, Pham, Kraut et al., 2003). Therefore, it does not appear to be a major contributor to the cognitive consequences of aging. Second, reductions in brain volume also reflect the contribution of neuronal and cellular changes besides neuronal loss, such as loss of synapses and receptors, neuroglia, myelin and vascular changes, with unclear implications for a reduction in cognitive performance attributed to aging.

Furthermore, neuronal loss could conceivably be plasticity-related and be associated with compensatory brain changes. Apoptosis or neuronal loss is prevalent during early development and is accompanied by changes in the dendritic branches of neurons, with associated synaptic changes following the principles of Hebbian learning (Changeaux & Danchin, 1976; Huttenlocher, 1990). Such changes result in a more efficient functioning of the remaining neuronal networks. Apoptosis in aging could serve the potentially protective function of removal of damaged cells from the brain, although such removal could be detrimental if many neurons get damaged due to age-intrinsic or age-extrinsic processes (see reviews by Zhang & Herman, 2002; Rutten, Korr, Steinbusch, & Schmitz, 2003).

Microscopic Anatomical Findings

Intraneuronal histological changes that are characteristic of dementia (Braak & Braak, 1997a) are also found in a proportion of healthy elderly persons, but their density and regional distribution are distinctly different. Neurofibrillary tangles (NFTs) and neuropil threads are the two main forms of neurofibrillary changes: NFTs are filaments that develop within the nerve cell body, and neuropil threads occur in the axon and dendrite of the neuron. Eventually, they distort the cytoskeleton, disrupt neuronal function, and trigger neuronal death (Braak & Braak, 1997b). Although the number of NFTs in the brains of nondemented persons increases with age, they remain sparse, and their density is much less than that in age-matched demented persons (Braak & Braak, 1997b; Schmitt, Davis, Wekstein et al., 2000). For instance, some NFTs may be found in the entorhinal cortex and the CA1 region of the hippocampus in the majority of nondemented elderly, although some older people remain free of such changes (Schmitt et al., 2000). NFTs are confined to the limbic system in nondemented elderly, but in persons with dementia they spread throughout the hippocampus and neocortex in a predictable and well-documented sequence (Braak & Braak, 1997a). Furthermore, the distribution of NFTs in the prefrontal cortex, an area that is progressively involved as AD worsens, is found only in clinically demented persons (Bussière, Gold, Kövari et al., 2003).

Age-Related Changes in Baseline Metabolic Rate

Reduced brain metabolism is an expected correlate of a reduction in brain volume and does not necessarily reflect an intrinsic metabolic decline of brain tissue in the elderly. Although early studies showed a reduction in cerebral blood flow and baseline metabolic rate in the elderly, healthy elderly persons do not differ from young persons when resting glucose metabolism is adjusted for global brain volume reduction (Meltzer, Cantwell, Greer et al., 2000; Ibáñez, Pietrini, Furey et al., 2004). Patients with AD, on the other hand, show a distinct pattern of regional hypometabolism even when activity levels are corrected for brain atrophy (Alavi, Newber, Souder, & Berlin, 1993; Meltzer, Zubieta, Brandt et al., 1996; Ibáñez, Pietrini, Alexander et al., 1998).

Age-Related Neurochemical Changes

Aging is associated with certain neurochemical changes, most notably a decrease in dopamine and norepinephrine systems (see Chapter 2). Dopamine levels decline in the striatum (e.g., Volkow, Gur, Wang et al., 1998) and are accompanied by a reduction in the numbers of both D1 and D2 dopamine receptors at an estimated rate of 5–10% per decade (reviewed by Arnsten, 1998a; Kaasinen & Rinne, 2002). Comparable rates of decline are reported for D1 and D2 receptors in the neocortex and thalamus (Kaasinen, Vilkman, Hietala et al., 2000; Kaasinen & Rinne, 2002), but D2 receptors decline faster in the frontal cortex than in the temporal cortex, at a rate between 11% and 14% per decade. The decrease cannot all be accounted for by cortical atrophy (Kaasinen et al., 2000), is correlated with reduced metabolism in the frontal cortex and anterior cingulate gyrus (Volkow, Logan, Fowler et al., 2000), and is associated with performance on tests of working memory and executive function (Arnsten, 1998a; Kaasinen & Rinne, 2002). The age-related decline in D2 receptors in the caudate and putamen is associated with motor performance, tests of attention and response inhibition (e.g., the Stroop Color-Word test), and tests of executive function (Volkow, Gur, Wang et al., 1998). Dopaminergic loss in nonpathologic aging could affect frontal function directly through a decrease in D2 receptors and indirectly through a disruption of frontostriatal pathways. The pattern of memory impairment associated with Parkinson disease, reviewed in Chapter 4, is characterized by attentional, working memory, and executive dysfunction, though at a considerably more severe level.

Age-Related Activation Changes

There have been several attempts to identify age-related changes in task-specific patterns of brain activity. Most functional neuroimaging studies have examined the activation of the brain during the performance of tasks of attention and memory, as deficits in these are the most frequent age-related symptoms. Both increased and reduced areas of activation have been observed in the brains of elderly persons when compared with those of young persons (Hazlett, Buchsbaum, Mohs et al., 1998; Schiavetto, Kohler, Grady et al., 2002; Cabeza, Daselaar, Dolcos et al., 2004), but interpretation of the significance of these differences in terms of memory processes is not at all transparent. Age-related decreases in activation do not necessarily reflect a processing deficiency, nor do age-related increases in activation reflect behavioral compensation.

CONCLUSIONS AND SPECULATIONS

Population-based studies on aging are likely to be contaminated by the presence of elderly individuals with prodromal dementia or individuals who suffer from other common medical conditions that are known to affect cognitive processes, such as untreated high blood pressure, depression, or subclinical vascular disease.

Disentangling cognitive dysfunction that is a consequence of subclinical neu-rodegenerative disorders, themselves age-related, from cognitive dysfunction that is a consequence of aging is not an easy task. But the few community-based stud-ies on successful aging indicate that it is possible to remain cognitively intact well into an advanced age. An easier distinction is between normal aging, which is commonly defined as the absence of specific diagnostic or medical conditions, and aging associated with a dementia (see Chapter 4).

Delayed recall performance is the best predictor of the onset of dementia in nondemented elderly persons. An anterograde episodic memory deficit is the earliest deficit in persons with prodromal AD, who are similar to healthy elderly in other domains (Petersen, Smith, Waring et al., 1999; Grundman, Petersen, Ferris et al., 2004). The decrease in delayed recall performance in prodromal AD is correlated with atrophy of the hippocampus and entorhinal cortex.

In aging, the encoding of information declines gradually, but the consolida-tion and retention of information are relatively preserved, whereas in early dementia both the encoding of information and its retention are significantly impaired.

We can summarize our conclusions on age-related memory decline by addressing the following four questions.

1. *To what degree is age-related memory decline characterized by deficits in differ-ent memory phenomena?*

   Nonpathological age-related memory decline is characterized by mild deficits in episodic memory, which are predominantly attributed to reduced primary memory functions. Context information, irrespective of its nature, is more vulnerable than content information, leading to difficulties with source memory. General information accrued from many related experiences that constitutes "timeless" elements of memory (semantic memories) is generally more resistant to the effects of aging.

2. *Is the deficit mostly anterograde, retrograde, or both?*

   Memory deficits associated with aging manifest in recently acquired episodic memories. Such memories are more susceptible to degradation or interference. Anterograde deficits are observed in both explicit (forgetting phone numbers and proper names) and implicit domains (learning new visuomotor skills). Ensuring that the information to be learned is properly encoded (by reducing distracting conditions and providing explicit memo-rization cues) renders the ability of the elderly to retrieve it after short delays only marginally worse compared with that of younger persons.

   Semantic memory is another phenomenon that remains relatively unim-paired in the elderly—a situation that parallels the preservation of temporal neocortex. In contrast, medial temporal lobe atrophy, even limited in degree and progressing very slowly during normal aging, as suggested by most studies (e.g., Murphy, DeCarli, McIntosh et al., 1996; Bigler, Blatter, Anderson et al., 1997; Resnick, Goldszal, Davatzikos et al., 2000; Van Petten, 2004), may be associated with the temporally graded retrograde episodic amnesia that is often found in the elderly (e.g., Petersen, Jack, Xu et al., 2000; Hackert, den Heijer, Oudkerk et al., 2002).

3. *Which memory functions or constituent operations are affected and to what degree?*

Source memory impairment can be attributed to a less distinctive encoding of information, primarily a diminished ability to form intentional associations between items, to impairment of strategic or effortful retrieval, or to a combination of the two factors. Primary memory functions that involve the manipulation of information and effortful retrieval are the most affected, whereas consolidation and storage deficits are mild for memories that have been adequately encoded.

4. *Given the above deficits and what is known about the pathophysiology of age-related memory impairment, what can be said about the nature of the memory functions and associated brain mechanisms?*

There is converging evidence for a systematic relationship between impaired memory functions and changes in associated brain mechanisms. Age-related reductions in primary memory capabilities are correlated with gross anatomical and neurochemical deterioration in the frontal-striatal system. As we saw in Chapter 2, this system is closely involved in the short-term maintenance of active representations of incoming information through rehearsal and in operations that lie at the core of working memory phenomena, such as the continuous monitoring, selection, and mental manipulation of items. The early and progressive loss of frontal lobe volume coincides with an age-related decline in attention and complex primary memory functions. Free-recall performance is expected to be particularly vulnerable to deterioration of prefrontal function, involving as it does deliberate, rather than automatically triggered, retrieval by current sensory input or strong thematic relations. Recognition, on the other hand, does not require effortful and deliberate retrieval of memories and remains relatively unaffected.

The concept of "cognitive reserve" has been proposed to explain the repeated observation that the relationship between the degree of brain pathology and the degree of cognitive impairment is not a direct or linear one. Cognitive reserve is a multidimensional construct and implies flexibility in solving a problem, as well as some redundancy in the organization of cognitive functions. Flexibility in problem solving and the employment of different strategies have been linked both to higher intellectual functioning and to higher educational attainment, and educational attainment is often used as proxy for intellectual functioning when the direct measurement of level of intelligence is not practical or feasible (see Stern, 2002, for a critical review of cognitive reserve). Cognitive reserve may allow the elderly to cope more successfully with age-related changes in brain and cognitive function and even cope better with brain pathology.

To illustrate the point, a large, population-based study of elderly persons showed that although severity of white matter lesions was not associated with education level or occupation, it was strongly associated with performance on tests of attention and speed in elderly persons with low education, but negligibly so in elderly persons with high education levels (Dufouil, Alpérovitch, & Tzourio, 2003). Thus, an educated elderly person with significant brain pathology may function very well, but a less educated elderly person with the same degree of pathology may experience difficulties in many domains.

But the neurobiological base of cognitive reserve is not known, and few studies have explicitly examined the contribution of cognitive reserve to age-related differences in the neurobiological substrate of memory. A person with more cognitive reserve might be expected to recruit an alternative network in order to perform a task, but the engagement of these networks may reflect compensatory changes rather than cognitive reserve (Stern, 2002; see also Buckner, 2004). More studies are clearly needed in this area, and disentangling compensation from reserve is not a straightforward proposition. Findings of an alternative activation pattern in the more educated elderly persons that is also associated with better memory performance on the experimental task and that is similar to the activation pattern of young persons, with ability measured independently of performance on the experimental task, would provide evidence for the mediation of cognitive reserve.

4

Amnesias Associated
with the Dementias

ALEXANDRA ECONOMOU, SOKRATIS G. PAPAGEORGIOU,
AND ANDREW C. PAPANICOLAOU

The family of disorders known as dementias derive their name from the most
conspicuous set of symptoms with which they are associated; that is, deficits in
mentation. Such deficits are secondary to a number of pathophysiological
processes like infections, metabolic deficiencies, autoimmune diseases, toxic
encephalopathies, hypothyroidism, trauma, and hydrocephalus, among others.
However, these secondary deficits are either reversible or, generally, not progressive. In the case of the dementias, on the other hand, the same deficits are
not just irreversible but, with the exception of vascular dementia, worsen
and progress over time, following the rhythm of the underlying pathophysiology.

The pathophysiological processes causing the dementias have been traditionally classified as primarily cortical or primarily subcortical, a distinction that is
not employed here, as it is not particularly informative and, in some cases, could
even be misleading. For example, although Alzheimer disease (AD) is usually
classified with cortical diseases, it also entails loss of cholinergic neurons in subcortical structures. Subcortical ischemic vascular dementia is typically classified
with the subcortical diseases, even though it is associated with atrophy of the
frontal cortex.

The cognitive deficit most apparent in most dementias is amnesia. The
amnesia varies depending on two factors: the stage of the pathology and the
brain structures compromised. The amnesic syndromes of the dementias
fall into two main classes: those characterized by deficits in secondary and
primary memory functions (or both); and those characterized by predominant deficits in primary memory, notably involving the operation of effortful retrieval.

The syndromes of the first class, characterized by deficits in both secondary and primary memory, result from AD, vascular dementia due to a strategic single infarct, or the "temporal" variant of frontotemporal dementia. Within these, the syndrome due to AD presents with selective anterograde episodic memory impairment, followed by retrograde episodic and semantic memory impairment, primary and secondary implicit memory deficits, and culminating in agnosia, aphasia, and apraxia. The amnesic syndrome resulting from vascular dementia due to a strategic single infarct often includes secondary memory symptomatology similar to that described for diencephalic amnesia and amnesia due to basal forebrain lesions (see Chapter 6). Finally, the syndrome characteristic of the temporal variant of frontotemporal dementia is that of semantic amnesia covered in Chapter 5.

The second class of amnesias consists of a set of similar syndromes, all featuring a predominant primary memory deficit and subcortical damage, mainly of the basal ganglia, as well as damage to the frontal lobes. The damage may be due to subcortical ischemia, Huntington disease, Parkinson disease, or atrophy of the frontal lobe. The profile of memory and cognitive impairment in these dementias is similar to that seen in other disorders that involve the prefrontal cortex.

Besides these two classes of dementia-related amnesic syndromes, there is a third one due to posterior cortical atrophy (PCA). This is a rare, progressive dementia, which is pathologically heterogeneous, but AD pathology appears to be its major cause. Other causes are Jakob-Creutzfeldt disease, subcortical gliosis, Pick disease, and corticobasal degeneration. Patients with PCA present with pronounced impairment in the visual domain, with preserved episodic memory and insight in the early stages of the disease. Case studies of patients with PCA, irrespective of etiology, show impairment in the visual domain including visual identification, matching, copying, optic apraxia and ataxia, simultagnosia, prosopagnosia, alexia, agraphia, constructional dyspraxia, Wernicke aphasia, anomia, acalculia, and right/left disorientation (Black, 1996; Ross, Graham, Stuart-Green et al., 1996; Ardila, Rosselli, Arvizu, & Kuljis, 1997; Hof, Vogt, Goethals & Santens, 2001; Boxer, Kramer, Du et al., 2003; Tang-Wai, Josephs, Boeve et al., 2003b). Although it could be argued that this dementia entails a semantic memory deficit, that deficit cannot be differentiated from the symptoms of agnosia that dominate its clinical picture. Therefore, we will not consider it further in this chapter.

Because all the syndromes mentioned above vary not only with the neuroanatomical location of the damage but also with the progression and spread of the degeneration, they are constantly becoming more severe and more pervasive, involving an ever-increasing number of cognitive functions, thus growing more diffuse and less distinct from each other. Consequently, in the following pages, although we will be commenting on their evolution, our description of each will be based on their appearance during the early stages of the dementing disease that causes them, when they are most distinct and their correct detection and diagnosis is of greatest pragmatic import.

ESTABLISHMENT OF THE SYMPTOMS

Syndromes of the First Class Involving Secondary and Primary Memory Systems

As mentioned above, three main amnesic syndromes sharing the feature of explicit memory deficits compose this class. They differ, mainly, in that the first, caused by AD, is progressive, whereas the second, caused by single thalamic infarcts, is not, and both differ from the third, caused by degeneration of neo-cortical temporal lobe regions, in that the third features most prominently semantic rather than episodic deficits. In the following paragraphs, the establishment of the symptoms that compose each of the three syndromes will be discussed, along with illustrative case reports, all of which are taken from the files of the first and second authors of this chapter.

The Amnesic Syndrome in Alzheimer Dementia

Case 1: Mild Alzheimer Disease

Ms. R is an 80-year-old, right-handed, retired attorney diagnosed with AD. She remains quite functional in her daily life, making use of compensatory strategies such as recording everything that she has to do, but she does require considerable supervision and does not live alone. Neuropsychological testing revealed significant impairment in immediate recall of both verbal and nonverbal material (Wechsler Memory Scale, Third Edition; WMS-III), with loss of the limited information that she was able to recall after a brief delay and poor recognition. Her working memory, on the other hand, was in the average range for her age. Performance on a list-learning test (California Verbal Learning Test; CVLT) showed very poor initial recall of the items and limited improvement across trials, as well as numerous intrusion errors in her delayed recall. Her ability to discriminate items from the specified list from items not on the list or items not presented previously was at chance. Performance in other domains was only mildly impaired or not impaired relative to norms (superior Vocabulary, average Matrix Reasoning and Judgment of Line Orientation [JLO], slightly impaired phonological and semantic fluency due to repetitions and errors, slow Digit Symbol performance, yet fast Symbol Copy relative to her age group). Ms. R is a person in the early stages of AD, with significant anterograde, episodic memory deficits. Her magnetic resonance imaging (MRI) scan showed bilateral temporal lobe atrophy, with widening of the sulci and the Sylvian fissure, and moderate hippocampal atrophy. Mild diffuse cortical atrophy, as shown in Figure 4–1, was also seen in the frontal and parietal cortex.

(Courtesy of Alexandra Economou)

Episodic Memory.   Patients with Alzheimer disease in the early stages, and persons with "amnesic" mild cognitive impairment (amnesic MCI), most of

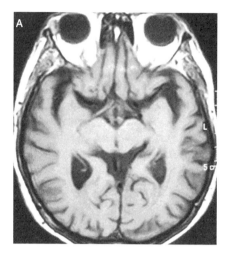
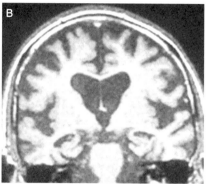

Figure 4–1 (A) An axial T1-weighted MRI slice showing bilateral temporal lobe atrophy in the hippocampus and the neocortex of the temporal lobe, with widening of the sulci and the Sylvian fissure. (B) A coronal T1-weighted brain MRI slice demonstrating moderate hippocampal atrophy and mild diffuse cortical atrophy in the frontal and temporal cortex. Note: The left hemisphere is shown on the right side of the image. (Courtesy of Sokratis G. Papageorgiou)

whom are considered to be in the predementia stage of AD, show a markedly reduced ability to retain new information. They have difficulty recalling the names of people, conversations, appointments, where they have parked their car or placed their keys, and often complain about their forgetfulness. The inability to recall episodic information after a delay, besides being the most salient deficit of patients with AD (Tröster, Butters, Salmon et al., 1993; Reed, Paller, & Mungas, 1998), is the most important predictor of who will develop AD among nondemented elderly persons (Masur, Sliwinski, Lipton et al., 1994; Tierney, Szalai, Snow et al., 1996; Chen, Ratcliff, Belle et al., 2000). The anterograde episodic memory impairment in AD is broad and not restricted to the verbal modality; however, we know much less about the sensitivity of visual memory measures in the early detection of the disease, aside from the fact that patients with mild AD are significantly impaired on visual recognition tasks (Barbeau, Didic, Tramoni et al., 2004). The performance of patients with amnesic MCI on delayed recall measures of episodic memory typically falls between the performance of patients with AD and that of nondemented elderly persons, but their performance in other cognitive domains is more like the performance of healthy elderly persons (Petersen, Smith, Waring et al., 1999; Petersen, Doody, & Kurz, 2001; Grundman, Petersen, Ferris et al., 2004).

Semantic Memory.   The spontaneous speech of patients with early AD tends to be vague, full of circumlocutions, empty phrases, and indefinite terms, and often contains semantically related but incorrect content words. This suggests that patients with AD suffer from a semantic memory deficit. Indeed, AD patients are impaired on a variety of tasks that require accessing semantic memories, such as basic word retrieval, retrieving exemplars of a semantic category, and naming objects. They are most impaired on tasks that require them to carry out a directed search, as in phonemic fluency tasks. They show a steady decline in semantic fluency as the disease progresses and exhibit word-finding difficulties in object naming and in naming to definitions. Vocabulary knowledge, however, is stable in the early course of the disease (Nebes, 1989).

Patients with AD show loss of appreciation of the features that distinguish concepts from one another, as measured by their listing of such features and by priming studies (Alathari, Ngo, & Dopkins, 2004). Furthermore, patients with AD organize concepts primarily on the basis of concrete features, whereas healthy elderly people tend to group concepts together on the basis of abstract conceptual attributes (Chan, Salmon, Nordin et al., 1998). The magnitude of the semantic deficit of patients with AD is affected by the level of severity of the disorder and the manner in which semantic knowledge is tested.

Patients with early AD, or even persons at risk for developing AD, show impairment in the ability to identify odors relative to healthy elderly (Nordin & Murphy, 1996; Murphy, Bacon, Bondi, & Salmon, 1998; Larsson, Semb, Winblad et al., 1999; Murphy, 1999; Gilbert, Barr, & Murphy, 2004). This deficit is not due to impaired sensory registration and is consistent with an impairment in semantic memory, that is, with progressive loss of knowledge about the smells (Larsson et al., 1999; Murphy, 1999; Gilbert et al., 2004). It is also a predictor of subsequent decline in verbal learning and memory, as well as global measures of cognition (Borenstein Graves, Bowen, Rajaram et al., 1999; Devanand, Michaels-Marston, Liu et al., 2000; Swan & Carmelli, 2002).

Implicit Memory.   AD is not associated with consistent perceptual implicit memory impairments (Meiran & Jelicic, 1995; Maki & Knopman, 1996; Camus, Nicolas, Wenisch et al., 2003). Many studies, however, have shown conceptual implicit memory impairments in AD patients. Impaired performance has been reported on implicit category exemplar generation, semantic decision, word-stem completion, and word-association tasks (Gabrieli, Vaidya, Stone et al., 1999; Lazzara, Yonelinas, & Ober, 2001). Intact performance on some conceptual implicit memory tasks by patients in the early stages of the disease suggests that lexical and conceptual processes in some cases are not impaired until later in the progression of the disease (Camus, Nicholas, Wenisch et al., 2003).

A particular form of implicit learning which is not assessed frequently is habit learning. This is the gradual improvement in performance across learning trials. Patients with AD are able to acquire the associations between cues and outcomes despite performance at chance level on a test of explicit memory for the training episode (Eldridge, Masterman, & Knowlton, 2002). Fear conditioning, another form of implicit memory, is impaired in patients with mild AD compared with elderly persons, after equating the two groups on their ability to produce unconditioned responses. The impairment in fear conditioning is consistent with AD neuropathology, which frequently involves the amygdala early in the disease (Hamann, Monarch, & Goldstein, 2002).

Primary Memory.   Patients with mild AD do not differ consistently from the healthy elderly on measures of primary memory, especially those assessing operations of short-term memory, but they do present deficits in measures of working memory, as evident from the nature of the explicit memory deficits described in the previous paragraphs.

Patients with AD have no difficulty with easy short-term memory operations such as holding and rehearsing of information (Perry, Watson, & Hodges, 2000; Swainson, Rogers, Sahakian et al., 2000; Baddeley, Baddeley, Bucks, & Wilcock, 2001; De Jager, Milwain, & Budge, 2002), but they experience increasing difficulty as the complexity of the putative operations or task demands increases. This is demonstrated in tasks that require divided attention and the simultaneous performance of two activities (Baddeley, Bressi, Della Sala et al., 1991, Perry et al., 2000; Baddeley et al., 2001). Dual-task performance is not affected in normal aging, provided that tasks are chosen so to involve different cognitive operations, and the level of difficulty is adjusted so to equate single-task performance across groups (Della Sala & Logie, 2001). As such, it can be used to discriminate between normally aging individuals and individuals likely to develop AD.

Impairment in immediate auditory recall in AD is related to deficits in working memory/executive functions, such as the inability to resist distraction or to manipulate information that is held in short-term memory rather than to reduced auditory memory span. Patients with mild to moderate AD are especially vulnerable to information overload inherent in supraspan tasks (Cherry, Buckwalter, & Henderson, 2002).

Tests of primary memory functions do not contribute significantly to the prediction of who will develop AD and when they will do so; these tests are much less important than tests of secondary memory functions (Masur, Sliwinski, Lipton et al., 1994; Tierney, Szalai, Snow et al., 1996; Fabrigoule, Rouch, Taberly et al., 1998; Chen, Ratcliff, Belle et al., 2000; Albert, Moss, Tanzi, & Jones, 2001). Performance in primary, short-term memory tasks is not a good predictor of subsequent AD diagnosis and may, in fact, be relatively good in persons with poor performance in secondary memory tasks (Linn, Wolf, Bachman et al., 1995). Persons with MCI, much like AD patients, decline most rapidly in episodic memory, next in primary memory, then in semantic memory, and finally, in perceptual speed. However, neither group differs from normal aged individuals in their rate of decline in short-term/working memory (Bennett, Wilson, Schneider et al., 2002).

The Evolution of the Syndrome Contingent on the Progression of the Disease. The well-specified and predictable sequence of pathophysiologic stages of AD described by Braak and Braak (1991) has led to efforts to stage the severity of the clinical symptoms. Global assessment measures, such as the Clinical

Dementia Rating scale (CDR; Morris, 1993), the Global Deterioration Scale (GDS; Reisberg, Ferris, de Leon, & Crook, 1982) and the Global Deterioration Scale/Functional Assessment Staging (GDS/FAST) system (see Auer & Reisberg, 1997) are useful in tracking the progression of AD because they describe its entire course. Changes in functional status using these measures are typically obtained from a collateral source, preferably someone who lives with the patient such as a spouse or offspring. Other more appropriate measures used for staging AD are longer measures of general cognitive function, such as the Mattis Dementia Rating Scale (DRS; Mattis, 1988) and the cognitive subscale of the Alzheimer Disease Assessment Scale (ADAS-Cog; Rosen, Mohs, & Davis, 1984).

The episodic memory deficit is the earliest and most prominent deficit in AD, with complex primary memory functions deteriorating next, followed by impairment in semantic and visuospatial functions (Perry & Hodges, 1999; Perry, Watson, & Hodges, 2000). The pattern of deficits in executive function is heterogeneous in AD patients with relatively focal deficits. Semantic deficits predominate over visuospatial deficits in most AD patients, yet a minority presents with marked visuospatial, but no semantic, deficits (Caine & Hodges, 2001). Tests of episodic memory are very sensitive in discriminating patients with even mild AD from the healthy elderly, but because floor effects are reached early in the course of the disease, they are not indicated for the staging of AD (Locascio, Crowdon, & Corkin, 1995). Naming and semantic fluency tests show a linear decline over time in AD relative to healthy elderly controls and are therefore more useful for staging dementia severity.

The Amnesic Syndrome in Single Infarct Dementia

Infarcts involving the thalamus or basal forebrain structures produce the corresponding syndromes of limbic amnesia, which are treated extensively in Chapter 6. In this section, we will comment on the syndrome resulting from single thalamic infarcts illustrated by a case report from our files.

Case 2: Strategic Thalamic Infarct Dementia

Mr. S, a 55-year-old, right-handed salesman with a junior high school education, sustained a bilateral thalamic infarct, which produced vertical gaze palsy, a severe memory impairment, and dysarthria. His computed tomography (CT) scan showed bilateral hypodensity in the midline and anterior parts of both thalami due to a bilateral thalamic infarct (Figure 4–2). Neuropsychological testing revealed very reduced immediate recall of two stories (WMS-III Logical Memory), with no retention of any of the information after a short delay and very impaired recognition. Performance on a list-learning task (CVLT) was similarly impaired, with no improvement after repetitions of the list, lack of semantic organization, loss of all of the information after a short delay, and very deficient recognition performance. What was of note in this patient's cued

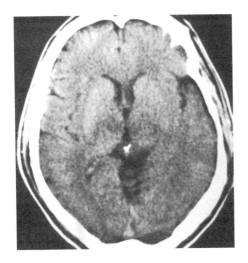

Figure 4–2 An axial brain CT scan slice of the patient, demonstrating a bilateral hypodensity in the midline and anterior part of both thalami due to a bilateral infarct. Note: The left hemisphere is shown on the right side of the image. (Courtesy of Sokratis G. Papageorgiou)

recall performance was the presence of numerous intrusion errors that were unrelated to the content of the list. Auditory working memory was very impaired. Mr. S was barely able to sequence one number and one letter, immediately losing track of the task (WMS-III Letter-Number Sequencing). Verbal fluency, phonemic and semantic, was extremely impaired over and above the contribution of the dysarthria. Mr. S shows dementia secondary to a strategic infarct in the thalamus. The superimposition of unrelated information on the patient's cued recall performance may indicate the presence of confabulations. (Courtesy of Alexandra Economou)

Vascular dementia encompasses several subtypes with heterogeneous clinical manifestation. Strategic single-infarct dementia, the subtype of vascular dementia with an abrupt onset that we are describing here, is attributed to a single infarct that is sufficient to lead to amnesia. It affects, albeit indirectly, cortical or subcortical areas that are critical to memory functions. Strategic infarct vascular dementia is often observed after infarcts or focal hemorrhages that involve the paramedian nuclei of the thalamus. Severe personality changes as well as a variety of neuropsychological impairments, including deficits of attention, primary and secondary memory deficits, and a decline in motivation, have been reported (Szirmai, Vastagh, Szombathelyi, & Kamondi, 2002). The secondary memory symptomatology associated with vascular dementia due to a single infarct is more extensively discussed in Chapter 6.

The Amnesic Syndrome in Frontotemporal Dementia, Temporal Variant

The amnesic syndrome resulting from damage to the temporal neocortex due to various causes, including neurodegenerative diseases, is extensively discussed in

Chapter 5. Here we present a brief account of the syndrome as it results from this form of degenerative disease.

Case 3: Frontotemporal Dementia, Temporal Variant

Mr. C, a 70-year-old, right-handed, retired fireman, complained of difficulty recalling names of people but not faces or places. He traced the onset of his difficulty to about 6 months earlier and insisted that his memory had been very good prior to that time. He is functional in his daily life. The neuropsychological evaluation revealed borderline performance on the Wechsler Adult Intelligence Scale, Third Edition (WAIS-III) Matrix Reasoning and Vocabulary Subtest. Mr. C had difficulty providing the meanings of common words and was unable to identify the similarity between objects and concepts on a concrete level (WAIS-III Similarities). His immediate recall of verbal material (WMS-III Logical Memory) was very deficient, with complete loss of the information after a delay and chance-level recognition performance. His visual memory was in the borderline range (WMS-III Visual Reproduction), with loss of all the information after a delay, but with recognition skills in the average range and adequate copying performance. His verbal working memory was also in the borderline range, but his visual working memory skills were average. Processing speed was very slow (WAIS-III Digit Symbol), including the simple copying of the symbols. Color naming on the Stroop test in the conflict condition was very slow with errors, but even his color naming in the simple condition was slow. Phonemic and semantic fluency was deficient. He showed great difficulty naming line drawings of animals and inanimate objects, even very common ones (Snodgrass & Vanderwart [1980] stimuli), with only slight improvement when given phonemic cues. He exhibited great difficulty on a picture description task (Boston Diagnostic Aphasia Examination Cookie Theft subtest), with circumlocutions and many paraphasic errors. Performance on a visual perception task that requires no construction (Judgment of Line Orientation;) was in the average range. His execution of a series of alternating hand movements was very impaired. His MRI scan showed severe atrophy of the left anterior temporal lobe (Figure 4–3). What is remarkable in this patient is the preservation of activities of daily living in the face of his deficient memory functioning. Independent daily living and behavior may be preserved longer in patients with temporal variant frontotemporal dementia (FTD) than in patients with AD, due to the nature of the memory deficits; in the advanced stage of the disease, however, the clinical picture can be indistinguishable from that of AD.

(Courtesy of Alexandra Economou)

Frontotemporal dementia of the temporal variant (tv-FTD) is a progressive disease that gives rise to the syndrome of semantic amnesia (covered extensively in Chapter 5). The recent consensus criteria for FTD (Neary, Snowden, Gustafson et al., 1998) include both cognitive and behavioral features of the disorder. Neary, Snowden, Gustafson et al. (1998) further subdivide the disease into

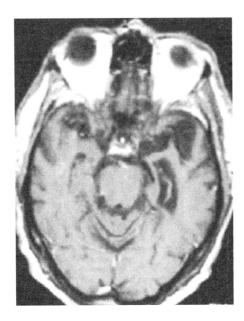

Figure 4–3 A T1-weighted axial MRI slice demonstrates severe atrophy of left anterior temporal lobe. Atrophy is most prominent in the temporal pole but extends to the hippocampus. Note: The left hemisphere is shown on the right side of the image. (Courtesy of Sokratis G. Papageorgiou)

three clinical syndromes: FTD, primary progressive aphasia (PPA), and semantic dementia. The classification reflects the clinical heterogeneity of FTD, which is determined by the relative involvement of the frontal and temporal lobes, as well as the right and left hemispheres. Predominantly frontal involvement (i.e., frontal variant FTD) is associated with behavioral abnormalities and with working memory and retrieval deficits. Predominantly left frontal involvement is associated with progressive loss of speech and nonfluent speech output (progressive aphasia), and predominantly left temporal involvement is associated with loss of knowledge of words and the meaning of objects (semantic dementia) (Rosen, Gorno-Tempini, Goldman et al., 2002b).

Mesulam, Grossman, Hillis et al. (2003) provided detailed descriptions of the two language syndrome of PPA. PPA is a progressive language disorder, with anomia as its most common sign. Many patients with PPA remain in an anomic phase, experiencing a gradual worsening of word-finding ability, whereas others develop agrammatism (inappropriate word order in speech and misuse of grammatical words) and/or comprehension deficits.

Syndromes of the Second Class Featuring Primary Memory Impairment

In this class, we have included amnesic syndromes characterized by working memory and retrieval deficits; that is, deficits of the primary memory system. First, we discuss the amnesic syndrome of subcortical ischemic vascular dementia, followed by a discussion of the amnesias associated with Parkinson disease, Huntington disease, corticobasal atrophy or degeneration, progressive supranuclear palsy, and the frontal variant of frontotemporal dementia.

Amnesic Syndrome in Subcortical Ischemic Dementia

Case 4: Subcortical Ischemic Vascular Dementia

Mr. B, a 69-year-old, right-handed architect, presented with disorientation and a decline in memory. Although he stated that he has kept a limited practice, he did not acknowledge any projects currently in progress upon questioning. He judged his memory difficulties to be mild and attributed them to tiredness and getting old. His wife, however, described the existence of considerable memory difficulties and complained that he behaves inappropriately toward her. During the interview, he was disoriented in time and gave the wrong date and month. The neuropsychological evaluation revealed deficient immediate recall of verbal and nonverbal information, with no recall of the information after a short delay (WMS-III). His poor immediate and delayed reproduction of the WMS-III designs contrasted with his perfect copying performance. His recall of a list of words from the CVLT was very poor, with numerous intrusions. Mr. B stated that he was unable to keep more than five words in his mind at a time. His recognition memory was very poor, with many false positive responses. Mr. B's short-term and working memory were also very limited. For example, he was able to tap only as many as four cubes forward and two cubes backward (WMS-III Spatial Span). He had difficulty with phonemic and especially with semantic fluency, made many perseverative errors, and halfway through the semantic fluency task he spontaneously switched categories from animals to food items. Tasks of executive function and processing speed showed striking deficits. Digit Symbol performance was extremely slow with many errors and contrasted with his very fast copying of the symbols. Performance on the Stroop task was very poor: he was unable to inhibit the effect of the printed words on his color-naming performance, despite efforts to do so ("blue, which is not the color blue but another color"). Performance on WMS-III Matrix Reasoning was very poor: He had difficulty maintaining the goal of the problems, asked for the instructions to be repeated, took a very long time to perform the task, and was unable to solve any problems requiring a solution beyond identification. His MRI scan showed diffuse periventricular white matter hyperintensities and lacunar microinfarcts, the characteristic imaging features of subcortical ischemic vascular dementia (SIVD), and a lacunar infarct in the head of the left caudate nucleus (Figure 4–4). A single photon emission computed tomography (SPECT) study (not shown) demonstrated bilateral parietal and left frontal and temporal hypoperfusion. A "patchy" distribution of hypoperfusion favors a diagnosis of vascular dementia.
(Courtesy of Alexandra Economou)

Mr. B showed deficits in almost all cognitive domains, with notable deficits in all primary memory and executive tasks. His reduced encoding, indicated by his poor performance on tests of immediate recall, is likely to have affected his delayed recall, though his ability to consolidate the information that he has encoded cannot be established because the memory tests did not specifically

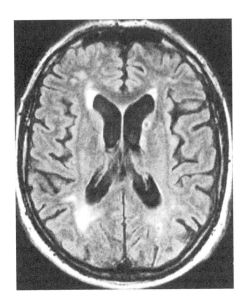

Figure 4-4 An axial brain proton density MRI slice, demonstrating diffuse periventricular white matter hyperintensities and lacunar microinfarcts, the characteristic imaging features of subcortical ischemic vascular dementia. Also note a lacunar infarct in the head of the left caudate nucleus. Note: The left hemisphere is shown on the right side of the image. (Courtesy of Sokratis G. Papageorgiou)

control for level of encoding. Patients with SIVD are more likely to have greater deficits in primary memory and executive function than patients with AD. The prominent deficit in AD is one of consolidating new material into long-term memory, which produces a rapid decay of the information and affects both recall and recognition of new material. Therefore, performance on tests of episodic memory, such as Logical Memory delayed recall (WMS-III), tends to be more impaired in AD than in SIVD but only when the deficit is mild (see Graham, Emery, & Hodges, 2004, for further discussion). With increased severity, the performance of both AD and SIVD patients is likely to reach floor levels, as in the case of Mr. B.

Subcortical ischemic vascular dementia is the most prevalent subtype of vascular dementia. It is characterized by pronounced primary memory impairment and executive dysfunction early in the course of the dementia, attributed to subcortical white matter and fronto-striatal involvement. Patients with SIVD show less impairment in episodic memory than patients with AD, with better recognition performance, and greater impairment in attention and executive functions (Lamar, Price, Davis et al., 2002; Yuspeh, Vanderploeg, Crowell, & Mullen, 2002; Graham, Emery, & Hodges, 2004). The pattern of impairment is more distinct in the early stages of the disease, provided care is taken to exclude patients with concurrent AD and significant white matter abnormalities. Vascular disease, especially with pathology characteristic of SIVD, frequently coexists with Alzheimer disease, and vascular and degenerative pathologies interact in terms of the clinical expression of cognitive impairment (Snowdon, Greiner, Mortimer et al., 1997; Esiri, Nagy, Smith et al., 1999). Mixed SIVD and AD is considered to be the most frequent form of dementia in the general population, with a higher frequency than AD and vascular dementia separately, which may explain in part the difficulty of many studies in demonstrating distinctive cognitive profiles in AD and SIVD (Graham, Emery, & Hodges, 2004). Performance on tasks of semantic memory does not distinguish the two types of dementia (Baillon, Muhommad, Marudkar et al., 2003; Graham, Emery, & Hodges, 2004).

Hachinski and Bowler (1993) have proposed the term "vascular cognitive impairment" to indicate cognitive impairment in persons with vascular disease who do not meet criteria for dementia. Vascular cognitive impairment is characterized by a specific cognitive profile of preserved episodic memory, with impairment in primary memory and executive functions. Clinically important cognitive impairments associated with vascular disease may not meet criteria for dementia, which are based on the concept of AD and therefore require the presence of prominent secondary memory impairment (O'Brien, Erkinjuntti, Reisberg et al., 2003).

The Amnesic Syndrome in Lewy Body Diseases

Case 5: Parkinson Disease Dementia

Ms. J, a 68-year-old homemaker with a high school education, suffers from Parkinson disease (PD), although with very mild motor symptoms. Her husband has noticed deficits in her memory lately, which she also acknowledges. For example, she forgets to turn the burner off after cooking. She has always been "absent-minded," but her ability to concentrate has declined to the point where she is now completely dependent on her husband for her everyday functioning. She is anxious and insecure about her memory ability and is very rigid in her daily routine. The neuropsychological evaluation revealed significant memory deficits, both visual and verbal. Her visual memory was affected by her poor visuospatial and construction abilities, which were evident in the much distorted copying of the WMS-III designs. Furthermore, she gave very few correct responses on a visual perception task that requires no construction (Judgment of Line Orientation). She recalled fewer elements from a story the second time it was read to her (WMS-III Logical Memory learning slope) but showed no loss of the material after a delay; in fact, her delayed recall was better than her immediate recall. Her immediate and delayed recall on a list-learning test (CVLT) were poor, but her performance improved with semantic cues, albeit with an increase in errors of intrusion. Her recognition of the items was very good, but her false positive responses reduced somewhat her ability to discriminate old from new information. Ms. J's working memory, both verbal and spatial, was very limited (WMS-III), and her phonemic and semantic fluency were reduced. Performance on WMS-III Matrix Reasoning was very poor. Her execution of a series of alternating hand movements was very impaired, and she could not maintain a sequence of three movements without a visual model. Digit Symbol performance was extremely slow with many errors, but the copying of the symbols was also slow. Color naming on the Stroop test in the conflict condition was impossible, because Ms. J could not inhibit the color named by the printed word. She reported fluctuations in her mood and acknowledged some depressive symptoms on the Beck Depression Inventory-II.

Ms. J shows reduced recall of the information and considerable primary memory and executive deficits, but her episodic memory is better, as indicated by her improvement with semantic support and better recognition memory. Her deficient visuospatial skills, which are associated with PD even in the early stages, have been linked to disruption in a functional circuit that involves the basal ganglia, frontal lobes, and parietal lobes (Crucian, Barrett, Schwartz et al., 2000), though the exact mechanism of the deficits is unclear.

(Courtesy of Alexandra Economou)

The amnesic syndrome in patients with Parkinson disease is similar to that of other dementias with frontostriatal involvement. Patients with PD, who do not meet criteria for dementia, exhibit a variety of attentional deficits, which are more prominent than their secondary memory deficits. Because a high percentage of patients with PD eventually develop dementia and because the current definition of dementia is biased toward secondary memory impairment, we will comment on the memory deficits of patients with PD who have developed dementia as well as patients with PD who have not reached the dementia stage.

Disruption of the Primary Memory System.   Attentional, working memory, and visual-perceptual dysfunction are prominent early in the course of dementia with Lewy bodies (DLB) and Parkinson disease dementia (PDD), two dementia syndromes with Lewy bodies as their pathophysiologic characteristic. The deficits in these domains are substantially greater than the deficits that are seen in AD patients, matched for overall dementia severity, whereas anterograde episodic memory is worse in AD (Shimomura, Mori, Yamashita et al., 1998). Fluctuations in cognitive function over time are attributed to shifts in degree of attention and alertness and are very common (Del Ser, McKeith, Anand et al., 2000; Calderon, Perry, Erzinclioglu et al., 2001; Serby & Samuels, 2001; Ballard, Aarsland, McKeith et al., 2002) but cannot be accounted for by lower general cognitive function (Ballard, Aarsland, McKeith et al., 2002).

Patients with PD without dementia manifest deficits in visuospatial attention, as measured by a visual delayed-response task (Postle, Jonides, Smith et al., 1997), and have difficulty with visual selective attention tasks, similar to patients with frontal lobe damage (Lee, Wild, Hollnagel, & Grafman, 1999). Furthermore, nondemented patients with PD and patients with SIVD show considerable deficits relative to both controls and patients with AD on a simplified version of the Rey Osterrieth Complex Figure (Freeman, Giovannetti, Lamar et al., 2000).

Disruption of the Secondary Memory System.   The secondary memory deficits of patients with DLB or PD with or without dementia, are much less prominent than their primary memory deficits and appear to be attributable to processing speed or working memory deficits. The means by which working memory dysfunction may lead to other memory problems is unclear and may include reduced encoding and/or retrieval disruption. When impairment is observed on immediate and delayed recall tasks, recognition is much less affected (Stebbins, Gabrieli, Masciari et al., 1999; Higginson, King, Levine et al.,

2003; Hamilton, Salmon, Galasko et al., 2004). Impairment in secondary memory includes deficient recognition memory for olfactory stimuli that cannot be attributed to odor detection impairment and is greater than the impairment observed in AD (Gilbert, Barr, & Murphy, 2004).

Implicit Memory.   PD patients show certain deficits in procedural learning, namely those that involve the gradual acquisition of a habit or a motor sequence. When the task inadvertently includes an explicit component, the impairment is not evident.

Patients with damage to the basal ganglia due to PD or Huntington disease (HD) exhibit severe deficits on probabilistic classification tests despite unimpaired performance on explicit memory tasks (Knowlton, Mangels, & Squire, 1996a; Knowlton, Squire, Paulsen et al., 1996b). Procedural learning can be dissociated from episodic learning, as evidenced by the ability of patients with PD and healthy controls to recall the task events subsequent to training but the inability of patients with AD to do so, despite the ability of the latter to acquire the associations between the cues and outcomes.

The most consistent procedural learning deficit involves motor learning tasks. Performance on one such task, the rotary pursuit task, is slower in PD patients relative to normal controls in the randomized condition. This condition requires the execution of multiple motor sequences. PD patients are unimpaired in the blocked condition, which requires the execution of one motor sequence (Haaland, Harrington, O'Brien & Hermanowicz, 1997). The Serial Reaction Time task (SRT; Nissen & Bullemer, 1987) is another widely employed tool for the assessment of motor procedural learning. It involves responding to visual stimuli, which appear sequentially at different locations on a computer screen, by pressing keys that spatially correspond to the stimulus locations. The task includes two learning measures: visuomotor learning, which entails learning of the associations between the stimuli and motor responses; and learning of the specific sequential pattern. Studies of patients with PD show inconsistent findings concerning sequence-specific learning and a small reduction in reaction times (RTs) during the initial training of the sequence, which suggests impaired visuomotor learning. Deficits in the performance of SRT task sequences are observed even when the motor demands are reduced. PD patients show a deficit in the implicit learning of both pairwise components and higher order information in a version of the SRT task that requires verbal rather than motor reponses (Smith & McDowall, 2004).

Another classic test of procedural learning is the mirror-reading task, which requires the reading of words reflected in a mirror. Some of the words are repeated over different trial blocks and others are not. Healthy persons read both repeated and new words faster with practice, which indicates the acquisition of a skill. Acquiring the skill, however, depends on both implicit and explicit processes. A modification of the mirror-reading task involves the reading of inverted words (e.g., ygoloruen). The changing of mirror words into inverted words allows the separation of the right-to-left visual scanning process, which is a "pure" procedural learning process, from explicit learning processes such as the explicit learning of letter-specific transformations or of the repeated words. PD patients show specific deficits in the procedural component of the tasks, the right-to-left visual scanning component, compared with normal controls (Koenig, Thomas-Antérion, & Laurent, 1999).

Patients with Parkinson disease frequently become dependent on their relatives or caregivers. Motor dysfunction is significantly related to the ability to carry out physical activities of daily living, such as eating and grooming, whereas performance on tests of working memory and sequencing is significantly related to the ability to carry out such daily activities as shopping and dialing a telephone (Cahn, Sullivan, Shear et al., 1998).

The Amnesic Syndrome in Huntington Disease

Similar to the other frontostriatal dementias, deficits in motor functions, speed of processing, and primary memory functions are prominent in the early stages of HD and show progressive decline (Watkins, Rogers, Lawrence et al., 2000; Bachoud-Lévi, Maison, Bartolomeo et al., 2001; Ho, Sahakian, Brown et al., 2003). Even early in the course of the disease, HD patients show selective deficits on tests of visuospatial planning, such as the one-touch computerized Tower of London test, compared with age- and IQ-matched controls (Watkins, Rogers, Lawrence et al., 2000).

Cognitive deterioration in HD mutation carriers who develop the disease may start very early. Even though the symptoms of HD are well characterized, the precise natural history of the disease is not known. Evidence for the progression of the disease in the early and middle stages comes from studies on the longitudinal performance of clinically asymptomatic persons carrying the HD gene, who have a virtually 100% lifetime risk of developing the disease, and from studies of early to moderate HD patients. Additional evidence for the earliest symptoms of HD comes from cross-sectional studies on the cognitive and motor performance of asymptomatic carriers of the HD mutation gene in relation to healthy controls who do not carry the HD gene.

The longitudinal performance of apparently asymptomatic carriers of the HD mutation gene is characterized by symptoms other than the classic choreiform movements and psychiatric manifestations. Measures of response inhibition (e.g., Stroop test), eye movements, motor planning (rapid alternating movements), psychomotor speed (e.g., Digit Symbol), verbal fluency, and primary memory (block span) are sensitive measures of cognitive decline in the asymptomatic gene carriers. Memory appears to show a more precipitous decline around the time of clinical onset of HD (Kirkwood, Siemers, Stout et al., 1999; Paulsen, Zhao, Stout et al., 2001; Snowden, Craufurd, Griffiths et al., 2001; Lemiere, Decruyenaere, Evers-Kiebooms et al., 2002; Snowden, Craufurd, Thompson, & Neary, 2002). Longitudinal performance of HD patients after clinical onset shows a significant and consistent decline in psychomotor skills (Bamford, Caine, Kido et al., 1995; Snowden, Craufurd, Griffiths et al., 2001) and in primary memory and executive functions, as measured by the Stroop test, Trail Making Test Part A, verbal fluency tasks, the Token Test, and a visual span test (Bachoud-Lévi, Maison, Bartolomeo et al., 2001; Snowden, Craufurd, Griffiths et al., 2001). However, decrements in performance of individual patients is often small, and interindividual and intraindividual variability in decline is high.

A longitudinal study of the evolution of cognitive decline in early to moderate HD patients (Ho, Sahakian, Brown et al., 2003) showed that tests tapping into psychomotor skill and primary memory, such as Trail Making Test Parts A and B, Stroop word reading, Stroop color naming, and Digit Symbol, show the greatest decline. The next most sensitive tests are those of executive function that tap into planning, such as the Tower of London test from the Cambridge Neuropsychological Test Automated Battery (CANTAB) battery. Next in sensitivity are phonemic and semantic fluency tests, tests of attention span, such as spatial span and digit span (forward and backwards), and tests of immediate memory. Visuospatial and semantic memory measures show no progressive decline. The ability to perform daily living activities correlates with the Tower of London test performance, rather than with motor performance. A test of planning, the Wisconsin Card Sorting Test (WCST), did not show any decline (Bachoud-Lévi, Maison, Bartolomeo et al. 2001; Snowden, Craufurd, Griffiths et al., 2001; Ho, Sahakian, Brown et al., 2003), and test performance actually improves with practice (Bachoud-Lévi, Maison, Bartolomeo et al., 2001), rendering this test inappropriate for longitudinal follow-up of HD.

The Amnesic Syndrome in Corticobasal Degeneration

Corticobasal degeneration (CBD) is an infrequent, but possibly underdiagnosed, progressive neurodegenerative disorder that typically presents with asymmetric cortical atrophy and asymmetric rigidity and apraxia. CBD overlaps significantly with primary progressive aphasia and frontal variant frontotemporal dementia (fv-FTD), and its extrapyramidal or apraxic symptoms may precede, follow, or appear simultaneously with the behavioral symptoms (Kertesz, Martinez-Lage, Davidson, & Munoz, 2000). Nonfluent aphasia may be a prominent, but underreported, symptom in CBD because language functions are not routinely evaluated in such patients; yet, language deficits may be common when there is left hemisphere involvement. Phonologic and spelling impairment appears to be prevalent even in the absence of aphasia, but semantic memory, as measured by naming tasks, may be normal. Other prominent deficits concern phonemic and semantic fluency, visual construction (copying of complex figures), and visuospatial performance (Frattali, Grafman, Patronas et al., 2000; Graham, Bak, Patterson, & Hodges, 2003).

The neuropsychological profile of patients with CBD overlaps significantly with that of patients with progressive supranuclear palsy (Pillon, Deweer, & Michon, 1994; Pillon, Blin, Vidailhet et al. 1995) and may, in rare cases, include symptoms typical of posterior cortical atrophy, such as visual agnosia, visuospatial dysfunction, and visual impairment (Tang-Wai, Josephs, Boeve et al. 2003b).

The Amnesic Syndrome in Progressive Supranuclear Palsy

Progressive supranuclear palsy (PSP) is a neurodegenerative disorder character-ized by neuronal loss and other pathological changes in the basal ganglia, brain stem, and cerebellar nuclei. Postural instability and vertical supranuclear gaze palsy appear early in the course of the disease and visual symptoms, especially apraxia of eyelid opening, are common and may be functionally disabling (Nath, Ben-Shlomo, Thomson et al., 2003). The clinical picture of PSP in its fully developed form is highly characteristic: The patient has a fixed "Mona Lisa" stare, displays a low frequency of blinking, and retracts his or her head. The patient's voice is reduced to a distinctive growl. He or she walks clumsily and unsteadily, with a tendency to topple backward. Clothes typically are soiled because the patient is unable to look down and has difficulty swallowing. Time to respond to questions is often lengthy (Burn & Lees, 2002).

Patients with PSP exhibit memory deficits characterized by impaired imme-diate memory, reduced learning with repetition, and an abnormal number of false alarms in recognition tests compared with age- and education-matched con-trols. Providing semantic cues during encoding and recall results in marked improvement. Patients with PSP and CBD show a similar neuropsychological profile of impairment, and both show an executive dysfunction that is more severe than that of AD patients (Pillon, Deweer, Michon, 1994; Pilion, Blin, Vidailhet et al., 1995).

Little is known about the natural history of the disease from prospective stud-ies. A retrospective study (Nath, Ben-Shlomo, Thomson et al., 2003) showed that mobility problems were the most common early symptoms of the disease, and visual and cognitive problems were also common. According to caregivers, motor and visual symptoms appear first and affect almost every patient. They are followed by emotional and personality problems, cognitive impairment, and sleep changes (Santacruz, Uttl, Litvan, & Grafman, 1998).

The Amnesic Syndrome in the Frontal Variant of Frontotemporal Dementia

Personality and behavioral changes are the earliest and most pervasive features of frontal variant frontotemporal dementia. These features set it apart from typical forms of AD that begin with a relatively selective anterograde episodic memory deficit. Because the brain areas affected in fv-FTD are the frontal lobes, the anterior temporal lobes, and the amygdala, the observed personality and behavioral changes ostensibly arise from a disruption of the role of these struc-tures in social functioning and emotional responsiveness. Secondary memory, on the other hand, is spared until the late stages of the disease. fv-FTD patients show a less distinct profile of neuropsychological impairment than tv-FTD and AD patients, characterized by a greater involvement of primary memory and executive functions, and may perform normally in all cognitive domains. The following case study illustrates some characteristics of the syndrome.

Case 6: Frontal Variant Frontotemporal Dementia

Mr. F, a 55-year-old systems analyst with a university degree in mathematics, came to the attention of the staff of a memory clinic because of memory and behavioral changes in the past 4 to 5 years, reported by his wife. She complained that when he pays for something he forgets to pick up the change and does not remember what he has to do during the course of the week. He does not benefit from written directions because he does not pay any attention to them. His wife is now completely in charge of the household finances because Mr. F appears totally unconcerned about the family's ability to meet its financial obligations. Although he does not take any initiative concerning household purchases or the handling of the finances, he can suddenly spend a large amount of money to satisfy a whim or give money to someone in need. For example, 5 years ago he bought a used car that does not even run, although he does not drive, and recently bought another used car, which he never drove, either. Nevertheless, Mr. F seems overconfident about his driving abilities. His personality seems to have undergone the greatest change. Although he claims to be very fond of his wife and is totally dependent on her, he shows indifference toward his family and knows very little about the lives of their two adult children. He has become socially isolated, with no friends of his own. In the past 3 years, he has become increasingly sleepy and inert at home. Mr. F also exhibits considerable collecting behavior. He has always been an avid collector of books, newspaper clippings, and periodicals, but this behavior is now exaggerated. He collects books and magazines from garbage bins and brings home useless, broken objects from his trips. He has a large collection of old TV sets that do not work and seems drawn to small metal objects, such as bottle caps, screws, and nails that he finds on the street. Mr. F explained that he does not throw away anything that might be of use. Although he calmly admitted to the bizarreness of this behavior, stating "I also find it sick," he accounted for it by saying that it might be related to a repressed wish to build a workshop at home. According to his wife, however, he is very awkward with his hands and has never shown any inclination to engage in household repairs. The neuropsychological evaluation revealed a superior Vocabulary score and average scores in Similarities, Matrix Reasoning, and Digit Symbol on the WAIS-III. His performance on the WMS-III was surprisingly intact, spanning from the average to the high average range, with no signs of memory loss over time. His CVLT performance was also above average. Verbal fluency, phonemic and semantic, was above average for his age. His performance on the Wisconsin Card Sorting Test was strikingly deficient, however: he made a very large number of perseverative responses and did not complete any categories. Mr. F's MRI showed mild atrophy of the frontal lobes, with widening of the sulci and enlargement of the subarachnoid space in the convexity of the skull as shown in Figure 4–5. A SPECT study showed hypoperfusion of the left frontal lobe.

Mr. F did not show any deficits in learning and memory, although some decline in working memory, attention, and abstract thinking may be inferred based on his estimated premorbid cognitive functioning. The complaints of his

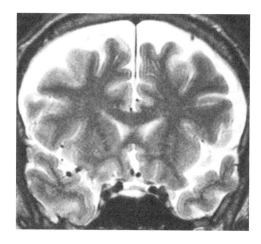

Figure 4–5 A coronal T2-weighted brain MRI slice of the patient demonstrates mild atrophy of the frontal lobes with widening of the cortical sulci and dilatation of the subarachnoid space at the convexity of the skull. Note: The left hemisphere is shown on the right side of the image. (Courtesy of Sokratis G. Papageorgiou

family about difficulties with everyday memory functioning may relate to impairment in primary memory, such as his apparent inability to focus on a task and to not get distracted. Mr. F's one notable deficit was in a test of planning and cognitive flexibility, which is sensitive to frontal dysfunction, namely, the WCST. Patients with frontotemporal dementia may not show any signs of memory or cognitive decline in the early stages of the disease, the only reliable indications being behavioral and personality changes. Interestingly, some of the behavioral and personality changes in Mr. F were very insidious because they were exaggerations of preexisting behavioral patterns, such as his collecting behavior and reduced involvement with family affairs.

(Courtesy of Alexandra Economou)

Retrospective examinations of the charts of autopsy-proven cases with FTD or AD, matched for level of dementia using the Mini-Mental State Examination (MMSE), highlight important differences in behavioral and neuropsychological profiles between patients with FTD and AD (Rascovsky, Salmon, Ho et al., 2002; Rosen, Hartikainen, Jagust et al., 2002c). A significantly larger proportion of patients with FTD than patients with AD show behavioral abnormalities, as well as extrapyramidal motor symptoms. Conversely, neuropsychological abnormalities are present in many patients with AD but in few patients with FTD. Social conduct disorders, hyperorality, akinesia, absence of amnesia, and absence of perceptual deficit correctly classified 93% of the patients with FTD and 97% of the patients with AD (Rosen, Hartikainen, Jagust et al. 2002c). Patients with FTD perform significantly worse on letter and category fluency tests but significantly better on the Mattis Dementia Rating Scale (DRS) memory subscale, the block design subtest, and the clock drawing test.

The personality profile of fv-FTD is distinct, according to converging evidence from investigations of the personality alterations, from retrospective reviews of the charts, and from caregivers' reports. Behavioral deficits are the hallmark of fv-FTD and include lack of insight and judgment, apathy, disinhibition, hyperphagia (overeating), speech abnormalities, lack of personal hygiene, and emotional unconcern, but symptoms of depression are reported to be rare (Kertesz, Martinez-Lage, Davidson et al., 2000; Miller, Diehl, Freedman et al., 2003). In addition to the Frontal Behavioral Inventory (Kertesz, Davidson, & Fox, 1997), another useful instrument for the assessment of behavioral changes is the Frontotemporal Behavioral Scale (Lebert, Pasquier, Souliez, & Petit, 1998). Neuropsychological functioning, including performance on tasks of executive function, may be strikingly intact in the early stages of the disease, despite prominent behavioral dysfunction and social and occupational impairment (e.g., Gregory, Serra-Mestres, & Hodges, 1999). Loss of insight, emotional detachment, and dissociation between intellectual functioning, as measured by formal assessment, and the ability to function in daily life, may characterize the disease in the early stages. Functional dependency, when present, is due more to behavioral disturbances than to memory and cognitive dysfunction.

EPIDEMIOLOGY AND PREDISPOSING FACTORS

Alzheimer Disease

Approximately 10% of persons older than 65 years suffer from some form of dementia (Evans, Funkenstein, Albert et al., 1989), and about 90% of those have AD either alone or in combination with other pathologies (Lim, Tsuang, Kukull et al., 1999). In addition to age, epidemiological studies conducted in recent years have identified numerous risk and protective factors. Gender is a well-known risk factor; the disease affects women 1.5 times as often as men, and AD remains more frequent in women even after correction for their greater longevity (Mendez & Cummings, 2003). In recent years, vascular risk factors such as diabetes, hypertension, heart disease, smoking, and elevated cholesterol have been related to an increased frequency not only of vascular dementia but also of AD (de la Torre, 2004).

Chronic use of statins (cholesterol-lowering agents), nonsteroidal anti-inflammatory drugs, and dietary fish oil rich in omega-3 fatty acids may have a protective action against AD. Low levels of education, lack of intellectual stimulation in midlife, lack of physical activity and hobbies have all been associated with an increased probability for developing AD (Snowdon, Kemper, Mortimer et al., 1996; Lindsay, Laurin, & Verreault, 2002), but a high level of education may delay the detection of the onset of the symptoms (Stern, Tang, Denaro, & Mayeux, 1995; Unverzagt, Hui, Farlow et al., 1998). Individuals with a first-degree relative with AD have a slightly increased risk of developing the disease compared with the general population. Most cases of AD, however, are sporadic, with a late onset, and familial cases of AD account for only 5% of the cases.

Vascular Dementias

Vascular dementia is the second or third leading cause of dementia, depending on the geographical location (Kase, Wolf, Chodosh et al., 1989; Kase, 1991;

Ebly, Parhad, Hogan, & Fung, 1994; Ott, Breteler, van Harskamp et al., 1995; Ikeda, Hokoishi, Maki et al., 2001; Knopman, Parisi, Boeve et al., 2003). An additional 11% to 43% of the dementia cases, however, may have mixed dementia (AD with vascular dementia) (Kase, 1991; Tatemichi, Desmond, Mayeux et al., 1992; Pohjasvaara, Erkinjuntti, Vataja, & Kaste, 1997; Barba, Martinez-Espinosa, Rodriguez-Garcia et al., 2000). Men are more commonly affected than women in most studies (e.g., Meyer, McClintic, Rogers et al., 1988; Kase, 1991; Rocca, Hofman, Brayne et al., 1991; Ott et al., 1995).

Up to two thirds of the cases of vascular dementia are classified as SIVD caused by small-vessel ischemic changes such as multiple lacunae and white matter lesions (Chui, 2001). SIVD is clinically homogenous and constitutes a major cause of cognitive impairment and dementia, especially in elderly patients. Multi-infarct dementia (due to multifocal large vessel thromboembolism) as well as dementia caused by strategically placed single infarcts are much less frequent. These different types of vascular dementia, however, can often coexist in the same patient. Genetic forms of vascular dementia are rare.

Dementia with Lewy Bodies

Dementia with Lewy bodies (DLB) represents the second most common category of degenerative dementias after AD, with as many as 20% of the dementia patients suffering from this disease. The disease is more prevalent in men than women, with the ratio being at least 2:1. DLB accounted for 10–15% of cases from a hospital-based autopsy series (McKeith, Mintzer, Aarsland et al., 2004). A community-based study of people over the age of 85 found that 5% of the population met the DLB clinical criteria, representing 22% of all dementia cases (Rahkonen, Eloniemi-Sulkava, Rissanen et al., 2003). The majority of patients with DLB also have some AD pathology, which explains why DLB was termed the Lewy body variant of AD until recently. Advanced age and the presence of the e4 allele of the apolipoprotein E (ApoE) gene are the only known risk factors for this disease, the latter possibly acting as an accelerator of cognitive decline (McKeith et al., 2004). There are rare familial cases of DLB, with diffuse Lewy bodies and neuronal loss in the CA2 and CA3 fields of the hippocampus, related to mutations involving the a-synuclein gene on chromosome 4 (McKeith et al., 2004).

Parkinson Dementia

Parkinson disease is one of the most frequent degenerative disorders, with a prevalence of 1–3% in people older than 55 years and a slight male predominance. Although cognitive deficits are a common characteristic of PD, dementia affects only a portion of PD patients, with an average frequency of 40% across studies (Aarsland, Anderson, Larsen et al., 2001; Emre, 2003a, 2003b). However, high rates of mortality and the institutionalization of PD patients with dementia may lead to underrepresentation of these patients in epidemiological surveys. The incidence of dementia in patients with PD exceeds that of comparable controls by about 4 to 6 times over the course of 5 years (Aarsland et al., 2001) and is strongly associated with age (Mayeux, Denaro, Hemenegildo et al., 1992; Marder, Tang, Cote et al., 1995; Katzen, Levin, & Llabre, 1998). Other factors contributing to higher prevalence of dementia in patients with PD are long disease duration, the akinetic-rigid form of the disease compared with the tremor form of the disease, the presence of depression, early autonomic failure, and poor response to dopaminergic treatment (Aarsland, Tandberg, Larsen, & Cummings, 1996).

Frontotemporal Dementia

Frontotemporal dementia is the fourth most common progressive dementia syndrome after AD, dementias with Lewy bodies (DLB and PDD), and vascular dementia. FTD represents a heterogeneous group of disorders with variable clinical and pathologic manifestations whose spectrum is composed of degeneration of the frontal lobes, the anterior temporal lobes, or both.

FTD appears to be relatively more prevalent in younger patients and is less common among individuals over the age of 70. In the two existing large-scale epidemiological studies, prevalence was 10.7 per 100,000 in the 50-60-year-old range (Stevens, van Duijn, Kamphorst et al., 1998) and 15 per 100,000 in the 45- to 65-year-old range (Ratnavalli, Brayne, Dawson, & Hodges, 2002), similar to the prevalence of AD for these age groups. A striking male preponderance with a ratio of 14:3 was found by Ratnavalli et al. (2002). Dementia with motor neuron disease is one of the more common variants of FTD (Neary, Snowden, Mann et al., 1990; Caselli, Windebank, Petersen et al., 1993). Although the underlying cause of FTD is unknown, genetic factors are strongly implicated, and FTD may occur as a familial disease with tau mutations (Heutink, Stevens, Rizzu et al., 1997; Pickering-Brown, Baker, Yen et al., 2000). Different clinical subtypes of FTD (frontal variant FTD, temporal variant FTD) have been found to have different tau and ApoE genotype frequencies, suggesting that these genes may influence the clinical presentation (Bird, Knopman, van Swieten et al., 2003).

Progressive Supranuclear Palsy

Two separate surveys in the United Kingdom found the age-adjusted population prevalence of progressive supranuclear palsy (PSP) to be approximately 5 per 100,000, about 3% to 5% of the prevalence of PD (Schrag, Ben-Shlomo, & Quinn, 1999; Nath, Ben-Shlomo, Thomson et al., 2001). Men appear to be slightly more frequently affected than women. Approximately half of the patients with progressive supranuclear palsy experience the initial symptoms during their sixties, one quarter during their fifties, and the other during their seventies (Maher & Lees, 1986; Golbe, Davis, Schoenberg, & Duvoisin, 1988).

Huntington Disease

Huntington disease is a progressive, autosomal dominant hereditary disease of the central nervous system characterized by motor disturbance (chorea), behavioral or psychiatric disturbance, and cognitive impairment. It usually manifests in early to middle adulthood.

DIFFERENTIAL DIAGNOSIS

The distinction between delirium-induced amnesia and dementia has important implications for treatment and is better documented for AD. The differentiation of dementia from depression-induced amnesia presents a challenge in the early stages of many dementia illnesses, especially in cases that are characterized by predominant primary memory impairment.

Dementia versus Delirium-Induced Amnesias

Delirium is a confusional state with an acute onset characterized by severe attentional impairment, fluctuating attention, and cognitive dysfunction. Confusional states may be caused by various conditions, the most common being toxic-metabolic encephalopathies (Mesulam, 2000, pp. 177–182). Delirium among older persons is frequent, ranging from 22% to 89% of hospitalized or community populations (Marcantonio, Simon, Bergmann et al., 2003). The usually acute onset of the symptoms and the transient nature of the dysfunction distinguish it from the irreversible and progressive cognitive changes of the dementias. Delirium symptoms, however, may be relatively long lasting, from 1 week up to 12 months after diagnosis, and recovery may never be complete (Marcantonio et al., 2003; McCusker, Cole, Dendukuri et al., 2003). The amnesia associated with Lewy body dementias is differentiated from the amnesia due to delirium mainly on the basis of the gradual worsening of the former. Furthermore, visual hallucinations in PDD and DLB are well formed and recurrent, unlike hallucinations in delirium (Popescu & Lippa, 2004).

Delirium may coexist with dementia, and a delirium superimposed on a preexisting dementia can give rise to a severe confusional state that is also known as "beclouded" dementia. The treatment of the toxic-metabolic encephalopathy can lead to an improvement of the confusional state, but the symptoms of the dementia will remain (Mesulam, 2000).

Dementia versus Depression-Induced Amnesia

The high prevalence of dementia and depression among the elderly raises two diagnostic issues: the differential diagnosis of dementia versus depression and the diagnosis of depression with dementia. Although depression and memory impairment are significantly related, the magnitude of the association between the two is small compared with the magnitude of the association between dementia and memory impairment (Hart, Kwentus, Hamer et al., 1987; Burt, Zembar, & Niederehe, 1995). But the degree of overlap between elderly persons with depression and patients in the very early stages of AD in terms of primary or secondary memory measures can be very high (e.g., Swainson, Rogers, Sahakian et al., 2000), rendering differential diagnosis quite challenging.

The second issue related to the diagnosis of amnesia due to both dementia and depression is the possibility that depression may be associated with the subsequent development of dementia (Devanand, Sano, Tang et al., 1996; Schmand,

Jonker, Geerlings, & Lindeboom, 1997; Jorm, 2000; Green, Cupples, Kurz et al., 2003; Kessing & Nilsson, 2003) and the cognitive decline of patients specific to the depression (Kessing & Nilsson, 2003). Individuals with depression and coexisting cognitive impairment are highly likely to have an underlying dementia (Knopman, Boland, Mosley et al., 2001). The evidence for an association of depression with dementia is particularly strong for the vascular dementias and dementias with Lewy bodies such as Parkinson disease. Vascular disease is associated with high rates of depression (Li, Meyer, & Thornby, 2001; Thomas, Kalaria, & O'Brien, 2004), and, according to the "vascular depression" hypothesis, the disease predisposes to, precipitates, or perpetuates depression (Alexopoulos, Meyers, Young et al., 1997; Jorm, 2000).

Depression is prevalent in AD in population studies (Lyketsos, Steinberg, Tschantz et al., 2000; Lyketsos, Lopez, Jones et al., 2002), and it is one of the most frequent comorbidities of AD, affecting as many as 50% of patients (Lyketsos & Olin, 2002). However, the diagnosis of depression in dementia presents a number of difficulties (Lee & Lyketsos, 2003), as both disorders share symptoms like psychomotor slowing and apathy. In some patients with AD, depressive symptoms fluctuate over time, and the manifestation of depressive symptoms may change with the progression of AD (Alexopoulos, 2003).

The presence of depression does not appear to worsen significantly the cognitive impairment of patients with dementia (Li et al., 2001; Berger, Fahlander, Wahlin, & Backman, 2002), but it contributes to earlier placement in a higher level of care (Lyketsos & Olin, 2002; Lee & Lyketsos, 2003). Treatment for the depression may improve the mood and everyday functioning of depressed patients with dementia but will not reverse their memory deficits.

Amnesia Due to Dementia versus Limbic Amnesia

In the preclinical or very early stage of AD, when damage is confined to the hippocampus and parahippocampal cortex, the memory impairment is relatively confined to a deficit in learning new events and resembles the anterograde episodic memory impairment due to damage to the limbic system. However, the nature of the onset of the memory impairment and the progression of symptoms can help with diagnosis, especially when the lesion is not clear on MRI as in the very early stages of AD or when lesions are restricted to a small portion of the hippocampus. As the pathology of AD progresses, other deficits become apparent, most notably deficits in primary memory that are related to the spread of the disease to areas beyond the medial temporal lobe or to disconnection of different cortical regions.

Other types of amnesia, such as transient global amnesia or transient epileptic amnesia, can be distinguished from dementia by virtue of their transience and/or the presence of a seizure disorder.

Dementia-Specific versus Predementia Amnesia (Amnesic MCI)

The National Institute of Nervous Diseases and Stroke-Alzheimer's Disease Related Disorders Association (NINDS-ADRDA) diagnostic criteria for probable

AD require (1) the presence of a dementia syndrome with an impairment in memory and in at least one more cognitive function (as defined also by the DSM-III or DSM-IV criteria; American Psychiatric Association, 1987, 1994), (2) an onset between 40 and 90 years of age and a progressive course, (3) the absence of delirium and of any other disease that could cause the disorder, and (4) a functional impairment in activities of daily living in relation to cognitive impairment (McKhann, Drachman, Folstein et al., 1984). Petersen's criteria for amnesic MCI (Petersen et al., 1999; Petersen, Doody, & Kurz, 2001), on the other hand, include (1) memory complaint, corroborated by an informant, (2) abnormal memory function in relation to age and education, (3) normal general cognitive function, as determined by a clinician's judgment based on a structured interview with the patient and an informant using the Clinical Dementia Rating scale (CDR; Morris, 1993), (4) minimal or no impairment in activities of daily living, as determined by a clinical interview with the patient and informant, and (5) insufficient impairment to meet the NINCDS-ADRDA diagnostic criteria for probable AD.

Amnesic MCI represents prodromal AD because the majority of amnesic MCI patients develop AD (Bozoki, Giordani, Heidebrink et al., 2001), even though the interval between onset of memory loss and actual functional decline may extend over several years. Based on the above criteria, a person with AD is more globally cognitively impaired than a person with MCI and also shows functional impairment in activities of daily living. Patients with mild AD and persons in the predementia stage of AD, however, may not differ in degree of secondary memory impairment. In persons of high premorbid ability, substantial impairment in memory may occur before a significant impairment in daily functioning becomes evident.

The major drawback of the NINCDS-ADRDA criteria is that a formal diagnosis of AD (probable AD) can be made only in the presence of dementia, whereas recent evidence suggests that AD can be accurately diagnosed in its predementia stage, that is, at the stage of amnesic MCI (Petersen, Doody, & Kurz, 2001; Petersen, Stevens, Ganguli et al., 2001; Grundman, Petersen, Ferris et al., 2004), which roughly corresponds to the terms "very early AD" or "questionable dementia" proposed by Morris, Storandt, Miller et al. (2001).

Differentiation Among the Amnesic Syndromes Due to the Different Dementias

The two classes of amnesic syndromes due to dementing diseases manifest different forms of memory impairment in the early stages: deficits primarily in secondary memory functions characterize the first class, whereas deficits in primary memory and executive functions characterize the second. The neuropsychological profile of HD, however, is similar to aspects of the neuropsychological profile of AD (Butters, Goldstein, Allen, & Shemansky, 1998), including deficits in visual recognition (Rosas, Liu, Hersch et al., 2002).

The presence of primary memory deficits may result in impairment in the spontaneous retrieval of episodic information and may give the impression of a deficit in secondary memory, but recognition of the material will be relatively intact. In cases of PDD or DLB with widespread AD pathology, the memory impairment will be consistent both with an episodic memory impairment and salient primary memory impairment, as well as fluctuating attention and a more severe clinical picture than in AD.

Differentiation Among Syndromes of the First Class

The amnesic syndrome due to strategic single thalamic infarct is distinct from that of AD and from that of tv-FTD in that unlike them it is nonprogressive and has a sudden onset. Next, the amnesic syndrome of tv-FTD can be readily distinguished from that of AD in that the most salient symptom in tv-FTD is a severe retrograde impairment in semantic memory, with relatively preserved episodic memory, whereas in AD the most salient symptom is a severe antero-grade deficit in episodic memory with a more subtle impairment in semantic memory. However, deficits in verbal processing abilities and word retrieval in persons with tv-FTD may contribute to reduced memory functioning in daily life and to the impression on the part of the relative or caregiver that the patient's verbal and nonverbal anterograde episodic memory are impaired.

Differentiation Among Syndromes of the Second Class

With the exception of the amnesic syndrome in dementia with Lewy bodies (DLB/PDD), which presents with fluctuating attention, the primary memory impairment of the other dementias that compose the second class is quite similar and appears to differ in degree only. The nonmemory symptoms of these demen-tias which include significant visuoconstructive deficits, visual hallucinations, REM sleep disorder, early symptoms of autonomic dysfunction, and parkinson-ian features (rigidity, resting tremor, bradykinesia, gait and postural abnormali-ties, and hypophonia) (Popescu & Lippa, 2004), contribute to the differential diagnosis. FTD with parkinsonism, however, is a common variant of FTD; atyp-ical parkinsonism syndromes such as FTD with parkinsonism and PSP must be excluded to diagnose PDD (see McKeith et al., 2004). Inappropriate social behav-ior is the hallmark of fv-FTD.

Progressive supranuclear palsy may be a fairly common disorder that is fre-quently misdiagnosed, especially as PD (Santacruz, Uttl, Litvan, Grafman et al., 1998). The presence of certain cardinal neurological symptoms, such as vertical supranuclear palsy or slowing of vertical saccades and postural instability, and the exclusion of others, described in the National Institute of Neurological Disorders and Stroke and Society for Progressive Supranuclear Palsy (NINDS-SPSP) diagnostic criteria (Litvan, Agid, Jankovic et al., 1996), distinguish PSP from other dementias. Neuropsychological assessment in the early stages may contribute to an accurate diagnosis. Patients with PSP have striking inertia and typically show significantly more apathy and disinhibition and a greater decline in attention and set shifting than patients with PD (Popescu & Lippa, 2004).

PATHOPHYSIOLOGY

In this section, we will describe the pathophysiology of the dementias rather than that of the several amnesic syndromes that are associated with each. The reason for this shift of emphasis is once again the availability of pathophysiological data for the dementias at large but not for the amnesic syndromes, specifically.

Alzheimer Disease

The AD brain is characterized by atrophy, narrowing of the gyri in the association cortices, widening of sulci and enlargement of the ventricles, and reduced overall weight. The neuropathological hallmarks of AD are the neuritic plaques (NP) and neurofibrillary tangles. NFTs are intracellular segregations of abnormal filaments, which consist primarily of phosphorylated tau (τ) protein and ubiquitin. They are found in the limbic regions, basal forebrain (nucleus basalis of Meynert), cerebral cortex, substantia nigra, the raphe nuclei, and the locus coeruleus. NFTs lead to disruption of neuronal function and even neuronal death. Neuritic plaques are extracellular formations made of neuronal and glial processes and extracellular amyloid, which are distributed predominantly in the hippocampus and amygdala but also throughout the cerebral cortex, striatum, and thalamus. The thinning and alteration of synapses around the plaque impair their function, leading to the clinical symptoms of AD. NFTs are also found in the normally aging brain but in much lower density. The pattern of emergence and extent of their distribution in AD is invariant and is included in the Braak and Braak (1991) staging criteria.

The initial episodic memory impairment in AD is attributed to transentorhinal neuropathology, which disrupts connections to and from the hippocampus (Garrard, Perry, & Hodges, 1997). The entorhinal cortex receives projections from widespread limbic and association cortical areas and gives rise to the perforant pathway, the major input to the hippocampus (Gómez-Isla, Price, McKeel et al., 1996). Pathological changes in the transentorhinal region disrupt connections to and from the hippocampus. Lesions along the perforant path disrupt the major input pathway of the hippocampus, and lesions in the CA1/subicular area disrupt the efferent projections of the hippocampus to widespread areas of the cerebral cortex. Nevertheless, correlation of NFT distribution with cognitive status is not perfect, and there are cases of cognitively healthy elderly individuals who receive a neuropathological diagnosis of AD postmortem.

In addition to neuronal loss and atrophy, there are several neurotransmitter changes in the AD brain. The cholinergic deficit plays a key role in amnesia and in the other cognitive deficits of the disease. The degree of the cholinergic reduction in the cortex is related to the degree of neuronal loss in the basal forebrain nuclei, the major source of acetylcholine (ACh) in the brain. Neurons of the nucleus basalis of Meynert produce choline acetyltransferase (ChAT), which is transferred to the synaptic end where it manufactures Ach, which is in turn released into the synapse and stimulates the postsynaptic cholinergic receptors.

Acetylcholinesterase (AChE) is the enzyme that eliminates ACh in the synapse. ACh is distributed from the nucleus basalis in a diffuse cholinergic projection system in the cerebral cortex. Neuronal death in the nucleus basalis leads to a reduction of ChAT production and a subsequent deficit in ACh production. In advanced AD, cholinergic activity is reduced to 80–90% in the hippocampus and other medial temporal regions, the parietal cortex, and the frontal cortex.

The disease-specific drugs in AD, the AchE inhibitors (AchE-Is), make more Ach available to stimulate postsynaptic cholinergic receptors by inhibiting AChE. As the neuropathological lesions affect specific areas in the brain, other neurotransmitters are also reduced. Lesions in the locus coeruleus and the raphe nuclei result in deficits in serotonin and norepinephrine, which are likely related to depression and the behavioral disorders in AD. A reduction of the dopamine D1 receptors of the striatum probably underlies the extrapyramidal symptoms. Receptors of GABA are also diminished, and reductions in somatostatin, substance P, corticotropin releasing factor, and vasopressin have been reported (Mendez & Cummings, 2003).

Vascular Dementias

Vascular dementia refers to dementia due to a variety of diseases of the cerebral vasculature, which consist of ischemic, hypoperfusive, or hemorrhagic brain lesions. The vascular diseases can result in multiple large infarcts, single infarcts, diffuse leukoaraiosis (white matter rarefaction), multiple small lacunar infarcts, inflammation of the brain vessels, and intraparenchymal hemorrhage.

Changes in cerebral microcirculation play a central role in the pathogenesis of SIVD. The changes are mainly related to aging, chronic arterial hypertension, and diabetes mellitus (Roman, Erkinjuntti, Wallin et al., 2002). Progressive occlusion of the small arteries (arterioles) of the brain leads to diffuse lesions and dementia. There is a fourfold increase of risk for dementia in patients with chronic untreated hypertension (Tzourio, Dufouil, Ducimetiere, & Alperovitch, 1999), which demonstrates a clear relation between vascular risk factors and dementia development.

White matter lesions are typically diffuse, include diffuse myelin pallor, astrocytic gliosis, and widening of perivascular spaces and lacunes. The accumulation of white matter lesions eventually leads to SIVD. A combination of small-vessel and large-vessel cerebrovascular disease in the same patient is common, though cortical and basal ganglia microinfarcts may not be apparent on MRI. In addition to widespread microinfarctions and lacunar strokes, ischemic injury can occur in the hippocampus, which could explain the episodic memory deficits observed in many patients with SIVD (Vinters, Ellis, Zarow et al., 2000). Severity of dementia in SIVD correlates strongly with degree of hippocampal and cerebral atrophy (Fein, Sclafani, Tanabe et al., 2000; Pohjasvaara, Mantyla, Salonen et al., 2000; Mungas, Jagust, Reed et al., 2001).

In SIVD, prefrontal-subcortical loops can be interrupted by lacunae in the striatum, globus pallidus, or thalamus, or by white matter lesions that disconnect the prefrontal or anterior cingulate cortices from their basal ganglia or their thal-amocortical connections (Cummings, 1993). The predominance of ischemic lesions in the frontal-subcortical-basal ganglionic area of the brain accounts for the prominent deficits in executive function, working memory, and retrieval in the clinical expression of SIVD. Interruption of the dorsolateral prefrontal cortex and its subcortical connections may be associated with executive dysfunction. Orbitofrontal-subcortical circuit interruption may account for the observed loss of inhibition, impulsivity, and personality change. Interruption of the anterior cingulate connections is associated with loss of motivation, abulia, and apathy (Royall, 2000).

Dementia with Lewy Bodies and PD

The clinical-pathological profile of DLB and PDD overlap considerably (Horimoto, Matsumoto, Nakazawa et al., 2003) and the differentiation of the two disorders is based on the time lapse between the appearance of dementia and the emergence of extrapyramidal symptoms. In DLB, dementia occurs before parkinsonism or shortly thereafter, whereas patients with PDD only meet the DSM-IV-TR criteria for dementia after the diagnosis of PD has been established, using the arbitrary but generally accepted clinical criterion of the presence of at least 12 months of motor symptoms only before dementia onset (McKeith et al., 2004). The biochemical differences between the two disorders, however, are not clear, and the clinical distinction is arbitrary. Differences in clinical symptoms may reflect the regional distribution of the pathology in identical disease processes (Popescu & Lippa, 2004).

The formation of Lewy bodies is the common cardinal feature of both syndromes. Lewy bodies are also a marker of PD. However, the amount and extent of their distribution differentiates PD from DLB. The amount and distribution of Lewy bodies underlies the clinical expression of the disease: brain-stem localization correlates with motor parkinsonism and cortical localization with dementia (Marti, Tolosa, & Campdelacreu, 2003). Whereas in PD Lewy bodies are few and localized in the substantia nigra, in DLB Lewy bodies are widely distributed in the substantia nigra, the locus coeruleus, the autonomic nervous system, the cholinergic nuclei of the basal forebrain, the hypothalamus, the cerebral cortex, and the spinal cord (Mendez & Cummings, 2003).

Neurochemistry studies have shown decreased concentrations of various neurotransmitters in DLB. There is reduced activity of choline acetyltransferase (ChAT) in the neocortex, but in contrast to AD, there is a more marked mid-frontal as opposed to hippocampal cholinergic deficit in DLB (Tiraboschi, Hansen, Alford et al., 2000). This could explain the prominent attentional deficit in patients with DLB when compared with patients with AD. Low levels of dopamine, serotonin, and norepinephrine have also been reported (Ohara & Kondo, 1998). The many neurotransmitter deficits found in demented patients with PD contribute to the different aspects of this syndrome. Dopaminergic deficits are thought to be related to working memory and executive dysfunction, cholinergic deficits to anterograde amnesia, and noradrenergic deficits to impaired attention (Emre, 2003a, 2003b).

Huntington Disease

In Huntington disease, the pathologic process is characterized by severe neuronal loss and gliosis in the caudate nucleus and putamen (Paulsen, Zhao, Stout et al., 2001). The finding of a posterior cortical degeneration early in the course of the disease (Rosas, Liu, Hersch et al., 2002) is consistent with the few neuropsychological investigations reporting impairments in visual recognition even relatively early in the disease (e.g., Jacobs, Sano, Dooneief et al., 1995). The extent of cortical involvement in the disease is consistent with a study showing that HD has a neuropsychological profile that is highly similar to that of the "classical" cortical dementia, AD, except for the presence of a prominent movement disorder: chorea (Butters, Goldstein, Allen, & Shemansky, 1998). The results suggest that cognitive dysfunction in HD is related not only to disruption of frontostriatal circuits but also to other less well-defined circuits involving posterior cortical areas.

Frontotemporal Dementia

Frontotemporal dementia is a heterogeneous disorder in terms of nosology. Postmortem gross anatomy studies reveal a lobar distribution of atrophy involving the frontal lobe, temporal lobe, or both. The orbitofrontal cortex and the anterior temporal cortex are the most affected areas (see also Chapter 5 on semantic amnesia). Three histopathological types of FTD have been described: (1) Pick Type A, or Pick disease, (2) Pick Type B, or dementia with swollen chromatolytic neurons, and (3) Pick Type C, or "dementia lacking distinct histology" (see Constantinidis, Richard, & Tissot, 1974; Knopman, Mastri, Frey et al., 1990; Hof, Bouras, Perl, & Morrison, 1994; Jellinger, 1994; Kertesz, Hudson, Mackenzie, & Munoz, 1994; Giannakopoulos, Hof, & Bouras, 1995; Delacourte, Robitaille, Sergeant et al., 1996; Kertesz & Munoz, 1998).

Corticobasal Atrophy or Degeneration

Pathologically, corticobasal degeneration has distinctive features that include prominent frontoparietal cortical atrophy and degeneration of the substantia nigra pars compacta. Pallidal, striatal lesions and lesions in the amygdala can also occur (Tsuchiya & Ikeda, 2002). Although the clinical presentation is initially asymmetric, postmortem pathological changes and cortical atrophy are symmetric with typically prominent atrophy of the precentral gyrus (Rebeiz, Kolodny, & Richardson, 1968; Gibb, Luthert, & Marsden, 1989; see Dickson, Bergeron, Chin et al., 2002, for the new minimal neuropathological criteria).

Recent advances in studies of tau protein demonstrate that corticobasal degeneration shares a common genetic background with progressive supranuclear palsy (Arvanitakis & Wszolek, 2001; Houlden, Baker, Morris et al., 2001).

Progressive Supranuclear Palsy

Progressive supranuclear palsy is a tauopathy, involving the abnormal formation of tau protein in the brain, of unknown etiology. Patients demonstrate atrophy in the upper part of the brain stem, which can be depicted in vivo by MRI (see Jellinger, Riederer, & Tomonaga, 1980; Hauw, Daniel, Dickson et al., 1994). The NFTs and tau proteins are similar but not identical to those found in AD and other diseases, and there are no amyloid deposition or apolipoprotein E allelic involvement (Anouti, Schmidt, Lyons et al., 1996). These differences suggest that PSP is a distinct disorder. Dementia in PSP is caused by lesions involving the mesodiencephalic region, which disrupt multiple subcortical neural circuits, especially the frontal-subcortical ones, and by the spread of the pathology to the frontal and temporal cortex.

PROGNOSIS AND TREATMENT

The focus of this section is the prognosis and treatment of the diseases rather than the treatment of the amnesic syndromes, as both prognosis and treatment of the memory disorder depend almost entirely on the course and treatment of the underlying disease.

Alzheimer Disease

The rate of decline is more marked for patients in the moderate stage of the disease and slower in the early and late stages, typically following an S–curve shape (Stern, Liu, Albert et al, 1996). The predementia stage (amnesic MCI or prodromal AD) has a slow progression to dementia in an average of 3 to 5 years. The mean survival for patients diagnosed with probable Alzheimer disease is about 8 to 10 years but may extend to 15 years and beyond (Jost & Grossberg, 1995). However, unusually short median survival rates of 4.2 years for men and 5.7 years for women were reported recently (Wolfson, Wolfson, Asgharian et al., 2001). The presence of extrapyramidal signs, gait disorders (Katzman, & Jackson, 1991; Larson, Shadlen, Wang et al., 2004), and comorbidities such as stroke, heart disease, and diabetes (Larson et al., 2004) shorten considerably the median survival rates. Prognosis depends on age, with younger patients having a more pronounced reduction in life expectancy, and on the stage of the disease as measured with the MMSE (Larson et al., 2004).

Pharmacological management of AD targets some of the cognitive deficits and the affective and behavioral symptoms of the disease. The newer acetylcholinesterase inhibitors donepezil, rivastigmine, and galantamine have been shown by several studies to improve cognition relative to placebo significantly in patients with AD (Rogers, Farlow, Doody et al., 1998; Tariot, Solomon, Morris et al., 2000; Scarpini, Scheltens, & Feldman, 2003). These drugs act by inhibiting acetylcholinesterase, the enzyme that eliminates acetylcholine in the synapse, making more acetylcholine available to stimulate postsynaptic cholinergic receptors and lessening the deficit in central cholinergic transmission caused by the degeneration of basal forebrain nuclei. The evaluation of the effects of the drugs on cognition in the different studies is based on a global measure of cognition, the ADAS-Cog (Alzheimer's Disease Assessment Scale-Cognitive portion), with no data concerning improvement of separate memory and cognitive functions. Initial improvement from baseline lasts an average of 6 to 12 months and is followed by a slow decline. About one third of AD patients, however, do not show benefit from cholinergic treatment, and it remains unknown what characteristics could differentiate "responders" from "nonresponders" (Scarpini et al., 2003). Recently, memantine, an N-methyl-D-aspartate (NMDA) inhibitor, has also been shown to be beneficial in the treatment of patients with AD either alone (Reisberg, Doody, & Stoffler, 2003) or in combination with donepezil (Tariot, Farlow, Grossberg et al., 2004).

Vascular Dementia

The progression of deficits in vascular dementia is generally slower than that of patients with AD. Prognosis is poor because of deterioration in cognitive functions. However, if prevention of further strokes or microvascular lesions can be achieved, then cognitive status is stabilized. Vascular dementia patients have higher mortality rates and lower life expectancy than nondemented stroke patients (Mendez & Cummings, 2003). Fifty percent of vascular dementia patients survive for approximately 6.7 years from the onset of symptoms, and less than 2% survive after 14 years from the onset of symptoms (Ostbye, Hill, & Steenhuis, 1999).

Vascular cognitive impairment without dementia can be regarded as a precursor of vascular dementia, as it increases the likelihood of subsequent dementia. In contrast to the well-known rates of progression of amnesic MCI to AD, however, little is known about the natural history and progression of vascular mild cognitive impairment to vascular dementia (O'Brien, Erkinjuntti, Reisberg et al., 2003).

The treatment of vascular dementia involves addressing the underlying cause and the management of acute stroke. Prevention strategies include the control of risk factors, such as hypertension, diabetes, and cigarette smoking. Secondary prevention strategies include carotid endarterectomy and anticoagulant therapy for atrial fibrillation. Many compounds have been proposed for the symptomatic treatment of cognitive dysfunction in vascular dementia, including vasodilators, nootropics "smart drugs", and antioxidants, with controversial results (O'Brien et al., 2003). Treatment with cholinesterase inhibitors has been shown to improve the cognitive symptoms of the disease, but guidelines for their application in specific patient subgroups remain to be established.

Dementias with Lewy Bodies

Dopamine replacement by L-dopa and dopaminergic agonists improves motor function and can slightly improve cognitive function, mainly by increasing psychomotor speed and arousal in DLB (Kulisevsky, 2000). Due to the marked cholinergic deficits in these patients, treatment with acetylcholinesterase inhibitors can be effective in improving the cognitive impairment and reducing the visual hallucinations, apathy, anxiety, and sleep disturbances (McKeith, Ballard, Perry et al., 2000; Samuel, Caligiuri, Galasko et al., 2000; Aarsland, Laake, Larsen, & Janvin, 2002; Edwards, Hershey, Wray et al., 2004). Treatment with acetylcholinesterase inhibitors is not associated with exacerbating the motor symptoms of the disease (Reading, Luce, & McKeith, 2001; Aarsland et al., 2002; Aarsland, Hutchinson, & Larsen, 2003; Giladi, Shabtai, Gurevich et al., 2003), but traditional neuroleptics, such as D2-receptor antagonists, should be avoided because they exacerbate parkinsonism.

Huntington Disease

Treatment of patients with Huntington disease consists of the pharmacological management of symptoms as well as the social, physical, and occupational management of this progressive disease that occurs in young to middle-aged patients. Classic neuroleptics have been shown to ameliorate both choreoathetosis and psychiatric symptoms, but high doses can result in deterioration of cognitive function and impair motor function and swallowing. The newer atypical neuroleptics clozapine, olanzapine, and risperidone have been shown to be effective for the treatment of both chorea and psychosis (Sajatovic, Verbanac, Ramirez, & Meltzer, 1991; Parsa, Szigethy, Voci, & Meltzer, 1997; Dipple, 1999). Other drugs such as lithium, carbamazepine, buspirone, and valproate have been used to treat irritability, aggressive behavior, and mania.

Frontotemporal Dementia

Disease duration in FTD is estimated to range from 8 to 11 years, although certain variants may have a shorter duration. FTD linked to chromosome 17 has an earlier onset and faster course. The course is also faster when FTD is associated with motor neuron disease (Pasquier, Lebert, Lavenu, & Petit, 1998).

No specific treatment exists for FTD, but specific symptoms can be successfully targeted. Symptoms attributed to a serotonergic deficit, such as disinhibition, carbohydrate craving, compulsions, irritability, and impulsivity (Litvan, 2001), may respond to SSRIs (Swartz, Miller, Lesser, & Darby, 1997) or trazodone, an atypical serotonergic agent (Pasquier, Fukui, Sarazin et al., 2003). The more severe behavioral disturbances of FTD, such as marked disinhibition and aggressive behavior, require treatment with major tranquilizers, preferably with the atypical ones, like risperidone, olanzapine, quetiapine, or with trazodone, because patients may manifest unusual hypersensitivity to classic neuroleptics.

Corticobasal Atrophy or Degeneration

There is no effective treatment for this rare disease.

Progressive Supranuclear Palsy

Treatment for this disease is purely symptomatic and remains unsatisfactory, as the disease progresses relentlessly (Kompoliti, Goetz, Litvan et al., 1998).

CONCLUSIONS AND SPECULATIONS

The amnesic syndromes produced by the various dementias reflect important differences in the types of memories and memory functions that are implicated early in their courses. The types of memories and other cognitive functions are correlated with the pathophysiologic processes that characterize them. We summarize our conclusions around the following questions.

1. *To what degree are the various amnesic syndromes produced by the dementias characterized by deficits in different types of memories?*

    Two of the dementias of the first class, AD and SIVD, show prominent episodic memory impairment, irrespective of modality, and lesser semantic memory impairment, whereas tv-FTD shows the opposite pattern of prominent semantic memory impairment and lesser episodic memory impairment. Implicit procedural and perceptual memories are relatively spared in the first class of syndromes.

    The amnesic syndromes produced by the second class of dementias show impairment in primary memory and deliberate, effortful retrieval, without salient impairment in episodic or semantic memory in the early stages. Episodic memories, however, are secondarily affected. Implicit procedural and perceptual memory deficits are notable in the second class of dementias, especially those that involve basal ganglia and cerebellar damage. Of the second class, however, HD shows a mixed amnesic syndrome with characteristics of both the first and the second class of dementias, namely difficulties with episodic memories and with primary memory functions.

    The episodic memory deficit of AD and strategic infarct vascular dementia due to thalamic lesions is anterograde, but a disruption of hippocampal function also typically results in some retrograde memory impairment. The consolidation of episodic memory, including autobiographical information, is thought to depend on the integrity of the hippocampus, at least initially. The hippocampus is involved in the rapid encoding of new information, which is subject to decay or interference caused by new learning. As episodic memories age, the hippocampus may become less critical for retrieval, while cortical areas such as the prefrontal and posterior cortex may become more engaged in the process of effortful retrieval (e.g., Petrides, 2000; Eichenbaum, 2004; Wiltgen, Brown, Talton, & Silva, 2004). Semantic memories may be more resistant to decay or interference by new learning than episodic memories because they are gradually incorporated into existing knowledge structures in the cortex and progressively may become independent of the hippocampus. Damage to neocortical sites results in impaired semantic memory, which is "timeless" and less dependent on the hippocampus for its activation.

2. *Which of the primary and secondary memory functions or constituent operations are affected and to what degree?*

In early AD, the primary memory function of encoding is affected to a lesser extent than the secondary memory functions of consolidation and storage. Even when the operation of encoding is controlled, decay is observed in the delayed recall of information, and the provision of retrieval support does not result in improvement. Within primary memory, the operation of holding the information in awareness or short-term memory is affected to a much lesser extent in AD than the more complex, effortful working memory operations of manipulating, selecting, and monitoring, which overlap with the so-called executive functions. In the dementias of the second class, on the other hand, even short-term memory may be affected early on, and the more complex working memory operations are always affected. Retrieval of information that has been encoded is deficient, especially if the retrieval process requires effort, but the provision of support usually results in improvement in performance. Secondary memory deficits for information that has been encoded are usually mild, as evidenced by relatively intact recognition performance, with the exception of HD, which shows a mixed pattern of impairment.

3. *Given the above questions and given what is known about the pathophysiology associated with each syndrome, what can be said about the nature of memory functions and its brain mechanisms?*

The gradual acquisition of memories and their integration within existing semantic structures are functions of the neocortex. This gradual acquisition of memories is essential for the discovery of generalities and the formation of knowledge structures in the form of semantic networks. When brain pathology involves damage to the neocortex, the knowledge structures, both verbal and nonverbal, become degraded or lost. The fast acquisition of episodic information, which is relational in nature, is critically dependent on the hippocampus. Such knowledge is flexible but easily disruptible because the consolidation and storage of knowledge into a more permanent state takes a long time. Without the contribution of the hippocampus, knowledge mediated by different cortical areas may not become integrated into conscious, explicit memory.

5

Semantic Amnesia

ANDREW C. PAPANICOLAOU,
REBECCA BILLINGSLEY-MARSHALL,
DAVID MOLFESE, AND BARBRA NOVAK

Semantic amnesia is a syndrome that results from temporal lobe lesions that are restricted to the neocortex and do not include the hippocampus or any other limbic areas. This syndrome was briefly discussed in the previous chapter, in the context of the temporal variant of frontotemporal dementia. Yet, several reasons compel us to revisit it here and devote a separate chapter to it. To begin with, the syndrome is not exclusively due to degenerative diseases; other, nonprogressive lesions may also cause it. More importantly, its nature raises basic questions: Is the syndrome distinct from other forms of loss of knowledge, namely aphasia and agnosia, and, if so, how? Do episodic and semantic memories entail the same or different sets of mnemonic operations and cerebral mechanisms, and how is the meaning of facts, concepts, and symbols coded and arranged in the cortex? These are questions, in short, that merit special treatment.

Semantic amnesia is the loss or the inaccessibility of facts and concepts that have been part of one's store of knowledge. It is, basically, retrograde in nature. Yet, its gradient is the opposite of that found in other organic amnesias in that recent memories are better preserved than older ones. It is also unlike most other organic amnesias in that episodic memories are not noticeably affected nor is the acquisition of new memories. It was first described methodically and so-named by Warrington in 1975 (Warrington, 1975), 3 years after Tulving's (1972) division of memory into semantic and episodic. The syndrome is also referred to as semantic dementia, as, in most cases, it is due to a dementing disease. However, that term may be more appropriate for the form of the syndrome in advanced stages of dementia and less for the syndrome itself, independently of its cause.

CLINICAL TESTING: ESTABLISHMENT OF SYMPTOMS

Semantic amnesia involves difficulties in remembering facts and names learned in the past, and it results from selective damage of the anterior, inferior, and lateral aspects of the temporal lobes bilaterally or only the left temporal lobe. Occasionally, however, the damage is not that selective. When it results from infections, like herpes encephalitis, or from traumatic injuries, it usually involves the medial aspect of the temporal lobes, in addition to their anterior and lateral aspects. When the damage is highly selective and localized to the anterior temporal neocortex only, as is typically the case early in the course of neurodegenerative diseases, the symptoms are also restricted to long-established semantic memories only. When the damage extends to the limbic region, the symptoms include loss of episodic memories in addition to semantic ones, and the deficits are anterograde as well as retrograde. If the lesions extend over areas other than the anterior, inferior, and lateral temporal, such as the posterior temporal, the parietal, or the occipital, the patients may present symptoms of receptive aphasia and agnosia, in addition to those of semantic amnesia.

The following three case studies illustrate the typical range of symptomatology that attends the various forms of pathophysiology and constitutes the semantic amnesia syndrome.

Case Study 1

A.M. (b. 1930) presented in April 1994 with a history of "loss of memory for words," which had progressed slowly over the previous 2 years. His wife has also noted a decline in his comprehension ability initially affecting less common words. Despite these problems, he still played golf (to a high standard) and tennis. He was still driving and able to find his way to various golf clubs alone and without difficulty. Day-to-day memory was also good, and when seen in the clinic he was able to relate—albeit with prominent word-finding difficulties—the details of their recent holiday in Australia and his latest golfing achievements. There had been only a slight change in personality at that time with mild disinhibition and a tendency to stick to fixed routines.

The following transcription illustrates that A.M.'s speech was fluent and without phonological or syntactic errors but strikingly devoid of content. It also shows his recall of undergoing a brain scan some 6 months previously.

> E: Can you tell me about a last time you were in hospital?
> AM: That was January, February, March, April, yes April last year, that was the first time, and eh, on the Monday, for example, they were checking all my whatsit, and that was the first time when my brain was, eh, shown, you know, you know that bit of the brain (indicates left), not that one, the other one was okay, but that was lousy, so they did that, and then like this (indicates scanning by moving his hands over his head) and probably I was a bit better than I am just now.

Formal neuropsychological testing in April 1994 revealed that A.M. was severely impaired on tests of picture naming. On the category fluency test, in which subjects are asked to generate exemplars from a range of semantic categories, within a set time, he was able to generate a few high-frequency animal names (cat, dog, horse) but no exemplars from more restricted categories such as birds or breeds of dog. He was only able to name 3 out of 48 black-and-white line drawings of highly familiar objects and animals from the Hodges and Patterson semantic battery (Hodges & Patterson, 1995). Most responses were vague circumlocutions such as "thing you use," but he also produced some category coordinate errors, such as horse for elephant. On a word-picture matching test, based on the same 48 items, in which A.M. had to point out a picture from 8 other exemplars (e.g., zebra from 8 other foreign animals), he scored 36 out of 48 (25 age-matched controls scored on average 47.4 ± 1.1). When asked to provide descriptions of the 48 items in the battery from their names, he produced very few details, most were vague or generic responses containing the superordinate category only ("a musical instrument," "in the sea," etc.). On the picture version of the Pyramid and Palm Trees Test, a measure of associative semantic knowledge in which the subject has to decide which of two pictures (a fir tree or a palm tree) goes best with a target picture (pyramid) (Howard & Patterson, 1992), A.M. scored 39 out of 52 when he first presented. Control subjects typically score close to ceiling on this test. On tests of reading, A.M. showed the typical pattern of surface dyslexia (Patterson & Hodges, 1992): normal ability to read aloud words with regular spelling to sound correspondence, but errors when reading aloud irregular words (pint, island, leopard, etc.).

By contrast, on nonsemantic tasks (such as copying the Rey Complex Figure), A.M.'s performance was faultless. When asked to reproduce the Rey Complex Figure after a 45-minute delay, A.M. scored well within the normal range. On nonverbal tests of problem-solving, such as Raven's Colored Matrices, a multiple- choice test of visual pattern matching that requires the subject to conceptualize spatial relationships, A.M. was also remarkably unimpaired. Auditory-verbal short-term memory was spared as judged by a digit span of six forward and four backward.

A.M. was tested approximately every 6 months over the next 3 years. A.M. was so profoundly anomic when he first presented that there was little room for further decline. On tests of comprehension, by contrast, there was a relentless drop; for instance, on the word-picture matching test, A.M.'s score fell from 36 to 5 out of 48 in November 1996 (controls: 47.4 ± 1.1). Likewise, on the pictorial version of the Pyramid and Palm Trees Test, his score fell progressively from 39 out of 52 to chance.

Despite this rapid loss of semantic knowledge, A.M. showed no significant decline on tests of nonverbal problem-solving or visual-spatial ability over the same time period. For instance, on Raven's Colored Matrices he still scored perfectly in November 1996.

A.M.'s impairment in semantic knowledge had a considerable impact on his everyday activities. On various occasions he misused objects (e.g., he placed a closed umbrella horizontally over his head during a rainstorm), selected an inappropriate item (e.g., bringing his wife, who was cleaning in the upstairs bathroom, the lawnmower instead of a ladder), and mistook various food items (e.g., on different occasions, A.M. put sugar into a glass of wine, orange juice into his lasagna, and ate a raw defrosting salmon steak with yoghurt). Activities that used to be commonplace acquired a new and frightening quality to him: on an airplane trip early in 1996, he became clearly distressed at his suitcase being X-rayed and refused to wear a seat belt in the airplane. After 1996, behavioral changes became more prominent with increasing social withdrawal, apathy, and disinhibition. Like another patient described by Hodges, Graham, & Patterson (1995), A.M. showed a fascinating mixture of "preserved and disturbed cognition." Hodges and colleagues' patient, J.L., would set the house clocks and his watch forward in his impatience to get to a favorite restaurant, not realizing the relationship between clock and world time. A.M. made similar apparently "insightful" attempts to get his own way. For example, his wife reported an incident in which she secretly removed his car keys from his key-ring to stop him taking the car for a drive. At this point, A.M. was obsessed with driving and very quickly noticed the missing keys. He solved the problem by taking his wife's car keys off her key-ring without her knowledge and going to the locksmiths, successfully, to get a new set cut. At no point did A.M. realize his wife had taken the keys from his key-ring. Despite virtually no language output and profound comprehension difficulties, he still retained some skills, for example, he continued to play sports (particularly golf) regularly each week, remembering correctly when he was to be picked up by his friends, until 1998 when he entered permanent nursing care.

Serial brain imaging using magnetic resonance imaging (MRI) images showed the pattern typical of semantic dementia, namely striking asymmetrical atrophy of the anterior temporal lobes involving the temporal pole, fusiform gyrus and infero-lateral region, but with relative sparing of the hippocampus.

In summary, A.M.'s case-history illustrates a number of the characteristic neuropsychological features of semantic dementia: (i) selective impairment of semantic memory causing severe anomia, impaired single-word comprehension, reduced generation of exemplars on category fluency tests, and an impoverished fund of general knowledge, (ii) surface dyslexia, (iii) relative sparing of syntactic and phonological aspects of language, (iv) normal perceptual skills and nonverbal problem-solving abilities, and (v) relatively preserved recent autobiographical and day-to-day (episodic) memory. (From Hodges & Graham, 2001, with permission of *Philosophical Transactions of The Royal Society: Biological Sciences*)

Case Study 2

L.A. is a 62-year-old housewife with a university degree in biological sciences, who in December 1984 suddenly presented an episode of headache, vomiting, and hyperpyrexia, followed by right-sided hemiparesis, jargon aphasia, and progressive consciousness disorders. She was admitted to the intensive care unit of the Catholic University of Rome, where a diagnosis of herpes simplex encephalitis was made, and treatment with acyclovir was started. About 2 months after the onset of the symptomatology, a thorough neuropsychological examination disclosed (1) intact attentional and perceptual skills, (2) fluent and informative speech, without phonemic and syntactic disorders but with occasional word-finding difficulties, (3) a severe amnesic syndrome, with very poor scores on verbal and nonverbal tests of long-term memory, (4) a category-specific semantic disorder selectively affecting living beings and food and sparing body parts and inanimate objects (Silveri & Gainotti, 1988).

This pattern of cognitive impairment has remained remarkably stable during the following years, allowing us, from 1989 to 1993, to undertake a more systematic investigation of the cognitive locus of lesion underlying her selective semantic disorder for living beings. At the same time, MRI scans taken in April 1991 have permitted a more detailed assessment of the anatomical lesions provoking this selective semantic impairment.

The lesions of patient L.A. bilaterally involved all the temporo-limbic structures, with a greater extension on the left side (where the polar temporal cortex, the amygdala, the entorhinal cortex, and the hippocampal formation were all extensively damaged) and a lesser involvement of the right side (where the lateral portion of the amygdala was relatively spared). However, the lesions were not restricted to the temporo-limbic structures but also involved other parts of the temporal lobes and in particular the inferior temporal cortex, which was completely destroyed on the left and only spared in its lateral parts on the right side. (From Gainotti & Silveri, 1996, with permission of *Cognitive Neuropsychology*)

Case Study 3

L.P. is a 44-year-old, right-handed woman with unremarkable medical history until the onset of the present disease. She had completed high school courses, getting a certificate as elementary school teacher, and had been working for 14 years as a secretary in a high school. She was married and had two children.

In late November 1984, the patient complained of malaise and headache and was feverish. On 30 November, she did not recognize her husband and children and had olfactive hallucinations; her speech was incoherent. Admitted to the hospital of another city, she was found to be anomic, without any abnormality of elementary neurological functions. She scored 34/36 on Raven Progressive Matrices . . . and was neither apraxic, nor acalculic. The patient remained feverish and hallucinated until 5 December, then gradually improved. . . . CT scan showed a mild hypodensity in the left posterior temporal lobe, and EEG showed a slow dysrythmia in the left temporo-occipital area following hyperpnea.

When the patient came back home (12 January 1985), she manifested difficulty in recognizing familiar persons, except her husband and children. She was unable to cook and to operate the washing machine but could tidy up the house, iron, sew, and drive. She was deeply depressed and in the first days stayed in bed most of time.

The patient was admitted to our department on 13 March 1985. Neurological examination showed a severe anomia on visual and verbal confrontation, but a much less marked impairment in running speech, which was fluent and constructed with correct sentences, in spite of some anomic blocks and very rare semantic paraphasias. Articulation and prosody were normal. She was well-groomed, communicative, eager to cooperate, appropriate in affect, and had full insight into her situation but was frustrated by her predicament and often wept in exasperation. Depression improved following medication with amitriptyline. During her stay in the hospital, she had a new CT scan, which was normal, except for a mild widening of the left temporal horn.

The patient was discharged after 15 days and followed over the successive months, first every week and then every 2 weeks for 1 year. The last control was carried out in July 1987, when an MRI was obtained. The T2-weighted images showed a wide and irregular area of increased signal intensity extending over the inferior and anterior part of the left temporal lobe above and laterally to the temporal horn, which was enlarged. The lesion involved the amygdala, the uncus, the hippocampus, the hippocampal gyrus, and the anterior part of the fusiform gyrus. In the upper cuts, it encroached upon the external capsule and the insular white matter. The frontal lobe and the language area of the temporal and parietal lobe were spared. On the right there were minimal signs of increased signal intensity in the white matter of the inferior temporal lobe.

Her neuropsychological status has remained substantially unchanged. After a few months she resumed her job, which mainly consisted of preparing forms to compute the monthly salary of teachers, taking into account how long they had been in the rolls (i.e., their coefficients). She used to automatically retrieve this information as soon as she read the teachers' names, but now they sounded new to her, and she had to wearily check any piece of information and was unable to carry out the task in a reasonable amount of time. When shopping, she encountered great difficulty in getting what she needed. She, or her mother-in-law, prepared a list, but this was of little help, because some of the written names were meaningless to her at the moment she read them. Moreover, she had forgotten the place where the different kinds of food were located and the physical appearance of their boxes or containers and thus she went on passing several times in front of the stands where they were kept without recognizing them. She resorted to the trick of collecting the front faces or tags of the food boxes and to try to match them with those kept on the shelves of the food store. A special problem was presented by vegetables packed up together, because she was afterward unable to identify those needed to prepare the "minestrone." She, therefore, always asked the greengrocer to pack these special vegetables apart.

Housework was, generally, performed appropriately. She was able to operate the washing machine and the dishwasher, to iron, to keep the house clean, to typewrite, and to drive. Also more unusual tasks, such as taking the curtains down from windows in order to wash them and then putting them back in place, were correctly performed. She had problems, however, in remembering where the house tools were located and in cooking.

One of the main problems of the patient, for which she greatly complained, was her failure to recognize well-known persons. When she returned to school, several teachers who had been working with her for years and knew of her disease came to her office to greet her, but to her great embarrassment she could not recognize them. For some of these people she had a sense of familiarity, though being unable to remember who they were; others looked completely unknown. This failure persisted and greatly hampered her working capacity. One day she met a woman who greeted her warm-heartedly and had a talk with her. She did not recognize the woman and asked her name. Upon telling her husband, she discovered that the woman was a friend, with whom she used to spend her New Year's Eve. There were persons she recognized and others, equally familiar, she did not. Recognition was particularly difficult for people met out of the environment in which they usually appeared. Relatives were all recognized. She identified the doctors with whom she had spent a long time in testing but not other doctors who had attended to her care during the time of her hospitalization. The psychologist was often not recognized, in contrast with a good recall of the details of her life (for instance, she remembered perfectly that the psychologist had changed the color of her hair a few days before). (From De Renzi, Liotti, & Nichelli, 1987, with permission of *Cortex*)

The symptoms that define the syndrome of semantic amnesia may be arranged in order of prominence as follows. The most prominent symptom is a retrograde loss or inaccessibility of semantic memories. In view of the fact that most semantic memories are verbally coded, this deficit presents typically as word-finding difficulty, difficulty in naming objects, difficulty or inability to remember and relate facts, and difficulty in understanding the meaning of words and concepts once known. These difficulties in verbal expression and in comprehension of verbally mediated facts and concepts are recognizably distinct from similar difficulties associated with either expressive or receptive aphasia secondary to frontal and posterior superior temporal (typically left) lobe lesions. Patients with expressive aphasia typically commit syntactic errors, yet patients with semantic amnesia seldomly do, except when the disease extends to frontal regions of the brain as is the case in the later stages of the temporal variant of frontotemporal dementia, one of the chief causes of semantic amnesia (Bishop, 1989; Hodges, Patterson, Oxbury et al., 1992; Tyler, Moss, Patterson et al., 1997). In fact, it appears that patients with semantic amnesia take advantage of their intact syntactic skills to clarify the forgotten meaning of words through their place and function in a sentence (Breedin & Saffran, 1999). Also, unlike patients with expressive aphasia, patients with semantic amnesia do not commit phonological errors (Snowden, Griffiths, & Neary, 1994) when they speak, in spite of their pronounced anomia. It is clear that their difficulty is with remembering the appropriate words with which to express themselves, which forces them either to use circumlocutions, omit the word they cannot find, or use superordinate category names, including expressions like "that thing" instead of the specific name of the item (Hodges & Patterson, 1996; Snowden, Neary, & Mann, 1996). Similarly, their difficulties in comprehension of speech are not due to lack of ability to make fine phonological distinctions (Knott, Patterson, & Hodges, 1997) but to their inability to access the meaning of words they hear. Moreover, though they may resemble dyslexic or agraphic patients in that they may present difficulties in reading and in writing, patients with semantic amnesia differ in that their difficulties vary directly with the frequency of word usage and, most tellingly, in that their errors in writing take the form of "regularization" to higher frequency words; that is, substitutions of low-frequency with high-frequency ones (McCarthy & Warrington, 1986; Diesfeldt, 1992; Patterson & Hodges, 1992; Lauro-Grotto, Piccini, & Shallice, 1997; Graham, Patterson, & Hodges, 2000).

Equally distinctive is the pattern of defective performance of semantic amnesia patients in word finding and usage. In cases where the syndrome is due to a degenerative disease, as the degeneration of the temporal cortex progresses, the frequency of usage of specific words decreases, and their substitution with more general words from superordinate categories increases. With progression of the pathology there appears to be a disproportionate elimination of nouns as compared with verbs from the patients' repertory. This phenomenon has been observed since the nineteenth century (e.g., Bergson, 1911) and has received various interpretations. One of the most current ones is the one proposed by Patterson and Hodges (2000) claiming that this phenomenon is a mere consequence of the fact that the verbs used by normal speakers (as for example in the context of the "Cookie Theft" subtest of the Boston Diagnostic Aphasia Examination (Goodglass & Kaplan, 1983) tend to be of higher frequency than the nouns that a description of the Cookie Theft would entail. An alternative interpretation is that the mnemonic traces representing nouns are located in the inferior temporal cortex, which may be affected by the disease first, whereas the traces representing verbs may be residing in areas affected at later stages of the disease, like the frontal lobes or in the superior aspects of the temporal lobes. The merit of alternative interpretations aside, the fact remains that at least in the context of formal testing with the Cookie Theft subtest, nouns tend to be depleted at a higher rate than verbs (Patterson & Hodges, 2000).

Patterns of decay, or inaccessibility of traces representing different types of verbal and nonverbal facts and concepts of much greater specificity than simply nouns and verbs, contingent on diverse lesion patterns, have also been proposed in support of alternative conjectures as to the spatial order in which these traces are arranged along the cortical surface. The observations that specific items of knowledge are either lost or inaccessible due to lesions of specific areas are quite old and not altogether infrequent (Nielsen, 1949), going back to at least the nineteenth century (Bergson, 1911). Specific details range from selective amnesia for faces and colors to hemisphere-specific deficits in knowledge of people versus objects, the former mostly due to right temporal pole lesions, and the latter due to lesions in either hemisphere (Tranel, Damasio & Damasio, 1997); selective deficits in recognizing famous people without any other category deficits, following right temporal lobe atrophy (Evans, Heggs, Antoun et al., 1995); gradients of difficulty, independent of lesion site, with abstract concepts being affected more than concrete ones (an observation also going back to the nineteenth century (Bergson, 1911); as well as gradients of difficulty in the opposite direction (Warrington, 1975; Warrington & Shallice, 1984). Also noted are selective deficits in remembering the names of "natural things" as opposed to artifacts (Farah, Hammond, Mehta, & Ratcliff, 1989; Farah, McMullen, & Meyer, 1991; Sirigu, Duhamel, & Poncet, 1991; Hart & Gordon, 1992; Laiacona, Barbarotto, & Capitani, 1993; Sheridan & Humphreys, 1993; Powell

& Davidoff, 1995; Damasio, Grabowski, Tranel et al., 1996; Laiacona, Capitani, & Barbarotto, 1997; Caramazza & Shelton, 1998); even more highly selective deficits concerning living things but not body parts, musical instruments and foods but not other "nonliving" entities (Gainotti, Silveri & Daniele, 1995); names of artifacts except for very large ones (Warrington & McCarthy, 1987); common and very familiar (to the patient) items used in hospitals but not any other items (Crosson, Moberg, Boone et al., 1997); verbs and not nouns, but also nouns more than verbs, depending on whether the lesion is frontal or temporal (Micelli, Silveri, Villa et al., 1984; Micelli, Silveri, Nocentini et al., 1988). In short, the patterns of selectivity are virtually inexhaustible.

Yet, there is no reason to doubt the accuracy of these observations as far as they go. The difficulty with them arises only when one is attempting to derive generalizations regarding the order in which the categories are represented along the cortical surface and when one attempts to identify the categories, so represented. It is difficult enough to match consistently lesion locations with particular categories of facts and concepts; but it is virtually impossible to certify that the deficits observed are indeed due to selective interference of the lesion with the category the observer postulates simply by using test items that belong to that nominal category. To be specific: a patient may be truly incapable of remembering a fact or concept belonging to category X, yet the reason for that selective deficit may have nothing or very little to do with the lesion affecting traces of tokens of category X. It may have much or everything to do with a host of other factors that are operative at the same time, starting with subject variables, like patient-specific familiarity with the particular set of test items, and ending with the very disturbing possibility that any item, any concept, may very well belong to a number of alternative and not mutually exclusive categories: the category of things that involve action (or not); the category of big (or small) objects; the category of objects rather than processes; of nouns versus function words; of usually moving or usually stationary things; of things of great evolutionary significance; of familiar, rare, bright, odorless things, ad infinitum.

Pointing out the difficulties involved in establishing category-specific deficits is not meant to imply that the issue of how traces of concepts and facts are arranged on the cortical mantle cannot be solved. In fact, there is every reason to hope that, once we learn how to obtain valid and reliable activation profiles of brain mechanisms through functional neuroimaging methods, the solution of this puzzle may arrive quite fast. Rather, by pointing out the difficulties, we wish to illustrate why the observations of selective semantic memory deficits, as they now stand, cannot provide answers to the question of cerebral representation of knowledge; why we ought to accept these data as they stand, without generalizing, and why we ought to assert simply that there is category-specificity, though we do not know if it follows particular rules or if it is idiosyncratic and patient-specific.

Additional symptoms that constitute the syndrome of semantic amnesia, detailed by Snowden, Neary, & Mann (1996) in their seminal paper, are changes in the patient's behavior and attitude, as a function of declining semantic memory, and therefore their capacity for comprehending the world around them: The settling of the patient into nearly ritualistic daily routines, including monitoring of time and clock watching; a narrowing of the repertory of daily activities; inordinate preoccupation with nonverbal activities like completing jigsaw puzzles; a change toward greater regimentation in eating habits and preferences for the same food over and over, and a rather curious development of a "sweet tooth," even by patients who did not particularly like sweets before.

More equivocal and much harder to establish is the symptom of retrograde episodic memory. Certainly, loss of recent episodic memories does not constitute a defining feature of semantic amnesia. Things are less certain about old episodic memories, partly because the veridicality of them is much more difficult to assess than that of semantic memories. It appears, nevertheless, that old episodic memories are more likely to be forgotten in semantic amnesia than more recent ones, a phenomenon radically different from that observed in limbic amnesia (see next chapter), in Alzheimer disease, or, for that matter, in most amnesias: a phenomenon moreover that was observed and reported in the eighteenth century by Theodule Ribot (1882) and which carries, since then, his name: Ribot's law. The implications of this "reverse" temporal gradient, true of episodic but also of semantic memory loss (Snowden, Griffith & Neary, 1996; Graham & Hodges, 1997; Hodges & Graham, 1998) will be dealt with later. At present, another even more disputable symptom of semantic amnesia ought to be considered: anterograde deficits. Unlike most other types of organic amnesia, semantic amnesia does not include an inability to acquire new information, especially nonverbal, and especially episodic (Warrington, 1975; Graham, Becker, & Hodges, 1997; Graham, Simons, Pratt et al., 2000b). Yet, new semantic memories are most certainly not acquired, a fact that presents difficulties with the assumption that we have adopted here, namely that semantic memories are episodic ones minus their "source" markings.

What is certainly true is that all symptoms of semantic amnesia, both the well-established and the less securely established ones, concern secondary memories. All primary memory operations, encoding, holding, and manipulating of items, are intact. A possible exception to that is retrieval, which may be compromised, as it can never be definitely demonstrated that an inability to remember is not a retrieval deficit. However, barring that logical caveat, it may be said with confidence that retrieval is also intact, except when the disease extends to the frontal cortex. Specifically, patients with semantic amnesia are not disoriented with respect to time, place, or person (Lauro-Grotto, Piccini, & Shallice, 1997), perform normally on tests of visuospatial function like the Rey Complex Figure test or Judgment of Line Orientation test, as well as on working memory and problem- solving tests like the Raven Colored Progressive Matrices (Hodges, Patterson, Oxbury, & Funnell, 1992; Hodges & Patterson, 1996; Snowden, Neary, & Mann, 1996). They also score within the normal range on the digit and corsi span tests (Patterson, Graham, & Hodges, 1994; Snowden, Griffith, & Neary, 1994; Knott, Patterson, & Hodges, 1997; Lauro-Grotto, Piccini, & Shallice, 1997).

In addition to the tests mentioned in the previous paragraph, the following are also used to specify the nature of the symptoms of semantic amnesia, chief among which is the test of "famous faces and events" (Leplow & Dierks, 1997;

Markowitsch, Calabrese, Neufeld et al., 1999; Snowden, Thompson, & Neary, 2004). More general tests of semantic knowledge for well-known facts and for object recognition include the "Hodges and Patterson semantic battery" (Hodges & Patterson, 1995), the Pyramids and Palm Trees Test (Howard & Patterson, 1992), and the Semantic General Knowledge Test (see Markowitsch, Calabrese, Neufeld et al., 1999). As described in Case 1 above (Hodges & Graham, 2001), the Hodges and Patterson semantic battery is used to test an individual's knowledge of 48 black-and-white line drawings of highly familiar objects and animals (Hodges & Patterson, 1995). The Pyramids and Palm Trees Test is a measure of associative semantic knowledge in which the patient is required to indicate which of two pictures (e.g., a fir tree or a palm tree) is most closely associated with a target picture (e.g., a pyramid) (Howard & Patterson, 1992). The Semantic General Knowledge Test (see Markowitsch, Calabrese, Neufeld et al., 1999) is a measure of semantic memory and includes questions about names of countries, cities, animals, currencies, and other general knowledge. Although individual test results may be compared with age-referenced norms, a problem with interpretation of the results of any remote memory test is an inability to know how well such semantic information was initially learned or remembered by the individual patient prior to the onset of the current symptoms.

The Autobiographical Memory Interview (AMI; Kopelman, Wilson, & Baddeley, 1989) was designed primarily to test retrograde episodic memory, but it also measures the ability to recall remote autobiographical semantic memories. Individuals are asked to recall events from two or three periods of their lives, including childhood, young adulthood, and later adulthood. They are also asked to recall, with as much detail as possible, some unique personal events, such as their wedding or graduation day. Questions about the individual's memory for personal facts are intended to be specific to information that the patient is known to have previously acquired, thereby avoiding the aforementioned problem associated with some memory tests of previously acquired, nonpersonal semantic knowledge.

The time of the onset of symptoms of semantic amnesia in a given patient may or may not be precisely known. The acquisition and retention of autobiographical and nonpersonal semantic information encountered after the onset of a brain insult or after the presentation of initial symptoms can be assessed through probing similar to the semistructured interview format of the AMI. Testing for knowledge of new vocabulary that has entered the cultural lexicon since the onset of the patient's brain damage is one way in which anterograde nonpersonal semantic memory may be assessed (Verfaellie, Koseff, & Alexander, 2000).

Anomia and semantic paraphasias, which are almost certain to be observed during the initial patient interview, may be assessed formally with a variety of tests. Naming problems are commonly assessed with the Boston Naming Test (Kaplan, Goodglass, & Weintraub, 1983), which consists of line drawings of high- to low-frequency objects. Impaired expressive naming skills may also be tested with category fluency tests in which a subject must generate exemplars of specific categories of items within a restricted time frame (the Controlled Oral

Word Association test; see Spreen & Strauss, 1998). Single-word comprehension may be tested with the Peabody Picture Vocabulary Test – Revised (Dunn & Dunn, 1981), which requires the patient to point to pictures denoting words spoken aloud by the examiner. Comprehension of oral phrases of increasing complexity can be assessed with the Token Test (Benton, Hamsher, Rey, & Sivan, 1994), which requires the patient to arrange groups of plastic tokens according to specific commands. Comprehensive batteries for testing language deficits, typically used in screenings for aphasia and which can be used in the assessment of patients with symptoms of semantic amnesia, include the Boston Diagnostic Aphasia Examination (Goodglass & Kaplan, 1983) and the Multilingual Aphasia Examination (Benton et al., 1994). These tests also include assessments of reading and written language skills, which may reveal the presence of surface dyslexia or dysgraphia, which, as mentioned above, are among the possible symptoms of semantic amnesia.

DIFFERENTIAL DIAGNOSIS

Semantic versus Other Organic Amnesias

Although semantic amnesia is a symptom that may be found in most organic amnesias, as a distinct syndrome it can be readily recognized and differentiated from all others. As mentioned in the previous section, there are two cardinal features of semantic amnesia that set it apart: first, a pronounced retrograde deficit for facts, concepts, and symbols but not episodes; and second, a retrograde gradient opposite of that found in all other amnesic syndromes, namely one that features greater loss of old and less of more recent memories. These two features suffice to differentiate semantic amnesia from all other organic syndromes, especially limbic amnesias (see next chapter), which are characterized by diametrically opposite features, namely a greater anterograde deficit, mostly involving episodes, and the typical gradient of retrograde deficits whereby newer memories are more readily forgotten than old ones.

Semantic Amnesia versus Aphasia and Agnosia

Less readily, one may differentiate between semantic amnesia on one hand and either aphasia or agnosia on the other. Part of the difficulty is due to the fact (discussed rather extensively in the first chapter) that definitions shift with the prevailing theoretical winds, and yesterday's aphasic symptom becomes a bona fide one of semantic amnesia today. Yet, certain conventions do remain more or less diachronically invariant: Receptive aphasia is characterized by loss of procedures for arriving at word meaning not by symptoms of forgetting of some words. Expressive aphasia is characterized by loss of procedures for producing words and grammatically correct sentence structures, not simply by groping for the right word, as in word-finding difficulty that characterizes spontaneous speech and performance in tasks, like object naming, in semantic amnesia. That is, amnesia can be distinguished from aphasia by the paucity of phonological and syntactic errors in the amnesic patient's performance in both receptive and expressive verbal tasks (Hodges & Graham, 2001; Caplan, 2003).

With agnosia, things become a bit more complicated because of definitional problems. The classification of agnosic deficits has been the subject of debate for more than a century (Bauer & Demery, 2003). What has been settled is that agnosias fall into two main types: perceptual or apperceptive on one hand and associative on the other. Individuals with perceptual agnosia show deficits of perception though their sensory functions are intact. (For example, in the visual modality, they show normal acuity, color vision, normal visual fields, and adequate motion detection.) Yet in spite of that, they are unable to copy, trace, or match line drawings or visual forms. They cannot perceive the object as a whole. Provided that we call apperceptive agnosia the condition that is characterized by a sensory-modality-specific perceptual deficit, it is always possible to tell apart whether patients are agnosic or amnesic by testing their knowledge through means that circumvent the particular sensory-modality-specific apperceptive deficit. For example, when a patient cannot recognize his wife when we show him her portrait, but does so as soon as she speaks, we call him agnosic. When, on the other hand, he fails to recognize her at all, even though he does not have other auditory perception deficits, then we may call him amnesic.

Certainly, most clinicians would not classify a patient as agnosic if under the above described conditions he fails to recognize a colleague he met once, a month ago, at a meeting. And the difference between the certainty of the latter, and the tentative nature of the former judgment, reflects the implicitly, but quite generally held notion that one of the differences between forgetting a fact and not really knowing it (between semantic amnesia and agnosia) is the degree of familiarity with that fact. As noted in the first chapter, such classificatory schemes are far from formal, logical, and categorical. Yet, they are retained in the hope that distinctions that feel right today may someday be justified as neuro-anatomically valid.

The tentative nature of classificatory judgments becomes even more obvious in cases where semantic amnesia is to be differentiated from the so-called associative agnosia where the deficit is not apperceptive, is not due to a sensory-modality-specific perceptual difficulty, but is due to difficulties that are referred to as "higher-order impairments of global visual search skills" whereby patients cannot readily form percepts of the entire object, but rather they attempt to form it through a laborious feature-by-feature construction. Here, it becomes clearly a matter of personal theoretical prejudice whether one wishes to state that the behavioral signs of experienced difficulties point to forgetting of the automatisms for object recognition, to forgetting of the meaning of the object, or to obliteration of any knowledge of it. That is, depending on one's implicit model of what the nature of the meaning of things is, and how it comes about that we recognize objects, one person may insist on calling the symptoms amnesic, and another agnosic. And it helps little to appeal to the site of lesion and if the lesion is closer to the parietal cortex to call the resulting symptom agnosic and if it is in the temporal cortex to call the symptom amnesic, because then, justification for so-naming things becomes circular. We only raise this issue here to alert the reader to the fact that such justifications are often used, but they are of the kind that generate more heat than light for understanding the disorder and, beyond it, the nature of memory and the nature of knowledge.

PATHOPHYSIOLOGY

As mentioned in the previous section of this chapter, the syndrome of semantic amnesia is produced typically by bilateral temporal lobe lesions extending posteriorly, inferiorly, and laterally from the poles but not medially, leaving the hippocampus and associated limbic structures relatively or practically intact. This pattern of damage may be produced by herpes encephalitis as in the case of Gainotti and Silveri (1996) presented above, by traumatic brain injury (Grossi, Trojano, Grasso, & Orsini, 1988), or radiation-induced necrosis (Kapur, Ellison, Parkin et al., 1994). However, in those cases the lesion pattern is likely to include parts of the medial temporal lobes, adding to the semantic syndrome features typical of limbic amnesia, specifically, anterograde episodic deficits. The typical neocortical temporal lesion pattern is most often the result of degenerative disease, notably the temporal variant of frontotemporal dementia (reviewed in the previous chapter), accounting for about 25% of all frontotemporal dementias (Hooten & Lyketsos, 1996) with another 50% of all cases additionally showing frontal lobe involvement. In the cases of primarily temporal lobe involvement, at least initially the damage appears to be unilateral, but on closer inspection, especially in later stages, the disease clearly involves both temporal lobes, albeit not always to the same extent (Figure 5-1) (Mummery, Patterson, Price et al., 2000).

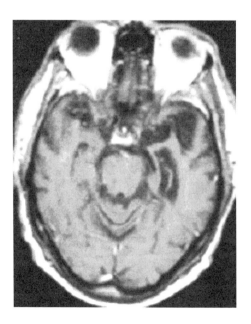

Figure 5–1 A case of a 72-year-old male with semantic dementia who showed atrophy of the left and right temporal poles, with greater atrophy in the left hemisphere. Note: The left hemisphere is shown on the right side of the image. (Courtesy of Sokratis G. Papageorgiou)

There appears to be a preponderance of cases presenting with greater left than right temporal lobe involvement. This disproportion may reflect the fact that left-sided damage typically results in more pronounced anomia, which renders the syndrome more apparent and consequently more likely to be investigated at a relatively early stage before the disease progresses and the semantic amnesia syndrome becomes, with increasing frontal lobe involvement, altered with the addition of primary memory deficits. As the disease progresses, degeneration of the adjacent frontal lobe, probably present from the beginning, but so slight as to be hardly discernible in the MRI, becomes more pronounced. When functional neuroimaging techniques are sufficiently improved, as preliminary evidence tends to indicate (Garrard & Hodges, 2000), functional changes in the same areas that show structural abnormalities may provide an early warning about the disease and may elucidate aspects of the mechanism that underlies the semantic deficits.

Anterior temporal neocortical damage can be caused by nonprogressive or progressive lesions. As in Case Study 2 presented above, herpes simplex encephalitis (HSE) can cause damage to the inferior temporal neocortex (Gainotti & Silveri, 1996), inferior and middle temporal gyri (Pietrini, Nertempi, Vaglia et al., 1988), and in medial, polar, and anterior infero-temporal structures bilaterally (Sirigu, Duhamel, & Poncet, 1991). Other nonprogressive causes of semantic amnesia include head injury (Grossi, Trojano, Grasso, & Orsini, 1988) and radiation-induced necrosis. Kapur, Ellison, Parkin et al. (1994), for example, reported a case in which experimental radiotherapy caused bilateral pathology of white matter and of neocortical temporal lobe structures. Their patient had particularly severe damage to anterior loci in the temporal lobes, with spared medial temporal lobe structures. Disruption of the posterior communicating artery is another nonprogressive cause of inferior temporal lobe damage (Sartori, Job, Miozzo et al., 1993).

PROGNOSIS AND TREATMENT

In those cases where the amnesic syndrome results from any of the nonprogressive lesions mentioned in the previous section, there is no change in the symptoms, whether positive or negative, after the subacute phase. But in most cases where the cause of damage is a progressive disease, the symptoms worsen following that progression. In the specific case of frontotemporal dementia, the time course of deterioration varies greatly from patient to patient, over a range of 3 to 14 years from symptom onset to the time the patient becomes untestable (Hodges, Patterson & Tyler, 1994; Hodges, Graham, & Patterson, 1995; Schwarz, De Bleser, Poeck, & Weis, 1998).

Although treatment options for semantic amnesia are limited, it has been observed (Snowden & Neary, 2002) that patients with semantic amnesia can relearn some of their lost vocabulary. Residual semantic knowledge as well as contextual knowledge (temporal order and spatial position) may facilitate the relearning of lost vocabulary items. Therefore, while there is no treatment for semantic amnesia, quality of life may be improved for a limited time by training patients to reacquire lost vocabulary.

CONCLUSIONS

The data on semantic amnesia that we have endeavored to summarize in this chapter do not warrant, of themselves, any secure inferences regarding which mnemonic operation or operations are compromised by temporal neocortical lesions. Consequently, they do not allow any inferences regarding what brain mechanisms might reside partly or entirely in the temporal neocortex. The reason for this is not only the incompleteness of the data but also the fact that such inferences are always codetermined by our implicit or explicit assumptions as to what encoding, consolidation, storage, retrieval, and their respective brain mechanisms are like.

For example, let us say that, following the lead of the overwhelming majority of researchers and theorists in the field, we too assume that semantic memory is not only a collection of memories but a "system" of memories, along with a complete set of the above-mentioned mnemonic operations (i.e., encoding, consolidation, storage, and retrieval) and their cerebral mechanisms. Having made this assumption, we have no choice but to conclude that the data indicate that any or all operations may be compromised by neocortical temporal lobe lesions, and that, possibly, the mechanisms of the entire semantic memory system, of encoding, retrieval, consolidation, and storage, is partly or entirely based on structures of the temporal neocortex. Of course, we would then have to attribute the fact that episodic memory remains relatively intact to the existence of a second memory "system." This second system, the episodic one, complete with all its contents (the episodic memories) and with its very own set of operations and mechanisms, resides either in the entire mesial aspect of the temporal lobes or, if we follow Vargha-Khadem, Gadian, Watkins et al. (1997) and Tulving and Markowitsch (1998), only in the hippocampus, since Vargha-Khadem and colleagues happen to believe that the rest of the mesial temporal lobe structures houses the semantic memory system.

Alternatively, let us say, that prompted by an urge to greater parsimony and by an unwillingness to substitute the fact of loss of specific memories with the hypothesis of loss of both memories and mnemonic operations, we assume that there is only one set of operations and mechanisms; that the same set constructs, maintains, and recalls all kinds of memories, both semantic and episodic, and that it is only the neuronal codes of these memories that reside in different neocortical regions. Under this alternative set of assumptions, the semantic amnesia data that we reviewed would constitute evidence that the temporal neocortex contains the codes or traces of semantic memories (facts, concepts, and symbols, verbal or otherwise), and that lesions degrade or destroy these traces and not any of the mnemonic mechanisms of encoding, retrieval, or consolidation.

Having in fact adopted the latter assumptions in this book, for the purpose of organizing and ordering the facts of amnesia (see Chapter 1), we may now consider how well that assumption accords with the data: The fact that patients with semantic amnesia retrieve memories (some semantic and most episodic) accords with the assumption that the lesions have not affected the retrieval mechanism. That mechanism may well reside in the prefrontal cortex, as it is only prefrontal lesions that interfere with all sorts of memories—not only semantic or only episodic (as do limbic lesions) or only items of spatial knowledge or knowledge of procedures (as do parietal, occipital, and frontal lesions). The fact that the retrograde amnesia gradient is the reverse of the one found in cases of limbic lesions and which is universally viewed as a sure sign of the consolidation operation provides supporting evidence that that operation (whether or not mediated by a limbic mechanism) is also not compromised. Finally, the fact that patients with semantic amnesia encode new information readily and have no short-term or working memory problems constitutes evidence that encoding, "holding," and all other primary memory operations and corresponding mechanisms are not compromised by temporal neocortex lesions. So what is compromised? Evidently, only the traces of a specific class of memories: the semantic ones.

Symbolic records or codes of items of information, whether neuronal or artificial, may not be retrievable either because they or their "addresses" have been permanently corrupted or decayed or temporarily interfered with by reversible causes. In the former case, the items of knowledge are irretrievably lost; in the latter case, access to them is refractory. Granted, one may never know with absolute certainty whether an item is lost or temporarily inaccessible, as it is always possible that the next attempt at its retrieval may be successful in spite of many (yet always finite in number) previous unsuccessful attempts. Yet, one may be certain that an item or a class of items is practically lost if one has exhausted all possible means at one's disposal for facilitating their retrieval.

Having some form or other of physical existence, traces must occupy some space; they must involve some molecular modifications of neurons that are extended in space. Two classes of physical form have been attributed to mnemonic traces. The one, derived by analogies from artificial forms of storage, photographs, records, CDs, and videotapes, is thought to involve a set of interconnected cells forming an assembly, a different one for each memory. In the other, proposed by Lashley (1950) as the only possibility after his unsuccessful search for localized "engrams" and modeled by Pribram (1971) after holograms and by some contemporary theorists after "parallel distributed" networks, envisions each trace, corresponding to each memory, is viewed as distributed over vast networks of neurons such that the same neurons contain aspects of all or most traces. This form of storage, however sophisticated, does not accord with the facts of "category specificity" that we have reviewed. That is, it does not accord with the fact that certain lesions, involving specific patches of cortex, result in irretrievability of certain categories of memories. And, it does not matter whether the same categories are always compromised by the same or different lesions or whether the semantic memories of different patients are organized and classified into the same set of categories or not: As long as the data of inaccessibility of certain items and not others, in a given patient, are accepted as factual, this form of "distributed" storage will not do.

Is then the alternative form, whereby each trace involves a particular set assembly, exclusive of all other traces, more serviceable? Certainly, it does accord with the facts of category specificity, but it creates a host of other problems: Take any "fact," such as the fact that Columbus discovered America. What makes that or any other fact meaningful is that it entails information about Columbus: that he is a particular man, in this case, and not the capital of the state of Ohio; information regarding what "to discover" means; and information about what is "America." Each of the constituent concepts out of which the fact is made enters into relations with an enormous number of separate facts and, for that matter, in relation with an incalculable number of different episodic memories. If we insist on the original specification that each fact must involve its own set of cells, the available number of cell assemblies will soon be exhausted. To address this and other impasses, a very old idea has been resurrected: the idea that all possible concepts (therefore facts and episodes) are made of a finite set of irreducibly simple features. Very much like the letters of the alphabet that suffice to produce an incalculable number of sentences, each with its own unique meaning, different aggregates of features may be said to suffice for all episodes, facts, concepts, and symbols that compose a person's total set of memories. All that is needed is a few operations or algorithms much like that of "retrieval," which would reassemble, on demand, particular facts or episodes using combinations of these elementary features, and the problem of storage is solved.

It is not our purpose here to review all the various models that have been and are continuously constructed in an effort to account for this and dozens of other aspects of human memory, but we will describe, by way of an example, one of the many intriguing ones that a literature search may uncover. This model (Lamb, 1999) concerns verbal concepts. According to it, a concept's entire network representation (lexeme) is widely distributed in the brain. Yet, the central node of the lexeme, the lemma, is localized in a particular area of the brain. The lemma carries no information; rather, the information is in the connections between the lemma and other nodes, including those dedicated to the phonological representations of the lexeme and the semantic representations of the lexeme, among others. These nodes are located in diverse areas of the brain in different cell assemblies—the phonological production node in the frontal lobe, the phonological recognition node in the posterior temporal lobe, the semantic node in the temporal lobe, and so on. All of the nodes connected to a specific lemma combine to form a lexeme. This model helps to explain how a patient with semantic amnesia can have a selective deficit of one category (e.g., nouns) while another category (e.g., verbs) remains unaffected. This relational network model goes beyond traditional connectionist theories in that it posits that concepts have not only distributed representations but also local representations. The local representations allow for selective category deficits such as nouns versus verbs, in which one category is selectively affected while the other is spared.

The virtues of this model are obvious and commendable. Its main difficulty, the same one that plagues all models of knowledge representation, may be summarized as follows: Were we to implement this model in a big enough computer, we would soon discover that on its hard disk we can fit entire encyclopedias and readily retrieve every lemma, every fact, and concept. But unless we, outside the computer, supply meaning to the retrieved items lighting up the computer screen, the items in themselves will remain meaningless. Which means, simply, that the model—and all others like it—are incomplete. They leave the central aspect of memories (i.e., their meaningfulness) unaddressed, while they account for the comparatively trivial aspect of how to preserve physical "signs" or "reminders" out of which a human being, by means of his knowledge of symbols, may easily reconstruct their meaning. A most vivid and entertaining description of the hopeless predicament of the theorist who tries to construct models of memory by means of neural networks, or any other physical code system that omits the component that accounts for how the meaning of the codes emerges, is to be found in the story the incomparable Garcia Márquez tells in his *One Hundred Years of Solitude* about the efforts of Aureliano and José Arcadio Buendia to fight the amnesia caused by the "insomnia plague" by means of a mechanism that would replace their affected brains: "One day," the story goes, Aureliano ". . . was looking for the small anvil that he used for laminating metals and he could not remember its name . . . ," whereupon his father, José Arcadio, told him the name, which he then wrote on a piece of paper and pasted it on the object. Later on, with the advance of insomnia, he found it necessary to label all the things he was forgetting, and he told his father of his method. Once the method was understood, his father went on and with a paintbrush marked every object in sight with its name, " . . . table, chair, clock . . . cow, goat, pig, cassava, caladium, banana . . . ," but he then realized that the time would soon come when, even though he could read off the names of objects, he would forget what the objects were about. To counter that eventuality he became more explicit: "The sign that he hung on the neck of the cow was an exemplary proof of the way in which the inhabitants of Macondo were prepared to fight against the loss of memory: 'This is a cow. She must be milked every morning . . . so that she will produce milk, and the milk must be boiled . . . .'" That way, Márquez continues, ". . . they went on living in a reality that was slipping away, momentarily captured by words, but which would escape irremediably when they forgot the values of the written letters."

The moral of this story is not whether modeling the emergence of meaning, out of reactivation of stored traces, is possible or impossible. Rather, the moral is that any model that does not include the reader and surveyor of the activated traces, the agent that confers meaning to those traces, is at best incomplete and of limited utility. But we will revisit this issue again in the concluding chapter of this book.

6

Limbic Amnesia

REBECCA BILLINGSLEY-MARSHALL,
PANAGIOTIS G. SIMOS, AND
ANDREW C. PAPANICOLAOU

Damage to the limbic system results in anterograde and retrograde deficits in explicit memory, with the most consistent symptom across patients being anterograde episodic amnesia. As described in Chapter 2, the limbic circuit that was characterized by Papez (1937) includes the medial temporal lobe structures (hippocampus, parahippocampal gyrus, entorhinal cortex, and perirhinal cortex), the mammillary bodies and mammillothalamic tract, and the anterior thalamus. The limbic system also includes the mediodorsal nucleus of the thalamus, the nuclei of the basal forebrain, and the amygdala. In this chapter, we describe, with the aid of several case studies, the clinical presentation typically associated with lesions in three sets of regions within the limbic system: the medial temporal lobes, the thalamic nuclei and the mammillary bodies (i.e., diencephalic structures), and the basal forebrain.

There is considerable overlap in the symptomatology associated with lesions in each of these three sectors of the limbic system and considerable individual variability. Nevertheless, the differences in the overall clinical presentation of patients who have sustained damage to each sector are sufficient to warrant a separate account.

Damage to medial temporal lobe structures can be caused by a variety of conditions, including stroke, viral infections, epilepsy, global hypoxia, and head injury. Diencephalic damage is most often caused by small vessel strokes, tumors, or progressive neuronal degeneration due to vitamin deficiency, and damage to the basal forebrain is most often caused by aneurysms at the anterior communicating artery. The most common effects of such damage are impairment in the ability to form new explicit memories (anterograde amnesia), accompanied by difficulties in remembering public and personal events and facts experienced before the onset of the lesions (retrograde amnesia). Additional deficits in primary memory functions are often present after diencephalic and basal forebrain damage, even in cases where damage to the frontal lobes is not apparent.

TESTING AND ESTABLISHMENT OF SYMPTOMS

The Symptoms of Medial Temporal Lobe Amnesia

The initial clinical presentation of patients after medial temporal lobe damage can be as variable as the disorders or events causing it. For instance, a patient with viral encephalitis will initially present with confusion, focal neurological signs, fever, and seizures. Conversely, an insidious case of cerebral ischemia may present only with amnesia. In view of the presence of transient symptoms not directly related to memory during the acute phase of the disease or injury, we will describe in this chapter the amnesia syndromes that appear later when the patient's condition has stabilized.

Depending on its severity and extent, damage to the medial temporal lobes results in both episodic and semantic anterograde memory deficits. Bilateral hippocampal damage results in a severe impairment in the acquisition of episodic memories, whether predominantly verbal or nonverbal, but unilateral damage tends to cause material-specific deficits, with left hippocampal damage producing mostly verbal and right hippocampal damage mostly nonverbal (figural, spatial) deficits. The ability to acquire new episodic memories is markedly impaired after damage restricted to the hippocampus (Shimamura & Squire, 1987; Cipolotti, Shallice, Chan et al., 2001). More extensive damage extending to surrounding structures, notably the parahippocampal gyrus, is more likely to impair semantic memory as well (Vargha-Khadem, Gadian, Watkins et al., 1997; Verfaellie, Koseff, & Alexander, 2000; Bayley & Squire, 2002).

Patients with limbic lesions, regardless of type and extent, score typically within the normal range or close to their estimated premorbid level on intelligence tests (Bauer, Grande, & Valenstein, 2003). A basic measure of patients' anterograde deficits is the difference between their intelligence quotient (IQ) and their Memory Quotient (MQ) (Scoville & Milner, 1957). In view of the fact that memory quotients rely heavily on verbal episodic memory, differences between IQ and performance on nonverbal memory tests should also be assessed. However, differences between intelligence and memory quotients must be interpreted with care because differences even of 20 points may not be indicative of a deficit, as in cases where an individual has exceptional IQ but only average memory. Moreover, in the case of younger children, age-appropriate norms are important for an accurate assessment of deficits.

Performance on tests of immediate memory, such as the Digit Span subtest of the Wechsler scales and the Corsi Blocks test (Kaplan, Fein, Morris, & Delis, 1991), is typically within normal limits in patients with medial temporal lobe lesions. This signals the absence of primary memory involvement. In contrast, measures of secondary memory show clear evidence of dysfunction. Bilateral damage to the hippocampus is sufficient to impair the capacity to recall or recognize studied verbal and nonverbal items (Manns, Hopkins, Reed et al., 2003), though in rare cases recognition ability may be relatively preserved as compared with recall ability (Vargha-Khadem, Gadian, & Mishkin, 2001; Mayes, Holdstock, Isaac et al., 2002), indicating that hippocampal lesions may interfere with consolidation as well as retrieval.

Formal assessment of a patient's anterograde episodic memory abilities typically involves the use of standardized memory assessment batteries, such as the Wechsler Memory Scale, Third Edition (WMS-III) (Wechsler, 2002). Performance on recall tests after a delay (typically 30–45 minutes) is considered a measure of the severity of the episodic deficits. In addition, the Rivermead Behavioral Memory Test (Wilson, Cockburn, Baddeley, & Hiorns, 1989) may be used to assess the extent to which daily life may be affected by a person's memory deficits. It requires prospective memory skills in which the examinee must remember the examiner's instructions to perform tasks when presented with various cues, such as the buzzing of a timer, a specific question, or the presentation of a cue such as an envelope. Other standardized batteries that contain subtests for the assessment of verbal and nonverbal recognition and recall abilities include the Children's Memory Scale (Cohen, 1997) for children of 5–16 years of age and the Denman Neuropsychology Memory Scale (Denman, 1984, 1987).

Individual memory tests (or subtests of memory batteries) that are reportedly highly sensitive to left medial temporal lobe damage include paired-associate recall tasks, such as the Paired Associates subtest of the WMS-III, and word-list learning tasks, such as the Rey Auditory Verbal Learning Test (RAVLT; Lezak, 1995) and the California Verbal Learning Test (CVLT [Delis, Kramer, Kaplan, & Ober, 1987b; Hermann, Seidenberg, Wyler et al., 1996] and CVLT, 2nd Edition [Delis, Kramer, Kaplan, & Ober, 2000]). Other tests commonly used to assess left medial temporal lobe damage are story memory tests, including the WMS-III Logical Memory subtest (Wechsler, 2002) and the Randt Memory Test (Randt & Brown, 1983).

For the assessment of nonverbal memory, the most often used instruments include face recognition tests (Denman, 1984, 1987; Beardsworth & Zaidel, 1994; Mabbott & Smith, 2003), spatial configuration recall and recognition tests (Smith & Milner, 1989), and recall of the Rey-Osterreith figure (Meyers & Meyers, 1995). Tests that do not require manual drawing may be a more accurate reflection of the patient's spatial (or otherwise nonverbal) memory function than those that require it. We note, however, that for adults with temporal lobe epilepsy, few nonverbal tasks have been identified that discriminate reliably between left and right hippocampal function preoperatively (Jones-Gotman, Smith, & Zatorre, 1993; Paradiso, Hermann, & Robinson, 1995).

Retrograde episodic and semantic amnesias have been observed in individuals with medial temporal lobe damage, but the extent of memory loss is variable. Some individuals show loss of episodic memories across time intervals, from early childhood to the time of the onset of damage (Cipolotti, Shallice, Chan et al., 2001), whereas others show virtually no retrograde amnesia. Still others have been reported to have a temporally graded memory loss, with earlier memories remembered better than more recent episodes, a pattern described by Ribot in his classic work on amnesia (Ribot, 1882).

Interpretation of results from "remote memory" tests is complicated by the fact that personal and public information about past events or facts may have been relearned (or learned for the first time) after the time period during which they took place (Bauer, Grande, & Valenstein, 2003; Lezak, 1995). Moreover, variability in patients' interests in, and exposure to, certain types of events (including fluctuations in such interests over the course of a single individual's life) compromises the value of all tests involving public occurrences, whether these are television programs, or names and faces of celebrities (Kapur, Thompson, Kartsounis, & Abbott, 1999). To overcome these difficulties, examiners may test for episodic and semantic memories of the person's own life experiences. Verification of the accuracy of a patient's autobiographical memories may be challenging, but the richness of detail and clarity of memories appear to differentiate those with retrograde amnesia from those with intact remote memories. Kopelman, Wilson, and Baddeley's (1989) Autobiographical Memory Interview (AMI) can be used to assess the quality of memories for personal facts and events. The first component of the AMI, the Autobiographical Incidents Schedule, is scored on the basis of the specificity of the patients' responses to questions about remote time periods in their life. The second component, the Personal Semantic Memory Schedule, is an assessment of the patients' memory for names, places, and dates. Childhood, early adult life, and recent events are the time periods included in each component of the AMI.

Specific and general conceptual knowledge can also be assessed with subtests of the Wechsler Adult Intelligence Scale, Third Edition (WAIS-III, Vocabulary, Comprehension, and Similarities; Wechsler, 1997), as well as with achievement tests. Scores on these subtests can be compared with premorbid estimates of IQ, such as those calculated with the Raven's Progressive Matrices (Raven, 1996) or the National Adult Reading Test (NART; Nelson, 1982), to identify discrepancies. Impairments of semantic memory may also be evident on naming, verbal fluency, and reading tasks, with some patients showing surface dyslexia (difficulty reading words with atypical print-to-sound pronunciations).

Amnesics with medial temporal lobe (and diencephalic) damage typically demonstrate normal memory on implicit tests of information they cannot recall or recognize on explicit tests (Moscovitch, 1982; Squire & Zola-Morgan, 1991; Squire, 1992a; Billingsley, McAndrews, & Smith, 2002; Moscovitch, Vriezen, Goshen-Gottstein, 1993). A variety of experimental tasks have been devised to probe for implicit memories. These include learning of both perceptual and motor skills, the ability to learn an artificial set of grammatical rules, and the ability to extract prototypical features in categorization tasks (Warrington & Weiskrantz, 1970; Moscovitch, Vriezen, & Goshen-Gottstein, 1993; Squire, Knowlton, & Musen, 1993; Knowlton, Squire, & Gluck, 1994; Squire & Zola, 1996).

To illustrate both the typical range of symptoms after medial temporal lobe damage and the ways of assessing them, we present below summaries and excerpts from three published case reports: Stefanacci, Buffalo, Schmock, and Squire (2000) described a 70-year-old patient diagnosed with herpes simplex encephalitis. His illness began with flu-like symptoms and an episode of memory loss (he could not remember the names of some family members) and appeared to recover in a few days. Although his illness was treated successfully, he continued to show stable, yet profound memory impairment when tested over a 6-year period. Magnetic resonance imaging (MRI) revealed severe bilateral damage involving the medial temporal lobes, including the amygdala, the entire hippocampus, entorhinal, and perirhinal cortices, and extending into the rostral fusiform gyrus and the rostral parahippocampal cortex. Quantitative measurements revealed volume loss in the insula and lateral temporal lobes (inferior, middle, and superior temporal gyri) and in his left parietal lobe. On neuropsychological tests:

> E.P. has normal or near-normal intellectual functions as measured by standard tests. His immediate memory and nondeclarative memory [for facts and events] are intact. In contrast, he has profound anterograde amnesia and is impaired on a wide variety of verbal and nonverbal tests of recall and recognition. He also has severe and extensive retrograde amnesia for facts and events, personal semantic knowledge, and autobiographical memory, but he appears fully capable of retrieving memories acquired in his early life, including detailed spatial memories of his childhood neighborhood. Finally, he is mildly impaired on tests of semantic knowledge, including tests of object naming, tests involving the detection and explanation of ambiguous sentences, and tests that asked about the features of common objects. (From Stefanacci, Buffalo, Schmolck, & Squire, 2000, with permission from *Journal of Neuroscience*)

Another report, by Cipolloti, Shallice, Chan et al. (2001) describes a 73-year-old retired chief engineer, who was reported by his wife as having an excellent memory before his illness. This patient developed profound anterograde and retrograde amnesia after a severe migraine attack and a series of three seizures that took place over a 4-day period. MRI studies revealed profound volume loss in the hippocampus bilaterally, including the CA1 region, and in the parahippocampal gyrus (greater on the left than on the right). There was also evidence for histological alterations in the remaining hippocampal tissue and in the left amygdala.

The patient demonstrated intact general intelligence, language, perception, and primary memory or "executive" functions, which remained stable over a 5-year period. Yet he was severely impaired on verbal and visual-spatial recognition and recall tests, with his performance on list learning, paired associative learning, complex figure, and face recognition tests showing severe deficits.

> The patient was completely unable to recall autobiographical episodes from his recent life and almost completely unable to recall autobiographical episodes from childhood and early adult life. Although he was able to produce a few pieces of personal semantic knowledge (e.g., his address when starting school but his address has remained the same throughout his life), he scored in the abnormal range for all three periods of his life. This shows that he had severe impairment of

both autobiographical and personal semantic memory from his childhood, early adult life, and recent life [and] there was no indication of a temporal gradient in his recall of personal semantic memories just as for the retrograde nonpersonal memory tasks. (From Cipolloti, Shallice, Chan et al., 2001, with permission of *Neuropsychologia*)

Finally, we present three cases of children with medial temporal damage incurred early in life that were described by Vargha-Khadem, Gadian, Watkins et al. (1997). The first patient, Beth, suffered anoxia during birth and generalized seizures over a 2- to 3-day period despite treatment with anticonvulsant medication. She showed full recovery within 2 weeks and did not display other neurological problems until she reached age 5 when memory difficulties were first noted on her entrance to school. The second patient, Jon, was delivered prematurely at 26 weeks of gestation and suffered from serious respiratory problems. Thereafter, he improved steadily and developed normally until, at the age of 4, he suffered two protracted convulsions. His memory impairment was first noted by his parents about a $1^1/_2$ years after the two long-lasting attacks. The third patient, Kate, was an average student until the age of 9, when she accidentally received a toxic dose of theophylline, a drug with which she was being treated for asthma. An acute episode of seizures, unconsciousness, and respiratory arrest ensued, from which she made a good physical recovery but which left her profoundly amnesic.

The patients were referred for evaluation in response to their parents' complaints that their children failed to remember events of daily life. They were experiencing difficulties in finding their way even in familiar surroundings and in remembering the location of objects around the house. They had to be constantly reminded of appointments and planned activities (prospective memory) and failed to remember daily events that had only recently occurred.

Three different MRI techniques that are very sensitive to temporal lobe pathology were used. Volumetric measurements showed that in each of the three patients, the hippocampi were abnormally small bilaterally, with volumes ranging from 43% to 61% of the mean value of normal individuals. T2 relaxometry indicated that the remaining hippocampal tissue was severely compromised in each case.

The parental reports were confirmed by results obtained from the Rivermead Behavioral Memory Test, where, out of a possible score of 12 and with a cutoff of impairment of nine correct items or less, Beth, Jon, and Kate obtained scores of 2, 3, and 4, respectively. Memory quotients obtained with the Wechsler Memory Scale (WMS) were 20 points (for Beth) and approximately 40 points (for Jon and Kate) below those predicted by their verbal IQs. All three patients performed near the lowest possible level on the delayed recall of stories and complex designs. All three patients performed poorly on other standardized verbal and nonverbal memory tests, including delayed recall of the word list contained in the Children's Auditory Verbal Learning Test and delayed reproduction of the Rey-Osterreith figure. By contrast, on immediate memory for the word list, as well as on digit span tests, all three patients performed within normal limits, a finding that is also characteristic of adult-onset medial temporal lobe amnesia.

Vargha-Khadem, Gadian, Watkins et al. (1997) concluded that:

> all three patients are not only competent in speech and language but have learned to read, write, and spell (with the exception of Jon's spelling) at levels that are commensurate with their VIQs. . . . With regard to the acquisition of factual knowledge, which is another hallmark of semantic memory, the vocabulary, information, and comprehension subtests of the VIQ scale are among the best indices available, and here, too, all three patients obtained scores within the normal range.
> (From Vargha-Khadem, Gadian, Watkins et al., 1997, with permission of *Science*)

These three cases of medial temporal damage restricted to the hippocampus have received much attention in the literature, and deservedly so, because they point to the possibility of accumulating knowledge without episodic memories of the circumstances surrounding its acquisition. This impressive fact may be variously interpreted. A common interpretation and one most commonly talked about by many commentators, including the authors of the report, is that the hippocampus supports an "episodic memory system" and the adjacent structures support an independent one for semantic memory. The merits of this interpretation are considered elsewhere in this volume (see chapter 1).

The Symptoms of Diencephalic Amnesia

Lesions to the thalamus, typically strokes, that affect the anterior and/or mediodorsal nuclei result in anterograde amnesia and sometimes in retrograde amnesia as well. However, retrograde amnesia is rarely the prevailing symptom (Miller, Caine, Harding, et al., 2001). Left-sided lesions are more often associated with verbal memory deficits and right-sided lesions with nonverbal ones (e.g., Ghika-Schmid & Bogousslavsky, 2000), although unilateral lesions can cause verbal and nonverbal deficits (Wallesch, Kornhuber, Brunner et al., 1983; Van der Werf, Weerts, Jolles et al., 1999). In the acute phase, patients typically present with somnolence, disorientation, limb and oculomotor disturbances, and less frequently with apathy, impaired thinking, and impaired verbal fluency. The latter set of symptoms are probably associated with damage to other thalamic nuclei or adjacent tissue, or due to interruption of frontal circuits connected to the damaged thalamic nuclei.

Anterograde amnesia accompanied by impairments in primary memory functions (such as impaired performance on digit span tests; Mayes, Daum, Markowisch, & Sauter, 1997) is commonly seen in alcoholic patients with "Korsakoff syndrome" involving degeneration of the anterior thalamus due to thiamine deficiency. Retrograde episodic and semantic amnesia is also present and tends to occur more often to Korsakoff patients than in patients with amnesia caused by vascular lesions. Given that most patients with Korsakoff disease are chronic alcoholics, their medical history likely contains hints of neuropsychological deficits prior to the onset of the disease, such as mild memory and attention problems or impairments in abstract reasoning or visuospatial performance (Grant, 1987; Parsons, Butters, & Nathan, 1987). Medical history may also reveal frequent "blackout" episodes accompanied by amnesia for events surrounding them. Persisting focal neurological signs (which may include ophthalmoplegia, nystagmus, ataxia, and gait disturbances, singly or in combination) are typically present along with signs of malnutrition and of thiamine deficiency. In the acute phase, the patient is often confused and disoriented. Following the acute phase of the crisis, which usually brings the typical Korsakoff patient to a health care facility, confabulation may be noted when verbal fluency resumes and confusion recedes. In its typical form, confabulation consists of coherent but fictitious stories in response to queries from the examiner. When the patients are probed about their story, they seem unaware of any problems with it and, showing a sincere and unpremeditated lack of concern, provide no indication that they intended deception.

In addition to amnesia and occasionally, confabulation, individuals with Korsakoff syndrome, and sometimes patients with thalamic stroke, often show impairments in primary memory and "executive" functions, such as monitoring of sensory input, organization and planning of ongoing activities, and appreciating the temporal order of external events (Moscovitch, 1982; Meudell, Mayes, Ostergaard, & Pickering, 1985; Squire, 1992b; Bauer, Grande, & Valenstein, 2003). Tests such as the Wisconsin Card Sorting Test and the Tower of London can be used to assess these impairments. The lack of appreciation of the temporal order of events often demonstrated by these patients may not simply be due to deficits of recognition (Squire, 1982), but deficits intrinsic to frontal-lobe mediated monitoring operations of the primary memory system (Moscovitch, 1982; Squire, 1982). Milner and colleagues (Petrides & Milner, 1982; Milner, Petrides, & Smith, 1985; McAndrews & Milner, 1991) have devised several experimental tasks to test for memory of temporal order, which they have shown to be worse in patients with damage to the frontal lobes than to other brain regions.

A graded memory loss for remote events, in which earlier events are remembered better than more recent episodes, is a commonly reported type of retrograde amnesia in Korsakoff patients (Squire, Haist, & Shimamura, 1989; Gade & Mortensen, 1990; Schnider, Gutbrod, Hess, & Schroth, 1996); but more severe, flat retrograde amnesia that encompasses very long periods of a patient's life has also been reported (Mair, Warrington, & Weiskrantz, 1979). In isolated cases, diencephalic amnesia associated with thalamic stroke or Korsakoff syndrome is also accompanied by anterograde (Exner, Weniger, & Irle, 2001) or retrograde procedural memory deficits (Miller, Caine, Harding et al., 2001). Three case studies of diencephalic amnesia, two cases associated with Korsakoff syndrome and one with a vascular thalamic lesion, are briefly described below.

The first patient reported by Mair, Warrington, & Weiskrantz (1979) was first evaluated for memory loss, numbness in the limbs, and vertigo. He had a history of diabetes, malnutrition, and alcohol abuse. Another episode of confusion and memory loss had apparently taken place 2 months prior to admission:

> On admission he was disoriented in time and in place and had a very severe memory impairment for past and ongoing events. He failed to learn the topography of the hospital ward and he did not learn to recognize the medical or nursing staff. He appeared to be aware of his memory deficit and at no time when he was under

observation was there any clear suggestion of confabulation. On questioning he appeared to have very little knowledge, if any, of events that had occurred during World War II. His behaviour on the ward was somewhat truculent and uncooperative; it was noted in the history obtained from his family that this personality trait was of long standing. "On examination there was nystagmus to the left and there was defective abduction of the left eye, giving him an uncrossed diplopia. There was bilateral weakness of the hip flexion and minimal impairment of co-ordination in the lower extremities, with absent deep tendon reflexes and flexor plantar responses. Sensation was impaired in a glove-and-stocking fashion on arms and legs, and there was also consistent impairment of superficial sensation, to a less severe degree, below the mid-thoracic region. His general nutrition appeared good; his liver and spleen were not palpable. On investigation a full blood count was normal although the ESR was slightly elevated at 27 mm.h. Serum electrolytes and urea were normal."
    (From Mair, Warrington, & Weiskrantz, 1979, with permission of *Brain*)

The second patient reported by Mair, Warrington, and Weiskrantz (1979) was a 50-year-old seaman who was admitted for headache. He also had a history of prolonged alcohol abuse.

On admission he was clearly disoriented in time and place and had a severe memory impairment for both past and ongoing events. He failed to learn his way around the ward and on neither his first nor his subsequent admission did he learn to recognize staff or other patients. He was fully aware of his memory deficit, frequently referring to his failure to recall events from all periods of his life. Confabulation was never observed on either admission. On questioning he said he remembered his experiences as a merchant seaman during World War II, but on closer questioning it was clear that his memory for events during that period was quite inaccurate and patchy.

Postmortem examination in both patients revealed:

marked gliosis, shrinkage and discoloration bilaterally in the medial nuclei of the mammillary bodies. In addition there was a thin band of gliosis bilaterally between the wall of the third ventricle and the medial dorsal nucleus, the rostral limit lying anterior to the medial dorsal nucleus. In the patient with no intellectual deterioration these were the only pathological changes that were seen. In neither patient was there evident local loss of nerve cells, gliosis or any other qualitative evidence of abnormality in the hippocampi, the white matter of the temporal lobes or the greater part of the medial dorsal nuclei, although it is difficult to be certain whether there was any overlap between the band of gliosis and the most medial region of the medial dorsal nucleus and other adjacent thalamic nuclei. In the other patient there was also a small zone of softening in the cerebellum and an increase in astrocytes in other regions of the cerebral hemispheres, including the basal ganglia, amygdala, and brain-stem, but without noticeable loss of cells. Both patients had had a relatively pure long-term memory impairment in the absence of other cognitive deficits and in the absence of a short-term memory impairment. Their retrograde amnesia for public events and famous faces had been measured and found to have extended backwards over at least twenty-five years. There was severe impairment in anterograde recognition memory for both verbal and non-verbal material. On a newly prepared memory quotient battery both patients had scored well below the bottom of the normal scale (less than 60, where 100 is the mean with a standard deviation of +/− 15). Both patients had also shown the characteristic differential improvement in retention when tested by cued recall and also the characteristic "prior learning effect," that is normal retention of one list of words when tested by cued recall but impaired retention of a second list sharing the same cues as the first list. There had been a slight but significant deterioration in intelligence in one patient in the two years prior to his death, although his IQ still fell within the normal range. The other patient remained undeteriorated until his death, and his IQ also was close to an estimated measure of his premorbid IQ.

(From Mair, Warrington, & Weiskrantz, 1979, with permission of *Brain*)

O'Connor, Verfaellie, and Cermak (1995) described a 49-year-old patient who developed amnesia associated with bilateral anterior thalamic infarcts after a cardiac catheterization procedure. Neuropsychological testing in the acute phase of the illness and three years later revealed essentially the same profile:

[His memory] deficits were more severe on verbal than nonverbal tasks. On list learning tasks, he demonstrated very slow learning across trials, with most of his performance accounted for by memory for the last item on the list. The presence of internal list structure and categorical cues did not improve his performance, suggesting impoverished encoding of the information. This was also evident on the Brown-Peterson Test: he was able to repeat three words perfectly when no interfering activity was imposed, but his performance declined rapidly when he was asked to count backwards for variable amounts of time. Of interest is the fact that C.W. also suffered a significant deficit in recognition memory for both verbal and nonverbal information. This suggests that his memory impairments are not due only to defective retrieval strategies, as is often seen in patients with frontal lobe lesions. . . . His general intelligence was in the low average range, with poorest performance on tests of general knowledge and abstract reasoning. This likely represents a decline from his premorbid level of functioning, which was estimated to be in the high average range. Language functioning, reading, spelling and perceptual abilities were intact. In contrast, attention span was impaired as was performance on tasks of cognitive flexibility.

Behavioral and personality changes were prominent in the acute phase and persisted during the next four years. In addition to his memory impairment for which the patient has only limited insight, he shows reduced motivation and initiative.

His family describes him as withdrawn and isolated at times, boisterous and socially inappropriate at other times. C.W. spends most of his time at home watching television, and even under the close supervision of his son, he has been unable to resume any work-related activities.

(From O'Connor, Verfaellie, & Cermak, 1995, with permission of the *Handbook for Memory Disorders*)

These case studies illustrate the severe anterograde and retrograde memory deficits that are associated with damage to the medial dorsal and anterior thalamic nuclei. Although there are some differences in the severity of the anterograde episodic memory deficits for verbal versus spatial information, both types of damage, the medial dorsal thalamic and mammillary body damage associated with Korsakoff syndrome and the relatively more circumscribed damage to the anterior thalamus reported by O'Connor, Verfaellie, & Cermak (1995), may lead to severe memory impairments for each type of material. The retrograde amnesia reported by Mair, Warrington, & Weiskrantz (1979), particularly for their second patient, was also severe, and appeared to encompass most if not all of the patient's episodic memory. Detailed testing of remote memory, however, was primarily limited to interviewing, which may not have revealed all of the patient's deficits or intact memories. Squire, Haist, & Shimamura (1989) have reported other patients with Korsakoff syndrome who had a graded memory loss for remote facts and events. Yet, given the problem in accurately assessing retrograde amnesia, establishing precisely the shape of its gradient is more often than not plainly impossible.

The Symptoms of Basal Forebrain Amnesia

Small, discrete lesions in the basal forebrain usually associated with rupture and/or repair of aneurysms of the anterior communicating artery are sufficient to cause anterograde and retrograde amnesia (Abe, Inokawa, Kashiwagi, & Yanagihara, 1998). This fact highlights the importance of connections between this region and the rest of the limbic system in sustaining the ability to form new and to retrieve old memories. Similar to reports of retrograde amnesia associated with diencephalic damage, the extent and nature of memory loss for events experienced before basal forebrain damage is variable but often pronounced (Bottger, Prosiegel, Steiger, & Yassouridis, 1998; Simard, Rouleau, Brosseau et al., 2003). There are reports of temporally graded memory loss similar to the impairment reported in Korsakoff syndrome, with greater deficits evident for more recent events in a person's life (Lindqvist & Norlen, 1966; Gade & Mortensen, 1990; Morris, Bowers, Chatterjee, & Heilman, 1992). Personality changes, including apathy and frequent confabulations, are common components of the clinical picture after the acute stage (DeLuca & Cicerone, 1991), which is typically characterized by confusion and disorientation. Amnesia associated with basal forebrain damage typically persists longer than the confabulations, which may be related to concomitant orbitofrontal damage (Baddeley & Wilson, 1986; Hashimoto, Tanka, & Nakano, 2000).

The following case report of amnesia after surgical repair of an anterior communicating artery aneurysm by Abe, Inokawa, Kashiwagi, & Yanagihara (1998) illustrates deficits that commonly occur following relatively restricted damage to the basal forebrain.

> A 61-year-old, right-handed high school teacher, who had taught science for more than 35 years and had had good memory function, experienced a sudden onset of weakness in the right upper and lower limbs in July 1993, but recovered the next day. He was admitted to a hospital and underwent MRI, which showed a small hemorrhage in the left external capsule. He underwent cerebral angiography, which showed an aneurysm 5 mm in diameter in the anterior communicating artery. He underwent surgical clipping of the aneurysm one month later. Immediately after the surgery, he developed disorientation and agitation. Although he became alert and oriented to person and place one month after the operation, he remained disoriented to date. He apparently had memory impairment at that time, but the details are not known to us. He had no motor or sensory deficits.

He visited the neurology outpatient service of the Osaka University Hospital four months after the operation. He was alert and did not have any focal neurological deficits. He did not seem to appreciate the graveness of his memory impairment. His language comprehension and expression were intact. He could repeat seven digits and perform serial subtraction without difficulty. He could learn five objects but he could recall only one of them after five minutes. During the interview, his recall was aided by cueing. Recall of his remote personal history was relatively preserved but the dates were mixed up, and he mistook recent personal episodes as remote ones. He did not have confabulation and remained silent when he could not answer a question. An EEG showed no abnormality.

A brain MRI performed 2 years later revealed a small discrete lesion in the basal forebrain slightly to the right of the midline, which appeared to encompass the diagonal band of Broca, the septal nucleus, the anterior hypothalamus, and the lamina terminalis. There was no evidence of other structural damage, but there were indications of reduced blood flow in the frontobasal area and the hippocampus, bilaterally. At the time of his first assessment:

his verbal IQ and nonverbal IQ fell within the normal range. The results of the Wisconsin Card Sorting Test, trail making test, word fluency, and go/no go task to measure frontal lobe function were normal. He obtained a verbal memory quotient of 69, whereas the non-verbal memory quotient was 104 on the Wechsler Memory Scale-Revised (WMS-R). He was able to repeat seven digits forward and five digits backward, indicating an intact attention span. Although he could learn four out of 10 easy paired associates, he could not learn any of the difficult word pairs. He was impaired on a word list learning task, recalling no more than nine out of 15 words. Although his recall of the word list dropped to zero after performing an interfering word list, he had recognition of 40 out of 50 words presented in a yes/no recognition paradigm. His recent non-verbal memory was relatively preserved. Immediate and delayed recall of the Benton visual retention test were moderately impaired. Memory for past public events . . . was within the normal range for the 1950s to the 1980s. He showed a limited period of retrograde amnesia for events before his operation. With the help of his family, a list for personal autobiographical memory was constructed with questions about significant personal events (for example, marriage, death, children's accomplishments). Although he could recall almost all events, he could not tag these events in sequence.

At a follow-up assessment 30 months later, the following was reported:

he showed mild improvement in memory performance, predominantly in non-verbal memory. Immediate and delayed recall of the Benton visual retention test fell within the normal range. Although his verbal memory quotient on the WMS-R increased from 69 to 82, it remained impaired compared with his non-verbal memory quotient of 108. He achieved normal maximal learning on a word list learning task, but he continued to show severely impaired delayed recall. On memory for past public events and personal autobiography, he could recall each event fairly well. However, he could not arrange these events in sequence and mistook the latest event from one having occurred years before.

(From Abe, Inokawa, Kashiwagi, & Yanagihara, 1998, with permission of the *Journal of Neurology, Neurosurgery, & Psychiatry*)

Taken together with previously described cases, this case demonstrates the variability in the nature of the amnesia that can result from basal forebrain lesions. Unlike other patients with basal forebrain damage, this patient did not show evidence of confabulation, his performance on primary memory or "executive" tasks was normal but he did show a profound episodic anterograde deficit. Although his memory for remote events was relatively intact, except for a limited period before his operation, he was unable to determine the accurate sequence of the remote episodes of his life.

PRECIPITATING FACTORS

There are many precipitating factors of damage to the limbic system. Epilepsy, hypoxia associated with cardiovascular arrest, stroke, viral infections such as encephalitis, and head trauma are the most common sources of damage to the medial temporal lobes. Diencephalic structures are usually damaged by stroke or tumors that develop around the walls of the third ventricle. Damage to the anterior and mediodorsal nuclei of the thalamus and the mammillary bodies is often caused by degenerative processes associated with thiamine deficiency in Korsakoff patients. Finally, ischemic damage caused by disruption of circulation in the anterior communicating artery is the most common cause of damage to basal forebrain structures. These most common precipitating factors of damage to the limbic system are each described in more detail below.

Epilepsy

The cumulative (lifetime) incidence of epilepsy in developed countries is estimated to be 3–4% (Hauser, Annegers, & Kurland, 1993), and in the United States, approximately 2000 patients undergo surgery for epilepsy every year (Engel, Wiebe, French et al., 2003). Analyses of large cohorts of children with febrile seizures indicate that epilepsy will develop in 2% to 10% of children who have febrile seizures (Annegers, Hauser, Shirts, & Kurland, 1987; Berg & Shinnar, 1996). Many of these children will develop temporal lobe epilepsy (TLE), which, regardless of age, is considered to be the most common epileptic syndrome.

In most TLE patients, the integrity of medial temporal structures is compromised, and evidence of necrosis is readily documented. Pathology is usually unilateral, but bilateral medial temporal lobe damage can be found in some cases. Numerous studies of adults with TLE have shown that hippocampal integrity has a significant impact on episodic anterograde and retrograde memory performance both pre- and postoperatively (Smith & Milner, 1981; McMillan, Powell, Janota, & Polkey, 1987; Oxbury & Oxbury, 1989; Smith & Milner, 1989; Saling, Berkovic, O'Shea et al., 1993; Helmstaedter, Grunwald, Lehnertz et al., 1997; Viskontas, McAndrews, & Moscovitch, 2000). Some investigations have found similar patterns of anterograde amnesia in pediatric TLE as in the adult population (Fedio & Mirsky, 1969; Jambaque, Dellatois, Dulac et al., 1993). Other studies of TLE in children have not shown material-specific patterns of memory deficits based on the side of the epileptogenic zone, as is typically found in adult TLE patients (Adams, Beardsworth, Oxbury et al., 1990; Akos Szabo, Wyllie, Stanford et al., 1998; Mabbott & Smith, 2003).

Cerebral Hypoxia and Hypoperfusion

Medial temporal lobe structures are particularly vulnerable to a sudden reduction in cerebral perfusion and oxygenation, which typically take place during cardiac and respiratory arrest. Figure 6–1 shows hippocampal atrophy in a 15-year-old female who experienced perinatal anoxia. One patient with severe anterograde amnesia who had experienced episodes of hypoxia and cardiorespiratory arrest was found at autopsy to have sustained pronounced loss of pyramidal cells restricted to the CA1 region of the hippocampus bilaterally (Zola-Morgan, Squire, & Amaral, 1986). Hypoxia leading to amnesia can also be a consequence of carbon monoxide poisoning, as well as hanging attempts (Kopelman, 2002a).

Regional, as opposed to global, hypoperfusion can occur during surgical repair of aneurysms. The functional integrity of basal forebrain structures is particularly vulnerable to local ischemia associated with the clipping of aneurysms in the anterior communicating artery. In some cases, basal forebrain damage takes place before surgery if the aneurysm ruptures. In addition to basal forebrain structures, orbitofrontal cortex may also sustain damage in such cases. With improvement in surgical techniques, the severity and extent of symptoms after surgery for aneurysm repair have been significantly reduced.

Viral Infections

Viral infections such as encephalitis and meningitis can affect the limbic system. Neuroradiological investigations of amnesia associated with meningitis have revealed damage to medial temporal lobe structures and the mammillary bodies

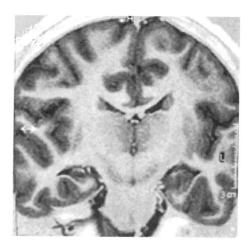

Figure 6–1 A coronal slice of an MRI showing right hippocampal atrophy in a 15-year-old female who experienced perinatal anoxia. Note: The right hemisphere is shown on the left side of the image. (Courtesy of Sokratis G. Papageorgiou)

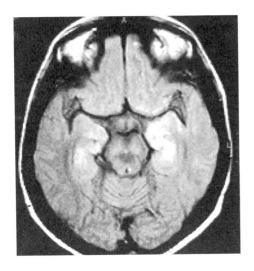

Figure 6–2 An axial slice of an MRI of the brain of a 42-year-old woman showing high signal intensity bilaterally in medial temporal cortex, including the hippocampus. (Courtesy of Sokratis G. Papageorgiou)

(Ceccaldi, Belleville, Royere, & Poncet, 1995), and permanent as well as transient episodic anterograde amnesias have been reported in cases of meningitis (Wilson & Baddeley, 1988; Ceccaldi, Belleville, Royere, & Poncet, 1995).

Medial temporal lobe damage is also a common consequence of herpes simplex encephalitis. Figure 6–2 shows an MRI of the brain of a 42-year-old woman who was diagnosed with the disease, presenting initially with headache, fever, nausea, seizures, and confusion. Despite the administration of antiviral agents that help control the course of the disease, the virus can cause inflammation and necrosis in inferior temporal and orbitofrontal regions. Severe signal alteration can be observed in the temporal lobes on MRI (Kopelman, 2002a). In some cases, the damage may be restricted to one hemisphere, but most commonly both hemispheres are involved. Structures affected include the hippocampus, the parahippocampal gyrus, the perirhinal cortex, the amygdala, and the temporal pole neocortex. Basal forebrain structures may also be affected in encephalitis, which may further exacerbate the severity of the amnesia (Kopelman, 2002a). Given the extensive nature of damage typically associated with herpes encephalitis, determining the site of damage responsible for a given memory deficit is often impossible.

Stroke

Ischemic infarcts and, less commonly, hemorrhagic strokes can each lead to an abrupt onset of amnesia if any of the three main sectors of the limbic system is damaged. Strokes involving the posterior cerebral artery can affect the posterior aspect of the hippocampus and the nearby medial temporal structures. Damage to the dorsomedial nucleus of the thalamus is typically associated with paramedian artery strokes, whereas damage to the anterior nucleus and the mammillothalamic tract can be caused by disruption of blood supply in the territory of the polar artery (Freitas & Bogousslavsky, 2002). Even small infarctions in the thalamus can result in severe, permanent deficits in anterograde episodic memory, but variable recovery patterns have been observed (Bauer, Grande, & Valenstein, 2003). As noted above, vascular insufficiency caused by rupture of aneurysms in the anterior communicating artery is one of the most common mechanisms of damage to the basal forebrain.

Traumatic Brain Injury

Medial temporal structures are also particularly vulnerable to head injury. The duration of amnesia after head injury correlates with the severity of the injury, typically defined by the period of unconsciousness assessed with the Glasgow Coma Scale (Levin, 1989). A detailed description of the memory and other neuropsychological deficits that are common after traumatic brain injury are provided in Chapter 7 and will therefore not be repeated here. However, head injury is noted here as a common precipitating factor for damage to the limbic system that can result in anterograde and retrograde memory deficits.

Thiamine Deficiency

Chronic alcohol abuse is the most common cause of severe thiamine (B1 vitamin) deficiency, the other being long-term parenteral nutrition. Thiamine deficiency is directly linked to widespread necrosis in the brain, which is particularly pronounced in the mediodorsal and anterior nuclei of the thalamus and the mammillary bodies. These and other lesions in the brain stem are characteristic of Wernicke encephalopathy, which presents with a constellation of focal neurological symptoms (Torvik, 1987). For reasons that are largely unknown, only some individuals with Wernicke encephalopathy develop amnesia (Korsakoff syndrome).

Other Causes

Structural damage to the medial temporal and other limbic structures can be caused by various types of tumors, which may or may not be associated with seizures. Tumors may impinge on the limbic structures critical for memory, affecting their function, sometimes temporarily (provided that surgical treatment occurs prior to onset of permanent structural damage), or they may infiltrate these structures and cause irreversible damage.

Other causes of limbic amnesia include autoimmune responses, such as those to systemic lupus erythematosus (SLE). Patients with SLE have been identified with isolated hippocampal damage and severe amnesia (Schnider, Bassetti, Schnider et al., 1995), but more widespread damage to the brain, associated with a host of neuropsychological problems, is more commonly reported (Skeel, Johnstone, Yangco, et al., 2000; Monastero, Bettini, Del Zotto et al., 2001; Leritz, Brandt, & Minor, 2002). Patients in whom the presence of antiphospholipid antibodies is detected may have more severe learning and memory problems, in addition to attention and visual-spatial processing deficits (Leritz, Brandt, & Minor, 2002).

DIFFERENTIAL DIAGNOSIS

Dementia versus Limbic Amnesia

Memory deficits associated with some forms of dementia present similarly to those that are associated with damage limited to the different sections of the limbic system. Differential diagnosis relies on at least three factors: imaging findings, the onset and course of the memory problems, and the existence of additional neuropsychological impairments.

Medial temporal lobe and diencephalic amnesias are typically accompanied by focal lesions that are visible on MRI. Progressive dementias, on the other hand, are not accompanied by focal lesions. However, in some cases of medial temporal lobe amnesia, structural lesions may be difficult to find, particularly when the damage is restricted to a small portion of the hippocampus or its surrounding cortex. Moreover, as reported by Markowitsch, Weber-Luxemburger, Ewald et al. (1997), pathology may not be evident on structural scans of the brain but only discernible by metabolic or perfusion imaging methods.

Memory problems have abrupt onset when damage is caused by viral infections (e.g., encephalitis), surgery, head trauma, or a cardiovascular event. Those associated with a progressive dementia, on the other hand, have a much more gradual and insidious onset. Typically, memory problems worsen over time in various types of dementia (see Chapter 4). In Alzheimer disease (AD), for example, patients often present with mild cognitive impairment (MCI), in which they demonstrate a memory deficit in the absence of other cognitive or functional impairment (Petersen, Smith, Waring et al., 1999; see Chapters 3 and 4) and later progress to severe impairment of memory and at least one other cognitive deficit (see Chapter 4). In addition, the onset of AD disease typically occurs between the ages of 40 and 90 years, whereas limbic amnesia may appear at any age.

It should be noted that progressive deterioration of memory may also occur after repeated (e.g., multiple consecutive) infarcts or chronic insults to medial temporal lobe structures like those caused by epileptic seizures or slow-growing tumors. Therefore, a critical aspect of differential diagnosis involves the existence of other deficits, such as expressive or receptive language deficits, apraxia, or executive function impairments, which suggest pathology beyond the limbic regions (see also sections on differential diagnosis of medial temporal versus diencephalic or basal forebrain damage, below).

In another common form of dementia (dementia with Lewy bodies), memory disturbances are not prevalent in the clinical presentation. Although this feature contrasts this form of dementia with medial temporal lobe amnesia, the presence of deficits in primary memory or "executive" functions presents obvious similarities with diencephalic and basal forebrain amnesias. The relative preservation of the ability to form and retrieve new memories clearly differentiates frontotemporal dementia from limbic amnesia. On the other hand, the clinical presentation and memory deficits in a form of subcortical dementia, progressive supranuclear palsy, share many features with the constellation of deficits after diencephalic damage (oculomotor deficits, apathy, abulia, "executive" function deficits, and anterograde amnesia).

Transient Global Amnesia versus Limbic Amnesia

As discussed in Chapter 8, transient global amnesia (TGA) has a sudden onset that resolves within a few hours and leaves behind a permanent memory gap for the events that transpired during the episode. Subtle memory and other cognitive deficits may persist months after the TGA episode, but these are far less severe than the amnesia that characterizes the episode itself. In contrast, amnesia resulting from limbic lesions tends to affect most aspects of a person's daily life over long periods of time.

Transient Epileptic Amnesia versus Limbic Amnesia

Like TGA, a distinguishing feature of transient epileptic amnesia (TEA) is its transience. TEA is characterized by a failure to incorporate events that occur during a nonconvulsive seizure into long-term memory (see Chapter 9). During the ictal phase of the seizure, the patient's cognitive functioning appears to be intact. Patients continue to engage in ongoing activity without interruption (Palmini, Gloor, & Jones-Gotman, 1992; Kapur, 1993), and the only behavioral indication of the ictal episode is the patient's subsequent report of amnesia regarding the preceding events. This clinical presentation differs markedly from limbic amnesia, which is most often permanent and affects most aspects of the patient's everyday life.

Diencephalic versus Medial Temporal Lobe Amnesia

By definition, the two types of amnesia are associated with distinct pathophysiology, and differential diagnosis can be based primarily on structural imaging findings. The most common precipitating factors are also largely different (e.g., degenerative processes are the pathophysiological substrate in diencephalic amnesia in Korsakoff syndrome, and epilepsy, hypoxia, and viral infections are among the most common conditions causing medial temporal lobe damage). Vascular diencephalic lesions are typically associated with focal neurological signs. For example, vertical gaze palsy (difficulty in moving the eyes upward and downward) is often seen after paramedian artery infarcts, and mild transient hemiparesis or hemianesthesia may accompany the memory disturbances associated with polar artery infarcts. Focal neurological signs are not typically present after selective insults to medial temporal structures.

In general, memory deficits resulting from damage to the diencephalon may appear very similar to deficits associated with medial temporal damage. Both types of damage can result in anterograde and retrograde impairments, although medial temporal lobe damage is more often associated with retrograde amnesia than diencephalic damage. Some studies examining the rate of forgetting of information over time, which involves episodic memory testing at multiple time points after a single study session, have shown that amnesics with medial temporal damage tend to demonstrate a more rapid forgetting rate than diencephalic amnesics (Huppert & Piercy, 1979; Squire, 1981; Martone, Butters, & Trauner, 1986). Subsequent studies, however, have failed to replicate these findings (Freed, Corkin, & Cohen, 1987; McKee & Squire, 1992).

Impaired performance on tasks requiring primary memory or executive functions, and difficulty appreciating the temporal order of external events, are usually found among patients with diencephalic amnesia and are much less common after medial temporal lobe damage (Meudell, Mayes, Ostergaard, & Pickering, 1985; Squire, 1992b; Bauer, Grande, & Valenstein, 2003). Executive function deficits are often attributed to concomitant damage to the frontal lobes in Korsakoff patients (Brokate, Hildebrandt, Eling et al., 2003), but they may be present after vascular lesions of the thalamus without apparent frontal pathology (Van der Werf, Jolles, Witter, & Uylings, 2003). Performance on "memory span" tests of primary memory function tends to be lower in patients with diencephalic amnesia (Mayes, Daum, Markowisch, & Sauter, 1997). In addition, source memory, or remembering the spatial and temporal context in which information was encountered, may be more impaired in diencephalic than medial temporal amnesics (Shimamura & Squire, 1987; Bauer, Grande, & Valenstein, 2003). Complex confabulations, which consist of errors of commission and not simple omissions of facts and details, have been reported in patients with diencephalic damage, but such symptoms are generally absent in patients with damage restricted to medial temporal lobe structures.

Basal Forebrain versus Diencephalic Amnesia

Differences in clinical presentation between patients with basal forebrain and diencephalic lesions, whether in terms of omission errors, confabulation, or impairments in "executive" functions (such as impaired planning ability, perseveration, and impulsivity) (Damasio, Graff-Radford, Eslinger, et al. 1985; Bottger, Prosiegel, Steiger, & Yassouridis, 1998), are practically impossible to detect. Like diencephalic damage, basal forebrain damage results in impairments for memory of temporal order (Damasio et al., 1985). But less like diencephalic lesions, basal forebrain lesions result in variable performance on memory tests from one instance to the next (Bauer et al., 2003) and occasionally in apathy and lack of concern for the amnesia (Phillips, Sangalang, & Sterns, 1987; Bauer et al., 2003).

Basal Forebrain versus Medial Temporal Amnesia

Basal forebrain damage is associated with a distinct clinical picture in the postacute phase of the illness, which includes personality changes, frequent confabulations, deficits in planning and decision making ability, impulsivity, and other likely signs of associated frontal lobe (primarily orbitofrontal) damage. This pattern of behavioral changes is not common in patients with medial temporal lobe damage. Deficits in primary memory or executive functions are especially common in patients with basal forebrain amnesia, (Diamond, DeLuca, Kim, & Kelley, 1997; Mavaddat, Kirkpatrick, Rogers, & Sahakian, 2000; Simard, Rouleau, Brosseau et al., 2003). Preservation of recognition ability relative to recall ability is often reported in basal forebrain amnesia (Damasio et al., 1985; Beeckmans, Vancoillie, & Michiels, 1998; Bottger et al., 1998; Simard, Rouleau, Brosseau et al., 2003) but is rarer after medial temporal lobe damage.

PATHOPHYSIOLOGY

Medial Temporal Lobe Amnesia

The precise location of damage of the medial aspect of the temporal lobes causing amnesia has been researched vigorously at least since publication of the report on patient H.M. by Scoville and Milner (1957). H.M. developed severe amnesia after bilateral surgical removal of his medial temporal lobes, which included the hippocampi, amygdala, and adjacent cortices. Until relatively recently, it was thought that the amygdala may play a role similar to that of the hippocampus and that damage to the amygdala may simply increase the impairment of explicit memory (Zola-Morgan & Squire, 1993). The amygdala is necessary for learning biologically significant and emotionally charged stimulus- reward contingencies, which is a function distinct from that of memory subserved by the hippocampus and other medial temporal structures. Individuals with bilateral or unilateral damage to the amygdala experience deficits in the perception of emotion-related stimuli that influence memory performance, but without concomitant hippocampal or other limbic damage, they do not have symptoms characteristic of limbic amnesia (Meletti, Benuzzi, Nichelli, & Tassinaria, 2003; Brierley, Medford, Shaw, & David, 2004; but also see Richter-Levin, 2004).

Even restricted hippocampal damage can produce a severe anterograde episodic memory impairment (e.g., Squire & Zola, 1996). However, the size or extent of hippocampal lesions does not consistently correlate with the severity of episodic memory impairment (Spiers, Maguire, & Burgess, 2001), and though unilateral left hippocampal damage most often leads to verbal and unilateral right hippocampal damage to nonverbal deficits, there are exceptions to this pattern (Spiers, Maguire, & Burgess, 2001). Restricted damage to the hippocampus incurred early in life may not impair the ability to acquire semantic memories (Butters, Glisky, & Schacter, 1993; Vargha-Khadem, Gadian, Watkins et al., 1997), but when the damage extends beyond the hippocampus proper to adjacent structures, a more severe impairment usually results that includes semantic amnesia (Westmacott & Moscovitch, 2001).

Extensive, bilateral damage restricted to the hippocampus is sufficient to cause retrograde episodic amnesia (Rempel-Clower, Zola, Squire, & Amaral, 1996), affecting both the ability for intentional retrieval of verbal and nonverbal material and the ability to judge whether a particular stimulus has been recently experienced (Manns, Hopkins, & Squire, 2003). The latter symptom is usually associated with prefrontal lesions (e.g., Petrides, 2000). Often, but not consistently, the medial temporal retrograde amnesia has the shape of the gradient described by Ribot's law (Ribot, 1882). These results notwithstanding, assessment of the precise role of hippocampus in memory is complicated, as we noted earlier, by the difficulties assessing retrograde amnesia (Warrington, 1996; Kapur, Thompson, Kartsounis, & Abbott, 1999; see "Clinical Testing" section).

Diencephalic Amnesia

There is ongoing debate regarding the precise role of the different diencephalic structures in memory. Although vascular lesions can be fairly discrete, the pattern of neuronal loss associated with Korsakoff syndrome is both complex and variable across patients. Patients with this syndrome show atrophy in the thalamus and mammillary bodies but also in the amygdala, the hippocampus, the white matter, the cerebellum, and the frontal lobes (Krill, Halliday, Svoboda, & Cartwright, 1997). The problem is further complicated by the following observations: First, chronic alcoholics who develop Wernicke encephalopathy without amnesia share many of the neuropathological abnormalities that characterize amnesic patients with Korsakoff syndrome (e.g., Davilla, Shear, Lane et al., 1994; Krill et al., 1997; Jauhar & Montaldi, 2000). Second, reductions in resting metabolic rate are often more extensive than neuropathological changes in Korsakoff patients (Aupee, Desgranges, Eustache et al., 2001; Reed, Lasserson, Marsden, et al., 2003). Third, the anterior and mediodorsal nuclei of the thalamus and the mammillary bodies are very closely connected to other structures known to be involved in memory functions, namely the frontal lobes and the hippocampus. Therefore, even selective damage to these diencephalic structures could impair memory by disrupting these larger circuits.

The results of recent studies of patients with thalamic stroke and of patients with Korsakoff syndrome that controlled for the effects of chronic alcohol abuse can be summarized as follows. First, medial temporal atrophy was not always present in Korsakoff patients (Squire, Amaral, & Press, 1990). When atrophy was present, the degree of volume reduction was not significantly different in chronic alcoholics with and without amnesia (Harding, Wong, Svoboda et al., 1997). Second, severe amnesia was not always present after isolated damage to the dorsomedial nucleus (Hodges & McCarthy, 1993) or the mammillary bodies (Hildebrandt, Muller, Bussmann-Mork et al., 2001). Third, the degree of atrophy of the dorsomedial nucleus and the mammillary bodies was not found to be significantly different between patients with Korsakoff and nonamnesic chronic alcoholics (Harding, Halliday, Caine, & Kril, 2000). In contrast, the degree of neuronal loss in the anterior nucleus of the thalamus was found to be significantly greater in the former compared with the latter group of patients.

The literature on the effects of restricted vascular damage to the mediodorsal nucleus on memory function is very limited. In most cases, concomitant damage to the anterior nucleus of the thalamus and/or medial temporal structures was present (see for instance, Cases 10, 13, 14, and 20 in Van der Werf, Jolles, Witter, & Uylings, 2003). In other reports, isolated mediodorsal thalamic infarcts (associated with paramedian artery stroke) were found to be associated with only mild memory deficits (von Cramon, Hebel, & Schur, 1985; Shuren, Jacobs, & Heilman, 1997). Mediodorsal lesions appear more closely linked to some of the associated acute symptoms of the diencephalic amnesia, namely, confusion, impaired attention, and somnolence (Donnal, Heinz, & Burger, 1990). In contrast, restricted damage to the anterior nuclei of the thalamus or the bundle that connects each nucleus with the ipsilateral mammillary body (the mammillothalamic tract) generally cause more selective memory deficits (Winocur, Oxbury, Roberts et al., 1984; von Cramon et al., 1985; Malamut, Graff-Radford, Chawluk et al., 1992; Van der Werf et al., 2003).

The pathophysiology of amnesia resulting from damage to the thalamus may depend, at least in part, on the connections between the thalamic nuclei and the medial temporal lobe (Aggleton & Sahgal, 1993; cited by Bauer et al., 2003). Thus, a disruption of fibers connecting the thalamus to the medial temporal lobe and to other limbic structures may contribute more than a single, focal lesion to the onset of amnesia. Disruption of connections between the mediodorsal and anterior nuclei of the thalamus with the frontal lobes may also contribute to the clinical picture of patients with diencephalic damage; at least one of the symptoms, confabulation, appears to be closely linked to frontal dysfunction (Benson, Djenderedjian, Miller et al., 1996).

Basal Forebrain Amnesia

The mechanism for the disturbance of memory that results from basal forebrain lesions appears to be related to the disruption of cholinergic transmission to other parts of the limbic system that are critical for memory retrieval (see Chapter 2). The basal forebrain consists of a number of different anatomic components, including the septal nuclei, the diagonal band of Broca, and the nucleus basalis of Meynert. Most cases of basal forebrain amnesia are accompanied by lesions that encompass more structures than those that comprise this region. Damage to ventral and medial aspects of the frontal lobes is especially common. Therefore, drawing conclusions about the precise pathophysiology of the amnesia in individual cases is difficult.

Connections between the basal forebrain nuclei and the medial temporal lobe also appear to be critical for the preservation of episodic memories. Cholinergic projections of the basal forebrain nuclei, in particular, are important for an intact memory function. Cholinergic neurons in the basal nucleus of Meynert of the basal forebrain project widely to other limbic structures and to the neocortex, while neurons in the medial septal nucleus and the diagonal band of Broca in the basal forebrain project directly to the hippocampus (Lewis & Shute, 1967; Mesulam, Mufson, Levey, & Wainer, 1983; summarized by Bauer et al., 2003). The important role of cholinergic projections in amnesic syndromes associated with damage to the basal forebrain is supported by reports of a selective loss of basal forebrain cholinergic neurons in patients with Korsakoff syndrome

(Butters, 1985; Butters & Stuss, 1989) and neuronal loss specifically in the basal nucleus of Meynert in individuals with Alzheimer disease (Whitehouse, Price, Clark, et al., 1981). There is some evidence that other neurotransmitters, like dopamine, may be associated with basal forebrain amnesia (Bauer et al., 2003; see also Chapter 2). As described in Chapter 2, it is also important to note the role of the fornix in amnesia. Lesions of the fornix, posterior to the anterior commissure, may disrupt fibers between the hippocampus and basal forebrain structures and can result in memory deficits (Aggleton, Desimone, & Mishkin, 1986; Gaffan & Parker, 1996; Aggleton, McMackin, Carpenter et al., 2000).

PROGNOSIS AND TREATMENT

Most forms of damage to the limbic system that cause amnesia are permanent. Studies of patients with intractable temporal lobe epilepsy who underwent surgery have shown that individuals who have better explicit memory performance and functional hippocampi prior to resection are at greater risk for anterograde episodic memory loss after standard anterior temporal lobectomy than those who demonstrate poorer episodic memory skills on standardized tests before resection (Chelune, Naugle, Luders, & Awad, 1991; Loring, Lee, Meador et al., 1991; Hermann, Wyler, Somes et al., 1992; Sperling, Saykin, Glosser et al., 1994). Surgical outcome after temporal lobectomy is less predictable for children than adults with TLE. Neither Lendt, Helmstaedter, and Elger (1999) nor Mabbott and Smith (2003) found verbal or figural memory deficits pre- or postoperatively in left or right TLE groups, but Adams, Beadsworth, Oxbury et al. (1990) found that, before surgery, children with left or right TLE were likely to show both verbal and nonverbal memory deficits. The presence of mesial temporal sclerosis may be a key factor in memory performance before and after surgical resection of the temporal lobe in childhood (Adams et al., 1990; Lendt, Helmstaedter, & Elger, 1999; Mabbott & Smith, 2003). Moreover, the status of anterograde episodic memory function pre- and postresection of the dominant temporal lobe appears to depend on the extent of the epileptogenic zone and the period of time in development in which seizures began (Seidenberg, Hermann, Schoenfeld et al., 1997). The onset of seizure activity early in life may not be as deleterious to memory if the seizures arise from a circumscribed zone and structures outside that zone have a capacity to support that function (Seidenberg et al., 1997).

A variety of techniques has been used to rehabilitate individuals with limbic amnesia. Compensatory approaches to rehabilitation consist of encouraging and training amnesic patients to use strategies to remember daily events and tasks, such as writing notes and using other assistive devices as memory aids. Pagers, personal electronic devices, timers, and personal computers are all aids that can be used to help amnesic patients remember to perform daily tasks (Wilson, Evans, Emslie, & Malinek, 1997; Wilson, Emslie, Quirk, & Evans, 2001).

Another approach to the rehabilitation of patients with limbic amnesia has been to use the patient's intact memory skills to aid explicit memory. Glisky and her colleagues examined whether intact implicit memory abilities can be used to enhance patients' performance on specific kinds of tasks. They showed that amnesic patients with damage to limbic structures were able to learn new material through procedural skill learning procedures and through the method of "vanishing cues," where the individual is provided less and less contextual information for rehearsing material to be learned over subsequent trials (Glisky, Schacter, & Tulving, 1986a, 1986b; Glisky & Schacter, 1988, 1989). With the latter method, amnesic patients without previous computer experience were taught to use computers for domain-specific tasks (Glisky et al., 1986a) and, as noted earlier, amnesics with hippocampal damage were taught new vocabulary related to a single theme (Butters, Glisky, & Schacter, 1993), demonstrating a preserved ability of these patients to acquire semantic knowledge.

Rehabilitative approaches that aim to improve explicit memory performance itself have proven to be effective in some individual amnesic patients (Wilson, 1998), but therapeutic efficacy for groups of patients with limbic amnesia has not been established. Many such restorative approaches have employed explicit rehearsal and repetition as a means of improving memory performance, and others have attempted to teach organizational and imagery strategies (Crovitz, Harvey, & Horn, 1979; Gianutsos & Gianutsos, 1979; summarized by Bauer et al., 2003). Other methods have focused on improving attentional skills as a way to facilitate better encoding of information (Sohlberg & Mateer, 1989).

Evidence suggestive of a relation between a selective loss of cholinergic neurons in the basal forebrain and anterograde amnesia led to the prescription of cholinergic enhancing agents for patients with Alzheimer disease (see also Chapter 4), resulting in moderate success in improving explicit memory in the early stages of the disease (Seltzer, Zolnouni, Nunez et al., 2004; see also Chapter 2). The efficacy of these agents in nondemented patients with limbic amnesia, however, has not been established. Nonetheless, there is some evidence that a combined approach involving agents that promote cholinergic transmission in conjunction with cognitive rehabilitation is particularly effective (León-Carrión, Dominguez-Roldan, Murillo-Cabezas et al., 2000). In agreement with the notion that dopamine transmission may be implicated in amnesia after basal forebrain damage, a selective dopamine agonist was found to improve memory in an amnesic patient with damage to the basal forebrain and caudate nucleus (Dobkin & Hanlon, 1993). Due to the scarcity of patients with selective damage to the basal forebrain, however, no large-scale drug studies have been reported.

SUMMARY OF FACTS AND DISCUSSION

The main feature of limbic amnesia is an anterograde episodic memory impairment, affecting both public and personal events encountered after the onset of the illness. These deficits tend to be modality-dependent when the damage to the medial temporal lobe and diencephalic structures is unilateral. Verbal memory tends to be more greatly affected by left-sided damage, whereas nonverbal memory for spatial position and faces tends to be more greatly affected by right-sided damage. The ability to learn new factual information, independent of its context, may be preserved after diencephalic damage and restricted medial temporal lobe damage (it is not known if this is the case for basal forebrain lesions as well).

The ability to retrieve information about personal and public events encountered prior to the onset of the disease may also be impaired in a much more consistent fashion after medial temporal damage than damage to the diencephalon or basal forebrain region. Typically, both effortful recall and recognition are impaired, although the latter is more likely to be preserved, to some extent, in diencephalic and basal forebrain amnesia. The ability to form and retrieve stored implicit memories generally remains intact.

Retrograde episodic and semantic amnesia often involve a temporal gradient in which recent memories of events are more affected than distant memories. Typically, the period prior to the onset of the disease for which the ability to retrieve memories of encountered events and facts is most affected extends for 10–20 years, although patients with either "steeper" or "flatter" temporal gradients have been described. It is unknown to what extent differences reported between patients with similar damage to limbic regions are due to the nature of the neuropsychological testing or lack thereof (Kapur, Thompson, Kartsounis, & Abbott, 1999), to individual differences in the brain mechanisms of these functions, or subtle differences in sites of brain damage.

The symptoms of limbic amnesia suggest impairments of primary and secondary memory functions, as those were defined in Chapter 1. Within primary memory, automatic retrieval, particularly recognition, and effortful retrieval, in the form of cued and free-recall, are impaired in limbic amnesia. In contrast, operations within primary memory that are not affected in limbic amnesia are encoding, holding in awareness (short-term memory), and rehearsal operations. The working memory function, on the other hand, is likely to be compromised by diencephalic and basal forebrain lesions. Within secondary memory or memory proper, consolidation of episodes appears to be consistently impaired, and storage of remote memories is often, but inconsistently, impaired. Confabulations characteristic of the early stages of basal forebrain amnesia and of diencephalic amnesia associated with Korsakoff syndrome may be construed as evidence for either transformation of stored traces or for faltering retrieval operations.

The available data on limbic amnesia have led to hypotheses about the nature of the neuronal mechanisms of memory. Long-term memory consolidation has been described as a process whereby memory traces are formed by the medial temporal lobe, after encoding become independent from it (Scoville & Milner, 1957; Squire, 1992b; Squire & Alvarez, 1995). According to this standard model of memory consolidation, the medial temporal lobe must be intact for the initial binding of information into a memory trace, but over time its role in sustaining the memory trace diminishes (Squire, 1992b). Most of the evidence for this view has come from reports of temporally graded retrograde amnesia. As described above, many patients with limbic damage have been reported to remember events from several years in the past but not those that occurred shortly before the onset of the lesion. The standard model posits, therefore, that over time, retrieval of episodic memories becomes independent of the hippocampus and solely dependent on neocortical association areas (Squire, 1992b).

According to a second proposal, known as "The Multiple Trace Theory" (Nadel & Moscovitch, 1997; Fujii, Moscovitch, & Nadel, 2000) retrieval of episodic memories is always dependent on the hippocampal system, defined by Nadel and Moscovitch (1997) as the CA fields, the dentate gyrus, the subiculum, and the entorhinal, perirhinal, and parahippocampal cortices. They suggested that temporal gradients of retrograde amnesia reported in human and animal investigations indicate not that the hippocampus becomes less essential to retrieval over time, but that there are more numerous neuronal "traces" of older memories in the hippocampus and in neocortex.

The multiple trace theory is at odds with the standard model of consolidation because it posits both that the hippocampus may be necessary for the retrieval of episodic information throughout life and that semantic and episodic memories are maintained separately in the brain over long time periods. Evidence for the independence of episodic and semantic memory traces (e.g., Warrington & McCarthy, 1988; Hodges, Patterson, Oxbury, and Funnell, 1992) appears to favor the multiple trace theory. However, the paucity of solid evidence regarding the shape of the retrograde amnesia gradient for episodes and for facts and concepts—on which we have commented frequently—is one of the factors that force us to defer judgment regarding the relative worth of either set of conjectures until the requisite facts become available or additional predictions unique to each proposal are clearly articulated and empirically evaluated.

7

Traumatic Amnesia

MARY H. KOSMIDIS, AIKATERINI GIAZKOULIDOU,
VASILIS P. BOZIKAS, AND ANDREW. C. PAPANICOLAOU

Any impact of sufficient magnitude to result in even momentary alteration in consciousness constitutes a traumatic brain injury (TBI). A blunt injury with no penetration of the skull is considered a closed head injury. Due to the nature of the mechanical forces involved in a closed head injury, the associated pattern of cognitive deficits is distinct from that observed in penetrating head injuries. Closed head injuries generally result in pervasive and diffuse deficits in addition to any focal impairment. In contrast, penetrating injuries (e.g., from a gunshot wound) may or may not lead to alteration or impairment of consciousness, depending on the severity and the location of the trauma. In this chapter, we will primarily discuss the impact of closed head injuries, as these are both more prevalent and more likely to affect memory.

Although TBI may lead to a broad range of cognitive deficits depending on the nature of the impact, the type of injury, and its severity, it is typically associated with a particular pattern of cognitive dysfunction. In the acute stage, this pattern is different from the long-term profile characteristic of survivors of TBI. Despite spontaneous recovery and improvement secondary to cognitive rehabilitation interventions, most survivors of a moderate to severe TBI will continue to experience cognitive problems in the long term.

The cognitive deficits observed in survivors of TBI can be grouped into four stages based on when they occurred in relation to the injury. The first stage consists of a period of alteration of consciousness or coma, which may occur upon, or soon after, impact. The second phase is characterized by a combination of cognitive and behavioral abnormalities, agitated psychomotor activity, an inability to recall or sequence events and/or acquire new information. These two phases, lasting several days, involve a form of posttraumatic delirium. They are followed by a 6- to

12-month period of rapid recovery of cognitive functioning, with stabilization of recovery over the next year. The fourth phase is characterized by permanent deficits in a variety of cognitive functions (e.g., speed of information processing, attention and vigilance, memory and new learning, verbal skills, executive functions, self-regulation of mood and emotional reactions, and awareness of one's limitations.

Memory is commonly the last cognitive function to show improvement after an acute trauma (Conkey, 1938), and patients often exhibit the features of an amnesic syndrome (Baddeley, Harris, Sunderland et al., 1987; Levin, Williams, Crofford et al., 1988). Some survivors experience a period of posttraumatic amnesia (PTA), with or without retrograde amnesia. Disproportionate retrograde amnesia has been described (see below), particularly in association with damage to the frontal or anterior temporal regions, and is usually associated with antero-grade amnesia: Forgetfulness is a common complaint even after a mild concussion (Lishman, 1988; Fleminger, 2000). Although recovery from mild head injury is expected to occur soon (within 1 to 3 months) after injury, some patients present with symptoms far beyond this time interval (Barth, Diamond, & Errico, 1996). Such cases of enduring disability may reflect, in part, unique characteristics of particular patients. In some cases, complaints may persist long after the settlement of any compensation issues (Merskey & Woodforde, 1972; Miller, 1979; Tarsh & Royston, 1985; Kopelman, 2002a), suggesting that they do not merely reflect litigation status.

Residual memory deficits are among the most common and debilitating consequences of head injury and may compromise an individual's daily routine (Wilson, 1994a; Wills, Clare, Shiel, & Wilson, 2000). Frequently, however, the assessment of memory impairment has proved challenging, as subjective memory complaints are often not commensurate with the results of objective memory tests (Kinsella, Murtagh, Landry et al., 1996). Conflicting findings in the literature may reflect the difference between the types of memory typically assessed in a research protocol or clinical evaluation and those related to everyday functioning. In addition to problems with attention, encoding, new learning, and prospective memory, many survivors of a TBI present with retrograde amnesia for personal events, which result in a feeling of "loss of self." In all cases, both diffuse and focal damage to the frontal system contribute to the memory impairment observed, as does damage to temporal lobe structures (Figure 7-1).

TESTING: ESTABLISHMENT OF THE SYMPTOMS

The cases described below are representative of the variety of memory problems observed in people with a TBI. Most often these involve primary memory difficulties, notably attentional, but are not confined to those. Although some survivors of moderate to severe TBI do not complain of retrograde amnesia for either public or autobiographical episodes and facts, those who do often show a reverse temporal gradient (with older memories more vulnerable) and may or may not have concurrent anterograde amnesia.

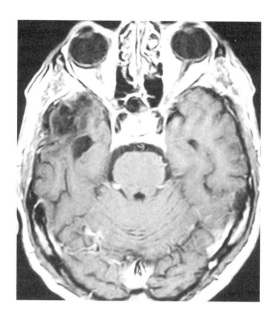

Figure 7–1 Magnetic resonance image of a 67-year-old man with contusions on the right frontal and temporal lobes due to a closed head injury. (Courtesy of Sokratis G. Papageorgiou)

Case 1

A 34-year-old physician had been in a head-on collision with a truck 6 years prior to the current evaluation, resulting in a severe TBI. Her injuries were in the left hemisphere including the cerebellum, and she was in a coma for 2 months. Her most recent magnetic resonance imaging (MRI) findings indicated "foci with an abnormal sign in the cerebral hemispheres, at the brain-stem formation and cerebellum, and normal ventricles. Disruption of the skull over the right frontal area, perhaps due to cranioplasty." A Doppler exam showed no significant disruption of blood flow. She reported a posttraumatic amnesia of about 6 months duration, which resulted in lost memories for events up to 1 year before and 6 months after the accident. Although she received 6 months of physical therapy and cognitive rehabilitation several months postinjury, 6 years later she still complained of memory problems. With the help of a friend, she retrained herself in her area of specialty so that she could begin to work privately. During the evaluation, she reported a good mood, but a limited social circle and social activities, which she attributed to her feeling awkward because she forgets social information (e.g., the names of new acquaintances). Despite her complaints of forgetting, she claimed that she does remember important information for which she feels responsible (e.g., her patients' histories and appointments), yet she cannot retain telephone numbers and names or even the plots of recently seen movies. She attributed her problems to not being observant. A neuropsychological evaluation revealed average attention and encoding skills (probably below her premorbid level), with poor performance when visuomotor responding was also required. Although unable to use learning strategies spontaneously, her performance improved when she was given cues. In the context of the evaluation, she was able to encode new information, as she demonstrated intact recognition, but had difficulty recalling this information (both auditory and visual). Memory for faces was in the borderline range on tests of immediate recall and low average on tests of delayed recall. Memory for pictures of everyday-type scenes was very low, as she retained neither the spatial information of the scenes nor their details. Her short-term memory was in the average range, but her secondary memory performance was in the mildly impaired range. Her implicit memory was not assessed due to fatigue (she declined). The patient had an overall profile of slowed cognitive processing, executive dysfunction, a tendency to sacrifice speed for accuracy to compensate for her impairment, and she was able to succeed on some tests with intense effort, leading to premature fatigue.

(Courtesy of Mary H. Kosmidis)

Case 2

Levine, Black, Cabeza et al. (1998) describe a patient, ML, who had isolated retrograde amnesia after a severe TBI, with relatively preserved anterograde memory. ML was densely amnesic for experiences predating his injury, including his childhood and early adult years. His retrograde amnesia did not have a temporal gradient. The isolated events that he did remember were without temporal, spatial, or emotional context. In contrast, he showed normal anterograde memory performance on a variety of standard tests of recall and recognition. The cognitive processes underlying this performance were examined with the "remember/know" technique, which permits separation of episodic from nonepisodic contributions to memory tests. The results demonstrated that the patient did not episodically reexperience postinjury events to the same extent as control examinees, although he could employ a feeling of familiarity to distinguish events he had experienced from those he had not experienced. His MRI showed damage to the right ventral frontal cortex and underlying white matter, including the uncinate fasciculus, a frontotemporal band of fibers previously hypothesized to mediate retrieval of specific events from one's personal past. Right frontal polar hypoactivation in response to episodic retrieval demands was noted when the patient was examined with a cognitive activation $H_2^{15}O$ positron emission tomography (PET) that reliably activated this frontal region in both healthy controls and patients with TBI carefully matched to the patient (but without isolated retrograde amnesia). The findings from this examination converge to suggest that ML has impaired autonoetic awareness attributable to right ventral frontal lobe injury, including a right frontal-temporal disconnection. Reorganized brain systems mediate certain preserved cognitive operations in ML but without the normal complement of information concerning the self with respect to both past and future.

(From Levine, Black, Cabeza et al., 1998, with the permission of *Brain*)

Case 3

This 45-year-old man was injured while driving on the highway. Upon regaining consciousness, he was disoriented with respect to time and place. Nine months after his injury, he sought treatment for his anterograde and retrograde memory problems. An MRI revealed right frontal white matter lesions, as well as in the genu and splenium, and a single photon emission computed tomography (SPECT) demonstrated mild hypoperfusion of the right anterior frontal lobe, temporal lobe, thalamus, and cerebellum, as well as of the left superior frontal and parietal lobes. A neuropsychological assessment suggested a selective memory problem, with intact abilities in other areas of cognitive functioning. This memory impairment included both anterograde and retrograde amnesia, the latter showing a negative temporal gradient for events extending approximately 10 years into the past. More detailed assessment of the retrograde amnesia revealed an interesting dissociation of public versus autobiographical memory processes, as well as of allocentric versus egocentric temporal judgments. Specifically, he had difficulty recalling public events, although he could recognize them, whereas he could both recall and recognize autobiographical events. His amnesia for public events showed a negative temporal gradient in both allocentric and egocentric temporal judgment, but his memory for autobiographical events was impaired only when dependent on making an allocentric temporal judgment, with intact egocentric temporal judgment. This pattern of findings suggests that his difficulty recalling public events may reflect deficits in retrieval strategies related to temporal context, particularly when this context is allocentric. It appears that the patient used egocentric (but not allocentric) temporal information adequately when trying to recall autobiographical memory.

(From Tsukiura, Otsuka, Miura et al., 2000, with the permission of *Brain and Cognition*)

Several injury-related factors have implications for establishing and assessing the symptoms of a TBI. Such factors have to do with the severity of the injury (i.e., mild, moderate, severe), the nature of the impact (i.e., acceleration, deceleration), and condition upon and soon after impact (i.e., length of unconsciousness, duration of PTA). We discuss each of these factors and their relationship to the cognitive status of the individual in the acute stage as well as to their long-term prognosis.

Severity of TBI

In an attempt to systematize a method of estimating TBI severity, several variables, and scales to assess them, have been developed. Typically, the depth of coma in the first 24 hours after injury and the duration of PTA are used to classify injuries as mild, moderate, or severe. A large number of cases of TBI are usually moderate to severe, with the rest being considered mild.

Unconsciousness Interval and Depth of Coma

Coma is defined as a period of unconsciousness or significant alteration of awareness. The depth of coma in the acute phase (i.e., during the first few hours after injury) is associated with outcome; thus, it serves as an early index of trauma severity. The most commonly used measure of depth of coma is the Glasgow

Coma Scale (GCS). This scale assesses several abilities (eye opening, motor response, and verbal response) and gives a quantifiable estimate of the depth of coma while enabling the clinician to track changes over time. Scores on this scale range from 3 to 15, with scores of 8 or less indicating severe injury, 9 to 12 indicating a moderate TBI, and 13 or more a mild injury (Jennett, Snoek, Bond, & Brooks, 1981).

Posttraumatic Amnesia

Posttraumatic amnesia is the period after the head injury during which the person is disoriented and has anterograde memory problems. Its duration is difficult to determine with accuracy (Russell, 1932; Symonds & Russell, 1943), as many individuals may have islands of memory (Russell & Nathan, 1946). In some patients, PTA may go unnoticed, with the exception of a gap in their memory for a given period of time. PTA is characterized by confusion, disorientation, restlessness, agitation, and, in some cases, confabulation.

The duration of PTA is typically measured with the Galveston Orientation and Amnesia Test (GOAT) (Levin, O'Donnell, & Grossman, 1979); this scale assesses orientation to person, place, time, and circumstances. It can be used repeatedly to track change over time. The GOAT assesses the ability to retrieve knowledge from before the injury as well as to acquire new information. The duration of PTA gives a more accurate indication of outcome than coma duration (Levin, Benton, & Grossman, 1982), as it is related to residual problems and long-term recovery of daily functioning (Dikmen, Machamer, Winn, & Temkin, 1995). The combination of GOAT and GCS scores yields the most accurate prognostic information. Although most closed head injuries lead to transient disruption of memory such as PTA, penetrating head injuries do not necessarily alter the individual's level of conscious awareness or the ability to remember new information (Russell & Nathan, 1946). In the rare instances of PTA after a penetrating head injury, it is either very brief (less than 24 hours) or very long and is associated with extensive damage to the brain.

Symptoms

Attention and Retrieval

Most symptoms of TBI involve primary memory functions. Therefore, we will begin this section by commenting first on the most prominent deficits and follow with a description of the types of memory experiences affected by TBI.

One of the most frequent and prominent features of TBI is disruption of brainstem structures and diffuse, bilateral, subcortical lesions. It is thus not surprising that survivors of a TBI often demonstrate decreased alertness, arousal, and sustained attention. Also common are difficulties with selective, alternating, and divided attention. Such difficulties are often severe enough to cause considerable subjective distress and to prevent patients from returning to their premorbid level of functioning (Mangels, Craik, Levine et al., 2002). Consequently, they may be partially responsible for the memory problems observed in these individuals

(Arciniegas, Adler, Topkoff et al., 1999). The pattern of attentional deficits after mild TBI resembles that of frontal dysfunction (Mangels et al., 2002).

The role of attentional impairments becomes more evident as task demands increase. In a study examining the effects of TBI on memory under increasingly challenging conditions (i.e., learning under focused and divided attention) (Mangels et al., 2002), TBI patients demonstrated intact performance on free-recall, context-cued recall, and recognition memory tests when items were encoded under focused attention. In contrast, their performance was impaired when items were encoded under divided attention.

There also appears to be a modality effect on early attentional processing. Whereas sensory processing of visual stimuli appears to be spared, higher order visual processing involved in the discrimination of stimulus features is compromised. In contrast, processing of auditory information (perception, identification, and categorization of stimuli) appears to be altered permanently. This finding may explain why TBI survivors have a persistent impairment of attention, concentration, and mental shifting (Solbakk, Reinvang, Nielsen & Sundet, 1999; Duncan, Kosmidis, & Mirsky, 2003). Tests requiring multitasking skills may be more similar to everyday activities and their demands and, thus, a more accurate reflection of their true abilities (Arciniegas et al., 1999).

The mechanism of the retrieval operation has been postulated to involve the frontal lobes (e.g., Petrides, 1996a, 2002). Frontal structures are involved in strategy formation, memory for temporal order, self-monitoring, and initiating retrieval. Individuals with TBI affecting frontal structures often exhibit decrements in the ability to retrieve stored information efficiently. They are particularly susceptible to memory errors of distortion and confabulation. They also demonstrate poor source memory (Shimamura & Squire, 1991), as we will explain in more detail in the next section of this chapter.

Types of Memories Affected by TBI

Semantic memories are often preserved in TBI, although new ones are acquired with difficulty, especially in the presence of anterograde episodic amnesia. The latter expresses itself in "prospective" and "source" memory difficulties.

One of the most frequent complaints of survivors of a TBI is impairment in prospective memory, that is in the ability to remember to carry out an action at a particular time in the future; which is more closely related to everyday functioning than performance on any formal tests (Wilson, 1986; Kinsella et al., 1996; Raskin & Sohlberg, 1996) and which, consequently, can have devastating effects in a patient's life (Mateer, Sohlberg, & Crinean, 1987; Groot, Wilson, Evans & Watson, 2002). Generally speaking, patients have more difficulty with remembering when to do something rather than what to do at the designated time (Groot et al., 2002), and their impaired performance has been attributed to a combination of attenuated speed of processing, attention, and executive functioning (Groot et al., 2002); that is, once again to functions of the primary memory system.

Difficulties with remembering "source" information have been associated with frontal damage, which is ubiquitous in TBI. Yet, information regarding source memory in TBI patients is scarce (Shimamura & Squire, 1991; Dywan, Segalowitz, Henderson, & Jacoby, 1993). More frequently found in the literature are discussions of retrograde amnesia, not only because of its frequent presence in TBI but also by virtue of the consequences in patients' daily lives.

The duration of retrograde amnesia may range from a few moments to several years. It occurs in most, but not all, cases where alteration of consciousness had been sufficiently severe to produce a short period of PTA (Russell & Nathan, 1946). The amnesia displays the typical temporal gradient, whereby information learned closer to the time of the injury is more likely to be lost than that farther back in the past (Levin, High, Meyers et al., 1985; Carlesimo, Sabbadini, Bombardi et al., 1998; Tsukiura et al., 2000).

Independent of the shape of the gradient, a loss of memory for past events and for information acquired over the course of an entire lifetime may be even more disruptive to the individual's adjustment to the new circumstances of daily living than difficulty with new knowledge (Carlesimo et al., 1998). A case illustrating the devastating effects of retrograde amnesia is that of the patient who, after a severe closed head injury, had no recollection that he was divorced and was distraught to learn of this after his injury (Sohlberg & Mateer, 2001).

Even after the resolution of PTA, retrograde amnesia remains highly prevalent in TBI patients (Goldberg, Antin, Bilder et al., 1981; Rousseaux, Delafosse, Cabaret et al., 1984; Laiacona, Barbarotto, & Capitani, 1993; Markowitsch, Calabrese, Liess et al., 1993a; Markowitsch, von Cramon, & Schuri, 1993b; Stracciari, Ghidoni, Guarino et al., 1994; Mattioli, Grassi, Perani et al., 1996; Tsukiura et al., 2000), and it may involve both autobiographical and semantic memories (Laiacona et al., 1993; Markowitsch et al., 1993a; Markowitsch et al., 1993b; Mattioli et al., 1996), only autobiographical (De Renzi, Lucchelli, Muggia & Spinnler, 1995), or only semantic ones (Grossi, Trojano, Grasso, & Orsini, 1988). In contrast to explicit memory, implicit memory is not impaired in survivors of a TBI (Cohen, Eichenbaum, Deacedo, & Corkin, 1985; Squire, 1992; Timmerman & Brouwer, 1999; Watt, Shores, & Kinoshita, 1999; Nissley & Schmitter-Edgecombe, 2002).

In addition to errors of omission, confabulations, that is errors of commission, are also common in TBI. In a study of patients with closed head injuries as well as those with penetrating injuries, Weinstein and Lyerly (1968) found confabulation in 60% of patients. An older study, however, reported transient confabulation in only 38 of 1931 cases of closed head injury studied during World War II (Whitty & Zangwill, 1977a). Although most cases of PTA might be accompanied by mild confabulation, more prominent confabulation may occur despite otherwise normal behavior or during a posttraumatic confusional state (Russell, 1935; Symonds, 1937; Whitty & Zangwill, 1977a). Typically, florid spontaneous confabulation is transient and limited to the postacute stage of recovery from severe TBI; but in some cases it may extend to several months postinjury. Individuals who confabulate usually have considerable frontal damage (Baddeley & Wilson, 1986). Investigators reporting a more extensive duration of confabulation or "reduplicative paramnesia," lasting for several weeks (Patterson & Zangwill, 1944) or several months (Benson, Gardner, & Meadows, 1976), attributed their patients' confusion to frontal dysfunction. More commonly, confabulation consists of modifying real experiences, such as placing actual events in the wrong temporal or spatial context.

Neuropsychiatric Sequelae of TBI

Mood Disorders

Prevalence rates of major depression during the first year after TBI have been estimated at about 18–26%. These rates increase after the first year postinjury, ranging from 38% to 59% (Fleminger, Oliver, Williams, & Evans, 2003). Mania is seen in about 9% of patients after TBI, a rate lower than that of depression, but much higher than in the general population (Jorge, Robinson, Starksein et al., 1993). Rates of suicide after brain injury are 2.7, 3.0, and 4.1 times the standard suicide rate for those with a skull fracture, concussion, and an intracerebral contusion or hemorrhage, respectively (Teasdale & Engberg, 2001). Moreover, in a sample of outpatients with TBI, 35% presented moderate to severe levels of hopelessness, 23% some suicidal ideation, and 18% had actually made a suicide attempt postinjury (Simpson & Tate, 2002).

Anxiety

All variants of anxiety disorders may be found in survivors of a TBI, including generalized anxiety disorder (2–28%), panic disorder (4–17%), phobic disorder (1–10%), and obsessive-compulsive disorder (2–15%) (Van Reekum, Bolago, Finlayson et al., 1996; Hibbard, Uysal, Kepler et al., 1998; Deb, Lyons & Koutzoukis, 1999; Koponen, Taiminen, Portin et al., 2002).

Psychosis

Psychosis after TBI can occur during the period of posttraumatic amnesia, as a complication of posttraumatic epilepsy, in the context of TBI-related mood disorders, or in association with a chronic schizophrenia-like syndrome (McAllister & Ferell, 2002). The percentage of TBI patients developing schizophrenia-like psychosis varies from 0.7 to 9.8 (Davison & Bagley, 1969). The more severe the injury, the greater is the likelihood of psychosis, and it appears that TBI can interact with genetic vulnerability to greatly increase the risk of developing such a disorder (McAllister & Ferell, 2002).

Apathy

Apathy or loss of motivation is frequently observed in TBI patients and is often associated with depression. In one study, 60 out of 84 brain-injured patients presented with both depression and apathy, while 10 out of 84 exhibited only apathy (Kant, Duffy, & Pivovarnik, 1998).

Postconcussion Syndrome

Postconcussional disorder is included in the DSM-IV (American Psychiatric Association, 1994) yet inadequately studied. Research criteria include a history of closed head trauma causing significant cerebral concussion (with loss of consciousness, posttraumatic amnesia, or posttraumatic onset of seizures), attention or memory impairment, and at least three of the following symptoms occurring after the trauma and lasting for a minimum of 3 months: fatigue, disordered sleep, headache, vertigo or dizziness, irritability or aggression, anxiety or depression or affective lability, changes in personality, and apathy. The International Classification of Diseases (ICD-10; World Health Organization, 1992) includes similar criteria for postconcussion syndrome, with the addition of the prerequisite of objective evidence of cognitive deficits. Among patients who have sustained a mild head injury resulting in loss of consciousness not exceeding 10 minutes, or amnesia for the event, and without objective or radiological findings, about half experience at least one postconcussion symptom at 1 month, 43% at 3 months, and 25% at 6 months after injury (Bazarian, Wong, Harris et al., 1999). In one outcome study, 7–8% of mild head trauma patients reported chronic symptoms, and 14% were considered disabled (Binder, 1997).

There has been considerable debate regarding the extent to which the etiology of postconcussion syndrome is primarily due to the physical damage per se (Levin, Williams, Eisenberg et al., 1992; Garnett, Blamire, Corkill et al., 2000a; Garnett, Blamire, Rajagopalan, et al., 2000b) or is reflective of the individual's emotional reaction (Lishman, 1988; Binder & Rohling, 1996; Hanks, Temkin, Machamer, & Dikmen, 1999; Sawchyn, Brulot, & Strauss, 2000). In an attempt to reconcile these two perspectives, King (2003) proposed that different periods of vulnerability exist in different cases, and possibly within a single individual at different times after the injury. Mild dysfunction is more common in the early days after mild head trauma, whereas psychological features can develop and/or preexisting psychological vulnerabilities may be activated subsequently (i.e., when the patient becomes concerned about the potential permanence of symptoms or when compensation claims predominate).

A growing literature attempts to explain the evolution and persistence of symptoms in patients who sustained a mild head injury (Gunstad & Suhr, 2002). It has been suggested that individuals with mild head injury report many symptoms because of a generalized expectation that they will experience negative consequences from their injury and because of subjective distress. Consequently, specific expectations about head injury may lead to the reporting of specific postconcussion symptoms.

Episodic Dyscontrol Syndrome

The core features of dyscontrol syndrome are sudden unpredictable outbursts of rage, which may be associated with severe physical aggression, destructiveness, or verbalized anger, described by others as out of character, with either a trivial or an unidentifiable trigger, terminating suddenly after only a few minutes, and typically accompanied by a sense of remorse. The frequency of these episodes vary from almost daily to once every few weeks or even months. The incidence of episodic dyscontrol syndrome has been estimated to be about 5.5% (Eames & Wood, 2003) among patients with TBI.

Insomnia

The postacute phase of TBI carries considerable risk for sleep problems; 28% of TBI patients have been found to suffer from insomnia, and an additional 14% suffer from poor sleep quality (Fichtenberg, Zafontes, Putnam et al., 2002).

PRECIPITATING FACTORS

Prevalence

The annual incidence of TBI in the United States is approximately 1.5 million per year (Thurman, Alverson, Dunn et al., 1999). Of these, 80,000 typically experience some degree of chronic disability (Frankowski, 1986). A recent report estimated the number of people in the United States who currently live with disabilities resulting from a TBI to be about 5.3 million (Thurman et al., 1999). TBI is a particularly significant health problem in children and adolescents, resulting in 400,000 annual emergency room visits and 29,000 hospitalizations in the United States for acute brain trauma in children under 15 years of age (Langlois & Gotsch, 2001).

The causes of TBI are often related to the demographic characteristics of the victim. Motor vehicle accidents are the most common cause of TBI, accounting for more than 48%, followed by falls (21%), violent attacks (12%), and sports- or recreation-related injuries (10%) (Kraus, Black, Hessol et al., 1984). A more recent report estimated sports-related brain injuries at approximately 18% of the TBI cases in the United States (Echemendia & Julia, 2001).

Gender differences are evident in the prevalence of TBI. Men are injured twice as frequently as women, and their injuries are more severe; the risk of fatal head injury among men is four times greater than in women. Certain age groups appear to be more susceptible to TBI. The incidence of head injury increases and peaks between the ages of 15 to 25, decreases, and rises again in the elderly (over 75 years of age) (Kraus et al., 1984; Sosin, Sniezek, & Thurman, 1996; Thurman et al., 1999). Children under the age of 5 years also have a higher than average risk for TBI, mainly due to falls (Kraus, Fife, & Conroy, 1987).

Among survivors of a TBI, the prevalence of alcohol and substance abuse is high (Kolakowsky-Hayner, Courley, Kreutzer et al., 1999; Bogner, Corrigan, Mysiw et al., 2001). In one study, approximately half the patients who were hospitalized or died after TBI were intoxicated at the time of the injury (Kraus, Morgenstern, Fife et al., 1989). Whereas alcohol and illicit drug use typically declines after injury, alcohol use tends to increase again over time (Taylor, Kreutzer, Demm & Meade, 2003).

PATHOPHYSIOLOGY

Pathological Processes

The pathophysiology of injury to the brain and its outcome are directly related to characteristics of the injury, such as type, severity, and area of the brain affected. A series of neuronal and vascular changes follow the impact, depending on the nature and direction of the initial mechanical forces. The physiological changes that occur are related to several factors (Sohlberg & Mateer, 2001): Deformation of the skull resulting from the forces related to the impact, either directly at the site of impact or at another site, may lead to fractures causing damage of brain tissue. Primary injury refers to the actual disruption of brain tissue at the time of the injury, which results in focal lesions, contusions, and/or diffuse axonal injury. Secondary injury results from biochemical changes secondary to the trauma, leading to metabolic and biochemical abnormalities. A series of cellular changes leads to cell death, receptor dysfunction, and calcium-mediated damage (Davis, 2000). Additional manifestations of injury are increased intracranial pressure, intracranial hemorrhage, cerebral edema, respiratory or cardiac failure, and ischemic brain damage (Bullock, Lyeth, & Muizelaar, 1999), leading to additional microscopic lesions, damage to nerve fibers (Strich, 1961), and connections to other parts of the brain (Levin et al., 1982). Such tissue damage may lead to ventricular enlargement; in fact, enlargement has been identified by computed tomography (CT) scans in 72% of patients with a severe closed head injury (Levin, Meyers, Grossman, & Sarwar, 1981), and hydrocephalus also sometimes occurs (Blatter, Bigler, Gale et al., 1997). A common delayed complication of the extensive cell death after head injury is posttraumatic epilepsy (Annegers, Hauser, Coan, & Rocca, 1998).

Given the vulnerability of the frontal and temporal regions and the hippocampus to injury, it is not surprising that primary memory problems, executive dysfunction, and changes in personality are some of the most frequent complaints after TBI (Fontaine, Azouvi, Remy et al., 1999; Van der Naalt, Van Zomeren, Sluiter, & Minderhoud, 1999; Palmese & Raskin, 2000; Bigler, 2001).

Mechanisms of Injury

Awareness of the biomechanics involved in closed head injury is important for understanding the areas of cognitive functioning that are affected. The mechanisms of injury involved in TBI depend on the motion of the head in relation to the object of impact. Impact deceleration results from the deceleration of the head's movement by an object that is stationary or is moving more slowly. Linear acceleration occurs when a moving object strikes a head that is stationary or moving more slowly than the object. In both cases, there is also rotational or angular acceleration involving a twisting of the head (Gurdjian & Webster, 1958; Ommaya & Gennarelli, 1974; Levin et al., 1982). The inertia of the moving head and brain results in a decreasing centripetal progression of strain from the outer surface of the brain to the midbrain and basal diencephalon (Ommaya & Gennarelli, 1974). In order for an alteration in consciousness to occur, the force of the shearing strain must reach the mesencephalic part of the brain stem (Ommaya & Gennarelli, 1974). This process may lead to stretching and shearing of fiber tracts or tearing of arteries and veins (e.g., hemorrhage), resulting in diffuse axonal injury (DAI) (Ommaya, 1984). DAI may range from mild, scattered shearing of axons in the parasagittal white matter of the cerebral hemispheres to severe, widespread axonal shearing in the cerebral hemispheres and hemorrhages from damaged capillaries (Gennarelli, Thibault, Adams et al., 1982). Focal cortical contusions are often not limited to the site of impact (coup) but may also affect the site opposite to that of impact (contrecoup), as the inertia of the brain leads to impact with the decelerating skull.

Various factors may affect the areas in which damage occurs. Mechanical forces, the location of bony protrusions of the skull, proximity to the falx cerebri and tentorium cerebelli, vascular anatomy, and differences in tissue densities may affect the direction of the strain and the susceptibility of particular brain regions. For example, parts of the cortex that are covered by rough surfaces (e.g., temporal lobes, orbital frontal cortex) are more susceptible to damage than areas covered by a smooth surface of the skull (e.g., occipital lobe) (Holbourn, 1943; Ommaya & Gennarelli, 1974; Umile, Plotki, & Sandel, 1998; Karli, Burke, Kim et al., 1999; Hofman, Stapert, van Kroonenburgh et al., 2001; Umile, Sandel, Alavi et al., 2002).

The location of the hippocampus near the base of the skull makes it particularly vulnerable to damage (Dixon, Taft, & Hayes, 1993; Conti, Raghupathi, Trojanowski, & McIntosh, 1998; Gale, Hopkins, Weaver et al., 1999; Tate & Bigler, 2000). Damage to the hippocampus leads to abnormal cholinergic functioning (Arciniegas et al. 1999), cell death, and hippocampal atrophy (Harding, Halliday, & Kril, 1998; Albensi, Knoblach, Chew et al., 2000; Pike, Zhao, Newcomb et al., 2000).

PROGNOSIS AND TREATMENT

Memory problems after mild TBI typically resolve within the first 1–3 months after the injury (Levin et al., 1992; Dikmen et al., 1995) but may persist up to a year (Bohnen, Jolles, Twijnstra et al., 1992; Ruff, Crouch, Troster et al., 1994) and be severe enough to be disabling (Ryan, Sautter, Capps et al., 1992). In contrast, memory impairment persists in the long term after moderate to severe TBI (Goldenberg, Oder, Spatt, & Podreka, 1992). Various interventions have been proposed for the rehabilitation of memory impairment in general and after TBI in particular. Optimal and theoretically based interventions take into account the types of memory that are often intact after TBI. The interventions most commonly used fall into three basic categories (Sohlberg & Mateer, 2001). The first category aims at restoring memory skills by improving underlying processes. This is frequently done by providing training through practice drills (Schacter & Glisky 1986) or through training patients in the use of specific mnemonic strategies involving mental imaging or prospective memory drills (Sohlberg, Mateer, & Geyer, 1985; Wilson, 1986).

The second category of interventions involves training patients in specific tasks with practical relevance to their daily functioning (Glisky & Schacter, 1989; Evans, Wilson, Schuri et al., 2000). Such interventions include mnemonic strategies for those types of information relevant to the patient and which may generalize to similar tasks (Glisky, Schacter, & Tulving, 1986a, 1986b; Glisky & Schacter, 1989; Brush & Camp, 1998a, 1998b; Sohlberg & Mateer, 2001).

The third category includes interventions that involve the use of external aids, such as electronic organizers and memory books (Harris, 1980; Glisky & Schacter, 1986a, 1986b; Wilson, 1991; Evans, Wilson, Needham, & Brentnall, 2003). These aids are geared toward compensating for impairment rather than restoring memory processes (Sohlberg, Todis, & Glang, 1998).

In addition to purely behavioral programs for memory rehabilitation, others have explored the effectiveness of combined pharmacological and neuropsychological interventions to help improve memory after TBI (León-Carrión, 1997; León-Carrión, Dominguez-Roldan, Murillo-Cabezas et al., 2000). The Combined Method (León-Carrión, 1997) is based on the model of physical therapy, which first seeks to resolve the underlying basis of any functional impairment. Thus, this method emphasizes the importance of understanding the pharmacodynamics of cognition in order to intervene on a behavioral level. According to this approach, rehabilitation specialists first attempt to restore cerebral blood flow through pharmacological treatment, then apply neuropsychological rehabilitation strategies targeting those cognitive functions that are impaired.

CONCLUSIONS

The memory deficits observed in TBI are significant but not ubiquitous. The nature of the impact and the mechanisms of injury in most cases of TBI and, more specifically, closed head injury, lead to both diffuse and circumscribed damage in the frontal and temporal regions. Not surprisingly, the types of memory disruption observed in TBI reflect this pattern of brain damage. Diffuse injury, especially that affecting the frontal lobes, may be responsible for impairments in attention and encoding, strategic processing and organization, or categorization of information. TBI patients appear to have difficulty with effortful retrieval, as this operation involves strategy formation skills, temporal ordering of events, and monitoring and may account for confabulations as well. Although semantic memories are typically unaffected, new information is not added easily due to anterograde, episodic memory problems. Perhaps the most disturbing

deficits to the survivor of a TBI are deficits in prospective memory, as these interfere with effective daily functioning, and retrograde amnesia, particularly of
autobiographical information, which disrupts one's sense of self.

The pattern of memory impairment in TBI highlights the role of multiple
brain regions in normal memory. The temporal gradient commonly observed in
retrograde amnesia is indicative of a disruption in the process of memory consolidation, a function probably mediated by the synergy of hippocampus and
mesial temporal lobes, which are typically affected in TBI. Yet, the relative
preservation of implicit memory such as procedural learning and priming, indicates the neuroanatomic independence of their mechanisms from those subserving the more purposeful, effortful memory functions. The temporal gradient
of retrograde amnesia reported in cases of TBI may extend over a period of many
years in the person's past. Although it is thought that transfer of memory trances
from the hippocampus to the neocortical areas responsible for their consolidation and storage is a process that occurs slowly over time, what is not clear is the
range of this time interval. The temporal range of the retrograde amnesia would
suggest that the process of memory consolidation may extend over many years, a
conclusion inconsistent with the one emerging from the profile of seizure-
related amnesia, which extends only hours or days into the past, suggesting a
much briefer consolidation process.

8

Transient Global Amnesia

PANAGIOTIS G. SIMOS AND
ANDREW C. PAPANICOLAOU

Transient global amnesia (TGA) is an apparently benign disorder of memory of unknown pathophysiology, affecting mostly middle-aged individuals of both genders. It has a sudden and disconcerting onset that resolves almost entirely within a few hours and rarely lasts more than 24 hours. There is usually a permanent memory gap for events that transpired during the episode and for the episode itself. It was first identified and given its current name in the 1950s (Fisher & Adams, 1958, 1964) when the first series of 17 patients were described in detail.

There can be no doubt that the condition occurred before it was identified, but most likely it was confused with the psychogenic or hysterical amnesias (Kapur, 1993). The confounding is understandable, as neither disorder is contingent on brain injuries, stroke, or any other obvious pathophysiological event, and both have a sudden onset. Understandable also is the confusion between TGA and transient epileptic amnesia, a condition that was identified as a separate clinical entity only since 1993 (Kapur, 1993). In the several hundred TGA cases that have been reported thus far, the onset of the condition was invariably sudden and has taken the patient by surprise. The individuals are almost always disoriented to time and place, depending on how familiar their surroundings are at the onset of the episode; but, unlike those suffering from psychogenic amnesia, they never become disoriented to person (Hodges & Ward, 1989). They realize immediately that something is wrong with them because they do not know the time or the date. Often, they realize that they do not know where they are, how or why they got there, and they typically ask friends, or whoever is around at the time, these questions. This repetitive questioning constitutes one of the cardinal features of the disorder and is one among many signs of the profound anterograde deficit that characterizes the disorder: The patients appear to forget the answers to their questions within minutes, although they are clearly able to attend to and comprehend them. Possibly, however, the reason for the repeated questioning is not, or is not exclusively, their inability to retain the answers but possibly an expression of perseveration common in frontal lobe pathology. The following observations argue that frontal lobe involvement may, in fact, be partially responsible for the disorder: The patients repeat the same questions even though the circumstances have changed, making the questions irrelevant or superfluous. Or, they may keep asking about their condition while they otherwise appear completely unconcerned about their disorder (Stillhard, Landis, Schiess et al., 1990). In addition, to repeated questioning patients may engage in apparently compulsive acts like washing their hands over and over (Caplan, 1990) or ascending and descending the same staircase (Mazzucchi, Moretti, Caffarra, & Parma, 1980). The precise significance of these repetitive behaviors is not clear, but they constitute one of the defining features of the disorder.

Upon questioning, whether informally or in the context of formal testing, it becomes rapidly apparent that patients also have a retrograde memory deficit (though not as severe as the anterograde deficit) that varies widely from a few hours to several years (Caffarra, Moretti, Mazzucchi, & Parma, 1981; Regard & Landis, 1984; Stracciari, Rebucci & Gallassi, 1987; Kritchevsky, Squire, & Zouzounis, 1988). In some cases, the retrograde amnesia is complete for a given time period preceding the onset of the attack, and patients feel that the present is contiguous with the (edge of that) gap, which may extend back over years (Caffarra et al., 1981; Kritchevsky & Squire, 1989). More often, the retrograde memory gap is not solid and continuous but patchy and without clear temporal limits, and the patients have an especially pronounced difficulty in correctly chronologically ordering those personal and public episodes that they manage to remember (Regard & Landis, 1984; Stracciari et al., 1987; Kritchevsky et al., 1988; Hodges & Ward, 1989).

In spite of the profound memory deficit, patients remain capable of performing complex tasks such as driving a car and can reason and converse normally. It has been reported that a patient, who happened to be a neurologist, was able to correctly diagnose his own condition (Miller, Petersen, Metter et al., 1987a). The perplexity that the patients experience at the onset of the amnesic attack may evolve into concern and anxiety or withdrawal, apathy, or even anosognosia (Regard & Landis, 1984; Stracciari et al., 1987; Kritchevsky et al., 1988; Hodges & Ward, 1989). In addition to these affective responses, patients often report somatic symptoms, like headache, sleeplessness, nausea, or dizziness (Caffarra et al., 1981; Kritchevsky & Squire, 1989; Kapur, 1993). All these symptoms, along with the amnesia, resolve, apparently spontaneously and completely, within 24 hours or less, leaving behind a permanent memory gap for events that transpired during the amnesic attack. Careful neuropsychological testing after the event sometimes reveals residual subclinical memory deficits that persist months after the attack (Mazzucchi et al., 1980; Caffarra et al., 1981; Regard & Landis, 1984;

Gallassi, Lorusso & Stracciari, 1986a; Hodges & Oxbury, 1990; Stillhard et al., 1990). Testing also shows that deficits are not just verbal or visuospatial, but kinesthetic, auditory (nonlinguistic), and olfactory (Mazzucchi et al., 1980). This perhaps constitutes a justification for continuing to use the adjective "global" to characterize the deficit, despite the fact that such a designation may be misleading in that it implies that the deficit encompasses all forms of memory, whereas the condition involves only anterograde (both semantic and episodic) and mainly episodic retrograde amnesia. A detailed account of specific facets of memory affected, as well as the degree of their affliction, is provided in the subsequent section, following a description of three cases that demonstrate the clinical features of TGA.

Case 1

LV, a 67-year-old retired telephonist, was observed during his first episode of TGA on 15 July 1985. He was generally fit and had no vascular risk factors. Ten years before he had suffered a major affective illness, since when he had remained on lithium without further psychiatric illness. He was a lifelong migraineur. Since retiring from full-time work at the age of 60, he had continued to work as a part-time gardener and handyman at a local convent. He was awaiting prostatic surgery but had had no other recent psychological stresses.

On the day of his attack he had been shopping in the morning. After lunch he had arranged to meet a nun at the railway station and transport her to the convent. This he did quite normally. He returned home at around 1530 and went out again without seeing his wife to mend a broken window in their garage. At 1645 he came into the house in a confused state, and said that he could not remember what he had been doing that day and he did not know if he was "coming or going." His wife rang the convent confirming that he had safely delivered the sister and after consulting their general practitioner he was transferred to the Radcliffe Infirmary.

On arrival, at 2000, he appeared quiet, vague, and perplexed. His speech and language were normal. He was oriented to place but did not know the day or month. After prompting he guessed the year to be 1985. He repeated every few minutes a stereotyped phrase: "By the way, let me tell you, there is a slight pressure on top of my head." His anterograde amnesia was profound: when given a simple eight-item name and address to recall he repeated it immediately, but after 2 minutes he had no recollection whatsoever of the task. Informal assessment suggested a retrograde amnesia of around 30 to 40 years. He had forgotten the birth of his grandchild 1 month before. He was unaware of his impending operation. He was unable to recall the Prime Minister. When asked if it was a man or a woman, he said that it was definitely a man (incorrect); when offered a choice of four names he selected the correct one. He was able to furnish details about his early life, war service, and post-war occupation. The general framework of his life appeared preserved. However, he was particularly confused about the sequence of events over the past two decades. There was no consistent or sharp cutoff point to his retrograde amnesia; for instance, he was able to recall his son's wedding 12 months before but not the assassination of President Kennedy.

By 7 hours postonset the retrograde amnesia had shrunk, he was able to remember his grandson's recent birth and also recall that he was due to meet someone from the train that day. Although there appeared to be no dense retrograde amnesia at this stage, his chronological sequencing of past public and personal events was still very poor. When given a list of nine post-war Prime Ministers, he was quite unable to place them in anything approaching the correct order. By 0230 the following morning his memory was clearly improving and he was able to lay down new memories.

The following day his family felt that he had returned to normal. He recalled events of the preceding day, up until 1330. The 2-hour permanent retrograde gap for events prior to the onset of the attack has not subsequently improved. An EEG performed that day was normal as were the following investigations: full blood count, biochemical screen, ECG, chest X-ray, and CT scan. Repeat neuropsychological assessment was performed at 24 hours, 1 week, 4 weeks, and 6 months postattack.

Summary: an unprovoked attack in a lifelong migraineur. During the attack he repeatedly complained of a pain on top of his head. The anterograde amnesia was profound and the retrograde memory loss extended back for approximately two decades but was patchy. A particular problem in sequencing past events was noted. There was a permanent retrograde gap of 2 hours.

(From Hodges, 1991, with the permission of W.B. Saunders)

Case 2

The second patient was a 75-year-old female retired tailor. Mild hypertension had been treated for ten years. She had suffered from frequent headaches and occasional attacks of migraine since youth. Thirty years earlier she had been admitted to a neurological hospital with a suspicion of meningitis because of severe headache. Ten years ago she had been hospitalized with a confusional state lasting two days. In April 1990, in the morning after returning by bus from an exhausting sightseeing trip to Budapest, she rose and breakfasted as usual. Her husband then left home to go shopping and when he came back he found her sitting on a chair and complaining, ". . . What's the matter with me? It's starting again, it's like last time." She repeatedly asked where she had been the last days and when she had returned home. When the answer was given she said, "Oh yes, I remember," but asked the same questions again shortly afterwards.

She was brought to the Neurology Department. When seen there two hours after her arrival she knew that she was in a hospital and that her relatives had brought her there. She knew the month but neither the year nor the day. She had no recollection at all of the time already spent in the hospital and did not recognize persons whom she had encountered during that time.

The patient knew that she had returned from a journey one day ago, but she was not sure whether she had been in Budapest or in Tyrol where she actually had spent her last winter holiday. When asked about both of these stays she confounded their circumstances and details. She could neither enumerate a single specific sight seen in Budapest nor recall the name of her hotel there. Her recall of previous hospitalizations and of recent and remote political events was similar in that she confounded their circumstances, and in that she was unable to enumerate specific details. A clear-cut temporal limit of this retrograde memory impairment could not be established, but recall of events up to 1950 appeared unimpaired and was not different from that given at follow-up.

During the examination she would remark with a frequency of up to twice a minute that she was now starting to have a little headache. Application of analgesics had no influence on the frequency of this complaint. When unable to answer a question she would invariably respond: "I don't know what was yesterday, but I do know what happened twenty years ago."

The neurological examination was normal. On neuropsychological examination spontaneous speech was also normal, and there was no apraxia. A copy of the Rey Figure was turned by 90 degrees, and the position of details was distorted. She did not recognize any of 30 concrete pictures and scored at chance on a multiple-choice recognition trial. Across five trials she could never repeat more than five words of a 12-word list. Fifteen minutes later she did not remember having heard a word list at all and was at chance level when identifying words from the list in the multiple choice task. Immediate recall of the Rey-Osterreith Figure was restricted to its gross outlines, and delayed recall impossible. On the procedural learning task her score improved across three trials, but after the last trial she thought that she had seen the digits only once or twice. Both verbal and design fluency were reduced and she produced multiple perseverations. On a card-sorting task she found only one out of six possible criteria and repeatedly used the same criterion three times in a row. In addition, she attempted two illogical sortings.

A SPECT was performed immediately after the neuropsychological examination. On the next day her memory improved. She had a complete amnesia for the first three to four hours of the attack and for the morning before. She had some vague recollections of the SPECT scan and of the neuropsychological tests preceding it. Recall of previous events was richer and more orderly than during the episode, but details were still lacking and she was insecure with respect to the distinction between events. She still repeatedly commented that the headache is starting now and that she did not know what was yesterday but did know what had happened twenty years ago; but the frequency of these repetitive comments was much lower than during the attack. Recognition memory for concrete pictures at the lower margin of the normal range. Learning and delayed recall of a 15-word list betrayed some storage in secondary memory but was still markedly reduced. When copying the Rey-Osterreith figure she duplicated one detail and omitted another, but preserved the main topological relationships and the orientation, and her score was in the normal range, while reproduction from memory was impoverished. Both verbal and design fluency were in the low normal range. On the procedural learning task her initial performance was better than the final performance of the previous day, which was reached only on the second trial.

At follow-up two weeks later, she claimed to have regained a recollection of the morning before the spell. Asked about her headache she said that she used to have headaches frequently but did not remember a particular aggravation during or after the attack. Her recall of previous events was chronologically correct without confusions, and she recalled without hesitation details she had been unable to remember during TGA. On neuropsychological examination, recognition memory for concrete pictures was perfect and she scored in the normal range on word-list learning and recall of a complex figure. Word fluency had improved while design fluency had remained the same. On the sorting task she now found two criteria and produced neither perseverations nor illogical sortings. On the procedural learning task she started at the final level of the last examination and improved further across three trials.

CT on the day of TGA was normal. SPECT done during the attack demonstrated bilateral hypoperfusion of both thalami and the left frontal and the left temporal lobes. The temporal hypoperfusion affected the medial temporal region; and there was some reduction of local HMPAO uptake in the right medial temporal region also noted. A follow-up SPECT two weeks later was normal.

(From Goldenberg, 1995, with the permission of John Wiley & Sons)

Case 3

A 48-year-old man developed global amnesia while undergoing an arteriographic evaluation for recurrent chest pain. Left ventriculography had been performed with a 40-ml injection of diatrizoate (Hypaque) sodium. Four injections (7 ml each) of diatrizoate meglumine and diatrizoate sodium (Renografin 76) into the left coronary artery and two injections (5 ml each) in to the right coronary artery had been performed without incident. The arterial pressure measurement through the catheter became damped four minutes later. Aspiration of the catheter was performed while it was in the aorta, and good pressure pulses could then be obtained. The patient began to complain that he did not know why he was there, and he did not know the physicians. He could not remember anything the physicians told him. He continued to talk and did not have any trouble with vision. His blood pressure was unchanged (110/80 mm Hg) from his prearteriogram recordings. Results of a detailed neurological examination about one hour after onset were entirely normal except for memory function. Though he was able to hold various types of memoranda for up to 30 seconds, he could not recall anything when the time duration exceeded one to two minutes. A standard test of memory function developed by one of us (E.C.S) was applied at this time and repeated at intervals until normal recent memory function was reestablished. Careful instructions were given before each test. The tests were applied as follows:

Olfactory Memory - The odor of cloves was presented, which he correctly identified with his eyes closed and recalled 30 seconds later. After a delay of approximately five minutes, he had no recollection of having perceived any odor, and he was unable to identify the correct odor previously presented when given three choices in identical unmarked bottles. Visual Memory - A picture of a cup, a small red-colored paper square, and a paper clip were presented. He correctly identified all of them and recall was intact at approximately 30 seconds. After approximately five minutes he had no spontaneous recall nor could he pick out the cup among three possible pictures of equal size. He did not recall the red square when three variously colored squares were presented. He did not recall the clip when three small object choices were presented.

Auditory Nonverbal Memory - He correctly identified the sound of paper being crumpled close to his ear (eyes closed), and recalled this at 30 seconds, but there was no spontaneous recall or ability to pick the correct sound from three noises presented five minutes later.

Tactile Memory - He correctly identified the size and shape of an aluminum square, but called it plastic. When he was asked if it might be metal, he agreed that it could be since it felt cold. He recalled the previously presented stimulus as plastic at 30 seconds, but after five minutes there was no spontaneous recall, and he failed when given three tactile choices. When given the same aluminum square, he again said it was plastic, but he was certain that he had never encountered it before.

Proprioceptive-Kinesthetic Memory - With eyes closed, he correctly identified a passive downward displacement of the right index finger and recalled the direction it had moved within 30 seconds. There was no spontaneous recall, and he failed to select the proper movement when offered several choices during testing five minutes later.

Auditory Verbal Memory - Digit span was seven numbers (forward) with no recall after five minutes. He could readily repeat the name of three objects and a name and address immediately, but there was no recall after five minutes.

Visual Verbal Memory - He was able to read correctly four printed words and to recall them immediately after finishing the series. After five minutes, no recall (either spontaneously or when presented with a group of 12 choices) was present.

Remote Memory - He recalled his present home address correctly (had lived there for 22 years), World War II, and the Korean Conflict, but he did not recall the more recent Vietnam War.

Throughout the examination he asked repeatedly, "What happened to me? Where am I?", despite the fact that he was given the same replies each time. Two hours later, the same series of tests was repeated with complete failure of recall of any items presented. It was found that he could retain most memoranda for only 30 to 45 seconds, with slightly longer retention for olfactory and proprioceptive-kinesthetic stimuli (one to two minutes). He was now able to recall the Vietnam War and the names of the presidential candidates in the last election (though he first selected Johnson, then changed to McGovern and Nixon). He was incorrect in stating that his brother had died during the Korean

Conflict (actually died in 1963 of acute myocardial infarction). He was again retested three hours later (now six hours after the onset of the attack). Though he still denied ever having seen the examiner before, he could correctly identify the name of the hospital and the approximate date for the first time. His retrograde amnesia had shrunk to two days (accuracy of his recall was checked with his wife and daughter). The same series of tests was then applied again, and he demonstrated normal recall on each test. Furthermore, he was no longer repeating his questions, but he was visibly more upset and concerned about what had happened during the past two days. Ten hours after the insult, he was able to recall events that occurred the evening before the angiogram. He still could not recall being taken from his room or any part of the cardiac angiography examination when he was last questioned 12 days after the onset of the memory loss. The first thing he seemed to recall after the resumption of his memory function was being asked to identify odors, a picture of a cup, and his wife's visit, which was approximately $5\frac{1}{2}$ hours after the onset of his difficulty. However, islands of amnesia persisted regarding some portions of this visit with his wife.

(From Shuttleworth & Wise, 1973, with permission of *Archives of Neurology*)

CLINICAL TESTING AND ESTABLISHMENT OF THE SYMPTOMS

Disorientation to time and place is a basic clinical feature of TGA. Therefore, the presence of attentional or other cognitive deficits that may contribute, to a greater or lesser degree, to the amnesic phenomena must be carefully evaluated. In formal testing with the forward digit span test, patients appeared to fall within normal limits (Hodges, 1994; Eustache, Desgranges, Laville et al., 1999), indicating that their attention and primary memory were intact. The results of the block-tapping test also showed that immediate spatial primary memory was intact (Hodges & Ward, 1989). Attention to verbal and visuospatial information appeared to be generally intact, as indicated by preserved repetition and complex-figure copying abilities (Regard & Landis, 1984; Hodges & Ward, 1989). There are, however, some questions regarding more complex working memory abilities: the same patients showed slightly reduced performance on the backward digit span test (Gallassi et al., 1986a; Quinette, Guillery, Desgranges et al., 2003).

As indicated in Chapter 1, working memory as currently defined is nearly synonymous to thinking. Is there then, any additional evidence that thinking may be partially impaired? There are several isolated reports that at least some TGA patients perform lower than expected on tests that involve complex thinking (tests that require mental suppression of irrelevant information, switching between different strategies for processing stimuli and selectively retrieving information). Thus, although patients may perform within normal limits on simple object naming tests (like the Boston Naming Test), they often show reduced performance on category fluency tasks. There are also reports of increased susceptibility to interference on the Stroop Test (Hodges, 1994), and on subspan list-learning tasks that entail variable recall delays during which the patient is asked to perform an interfering task (Regard & Landis, 1984; Hodges & Ward, 1989; Stillhard et al., 1990), such as the Brown-Peterson task (Quinette et al., 2003). These findings, along with the general propensity of TGA patients to perseverate in their responses, indicate frontal lobe dysfunction. Yet, clearly, frontal involvement could not account for all symptoms of the condition. In fact, it remains unclear whether working memory dysfunction is a cardinal feature of TGA. In conclusion, whereas perception, language, and attention seem to be unaffected, there are some indications that demanding working memory tasks may reveal deficits in some patients. But there is no question that retrograde long-term memory and especially anterograde memory are affected.

As mentioned earlier, there are indications that verbal as well as visuospatial, olfactory, tactile, and kinesthetic episodes cannot be retained beyond a few minutes by TGA patients. Verbal learning (i.e., retaining verbal episodes) is clearly defective as assessed by immediate and delayed recall for stories (Kritchevsky et al., 1988; Eustache, Desgranges, & Lalevee, 1998) and by the associated word-pairs subtests of the Wechsler Memory Scale (Stillhard et al., 1990). These deficits are particularly dramatic when the experimental procedure ensures that patients have processed the word stimuli adequately for meaning and can accurately recall them immediately after presentation. Performance on such tasks as the drilled word list learning task (Eustache et al., 1999; a variant of Grober and Buschke's procedure, (Grober & Buschke, 1987) demonstrates the speed of anterograde forgetting in TGA patients. Anterograde forgetting is also present for nonverbal information, as assessed by the delayed reproduction of the Rey-Osterrieth Complex Figure (Kritchevsky, Zouzounis, & Squire, 1997) or the supraspan block-tapping test used by Hodges & Ward (1989).

As mentioned before, anterograde amnesia is by definition episodic. Therefore, the question of possible semantic, implicit procedural, and implicit non-procedural memory deficits in TGA is one regarding retrograde memory. The retrograde memory deficit for semantic information is rather unlikely except possibly in demanding working memory or thinking (problem-solving) tasks that require rapid access to semantic information. Equally unlikely are subclinical deficits in procedural implicit memory, since complex yet highly practical and normally nondemanding skills, like driving, are carried out by TGA patients. Although implicit nonprocedural memory abilities have not been studied extensively in TGA, verbal priming (using word-stem completion and familiarity recognition tasks) was found to be intact in two patients (Kapur, Abbott, Footitt, & Millar, 1996; Eustache, Desgranges, Petit-Taboue et al., 1997).

In contrast to retrograde semantic and implicit memory, episodic memory of past events is substantially affected in TGA. As mentioned before, retrograde amnesia is sometimes patchy, with gaps extending many years back, and in other cases it is limited to a given time period. Formal evaluation of autobiographical episodic memory using the Crovitz test of remote personal memory (Crovitz, Harvey, & McClanahan, 1981) has revealed substantial memory gaps in the majority of patients studied (Hodges & Ward, 1989; Kopelman, Wilson, &

Baddeley, 1989; Kritchevsky et al., 1997). However, there were marked, individual differences in performance, underlining the need for more flexible, informal interviewing procedures, such as the Autobiographical Memory Interview (Evans, Wilson, Wraight, & Hodges, 1993). Retrograde memory for public episodes (famous faces and events) was evaluated in the same patients. Again, most patients had great difficulty recollecting public events or famous faces. Although there were some indications for a temporal gradient in the patients' retrograde memory deficits (there was a tendency for older episodes to be better remembered than newer episodes), the presence of marked individual differences obscured the possible temporal gradient.

PRECIPITATING FACTORS

Epidemiology

Based on large patient series in several Western countries, annual incidence rates in the general population range from 3 to 10 cases per 100,000 (Hinge, Jensen, Kjaer et al., 1986; Miller et al., 1987a; Koski & Marttila, 1990; Lauria, Gentile, Fassetta et al., 1997). The age range in these patient samples is rather broad (21–85 years), but only about 5% of the patients were under the age of 40 (the mode was between 60 and 70 years, with a mean of 63 years). Accordingly, the incidence of TGA among patients older than 50 years has been reported to be as high as 23.5 per 100,000 per year (Miller et al., 1987a). Interestingly, the proportion of cases declines beyond the eighth decade of life, in contrast with the cerebrovascular incident rate, which increases continuously with age. Very important to note is the fact that most patients experience only one episode, a feature that helps differentiate between TGA and transient epileptic amnesia.

Physiological Risk Variables

Although no single physiological factor is identified as the single most important one, in all TGA cases at least two have been observed in a significant proportion of patients: vascular disease and migraine.

　The incidence of hypertension has been found to vary from 13% (Crowell, Stump, Biller et al., 1984; Kushner & Hauser, 1985; Colombo & Scarpa, 1988; Guidotti, Anzalone, Morabito, & Landi, 1989) to 50% (Mumenthaler & Treig, 1984; Matias-Guiu, Colomer, Segura & Codina, 1986; Miller, Yanagihara, Petersen, & Klass, 1987b; Hodges & Warlow, 1990a) among TGA patients. In most reported studies, hypertension characterized between 25% and 35% of the patients (Miller et al., 1987a). This has led to the hypothesis that TGA has a cerebrovascular etiology, may be due to transient ischemic attacks (TIAs) and to the possibility that the incidence of TGA may presage further cerebrovascular incidents. However, recent consensus is that vascular problems are no greater in patients who had a TGA episode than in the general population and that the prognosis of TGA patients is excellent as far as cerebrovascular morbidity or mortality is concerned (Hodges & Warlow, 1990a; Melo, Ferro, & Ferro, 1992; Zorzon, Antonutti, Mase et al., 1995).

Another possible predisposing physiological factor is migraine headache, as an estimated 20% of TGA patients suffer from migraines (Hodges & Warlow, 1990a; Zorzon et al., 1995), whereas the incidence of migraine in the general population is much lower. Yet the fact remains that most TGA patients (about 80%) do not have a history of migraine and, conversely, a much smaller proportion of migraine sufferers ever develop TGA. More systematic studies also question the proposed causal link between migraine and TGA, suggesting that the observed comorbidity may be simply due to a common physiological substrate (Schmidtke & Ehmsen, 1998).

Situational Variables

Several antecedent events have been reported with TGA. They usually involve physical exertion, sexual intercourse, or emotional stressors (Hodges & Warlow, 1990a; Miller et al., 1987a). For most patients, however, no situational variables are identified. An interesting variant of TGA has also been reported in a series of nine younger patients sustaining mild head injury without loss of consciousness or other neurological symptoms (Haas & Ross, 1986). Especially noteworthy is the medical procedure of angiography, which results with a certain probability in TGA or TGA-like episodes. The significance of these predisposing factors for the search of the pathophysiological mechanism of TGA will be considered in a subsequent section.

DIFFERENTIAL DIAGNOSIS

To identify cases of TGA and to differentiate them from other types of amnesia, whether transient or enduring, are especially daunting tasks, as the diagnosis can only be made on the basis of the clinical presentation; and it cannot be subsequently verified by laboratory studies given that no known physiological cause for the condition exists. Laboratory evidence can only be used to exclude some amnesia cases from being further considered as instances of TGA.

This being the case, establishment of rigid diagnostic criteria has been especially important for this condition. In fact, lack of such criteria until recently resulted in many misdiagnoses, held back the establishment of the condition as an independent clinical entity, and resulted in the survival of several hypotheses regarding the pathophysiology of the condition, which in retrospect appear clearly wrong (Hodges, 1991). For example, if amnesia cases with neurological symptoms and signs in addition to amnesia are included in the diagnosis of TGA (as was occasionally the case in the past), the hypothesis of the cerebrovascular origin of the condition would appear viable. In contrast, if additional neurological symptoms and signs are exclusion criteria, the likelihood of finding evidence of cerebrovascular pathology among TGA patients is dramatically reduced, as is the viability of the hypothesis that TGA is due to thromboembolic episodes.

Rigorous diagnostic criteria were proposed in the mid-1980s and were adopted in a number of TGA studies involving large patient series (Caplan, 1985; Hodges & Warlow, 1990a, 1990b). The criteria are as follows:

1. An attack must be witnessed by an observer who can provide additional information.
2. Anterograde amnesia must be present.
3. There is no clouding of consciousness or loss of personal identity (i.e., patients must know their names).
4. Cognitive impairment is limited to amnesia, without apraxia or aphasia.
5. There is no recent history of head trauma and no history of seizures in the preceding 2 years.
6. There are no focal neurologic signs and no epileptic features.

TGA versus Psychogenic Amnesia

Psychogenic amnesia (also known as hysterical amnesia) has features in common with TGA. For instance, both have a sudden onset unaccompanied by any obvious relevant physiological signs. Yet they can be distinguished on the basis of the following characteristics: A prominent feature of psychogenic fugue is disorientation to person (see Chapter 11). Patients typically travel away from home, appear unable to recall their previous identity, and, in some cases, they may even assume a new identity. This feature is not present in TGA. In contrast, one of the most prominent features of TGA is disorientation to time and, most often, to place, which may be the reason for the almost compulsive questioning of TGA patients about their circumstances. No such repetitive questioning is a feature of psychogenic fugue.

Anterograde amnesia is a most conspicuous defining feature of TGA (second criterion). In contrast, patients with psychogenic memory disturbances are usually able to retain new episodes (Kritchevsky et al., 1997). It is this ability that allows patients with psychogenic fugue to establish a new personal history and thus cope with life. Retrograde amnesia, especially for autobiographic episodes and facts extending over the patient's entire past, is a cardinal feature of psychogenic memory disturbances but is not nearly as profound in TGA.

The duration of TGA cannot exceed a 24-hour period, and it normally lasts less than 12 hours, whereas fugues can last days, weeks, or months. Besides the above points of difference with respect to clinical features, TGA and psychogenic memory disturbances also differ in some epidemiological features and precipitating factors. As mentioned in the overview above, TGA is an affliction of middle age and rarely strikes people under 40 years of age. Psychogenic amnesia, on the other hand, is likely to afflict young adults and adolescents. Moreover, TGA is not specifically an affliction of people with personality disorders, social and psychological problems, and is not preceded by profound and enduring psychological stress. In contrast, psychogenic fugue is typically associated with psychosocial precipitating factors and usually afflicts people with personality or social problems (Abeles & Schilder, 1935; Kanzer, 1939; Sargent & Slater,

1940–1941; Parfitt & Gall, 1944; Wilson, Rupp, & Wilson, 1950; Berrington, Liddell, & Foulds, 1956). Moreover, psychogenic amnesia almost invariably follows acute psychological stress. Psychogenic memory disturbances are not triggered by physical exertion, nor are they followed by normal sympathetic activation (e.g., sexual intercourse), as TGA episodes often are. Finally, whereas TGA rarely recurs, psychogenic fugues (but not psychogenic amnesia) have been found to recur in many cases (Berrington et al., 1956).

TGA versus Transient Epileptic Amnesia

The rate and frequency of recurrence are the features that differentiate TGA from transient epileptic amnesia, a condition that can easily be confounded with TGA (see Chapter 9). Unlike the overwhelming majority of TGA patients who experience only one episode of memory loss, the majority of patients with transient epileptic amnesia (TEA) experience recurrence of the episodes. Moreover, unlike the low frequency of recurrence of TGA (usually two TGA episodes), TEA recurs much more frequently, often several episodes in a single year. The duration of TEA is usually less than 1 hour, in contrast to the average duration of 4–6 hours for TGA. Whereas TGA is likely to follow strenuous physical exertion, TEA tends to appear after the patient awakens from sleep.

Additional signs and symptoms such as complex partial seizures, prominent déjà vu, and interictal epileptiform activity on EEG are by definition exclusionary features in TGA. It should be noted, however, that nonspecific EEG abnormalities, consisting primarily of diffuse slowing, are not uncommon among patients examined after a TGA episode (Tharp, 1969; Greene & Bennett, 1974; Rowan & Protass, 1979; Miller et al., 1987b).

TGA versus Amnesias Secondary to Migraine, Drugs, Head Injury, and Cerebrovascular Disease

Given the fact that migraine is a condition shared by many TGA patients and that migraine may induce amnesia, it is important to separate those amnesia cases from pure TGA. In addition to migraine, drugs (either recreationally taken or prescribed for the treatment of other conditions, such as anxiety or depression), head injury, and cerebrovascular episodes may also precipitate amnesias, which do not qualify as instances of TGA.

The patient's history is the most accurate basis for distinguishing TGA from these forms of symptomatic amnesia. In addition, migraine, drug overdose, and head injury may result in anterograde amnesia, but secondary to acute confusion, and an inability to attend to and encode events. Chronic use of drugs is associated either with other cognitive signs and symptoms like depression or other neurological signs and symptoms that automatically invalidate the diagnosis of TGA (Criteria 4 and 5). Cholinergic antagonists and benzodiazepines are known to interfere with memory (see Chapter 2). Therefore, amnesias resulting from their use are secondary to those known pharmacological factors and therefore are not instances of TGA.

Migraine and cerebrovascular episodes result in other neurological signs and symptoms in addition to possible transient global amnesia. Migraine is typically accompanied by severe headache and nausea. On the other hand, cerebrovascular episodes associated with memory dysfunction are typically accompanied by focal neurological signs caused by disruption of the posterior cerebral circulation. In both cases, the signs and symptoms accompanying the memory dysfunction would disqualify the amnesia episodes as instances of TGA on the basis of the fourth and fifth criteria. Moreover, as will be discussed in the next section, TGA is not associated with other risk factors for vascular disease such as hypertension, heart disease, and diabetes.

Finally, a host of other neurological conditions like tumors, encephalitis, neurosyphillis, cerebral or subarachnoid hemorrhage, subdural or intraventricular hematomas, and hydrocephalus may produce transient loss of memory (Aimard, Trillet, Perroudon et al., 1971; Heon, Reiher, Dilenge, & Lamarche, 1972; Hartley, Heilman, & Garcia-Bengochea, 1974; Boudin, Pepin, Mikol et al., 1975; Lisak & Zimmerman, 1977; Rosenberg, 1979; Shuping, Toole, & Alexander, 1980; Landi, Guisti, & Guidotti, 1982; Findler, Feinsod, Lijovetzky, & Hadani, 1983; Pommer, Pilz, & Harrer, 1983; Ross, 1983; Sandyk, 1984; Chatham & Brillman, 1985; Meador, Adams, & Flanigan, 1985; Collins & Freeman, 1986; Giroud, Guard, & Dumas, 1987; Jacome & Yanez, 1988). Yet all cases of amnesia arising from these conditions can be excluded from the category of TGA because they are all associated with additional signs and symptoms.

TGA versus Amnesia Secondary to Angiography

Angiography may result in the inadvertent production of emboli and may result in several hours of a TGA (or TGA-like) episode (see Case 3 above).

The fact that both cerebral and cardiac angiography have been complicated by occasional, yet definite, TGA-like episodes has been known for a long time (Hauge, 1954; Whishart, 1971; Shuttleworth & Wise, 1973; Wales & Nov, 1981; Cochran, Morrell, Huckman, & Cochran, 1982; Haas, 1983; Pexman & Coates, 1983; Giang & Kido, 1989). What is not known, however, is whether the amnesic effects were due to transient embolization in the posterior circulation, as appears to have been the case recounted above, or due to the drugs given to patients before or during the procedure (Hodges, 1991). If the latter, then amnesia secondary to angiography must be distinguished from TGA for the same reason that amnesias secondary to drugs have been. However, we may then overlook the possibility that the proximal cause of TGA might be transient inhibition of the cholinergic system of the hippocampus triggered by medications administered during angiography. If the former explanation is correct, then all TGAs may be attributed to momentary ischemia in the posterior circulation vessels, which irrigate the hippocampus and/or the thalamus. In that case, we may have to explain how brief episodes of ischemia, which are not sufficient to produce focal neurological signs and symptoms associated with TIAs, can nevertheless profoundly disrupt the mechanisms of memory for several hours.

PATHOPHYSIOLOGY

It was commented above, in the introductory section of this chapter, that the pathophysiology of TGA is unknown. Yet unlike the case of psychogenic amnesia, no observer has characterized TGA as psychogenic. This is because, first, no psychological triggers appear to predate its onset; second, the symptoms have an uncanny resemblance to those resulting from frontal lobe lesions (and to a lesser extent diencephalic or mesial temporal ones), albeit they are reversible; and third, because the first reported TGA cases appeared to be associated with transient ischemic attacks, as in Case 3 reproduced above, or with what appeared to be temporal lobe epilepsy (Kapur, 1993).

Even though no progress has been made toward identifying the physiological causes of TGA since its identification as a separate syndrome, it is clear that these unknown pathophysiological changes must be reversible. This requirement invalidates the notion that TIAs cause TGA. It is also likely that these reversible changes involve the mesial temporal lobe and/or diencephalic regions. Thus, the anterograde amnesia observed in TGA is very similar to that found after bilateral mesial temporal lobe damage, caused by surgery, ischemia, encephalitis, or microhemorrhages as in Korsakoff syndrome (Milner, Corkin & Teuber, 1968; Cermak & O'Connor, 1983; Butters, 1985; Warrington & McCarthy, 1988; Squire, Haist, & Shimamura, 1989; Sullivan & Marsh, 2003).

One unvarying feature of TGA is the permanent memory gap for events transpiring during the episode after complete recovery from the condition. Such a gap could not be attributed to a malfunction of the retrieval mechanism, as there is complete recovery from retrograde amnesia up to the onset of the condition. There is also no evidence of any difficulty with retrieving episodes either before the TGA onset or after its resolution. In view of the fairly well-documented role of mesial temporal lobe structures for memory of new episodes (Squire & Zola, 1997; see Chapter 6), the permanent loss of memory for events experienced during the TGA episode points to a transient dysfunction of this region. On the other hand, lesions affecting different parts of the thalamus can lead to selective anterograde amnesia (Malamut, Graff-Radford, Chawluk et al., 1992), selective retrograde amnesia (Miller, Caine, Harding et al., 2001), or to combined anterograde and retrograde memory disturbances (von Cramon, Hebel, & Schuri, 1985; Graff-Radford, Tranel, Van Hoesen, & Brandt, 1990; Hodges & McCarthy, 1993).

Electrophysiological testing during TGA has failed to disclose any abnormalities or may show, at best, nonspecific abnormalities. The exception is where memory deficits are associated with temporal lobe epilepsy, in which case the condition is not TGA but epileptic amnesia (see Chapter 9) (Tharp, 1969; Greene & Bennett, 1974; Rowan & Protass, 1979; Miller et al., 1987b, Zorzon et al., 1995). Structural scanning (CT or MRI) during TGA is also negative except in cases where the amnesic episode is secondary to a lesion of sudden onset (whether traumatic or vascular), in which case the amnesia is not of the TGA variety. The few studies of functional imaging during TGA, using single photon emission computed tomography (SPECT) or positron emission tomography (PET), indicate hypoperfusion during the acute phase in the temporal lobes (including their mesial aspects) mostly bilaterally (Stillhard et al., 1990; Tanabe, Hashikawa, Nakagawa et al., 1991; Evans et al., 1993; Schmidtke, Reinhardt, & Krause, 1998). Occasionally, the hypoperfusion is more evident in one hemisphere (though this asymmetry is not consistently associated with preponderance of amnesia for verbal versus nonverbal episodes) and less frequently in one or both frontal lobes (Baron, Petit-Taboue, Le Doze et al., 1994; Schmidtke et al., 1998). Reduced blood flow in diencephalic regions has also been reported (Goldenberg, Podreka, Pfaffelmeyer et al., 1991; Baron et al., 1994).

The functional imaging data lend credence to the often-voiced conjecture that something is wrong during a TGA episode, with the temporal or, in some cases, with the frontal lobes. Four explanations have thus far been offered: TIAs, epilepsy, spreading depression (wave of depolarization progressing across cortex at 3–5 mm/min) associated with aura or migraine headaches, and transient venous ischemia.

Temporal lobe epilepsy, as a possible cause of TGA, was suspected when EEG abnormalities were found in a number of early case studies (Lou, 1968; Tharp, 1969; Steinmetz & Vroom, 1972; Greene & Bennett, 1974; Gilbert, 1978; Rowan & Protass, 1979; Deisenhammer, 1981) and because of the fact that temporal lobe seizures can cause reversible memory deficits (see Chapter 9). However, epilepsy could not account for TGA because epilepsy results in repeated episodes of transient amnesia, not just the one or occasionally two episodes that characterize TGA. Indeed, frequency of amnesic episodes is one feature that distinguishes epileptic from transient global amnesia (see "Differential Diagnosis" section, above). Moreover, no EEG evidence of temporal lobe epilepsy is found in TGA, and the usual features of epileptic seizures are not present. EEG recordings during TGA are rarely indicative of pathology (Jacome, 1989). Of course, one can always maintain that a form of abnormal epileptiform discharges in the medial temporal lobes invisible to surface EEG is causing TGA, but this contention is beyond empirical verification.

TIAs due to infarction of the posterior cerebral arteries that supply part of the limbic memory circuit could produce amnesia, both retrograde and anterograde in nature (Graff-Radford et al., 1990; Hodges & McCarthy, 1993), by reducing blood flow in the mesial temporal region, a feature that the functional imaging data often show in TGA. Ischemia would also explain the observation that arteriographic procedures, as in Case 3, could result in TGA. Yet, several facts render this explanation untenable: TGA may be a complication after angiography, suggesting that an embolus caused a TIA. However, in more than 3000 cases of angiography, the incidence of TGA was no higher than its base rate in the population (Hodges & Warlow, 1990a). Amnesia during TIA is accompanied by other signs and symptoms (e.g., vertigo, diplopia, etc.) not seen during TGA, which differentiate the two syndromes (see "Differential Diagnosis" above). Finally, TIAs recur, causing additional morbidity and mortality, whereas TGA has a benign prognosis (Hodges & Warlow, 1990a, 1990b; Melo et al., 1992; Zorzon et al., 1995).

Migraine was thought to be a cause of TGA for several reasons: First, its relative prevalence in TGA (estimated to vary anywhere from 2% to 30%; Hodges & Warlow, 1990a, 1990b; Zorzon et al., 1995) was noted quite early (Poser & Ziegler, 1960; Fisher & Adams, 1964; Evans, 1966; Whitty, 1977b). Second, migraine-like symptoms, notably headache, are present in between 17% to 58% of TGA episodes (Hodges & Warlow, 1990a, 1990b). Third, migraine and TGA present similar profiles of blood flow anomalies (hypoperfusion) as determined by functional imaging studies, especially in the temporal lobes and in the distribution of the posterior cerebral arteries (Norris, Hachinski, & Cooper, 1975; Mathew, Hrastnik, & Meyer, 1976; Lauritzen, Skyhoj Olsen, Lassen, & Paulson, 1983a). Two mechanisms have been proposed linking migraine and TGA and are supported by functional imaging data. The first is vasoconstriction resulting in temporary ischemia that would cause both the migraine symptoms and TGA. The second is spreading depression. This phenomenon entails neuronal depolarization, resulting in depression of normal EEG rhythms, and is followed by a decrease in blood flow persisting for as long as 1 hour (Lauritzen et al., 1983a; Lauritzen, Skyhoj Olsen, Lassen, & Paulson, 1983b). It can be triggered by sensory stimulation in animals and, when present in the hippocampus, causes reversible (functional) ablation with attendant amnesia (Bures, Buresova, & Krivanek, 1974). The hypothesis is that spreading depression occurs during a migraine episode and accounts for blood flow changes and memory disturbances observed during a migraine attack (Olesen & Jorgensen, 1986). Moreover, it is speculated that intense volleys of sensory input to the hippocampus trigger release of glutamate, which is shown to produce spreading depression in experimental animals (Bures et al., 1974). Yet, the evidence in favor of a causal connection between TGA and migraine is tentative, as are the two specific physiological mechanisms that were proposed to account for both syndromes. Moreover, the fact remains that the majority of TGA episodes are not accompanied by migraine or by EEG changes (which are a sign of spreading depression).

The fourth and most recent pathophysiological explanation of TGA also invokes a vascular mechanism—one triggered by a transient disruption in the venous system. It supposes that all precipitating factors of TGA would be expected to cause an increased return of venous blood to the superior vena cava. This may be caused by intense physical exertion that would entail increased arterial flow to the arms or by immersion in cold water, which may produce the diving reflex (bradycardia, peripheral vasoconstriction, and apnea). This response involves sympathetic activation, which in turn involves increases in central venous pressure due to diversion of arterial blood from the periphery to the core. Emotional arousal (for instance, during sexual intercourse) is also associated with increased venous return because it also requires sympathetic activation. In all such cases, a Valsalva-like maneuver takes place, eventually causing transient cerebral ischemia. The maneuver consists of a forceful expiration against a closed glottis, as for example during coughing, heavy lifting, straining to defecate, sexual intercourse, sawing, or pumping. Such forceful expiration leads to increased intrathoracic pressure, reduction of the diameter of the superior vena cava, and decreased venous return to the heart. Subsequently, venous flow from the internal jugular veins to the superior vena cava is reduced, leading to an increase in pressure in the cerebral venous system (venous hypertension), which then results in cerebral ischemia by slowing delivery of arterial blood to brain structures. Obstruction of venous return from the brain can be momentary, affecting cerebral blood flow to limbic structures, ultimately causing TGA. The likelihood that these structures would be affected is upheld by the fact that they depend for venous drainage on the vein of Galen, which drains ultimately into the internal jugular veins.

Although this hypothesis is attractive, it rests on the assumption that momentary disruption of blood supply is sufficient to disrupt the limbic mechanism of memory for hours after the ischemic incident. The assumption may be reasonable given that transient thromboembolic ischemia during angiography (see Case 3 above) also disrupts memory for hours. Whatever the underlying cause of the regional disruption of blood supply, it is possible that it triggers neurochemical events, such as the release of glutamate in the hippocampus, which may in turn last for several hours. The combined effects of vascular insufficiency and secondary neuronal processes may account for both the transient nature of the deficit in memory function and the permanent inability to recollect any of the events experienced during the TGA incident.

PROGNOSIS AND TREATMENT

If cases of amnesia due to thromboembolic events are excluded from the TGA diagnostic category, the TGA episode itself has an excellent prognosis and does not predict higher morbidity or mortality for TGA patients than expected for age-matched individuals in the population (Hodges & Warlow, 1990a, 1990b; Melo et al., 1992; Zorzon et al., 1995). Moreover, the majority of patients experience only one TGA episode.

As mentioned repeatedly, the episode itself is of relatively short duration, usually 4 to 6 hours, rarely over 12 hours, and never longer than 24 hours. It was also mentioned, however, that resolution of TGA within these time limits results in dramatic improvement of memory to levels that, from a clinical viewpoint, would not be considered pathological. Nevertheless, formal neuropsychological testing discloses some residual memory deficits that persist for weeks or months after the episode (Mazzucchi et al., 1980; Caffarra et al., 1981; Regard & Landis, 1984; Gallassi et al., 1986a; Hodges & Oxbury, 1990; Stillhard et al., 1990). The deficits are both verbal and nonverbal and mostly anterograde. Retrograde residual deficits may be hard to assess owing to the poor quality of the tests specifically designed for that purpose. Besides those subclinical deficits, the patients are permanently amnesic for events that transpired during the episode.

Given the benign prognosis of TGA, the shortness of its acute and clinically significant phase, and the fact that its pathophysiology remains hidden, providing no treatment is neither unreasonable nor particularly undesirable. During the episode, the patient needs reassurance, which includes patiently answering repeated questions. Although no semantic or procedural memory deficits are present during the episode, the patient ought to remain under observation and undergo careful examination either during or soon after the resolution of the acute stage to exclude epilepsy, cerebrovascular insults, or other causes of the condition. The patients with documented TGA should be reassured that the likelihood of repetition of the episode is small, and they should be informed that they will have a permanent memory gap for the episode itself.

SUMMARY

TGA incidents are characterized by acute onset, severe anterograde amnesia for verbal and nonverbal material, and retrograde amnesia that affects both public and personal events. The temporal extent of the retrograde amnesia is variable, ranging from an apparently complete inability to recall any episodes experienced during two or more decades preceding the TGA incident to the presence of gaps in the continuum of past events. Amnesia manifests with a profound disorientation to time and place, while the sense of personal identity is preserved throughout the incident. Immediate memory is intact, and deficits in thinking, planning, and organizational abilities, if present, are only subtle. Although there are some indications for a temporal gradient in the retrograde memory deficit (Kritchevsky et al., 1997) (better recollection for more distant events), a gradient entailing faster return of distant memories appears more likely (Hodges & Ward, 1989; Guillery-Girard, Desgranges, Urban et al., 2004). Despite an explicit memory deficit, procedural knowledge acquired prior to the incident remains largely intact. To our knowledge, implicit nonprocedural memory for events experienced prior to the TGA incident has not been systematically examined.

The inability to recall or recognize newly presented material during the TGA incident, and the permanent inability to recollect the incident itself after its resolution, suggest that at least one of the core underlying deficits in TGA is a dysfunction in the brain mechanism that is responsible for the formation of new memories. The cognitive impairment responsible for the retrograde amnesia is less evident. One possibility is that retrograde amnesia is caused by dysfunction of the brain mechanism responsible for retrieval. This hypothesis is concordant with the presence of other "frontal" symptoms characteristic of the disorder.

9

Transient Epileptic Amnesia

MARY H. KOSMIDIS AND
ANDREW C. PAPANICOLAOU

Transient epileptic amnesia (TEA; a term coined by Kapur, 1993) is a unique and perhaps underdiagnosed seizure disorder. It is characterized by a failure to incorporate into long-term memory any events that occurred during the seizure (Mendes, 2002). What is remarkable about the disorder is that cognitive function appears to be intact during the ictal phase. In fact, reliable observers have reported no obvious indication of dysfunction, as patients continued to engage in ongoing activity without interruption (Palmini, Gloor, & Jones-Gotman, 1992; Kapur, 1993). In these accounts, the only behavioral indications of the ictal episode were subsequent reports of amnesia regarding the events, usually manifested as repetitive questioning regarding the amnesic period.

Reports of amnesia for brief periods during which activity proceeded without interruption, although rare, have appeared in the literature over the past 100 years and have associated these episodes with temporal lobe epilepsy (cf. Zeman, Boniface, & Hodges, 1998). A more recent report of several cases of TEA supported this association by demonstrating mesial temporal lobe epilepsy (MTLE) and the typical signs of seizure disorder in the same patients (Palmini et al., 1992). The variability in the clinical profile of these patients makes diagnosis difficult. Whereas many investigators have suggested that this type of seizure is usually accompanied by other seizures as well (Gallassi, Morreale, Lorusso et al., 1988; Bridgman, Malamut, Sperling et al., 1989; Gallassi, Morreale, Di Sarro, & Lugaresi, 1992; Lee, Lee, Hwang et al., 1992; Palmini et al., 1992; Kapur, 1993; Kopelman, Panayiotopoulos, & Lewis, 1994b; Rabinowicz, Starkstein, Leiguarda, & Coleman, 2000; Corridan, Leung, & Jenkins, 2001); several researchers have reported cases in which this seizure type was the only symptom (cf. Zeman et al., 1998). In fact, seizures that lead to amnesia could easily be misdiagnosed as transient global amnesia (TGA) (Hodges, 1991) or psychogenic amnesia (Kopelman et al., 1994b).

The following case reports afford representative descriptions of patients with TEA.

Case Study 1

A 45-year-old man with a 20-year history of complex partial seizures, some with secondary generalization, was seen because of an increase in the number of his habitual seizures. He had been taking inappropriately low doses of three antiepileptic drugs (AEDs) for years. Two of these drugs were slowly withdrawn and carbamazepine (CBZ) was increased up to 1400 mg/day. After 4 months he went on carbamazepine monotherapy. Two months later he was free of his habitual seizures, but started noticing a new sort of "blank spell." He described that 15 days before, he had arrived home, but with no idea of his journey. The following day he asked a colleague, who usually traveled with him, what had happened the day before. His colleague explained that they had taken the usual bus and they had discussed a football match on their way home. His friend was interviewed afterwards. He remarked that the patient was completely normal during their conversation and he did not show any subtle signs of impaired consciousness. The patient was completely amnesic for the entire period. He was also unable to remember how he arrived home. Following a further increment in CBZ the "blank spell" decreased in frequency although it did not stop completely. He has been followed for seven years without any significant change in the number of the "blank spells" (TEA) but he is now free of secondary generalized seizures and has one or two partial complex seizures/year.

(From Mendes, 2002, with permission from *Seizure*)

Case Study 2

A 71-year old woman presented with a 6-month history of four episodes of "completely forgetting." One of these episodes was witnessed by the caretaker of her apartment building and the second indirectly by her son, during a phone call. In the first episode she went to a shop on a Saturday morning, as was her usual practice. When she arrived home the caretaker helped her carry her bags to her flat. Inside the lift she talked normally, without any sign of impaired consciousness or prolonged reaction time. In her flat while unpacking the bags, she suddenly asked the caretaker: "Who has bought these? Who went to the supermarket?" The caretaker replied: "You did Miss, as you usually do on Saturday mornings." She repeatedly said: "Are you sure that I did? I cannot remember leaving my house today! What is happening to me?" The witness reported that, apart from her dazed appearance and repeated queries at the end of the episode, her behavior was completely normal. She confirmed that she went to the shop by comparing the bill with the value in her checkbook. There was no clue of any alteration in her behavior or awareness during the time he observed her. The second episode happened while she was phoning her son. They talked for approximately 40 minutes. She made arrangements for visiting him on the next weekend. Her son reported that she spoke normally, again without any delay in replying. During the call she did not show any sign of losing track of the conversation. Two days later, the son phoned to confirm her visit and discovered that she was amnesic for the whole event. She vigorously denied having phoned him and making arrangements for the visit. During the next two months she experienced two more episodes, one documented by a friend during a phone call, the last one was again witnessed by the caretaker. She was able to remember that she had forgotten what she had done before in episodes one, two and four and that she had repeatedly asked the caretaker. Her EEGs and brain MRI scan were normal; although no detailed assessment of the hippocampus was undertaken. The possible diagnosis was discussed, carbamazepine was introduced and titrated up to 600 mg daily. She has been followed for 3 years with no further episodes. No cognitive decline was observed, as assessed by a Mini-Mental State Examination (MMSE), although she has always complained about memory impairment. She continued to live alone and independently when she was last seen.

(From Mendes, 2002, with the permission of *Seizure*)

Case Study 3

A 74-year-old man presented with a two-month history of three episodes of "forgetting and a little confusion" that lasted for almost one hour. Three of these episodes were witnessed by two different observers. Both were interviewed separately and confirmed that, besides his dazed appearance and repetitive questioning at the end of the episode, he appeared normal for the period that he was amnesic. In the first episode he and his wife had left their house to visit a friend. After almost one hour walking and talking normally, he suddenly asked her "where are we now? Why did we come here?" He then became perplexed and asked the same question many times. He remembered having asked her these questions and that he did not know what they were going to do. The two other episodes were similar. A MRI scan was normal, although hippocampal volumes were not measured. He had two normal awake EEGs and only one demonstrated nonspecific intermittent slowing (rare) over the frontotemporal regions, without any side emphasis. The possible diagnosis was discussed and he decided to take 250 mg of phenytoin. He has been followed for 3 years. After one year free of episodes, he decided to stop the phenytoin because he would like to drink alcohol during the Christmas period. Two weeks later he experienced a further episode, lasting almost one hour. He recommenced his AED again and thereafter had no further episodes.

(From Mendes, 2002, with the permission of *Seizure*)

The patients described in the case studies failed to show any seizures or indications of cognitive decline on multiple follow-up assessments over several years (Mendes, 2002). Two of the three patients were aware of the fact that they had had an amnesic episode; in fact, this awareness apparently led to the termination of the episodes.

All patients were concerned about losing their memory and complained of memory problems. Their structural imaging was normal (one patient underwent computed tomography [CT] and the other two underwent magnetic resonance imaging [MRI]).

TESTING AND ESTABLISHMENT OF SYMPTOMS

Only one study has reported neuropsychological evaluations of a group of patients with TEA (Zeman et al., 1998). This evaluation, which targeted memory skills alone, included measures of both anterograde and retrograde memory. Table 9–1 (Zeman et al., 1998) lists the tests administered and the performance

Table 9–1 Neuropsychological Test Results

	TEA mean (SD)	Controls mean (SD)
Anterograde memory tests (Maximum score in parenthesis)		
Age	65 (9)	70 (8)
Education (y)	12 (2)	11 (2)
NART	115 (6)	119 (7)
Story recall WMS		
Immediate (21)	13 (4)	12 (4)
Delayed (21)	10 (3)	9 (3)
Rey-Ostereith figure		
Copy (36)	35 (1)	34 (3)
Delayed recall (36)	20 (4)	15 (8)
Recognition memory test		
Words (50)	46 (3)	47 (3)
Faces (50)	43 (4)	44 (4)
Retrograde memory tests (Maximum scores in parenthesis)		
Famous faces test		
Recognition (50)	47 (2)	43 (7)
Identification (50)	38 (5)	39 (9)
Naming (50)	26 (10)	31 (4)
Famous names test		
Recognition (50)	49 (1)	50 (1)
Identification (50)	46 (2)	49 (1)
Autobiographical memory interview		
Personal semantic		
Childhood (21)	19 (2)	20 (2)
Early adulthood (21)	18 (2)	20 (2)
Late adulthood (21)	20 (2)	20 (1)
Personal incident		
Childhood (9)	8 (2)	7 (2)
Early adulthood (9)	7 (2)	8 (2)
Late adulthood (9)	7 (3)	7 (2)

NART, National Adult Reading Test; WMS, Wechsler Memory Scale.

From Zeman, Boniface, & Hodges, 1998, with permission of *Journal of Neurology, Neurosurgery and Psychiatry*.

of that patient group relative to that of a healthy control group. As a group, the patients with TEA did not differ from the controls in either demographic characteristics or neuropsychological test performance. An analysis of individual test scores, however, yielded a different pattern. Seven of the 10 patients evaluated had scored more than two standard deviations below the mean of the control group on at least one test, suggesting impairment in the particular skill being measured. All but one of the tests revealing impairment had measured retrograde memory; the others measured anterograde memory (Zeman et al., 1998). Thus, the overall profile of patients with TEA was misleading in that it appeared normal with respect to memory functioning, when, in fact, most individuals in this sample had some memory impairment.

Interestingly, patients' memory deficits were not limited to the ictal events but appeared to be long-standing. In addition to their scores on objective memory tests, patients also reported subjective complaints of remote memory impairment (Zeman et al., 1998; Mendes, 2002). Table 9–2 shows the clinical profile of the patients in the same study (Zeman et al., 1998).

Seven of the 10 patients reported an inability to recall personal information or events. The impairment had a temporal gradient with extensive amnesia for more recent events but less so for those in the distant past. In most cases, the impairment affected recall for episodes, which predated the clinical onset of TEA by many months or even years. This pattern is suggestive of bilateral hippocampal dysfunction subsequent to the attacks (Zeman et al., 1998).

Beyond their complaints of retrograde memory problems, patients reported other types of amnesia (Zeman et al., 1998). Six patients reported difficulty recognizing familiar landmarks and routes, suggesting topographical amnesia (an inability to remember topographical relationships between landmarks that can be identified individually). Three complained of difficulty in recalling the names of people they had known for many years, and two complained of a loss of procedural memory regarding a presumably overlearned work-related technique (although these are not specified in the study). Only one, however, complained of an impairment of everyday memory. At least one case study described a patient who presented with two episodes of transient anomia for his children's names as the only clinical manifestation of his TEA (Ghika-Schmid & Nater, 2003).

In their study of 10 patients with TEA, Zeman and his colleagues (1998) noted the characteristic features of these episodes. Based on patient reports, they concluded that TEA attacks occur rather frequently: nine attacks over a 3-year period, or an average of three per year. TEA episodes are also relatively brief in duration, with many lasting less than 1 hour (Mendes, 2002), although in some cases they lasted several hours or days. Zeman and his colleagues (1998) reported that, at the time of diagnosis, their patients already had a history of amnesic episodes ranging from 4 months to 14 years, with a mean duration of illness of 3 years. Although retrograde amnesia subsequent to the attacks was usually brief, all patients reported some episodes when it extended over several months, with six patients reporting that it had extended over many years.

Table 9–2 Current Series: Clinical, EEG, and Neuropsychological Features

Case	Age	Sex	History (Duration)	Attacks	Attack (Duration)	Repetitive Questioning	Sleep Related	EEG Findings	Rx Response	Other Epilepsy	TEA Aura	Focal Retrograde Amnesia
1	63	M	3 y	20	1 h	+	+	–	+ CBZ	sps	+/–	+
2	49	M	4 mo	12	<1 h	+	+	+Bilateral	+ CBZ	sps	+/–	+
3	68	M	8 mo	5	h to days	+	+	+Bilateral	+ SVP	sps,cps	–	+
4	66	F	1+	5	<1 h ≥1 h	+	+	+L	E CBZ	–	–	–
5	79	M	15 mo	3	h to days	+	+	+Bilateral	E CBZ	–	–	+
6	70	M	2 y	13	<1 h	+	+	Polyr	No Rx	sps	+/–	–
7	73	M	6 mo	5	1 to 2 h	–	+	Polyr	+ P	–	–	–
8	60	M	6 mo	3	<1 h ≥1 h	+	+	–	+ SVP	tcl	–	+
9	69	M	4 mo	3	<1 h	+	+	–	+ CBZ	cps	+/–	+
10	56	M	9 mo	20	<1 h	+	+	–	+ CBZ	cps, tcl	–	+

EEG, electroencephalograph; Polyr, polyrhythmic abnormalities present; Rx response, treatment response (+, abolition or substantial reduction of episodes; E, equivocal reduction, CBZ, carbamazepine; P, phenytoin, SVP, sodium valproate); sps, simple partial seizures; cps, complex partial seizures; tcl, tonic-clonic seizures; transient epileptic amnesia (TEA) aura, occurrence of co-occurring seizure type as prodrome of amnesic episode (+, co-occurring seizure type always precedes TEA; +/–, co-occurring seizure type sometimes precedes TEA; –, no co-occurring seizure type).

From Zeman, Boniface, & Hodges, 1998, with permission of *Journal of Neurology, Neurosurgery and Psychiatry*.

One characteristic of TEA is that episodes appear to be sleep-related. All patients in the Zeman and colleagues study (1998) reported at least one attack upon awakening, with most describing episodes on awakening as a frequent occurrence. Therefore, amnesic episodes that occur upon awakening are considered to be a distinguishing feature of TEA.

Another potentially distinguishing feature of TEA is the patients' repeated questioning of an observer. Nine of the 10 patients in the Zeman and colleagues (1998) study had questioned a companion repeatedly after an episode regarding the events that took place during their amnesic period. This is in contrast, however, to Kapur's (1993) finding that repeated questioning was not a typical feature of TEA.

A final distinguishing characteristic of TEA is the patients' response to anticonvulsant medication. Although medication response is generally not an appropriate diagnostic criterion, the fact remains that most patients who underwent treatment with anticonvulsant drugs showed improvement (for a review of published reports, see Zeman et al., 1998). Of course, there is an inherent selection bias in this group in that they presented for treatment.

Table 9–3 (Zeman et al., 1998) lists previously published reports of cases with TEA and summarizes their clinical, electrophysiological, and neuropsychological features. Overall, these reports are in concordance with each other with respect to these features: Most patients reported episodes upon awakening, had positive response to anticonvulsant medication, abnormal EEG findings and other types of epileptic seizures, and impaired memory according to self-report or formal testing. An exception to this otherwise uniform symptomatology was introduced by four patients for whom the amnesic episodes always followed complex partial seizures (Gallassi, Pazzaglia, Lorusso, & Morreale, 1986b; Gallassi & Morreale, 1990; Stracciari, Ciucci, Bianchedi, & Rebucci, 1990).

PRECIPITATING FACTORS

The prevalence of TEA is higher in men (12 of 20 cases reported in case studies; 9 out of 10 cases reported by Zeman et al., 1998) relative to women. The typical age of onset is in later life (Hodges & Warlow, 1990a) between the ages of 49 and 73 years (Zeman et al., 1998); however, there exist reported cases of an 11-year-old girl (Deisenhammer, 1981) and a 37-year-old man (Ghika-Schmid & Nater, 2003).

A common risk factor for TEA is a history of cardiovascular disorder (Hodges & Warlow, 1990a; Zeman et al., 1998). It is hypothesized that the hypoxia induced in individuals with cardiovascular disorder may damage the mesial temporal lobes, thus inducing epileptic activity. Two other possible factors are head injury and tumors: reported cases had severe head injuries with loss of consciousness in early adulthood, with negligible to minimal posttraumatic amnesia (Zeman et al., 1998), another two had tumors (Meador, Adams, & Flanigan, 1985; Shuping, Toole, & Alexander, 1980), one had experienced focal infarction

Table 9–3 Previously Reported Cases: Clinical, EEG, and Neuropsychological Features

Reference	Age	Sex	History (Duration)	Attacks (n)	Attack (Duration)	Repetitive Questioning	Sleep Related	EEG Findings	Rx Response	Other Epilepsy	TEA Aura	Focal Retrograde Amnesia	Memory Tests
Lou (1968)	61	M	?	9	15 min ≥ h	+	+	+R	+ OXZ	–	–	–	Ant
Shuping et al. (1980)	60	M	?	3	< 1 h	?	?	–	–	tcl	–	–	ND
Deisenhammer (1981)	11	F	1 mo	4	< 1 h	+	+	+R	+ CBZ	–	–	–	ND
Dugan et al. (1981)	82	M	2 mo	3	3 to 4 h	+	?	+Bilateral	+ P	–	–	–	ND
Pritchard et al. (1985)													
i	65	M	4 y	10	< 15 min	–	?	+Bilateral	+ P	–	–	?	ND
ii	64	M	6 mo	3	1 to 24 h	–	?	+Bilateral	+ CBZ	–	–	?	ND
Meador et al. (1985)	47	F	10 mo	2	< 1 h	–	–	+Bilateral	+ P/surg	cps	–	–	Normal
Galassi et al. (1986b)	67	M	2 y	25	< 1 h	+	+	ThetaR	E P	sps/cps	+	Imp mem	Verb
Gallassi et al. (1988)													
i	70	F	3 y	2 to 3/week	< 1 h	+	?	+R	+ CBZ	cps	+	Imp mem	Vis/verb
ii	66	M	2 y	1/mo	< 1 h	+	?	ThetaL	+ CBZ	cps	+	Imp mem	Verb
Miller et al. (1987b)													
i	62	M	14 mo	8	< 30 min	+	+	+Bilateral	+ P	–	–	–	ND
ii	22	?	Weeks	Several	< 1 h	?	?	+L	+ ?	cps	+/–	?	ND
Stracciari et al. (1987)	70	F	8 m	8	10 min to 7 h	+	–	+L	+ CBZ	cps	+/–	Imp mem	Vis/verb

(continued on the following page)

197

Table 9–3 Previously Reported Cases: Clinical, EEG, and Neuropsychological Features *(Continued)*

Reference	Age	Sex	History (Duration)	Attacks (n)	Attack (Duration)	Repetitive Questioning	Sleep Related	EEG Findings	Rx Response	Other Epilepsy	TEA Aura	Focal Retrograde Amnesia	Memory Tests
Kapur (1989)	74	M	5 y	20	30 min ≥ h	?	+	+Bilateral	?	cps	+/–	+	Retro
Kapur (1993)													
i	63	F	3 y	35	min ≥ h	–	?	ThetaL	+ SVP	cps	+/–	Imp mem	Vis/retro
ii	67	F	4 mo	6	30 min to 1 h	–	?	ThetaL	+ P	–	–	–	Normal
iii	28	M	?	20	1 to 2/day	+	+	+Bilateral	+ CBZ/P	cps	+/–	?	Vis/verb
iv	61	F	?	2	min	?	+	+L	+ CBZ	cps	+/–	Imp mem	?
v	60	M	3 y	Many	10 to 15 min	+	?	+Bilateral	+ CBZ	sps, cps	+	?	Verb
vi	54	M	21 months	8	30 min to 1 h	+	?	+Bilateral	+ P	cps	+/–	+	Ant
Vuilleumier et al. (1996)	41	F	≥ 20 y	Many	Hours	–	+	+Bilateral	+ CBZ	sps	+	–	Normal

EEG, electroencephalograph; Rx response, treatment response (+, abolition or substantial reduction of episodes; E, equivocal reduction; CBZ, carbamazepine; P, phenytoin; SVP, sodium valproate; OXZ, oxazepam; surg, surgery); other epilepsy, other co-occurring seizure types (sps, simple partial seizures; cps, complex partial seizures; tcl, tonic-clonic seizures); transient epileptic amnesia (TEA) aura, occurrence of co-occurring seizure type as prodrome of amnesic episode (+, co-occurring seizure type always precedes TEA; +/–, co-occurring seizure type sometimes precedes TEA; –, no co-occurring seizure type); Imp mem, complaint of impaired memory not further specified; vis/verb, deficits on tests of anterograde visual/verbal memory; ant, anterograde memory impairment not further specified; retro, deficits on tests of retrograde memory; ND, not defined.

From Zeman, Boniface, & Hodges, 1998, with permission of *Journal of Neurology, Neurosurgery, and Psychiatry.*

of the posterior corpus callosum and another focal atrophy of the right hippocampus (Zeman et al., 1998).

DIFFERENTIAL DIAGNOSIS

There is now considerable evidence that supports the existence of TEA as a distinct neurological entity (Zeman et al., 1998). TEA often coexists with complex partial seizures of temporal lobe origin (Penfield & Mathieson, 1974; Pritchard, Holmstrom, Roitzsch, & Giacinto, 1985; Palmini et al., 1992; Kapur, 1993), while several reports have claimed that ictal amnesia is the main clinical feature of this disorder (Penfield & Mathieson, 1974; Pritchard et al., 1985; Gallassi et al., 1988; Palmini et al., 1992). Another view is that these seizures should be classified as mesial temporal lobe epilepsy, as on close inspection of the descriptions of ictal behavior, they showed classic signs of this type of epilepsy (Mendes, 2002).

In order to differentiate TEA from other possible diagnoses, Zeman and his colleagues (1998) have proposed three criteria: patients with transient amnesic episodes must demonstrate epileptiform discharges on EEG, have concurrent onset of other seizure types, and have a response to anticonvulsant pharmacotherapy. The authors based their proposition that TEA is a distinct neurological entity on the observation that two of their patients satisfied all three criteria; the rest satisfied either one or two of the criteria. Despite some differences, they concluded that all three groups of patients shared a common mechanism with respect to their transient amnesia, as was evidenced by the fact that the clinical features of their attacks were identical (Zeman et al., 1998).

To date, more than 30 patients have been described either in single case or group studies, who fulfill some of the diagnostic criteria proposed for TEA (Penfield & Mathieson, 1974; Rowan & Protass, 1979; Pritchard et al., 1985; Gallassi et al., 1988; Bridgman et al., 1989; Gallassi et al., 1992; Lee et al., 1992; Palmini et al., 1992; Kapur, 1993; Kopelman et al., 1994b; Zeman et al., 1998; Rabinowicz et al., 2000; Corridan et al., 2001; Ghika-Schmid & Nater, 2003). The criteria proposed by several researchers are as follows: (a) recurrent episodes of transient amnesia witnessed by an observer, who confirms that the patient's cognitive functions, other than memory, are intact during the episodes; (b) evidence supporting a diagnosis of epilepsy, as shown by an awake or sleeping EEG, or the co-occurrence of other types of seizures; or (c) a positive response to anticonvulsant medication (Hodges & Warlow, 1990a; Palmini et al., 1992; Kapur, 1993; Zeman et al., 1998).

Nevertheless, diagnosing TEA continues to be difficult. On the one hand, many neurologists may be unaware of TEA as a separate diagnostic entity; consequently, they may fail to request the background information necessary to rule it out. On the other hand, patients often neglect to report transient amnesic episodes because they do not perceive a relationship between these episodes of forgetting and their seizures (Thompson & Corcoran, 1992), perhaps attributing them to the aging process or their anticonvulsant medication (Zeman et al.,

1998). Therefore, a diagnosis of TEA often requires a follow-up period to confirm that there have been no more episodes and that the anticonvulsant medications have resulted in improvement. Consequently, the diagnosis can only be made retrospectively or by inquiring specifically for such episodes in prospective studies.

There are several major concerns in making a diagnosis of TEA. Perhaps the most critical is differentiating it from TGA (Hodges & Warlow, 1990a) (see Chapter 8). Other potential differential diagnoses are somatization disorder with pseudo-neurologic symptoms (Betts, 1998); that is, amnesia, and dissociative amnesia (Thomas & Trimble, 1998). Nevertheless, TEA can be distinguished from other possible diagnoses on the basis of its characteristic features, one of which is its epileptic origin. Also, TEA differs from TGA on several features related to the occurrence of the amnesic episodes. Relative to TGA attacks, TEA episodes are much more frequent (Hodges, 1991), briefer (Mendes, 2002), and often occur upon awakening.

Another feature that may distinguish TEA from TGA is the patient's recollection of the attack. After a TEA episode, patients are often able to recall some of the details. In fact, Zeman and his colleagues (1998) reported that half of their patients with TEA could partially recall their attacks. In particular, they were "able to remember not being able to remember" (p. 440) events during the episodes.

There are contradictory reports regarding whether transient amnesia is the sole manifestation of epilepsy (Zeman et al., 1998), whereas others report that patients with temporal lobe epilepsy exhibit seizures other than the amnesic type (Palmini et al., 1992). In any case, temporal lobe epilepsy is an important diagnosis to consider in patients with brief recurrent episodes of amnesia, especially if they occur upon awakening. This is particularly important in light of findings of Hodges (1991), who reported that 7% of patients diagnosed with TGA later developed epilepsy of complex partial seizure type; and in another investigation, one of five patients with a diagnosis of TGA had epilepsy (Melo, 1994).

With the exception of one investigation (Zeman et al., 1998), no studies have addressed the issue of psychiatric comorbidity in their cases of patients with TEA. Zeman and his colleagues (1998) found that almost half of their patients (4 of 10) had either a definite (two patients) or a possible (two patients) history of a psychiatric disorder. More studies are needed to clarify the frequency and the role of psychiatric comorbidity in patients with TEA.

PATHOPHYSIOLOGY

The role of the medial temporal lobes in information acquisition and storage is now widely accepted (Squire & Alvarez, 1995), as is that of neocortical areas in the storage of autobiographical and semantic memories (Alvarez & Squire, 1994; McClelland, McNaughton, & O'Reilly, 1995; Murre, 1997; Graham & Hodges, 1997). Consequently, it is very likely that dysfunction in these regions could account for the clinical picture of TEA (Zeman et al., 1998). Investigations using depth electrodes have confirmed speculations expressed in studies using surface EEG that the mesial temporal areas are the source of the epileptiform activity (Morrell, 1980; Bridgman et al., 1989; Lee et al., 1992; Palmini et al., 1992). These data, combined with the clinical features of the seizures in TEA, provide strong support for mesial temporal lobe involvement.

One feature of TEA that remains unclear is whether the amnesic episodes occur during the ictal phase or subsequent to it. There are accounts in the literature of both ictal and postictal amnesia. More specifically, Palmini et al. (1992) described a case in which anterograde amnesia followed a brief epileptic seizure in both mesial temporal lobes. The patient had no recall of a telephone conversation during this episode. Other studies have demonstrated that transient temporal lobe seizures can disrupt recently encoded information, such as the recall of a list of words learned just before a unilateral hippocampal seizure (Bridgman et al., 1989). In fact, in an investigation of the effects of stimulating the mesial temporal regions, Halgren, Wilson, and Stapleton (1985) demonstrated that information acquisition and retrieval can be disrupted without affecting other cognitive functions.

Another question that has not been answered adequately is whether long periods of amnesia can be attributed to ictal or postictal activity. Several cases support each possibility. One case report (Lee et al., 1992) described a 38-year-old woman with a 12-day episode of continuous anterograde amnesia, including some retrograde amnesia, during a partial seizure. Recordings by nasopharyngeal electrodes showed frequent spikes in the mesial temporal lobes bilaterally. The authors concluded that intermittent temporal lobe discharges might appear as ictal amnesia that closely resembles TGA. In another case, a 41-year-old woman with a long history of repeated retrograde amnesia episodes (Vuilleumier, Desplane, & Regli, 1996) described experiencing an epigastric aura before her episodes, which frequently occurred shortly after awakening from sleep. One of her attacks during an EEG recording session was characterized by generalized epileptiform spikes with frontotemporal phase reversal. When treated intravenously with clonazepam, she demonstrated clear recall even for the ictal events. Other investigators (Morrell, 1980; Tassinari, Ciarmatori, Alesi et al., 1991) have described similar cases of amnesic episodes in the absence of epileptiform activity.

Memory problems in patients with TEA are not limited to the actual occurrence of an episode but may persist between episodes (Gallassi et al., 1988; Kapur, 1989; Stracciari et al., 1990; Kopelman et al., 1994b; Zeman et al., 1998). Zeman and his colleagues (1998) reported retrograde memory disturbance in their patients, who as a group performed in the normal range on neuropsychological tests. Individual analysis of test performance showed retrograde memory deficits in half of their patients, with one showing anterograde memory impairment. Poor retrograde memory with intact anterograde memory in TEA has been reported in another study as well (Kapur, 1989). In contrast, another patient had borderline scores on retrograde memory with poor anterograde memory (Kopelman et al., 1994b). The lack of consistency in these findings may be a reflection of the inconsistent nature of the impairment, as patients often report gaps in their autobiographical memory rather than graded amnesia. In fact, one patient (Zeman et al., 1998) showed profound autobiographical memory gaps for the 30-year period preceding the evaluation.

Nearly all studies of TEA, whether single case reports or group investigations, have reported EEG abnormalities in their patients (Lou, 1968; Shuping, Toole, & Alexander, 1980; Deisenhammer, 1981; Dugan, Nordgren, & O'Leary, 1981; Meador et al., 1985; Pritchard et al., 1985; Galassi et al., 1986b; Miller, Yanagihara, Petersen, & Klass, 1987b; Stracciari et al., 1990; Galassi et al., 1992; Kapur, 1993; Zeman et al., 1998; Ghika-Schmid & Nater, 2003) (see Tables 9–2 and 9–3). At least half of these patients presented with bilateral anterior or mesial temporal abnormalities. Fewer demonstrated either right or left temporal discharges. Very few patients had a normal EEG.

Zeman and his colleagues (1998) reported structural neuroimaging findings for their sample of TEA patients. All but one patient had a CT scan; all were within normal limits. Four patients underwent MRI. These were normal in two patients, while in one patient there was evidence of posterior corpus callosum focal infarction, and in another patient there was right anterior and mid-hippocampal focal atrophy. Two patients had a single photon emission computed tomography (SPECT) scan, which indicated mild frontal lobe hypoperfusion in both cases. There is only one report of mildly decreased left hippocampal volume (Ghika-Schmid & Nater, 2003).

PROGNOSIS AND TREATMENT

There are no reports of systematic investigations regarding the treatment and prognosis for patients with TEA. Those studies exploring the clinical characteristics of the disorder, however, have shown that most patients respond positively to the use of anticonvulsant medications. Pharmacological treatment achieved either total cessation of episodes or a notable decrease in frequency (Zeman et al., 1998; Mendes, 2002).

SUMMARY

TEA is a disorder difficult to diagnose, as it is characterized by transient episodes of amnesia, which take place while the patient, according to witnesses, behaves normally. Patients often are aware of their lapse in memory and, upon examination, present some anterograde, but primarily retrograde, amnesia for specific events, without a temporal gradient. The amnesia is not limited to the ictal and postictal phase but sometimes extends to periods predating the onset of the disorder by many years. Bilateral hippocampal epileptiform activity has been implicated in the clinical symptoms of TEA. Episodes are typically frequent and brief, often occur upon awakening, are followed by repeated questioning on the part of the patient (reminiscent of TGA; see previous chapter), respond to anticonvulsant medications, and often coexist with other types of seizures as well. TEA is most frequent in older men and in the elderly. Although its etiology has yet to be determined, risk factors include cardiovascular disease, head trauma, tumor, infarct, and atrophy of the brain. Neurophysiological and neuroimaging studies have revealed abnormal EEG activity, usually in the mesial temporal region, bilaterally.

Based on the clinical profile of patients, TEA is considered a type of temporal lobe epilepsy disorder. It often occurs in people with a history of complex partial seizures in temporal regions and ictal amnesia, the main clinical feature of mesial temporal lobe epilepsy. Although the medial temporal areas are clearly involved, what remains unclear is whether the epileptic activity responsible for the transient amnesic attacks is recent, current, or both. It appears that brief and long antero-grade and retrograde amnesic episodes may reflect an ictal state, whereas longer amnesic episodes may reflect postictal activity, although at this point this is merely speculation. What is certain, however, is that most patients exhibit persistent retrograde memory problems. Although no studies have explored its prognosis in a systematic fashion, it is clear that these patients respond well to anticonvulsant medication. Most reports in the literature cite significant reduction or even cessation of the amnesic attacks with pharmacotherapy.

Although apparently paradoxical, the observation of normal and purposeful behavior during a temporal lobe seizure can be explained by understanding the pathophysiology of the TEA. To the extent that it can be attributed to a seizure restricted only to the hippocampi bilaterally (Palmini et al., 1992), its clinical manifestation would consist of a failure to transfer episodes happening during ictus into long-term memory (Mendes, 2002) and, as long as the epileptiform discharge does not spread to other brain areas, there would be no concurrent behavioral abnormalities. Presumably, patients are not able to encode these episodes into long-term memory during hippocampal seizures (Manes et al., 2001; Mendes, 2002), and this results in the gaps in autobiographical memory often reported (Zeman et al., 1998). Because autobiographical memories are likely to involve both verbal and visual aspects (Bergin, Thompson, Baxendale et al., 2000), amnesia for autobiographical information would imply bilateral hippocampal dysfunction (Bridgman et al., 1989; Palmini et al., 1992; Shulz et al., 1995; Zeman et al., 1998; Bergin et al., 2000; Manes, Hodges, Graham, & Zeman, 2001).

Another possibility, that TEA may involve decay of already consolidated traces is supported by complaints patients sometimes voice about a sudden loss of once intact memories such as those for very familiar places and faces, as well as overlearned work-related skills (Zeman et al., 1998). But semantic memory deficits imply spread of ictal activity to temporal neocortical structures, because the latter are implicated as the locus of storage of semantic memories (see Chapter 5 and Martin et al., 1991; Evans, Heggs, Antoun, & Hodges, 1995; Patterson & Hodges, 1995; Garrard, Perry, & Hodges, 1997). However, lack of sufficient evidence renders all theorism about what mnemonic functions are compromised in TEA quite premature.

10

Electroconvulsive Therapy–Induced Amnesia

MARY H. KOSMIDIS AND
ANDREW C. PAPANICOLAOU

Despite its negative portrayal in popular movies as a controlling, even punitive, treatment for patients with psychiatric disorders (e.g., *One Flew Over the Cuckoo's Nest*), electroconvulsive therapy (ECT) is actually one of the safest and most effective treatments for severe depression (Weiner, 1984; National Institutes of Health [NIH], 1985; Devanand, Dwork, Hutchinson et al., 1994; American Psychiatric Association, 2001), as well as psychotic depression (Fink, 1977; Scovern & Kilmann, 1980; Weiner, 1984; NIH, 1985). Used as a last resort for those who have not responded adequately to antidepressant medications, it is at least as effective, if not superior to, some antidepressant medications (Greenblatt, 1977; Fink, 1978; Scovern & Kilmann, 1980; NIH, 1985). Nevertheless, potential side-effects related to memory disruption have led to controversy about its use.

The procedure, which occurs under general anesthesia, involves the application of electrodes to the head in order to induce a seizure. In the 60 years that have elapsed since its introduction, technological and methodological advances (i.e., brief pulse shocks, dose titration, suprathreshold doses, concurrent electroencephalographic (EEG) monitoring, hyperoxygenation, general anesthesia) have increased its effectiveness and safety and reduced potential side-effects. Concerns regarding the ethical acceptability of this treatment method have focused on its association with subsequent amnesia and its potential for causing permanent brain damage. Postictal effects, such as disorientation (Calev, Cohen, Tubi et al., 1991), and soft neurological signs, such as headaches, confusion, psychomotor slowing (Tubi, Calev, Nigal et al., 1993), resolve after the acute phase. What persists beyond the acute phase, thus fueling the controversy, is impairment in higher cognitive functions, primarily memory. Although there is no question that ECT is associated with memory loss, primarily retrograde, several issues remain unclear. Is the memory loss induced by ECT permanent or merely transient? Does ECT cause structural brain damage or merely functional disruption? Because ECT is delivered to the severely, and, often, chronically depressed, are the memory problems observed after treatment due to the ECT procedure itself or due to the pretreatment severity of the depression or other psychopathology? How does ECT affect new learning?

In this chapter, we will review the recent evidence of memory impairments associated with ECT and we will explore their nature. Moreover, we will address the neurophysiological mechanisms that may underlie ECT-induced memory disruption and discuss the evidence of (or lack thereof) structural brain damage caused by the procedure.

TESTING AND ESTABLISHMENT OF SYMPTOMS

The following reports highlight the cognitive improvement typically observed after a course of ECT, as well as the complexity of such cases.

Case Study 1

A.C., a 75-year-old woman with an 8th grade education and a diagnosis of bipolar disorder, was transferred from the hospital in which she had been treated to another in order to be evaluated for a course of ECT. She presented with depressed mood, appeared very agitated, had reduced appetite and difficulties sleeping, and reported a sense of hopelessness. This patient had undergone a course of ECT about 20 years previous to the current treatment, during which time she went into asystole and became tachycardic. Her current treatment consisted of eight sessions of bilateral ECT. Her pre-ECT neuropsychological assessment indicated low energy and motivation levels, as she declined some tests due to an inability to mobilize herself, fatigue, and "difficulty concentrating." Overall, her neuropsychological performance was clearly in the impaired range on measures of confrontation naming, attention span, vocabulary, visuospatial perception and construction, yielding an overall level of intellectual functioning in the very low range (Full-Scale IQ [FSIQ] = 68). Her Mini-Mental State Exam (MMSE) was also low (= 20), as was her verbal fluency (< 4th percentile), and finger tapping (dominant hand = 6.2, nondominant hand = 5.8). She declined to attempt several tests (verbal and visual memory tests, attention tests, Beck Depression Inventory [BDI]). Neuropsychological testing after a course of ECT indicated considerable improvement in her cognitive functioning, as well as in her mood, although her scores on cognitive tests were still generally in the impaired range (MMSE = 17, memory for short stories = 6 of 50, finger tapping: dominant hand = 31.4, nondominant hand = 28.8, Paced Auditory Serial Addition Test [PASAT] = 13%). Only her overall score on intellectual functioning increased considerably, placing her in the low average range (FSIQ = 82; judging from her level of education, this score may approximate her premorbid level). There was no improvement on verbal fluency (< 4th percentile) and confrontation naming, both of which remained in the impaired range.

(Courtesy of Linas Bieliauskas)

Case Study 2

H.M., a 74-year-old woman with a 12th grade education, was hospitalized for severe depression. She also had a 2-year history of cognitive difficulties with motoric slowness and stiffness, possibly due to a diagnosis of Parkinson disease (PD). She underwent a neuropsychological assessment before commencement of a course of ECT and on two occasions posttreatment (1 month and 3 months later). Her performance on neuropsychological tests before ECT indicated intellectual functioning and attention span at the borderline range, moderately impaired MMSE score and confrontation naming, severely impaired serial list learning, story recall, and verbal fluency, but low average visuospatial learning and average reading. Her score on the BDI (= 74) was in the severe range. On her first evaluation post-ECT, her BDI score improved considerably (= 12) and placed her in the mildly depressed range, yet her affect remained flat and her mood depressed. With respect to her cognitive functioning, she showed some improvement in attention span only. All other scores remained stable, with the exception of visuospatial learning, which decreased and reached the severely impaired level. Her clinical picture (bradyphrenic and bradykinetic) was consistent with her suspected diagnosis of PD. A second follow-up assessment showed mild improvement in her overall level of intellectual functioning, placing her in the average range, memory scores in the low average range, and improvement on the MMSE overall, but with problems with attention and delayed recall of verbal information. She also improved on confrontation naming and on verbal and visuospatial recent memory and recognition, although her scores remained in the mildly impaired range. Even at the 3-month follow-up, her manual speed was slow and she exhibited mild-to-moderate depression. On a more positive note, she demonstrated low average abilities on visuospatial construction and arithmetic calculation and scored in the average range on attention span, social judgment, and word knowledge.

(Courtesy of Linas Bieliauskas)

The first of the above cases illustrates the severity of the depression and the inability to mobilize and complete simple tasks, as the patient was unable to complete the battery and declined to attempt several tests. On assessment after a course of ECT, she was able to attempt the full battery administered to her. Performance on the tests that she had completed before indicated some improvement on several cognitive functions, although they were still in the very low range. The second case illustrates two points. First, it is an example of improvement over time post-ECT. Second, many patients receiving ECT for depression may have other diagnoses as well, which may also contribute to cognitive impairment. Although it is possible that her cognitive deficits before and immediately after her course of treatment reflect the acute effect of ECT and pharmacotherapy, her clinical profile may be attributable more to a dementia associated with PD.

The cases described highlight some of the difficulties in assessing the effects of ECT on memory. The most obvious is the influence of the concomitant depression. In fact, one of the challenges in differentiating the influence of ECT on memory from that of depression is that memory assessment scores reflect not only the effects of ECT but also of depression, which is known to affect primary memory especially (Sackheim, Freeman, McElhiney et al, 1992). Nevertheless, at least one study has reported persistent memory problems even when controlling for depression and did not attribute memory disruption to the ECT (Freeman, Weeks, & Kendell, 1980).

Improvement in cognitive functioning after ECT is not surprising. Patients with major depression generally demonstrate poor performance in several cognitive domains, such as attention, memory, and visuoperceptual ability. As the severity of depression abates over the course of several ECT sessions, so might any cognitive problems that existed pretreatment (Taylor & Abrams, 1985). At least one study, however, reported a dissociation between recovery from depression and improvement in cognitive function in the early subacute phase after a course of ECT, consistent with the claim that ECT affects primary memory functions adversely (Calev, Gaudino, Squires et al., 1995).

Another difficulty in evaluating the effects of ECT on memory is the wide variability in the measures used to assess memory across studies. Traditional neuropsychological testing of cognitive functions after a course of ECT treatment has generally supported the view that negative but transient changes in cognitive functions do occur. Such studies have employed either measures of overall cognitive functioning, such as intelligence scales, fixed composite batteries, and mental status examinations, or specific measures of memory. Although most of them do report impaired cognitive functioning after a course of ECT, they also report that such impairment usually resolves within a few weeks or months. In addition, as mentioned previously, many studies have also shown improved cognitive performance most likely due to improvement in depressive symptomatology.

A third factor that has led to great variability in research findings is the difference in specific techniques used to induce the shock treatment. Comparisons of the cognitive effects of ECT on patients undergoing unilateral versus bilateral electrode placement have been mixed. Right unilateral electrode placement has been found to be associated with greater increases in Full-Scale IQ (FSIQ) than bilateral electrode placement (Sackeim, Freeman, McElhiney et al., 1992) but other studies have found no differences between bilateral and unilateral ECTs (Taylor & Abrams, 1985). In a study comparing the effects of ECT delivered to the dominant hemisphere versus nondominant hemisphere, the investigators reported temporary memory problems in the former group (i.e., impaired memory for short stories) but improved scores on some functions assessed by a composite neuropsychological test battery in the former group. In either case (e.g., unilateral vs. bilateral ECT), impairments appear to be transient (Small, Small, Milstein, & Moore, 1972). The variability in these findings may reflect several factors: differences in the specific cognitive measures used, the extensiveness of the neuropsychological batteries, the specific ECT techniques used (e.g., intensity of electric discharge), as well as clinical factors, such as the severity of depression and response to pretreatment medications.

Subjective Memory Complaints

Many investigations have explored subjective reports of memory impairment in patients receiving ECT. Such complaints are mainly related to loss of autobiographical memories (Rose, Wykes, Leese et al., 2003), as well as of impersonal information such as knowledge of public events (Squire, Slater, & Miller, 1981), rather than to difficulties with new learning. But improvement of memory functioning after ECT has also been reported by the patients, possibly reflecting improvement of affect after ECT treatment (Squire et al., 1981; Prudic, Peyser, & Sackeim, 2000).

The duration of subjective memory problems may vary from several months to several years. In one study, subjective memory complaints persisted as long as 3 years posttreatment (Squire & Chase, 1975). Interestingly, subjective complaints of memory problems often do not coincide with the results of objective assessment. An investigation of both objective and subjective reports of memory disruption in the same patients yielded continued subjective complaints of memory problems, despite the lack of objective evidence to that effect, 6–9 months after bilateral ECT (Squire & Chase, 1975). This discrepancy raises several questions regarding the basis of such reports.

Several hypotheses have been offered to explain the discrepancy between objective and subjective memory deficits. One suggestion is that patients become frustrated by their persistent amnesia of events around the time of ECT and generalize from this memory gap to memory at large (Squire & Slater, 1983). Another possibility is that patients are influenced by the unsubstantiated, yet popular, impression that ECT erases memories, or even by their own, earlier (albeit currently resolved) memory problems. Consequently, they may be more sensitive to any lapses of memory, which might actually reflect ordinary or depression-related forgetting, and attribute them to the ECT (Squire & Slater, 1983; Squire, 1986). The scale that is often used to measure subjective memory complaints, the Squire Subjective Memory Questionnaire (SSMQ), assesses feelings associated with subjective memory efficacy and, as expected, is influenced by mood. It is possible that subjective complaints are influenced more by factors such as ease of retrieval and confidence in one's memory abilities than by actual abilities.

Objective Studies of ECT Effects on Memory

Acute Effects of ECT

Assessment of the actual extent of retrograde amnesia after a course of ECT is limited by the necessity of using information from the past that is easily accessible to the experimenters. In a study exploring memory for familiar television programs, investigators found that the amnesia resolved 7 months after ECT (Squire et al., 1981). Unlike amnesia for public events, however, amnesia for autobiographical material has been found to persist beyond 6 months after ECT (Squire, 1986; Weiner, Rogers, Davidson, & Squire, 1986). But the opposite pattern has also been reported, wherein the loss of personal memories had resolved at 7-month follow-up (Lisanby, Maddox, Prudic et al., 2000). At 3-year follow-up, ECT patients still had trouble remembering events that occurred 6 months before and 2 months after treatment. In fact, the resolution of memory gaps appears to be related to the individual's mental status before treatment and the level of disorientation after ECT (Sobin, Sackeim, Prudic et al., 1995).

Experimental evidence of memory loss subsequent to ECT emerges from studies that have used prospective objective measurements, including pretreatment learning trials, with posttreatment recall, priming, or recognition tests. In one such study, it was found that information presented 20–60 minutes before ECT was recalled more accurately than information presented within the 10-minute period preceding the session (Daniel & Crovitz, 1983a, 1983b). The same study showed worse recall immediately after treatment as compared with delayed recall.

Other studies have suggested that implicit learning but not explicit learning remains relatively intact after ECT. Dorfman, Kihlstrom, Cork, and Misiaszek (1995) reported intact priming on word-stem completion trials of a word-list learning test but impaired recall and recognition of the same. Other studies reported initial impairment in memory for general information, delayed recall of paired words and short stories, and in implicit learning. The aforementioned memory difficulties improved by 1-month follow-up assessment.

Reports of objective and subjective memory problems after ECT appear to be consistent across various types of memory measures, at least for the first month post-ECT. Most studies have reported a decline in memory processing shortly after ECT, particularly anterograde memory (Steif, Sackeim, Portney et al., 1986; Ng, Schweitzer, Alexopoulos et al., 2000). In one study, verbal learning decreased by 50% immediately after a completed course of ECT as compared with pre-ECT verbal learning scores. Figural learning did not change significantly overall (pre- vs. posttreatment) or when dose of electrical charge was manipulated. Although there were no differences between depressed patients with and without ECT in delayed verbal recall, ECT patients did more poorly on primary memory tests than those depressed patients who did not receive ECT (Datto, Levy, Miller, & Katz, 2001).

Several studies have addressed the potential relationship between severity of memory problems and number of ECT sessions. One of these found no cumulative deficits over the course of several ECT sessions (Sackeim, Decina, Prohovnik et al., 1986), whereas most studies did find cumulative memory problems with increasing number of treatments (see Sackeim et al., 1992), particularly at the completion of treatment and at 1-month follow-up (Steif et al., 1986; Ng et al., 2000). Another factor that appears to influence the severity of post-ECT memory impairment is the level of pre-ECT cognitive status. Those patients with lower MMSE scores before ECT were found to be more impaired at 2-month post-ECT follow-up with respect to duration and level of disorientation and retrograde amnesia than those with higher pretreatment MMSE scores (Sobin et al., 1995).

Chronic Effects of ECT

Most studies (Rami-Gonzalez, Salamero, Boget et al., 2003) report a return of lost memories by about 6 months posttreatment, occasionally accompanied by a permanent gap for events that took place during the 1 to 2 weeks that preceded a course of ECT (Benbow, 1989) or during the treatment period (Squire et al., 1981). This latter observation suggests that the ongoing ECT may have interfered with the consolidation of information encoded at that time. The preponderance of data support the contention that a standard course of ECT leaves little or no enduring cognitive side effects (Calev et al., 1995). Some patients, however, complain of persistent retrograde or anterograde memory problems (Squire et al., 1981). Other cognitive abilities are generally unaffected (Calev et al., 1995; Pisvejc, Hyrman, Sikora et al., 1998) or improve 1 week after ECT (attention, reaction times, immediate learning) (Weeks, Freeman, & Kendell, 1980; Sobin et al., 1995).

Reports of impairment in new learning are encouraging. Most suggest a return to normal, pre-ECT levels within a few days to a few weeks after the last treatment session (Fink, 1978; Jackson, 1978; NIH, 1985; Sackeim et al., 1986; Ng et al., 2000). In a review of the literature (Turek & Hanlon, 1977), the authors reported that most studies found no memory impairment after 6 months and no residual memory problems after 5 years. Therefore, concerns about long-term or permanent effects of ECT on learning remain largely unsubstantiated. Finally, it appears that impairment in anterograde memory post-ECT is greater shortly after treatment but decreases rapidly over time (Sackeim, Prudic, Devanand et al., 1993; Lewis & Kopelman, 1998; Ng et al., 2000).

PATHOPHYSIOLOGY AND THE IMPACT OF TECHNOLOGICAL ADVANCES ON ECT-RELATED AMNESIA

To a large extent, impressions of the adverse effects of ECT on memory have been formed by early reports when ECT techniques had not been refined. The implementation of newer, modified techniques (since the 1970s) has led to a marked decrease in cognitive side effects. In fact, the fewer memory problems reported by more recent studies could be a reflection of increased precision in the measurement of memory and/or the use of brief pulse current (Prudic et al., 2000) and unilateral ECT (Sackeim et al., 1986; Sobin et al., 1995; Lisanby et al., 2000; Sackeim, Prudic, & Devanand, 2000). There is a consensus that brief pulse current causes less memory and cognitive impairment than sine wave current (NIH, 1985; Squire, 1986; Sackeim et al., 1992; Prudic et al., 2000), although contradictory studies do exist (Cameron, 1994; Prudic et al., 2000). Patients who have undergone brief pulse ECT are disoriented for a shorter period of time than those who experienced sine wave ECT (Sackeim et al., 1992); in fact, sine wave ECT sometimes induces persistent disorientation between treatments. Additional features of ECT administration that reduce memory side-effects are use of anesthesia and hyperoxygenation (Devanand et al., 1994).

The differential effects of electrode placement on amnesia have received considerable attention. Overall, bilateral electrode placement has been associated with greater anterograde and retrograde amnesia as compared with unilateral electrode placement (Sackeim et al., 1986; Squire, 1986; Sobin et al., 1995; Lisanby et al., 2000; Sackeim et al., 2000). Verbal memory appears to be affected after bilateral ECT and less affected by nondominant hemisphere unilateral ECT (Squire & Chase, 1975; Weiner, 1984; Squire, 1986; Kroessler & Fogel, 1993). The drawback, however, to the use of unilateral ECT is that it is less effective than bilateral ECT in reducing the depressive symptoms (NIH, 1985; Taylor & Abrams, 1985; Kroessler & Fogel, 1993). At least one study found equivalent clinical effectiveness in unilateral and bilateral ECT but more memory complaints in bilateral, as compared with unilateral, ECT (Rosenberg & Pettinati, 1984). As expected, bilateral or dominant-side ECT reduces verbal and nonverbal memory (Fromm-Auch, 1982). In contrast, verbal memory remains intact or improves with nondominant unilateral ECT, but nonverbal memory deteriorates with 1–4 treatment sessions (Fromm-Auch, 1982) and begins to improve after 5 sessions.

Although many studies have investigated the adverse influence of ECT on memory, few have explored the neurophysiological mechanisms mediating the observed memory impairment. In a recent study of the effects of ECT on learning and memory (Frasca, Iodice, McCall, & Vaughn, 2003), the decline observed in learning after ECT was attributed to a disruption of encoding and working memory (Squire, Knowlton, & Musen, 1993; Moscovitch, 1995) and focal attention (D'Esposito, Detre, Alsop et al., 1995). Investigators have suggested that ECT-induced memory impairment results from the disruption of transient electrical conductance patterns in the brain and the subsequent disruption of the consolidation process of newly encoded items (Frith, Stenven, Johnstone et al., 1983; Hasse-Sander, Muller, Schuring et al., 1988).

Other investigators have explored the role of neurochemical processes in ECT-induced memory problems. More specifically, they have attributed these problems to the overstimulation of the glutamate receptor, N-methyl-D-aspartate (NMDA), during ECT (Stewart & Reid, 1993; Chamberlin & Tsai, 1998). Under normal circumstances, glutamate, an excitatory neurotransmitter found in brain areas like the hippocampus that form part of memory mechanisms, increases the effectiveness of hippocampal synapses when it interacts with NMDA receptors (Cotman, Monaghan, & Ganong, 1988; Chamberlin & Tsai, 1998). Consequently, ECT may lead to memory impairment because it reduces the long-term potentiation in the hippocampus (Stewart & Reid, 1993; Stewart, Jeffery, & Reid, 1994). The involvement of the NMDA receptor is also suggested by findings of memory dysfunction associated with epileptic seizures (Cotman et al., 1988; Sutula, Koch, Golarai et al., 1996). Other researchers have suggested that the excessive release of excitatory amino acids leading to the activation of NMDA receptors subsequently decreases cholinergic transmission and increases cerebral blood pressure, which in turn results in memory dysfunction (Rami-Gonzalez et al., 2003).

A question that emerges related to the neurophysiological effects of ECT is whether these exogenously induced seizures actually cause neuronal damage. One study explored this hypothesis as well as the hypothesis of disruption of the blood-brain barrier but found no evidence of neuronal or glial damage or blood-brain barrier dysfunction after ECT (Zachrisson, Balldin, Ekman et al., 2000).

Explorations of the brain regions involved in both the therapeutic effects of ECT and its cognitive side-effects are limited. A recent study compared cerebral blood flow (CBF) scans during bifrontal versus bitemporal ECT. Bifrontal ECT was associated with increased CBF in prefrontal and anterior cingulate regions, whereas bitemporal ECT was associated with increased CBF in lateral frontal and anterior temporal lobes (Blumenfeld, McNally, Ostroff, & Zubal, 2003). The greater increase in prefrontal activation relative to that in the temporal lobes during bifrontal ECT may be responsible for the improved therapeutic response and the reduced adverse effects on memory relative to bitemporal ECT (Nobler, Sackeim, Prohovnik et al., 1994; Drevets, Price, Simpson et al., 1997; Heikman, Salmelin, Makela et al., 2001; Nobler, Oquendo, Kegeles et al., 2001; Blumenfeld et al., 2003).

The mechanism of the antidepressant efficacy of ECT is unknown. Some have suggested that it may be related to the modulation of prefrontal cortical (Nobler et al., 2001) or cingulate (Drevets et al., 1997) circuits. These regions show increased CBF during ECT-induced seizures. This finding is consistent with reports of increased CBF during epileptic seizures followed by postictal decrease (Newton, Berkovic, Austin et al., 1992; Duncan, Patterson, Roerts et al., 1993; Zubal, Spanaki, MacMullan et al., 1999). In light of decreased prefrontal CBF in patients with depression (Drevet et al., 1997), the observed CBF changes after ECT may reflect the therapeutic influence of this method.

PROGNOSIS AND TREATMENT

ECT-induced memory dysfunction appears to be transient in most cases. Although the ability to learn new material typically returns, memory for the period around the ECT may not, as the induced seizures most likely interrupted the process of consolidation. Some gaps in retrograde memory may persist, and subjective complaints of memory difficulties are not uncommon even in the long term. Therefore, treatment could focus on education regarding the types of memory difficulties typically encountered after a course of ECT. This approach, including supportive counseling, might help to reduce patients' subjective complaints, which are often disproportionate to objective indices of memory impairment. As the neurophysiological mechanisms of memory disruption secondary to ECT are elucidated, preventive pharmacological intervention may become a possibility. Certainly, advances in the technology of ECT have already reduced memory side-effects while increasing clinical efficacy.

CONCLUSIONS

The typical pattern of memory impairment after ECT implicates a disruption of the process of consolidation of newly learned information during the induced seizures as the core problem in memory-related side effects. This is most evident in the permanent gap for events that occur during the course of treatment. This contention is also supported by the temporal gradient of the retrograde amnesia typically observed, whereby events that occurred very close in time to the onset of ECT (i.e., 10 minutes before) were less likely to be remembered than events that occurred earlier (20–60 minutes before).

Despite temporary memory disruption, patients who have undergone ECT overall have experienced improvement in both their depression and their memory. ECT is a safe and effective approach for the treatment of moderate to severe depression. Its memory-related side effects are temporary and reflective of a disruption in the process of consolidation of new information. In the long term, however, ECT results in clinical as well as cognitive improvement. To date, there is no evidence that ECT causes structural brain damage. Future controlled experiments and meta-analytic studies are needed to confirm the nature and mechanisms of transient memory impairments related to ECT.

11

Psychogenic Amnesias

IOANNA SAVVIDOU, VASILIS P. BOZIKAS, AND
ANDREW C. PAPANICOLAOU

Psychogenic amnesias are all retrograde in nature and usually involve reversible loss of autobiographical memories. As their name implies, they are believed to have psychological causes, a belief justified by the fact that they do not entail gross anatomical lesions. Because they are not precipitated by an apparent "physical" cause as are the other amnesias, and given that they are highly selective, involving only personal memories, they are fascinating to both scientists and laymen alike. Yet, in spite of the fascination they inspire, their nature and cerebral mechanisms still remain largely obscure.

Psychogenic amnesias are also called functional amnesias (Kihlstrom & Schacter, 1995) and are classified with the dissociative disorders (DD) in the *Diagnostic and Statistical Manual of Mental Disorders – Fourth Edition* (DSM-IV; American Psychiatric Association, 1994) and in the *International Classification of Diseases – Tenth Edition* (ICD-10; World Health Organization, 1992). The essential feature of dissociative disorders is a disruption in the usually integrated functions of consciousness, autobiographical memory, identity, and perception (DSM-IV).

Dissociative symptoms are not confined to memory. Rather, their various combinations result in several related disorders, namely, dissociative amnesia (DA), dissociative fugue (DF), dissociative identity disorder (DID), depersonalization disorder (DPD), and dissociative disorder not otherwise specified (DDNOS). All the disorders appear to result from a single or a series of psychologically traumatic or stressful events. These events may occur shortly before the onset of symptoms or have occurred sometime in the patient's past, often during childhood. The events often involve sexual or physical abuse, kidnapping, rape, incest, combat experiences, or witnessing of violent scenes.

The most intriguing aspect of the amnesia they cause is its selectivity. No other amnesic syndrome presents such specificity, whereby the suppressed memories are strictly autobiographical or context-specific. When all, or almost all, autobiographical memories are suppressed (as happens in the generalized type of DA and in DF), we are hard pressed to imagine what that subjective experience of the patient might be like. How do people in such cases make do without a personal history and, therefore, identity, or with one that is entirely "made up" and then adopted as real?

This loss of the sense of self is called "disorientation to person" and has quite a different quality from disorientation to place or time, both of which occur to varying degrees in many types of organic amnesia and are sometimes experienced by individuals with otherwise intact memory. Disorientation to person, on the other hand, only occurs in the presence of extensive organic pathology, such as advanced stages of dementia, delirium, or in the acute stages of traumatic brain injury (TBI). Thus, when a person forgets his identity in the absence of any discernible lesion or disruption in physical vigor or health, as happens in "fugue" and "generalized dissociative amnesia," the phenomenon cannot but appear awesome and strange. This fascination has inspired such imaginative works as R.L. Stevenson's *Dr. Jekyll and Mr. Hyde* and A. Hitchcock's film *Spellbound*. Earlier indications of this fascination appear in Greek and Roman literature, as well as in the Bible. Paracelcus in the seventeenth century, Eberhard Gmelin in the eighteenth century, and Benjamin Rush, the father of American Psychiatry in the early nineteenth century, all commented on identity alterations involving autobiographic memory loss. However, systematic examination and integration of these phenomena into theories of human mentation did not flourish until later in the nineteenth century with Pierre Janet, Jean Charcot, Joseph Breuer, Sigmund Freud, and Paul Briquet in Europe and Morton Prince and William James, among others, in the United States. (Tissie, 1887; Janet, 1889; James, 1890; Raymond, 1895; Dugas, 1898; Janet, 1907; Breuer & Freud, 1955; Ellenberger, 1970; Goldstein, 1985; Nemiah, 1989; Hacking, 1996; Putnam & Loewenstein, 2000; Brown, 2003).

For the purposes of the current discussion, we may consider the dissociative disorders arranged along a continuum. At one end of that continuum we may place dissociative amnesia, which is characterized by suppression and the unavailability of autobiographical memories. On the other end we may place dissociative identity disorders and other personality disturbances such as depersonalization, which primarily involve amnesic errors of commission rather than omission. Finally, we may place the disorder of dissociative fugue somewhere in the middle of the continuum, as it appears to involve both suppression of actual autobiographical memories and confabulation, enabling the fugue patient to adopt a fictitious set of alternative autobiographical memories. We will review all three types in the following pages.

Establishment of Symptoms

Clinical Features of Dissociative Amnesia

Dissociative amnesia usually follows a traumatic event and is characterized by an inability to recall important personal information or recent events and is too pronounced to be attributed to ordinary forgetfulness or fatigue. The disorder is not due to a general medical condition or to the direct physiological effects of a substance (DSM-IV [American Psychiatric Association, 1994]; ICD-10 [World Health Organization, 1992]). The DSM-IV describes five types of dissociative amnesias: (1) localized amnesia, when the patient fails to recall events that occurred during a circumscribed period of time, usually within the first few hours after a stressful event; (2) selective amnesia, when the patient fails to recall some, but not all, of the events during a circumscribed period of time; (3) generalized amnesia, when failure to recall encompasses the person's entire life; (4) continuous amnesia, when the patient is unable to recall events subsequent to a specific time up to and including the present; and (5) systematized amnesia, when the patient fails to recall certain categories of information, such as memories relating to one's family. The latter three types are rather rare and may suggest the presence of a more complex dissociative disorder, such as dissociative identity disorder.

With the exception of generalized amnesia where the problems are quite obvious, dissociative amnesias are among the most difficult disorders to diagnose. This is because patients become aware of the disorder only when it causes disruptions in their social and occupational life. Signs indicative of the presence of dissociative amnesia include possession of unfamiliar objects that cannot be accounted for, denial of one's own acts, and other evidence of inconsistencies on the part of the patient. Many patients develop adaptive strategies or resort to confabulations to compensate for their memory loss (Steinberg, 2000b, 2000c). Clinically, they may present with confusion, symptoms of depression, anxiety, inability to concentrate, or a history of memory gaps—the frequency and extent of which they are incapable of determining. The onset is typically acute in wartime, after natural disasters, or after extreme emotional trauma (Steinberg, 2000b, 2000c). The memory of the traumatic event is suppressed, but sensory cues, such as smells or fragmentary images of objects or sounds directly or indirectly associated with the event, may bring about anxiety reactions that imply that that the memory for the event, although inaccessible, is nevertheless preserved.

Although there may be some posttraumatic amnesia for the time interval after the traumatic event, the amnesia is mostly retrograde in nature. There are no disturbances in general cognitive or language functioning, and the ability to acquire new explicit and procedural memories remains intact (Kihlstrom & Schacter, 1995; Dalla Barba, Mantovan, Ferruzza, & Denes, 1997; Kopelman, 2002a). The fact that the amnesia is reversible, either spontaneously or after psychotherapeutic intervention, implies that the deficit involves the operation of retrieval rather than those of encoding, consolidation, or storage (Kihlstrom & Schacter, 2000), which is the case in all other forms of psychogenic amnesia.

The following is a case study illustrating a woman's experience of psychogenic amnesia.

Case Study 1

A 33-year-old right-handed female patient was referred to the local hospital because she complained of having lost her memory. Before the onset, she had been troubled by personal financial and possibly legal problems. She tried to commit suicide by overdosing on hypnotic drugs and was admitted to the hospital. Upon regaining consciousness, she had lost all her long-term memory, including her own name or identity. After a month, she was transferred to the neuropsychiatry setup. A physical examination revealed no abnormalities. Brain CT and MRI scans revealed no brain damage. She was alert, attentive, and oriented. Spontaneous speech, comprehension, repetition, and naming were normal, as were calculation, mapping, praxis, right-left orientation, and finger naming. All other neurological parameters were normal except for the persistent memory disturbance. After she acquired portions of her autobiographical memory and recalled famous events and facts, she still had difficulty in retrieving long-term memories. Even when she could remember a past event, she was unsure whether or not it indeed reflected her past. She met the DSM-IV criteria and was diagnosed as having psychogenic amnesia (dissociative amnesia).

A more extensive neuropsychological evaluation performed 2 months after onset displayed no remarkable abnormalities except for retrograde amnesia. The patient was alert, attentive, socially appropriate, and had normal digit span performance (seven digits forward, four backward). Intellectual functioning assessed by the WAIS-R (Wechsler, 1981) and RCPM (Raven, 1958) tests was adequate. Word fluency was normal, and all language and language-related functions were intact. The patient had no anterograde memory deficits. Results with the RAVLT-R (Spreen & Strauss, 1991) and the Rey–Osterrieth Figure were normal (Lezak, 1983), and performance on the WMS-R (Wechsler, 1987) was also excellent.

Autobiographical memory for events before her illness was assessed by a structured interview covering past personal events. The items selected for this interview covered educational experiences, occupational history, births, deaths, and other events within her family. In this test, difficulties appeared. For example, she could not remember the name of her brother, the death of her grandfather, or the divorce of her parents. In addition, she was shown pictures of famous faces or events and asked to name the pictured subject. Even when she could recognize them, she was often unsure whether or not these facts indeed reflected the past. The same tests were also administered to the patient 1 year after onset. By that time, the patient had regained most of her memories and had no difficulties in the structured interview covering past personal events and the famous faces or events test (96%). However, even during recovery, she often stated that she had relearned past events.

(From Yasuno, Nishikawa, Ikejiri et al., 2000, with the permission of *Psychiatry Research Neuroimaging*)

Clinical Features of Dissociative Fugue

Dissociative fugue (DF) is a rare disorder characterized by sudden and unexpected travel away from one's home or usual place of work. During such travel, patients are unable to recall their past and are either confused about their personal identity or assume a new one. Confusion may be present during short fugue episodes, but in more prolonged episodes the patient usually takes on a new identity with different personality features. Fugue episodes may last from less than an hour to a year or more but generally last days or weeks. During the episode, the patients act normally, without raising suspicions among their new acquaintances (Kopelman, 1995a; Coons, 2000; Kihlstrom & Schacter, 2000; Kopelman, 2002b).

The disorder is usually associated with periods of suspected or documented stress, such as may arise with the assumption of new responsibilities, the emergence of legal difficulties, divorce, bankruptcy, or enlistment in the army during wartime. Sometimes, the fugue appears to protect the patient from suicidal thoughts by suppressing them along with other personality features and traits.

Although there are no unequivocal answers to questions regarding the precise nature and extent of autobiographical memory suppression and alteration in fugue, some general features of the memory deficit are known. Suppression of remote autobiographical memories—both episodic and semantic in nature (e.g., the patient's name, or information regarding relatives, or places the patient lived)—is certainly involved. However, patients appear to maintain some fragments of their autobiographical memories and are able to recall some information on demand, especially memories about happy periods of their lives (Schacter, Wang, & Tulving et al., 1982; Kihlstrom & Schacter, 2000). On the other hand, the patients' general knowledge about the world, such as information about famous people or events of past decades, is spared (Markowitsch, Fink, & Thöne et al., 1997; Glisky, Ryan, & Reminger et al., 2004), but this finding is somewhat controversial (Kopelman, Christensen, & Puffet et al., 1994a; Kritchevsky, Chang, & Squire, 2004). Vocabulary also remains intact as measured with the verbal scale of the WAIS (Schacter et al., 1982; Kihlstrom & Schacter, 2000). Working memory and executive functions are generally preserved, but this observation has not been systematically investigated and confirmed (Kihlstrom & Schacter, 2000), and some investigators (Kopelman et al., 1994a; Glisky et al., 2004) have even reported that fugue patients may experience difficulties with executive functions. Such deficits may be reflected in Full-Scale IQ decrements during the fugue, as compared to the IQ scores obtained after recovery (Schacter et al., 1982; Kaszniak, Nussbaum, Berren, & Santiago, 1988; Kihlstrom & Schacter, 2000).

Deficits in semantic and episodic memory are largely retrograde, whereas the ability to acquire new information remains intact. Therefore, performance on typical memory tests (California Verbal Learning Test, CVLT [Delis, Kramer, Kaplan & Ober, 1987a]) is normal or only slightly affected (Kopelman et al., 1994a, 1994b; Kritchevsky, Zouzounis, & Squire, 1997; Markowitsch et al., 1997; Glisky et al., 2004; Kritchevsky et al., 2004). Some patients present difficulties in anterograde memory as well, but these are mostly attributable to general cognitive difficulties or to depressed mood during the period that memory impairment is prominent (Schacter et al., 1982; Kihlstrom & Schacter, 2000).

During the fugue, retrograde amnesia for autobiographical information is found for the true personality. After recovery, subjects can remember their life before the fugue, but this time they suffer amnesia for the period of the fugue and/or for traumatic events that occurred shortly before the fugue. The continuity of the true autobiography is thus restored, and the circumscribed period of the fugue is forgotten. Before full recovery, some patients may go through a period during which they are amnesic about their past but acknowledge their amnesia and seek help at police stations or hospitals. In many cases there are some islands of memory, awareness of some aspects of the past, or a vague sense of familiarity (Kopelman et al., 1994a, 1994b; Kopelman, 2002; Glisky et al., 2004), indicating the preservation of autobiographical information that cannot be consciously recalled (Glisky et al., 2004). This phase ends spontaneously or after a triggering event, such as the presence of a familiar face, or with therapeutic interventions, such as hypnosis. After recovery, the individual may not be able to remember the actual fugue phase, but they have memory of the second phase during which they felt confused and sought help (Coons, 2000; Kihlstrom & Schacter, 2000).

Whether the "new" identity that patients assume during fugue states differs from the previous one when it comes to implicit memory remains an open question. Do these patients exhibit the same ways of walking and talking, have the same preferences, and sensorimotor patterns that, after years of repetition, come to constitute their special personal characteristics? Some cases of impaired procedural memory have been reported, for example, the case of patient N.N. (Markowitsch et al., 1997) who knew how to drive but was unable to do so during the fugue. He also forgot how to perform his old trade and practiced another one during the fugue. Still, the preponderance of evidence suggests that procedural memory is preserved during the fugue (Kihlstrom & Schacter, 1995). Glisky and colleagues' (2004) patient F.F., who has been studied in detail (see case report below), had lost the ability to speak his native language, German, during the fugue, but retained implicit knowledge of the structure of the language, a fact that suggests implicit memory preservation. A further indication of implicit memory preservation is the fact that F.F. still knew how to operate computers during the fugue state as he did before.

Case Study 2

Patient F.F., a 33-year-old male, entered a motel and asked a clerk to call the police, stating that he believed he had been pushed out of a van by two men. He claimed not to know who or where he was. The police took him to the medical centre and he was admitted to the psychiatric ward of the hospital. Although he spoke English with a German accent, he claimed not to have any knowledge of German. He gave medical staff a name, which he thought might be his first name; this name proved to be correct. A few days later he was identified by two women, who had seen a photograph of him on television. They mentioned that he had come from Germany three months previously and that he had a considerable sum of money. A roommate was also found and asked to come to the hospital to identify the patient. He reported that the two of them had had a disagreement and that he had asked the patient to leave; he stated that he had thrown all of F.F.'s possessions out of the house. The patient seemed to be afraid of the roommate and said that he thought that the roommate might have shot at him at one time. The patient's passport was found when his living quarters were searched and it was confirmed that he was a German citizen and that his temporary visa into the United States had expired almost a month previously.

Over the next few days F.F. acquired considerable information of his personal past, but he claimed to have no memories of his childhood, his family members, any schools he attended, any jobs he had held or any people he may have known. However, he had considerable knowledge of computers and thought that he might have been involved with technology. This assumption proved to be true. Additionally, when doctors mentioned the possibility of doing a brain scan using MRI, he recalled having been in an MRI scanner, which he was able to describe in considerable detail; he also recalled that this procedure followed a motorcycle accident, although he was unable to describe any details of the accident.

The MRI scan showed no evidence of brain insult. His Full-Scale IQ was 113 (verbal IQ of 95 and performance IQ of 133). The comparably lower score on the verbal scale, however, might reflect the fact that English was his second language. At neuropsychological testing he exhibited a high level of performance on anterograde episodic memory (verbal/auditory memory was in the superior range, compared to only average levels of performance on visual memory) and normal semantic memory. He showed a similar discrepancy between verbal and visuospatial tasks on working memory tasks. On other tests of frontal function, he performed below expectations given his performance on the IQ and memory tests. Experiments designed to test his knowledge of the German language showed that he had implicit knowledge of the semantic and associative structure of the German language.

Electrophysiological testing provided evidence that he retained implicit knowledge of autobiographical information in the absence of explicit knowledge.

The patient was examined with fMRI during a lexical decision task using German and English words and non-words, in which he exhibited a striking difference in the ratio of frontal to parietal activation compared to normal bilingual German-English speaking controls, with more extensive activation in parietal than frontal regions.

Information from relatives in Germany revealed that F.F. had disappeared from his home in Germany some 4 months previously, during a stressful period of time, when he was facing financial problems. According to additional information provided by the patient himself after his return to Germany, he had suffered psychologically and physically stressful events in the previous year, including a serious motorcycle accident, problems with his business and impending divorce from his wife. In that context he moved to the United States to start anew. He was in the process of upgrading his tourist visa to a 6-year work visa when, for reasons he later could not explain, he decided instead to obtain false papers and run away again. It was at this point that he was driven to an unknown location by his roommate, robbed of his money and all other possessions, and shot at as he fled. After this incident and until he reached the motel he wandered for an indeterminate length of time, confused and not knowing who he was. After the disclosure of his identity the patient returned voluntarily to Germany. There, he was arrested, possibly for financial problems, and he was given 18 months probation. Ten days after his admission to the hospital he began to speak German again, but at a later interview he indicated that he continued to have problems speaking German fluently for about 5 weeks after having returned to Germany.

(From Glisky et al., 2004, with permission of *Neuropsychologia*)

Clinical Features of DID and Other Dissociative Disorders

Dissociative identity disorder (DID) is the most severe and well-known of the dissociative disorders and results in mostly errors of commission rather than omission. DID (formerly called multiple personality disorder) is characterized by the presence of two or more distinct identities, or "alters," which control the behavior of the person. The disorder is not due to direct physiological effects of a substance or other medical condition (DSM-IV [American Psychiatric Association, 1994]; ICD-10 [World Health Organization, 1992]).

According to Putnam (1989), the alters are experienced as being separate personalities, each with their own name, gender, age, personal history, and intentions (Putnam & Loewenstein, 2000). The disorder is often accompanied by depersonalization and/or derealization. That is, patients may feel disconnected from themselves and others and experience the world as distant and unreal. They may also experience auditory or visual hallucinations.

During personality alterations, psychological as well as sensorimotor and physiological changes occur. Accordingly, patients may manifest changes in their manner of speaking, dialect, voice, posture, handedness, and writing. Laboratory findings include variations across alters in autonomic and endocrine function. In addition, differences in visual acuity and visual evoked potentials, pain tolerance, symptoms of asthma, sensitivity to allergens and medications, response of blood glucose to insulin, thyroid function, cerebral electrical activity and regional cerebral blood flow, and skin temperature and galvanic skin response may be present (Miller & Triggiano, 1992; McFadden & Woitalla, 1993; Birnbaum & Thomann, 1996).

The number of alters may range from two to more than a hundred but most commonly are reported to vary from 10 to 15. Often, the alters are personalities of children or persons of a different age than the patient (Ross, Norton, & Wozney, 1989b). In cases of children with this disorder, alters with animal characteristics have been described as well (Lewis & Yeager, 1996). Alterations of identity are usually sudden after stressful experiences but may also be gradual. Momentary changes in facial expressions or voice, bursts of rapid blinking, or abrupt shifts in the train of thought may indicate a personality alteration (Ross et al., 1989b; Putnam & Loewenstein, 2000).

The main amnesic feature of this disorder is suppression and alteration of autobiographical memory (Kihlstrom & Schacter, 1995). Specific memories, particularly emotionally charged ones, can be recalled by those personalities who initially acquired them. This leads to dissociative states, in which alter egos are separated from each other by amnesia.

Amnesia may be asymmetrical, in that one personality may have no knowledge of the activities of another, or the latter may have full memory access to the activities of the former. Personalities with more complete access to traumatic memories are usually the more aggressive ones, or those that protect and guide the patient. Autobiographical memory gaps may involve recent or remote events, depending on the personality that presents them. The patient (the primary personality) may have memory gaps for long periods of his or her childhood, adolescence, or even adult life. Van der Hart and Nijenhuis (2001) have argued that psychogenic amnesias not only involve suppression of episodic and semantic memory, but in many instances may encompass varying degrees of procedural memory. Changes in the tone of voice or manner of speaking, handwriting, handedness, walking, affect, habits and tics, in addition to the changes in autonomic endocrine and immune responses mentioned above, certainly suggest pervasive disturbances of implicit memories, but this is not a feature found in all DID cases (Ludwig, Brandsma, & Wilbur et al., 1972; Silberman, Putnam, & Weingartner et al., 1985; Kihlstrom & Schacter, 1995; Eich, McCaulay, Lowenstein, & Dihle, 1996; Dorahy, 2001; Elzinga, Phaf, Ardon, & van Dyck, 2003).

The following case study illustrates the foregoing description of DID.

Case Study 3

A 15-year-old patient was referred for treatment because of his refusal to speak at school. His high school counselor noted that he had not spoken a word to anyone since his enrollment 2 years earlier. On occasion, however, he would attempt to communicate at school with written messages. The patient spoke fluent English at home and obtained high scores on standardized reading tests. He denied that he felt discomfort in speaking at school, insisting instead that he had "nothing to tell." Because he had an intense dislike of going out in public, the diagnosis of social phobia was not ruled out.

At initial evaluation: The patient was physically and sexually abused during infancy. At the age of 4, he was placed under the care of a single guardian after having witnessed the brutal murders of his sibling and friend. Although he later learned about the deaths from his guardian, the patient had no conscious memories of the murders or abuse. The early abuse and trauma raised questions about whether the patient had had reactive attachment and/or posttraumatic stress disorder in infancy or early childhood. However, these diagnoses were deferred because of the paucity of details about the patient's early reactions to the experiences.

From the start, the patient's relationship to his guardian was distant, due in part to the guardian's lack of involvement in the patient's life. The patient himself was described as "shy." As a child, he had considerable social inhibitions; for instance, he would hide under tables when taken to visit acquaintances.

Although his language development was apparently normal, from a young age he was reluctant to talk. He spoke to his guardian, however, and to selected children and teachers at school. His reticence to talk was exacerbated when he entered high school. At that time, he refused to speak altogether.

Treatment and progress: The patient was treated in individual psychotherapy for 4 years. Therapy was initially constrained by the patient's reluctance to reveal much about himself. In addition to mutism, weekly therapy notes documented social fears, depressive symptoms, and brief dissociative states. Because the patient failed to improve after 18 months of therapy, psychological testing was requested to clarify the differential diagnosis.

During testing, the patient made several drawings. His picture of a human face split down the middle was striking: The left side showed no emotion whatsoever. The right side, however, depicted a face tormented in agony. The patient subsequently expressed worries about being crazy. When he was assured that it was safe to talk, he revealed that voices often "fought" in his head.

A different personality state ("identity") attended the next session and flatly let the psychologist know that her belated arrival irritated him. "Harlequin" was grandiose and talkative. He "stepped in" to help, he said, because the patient was so pitiful. During the next few months, five separate identities were observed: In addition to the boy and Harlequin, there was an old man, who calmed the boy's fears; "Joey," an evil alter, and "Earl," a small child who feared death.

Dissociative identity disorder is thought to develop when a child cannot flee from overwhelming violence or trauma. In the present case, the patient's amnesia about his past combined with the emergence of several identities with different voices, presentations, and ways of thinking about the self and environment led to a diagnosis of dissociative identity disorder (DID).

After DID was diagnosed, therapy focused on helping the identities recognize and relinquish internal bans on thinking, feeling, and memory. Thus, the therapist often inquired into reasons for the censorship, assuring the identities that they would not be blamed or harmed for speaking. As the identities began to relax their vigilance, the therapist encouraged them to explore how emerging feelings and memories might be linked to prior experiences and trauma. Since identities often worked on different memories and assumptions, they were highly polarized. The patient's identities frequently vied for control during therapy. They seemed to monitor what the patient said, what he did, and what he recalled. On one occasion, the therapist mistakenly revealed information from the patient's childhood about which the patient had no conscious knowledge. Harlequin immediately appeared, screaming "emergency!" He proceeded to scold the therapist, stating that the patient could not yet tolerate that information. He was now obliged, he sighed, to make the patient forget what he had heard. When the patient later emerged, he recalled nothing and had difficulty hearing what the therapist said. On another occasion, the therapist asked the patient how he might change his feeling of helplessness at school. His hands immediately became limp, suggesting that another identity was controlling their very ability to move. At that time, the patient was unable to grasp or to even hold an object in his palm. Yet, when Joey emerged soon after, he stretched his fingers and grasped an object. The patient's identities often insisted on placing tape over the keyhole of the door during therapy. On other occasions, the identities seemed paranoid and mentioned fears of being followed. It is noteworthy that the patient had obsessive symptoms. For example, at times it took him more than an hour to leave home because he had to check repeatedly to confirm that the oven was off.

After the therapist gained the trust of the identities, they revealed that as a child, the patient had been subjected to repeated sexual and physical abuse and that he had observed the brutal murders of his sibling and friend. Harlequin reported that the patient was afraid to cry for help out of fear that he would be killed, too. As details of the murders emerged, an identity told the therapist in a small, taut voice that the murderer threatened to "get" the patient if he ever told anyone what he saw. The patient promised the murderer never to speak of the murders. The reason for the patient's mutism in adolescence also emerged in therapy. Just before the patient entered high school, his best friend was murdered. An identity told the therapist that he thought it best to "shut the boy up completely" to save him from death, too. The patient's guardian was unaware of the murder or of its links to the patient's mutism.

(From Jacobsen, 1995, with the permission of *Journal of the American Academy of Child and Adolescent Psychiatry*)

The memory deficits in depersonalization disorder and other similar conditions summarized below are very similar to those found in cases of DID but are by no means identical. Depersonalization is characterized by the persistent or recurrent experience of feeling detached or alienated from one's self. The body may seem to belong to a stranger, and the patient may feel as if he or she is acting in a movie or in a dream. Other experiences of depersonalization include the sense that one is an outside observer of one's mental processes or of one's body, emotional and mental "numbness," lack of emotional control, and not recognizing oneself in the mirror. Sometimes sensory anesthesia may be present, producing the feeling of not having control over one's own actions and speech or of being an automaton. The disorder may be accompanied by derealization, the sense that the world around is unreal.

Similar distortions of memory that accompany other dissociative disorders are seen in different cultures like amok and bebainan (Indonesia), latah (Malaysia), ataque de nervios (Latin America), pibloktoq (Northern Greenland), possession trance (India), and Ganser syndrome in Western cultures. Patients presenting with Ganser syndrome have knowledge of basic information like their names, but they give approximate answers to other personal questions, such as their age, address, or occupation. They also give approximate answers to simple questions like object naming (e.g., they would call a pen shown to them, a pencil) or to questions of arithmetic (e.g., they would answer that 3 + 1 equals 5). They may also present with disorientation, clouding of consciousness, amnesia for events prior to the onset of the condition, amnesia for events occurring during the episode, and, typically, amnesia of the episode as they recover from it

(Simeon & Hollander, 2000). Such characteristics are revealed in the case study below.

Case Study 4

C is a 12-year-old boy who presented to a local emergency department 3 hours after a bullying incident at school in which he received a minor head injury. He presented in a bizarre fashion, screaming and shouting, failing to recognize those people most familiar to him.

C lives with his mother and stepfather and two younger brothers. C's natural father does not live locally but has contact with all three boys on regular access weekends. Relations between C's mother and father are tense and at times C has become a messenger between them. There is no family history of any psychiatric problems. C was born of a normal pregnancy by forceps delivery. Soon after birth he was reported to have breathing problems and jaundice and spent his first 2 days on the local special care baby unit. He is reported to have been rather slow in development, walking at 18 months and not talking until after his second birthday. He was investigated for mild hearing loss at one stage and received help by a speech therapist before beginning school.

At school he has never been reported to have had any learning difficulties nor received any special help. He is, however, reported to find reading slightly more difficult than his peer group. His younger brother has specific reading retardation and has received help for this condition. Prior to the incident C's teachers described him as a model pupil, with no behavioral problems. He is described as outgoing, with a strong sense of fair play, and he has plenty of friends. He is a keen sportsman, playing for local football and cricket teams. While at school, C was involved in an episode of bullying. His head was banged on the wall approximately five times. There was no loss of consciousness, but he was sent by his teacher to visit the school nurse, who put him back to class. One hour later, C went to do his paper route, but he felt sick and dizzy and felt a pain in his head. When his parents returned from work one hour later, they discovered that he had vomited. They took him to the local emergency department, and on the way he became drowsy.

Assessment and progress: In the emergency department he claimed not to recognize anyone, and he was seen trying to eat his shoe. Neurological examination results were otherwise normal. There was no evidence of external injury and no clouding of consciousness. After admission he was assessed by the neurosurgical team. Upon examination he was found to have slurred speech, appeared indifferent to his problems, and demonstrated an apparent global memory deficit. He could not remember names of objects or their uses (e.g., that forks are used for eating) and appeared not to recognize his parents. He had a Glasgow Coma Scale score of 15, no papilloedema, no visual disturbance, and normal reflexes, power, sensation, and tone. A computed tomographic head scan showed no abnormalities. It was strongly felt that C's problems were likely to be functional in origin, and 2 days after admission C was referred to the liaison child psychiatry team.

Background history was obtained from C's family and the ward staff. While on the ward C was initially unable to use a knife and fork; to flush a toilet; or to walk; he was seen trying to eat an unpeeled banana, and instead of brushing his teeth he would brush his tongue. His speech was very stilted, demonstrating intermittent word-finding difficulties. He was unable to recognize his brothers when they first visited him on the ward. On direct examination 48 hours after the incident, C was fully alert and orientated. He was walking in an odd, shuffling manner. He was able to recount details of the bullying incident, although he complained of having no memory of events in his life prior to this incident. He called the hospital "home." He was unable to name simple pictures of a dog or a cat. When asked how many legs a cat had, he answered "two"; when asked how many legs he had, he answered "four." When counting the number of objects on a page he would pass over the correct answer. When his short-term memory was tested, he was able to remember only one of three objects at 5 minutes, but while on the ward he showed the ability to remember everything that was presented to him. C retained his ability to play computer games with his premorbid level of skill.

Over the next 4 days, C showed a global improvement in his level of functioning. He was able to retain the skills of all newly taught tasks, such as eating and walking. When prompted, however, he still complained of no memory of any events in his life prior to the incident. Apart from being occasionally fearful of some new stimuli, such as flushing the toilet, he still appeared indifferent to his condition.

Five days after admission he returned home. On arrival he was unable to find his way around the house. He did not know where his bedroom or the toilet was. He showed no recognition of his friends from school who visited him, but he enjoyed playing football in the garden with his brothers.

In view of the lack of any evidence of severe trauma, the clinical picture of inconsistent performance, approximate answers, approximate movements, la belle indifference, and somatic conversion symptoms, a working diagnosis of a dissociative amnesia with features of Ganser syndrome was made. The differential diagnosis at this point included an organic amnesic syndrome due to the mild head injury, a prolonged mild delirium, and a factitious disorder.

(From Miller, Bramble, & Buxton, 1997, with the permission of *Journal of the American Academy of Child & Adolescent Psychiatry*)

Other memory disturbances, such as the paramnesias, involve experiences of déjà vu, the uncanny feeling of a new situation as a familiar one, and jamais vu, when a familiar experience feels new. These phenomena may be observed in association with complex partial seizures, in diverse mental disorders, and also in neurologically intact individuals during periods of stress. Although they are often combined with depersonalization, these symptoms are considered to constitute distinct entities (Nemiah, 1989). Déjà vu experiences may occur with intact reality testing, or they may be delusionally expressed. A similar condition, referred to as "reduplicative paramnesia" is a condition in which the individual delusionally misidentifies a place as a familiar one. Recently, this term has been expanded to include the delusional reduplication of time and person as well (Sno, Linszen, & de Jonghe, 1992).

TESTING AND ESTABLISHMENT OF SYMPTOMS

A useful tool for the assessment of memory disturbances in dissociative disorders is the Structured Clinical Interview for DSM-IV Dissociative Disorders-Revised (SCID-D-R; Steinberg, 1994; 2000c). It consists of 276 items that assess symptoms of amnesia, depersonalization, derealization, identity confusion, and identity alteration. Other diagnostic tools include the Dissociative Disorders Interview Schedule (DDIS; Ross, 1990) and the Dissociative Experience Scale (DES; Bernstein & Putnam, 1986; Van Ijzendoorn & Schuengel, 1996), with 28 items that assess dissociative symptoms. The Child Dissociative Checklist (Putnam, Helmers, & Trickett, 1993) is useful for the assessment of children, and the Adolescent Dissociative Experiences Scale (A-DES; Armstrong, Putnam & Carlson, 1997) is used for adolescents. The A-DES consists of several questions about different experiences that the adolescent may have had and has a Likert scale from 0 (never) to 10 (always) for the frequency of the experience. The Dissociative Experiences Scale-Taxon, (DES-T; Waller & Ross, 1997) is a brief tool with 8 items that help distinguish between pathological and non-pathological types of dissociation.

Autobiographical memory can be assessed with the Crovitz test (Crovitz & Schiffman, 1974) and the Autobiographical Memory Interview (AMI; Kopelman, Wilson, & Baddeley, 1990), a semistructured interview in which patients are asked to recall events from their childhood, their early adult life, and their current life. Despite the available array of assessment tools, however, there are no clear-cut diagnostic indicators to distinguish malingering from dissociative amnesia. For this reason, clinicians often rely on the presence of inconsistent performance, such as failure on relatively easy items of IQ and memory tests, disproportionate impairment in recognition memory tests relative to recall measures, or failure to exhibit normal psychological phenomena, such as priming or procedural memory, for distinguishing signs (Kopelman, 1995a).

PRECIPITATING FACTORS

Epidemiology

The prevalence of dissociative disorders in psychiatric inpatients has been estimated at 5–17%. Studies conducted in European countries show the lowest prevalence (4.3–8.2%) (Modestin, Ebner, Junghan, & Erni, 1996; Friedl & Draijer, 2000; Gast, Rodewald, Viola, & Emrich, 2001), whereas much higher rates are reported in North America (15–17%) (Saxe, Van der Kolk, & Berkowitz et al., 1993; Horen, Leichner, & Lawson, 1995) and in Turkey (10.2%) (Tutkun, Sar, Yargic et al., 1998).

There is no sufficient evidence regarding the frequency of occurrence of dissociative amnesia. Studies show an equal sex ratio and a wide age distribution, with a peak incidence in the third and fourth decades of life (Steinberg, 2000b, 2000c). Fugue, on the other hand, is quite rare. Its prevalence in the general population has been estimated at 0.2%. However, it increases during stressful periods, such as wartime or natural disasters, or during social and religious upheavals (American Psychiatric Association, 1994). Studies conducted during World War II showed a high prevalence of all dissociative disorders, but the accuracy of these estimates is compromised by the different diagnostic conventions of the time and by the fact that they were, in many instances, gender biased in that they included mostly men. Fugue, though it does occur among children and adolescents, is most often found in adults in the second, third, and fourth decades of life. It is possible that fugue episodes in children are limited by their inability to arrange for independent transportation. There is not sufficient evidence regarding the gender distribution of the disorder (Coons, 2000).

Depersonalization as a symptom is very common in the general population. Fifty percent of adults have experienced at least one brief episode of depersonalization, usually under stressful conditions (Nemiah, 1989). In rural populations, the reported yearly prevalence was estimated at about 14.5% and of derealization at 19% (Aderibigbe, Bloch, & Walker, 2001). Depersonalization is the third most common psychiatric symptom, after depression and anxiety, and it is reported by 80% of psychiatric patients (Steinberg, 2000b). Higher rates of depersonalization or derealization are found in women and young adults (Nemiah, 1989; Aderibigbe et al., 2001).

The prevalence of the other dissociative conditions reviewed has been estimated at 2–19.3% (Saxe et al., 1993; Horen et al., 1995; Latz, Kramer, & Hughes, 1995; Modestin et al., 1996; Tutkun et al., 1998; Friedl & Draijer, 2000; Gast et al., 2001). Dissociative trance disorders have been described in various cultural contexts. Their frequency of occurrence decreases with an increase in industrialization, whereas it remains high among ethnic minorities that retain their cultural traditions.

Precipitating Factors and Comorbidities

Three major precipitating factors for the development of dissociative episodes have been reported: intensely stressful events, depressive mood, and a history of transient organic amnesia (Kopelman, 1995a, 2002b). Dissociative disorders often occur in combination with other psychiatric or general medical conditions. Patients with dissociative amnesia may also report symptoms of depression, anxiety, depersonalization, trance states, analgesia, and spontaneous age regression. They may exhibit aggressive impulses, self-mutilation, and suicidal impulses and acts. They may also have symptoms that meet criteria for conversion disorder, posttraumatic stress disorder (PTSD), a mood disorder, a substance-related disorder, or a personality disorder (DSM-IV [American Psychological Association, 1994]). In cases of fugue, there may be comorbidity with mood disorders, PTSD, and alcohol or other substance abuse (DSM-IV). Patients with DID may often present with depression (Kopelman, 2000, 2002b) and borderline personality disorder (Kluft, 1991b). In a study conducted by Dell (1998), DID patients presented personality traits similar to patients with PTSD (i.e., avoidant [76%], self-defeating [68%], borderline [53%], and passive-aggressive [45%]). They may also meet criteria for eating disorders, sleep disorders, sexual disorders, or somatoform disorders and may manifest self-destructive or risk-seeking behaviors, substance abuse, aggression, and abusive behavior toward their children.

Most cases with Ganser syndrome present comorbidity with other mental and organic disorders. The syndrome may be a prelude to a severe psychiatric disorder. However, it constitutes a separate diagnosis, as the underlying disorders cannot sufficiently account for its clinical picture. Rather, the underlying disorder may serve as an acute stressor that provides the ground upon which the syndrome's dissociative aspects are overlaid (Simeon & Hollander, 2000).

Situational Variables

Cultural context plays a critical role in the development of dissociative disorders. Dissociative phenomena encompass elements from cultural and religious beliefs and practices and are more common in third-world countries. In some cultures and religions, self-induced experiences of depersonalization and derealization appear in the context of meditation and self-suggestion. Additionally, dominant conceptions about medicine and psychotherapy, especially those influenced by Freudian ideas and psychoanalysis, may affect the emphasis placed on dissociative phenomena or even contribute to their development in some instances. Finally, it has been suggested that the identity disorders in particular are iatrogenic, or "side effects" of psychotherapy. This view maintains that alternate personality states are created rather than revealed by the therapist (Spanos, Burgess, Burgess et al., 1994; Schacter, 1996; Kihlstrom & Schacter, 2000). According to this view, social and cultural influences, in combination with the psychotherapist's expectations and the patient's expectations from psychotherapy or medicine in general, contribute to the genesis of the disorder or to its misdiagnosis.

DIFFERENTIAL DIAGNOSIS

As mentioned in the introductory section of this chapter, two cardinal features differentiate psychogenic from organic amnesias: the retrograde suppression or distortion of only autobiographical explicit memories and the absence of gross anatomical lesions or obvious changes in brain physiology. All permanent forms of organic amnesia can be readily differentiated from psychogenic ones. Limbic amnesia, for example, features prominent anterograde deficits, which do not occur in psychogenic amnesias. Even thalamic amnesia, occurring in the context of Korsakoff syndrome and entailing depersonalization and confusion, can be distinguished from the functional amnesias in that it always involves anterograde deficits. The same holds true for traumatic amnesia and amnesias associated with the dementias.

More challenging is the differentiation of functional amnesia from reversible organic amnesias. Helpful markers for the differential diagnosis of psychogenic from transient global amnesia are the rate and the circumstances of the onset of the disorder. In addition, in transient global amnesia the patient often asks questions, such as "where am I?" or "what am I doing here?" These questions are generally not encountered in psychogenic amnesias. When episodes of transient global amnesia are brief (up to an hour) and recurring, they are more likely to have an epileptic basis (Kopelman, 2002b). Episodes that have an acute onset and short duration may be accompanied by motor abnormalities and almost always by abnormal EEG findings. Seizure episodes are generally brief and do not involve the emergence of an alternate identity state.

Alcohol blackouts (i.e., periods of memory loss during alcohol intoxication) consist of partial or total amnesia for the events that occurred during the intoxication and may be mistaken for dissociative states. These can be readily differentiated on the basis of the clinical history of alcohol intake and blood alcohol concentrations drawn during acute intoxication. The clinician, however, should bear in mind that dissociative fugues and alcohol blackouts may coexist in the same patient (American Psychological Association, 1994; Coons, 2000). Similarly, other dissociative symptoms, such as depersonalization, may be exacerbated by substance use.

PATHOPHYSIOLOGY

There is no known pathophysiology for psychogenic amnesias. A diagnosis of dissociative amnesia is made after the patient has been physically examined and any other underlying neurological, psychiatric, or medical abnormalities have been ruled out. This, of course, simply indicates the absence of obvious structural abnormalities and disease. It does not, however, rule out the possibility that psychogenic amnesias may be related to physiological processes. Although the latter has yet to be determined conclusively, the idea that functional lesions (i.e., aberrations in neurophysiological processes) are as real as structural ones has been revitalized since it has become possible to register these using functional neuroimaging techniques.

In order to explain amnesic disorders that frequently accompany minor cerebral or physical injuries as well as states of psychological stress, the term "mnestic block syndrome" has been proposed (Markowitsch, 1999b, 2000, 2002). It has been suggested that both psychogenic and organic amnesia for autobiographical and, consequently, largely emotional material are the result of a similar mechanism, with the difference being that the former is produced by biochemical lesions, whereas the latter results from "mechanical" brain lesions (Markowitsch, 1996).

Mnestic block syndrome may develop after single exposure or repetitive exposures to psychologically stressful situations, which leads first to a change in stress hormone levels and neurotransmitters in the brain, and then to changes in the metabolism of cerebral areas responsible for the mnemonic processing of episodic autobiographical information (mainly right frontotemporal and adjacent limbic areas) (Markowitsch, 2000, 2002, 2003). As discussed in Chapter 2, high stress levels have a negative effect on the hippocampus and the limbic system, resulting in memory loss that may vary from mild to severe (Sapolsky, 1996; Bremner, 1999; Joseph, 1999). However, exactly how autobiographical memory suppression and alteration is related to brain physiology is currently an open question that hopefully will be answered by functional neuroimaging, as pioneering studies in this field have begun to suggest.

PROGNOSIS AND TREATMENT

Clinical Course

Clinical course and prognosis varies depending on the type of dissociative disorder and the severity of symptoms. Fugue episodes vary in duration from a few days to years, even though the patient may have been found and returned to a familiar environment (Schacter et al., 1982; Kopelman et al., 1994a). The course of the disorder is usually chronic, with recurrent episodes that fluctuate in severity. Typically, problems are detected when patients themselves realize their memory deficit or when they fail to provide appropriate answers to questions posed to them by police or medical staff regarding their identity, their history, and their recent activities.

Dissociative amnesia and fugue are usually fully reversible, especially when their onset is sudden after severe psychosocial stressors. In many cases, recovery is spontaneous when the patient, after being diagnosed, is brought into contact with his or her family and friends (Schacter et al., 1982). In some cases, the patient's memory and identity return suddenly, whereas in others memory recovers gradually (Kihlstrom & Schacter, 1995). Nevertheless, there are descriptions of cases where the loss of memory or identity is never restored (Treadwell, McCloskey, Gordon, & Cohen, 1992; Markowitsch et al., 1997).

The clinical course of dissociative identity disorder fluctuates and tends to be chronic and recurrent. It may be continuous or return sporadically. After age 40, the disorder usually subsides, although relapses may occur during periods of stress or as a result of substance abuse. When the disorder is diagnosed early in childhood and the child is removed from the stressful environment, the prognosis is generally good. In adolescence, however, alter personality states become more distinct and more autonomous. The prognosis of adult patients is better than that of adolescents but poorer than that of children. In The Netherlands, a review of 101 cases of dissociative identity disorders treated with psychotherapy on an outpatient basis for an average of 6 years showed that improvement was related to the intensity of treatment, with the more comprehensive therapies having better outcomes (Groenndijk & van der Hart, 1995). Another study that followed 54 inpatients found an improvement in dissociative symptoms and comorbid disorders 2 years after discharge (Ellason & Ross, 1997).

Depersonalization has a chronic course in about 50% of cases, causing variable functional impairment (Steinberg, 1991). The age and mode of onset of the other dissociative disorders, like trance, vary. They last from minutes to hours. Possession trance episodes may be recurrent, with a different power "overcoming" the individual each time, and they may continue for days or weeks, as long as the stressor persists. Complications of these dissociative disorders include suicide, self-destructive behaviors, and accidents. Comorbid anxiety disorders may contribute to morbidity and mortality through neuroendocrine and neuroimmune mechanisms or by direct neural stimulation (e.g., hypertension or cardiac arrhythmia) (American Psychological Association, 1994).

Treatment

Essential for the treatment of dissociative disorders is the removal of the stressor and the provision of a structured, protective, and supportive environment. These measures, in combination with treatment of comorbid conditions, may lead to the prompt resolution of symptoms. The treatment itself is mainly based on psychotherapy of psychoanalytic or other orientation (Putnam & Loewenstein, 1993). In the context of therapy, recovery of procedural and semantic memory seems to happen before recovering episodic autobiographical memories (van der Hart & Nijenhuis, 2001). A recent psychotherapeutic approach to trauma, "recovered memory therapy," aims at the recovery of memories for traumatic events, in order to prevent their intrusion into the person's life through implicit memory in the form of such symptoms as acting out, manifestations of somatization, or self-destructive behavior. However, recovered memory therapies, like functional memory disorders themselves, remain extremely controversial (Kihlstrom & Schacter, 2000).

Psychoanalytic Therapy

Psychoanalytic psychotherapy of dissociative identity disorder, if used (Kluft, 1991a, 1991b; Loewenstein & Ross, 1992; Gabbard, 1994), may address the entire set of personalities. The therapist maintains an impartial position toward the different personalities and provides the opportunity for them to be explored and integrated. Patients with dissociative identity disorder often manifest a complex and multilayered transference involving all the alter states. Commonly, transference is dominated by themes of trauma and abuse, where the therapist is often viewed as abusive, uninvolved, or as a helpless victim like the patient. Consequently, countertransference reactions are strong and frequently result in burnout (Coons, 1986; Gabbard, 1994).

Group Therapy

Group therapy is not usually seen as a viable primary modality for therapy of DID, but if used, patients should be carefully selected, and the intervention should focus on problem-solving strategies. Group therapy may or may not be combined with individual psychotherapy, and it can be of psychotherapeutic, supportive or psychoeducational orientation or aimed at the socialization of patients who have been removed from their families because of abuse (Dallam

& Manderino, 1997). Group psychotherapy has been reported as successful in veterans of war and victims of childhood abuse (Buchele, 1993).

Family Therapy

Family or couples therapy can enhance long-term stabilization, provide support for spouses or children living with the patient, and address dysfunctional patterns of behavior or practices of abuse (Porter, Kelly, & Grame, 1993).

Cognitive-Behavior Therapy

Cognitive-behavioral exercises can enhance semantic and procedural memory, whereas the reactivation and integration of episodic memories, especially of those that bring about intense emotional arousal, may require sustained therapeutic intervention. The goal of these exercises is the integration of the alter personalities into one mainstream of consciousness and the empowerment of the patient (Fine, 1999).

Hypnosis

In general, the contribution of hypnosis in the recovery of memory is controversial (Kihlstrom & Eich, 1994; Kihlstrom, 1998; Piper, 1993). The method referred to as "recovered memory therapy" through hypnosis, which is usually applied to victims of incest, or sexual abuse, lacks scientific basis (Kihlstrom, 1994). Hypnosis may help with retrieval of information and with reintegration of dissociated material. However, after hypnosis, amnesia may return. Similar objections have been expressed against "barbiturate-assisted interviews" (Piper, 1993; Kihlstrom, 1998). It has been suggested that the use of medications, such as sodium amytal and benzodiazepines, facilitates the psychiatric interview, but this practice is highly controversial. Techniques such as guided imagery and dream interpretation are not recommended, as they may lead to memory distortion or fabrication of false memories, given that the suggestibility of patients increases under these circumstances (Gudjonsson & Clark, 1986).

Counseling

Counseling helps the patient recognize what precipitates episodes, how they evolve, their defensive nature, and how symptoms can be alleviated. The aim of this method is to help the patients gain control over their symptoms. This counseling approach, referred to as "psychoeducation," is recommended mainly for the treatment of depersonalization disorder (Steinberg, 2000b).

Pharmacotherapy

With respect to pharmacotherapy, there are no studies in support of the use of a specific agent. However, medications are of use in cases of comorbidity or for the management of specific symptoms, such as sleep disturbances, affective symptoms, anxiety, obsessions or compulsions, and symptoms of posttraumatic stress disorder (i.e., intrusive and hyperarousal symptoms) (Loewenstein, 1991; Putnam & Loewenstein, 1993). In addition, while the usefulness of pharmacological treatments has not been firmly established for symptoms of depersonalization, there are case reports of patients who improved with treatment using desipramine, fluoxetine, or clonazepam (Noyes, Kuperman, & Olson, 1987; Hollander, Fairbanks, Decaria, & Liebowitz, 1989).

SUMMARY AND SPECULATION

Three fundamental features of all psychogenic amnesias are beyond dispute. First, they are all exclusively retrograde in nature. Anterograde difficulties that may be present in some cases are almost certainly due to comorbid conditions like depressed affect, anxiety, and inattention due to lack of motivation. Second, all psychogenic amnesias are highly selective, involving almost exclusively autobiographical memories, either entirely explicit, or both explicit and implicit in nature. Third, the deficits are reversible.

The fact that suppressed or distorted memories are reinstated indicates that the mnemonic function compromised in all cases is retrieval rather than encoding, consolidation and storage, or executive functions that operate on retrieved as well as new information. This being the case, the pathophysiological conditions associated with the amnesic and confabulatory symptoms most likely involve prefrontal cortical circuitry. It remains to be seen whether functional neuroimaging will verify this contention and elucidate the nature of the "functional" lesions that underlie these disorders.

12

Notes for a Theory of Memory

ANDREW C. PAPANICOLAOU

Our primary aim in this book has been to identify and segregate the symptoms and the signs of amnesia into distinct syndromes in order to create a practical guide for the clinician. A secondary aim was to provide a service to the theorists who would have to accommodate such facts into any model of memory if the latter were to be complete. But the construction of such a model was never in the blueprints of this work—which is one of the reasons for the rather vague and noncommittal title of this concluding chapter. A second reason for it is the incompleteness of the factual record as it now stands; the many gaps in our understanding of the nature of the phenomena of memory and of the amnesias. And, to the degree that theories must be about phenomena, a theory of memory at this point would be, in all probability, a precarious one, having to rest at least partially on the quicksands of conjecture rather than on solid factual foundations.

Reluctance to theorize, however, did not blind us to the necessity of using some theoretical framework, however rudimentary, broad, and informal, in order to identify, select, and order the empirical data. The framework we chose encompasses most reasonable working hypotheses that are widely accepted today, and it is laid out in the first and second chapters of this book. The question now is whether and how should that framework be modified, in light of the empirical data reviewed in Chapters 3 through 11 and in light of other considerations of a methodological nature to which we have alluded throughout the book. However, keeping to our original plan for the reasons mentioned above, we will not respond to that question by proposing a theory but by offering some hints as to what some of the prerequisites of such a theory may be, as well as what phenomena it ought to account for, and do so in a reasonably parsimonious manner.

PARSIMONY

Parsimony seems to be a virtue of only marginal appeal to contemporary theorists. Rather, as it was commented on in the concluding segment of Chapter 5, the prevailing tendency is for theorists to postulate cognitive operations and cerebral mechanisms in abundance and with an abandon hardly called for by the empirical observations.

It appears, however, that these empirical observations, the bulk of which we have summarized in the previous pages, could be accommodated in the context of a model that postulates a single set of mnemonic operations (encoding, consolidation, storage and retrieval), therefore a single set of corresponding brain mechanisms, sufficient for creating all types of memory phenomena, whether episodic or semantic. To such a model, the fact that some lesions affect semantic memories and other lesions only episodic memories would pose no real problem. Most certainly, this fact does not compel us to posit a separate system of memory traces and mechanisms in the temporal neocortex to account for semantic deficits and yet another one, in the hippocampus this time, to account for episodic deficits. In the context of the more parsimonious alternative suggested here, it could be said that lesions in the lateral aspects of the temporal lobes would simply interfere with the traces of semantic memories and lesions in the hippocampus with parts of the neuronal code of episodic memories.

ENCODING AND RETRIEVAL

Moreover, we could in the interest of greater parsimony posit that the mechanism of encoding is largely overlapping with that of retrieval. In fact, it appears that most relevant data, phenomenological and clinical, would favor the notion of a largely shared set of cerebral mechanisms for these two mnemonic functions. Let us review very briefly some of these: It is de facto and by definition the case that all memories begin their career in the form of episodes. There is not a single bit of information that is not acquired in particular and unique context and circumstances. This is the case not only of information that reaches us through the senses. It is also the case for ideas and abstract concepts that we acquire or (for those of Platonic leanings) "recollect" or rediscover. No less than percepts, those ideas are also acquired or discovered for the first time under particular and specific circumstances, in the context of a particular and unique "psychological present."

Now, the very first neural code of the very first encounter of any episode must consist of a unique temporal ordering of the following two items: first, of the activation patterns corresponding to current sensory inputs and to every single aspect of the psychological present including its hedonic valence, or emotional coloring; second, of the set of activated traces corresponding to already available concepts or percepts (for as we will comment in more detail below, we recognize sensory inputs as instances of particular types of percepts and that requires activation of traces representing these types). Remembering that episode an hour or a year later entails reactivating in the same temporal order a sufficient number of the same or similar neural codes if we are to recognize that experience as a veridical memory; that is, as a reconstruction of a bygone psychological present. If this is indeed the case, there is no need to postulate that the neural algorithms of encoding and those of retrieval make use of different brain structures and different sets of stored traces. Instead, it appears that a more parsimonious arrangement of the necessary functions and mechanisms would be one with the general features outlined in the sections below.

THE ANTERIOR-POSTERIOR SPECIALIZATION GRADIENT

It appears, in the first place, that there may be minimum overlap between brain structures supporting the mechanisms of the mnemonic functions of operations and structures serving as repositories of memory traces. Specifically it appears that with the exception of consolidation, which may be partially mediated by temporal lobe structures (the hippocampus in particular), all other mnemonic operations that result in conscious experiences are mediated by prefrontal regions, whereas the temporal and posterior neocortex serve, primarily, for the storage of traces representing experiences.

Conscious experiences composing the stream of consciousness are of two main kinds: episodes strung in a temporal series and the individual percepts and concepts, intentions and actions, that compose them. The latter, apprehended individually as separate entities, appear to be atemporal by virtue of being created automatically and effortlessly, although they do occupy an objective duration. A stereotyped verbal expression like "good morning" feels as instantaneous as the visual experience of any object. Nevertheless, both involve a sequencing and coordination of subsidiary processes, but by virtue of repetition, awareness of the sequences has been substituted by the impression of instantaneity. Yet, unlike the utterance where we can plainly see that what has been sequenced is a set of articulatory acts, in the case of concepts and percepts it is not obvious what it is, exactly, that is sequenced and coordinated. We postulate therefore, following numerous theorists on the subject, a set of elementary features. We further postulate that having a perceptual experience and becoming conscious of a concept involves coordinated activation of nascent traces representing such elementary features. During development, assembling these features is an effortful and deliberate process largely mediated by prefrontal mechanisms; but once conceptual development is complete, the coordinated arrangement of constituent features becomes largely independent of prefrontal mechanisms and almost exclusively mediated by the same cortical regions that retain the traces of these elementary constituent features (i.e., the temporal and posterior cortex) and feels instantaneous, effortless, atemporal, and automatic.

Episodes, on the other hand, always involve awareness of the sequencing and coordination of constituent percepts, concepts, intentions, and acts. This being the case, they must always require the contribution of the prefrontal cortex. And, given that the psychological present consists of a ceaseless parade of episodes, all conscious awareness, orientation to time, place, and person would, consequently, require the mediation of the prefrontal cortex. Consequently also, frontal lobe pathology or suboptimal function should result (and does) in disorientation, confusion, aboulia, and ultimately loss of the sense of self. In contrast, pathology of the posterior cortex should (and does) result in inability to activate and assemble automatically features resulting in percepts and concepts or automated action sequences (i.e., agnosia, semantic amnesia, apraxia) but not in confusion and disorientation or inability to form new automatisms.

Another idea suggested by both the objective data and by plain common sense is the one alluded to before that the mechanisms of deliberate encoding and retrieval ought to be largely overlapping. This must be the case if construction of a new episode, or reconstruction of an old one, involves the ordering of activated neuronal codes. In both cases, most of the neuronal codes activated are of already stored experiential elements, as perceiving or recognizing is basically ascertaining that a set of sensory inputs is a token of a specific configuration of elements that constitute the type of thing recognized or perceived. The difference then between retrieval and encoding consists in the presence of sensory input in the latter case—a relatively minor difference considering that in both cases there is activation of mnemonic traces and constructing of experiences through their assembly; that is, through retrieval.

Were the suggestions offered here of any objective value, it would follow that the difference among episodes remembered, much like the difference among concepts, would mainly consist in different orderings of their constituent elements. That is, ordering of percepts and concepts in the case of episodes and ordering of elementary features in the case of percepts and concepts. In either case, however, a mechanism for keeping track of the requisite order of activation of traces in each case is required. Now if forgetting of semantic memories is inaccessibility of the order in which features are to be activated, and forgetting of episodes inaccessibility of the order in which concepts and percepts is to be arranged, it would seem that the mechanism of ordering to create concepts resides along with the traces of constituent features in the temporal and posterior neocortex and the one for ordering percepts and concepts to re-create episodes in mesial temporal lobe structures and diencephalic structures.

CONSOLIDATION

Should a cohesive theory of memory provide for an operation and a cerebral mechanism for "consolidation" as most current theories do, and should it implicate the hippocampus as they all do?

It could hardly be questioned that interference with brain physiology, whether focal or diffuse, results in an inability to encode and retrieve (or only retrieve) events transpiring during or after the interference. This fact requires that we at least consider two forms of neural codes for each new episode: the one that survives for a few minutes, if not hours, after the termination of the experience it represents and which possibly consists in a Hebbian pattern of reverberating activity in a cell assembly; and the second one involving a more permanent code, a code that can remain dormant and be activated only occasionally, such as those that may be constructed by patterns of synaptic modification (see Chapter 2). Consolidation refers to the process of solidifying the latter traces. But whether or not this process is gradual, whether or not it transpires in the hippocampus, or the hippocampus and elsewhere, and what its precise nature might be, remains largely a matter of conjecture for many reasons. One of them is lack of precise information regarding the shape of retrograde amnesia gradients for various types of memories. In spite of the wide acceptance of Ribot's law, no unequivocal data on retrograde amnesia gradients exist to illuminate the nature of the consolidation process. Specifically, common experience tells us that with the passage of time we tend to forget more and more facts and episodes and even automated habits. Common experience, in other words, testifies to the existence of a temporal gradient opposite to that specified by Ribot's law, which is also based on equally loud testimony of our common knowledge and experience. Are both gradients true, but each of them true for only specific types of memories, such as memories we tend to rehearse often versus memories we tend not to rehearse? Or is the one true mostly for episodic and the other true mostly for fact and concept memories? And are these two types of memories really distinct, given that the older they become, the harder it is for us to tell with confidence that what we remember is the original episode and not its nth reconstruction, as the feeling of "being there," so unmistakable for newer memories, becomes so ambivalent for many old ones? Moreover, how can we be sure that it is possible to establish the precise shape of the retrograde amnesia gradient, let alone different gradients for episodic and semantic memories, in the presence of the many methodological difficulties we have mentioned throughout the book?

STORAGE

The situation is not altogether different when it comes to the issue of what is stored and how. As far as phenomenal experience goes, the entire stream of consciousness could be said to be somehow retained. For even when encoding is incidental, as when attention is focused on a particular task to the exclusion of all other aspects of the environment, it is often possible to retrieve nonattended aspects of that environment—the color of the carpet in a room, for example, that you could swear you had not noticed. And how many times are we surprised by the unexpected emergence of an insignificant bit of our personal past, the memory of the bend on a path we had taken on a run as children, the sound of the evening bell in a town we had been through once, and except for that bell toll, we would not have known that it ever existed?

Certainly, retaining the entire stream of consciousness, along with its shadowy fringes, would place an undue burden on the limited number of hippocampal or neocortical circuits and synapses. But it would do so only if we were to adopt a particular theory regarding information storage, namely the one suggested by the familiar hard disks and CDs, rather than some other form of storage, not yet discovered, but of the kind that allows whole libraries to be stored in vanishingly small bits of matter. Should a theory of memory, therefore, provide for storage of all experience as the one proposed, in all seriousness, by the philosopher–laureate Henri Bergson (see, e.g., Bergson, 1911)?

AND WHO INTERPRETS THE ACTIVATED TRACES?

It appears that no theory can afford to omit account of a mechanism that acts as an agent that, besides activating dormant traces of past episodes, surveys and interprets them as well. Yet theorists do omit such an agent because its presence in the biological machinery of the brain has always been a scandal, though they omit it at the cost of creating incomplete theories. Of course, it is always possible to claim that experiential facts that suggest the necessity of an agency are illusory: It is possible, for example, to claim that the inability to revisit a personal memory where, if your former self is included, it is viewed from the outside, as by another person, does not really suggest a real present-time surveyor divorced from the bearer of the memory and the participant in the original scene. But the claim is rather useless because we can dispense with the viewer and appraiser of activated mnemonic traces only at the expense of finding ourselves against the blind wall of another impasse: the impasse that was graphically depicted in Garcia Márquez's story of the insomnia plague mentioned in Chapter 5. This same impasse has been articulated by philosophers like Merleau-Ponty (1945) and more recently by memory experts like Dalla Barba (2002). The impasse results from the fact that mnemonic traces in themselves are signs to be interpreted by an intelligent agent much like the verbal signs pasted on the utensils and the animals of the amnesics of Márquez's fabled Macondo. It is always an agent or agency that is "reminded" by the signs, by the electrochemical activation patterns, in the case of memories, of the significance they represent. The significance is not in the signs, in the traces. The significance is outside them. It is the result of the interaction between them and the agent, just like the meaning of the word "cow" pasted on Buendia's animal is the result of the interaction between the letters written on the card and Buendia's mind and not in the letters, the signs themselves.

Now, the cardinal feature of episodes qua episodes is their quality of "pastness"; the quality that sets them clearly apart from new experiences. Is that quality inherent in the traces that represent them? One could certainly propose, and many implicitly do so, that the sign or "tag" of pastness may be attached to all traces of past experiences. But these signs or tags, no more and no less than all other traces, even when activated and made "visible," are bound to remain mute with respect to their being memories and memories of particular experience, in the absence of a reader that would read and interpret them. Were we now to postulate a "reader" and "interpreter" in the form of algorithms "running" in the prefrontal lobes; say, were we, in other words, to personify the "executive" function, we would do no more than simply to transpose the problem rather than to solve it. Because our "executive" is of exactly the same nature and substance as the activated traces she is supposed to read and interpret; namely, she is a set of electrochemical signals, that is to say signs, to be read and interpreted. Certainly, we can decree that these particular patterns of electrochemical activity representing the agent, this orchestrated movement of ions in cell dendrites and axons and in synaptic clefts, is not only a set of structured movements of ions but also a self-knowing intelligent agent capable of also knowing the meaning of other ion movement patterns of identical nature and judging them to be the signs of past as opposed to current experiences, and also understanding what the experiences are about. But such a decree would clearly be no less arbitrary, and possibly more counterintuitive than its alternative: the injecting of a conscious ghost in the machinery of the brain.

But let us turn right around and exit this cul-de-sac; let us consider, instead of the meaning of episodes, the meaning of their constituent items, and see whether that way we may dispense with the need of agencies and agents, as we have posited that percepts and concepts arise effortlessly and automatically in consciousness.

We have been maintaining, as several experts do, that episodes are unique and unrepeatable arrangements of percepts and concepts already formed; that the meaningfulness of episodes consists precisely in this unique arrangement. As for the meaning of the constituents of the episode, the percepts and the concepts, we maintain it is not explicitly but only implicitly appreciated, and we only become focally aware of it if the particular concept or precept is incongruous with the rest of the episode or if we must isolate it and consider it separately. For example, the episodic experience of the phrase "How is it going?" does not entail explicit awareness of any of the constituent words taken in isolation. But we do become focally aware of what that "going" means in that context if we have just begun acquiring the English language or if we have to translate it into another language. Under such circumstances, we discover that the meaning of isolated concrete concepts that immediately arise in mind consists in a concrete image or a token of the concept and that of abstract ones like "justice" or "and" or "however" in a particular diffuse attitude that is nevertheless specific to each.

It is precisely this ability of using concepts correctly in the context of episodes without being explicitly or focally aware of their meaning that raises the possibility that automatic activation of the traces that constitute a concept suffices, even in the absence of an agent or agency, to render them meaningful. A superficial look at the amnesia data may tempt us to interpret them as supportive of this possibility. Certainly, semantic amnesia does not bring about episodic amnesia. That is, the meaning of episodes can be appreciated explicitly, or so it appears, although the meaning of concepts is lost. Only, of course, it is not the meaning of all concepts that is lost in semantic amnesia. Sufficient numbers of them are still accessible out of which episodes can be created (or re-created). The data on amnesia, therefore, may not help us answer the question. The answer, if one is to be had, likely lies elsewhere, and it has much to do with the notion of meaning itself whether explicit or implicit: From a phenomenological perspective, the meaning of concepts, we have said, consists in awareness of images, percepts, or diffuse attitudes. Now diffuse attitudes may be said to constitute not only the explicit meaning of abstract concepts or function words like "however" but also the implicit meaning of all concepts correctly used and of which we may not be explicitly aware. The meaning of "going" in the phrase "How is it going?" may not be explicitly appreciated by the expert speaker of American English, but its correctness is nevertheless consciously sensed in the form of the diffuse feeling or attitude of "fitness" it engenders. Whether implicit or explicit, in other words, the meaning of concepts and precepts is a form of experience.

We turn now to the physiological counterpart of such experiences: The meaning of the activated traces or the neural code of a concept consists, we have said, in the evocation of "images" or general "attitudes." Each of these, of course, cannot be anything but another pattern of ionic movements identical in nature to those that constitute the concept, whose meaning they, presumably, furnish once activated. Thus stated, the circularity of the description becomes obvious, and unless we invoke, again, an agent to intercept and interpret (i.e., turn into experience) the neuronal activity patterns, meaning can only be said to arise magically out of that molecular movement. To invoke, once again, executive algorithms that would interpret the activated traces is, as it was just shown, useless, in that it would simply add another molecular movement pattern to the rest. And, to simply decree that this last molecular movement pattern besides being molecular is also a knowing, conscious one is, as clearly, utterly arbitrary. It appears then that we have no choice but to leave this issue to loiter, like many another, as a humble suppliant begging admission at the gates of Metaphysics.

Appendix of Neuropsychological Tests

DAVID W. LORING

Activities of daily living (ADLs) (also called Katz ADL). This is a measure of the ability to function in an independent (or semi-independent) environment. The Katz ADL measures the ability to perform in six areas including bathing, dressing, toileting, transferring, continence, and feeding. Each area is scored in which 6 indicates full functioning, 4 reflects moderate impairment, and 2 or less reflects severe functional impairment. [Katz, S., Ford, A.B., Moskowitz, R.W., Jackson, B.A., Jaffe, M.W. (1963). Studies of illness in the aged. The index of ADL: A standardized measure of biological and psychosocial function. *JAMA,* 185, 914–919]

Alternating hand movements (rapid alternating movements). A measure of adiadochokinesia, patients are typically asked to slap the palm and then the back of their hand repeatedly on their leg (i.e., pronation-supination of hands), although alternating opening and clenching of the hand is also common. Adiadochokinesia is typically associated with cerebellar lesions but may also be present in frontal lobe injury or basal ganglia disease.

Alzheimer's Disease Assessment Scale – Cognitive subscale (ADAS-Cog). This is an extended mental status examination that assesses language, memory, praxis, and orientation, with most individual items scored on a 1–5 point scale. The total ADAS-Cog score ranges from 0 to 70. [Rosen, W.G., Mohs, R.C., Davis, K.L. (1984). A new rating scale for Alzheimer's disease. *Am J Psychiatry,* 141, 1356–1364]

Autobiographical Memory Interview (AMI). The AMI is a measure of retrograde amnesia that employs a semistructured interview to assess the recall of personal events. Personal Semantic items include questions from childhood (e.g., names of schools or teachers), early adult life (e.g., name of first employer), and the more recent past (e.g., holidays, previous hospitalizations). An Autobiographical Incidents schedule is used to test recall of specific events that occurred during the same three time periods (e.g., description of an incident from primary school, from first job). [Kopelman, M.D, Wilson, B.A., Baddeley, A.D. (1990). The Autobiographical Memory Interview. Bury St. Edmunds, England: Thames Valley Test Company]

Beck Depression Inventory (BDI-II). A 21-item questionnaire of dysphoria and stress-related complaints. Each item is rated by the patient on a 0–3 scale. Although not diagnostic of depression, the BDI-II is in widespread research use and measures mood, sense of failure and worthlessness, sleep, indecisiveness and concentration difficulty, work inhibition, and appetite. No fixed classification exists, but cut score guidelines are suggested, and the BDI-II score is the sum of all of the individual statement ratings. [Beck, A.T. (1996). BDI-II, Beck Depression Inventory: Manual. San Antonio, Tex.: The Psychological Corporation]

Benton Visual Retention Test (BVRT). The BVRT measures visual perception, short-term visual memory and visual attention, and visuoconstructional ability. Either 2 or 3 simple geometric designs (2–3 per card) are presented simultaneously for either 5 or 10 seconds, and the subject is then asked to draw the designs from memory. A 15-second delayed memory condition may also be selected. Multiple forms exist, making this test attractive for repeated assessment, and each form contains 10 stimulus sets. The BVRT can be scored based on either number of design sets (stimulus reproductions of 2 or 3 designs) and complete reproductions without error or based on the numbers of reproduction errors produced. [Benton, A.L. (1974). Revised Visual Retention Test: Clinical and Experimental Applications (4th edition). New York: The Psychological Corporation. Sivan, A.B. (1992). Benton Visual Retention Test (5th edition). San Antonio, Tex.: The Psychological Corporation]

Boston Diagnostic Aphasia Examination (BDAE). A language battery designed to assess a broad range of language and linguistic functions often associated with left hemisphere impairment. Language is tested through different perceptual modalities (e.g., auditory, visual, gestural), processing functions (e.g., comprehension, analysis, problem-solving), and types of response (e.g., writing, articulation, manipulation). The battery consists of five sections: Conversational and Expository Speech, Auditory Comprehension, Oral Expression, Understanding Written Language, and Writing. An Aphasia Severity Rating is made based on performance on a semistructured interview and open-ended conversation. Formal subtests are scored for accuracy, and qualitative speech characteristics are rated. [Goodglass, H., Kaplan, E., & Barresi, B. (2000). The Boston Diagnostic Aphasia Examination (BDAE-3) (3rd edition). Philadelphia: Lippincott Williams & Wilkins]

Boston Naming Test (BNT). The BNT is a confrontation naming task in which line-drawn pictures serve as the stimuli, and the subject is asked to name the object. Semantic cues may be given to insure that perceptual errors such as an obvious misperception are not preventing the subject from correctly naming the picture. Phonemic cues consisting of the initial sound are given after naming failure, but correct responses after phonemic cuing are not included in the total score. [Kaplan, E.F., Goodglass, H., Weintraub, S. (1983). The Boston Naming Test (2nd edition). Philadelphia: Lea & Febiger]

Brown-Peterson distractor task. Memory procedure designed to assess retention of small amounts of information across a short distractor period (e.g., counting backward by 3s or 7s). This is often considered a short-term memory task because it employs maximum retention intervals of 45–60 seconds and does not test for retention of information over longer delays. The Brown-Peterson technique has been a popular approach to investigate the memory impairment associated with Korsakoff syndrome. This is the basic format for auditory consonant trigram testing, which is sensitive to certain types of frontal lobe dysfunction. [Brown, J. (1958). Some tests of the decay of immediate memory. *Q J Exp Psychol*, 10, 12–21. Peterson, L.R., Peterson, M.J. (1959). Short-term retention of individual verbal items. *J Exp Psychol*, 58, 193–198]

California Verbal Learning Test (CVLT). A serial word list learning task that is patterned in format after the Rey Auditory Verbal Learning Test. The CVLT consists of 16 words from 4 semantic categories (i.e., spices and herbs, fruits, tools, and clothing) that are presented as a "shopping list." The use of semantic categories permits the study of semantic clustering effects in patient learning and recall. After learning trials using the "Monday list," a single trial with a second list of words is administered ("Tuesday list") and consists of names of fruits, and spices and herbs, and new categories of fish and kitchen utensils. Free recall of the original Monday list is then obtained. Semantic cues are then provided. After a delay of approximately 20 minutes, free and cued recall and recognition is tested. Consecutive recall of words from the same semantic category (semantic clustering) reflects organization based on semantic word features. [Delis, D.C., Kramer, J.H., Kaplan, E., Ober, B.A. (1987). California Verbal Learning Test: Adult Version. Manual. San Antonio, Tex.: The Psychological Corporation]

Cambridge Neuropsychological Test Automated Battery (CANTAB). CANTAB is a computerized neuropsychological assessment battery that is used to measure cognitive changes caused by a variety of central nervous system disorders. CANTAB consists of 13 subtests that assess motor skill, visual attention, memory, planning, and working memory. All task stimuli are nonverbal, consisting of geometric designs or simple shapes, and the only language proficiency necessary is to understand task instructions. Many of the tests were developed from the kinds of tests used in lesion and drug studies with animals. CANTAB PAL is a subtest of visuospatial paired associates learning, which is used in the early detection of Alzheimer disease. [Sahakian, B.J., Owen, A.M. (1992). Computerized assessment in neuropsychiatry using CANTAB: discussion paper. *J R Soc Med*, 85, 399–402. Robbins, T., James, M., Owen, A. Sahakian, B., McInnes, L., Rabbitt, P. (1994). Cambridge Neuropsychological Test Automated Battery (CANTAB): A factor analytic study of a large sample of normal elderly volunteers. *Dementia*, 5, 266–281]

Cancellation tasks. A family of tasks to measure attention/psychomotor speed or hemispatial neglect that require the subject to mark specific stimuli from a larger stimulus array. Multiple variations of this task exist and may consist of letters or shapes. Rows containing letters are often presented on a sheet of paper, and the task is to cross out certain letters on the entire sheet. In some versions, the same target letter is used for the entire test, and in other versions, different target letters are crossed out in different rows. Patients with attentional deficits display inconsistent target responding throughout the test, and patients with processing inefficiencies require longer time to completion. Patients with hemispatial inattention tend to perform less well with stimuli on the side of the page corresponding to their neglect.

Children's Auditory Verbal Learning Test. This is a pediatric word learning task patterned after the Rey Auditory Verbal Learning Task. A word list is presented for 5 trials in a standard list learning format. A second list is then presented as an interference task, and free-recall for the interference task is tested followed by recall for words on the original list. Delayed recall and recognition are also obtained. [Talley, J.N. (1993). Children's Auditory Verbal Learning Test-2 (CAVLT-2). Lutz, Fla.: Psychological Assessment Resources]

Children's Memory Scale. A battery of tests designed as a downward extension of the Wechsler Memory Scale. It consists of six core subtests to assess verbal and visual learning and memory, as well as attention. Two supplemental subtests may be given. The test is intended for children age 5–16 years. [Cohen, M.J. (1997). Children's Memory Scale. San Antonio, Tex.: The Psychological Corporation]

Clinical Dementia Rating (CDR). Formally called the Washington University Clinical Dementia Rating Scale, the CDR is a widely used rating scale based on a semistructured interview to measure disease severity and progression. Status in six cognitive-functional categories is rated: Memory, Orientation, Judgment, Community Affairs, Home and Hobbies, and Personal Care. Each area is rated on a 3-point scale [0 = Normal (no significant problem), 0.5 = Questionable Impairment (more than just normal aging), 1 = Mild Impairment (mildly impaired relative to peers), 2 = Moderate Impairment, 3 = Severe Impairment]. These category scores (or "box scores") are then analyzed using special scoring rules to determine a final, overall CDR score. Patients with scores of 1 or greater demonstrate clear evidence of dementia, whereas a score of 0.5 reflects only mild impairment [Morris, J.C. (1993). The Clinical Dementia Rating (CDR): Current version and scoring rules. *Neurology*, 43(11), 2412–2414]

Clock drawing. Clock drawing tests both planning and visual-constructional ability and is often used as a screening measure for dementia or hemispatial inattention. Many different approaches exist. Patients may be given a large open circle and asked to fill in numbers or may be instructed to begin by drawing a circle and then draw a clock face with standard numbering. The relative number positions reflect planning, and errors may involve number perseveration or hemispatial inattention. Patients are also asked to draw the clock hands to indicate a particular time.

Computerized Tower of London test (from CANTAB). Called the "Stockings of Cambridge" in the CANTAB battery, the Computerized Tower of London is a spatial planning test. Tower of London measures cognitive aspects of planning essential for normal executive control over action. On the computer monitor, two sets of three colored balls are displayed and appear to be hanging in stockings. Subjects rearrange the balls in the bottom display such that their positions match the model arrangement on the top half of the screen. Planning ability is reflected by the time prior to the first move and subsequent time between individual moves in the sequence.

Controlled Oral Word Association (COWA). This is a test of verbal generative fluency in which words beginning with a specific target letter of the alphabet are generated during a 60-second interval. Three trials are administered, with the target letters being either C-F-L or P-R-W. This task is often contrasted with performance on semantic fluency tasks. This task is sometimes called letter fluency. [Benton, A.L., Hamsher, K.D., Sivan, A.B. (1994). Multilingual Aphasia Examination–Third Edition. Odessa, Fla.: Psychological Assessment Resources]

Corsi block tapping test. This task measures spatial learning, and is a visual analogue of Hebb's Recurring Digit Test. The subject asked to reproduce various span sequenced tapped out on small blocks by the examiner, and the span length of the sequences exceed the subject's spatial span by one block. Unknown to the subject, the same spatial sequence is repeated every third trial, and the task is to determine how quickly the patient learns the repeated sequence [Corsi, P.M. (1972). Human memory and the medial temporal region of the brain. Unpublished doctoral thesis, McGill University, Montreal, Quebec, Canada]

Crovitz test of remote personal memory. This is a test of remote memory based on an approach developed by Galton (1879) in which a particular stimulus word serves as a cue to elicit recall of an autobiographical event. Subjects are provided a list of cue words (e.g., garden, break, happy) and are required to describe an incident from their personal memory relating to each word. Scoring is based on the descriptive richness of each memory produced and its specificity [Galton, F. (1879). Psychometric experiments. Brain, 2, 148–162. Crovitz, H., Unconstrained search in long-term memory. Paper presented at the meeting of the Psychonomic Society, St. Louis, Mo., 1973. Crovitz, H.F., Schiffman, H. (1974). Frequency of episodic memories as a function of their age. *Bull Psychonom Soc*, 4, 517–518]

Denman Neuropsychology Memory Scale A clinical memory test that contains 11 subtests to evaluate immediate and delayed verbal and nonverbal memory. It is similar in format to the Wechsler Memory Scale (WMS) but contains several tasks without a WMS analogue, including a memory for faces subtest, a musical tone differentiation task, and the Rey-Osterreith Complex Figure. [Denman, S.B. (1987). Denman Neuropsychology Memory Scale. Charleston, S.C.: S.B. Denman]

Digit span. This is a test of auditory span based on the ability to repeat a series of numbers of increasing lengths. The ability both to repeat numbers immediately after their presentation and to repeat them in reversed serial order are typically both tested. Digit span, particularly backward digit span, is regarded by many as the prototypic neuropsychological test of mental tracking or working memory. Digit span tasks are part of a variety of procedures including the Wechsler Adult Intelligence Scales (WAIS) and its revisions, the Wechsler Intelligence Scale for Children (WISC) and its revisions, Wechsler Memory Scale (WMS) and its revisions, and Children's Memory Scale (CMS).

Dissociative Disorders Interview Schedule. The Dissociative Disorders Interview Schedule (DDIS) is a structured interview to establish a DSM-IV diagnosis of somatization disorder, borderline personality disorder, and major depressive disorder, or any of the various dissociative disorders. It inquires about positive symptoms of schizophrenia, extrasensory experiences, substance abuse, and other items relevant to the dissociative disorders. There is no overall summary score for the entire interview. [Ross, C.A., Heber, S., Anderson, G. (1990). The Dissociative Disorders Interview Schedule. *Am J Psychiatry*, 147, 1698–1699]

Dissociative Experience Scale. The Dissociative Experience Scale (DES) is a 28-item, self-administered inventory to measure the frequency of dissociative experiences [Bernstein, E.M., Putnam, F.W. (1986). Development, reliability, and validity of a dissociation scale. *J Nerv Ment Dis*, 174(12), 727–735]

Famous Faces Test. A measure of remote memory that assesses the ability to recognize photographs of individuals who achieved fame in each of six decades from the 1920s to 1970s. In addition to standard face recognition, photographs taken when the individuals were young are also paired with photographs of the same people who were still famous when they were old (e.g., Charlie

Chaplin) [Albert, M.S., Butters, N., Levin, J. (1979). Temporal gradients in the retrograde amnesia of patients with alcoholic Korsakoff's disease. *Arch Neurol*, 36, 211–216]

Finger tapping. A measure of fine motor speed in which the index finger is tapped as quickly as possible against a response key that is attached either to a mechanical counter or an electronic counter. Five trials of 10 seconds each that do not deviate by more than 10% are usually obtained for each hand; however, variability exists in test administration from 3 to 10 trials.

Frontal Behavioral Inventory. This is a 24-item questionnaire assessing negative behaviors including apathy, aspontaneity, indifference, inflexibility, concreteness, personal neglect, disorganization, inattention, loss of insight, logopenia, verbal apraxia, and alien hand, as well as positive behaviors including perseveration, irritability, excessive or childish jocularity, irresponsibility, inappropriateness, impulsivity, restlessness, aggression, hyperorality, hypersexuality, utilization behavior, and incontinence. The Frontal Behavioral Inventory may assist in the differential diagnosis of frontotemporal dementia. [Kertesz, A., Nadkarni, N., Davidson, W., Thomas, A. W. (2000). *J Int Neuropsychol Soc*, 6(4), 460–468]

Frontotemporal Behavioral Scale. This is a structured interview containing many items from the Lund-Manchester Consensus but with additional items such as irritability, tendency to sleep in the absence of stimulation, and emotional lability. Content areas assessed are Self-monitoring, Self-neglect, Self-centered, and Mood. Although there are many specific examples of abnormal behavior within each of the four content areas, each area is scored as impaired (e.g., score of 1) regardless of the number of abnormal behaviors within that content area. [Lebert, F., Pasquier, F., Souliez, L., & Petit, H. (1998). Frontotemporal behavioral scale. *Alzheimer Dis Assoc Disord*, 12(4), 335–339]

Functional Assessment Staging (FAST). This is a dementia rating scale that can be used as part of the Global Deterioration Scales. The FAST rates functional change in 7 major stages, with 16 successive stages and substages. The FAST identifies 11 substages from the later stages of the GDS, making it useful for staging severe dementia. [Reisberg B. (1988). Functional assessment staging (FAST). *Psychopharmacol Bull*, 24, 653–659]

Galveston Orientation and Amnesia Test (GOAT). This is a mental status examination designed to assess the duration of disorientation, or posttraumatic amnesia, after traumatic brain injury. The GOAT is designed for repeated assessment. The GOAT consists of orientation (e.g., person, place, and time) and also assesses the last event before the accident and the first memory after the accident. [Levin, H.S., O'Donnell, V.M., Grossman, R.G. (1979). The Galveston Orientation and Amnesia Test: A practical scale to assess cognition after head injury. *J Nervous Mental Dis*, 167, 675–684]

Glasgow Coma Scale (GCS). This is a measure of coma severity (i.e., level of consciousness) based on patient responsiveness in three dimensions (best eye response, best verbal response, best motor response). The sum of the three scales ranges from 3 to 15. Scores of 8 or less are indicative of coma; scores of 9–14 indicate various degrees of posttraumatic amnesia. Although not universally accepted, scores of 9–12 are generally considered to be moderate injuries, and scores of 13–15 are considered mild injuries. [Teasdale, G., Jennett, B. (1974). Assessment of coma and impaired consciousness: A practical scale. *Lancet*, 2, 81–84]

Global Deterioration Scale (GDS). This scale is part of the Global Deterioration Scale Staging System. The GDS consists of several major clinically distinguishable dementia stages, ranging from normal cognitive abilities to severe dementia. Examples within each of the seven content areas assist in determining the proper deterioration[s] stage. [Reisberg B., Ferris S.H., de Leon, M.J., Crook, T. (1982). Global Deterioration Scale (GDS) for assessment of primary degenerative dementia. *Am J Psychiatry*, 139, 1136–1139]

Hamilton Rating Scale for Depression. A measure of depression in which depressive symptoms are rated on a 3- or 5-point scale. It differs from other rating scales such as the Beck Depression Inventory in that the scale is filled out by an observer or interviewer. This test has been revised and different versions exist [Hamilton, M. (1967). Development of a rating scale for primary depressive illness. *Br J Social Clin Psychol*, 6, 278–296]

Hodges and Patterson semantic battery. A test of semantic memory in which category fluency is tested by having the patient generate words within the following semantic categories: animals, birds, water creatures, household items, vehicles, and musical instruments. [Hodges, J.R., Patterson, K. (1995). Is semantic memory consistently impaired early in the course of Alzheimer's disease? Neuroanatomical and diagnostic implications. *Neuropsychologia*, 33, 441–459]

Judgment of Line Orientation (JLO). A test of visual spatial processing containing stimulus materials of two spokes of a semicircular wheel that point in different directions. The task is to identify which lines of the entire semicircle containing 11 lines are pointing in the same direction (i.e., have the same spatial orientation) as the stimuli, and performance on 30 test items is obtained. JLO is thought to be a selectively sensitive measure of right hemisphere impairment [Benton, A.L., Sivan, A.B., Hamsher, K. deS., Varney, N.R., Spreen, O. (1994). Contributions to Neuropsychological Assessment. A clinical manual (2nd edition). New York: Oxford University Press]

Mattis Dementia Rating Scale (DRS). Scale developed for use in a geriatric population for assessing five cognitive domains that are commonly impaired in various dementias: attention, initiation/perseveration, construction, conceptual, and memory. Although called a rating scale, this procedure is more accurately viewed as a structured, extended mental status examination. [Mattis, S. (1988). Dementia Rating Scale: Professional Manual. Odessa, Fla.: Psychological Assessment Resources]

Mini-Mental State Examination (MMSE). Often simply called either the Folstein after its developer or the Mini-mental, the MMSE is a measure of mental status that assesses memory, orientation, visual-spatial copying, and language. The MMSE is useful as a screening test for moderate Alzheimer disease, but it is not sensitive to more subtle impairment. [Folstein, M.F., Folstein, S.E., McHugh, P.R. (1975). Mini-Mental State: A practical method for grading the cognitive state of outpatients for the clinician. *J Psychiatric Res*, 12, 189–198]

Multilingual Aphasia Examination. Language battery used to assess receptive, expressive, and repetition skills. Included are Visual Naming, Sentence Repetition, Controlled Oral Word Association, Token Test, Aural Comprehension of Words and Phrases, and Reading Comprehension of Words and Phrases. In addition, there is a spelling subtest with response modes: oral, written, and block spelling (i.e., use of plastic letters). This test was developed in the Benton Neuropsychology Laboratory. [Benton, A., Hamsher, K. deS. (1989). Multilingual Aphasia Examination. Iowa City, Iowa: AJA Associates]

National Adult Reading Test (NART). A reading test of irregularly spelled words used to estimate premorbid cognitive functioning that was developed in England. [Nelson, H.E. (1982). National Adult Reading Test (NART): Test Manual. Windsor, England: NFER]

n-back task. A measure of working memory in which stimuli are presented serially, and the subject is to identify a stimulus that occurred "n" steps back from the current stimulus. Different versions have included numbers, works, pictures, and spatial location.

Peabody Picture Vocabulary Test (PPVT). This is a measure of receptive vocabulary in which a word is read to the subject, and a drawing that best depicts the word is selected from a four-picture multiple-choice array. [Dunn, L.M., Dunn, L.M. (1997). Peabody Picture Vocabulary Test-Third Edition. Circle Pines, Minn.: American Guidance Service]

Pursuit Rotor Task. Manual tracking task used in the assessment of procedural learning skills. Two commonly used pursuit rotor tasks are produced by Lafayette Instrument Company and the Vienna Test System.

Pyramid and Palm Trees Test. A measure of picture and word recognition that requires knowledge of item similarity, either by property or by association. The format is the same for both pictures and words: a stimulus is presented and one of two choices is made. For example, a pyramid must be matched with either a palm tree or a pine tree. [Howard, D., Patterson, K.E. (1992). The Pyramids and Palm Tress Test. Bury St. Edmunds, Suffolk, England: Thames Valley Test Company]

Randt Memory Test. This test was designed for repeated assessments and has five different forms that have been shown to be comparable overall. Unlike many other memory tests, the Randt has a 24-hour telephone interview to assess long delayed recall. There are seven subtests: general information, a five-item list-learning task, digit memory span, six paired-associates, paragraph recall, picture recognition and verbal recall, and incidental learning. The major summary scores are Acquisition and Recall (AR) and Delayed Memory (DM). [Randt, C.T., Brown, E.R., Osborne, D.J. (1980). A memory test for longitudinal measurement of mild to moderate deficits. *Clin Neuropsychol, 2,* 184–194]

Raven's Progressive Matrices (standard and colored). The Raven Matrices are multiple-choice tests of visual-spatial ability and reasoning consisting of a series of visual patterns and analogies. The test requires the conceptualization of spatial, design, and numerical relationships. The Colored Progressive Matrices are easier and intended for children from 5 to 11 years and for adults 65 years and older. The Standard Progressive Matrices is generally employed for ages 8–65 years. [Raven, J.C., Court, J.H., Raven, J. (1982). Manual for Raven's Progressive Matrices and Vocabulary Scales. London, England: H.K. Lewis and Company Ltd.]

Recognition Memory Test. Also called the Warrington Recognition Memory test, this is a test of verbal and nonverbal memory using single words and unfamiliar male faces. After presentation of 50 verbal or nonverbal stimuli, subjects are tested with a two-alternative forced-choice recognition task in which the target is paired with a single distractor. As with other forced-choice measures, this test may also be used in symptom validity testing. [Warrington, E.K. (1984). Recognition Memory Test Manual. Windsor, Berkshire, England: NFER-Nelson]

Rey Auditory Verbal Learning Test (AVLT). This is a serial word list learning task in which 15 words are presented over five learning trials. After the final learning trial, a new list of 15 words is presented. Recall of the second list is measured, and then the subject recalls as many words as possible from the original list. A 20- to 30-minute delayed recall trial and a recognition memory trial, using either a story or word-list format, can also be given [Rey, A. (1958). L'examen clinique en psychologie. Paris: Press Universitaire de France]

Rey-Osterreith Complex Figure (ROCF). The ROCF is a measure of visual-spatial constructional skill and visual memory developed by Rey (1941) and standardized by Osterrieth (1944). The figure is first copied and this provides information about constructional ability. Memory is assessed by using immediate recall, delayed recall, or both. In addition, recognition memory may be assessed with several administration versions. An alternative complex figure was developed by Taylor (Taylor Complex Figure). [Osterrieth, P.A. (1944). Le test de copie d'une figure complex: Contribution a l'etude de la perception et de la memoire. Archives de Psychologie, 30, 286–356. Rey, A. (1941). L'examen psychologique dans les cas d'encephalopathie traumatique. Archives de Psychologie, 28, 286–340. Taylor, L.B. (1969). Localization of cerebral lesions by psychological testing. *Clin Neurosurg*, 16, 269–287]

Rivermead Behavioral Memory Test (RBMT). This is a test of "everyday memory" such as the ability to associate a name with a face. Other examples of everyday memory items include the ability to remember where a personal item has been hidden, the ability to remember an appointment or to deliver a message (Rivermead Behavioral Memory Test for Children [RBMT-C]). [Wilson, B., Cockburn, J., Baddeley, A. The Rivermead Behavioural Memory Test. England: Thames Valley Test Company]

Squire Subjective Memory Questionnaire. This is a measure of subjective memory impairment requiring the patient to assess the current memory function. It was developed to assess memory change after ECT. [Squire, L.R., Wetzel, C.D., Slater, P.C. (1979). Memory complaint after electroconvulsive therapy: assessment with a new self-rating instrument. *Biol Psychiatry*, 14, 791–801]

Stroop Color-Word Interference Test. A task consisting of color names printed in nonmatching colored ink (e.g., RED printed in blue ink). Reading the color names (e.g., RED, GREEN, BLUE) regardless of ink color used for printing is reliably faster and more accurate than identifying the ink color while ignoring the spelled color name (i.e., the interference or inhibition condition). Many different versions of this paradigm exist for experimental and clinical purposes, most of which also measure how quickly color names can be read when they are printed in dark ink and how quickly ink color can be identified when items contain minimal verbal content (e.g., XXXX printed in different colors). Various scoring schemes have been proposed, including time difference scores between the reading and "inhibition" tasks, and a ratio index of interference is commonly used. The inhibition effect is sensitive to brain damage. Diminished performance, however, has also been reported in depressed and anxious patients. [Stroop, J.R. (1935). Studies of interference in serial verbal reactions. *J Exp Psychol*, 18, 643–662]

Structured Clinical Interview for DSM-IV® Dissociative Disorders. This is a structured clinical interview that assesses 33 Axis I diagnoses in adults. Specialized editions and modules have been developed for specific disorders (e.g., dissociative disorders, panic disorder, and posttraumatic stress disorder) and particular patient populations (e.g., veterans, human immunodeficiency virus infection, and nonpsychiatric patients). The SCID-II is a companion instrument that assesses the Axis II Personality Disorders.

Token Test. This is a measure of auditory comprehension in which the subject is asked to execute commands of increasing length and complexity using small plastic or wooden tokens that vary in color, shape, and size. [De Renzi, E., Vignolo, L. (1962). The Token Test: a sensitive test to detect receptive disturbances in aphasics. *Brain*, 85, 665–678]

Tower of Hanoi/Tower of London. These tests are both problem-solving tasks used to assess frontal lobe dysfunction and residual learning capability. Although these versions differ with respect to complexity, they all involve moving different colored rings (or beads) from their positions on vertical sticks to other specific locations in the fewest number of moves. [Shallice, T. (1982). Specific impairments of planning. *Philos Trans R Soc London*, 298, 199–209]

Trail Making Test. This is a measure of visual scanning speed that has two parts. Part A consists of 25 circles numbered from 1 to 25 that are distributed on a piece of paper, and the task is to connect the circles from 1 to 25 as quickly as possible. Part B consists of 25 circles with numbers 1 to 13 and letters A to L, and the subject is to alternate between the numbers and letters in an ascending sequence (e.g., 1-A-2-B, etc.). [Author. (1944). Army Individual Test Battery. Manual of Directions and Scorings. Washington, D.C.: U.S. War Department, Adjutant General's Office. Armitage, S.G. (1946). An analysis of certain psychological tests for the evaluation of brain injury. *Psychol Monogr*, 60, (Whole No. 277)]

Verbal and Design Fluency. A family of tests developed as nonverbal analogues to verbal fluency tests (e.g., Controlled Oral Word Association) in which geometric designs or figures are generated within a specified period, usually 1–3 minutes. Jones-Gotman and Milner produced the first formal figural fluency measure, Design Fluency, in which nonsense figures are generated. Regard and Strauss developed the Five-Point Test in which 5-dot matrices are presented, and the subject produces different shapes by connecting different dot arrangements within the rectangle. The Ruff Figure Fluency Test is a modification of the Five-Point Test that contains distractors, or variations of the dot matrix pattern. Glosser and Goodglass's Graphic Pattern Generation consists of four different 5-dot matrices; subjects are instructed to draw different patterns by connecting the dots using four lines only. [Glosser, G., Goodglass, H. (1990). Disorders in executive control functions among aphasic and other brain-damaged patients. J Clin Exp Neuropsychol, 12, 485–501. Jones-Gotman, M., Milner, B. (1977). Design fluency: the invention of nonsense drawings after focal cortical lesions. Neuropsychologia, 15, 653–674. Regard, M., Strauss, E., Knapp, P. (1982). Children's production of verbal and non-verbal fluency tasks. Perceptual and Motor Skills, 55, 839–844. Ruff, R. (1988). Ruff Figural Fluency Test. San Diego: Neuropsychological Resources]

Verbal fluency, phonemic and semantic. These are two variations of fluency tasks in which subject generates words within a prescribed time limit, usually 60 seconds. The phonemic fluency task has the patients generate as many words as possible that begin with a specific letter of the alphabet, and F-A-S are commonly used. The semantic task requires the subject to give examples of a target category (e.g., animals, foods) within the specified limited time. Some evidence suggests that semantic fluency is more greatly impaired than letter fluency in Alzheimer disease.

Wechsler Adult Intelligence Scale (WAIS, WAIS-R, WAIS-III). The Wechsler Adult Intelligence Scale and its revisions are the most widely used tests of general cognitive abilities. The WAIS consists of multiple subtests that are combined to generate a Verbal IQ, Performance IQ, and Full-Scale IQ, and in the most recent edition, factor scores including Verbal Comprehension, Working Memory, Perceptual Organization, and Processing Speed. [Wechsler, D. (1997). Wechsler Adult Intelligence Scale–Third Edition. San Antonio, Tex.: The Psychological Corporation]

Wechsler Intelligence Scale for Children. The Wechsler Intelligence Scale for Children (WISC) and its revisions are a downward extension of the WAIS producing measures of Verbal IQ, Performance IQ, and Full-Scale IQ. It is appropriate for use with children ranging in age from 6 to 16 years. [Wechsler, D. (1991). Wechsler Intelligence Scale for Children–Third Edition. San Antonio, Tex.: The Psychological Corporation]

Wechsler Memory Scale (WMS; WMS-R; WMS-III). The Wechsler Memory Scale is among the most widely used memory test batteries. The original memory scale was criticized for including information such as orientation in the summary score, the Memory Quotient (MQ), and for considering memory to be a unitary construct. The Wechsler Memory Scale–Revised (WMS-R) separated verbal from visual memory and addressed many of the problems with the original version, although it, too, was criticized, in part due to its standardization on relatively few subjects. The Wechsler Memory Scale-III (WMS-III) provides a larger pool of tests so that summary scores can be developed from measures with demonstrated sensitivity to brain impairment. The WMS-III has 11 subtests: 6 compose the core battery and 5 are considered supplemental. The WMS-III is used to explore three general content areas: verbal auditory memory, visual nonverbal memory, and attention and concentration. The Auditory/Verbal Memory Domain consists of Logical Memory, Verbal Paired Associates, and Word List. Logical Memory is a prose passage recall task for two paragraphs, and the second paragraph is presented twice, and thus contains two learning trials. Verbal Paired Associates is a paired associate task containing only difficult word-pair associations. Word List is a supplemental test that contains an interference task in addition to standard learning trials. The Visual/Nonverbal Memory Domain contains Visual Reproduction, Memory for Faces, Dots, and Family Pictures. Visual Reproduction is a supplemental test for the WMS-III, and assesses recall of simple geometric designs. Memory for Faces is a measure of nonverbal memory for faces, Dots assesses spatial location memory, and Family Pictures tests memory for everyday activities. The Attention/Concentration Domain contains

Mental Control, Spatial Span, Digit Span, and Letter-Number Span. Mental Control is a measure of mental tracking and manipulation of familiar sequences and is a supplemental test; Digit Span and Spatial Span are traditional measures of length of auditory and visual working memory; Letter-Number Sequencing is a task in which letters and numbers are presented in a mixed-up order, and the task is to first state the numbers in ascending order and then to state the letters in alphabetical order. [Wechsler, D. (1997). Wechsler Memory Scale–Third Edition. San Antonio, Tex.: The Psychological Corporation]

Westmead PTA Scale. This is a measure of posttraumatic amnesia (PTA) that consists of seven orientation questions and five memory items. A patient is considered to have emerged from PTA if they can achieve a perfect score on the Westmead PTA Scale for 3 consecutive days. PTA is judged to have ended on the first of the 3 consecutive days of perfect recall. [Shores, E.A., Marosszeky, J.E., Sandanam, J., Batchelor, J. (1986). Preliminary validation of a clinical scale for measuring the duration of post-traumatic amnesia. *Med J Aust*, 144(11), 569–572]

Wisconsin Card Sorting Test (WCST). The WCST is used to assess hypothesis testing, abstract reasoning, and ability to shift and maintain the cognitive processes necessary for correct responding. Each card contains one to four symbols (triangle, star, cross, circle) printed in red, green, yellow, or blue. The subject is asked to place each card under one of four other cards—one red triangle, two green stars, three yellow crosses, and four blue circles—according to a principle that must be deduced from examiner feedback indicating whether or not the cards have been correctly sorted. The sorting principle changes multiple times during the test. Difficulty in changing sorting strategy, difficulty in maintaining a new sorting strategy after it has shifted, and the tendency to make perseverative responses are measured. The WCST is often regarded as a test of frontal lobe function. Performance, however, may be disrupted by both anterior and posterior cerebral regions and may be unaffected by large frontal lobe lesions. Thus, the WCST is better viewed as a complex measure of executive functioning that is not linked to a single brain region but rather relies on the integration of multiple neural areas, including frontal lobes. [Grant, D.A., Berg, E.A. (1948). A behavioral analysis of degree of impairment and ease of shifting to new responses in a Weigl-type card sorting problem. J Exp Psychol, 39, 404–411. Nelson, H.E. (1976). A modified card sorting test sensitive to frontal lobe defects. *Cortex*, 12, 313–324]

References

Aarsland, D., K. Andersen, J. P. Larsen, et al. 2001. Risk of dementia in Parkinson's disease: A community-based, prospective study. *Neurology* 56(6):730–736.

Aarsland, D., M. Hutchinson, J. P. Larsen. 2003. Cognitive, psychiatric and motor response to galantamine in Parkinson's disease with dementia. *Int J Geriatr Psychiatry* 18(10):937–941.

Aarsland, D., K. Laake, J. P. Larsen, C. Janvin. 2002. Donepezil for cognitive impairment in Parkinson's disease: A randomised controlled study. *J Neurol Neurosurg Psychiatry* 72(6):708–712.

Aarsland, D., E. Tandberg, J. P. Larsen, J. L. Cummings. 1996. Frequency of dementia in Parkinson disease. *Arch Neurol* 53(6):538–542.

Abe, K., M. Inokawa, A. Kashiwagi, T. Yanagihara. 1998. Amnesia after a discrete basal forebrain lesion. *J Neurol Neurosurg Psychiatry* 65(1):126–130.

Abeles, M., P. Schilder. Psychogenic loss of personal identity. *Arch Neurol Psychiatry* 34:587–604, 1935.

Adams, C. B. T., E. D. Beardsworth, S. M. Oxbury, et al. 1990. Temporal lobectomy in 44 children: Outcome and neuropsychological follow-up. *J Epilepsy* 3:157–168.

Aderibigbe, Y. A., R. M. Bloch, W. R. Walker. 2001. Prevalence of depersonalization and derealization experiences in a rural population. *Soc Psychiatry Psychiatr Epidemiol* 36:63–69.

Adolphs, R., N. L. Denburg, D. Tranel. 2001. *Behav Neurosci* 115:983–992.

Adolphs, R., D. Tranel, S. Hamann, et al. 1999. Recognition of facial emotion in nine individuals with bilateral amygdala damage. *Neuropsychologia* 37:111–1117.

Aggleton, J. P., R. Desimone, M. Mishkin. 1986. The origin, course, and termination of the hippocampothalamic projections in the macaque. *J Comp Neurol* 243:409–421.

Aggleton, J. P., D. McMackin, K. Carpenter, et al. 2000. Differential cognitive effects of colloid cysts in the third ventricle that spare or compromise the fornix. *Brain* 123:800–815.

257

Aggleton, J. P., A. Sahgal. 1993. The contribution of the anterior thalamic nuclei to anterograde amnesia. *Neuropsychologia* 31:1001–1019.

Aimard, G., M. Trillet, C. Perroudon, et al. 1971. Ictus amnesique symptomatique d un glioblastome interessant le trigone. *Revue Neurol (Paris)* 124:392–396.

Akos Szabo, C., E. Wyllie, L. D. Stanford, et al. 1998. Neuropsychological effect of temporal lobe resection in preadolescent children with epilepsy. *Epilepsia* 39:814–819.

Alathari, L., C. T. Ngo, S. Dopkins. 2004. Loss of distinctive features and a broader pattern of priming in Alzheimer's disease. *Neuropsychology* 18:603–612.

Alavi, A., A. B. Newber, E. Souder, J. A. Berlin. 1993. Quantitative analysis of PET and MRI data in normal aging and Alzheimer's disease: Atrophy weighted total brain metabolism and absolute whole brain metabolism as reliable discriminators. *J Nucl Med* 34:1681–1687.

Albensi, B. C., S. M. Knoblach, B. G. M. Chew, et al. 2000. Diffusion and high resolution MRI of traumatic brain injury in rats: Time course and correlation with histology. *Exp Neurol* 162:61–72.

Albert, M. S., M. B. Moss, R. Tanzi, K. Jones. 2001. Preclinical prediction of AD using neuropsychological tests. *J Int Neuropsychological Soc* 7:631–639.

Alexopoulos, G. S. 2003. Vascular disease, depression, and dementia. *J Am Geriatr Soc* 51:1178–1180.

Alexopoulos, G. S., B. S. Meyers, R. C. Young, et al. 1997. The "vascular depression" hypothesis. *Arch Gen Psychiatry* 54:915–922.

Alvarez, P., L. R. Squire. 1994. Memory consolidation and the medial temporal lobe: A simple network model. *Proc Natl Acad Sci U S A* 91:7041–7045.

American Psychiatric Association. 1987. *Diagnostic and Statistical Manual of Mental Disorders*, 3rd ed., revised (DSM-III-R). Washington, D.C., American Psychiatric Association.

American Psychiatric Association. 1994. *Diagnostic and Statistical Manual of Mental Disorders*, 4th ed. (DSM-IV). Washington, D.C., American Psychiatric Association.

American Psychiatric Association. 2001. *The Practice of ECT. Recommendations for Treatment, Training, and Privileging*, 2nd ed. A task force report of the American Psychiatric Association. Washington, D.C., American Psychiatric Association.

Andersen, B. B., H. J. Gundersen, B. Pakkenberg. 2003. Aging of the human cerebellum: A stereolocial study. *J Comp Neurol* 466(3):356–365.

Anderson, N. D., F. I. M. Craik, M. Naveh-Benjamin. 1998. The attentional demands of encoding and retrieval in younger and older adults: 1. Evidence from divided attention costs. *Psychol Aging* 13(3):405–423.

Annegers, J. F., W. A. Hauser, S. P. Coan, W. A. Rocca. 1998. A population-based study of seizures after traumatic brain injuries. *New Engl J Med* 378:2024.

Annegers, J. F., W. A. Hauser, S. B. Shirts, L. T. Kurland. 1987. Factors prognostic of unprovoked seizures after febrile convulsions. *New Engl J Med* 316:493–498.

Anouti, A., K. Schmidt, K. E. Lyons, et al. 1996. Normal distribution of apolipoprotein E alleles in progressive supranuclear palsy. *Neurology* 46(4):1156–1157.

Anstey, K. J., S. M. Hofer, M. A. Luszcz. 2003. A latent growth curve analysis of late-life sensory and cognitive function over 8 years: Evidence for specific and common factors underlying change. *Psychol Aging* 18:714–726.

Arciniegas, D., L. Adler, J. Topkoff, et al. 1999. Attention and memory dysfunction after traumatic brain injury: Cholinergic mechanisms, sensory gating, and a hypothesis for further investigation. *Brain Inj* 13:1–13.

Armstrong, J. G., F. W. Putnam, E. B. Carlson, et al. 1997. Development and validation of a measure of adolescent dissociation: The Adolescent Dissociative Experiences Scale. *J Nerve Ment Dis* 185:491–497.

Ardila, A., M. Rosselli, L. Arvizu, R. O. Kuljis. 1997. Alexia and agraphia in posterior cortical atrophy. *Neuropsychiatry Neuropsychol Behav Neurol* 10:52–59.

Arnsten, A. F. 1998a. Catecholamine modulation of prefrontal cortical cognitive function. *Trends Cogn Sci* 2:436–447.

Arnsten, A. F. 1998b. The biology of being frazzled. *Science* 280(5370):1711–1712.

Arnsten, A. F., Contant, T. A. 1992. Alpha-2 adrenergic agonists decrease distractibility in aged monkeys performing the delayed response task. *Psychopharmacology (Berlin)* 108(1–2):159–169.

Arvanitakis, Z., Z. K. Wszolek. 2001. Recent advances in the understanding of tau protein and movement disorders. *Curr Opin Neurol* 14(4):491–497.

Auer, S., B. C. Reisberg. 1997. The GDS/FAST staging system. *Int Psychogeriatr* 9(Suppl) 1:167–171.

Aupee, A. M., B. Desgranges, F. Eustache, C. Lalevee, et al. 2001. Voxel-based mapping of brain hypometabolism in permanent amnesia with PET. *Neuroimage* 13(6 Pt 1): 1164–1173.

Bachoud-Lévi, A. C., P. Maison, P. Bartolomeo, et al. 2001. Retest effects and cognitive decline in longitudinal follow-up of patients with early HD. *Neurology* 56: 1052–1058.

Baddeley, A. D., A. H. Baddeley, R. S. Bucks, G. K. Wilcock. 2001. Attentional control in Alzheimer's disease. *Brain* 124:1492–1508.

Baddeley, A. D., S. Bressi, S. Della Sala, et al. 1991. The decline of working memory in Alzheimer's disease: A longitudinal study. *Brain* 114(Pt 6):2521–2542.

Baddeley, A. D., J. E. Harris, A. Sunderland, et al. 1987. Closed head injury and memory. In: *Neurobehavioural Recovery from Head Injury*, H. Levin, ed. Oxford, Oxford University Press, pp. 295–317.

Baddeley, A. D., B. A. Wilson. 1986. Amnesia autobiographical memory and confabulation. In: *Autobiographical Memory*, D. C. Rubin, ed. Cambridge, Mass., Cambridge University Press, pp. 225–252.

Baddeley, A. D., B. A. Wilson, F. N. Watts, eds. 1995. *Handbook of Memory Disorders*. West Sussex, England, John Wiley & Sons.

Baillon, S., S. Muhommad, M. Marudkar, et al. 2003. Neuropsychological performance in Alzheimer's disease and vascular dementia: Comparisons in a memory clinic population. *Int J Geriatr Psychiatry* 18:602–608.

Ballard, C. G., D. Aarsland, I. McKeith, et al. 2002. Fluctuations in attention: PD dementia vs DLB with parkinsonism. *Neurology* 59:1714–1720.

Bamford, K. A., E. D. Caine, D. K. Kido, et al. 1995. A prospective evaluation of cognitive decline in early Huntington's disease: functional and radiographic correlates. *Neurology* 45:1867–1973.

Barba, R., S. Martines-Espinosa, E. Rodriguez-Garcia, et al. 2000. Poststroke dementia: Clinical features and risk factors. *Stroke* 31:1494–1501.

Barbeau, E., M. Didic, E. Tramoni, et al. 2004. Evaluation of visual recognition memory in MCI patients. *Neurology* 62:1317–1322.

Baron, J. C., M. C. Petit-Taboue, F. Le Doze, et al. 1994. Right frontal cortex hypometabolism in transient global amnesia: A PET study. *Brain* 117:545–552.

Barros, D. M., L. A. Izquierdo, T. Mello e Souza, et al. 2000. Molecular signaling pathways in the cerebral cortex are required for retrieval of one-trial avoidance learning in rats. *Behav Brain Res* 114:183–192.

Barth, J. T., A. Diamond, A. Errico. 1996. Mild head injury and post concussion syndrome: Does anyone really suffer? *Clin Electroencephalogr* 27:183–186.

Bartlett, F. C. 1995. *Remembering: A Study in Experimental and Social Psychology.* New York, Cambridge University Press.

Bartzokis, G., D. Sultzer, P. H. Lu, et al. 2004. Heterogeneous age-related breakdown of white matter structural integrity: Implications for cortical "disconnection" in aging and Alzheimer's disease. *Neurobiol Aging* 25:843–851.

Bauer, R. M., J. A. Demery. 2003. Agnosia. In: *Clinical Neuropsychology,* Fourth ed., K. M. Heilman, E. Valenstein, eds. New York, Oxford University Press, pp. 236–295.

Bauer, R. M., L. Grande, E. Valenstein. 2003. Amnesic disorders. In: *Clinical Neuropsychology,* Fourth ed., K. M. Heilman, E. Valenstein, eds. New York, Oxford University Press, pp. 495–573.

Bayen, U. J., M. P. Phelps, J. Spaniol. 2000. Age-related differences in the use of contextual information in recognition memory: A global matching approach. *J Gerontol B Psychol Sci Soc Sci* 55:131–141.

Bayley, P. J., L. R. Squire. 2002. Medial temporal lobe amnesia: Gradual acquisition of factual information by nondeclarative memory. *J Neurosci* 22(13):5741–5748.

Bazarian, J. J., T. Wong, M. Harris, et al. 1999. Epidemiology and predictors of postconcussive syndrome after minor head injury in an emergency population. *Brain Inj* 13:17–189.

Beardsworth, E. D., D. W. Zaidel. 1994. Memory for faces in epileptic children before and after brain surgery. *J Clin Exp Neuropsychol* 16:589–596.

Bechara, A., H. Damasio, A. R. Damasio. 2003. Role of the amygdala in decision-making. *Ann N Y Acad Sci* 985:356–69.

Beeckmans, K., P. Vancoillie, K. Michiels. 1998. Neuropsychological deficits in patients with an anterior communicating artery syndrome: A multiple case study. *Acta Neurol Belg* 98(3):266–278.

Belleville, S., I. Peretz, M. Arguin. 1992. Contribution of articulatory rehearsal to short-term memory: Evidence from a case of selective disruption. *Brain Lang* 43(4):713–746.

Benbow, S. M. 1989. The role of electroconvulsive therapy in the treatment of depressive illness in old age. *Br J Psychiatry* 155:147–152.

Benjamin, A. S. 2001. On the dual effects of repetition on false recognition. *J Exp Psychol Learn Mem Cogn* 27:941–947.

Bennett, D. A., R. S. Wilson, J. A. Schneider, et al. 2002. Natural history of mild cognitive impairment in older persons. *Neurology* 59:19–205.

Benson, D. F., A. Djenderedjian, B. L. Miller, et al. 1996. Neural basis of confabulation. *Neurology* 46:1239–1243.

Benson, D. F., H. Gardner, J. C. Meadows. 1976. Reduplicative paramnesia. *Neurology* 26:147–151.

Benton, A. L., K. deS. Hamsher, G. J. Rey, A. B. Sivan. 1994. *Multilingual Aphasia Examination,* 3rd ed. Iowa City, Iowa, AJA Associates.

Berchtold, N. C., C. W. Cotman. 1998. Evolution in the conceptualisation of dementia and Alzheimer's disease: Greco-Roman period to the 1960s. *Neurobiol Aging* 19:173–189.

Berg, A. T., S. Shinnar. 1996. Unprovoked seizures in children with febrile seizures: Short term outcomes. *Neurology* 47:562–568.

Berger, A. K., K. Fahlander, A. Wahlin, L. Backman. 2002. Negligible effects of depression on verbal and spatial performance in Alzheimer's disease. *Dement Geriatr Cogn Disord* 13:1–7.

Bergin, P. S., P. J. Thompson, S. A. Baxendale, et al. 2000. Remote memory in epilepsy. *Epilepsia* 41:231–239.

Bergson, H. 1911. *Matter and Memory*, translated by Nancy Margaret Paul and W. Scott Palmer. London, George Allen and Unwin.

Bernstein, E. M., F. W. Putnam. 1986. Development, reliability, and validity of a dissociation scale. *J Nerv Ment Dis* 174:727–735.

Berrington, W. P., D. W. Liddell, G. A. Foulds. 1956. A re-evaluation of the fugue. *J Ment Sci* 102:281–286.

Betts, T. 1998. Conversion disorders. In: *Epilepsy: A Comprehensive Textbook*, Vol. 3. J. Engel Jr., T. A. Pedley, eds. Philadelphia, Lippincott-Raven, pp. 2775–2783.

Bigler, E. D. 2001. The lesion(s) in traumatic brain injury: Implications for clinical neuropsychology. *Arch Clin Neuropsychol* 16:95–131.

Bigler, E. D., D. D. Blatter, A. V. Anderson, et al. 1997. Hippocampal volume in normal aging and traumatic brain injury. *Am J Neuroradiol* 18:11–23.

Billingsley, R. L., M. P. McAndrews, M. L. Smith. 2002. Intact perceptual and conceptual priming in temporal lobe epilepsy: Neuroanatomical and methodological implications. *Neuropsychology* 16:92–101.

Binder, L. M. 1997. A review of mild head trauma. Part II: Clinical implications. *J Clin Exp Neuropsychol* 19(3):432–457.

Binder, L. M., M. L. Rohling. 1996. Money matters: Meta-analytic review of the effects of financial incentives on recovery after closed head injury. *Am J Psychiatry* 153: 7–10.

Bird, T., D. Knopman, J. van Swieten, et al. 2003. Epidemiology and genetics of frontotemporal dementia/Pick's disease. *Ann Neurol* 54(Suppl 5): S29–31.

Birnbaum, M. H., K. Thomann. 1996. Visual function in multiple personality disorder. *J Am Optom Assoc* 67:327–334.

Bishop, D. V. M. 1989. *Test for the Reception of Grammar*. Manchester, U.K., Medical Research Council.

Black, S. E. 1996. Focal cortical atrophy syndromes. *Brain Cogn* 31:188–229.

Blatter, D. D., E. D. Bigler, S. D. Gale, et al. 1997. MR-based brain and cerebrospinal fluid measurement after traumatic brain injury: Correlation with neuropsychological outcome. *Am J Neuroradiol* 18:1–10.

Blumenfeld, H., K. A. McNally, R. B. Ostroff, I. G. Zubal. 2003. Targeted prefrontal cortical activation with bifrontal ECT. *Psychiatry Res* 123:165–170.

Bogerts, B., J. A. Lieberman, M. Ashtari. 1993. Hippocampus-amygdala volumes and psychopathology in chronic schizophrenia. *Biol Psychiatry* 33(4):236–246.

Bogner, J. A., J. D. Corrigan, W. Mysiw, et al. 2001. A comparison of substance abuse and violence in the prediction of long-term rehabilitation outcomes after traumatic brain injury. *Arch Phys Med Rehabil* 82:571–577.

Bohnen, N., J. Jolles, A. Twijnstra, et al. 1992. Coping styles, cortisol reactivity and performance in a vigilance task of patients with persistent postconcussion symptoms after a mild head injury. *Int J Neurosci* 64:97–105.

Borenstein Graves, A., J. D. Bowen, L. Rajaram, et al. 1999. Impaired olfaction as a marker for cognitive decline. *Neurology* 53:1480–1487.

Bottger, S., M. Prosiegel, H. J. Steiger, A. Yassouridis. 1998. Neurobehavioural disturbances, rehabilitation outcome, and lesion site in patients after rupture and repair of anterior communicating artery aneurysm. *J Neurol Neurosurg Psychiatry* 65(1): 93–102.

Boudin, G., B. Pepin, J. Mikol, et al. 1975. Gliome du systeme limbique posterieur, revele par une amnésie globale transitoire. *Revue Neurol (Paris)* 131:157–163.

Boxer, A. L., J. H. Kramer, A. T. Du, et al. 2003. Focal right interotemporal atrophy in AD with disproportionate visual constructive impairment. *Neurology* 61:1485–1491.

Bozoki, A., B. Giordani, J. L. Heidebrink, et al. 2001. Mild cognitive impairment predicts dementia in nondemented elderly patients with memory loss. *Arch Neurol* 58: 411–416.

Braak, H., E. Braak. 1991. Neuropathological stageing of Alzheimer-related changes. *Acta Neuropathol (Berlin)* 82:239–259.

Braak, H., E. Braak. 1997a. Diagnostic criteria for neuropathologic assessment of Alzheimer's disease. *Neurobiol Aging* 18:S85–S88.

Braak, H., E. Braak. 1997b. Frequency of stages of Alzheimer-related lesions in different age categories. *Neurobiol Aging* 18:351–357.

Braver, T. S., J. D. Cohen, L. E. Nystrom, et al. 1997. A parametric study of prefrontal cortex involvement in human working memory. *Neuroimage* 5(1):49–62.

Breedin S. D., E. M. Saffran. 1999. Sentence processing in the face of semantic loss: A case study. *J Exp Psychol Gen* 128:547–562.

Bremner, J. D. 1999. Does stress damage the brain? *Biol Psychiatry* 45:797–805.

Bremner, J. D., P. Randall, T. M. Scott, et al. 1995. MRI-based measurement of hippocampal volume in patients with combat-related posttraumatic stress disorder. *Am J Psychiatry* 152(7):973–981.

Breuer, J., S. Freud. 1955. Studies on Hysteria. In: *The Standard Edition of the Complete Psychological Works of Sigmund Freud*, Vol 2., J. Strachey, ed. London, Hogarth Press (Original work published 1893–1895).

Bridgman, P. A., M. A. Malamut, M. R. Sperling, et al. 1989. Memory during subclinical hippocampal seizures. *Neurology* 39:853–856.

Brierley, B., N. Medford, P. Shaw, A. S. David. 2004. Emotional memory and perception in temporal lobectomy patients with amygdala damage. *J Neurol Neurosurg Psychiatry* 75(4):593–599.

Brindley, D. N., Y. Rolland. 1989. Possible connections between stress, diabetes, obesity, hypertension and altered lipoprotein metabolism that may result in atherosclerosis. *Clin Sci (Lond)* 77(5):453–461.

Brokate, B., H. Hildebrandt, P. Eling, et al. 2003. Frontal lobe dysfunctions in Korsakoff's syndrome and chronic alcoholism: Continuity or discontinuity? *Neuropsychology* 17: 420–428.

Brown, M. W., J. Brown, J. B. Bowes. 1989. Absence of priming coupled with substantially preserved recognition in lorazepam-induced amnesia. *Q J Exp Psychol A* 41(3):599–617.

Brown, E. M., P. Janet, F. 2003. Artificielle. Multiple Personality in a nineteenth-century guise. *J Hist Behav Sci* 39:279–288.

Brown, A. S., E. M. Jones, T. L. Davis. 1995. Age differences in conversational source monitoring. *Psychol Aging* 10:111–122.

Brown, S. E., J. A. Rush, B. S. McEwen. 1999. Hippocampal remodeling and damage by corticosteroids: Implications for mood disorders. *Neuropsychopharmacology* 21: 474–484.

Brush, J. A., C. J. Camp. 1998a. Spaced retrieval during dysphagia therapy: A case study. *Clin Gerontol* 19:96–99.

Brush, J. A., C. J. Camp. 1998b. Using spaced retrieval as an intervention during speech-language therapy. *Clin Gerontol* 19:51–64.

Buchanan, T. W., Lovallo, W. R. 2001. Enhanced memory for emotional material following stress-level cortisol treatment in humans. *Psychoneuroendocrinology* 26(3): 307–17.

Buchele, B. J. 1993. Group psychotherapy for persons with multiple personality and dissociative disorders. *Bull Menninger Clin* 57:362–370.

Buckner, R. L. 2004. Memory and executive function in aging and AD: Multiple factors that cause decline and reserve factors that compensate. *Neuron* 44:195–208.

Bullock, M. R., B. G. Lyeth, J. P. Muizelaar. 1999. Current status of neuroprotection trials for traumatic brain injury: Lessons from animal models and clinical studies. *Neurosurgery* 45:207–217.

Bures, J., O. Buresova, J. Krivanek. 1974. *The mechanisms and applications of Leào's spreading depression of electroencephalographic activity*, New York, Academic Press.

Burn, D. J., A. J. Lees. 2002. Progressive supranuclear palsy: Where are we now? *Lancet Neurol* 1:359–369.

Burt, D. B., M. J. Zembar, G. Niederehe. 1995. Depression and memory impairment: A meta-analysis of the association, its pattern, and specificity. *Psychol Bull* 117: 285–305.

Buschke, H., M. J. Sliwinski, G. Kuslansky, R. B. Lipton. 1997. Diagnosis of early dementia by the Double Memory Test: Encoding specificity improves diagnostic sensitivity and specificity. *Neurology* 48:989–997.

Bussière, T., G. Gold, E. Kövari, et al. 2003. Stereologic analysis of neurofibrillary tangle formation in prefrontal cortex area 9 in aging and Alzheimer's disease. *Neuroscience* 117:571–592.

Butters, N. 1985. Alcoholic Korsakoff syndrome: Some unresolved issues concerning etiology, neuropathology, and cognitive deficits. *J Clin Exp Neuropsychol* 7:181–210.

Butters, M. A., E. L. Glisky, D. L. Schacter. 1993. Transfer of new learning in memory impaired patients. *J Clin Exp Neuropsychol* 15:219–230.

Butters, M. A., G. Goldstein, D. N. Allen, W. J. Shemansky. 1998. Neuropsychological similarities and differences among Huntington's disease, multiple sclerosis, and cortical dementia. *Arch Clin Neuropsychol* 13:721–735.

Butters, N., D. T. Stuss. 1989. Diencephalic amnesia. In: *Handbook of Neuropsychology*, Vol. 3, 2nd ed., F. Boller, J. Grafman, eds. Amsterdam, Elsevier, pp. 107–148.

Cabeza, R., S. M. Daselaar, F. Dolcos, et al. 2004. Task-independent and task-specific age effects on brain activity during working memory, visual attention and episodic retrieval. *Cereb Cortex* 14:364–375.

Caffarra, P., G. Moretti, A. Mazzucchi, M. Parma. 1981. Neuropsychological testing during a transient global amnesia episode and its follow-up. *Acta Neurol Scand* 63: 44–50.

Cahill, L., L. Gorski, K. Le. 2003. Enhanced human memory consolidation with post-learning stress: Interaction with the degree of arousal at encoding. *Learn Mem* 10(4):270–274.

Cahill, L., B. Prins, M. Weber, J. L. McGaugh. 1994. Beta-adrenergic activation and memory for emotional events. *Nature* 371(6499):702–704.

Cahn, D. A., E. V. Sullivan, P. Shear, et al. 1998. Differential contributions of cognitive and motor component processes to physical and instrumental activities of daily living in Parkinson's disease. *Arch Clin Neuropsychology* 13:575–583.

Caine, D., J. R. Hodges. 2001. Heterogeneity of semantic and visuospatial deficits in early Alzheimer's disease. *Neuropsychology* 15:155–164.

Calderon, J., R. J. Perry, S. W. Erzinclioglu, et al. 2001. Perception, attention, and working memory are disproportionately impaired in dementia with Lewy bodies compared with Alzheimer's disease. *J Neurol Neurosurg Psychiatry* 70:157–164.

Calev, A., R. Cohen, N. Tubi, et al. 1991. Disorientation and bilateral moderately suprathreshold titrated ECT. *Convulsive Therapy* 7:99–110.

Calev, A., E. Gaudino, N. K. Squires, et al. 1995. ECT and non-memory cognition: A review. *Br J Clin Psychol* 34:505–515.

Cameron, D. G. 1994. ECT: Sham statistics, the myth of convulsive therapy and the case for consumer misinformation. *J Mind Behav* 15(1/2):177–198.

Campo, P., F. Maestu, T. Ortiz, et al. 2005. Time modulated prefrontal and parietal activity during the maintenance of integrated information as revealed by magnetoencephalography. *Cereb Cortex* 15(2):123–130.

Camus, A. 1942. *The Stranger*. New York, Vintage.

Camus, J. F., S. Nicolas, E. Wenisch, et al. 2003. Implicit memory for words presented in short text is preserved in Alzheimer's disease. *Psychol Med* 33:169–174.

Caplan, D. 2003. Aphasic syndromes. In: *Clinical Neuropsychology*, Fourth ed., K. M. Heilman, E. Valenstein, eds. New York, Oxford University Press, pp. 61–91.

Caplan, L. R. 1985. Transient global amnesia. In: *Handbook of Clinical Neurology*, Vol. 1., P. J. Vinken, G. W. Bruyn, H. L. Klawans, eds. Amsterdam, Elsevier Science.

Caplan, L. R. 1990. Transient global amnesia: Characteristic features and overview. In: *Transient Global Amnesia and Related Disorders*, H. J. Markowitsch, ed. New York, Hogrefe & Huber, pp. 15–27.

Caramazza, A., J. R. Shelton. 1998. Domain-specific knowledge systems in the brain: the animate-inanimate distinction. *J Cogn Neurosci* 10:1–34.

Carlesimo, G. A., M. Sabbadini, P. Bombardi, et al. 1998. Retrograde memory deficits in severe closed-head injury patients. *Cortex* 34:1–23.

Caselli, R. J., A. J. Windebank, R. C. Petersen, et al. 1993. Rapidly progressive aphasic dementia and motor neuron disease. Ann Neurol 33(2):200–207.

Castner, S. A., P. S. Goldman-Rakic. 2004. Enhancement of working memory in aged monkeys by a sensitizing regimen of dopamine D1 receptor stimulation. *J Neurosci* 24(6):1446–1450.

Cave, C. B., L. R. Squire. 1992. Intact verbal and nonverbal short-term memory following damage to the human hippocampus. *Hippocampus* 2:151–163.

Ceccaldi, M., S. Belleville, M. L. Royere, M. Poncet. 1995. A pure reversible amnesic syndrome following tuberculous meningoencephalitis. *Eur Neurol* 35:363–367.

Cermak, L. S., ed. 2000. Memory and Its Disorders. *Handbook of Neuropsychology*, Vol. 2, 2nd ed. Amsterdam, Elsevier.

Cermak, L. S., M. O'Connor. 1983. The anterograde and retrograde retrieval ability of a patient with amnesia due to encephalitis. *Neuropsychologia* 21:213–214.

Chamberlin, E., G. E. Tsai. 1998. A glutamatergic model of ECT-induced memory dysfunction. *Harv Rev Psychiatry* 5:307–317.

Chan, D., D. Salmon, S. Nordin, et al. 1998. Abnormality of semantic network in patients with Alzheimer's disease: Evidence from verbal, perceptual, and olfactory domains. *Ann N Y Acad Sci* 855:681–685.

Changeaux, J., A. Danchin. 1976. Selective stabilization of developing synapses as a mechanism for the specification of neuronal networks. *Nature* 264:705–712.

Chatham, P. E., J. Brillman. 1985. Transient global amnesia associated with bilateral subdural hematomas. *Neurosurgery* 17:971–973.

Chelune, G. J., R. I. Naugle, H. Luders, I. A. Awad. 1991. Prediction of cognitive change as a function of preoperative ability status among temporal lobectomy patients seen at 6 month follow-up. *Neurology* 41:399–404.

Chen, P., G. Ratcliff, S. H. Belle, et al. 2000. Cognitive tests that best discriminate between presymptomatic AD and those who remain nondemented. *Neurology* 55:1847–1853.

Cherry, B. J., J. G. Buckwalter, V. W. Henderson. 2002. Better preservation of memory span relative to supraspan immediate recall in Alzheimer's disease. *Neuropsychologia* 40:846–852.

Chetelat, G., J. C. Baron. 2003. Early diagnosis of Alzheimer's disease: Contribution of structural neuroimaging. *Neuroimage* 18:525–541.

Chui, H. 2001. Dementia due to subcortical ischemic vascular disease. *Clin Cornerstone* 3(4):40–51.

Cipolotti, L., T. Shallice, D. Chan, et al. 2001. Long-term retrograde amnesia. . .the crucial role of the hippocampus. *Neuropsychologia* 39(2):151–172.

Cochran, J. W., F. Morrell, M. S. Huckman, E. J. Cochran. 1982. Transient global amnesia after cerebral angiography: report of seven cases. *Arch Neurology* 39:593–594.

Coffey, C. E., W. E. Wilkinson, R. D. Weiner, et al. 1993. Quantitative cerebral anatomy in depression. A controlled magnetic resonance imaging study. *Arch Gen Psychiatry* 50(1):7–16.

Cohen, M. *Children's Memory Scale*. 1997. San Antonio, Tex., Harcourt Assessment, Inc..

Cohen, N. J., H. Eichenbaum, B. S. Deacedo, S. Corkin. 1985. Different memory systems underlying acquisition of procedural and declarative knowledge. *Ann N Y Acad Sci* 444:54–71.

Cohen, J. D., W. M. Perlstein, T. S. Braver, et al. 1997. Temporal dynamics of brain activation during a working memory task. *Nature* 386:604–608.

Collins, M. P., J. W. Freeman. 1986. Meningioma and transient global amnesia: Another report. *Neurology* 36:594.

Colombo, A., M. Scarpa. 1988. Transient global amnesia: Pathogenesis and prognosis. *Eur Neurol* 28(2):111–114.

Comijs, H. C., M. G. Dik, D. J. Deeg, C. Jonker. 2004. The course of cognitive decline in older persons: Results from the longitudinal aging study Amsterdam. *Dement Geriatr Cogn Disord* 17:136–142.

Conkey, R. C. 1938. Psychological changes associated with head injuries. *Arch Psychol* 32:1–62.

Constantinidis, J., J. Richard, R. Tissot. 1974. Pick's disease. Histological and clinical correlations. *Eur Neurol* 11(4):208–217.

Conti, A. C., R. Raghupathi, J. Q. Trojanowski, T. K. McIntosh. 1998. Experimental brain injury induces regionally distinct apoptosis during the acute and delayed posttraumatic period. *J Neuroscie* 18:5663–5672.

Convit, A., M. J. de Leon, C. Tarshish, et al. 1995. Hippocampal volume losses in minimally impaired elderly. *Lancet* 345(8944):266.

Convit, A., M. J. de Leon, C. Tarshish, et al. 1997. Specific hippocampal volume reduction in individuals at risk for Alzheimer's disease. *Neurobiol Aging* 18:131–138.

Conway, M. A., C. W. Pleydell-Pearce. 2000. The construction of autobiographical memories in the self-memory system. *Psychol Rev* 107:261–288.

Cools, R., E. Stefanova, R. A. Barker, et al. 2002. Dopaminergic modulation of high-level cognition in Parkinson's disease: The role of the prefrontal cortex revealed by PET. *Brain* 125:584–94.

Coons, P. M. 1986. Dissociative disorders: Diagnosis and treatment. *Indiana Med* 79: 410–415.

Coons, P. M. 2000. Dissociative fugue. In: *Kaplan and Sadock's Comprehensive Textbook of Psychiatry*, H. I. Kaplan, B. J. Sadock, eds. Philadelphia, Lippincott Williams & Wilkins, pp. 1548–1552.

Corbetta, M., F. M. Miezin, S. Dobmeyer, et al. 1991. Selective and divided attention during visual discriminations of shape, color, and speed: Functional anatomy by positron emission tomography. *J Neurosci* 11:2383–2402.

Corridan, B. J., S. N. M. Leung, I. H. Jenkins. 2001. A case of sleeping and forgetting. *Lancet* 3547:524.

Costa, A., A. Peppe, G. Dell'Agnello, et al. 2003. Dopaminergic modulation of visual-spatial working memory in Parkinson's disease. *Dement Geriatr Cogn Disord* 15(2): 55–66.

Cotman, C. W., D. T. Monaghan, A. H. Ganong. 1998. Excitatory amino acid neuro-transmission: NMDA receptos and Hebb-type synaptic plasticity. *Annu Rev Neurosci* 11:61–80.

Crook, T., R. T. Bartus, S. H. Ferris, et al. 1986. Age-associated memory impairment: Proposed diagnostic criteria and measures of clinical change. Report of a NIMH Work Group. *Dev Neuropsychol* 2:261–276.

Crosson, B., P. J. Moberg, J. R. Boone, et al. 1997. Category-specific naming deficit for medical terms after dominant thalamic/capsular haemorrhage. *Brain Lang* 60:407–442.

Crovitz, H. F., H. Schiffman. 1974. Frequency of episodic memories as a function of age. *Bull Psychonomic Soc* 5:517–518.

Crovitz, H. F., M. T. Harvey, R. W. Horn. 1979. Problems in the acquisition of imaging mnemonics: Three brain damaged cases. *Cortex*, *15*, 225–234.

Crovitz, H. F., M. T. Harvey, S. McClanahan. 1981. Hidden memory: a rapid method for the study of amnesia using perceptual learning. *Cortex* 17:273–278.

Crowell, G. F., D. A. Stump, J. Biller, et al. 1984. The transient global amnesia-migraine connection. *Arch Neurol* 41:75–79.

Crucian, G. P., A. M. Barrett, R. L. Schwartz, et al. 2000. Cognitive and vestibulo-proprioceptive components of spatial ability in Parkinson's disease. *Neuropsychologia* 38:757–767.

Cummings, J. L. 1993. Frontal-subcortical circuits and human behavior. *Arch Neurol* 50(8):873–880.

D' Esposito, M., J. Detre, D. Alsop, et al. 1995. The neural basis of the central executive system of working memory. *Nature* 378:279–281.

D' Esposito, M., B. R. Postle. 1999. The dependence of span and delayed-response performance on prefrontal cortex. *Neuropsychologia* 37(11):1303–1315.

Dalla Barba, G. 2002. Beyond the memory-trace paradox and the fallacy of the homuncu-lus. *J Consciousness Studies* 8:51–78.

Dalla Barba, G., M. C. Mantovan, E. Ferruzza, G. Denes. 1997. Remembering and knowing the past: A case study of isolated retrograde amnesia. *Cortex* 33:14–154.

Dallam, S., M. A. Manderino. 1997. 'Free to be' peer group supports patients with MPD/DD. *J Psychosoc Nurs Ment Health Serv* 35:22–27.

Damasio, A. R., N. R. Graff-Radford, P. J. Eslinger, et al. 1985. Amnesia following basal forebrain lesions. *Arch Neurol* 42:263–271.

Damasio, H., T. J. Grabowski, D. Tranel, et al. 1996. A neural basis for lexical retrieval. *Nature* 380:499–505.

Daniel, W. E., H. F. Crovitz. 1983a. Acute memory impairment following electrocon-vulsive therapy, I: Effects of electrical stimulus wave-form and number of treatments. *Acta Psychiatr Scand* 67:1–7.

Daniel, W. E., H. F. Crovitz. 1983b. Acute memory impairment following electrocon-vulsive therapy, II: Effects of electrical stimulus wave-form and number of treat-ments. *Acta Psychiatr Scand* 67:57–68.

Daselaar, S. M., D. J. Veltman, S. A. Rombouts, et al. 2003. Neuroanatomical corre-lates of episodic encoding and retrieval in young and elderly subjects. *Brain* 126: 43–56.

Dash, P. K., A. E. Hebert, J. D. Runyan. 2004. A unified theory for systems and cellular memory consolidation. *Brain Res Rev* 45:30–37.

Datto, C. J., S. Levy, D. S. Miller, I. R. Katz. 2001. Impact of maintenance ECT on concentration and memory. *J ECT* 17:170–174.

Davila, M. D., P. K. Shear, B. Lane, et al. 1994. Mammillary body and cerebellar shrinkage in chronic alcoholics: An MRI and neuropsychological study. *Neuropsychology* 8(3):433–444.

Davis, A. E. 2000. Mechanisms of traumatic brain injury: Biomechanical, structural and cellular considerations. *Crit Care Nurs Q* 23:1–13.

Davis, H. P., S. A. Small, Y. Stern, et al. 2003. Acquisition, recall, and forgetting of verbal information in long-term memory by young, middle-aged and elderly individuals. *Cortex* 39:1063–1091.

Davison, K., C. R. Bagley. 1969. Schizophrenia-like psychosis associated with organic disorders of the central nervous system. *Br J Psychiatry* 114(Suppl):113–184.

Day, M., R. Langston, R. G. Morris. 2003. Glutamate-receptor-mediated encoding and retrieval of paired-associate learning. *Nature* 424(6945):205–9.

De Jager, C. A., E. Milwain, M. Budge. 2002. Early detection of isolated memory deficits in the elderly: The need for more sensitive neuropsychological tests. *Psychol Med* 32:483–491.

de la Torre, J. C. 2004. Is Alzheimer's disease a neurodegenerative or a vascular disorder? Data, dogma, and dialectics. *Lancet Neurol* 3:184–190.

De Leon, M. J., A. E. George, J. Golomb, et al. 1997. Frequency of hippocampal formation atrophy in normal aging and Alzheimer's disease. *Neurobiol Aging* 18:1–11.

De Renzi, E., M. Liotti, P. Nichelli. 1987. Semantic amnesia with preservation of autobiographic memory. A case report. *Cortex* 23:575–597.

De Renzi, E., F. Lucchelli, S. Muggia, H. Spinnler. 1995. Persistent retrograde amnesia following a minor trauma. *Cortex* 31:531–542.

Deb, S., I. Lyons, C. Koutzoukis. 1999. Neurobehavioral symptoms one year after a head injury. *Br J Psychiatry* 174:360–365.

DeCarli, C., J. Massaro, D. Harvey, et al. 2005. Measures of brain morphometry and infarction in the Framingham Heart Study: Establishing what is normal. *Neurobiol Aging* 26:491–510.

Dehon, H., S. Brédart. 2004. False memories: Young and old adults think of semantic associates at the same rate but young adults are more successful at source monitoring. *Psychol Aging* 19:191–197.

Deisenhammer, E. 1981. Transient global amnesia as an epileptic manifestation. *J Neurol (Berlin)* 225:289–292.

DeKosky, S. T., R. E. Harbaugh, F. A. Schmitt, et al. 1992. Cortical biopsy in Alzheimer's disease: diagnostic accuracy and neurochemical, neuropathological and cognitive correlations. *Ann Neurol* 32:625–632.

Del Ser, T., I. McKeith, R. Anand, et al. 2000. Dementia with Lewy bodies: Findings from an international multicentre study. *Int J Geriatr Psychiatry* 15:1034–1045.

Delacourte, A., Y. Robitaille, N. Sergeant, et al. 1996. Specific pathological Tau protein variants characterize Pick's disease. *J Neuropathol Exp Neurol* 55(2):159–168.

Delis, D. C., J. H. Kramer, E. Kaplan, B. A. Ober. 1987a. *California Verbal Learning Test: Adult Version Manual*. San Antonio, Tex., The Psychological Corporation.

Delis, D. C., J. H. Kramer, E. Kaplan, B. A. Ober. 1987b. *California Verbal Learning Test (CVLT): Research Edition*. New York, The Psychological Corporation.

Delis, D. C., J. H. Kramer, E. Kaplan, B. A. Ober. 2000. *California Verbal Learning Test – Second Edition*. San Antonio, Tex., The Psychological Corporation.

Dell, P. F. 1998. Axis II pathology in outpatients with dissociative identity disorder. *J Nerv Ment Dis* 186:352–356.

Della Sala, S., R. H. Logie. 2001. Theoretical and practical implications of dual-task performance in Alzheimer's disease. *Brain* 124:1479–1481.

DeLuca, J., K. D. Cicerone. 1991. Confabulation following aneurysm of the anterior communicating artery. *Cortex* 27(3):417–423.

Denman, S. 1984. *Denman Neuropsychology Memory Scale*. Charleston, S.C., S.B. Denman.

Denman, S. 1987. *Denman Neuropsychology Memory Scale*. Charleston, S.C., Sydney B. Denman.

Devanand, D. P., A. J. Dwork, E. R. Hutchinson, et al. 1994. Does ECT alter brain structure? *Am J Psychiatry* 151:957–970.

Devanand, D. P., K. S. Michaels-Marston, X. Liu, et al. 2000. Olfactory deficits in patients with mild cognitive impairment predict Alzheimer's desease at follow-up. *Am J Psychiatry* 157:1399–1405.

Devanand, D. P., M. Sano, M. X. Tang, et al. 1996. Depressed mood and the incidence of Alzheimer's disease in the elderly living in the community. *Arch Gen Psychiatry* 53:175–182.

Diamond, B. J., J. DeLuca, H. Kim, S. M. Kelley. 1997. The question of disproportionate impairments in visual and auditory information processing in multiple sclerosis. *J Clin Exp Neuropsychol* 19(1):34–42.

Dickerson, B. C., I. Goncharova, M. P. Sullivan, et al. 2001. MRI-derived entorhinal and hippocampal atrophy in incipient and very mild Alzheimer's disease. *Neurobiol Aging* 22:747–754.

Dickson, D. W., C. Bergeron, S. S. Chin, et al. 2002. Office of Rare Diseases neuropathologic criteria for corticobasal degeneration. *J Neuropathol Exp Neurol* 61 (11):935–946.

Diesfeldt, H. F. A. 1992. Impaired and preserved semantic memory functions in dementia. In: *Memory Functioning in Dementia*, L. Backman, ed. Amsterdam, Elsevier, 1992.

Dik, M. G., C. Jonker, H. C. Comijs, et al. 2001. Memory complaints and APOE-epsilon4 accelerate cognitive decline in cognitively normal elderly. *Neurology* 57:2217–2222.

Dikmen, S., J. E. Machamer, H. R. Winn, N. R. Temkin. 1995. Neuropsychologic outcome at 1 year post head injury. *Neuropsychology* 9:80–90.

Dipple, H. C. 1999. The use of olanzapine for movement disorder in Huntington's disease: A first case report. *J Neurol Neurosurg Psychiatry* 67(1):123–124.

Dixon, C., W. Taft, R. Hayes. 1993. Mechanisms of mild traumatic brain injury. *J Head Trauma Rehabil* 8:1–12.

Dobkin, B. H., R. Hanlon. 1993. Dopamine agonist treatment of antegrade amnesia from a mediobasal forebrain injury. *Ann Neurol* 33:313–316.

Donnal, J. F., E. R. Heinz, P. C. Burger. 1990. MR of reversible thalamic lesions in Wernicke syndrome. *Am J Neuroradiol* 11:893–894.

Dorahy, M. J. 2001. Dissociative identity disorder and memory dysfunction: The current state of experimental research and its future directions. *Clin Psychol Rev* 21: 771–795.

Dorfman, J., J. F. Kihlstrom, R. C. Cork, J. Misiaszek. 1995. Priming and recognition in ECT-induced amnesia. *Psychon Bull Rev* 2:244–248.

Drachman, D. A. 1977. Memory and cognitive function in man: Does the cholinergic system have a specific role? *Neurology* 27(8):783–790.

Drachman, D. A., J. Leavitt. 1974. Human memory and the cholinergic system. A relationship to aging? *Arch Neurol* 30(2):113–121.

Drevets, W. C., J. L. Price, J. R. Simpson, et al. 1997. Subgenual prefrontal cortex abnormalities in mood disorder. *Nature* 386:824–827.

Du, A. T., N. Schuff, X. P. Zhu, et al. 2003. Atrophy rates of entorhinal cortex in AD and normal aging. *Neurology* 60:481–486.

Dufouil, C., A. Alperovitch, C. Tzourio. 2003. Influence of education on the relationship between white matter lesions and cognition. *Neurology* 60:831–836.

Dugan, T. M., R. E. Nordgren, P. O'Leary. 1981. Transient global amnesia associated with bradycardia and temporal lobe spikes. *Cortex* 17:633–638.

Dugas, L. 1898. Un cas de depersonnalisation. *Revue Philosophique* 45:500–507 (translated by M. Sierra, G.E. Berrios, 1996, in *History of Psychiatry* 7:451–461).

Dumas, J. A., M. Hartman. 2003. Adult age differences in temporal and item memory. *Psychol Aging* 18:573–586.

Duncan, C. C., M. H. Kosmidis, A. F. Mirsky. 2003. Event-related potential assessment of information processing after closed head injury. *Psychophysiology* 40:45–59.

Duncan, C. C., M. H. Kosmidis, A. F. Mirsky. 2005. Closed head injury-related information processing deficits: An event-related potential analysis. *Int J Psychophysiol* (in press).

Duncan, R., J. Patterson, R. Roerts, et al. 1993. Ictal/postictal SPECT in the pre-surgical localisation of complex partial seizures. *J Neurol Neurosurg Psychiatry* 56:141–148.

Dunn, L. M., E. S. Dunn. *Peabody Picture Vocabulary Test – Revised*. Circle Pines, Minn., American Guidance Service.

Durstewitz, D., J. K. Seamans, T. J. Sejnowski. 2000. Dopamine-mediated stabilization of delay-period activity in a network model of prefrontal cortex. *J Neurophysiol* 83(3):1733–1750.

Dywan, J., S. J. Segalowitz, D. Henderson, L. Jacoby. 1993. Memory for source after traumatic brain injury. *Brain Cogn* 21:20–43.

Eames, P., R. L. Wood. 2003. Disorders of behaviour and affect after acquired brain injury. *Neuropsychol Rehabil* 13:241–258.

Ebly, E. M., I. M. Parhad, D. B. Hogan, T. S. Fung. 1994. Prevalence and types of dementia in the very old: Results from the Canadian Study of Health and Aging. *Neurology* 44(9):1593–600.

Echemendia, R. J., L. J. Julia. 2001. Mild traumatic brain injury in sports: Neuropsychology's contribution to a developing field. *Neuropsychol Rev* 11:69–88.

Edwards, K. R., L. Hershey, L. Wray, et al. 2004. Efficacy and safety of galantamine in patients with dementia with Lewy bodies: A 12-week interim analysis. *Dement Geriatr Cogn Disord* 17(Suppl 1):40–48.

Eich, E., D. McCaulay, R. J. Lowenstein, P. H. Dihle. 1996. Memory, amnesia, and dissociative identity disorder. *Psychol Sci* 8:417–422.

Eichenbaum, H. 2004. Hippocampus: Cognitive processes and neural representations that underlie declarative memory. *Neuron* 44:109–120.

Einstein, G. O., M. A. McDaniel, M. Manzi, et al. 2000. Prospective memory and aging: Forgetting intentions over short delays. *Psychol Aging* 15:671–683.

Eldridge, L. L., D. Masterman, B. J. Knowlton. 2002. Intact implicit learning in Alzheimer's disease. *Behav Neurosci* 116:722–726.

Ellason, J. W., C. A. Ross. 1997. Two-year follow-up of inpatients with dissociative identity disorder. *Am J Psychiatry* 154:832–839.

Ellenberger, H. F. 1970. *The Discovery of the Unconscious: The History and Evolution of Dynamic Psychiatry*. New York, Basic Books.

Elzinga, B. M., R. H. Phaf, A. M. Ardon, R. van Dyck. 2003. Directed forgetting between, but not within, dissociative personality states. *J Abnorm Psychol* 112(2):237–243.

Emre, M. 2003a. What causes dementia in Parkinson's Disease? *Mov Disorders* 18 (Suppl 6):563–571.

Emre, M. 2003b. What causes mental dysfunction in Parkinson's disease? *Mov Disorders* 18(Suppl 6):S63–71.

Engel, J., S. Wiebe, J. French, et al. 2003. Practice parameter: Temporal lobe and localized resections for epilepsy. *Neurology* 60:538–547.

Erickson K., W. Drevets, J. Schulkin. 2003. Glucocorticoid regulation of diverse cognitive functions in normal and pathological emotional states. *Neurosci Biobehav Rev* 27(3):233–246.

Esiri, M. M., Z. Nagy, M. Z. Smith, et al. 1999. Gerebrovascular disease and threshold for dementia in the early stages of Alzheimer's disease. *Lancet* 354:919–920.

Eustache, F., B. Desgranges, C. Lalevee. 1998. Clinical evaluation of memory. *Rev Neurol (Paris)* 154(Suppl 2):S18–32.

Eustache, F., B. Desgranges, P. Laville, et al. 1999. Episodic memory in transient global amnesia: Encoding, storage, or retrieval deficit? *J Neurol Neurosurg Psychiatry* 66:148–154.

Eustache, F., B. Desgranges, M. C. Petit-Taboue, et al. 1997. Transient global amnesia: Implicit/explicit memory dissociation and PET assessment of brain perfusion and oxygen metabolism in the acute stage. *J Neurol Neurosurg Psychiatry* 63:357–367.

Evans, D. A., H. H. Funkenstein, M. S. Albert, et al. 1989. Prevalence of Alzheimer's disease in a community population of older persons. Higher than previously reported. *JAMA* 262(18):2551–2556.

Evans, J., B. Wilson, E. P. Wraight, J. R. Hodges. 1993. Neuropsychological and SPECT scan findings during and after transient global amnesia: evidence for the differential impairment of remote episodic memory. *J Neurol Neurosurg Psychiatry* 56: 1227–1230.

Evans, J. H. 1966. Transient loss of memory, an organic mental syndrome. *Brain* 89: 539–548.

Evans, J. J., A. J. Heggs, N. Antoun, J. R. Hodges. 1995. Progressive prosopagnosia associated with selective right temporal lobe atrophy: A new syndrome? *Brain* 118:1–13.

Evans, J. J., B. A. Wilson, P. Needham, S. Brentnall. 2003. Who makes good use of memory aids? Results of a survey of people with acquired brain injury. *J Int Neuropsychol Soc* 9:925–935.

Evans, J. J., B. A. Wilson, U. Schuri, et al. 2000. A comparison of "errorless" and "trial-and-error" learning methods for teaching individuals with acquired memory deficits. *Neuropsychol Rehabil* 10:67–101.

Exner, C., G. Weniger, E. Irle. 2001. Implicit and explicit memory after focal thalamic lesions. *Neurology* 57:2054–2063.

Fabrigoule, C., I. Rouch, A. Taberly, et al. 1998. Cognitive process in preclinical phase of dementia. *Brain* 121:135–141.

Fang, J. C., Hinrichs JV, Ghoneim MM. 1987. Diazepam and memory: Evidence for spared memory function. *Pharmacol Biochem Behav* 28(3):347–52.

Farah, M. J., K. M. Hammond, Z. Mehta, G. Ratcliff. 1989. Category-specificity and modality-specificity in semantic memory. *Neuropsychologia* 27:193–200.

Farah, M. J., P. A. McMullen, M. M. Meyer. 1991. Can recognition of living things be selectively impaired? *Neuropsychologia* 29:185–193.

Fedio, P., A. F. Mirsky. 1969. Selective intellectual deficits in children with temporal lobe or centrencephalic epilepsy. *Neuropsychologia* 7:287–300.

Fein, G., V. Di Sclafani, J. Tanabe, et al. 2000. Hippocampal and cortical atrophy predict dementia in subcortical ischemic vascular disease. *Neurology* 55(11):1626–1635.

Ferguson, S., S. Hashtroudi, M. K. Johnson. 1992. Age differences in using source-relevant cues. *Psychol Aging* 7:443–452.

Fibiger H. C. Cholinergic mechanisms in learning, memory and dementia: A review of recent evidence. *Trends Neurosci* 14(6):220–223.

Fichtenberg, N. L., R. D. Zafontes, S. Putnam, et al. 2002. Insomnia in a post-acute brain injury sample. *Brain Inj* 16:197–206.

File S.E., R. G. Lister. 1982. Do lorazeam-induced deficits in learning result from impaired rehearsal, reduced motivation or increased sedation? *Br J Clin Pharmacol* 14(4):545–550.

Findler, G., M. Feinsod, G. Lijovetzky, M. Hadani. 1983. Transient global amnesia associated with a single metastasis in the non-dominant hemisphere. *J Neurosurg* 58:303–305.

Fine, C. G. 1999. The tactical-integration model for the treatment of dissociative identity disorder and allied dissociative disorders. *Am J Psychother* 53:361–376.

Fink, M. 1977. Myths of "Shock Therapy". *Am J Psychiatry* 134:991–996.

Fink, M. 1978. Efficacy and safety of induced seizures (EST) in man. *Compr Psychiatry* 19:1–18.

Fisher, C. M., R. D. Adams. 1958. Transient global amnesia. *Trans Am Neurolog Assoc* 83:143–146.

Fisher, C. M., R. D. Adams. 1964. Transient global amnesia. *Acta Neurol Scand* 40(Suppl 9):1–83.

Fleischman, D. A., J. D. E. Gabrieli. 1998. Repetition priming in normal aging and Alzheimer's disease: A review of findings and theories. *Psychol Aging* 13:88–119.

Fleminger, S. 2000. Difficult clinical problems in psychiatry. *J Neurol Neurosurg Psychiatry* 68:123H.

Fleminger, S., D. L. Oliver, W. H. Williams, J. Evans. 2003. The neuropsychiatry of depression after brain injury. *Neuropsychol Rehabil* 13:65–87.

Fontaine, A., P. Azouvi, P. Remy, et al. 1999. Functional anatomy of neuropsychological deficits after severe traumatic brain injury. *Neurology* 53(9):1963–1968.

Fontbonne, A., C. Berr, P. Ducimetiere, A. Alperovitch. 2001. Changes in cognitive abilities over a 4-year period are unfavorably affected in elderly diabetic subjects: Results of the Epidemiology of Vascular Aging Study. *Diabetes Care* 24:366–370.

Frankowski, R. F. 1986. Descriptive epidemiologic studies of head injury in the United States: 1974–1984. *Adv Psychosom Med* 16:153–172.

Frasca, T. A., A. Iodice, W. McCall, M. D. Vaughn. 2003. The relationship between changes in learning and memory after right unilateral electroconvulsive therapy. *J ECT* 19:148–150.

Frattali, C. M., J. Grafman, N. Patronas, et al. 2000. Language disturbances in corticobasal degeneration. *Neurology* 54:990–992.

Freed, D. M., S. Corkin, N. J. Cohen. 1987. Forgetting in H.M.: A second look. *Neuropsychologia* 25:461–471.

Freeman, C. P., D. Weeks, R. E. Kendell. 1980. ECT II: Patients who complain. *Br J Psychiatry* 137:17–25.

Freeman, R. Q., T. Giovannetti, M. Lamar, et al. 2000. Visuoconstructional problems in dementia: Contributions of executive systems functions. *Neuropsychology* 14:415–426.

Friedl, M., N. Draijer. 2000. Dissociative disorders in Dutch psychiatric inpatients. *Am J Psychiatry* 157:1012–1013.

Frith, C. D., S. M. Stenven, E. C. Johnstone, et al. 1983. Effects of ECT and depression on various aspects of memory. *Br J Psychiatry* 142:610–617.

Fromm-Auch, D. 1982. Comparison of unilateral and bilateral ECT: Evidence for selective memory impairment. *Br J Psychiatry* 141:608–613.

Fujii, T., M. Moscovitch, L. Nadel. 2000. Memory consolidation, retrograde amnesia and the temporal lobes. In L. S. Cermak, ed., *Handbook of Neuropsychology*, Vol. 2. Amsterdam, Elsevier, pp. 199–226.

Fukuzako H., T. Fukazako, T. Hashiguchi, et al. 1996. Reduction in hippocampal formation volume is caused mainly by its shortening in chronic schizophrenia: assessment by MRI. *Biol Psychiatry* 39(11):938–945.

Furey M. L., P. Pietrini, J. V. Haxby. 2000. Cholinergic enhancement and increased selectivity of perceptual processing during working memory. *Science* 290(5500):2315–2319.

Fuster, J. M. 1990. Behavioral electrophysiology of the prefrontal cortex of the primate. *Prog Brain Res* 85:313–323.

Fuster, J. M. 2001. The prefrontal cortex—An update: Time is of the essence. *Neuron* 30:319–333.

Fuster, J. M., G. E. Alexander. 1971. Neuron activity related to short-term memory. *Science* 173:652–654.

Gabbard, G. O. 1994. *Psychodynamic Psychiatry in Clinical Practice: The DSM-IV Edition*. Washington, D.C., American Psychiatric Press.

Gabrieli, J. D., C. J. Vaidya, M. Stone, et al. 1999. Convergent behavioral and neuropsychological evidence for a distinction between identification and production forms of repetition priming. *J Exp Psychol Gen* 128:479–98.

Gade, A., E. L. Mortensen. 1990. Temporal gradient in the remote memory impairment of amnesic patients with lesions in the basal forebrain. *Neuropsychologia* 28:985–1001.

Gaffan, D., A. Parker. 1996. Interaction of perirhinal cortex with the fornix-fimbria: memory for objects and "object-in-place" memory. *J Neurosci* 16:5864–5869.

Gainotti, G., M. C. Silveri. 1996. Cognitive and anatomical locus of lesion in a patient with a category-specific semantic impairment for living beings. *Cogn Neuropsychol* 13:357–389.

Gainotti, G., M. C. Silveri, A. Daniele, L. Giustolisi. 1995. Neuroanatomical correlates of category specific semantic disorders: A critical survey. *Memory* 3:247–264.

Gale, S., R. Hopkins, L. Weaver, et al. 1999. MRI, quantitative MRI, SPECT, and neuropsychological findings following carbon monoxide poisoning. *Brain Inj* 13(4):229–243.

Gallassi, R., S. Lorusso, A. Stracciari. 1986a. Neuropsychological findings during a transient global amnesia attack and its follow-up. *Ital J Neurol Sci* 7:45–49.

Gallassi, R., A. Morreale. 1990. Transient global amnesia and epilepsy. In: *Transient Global Amnesia and Related Disorders*, H. J. Markowitsch, ed. Toronto, Hogrefe and Huber.

Gallassi, R., A. Morreale, R. Di Sarro, E. Lugaresi. 1992. Epileptic amnesic syndrome. *Epilepsia* 33(Suppl 6):S21–S25.

Gallassi, R., A. Morreale, S. Lorusso, et al. 1988. Epilepsy presenting as a memory disturbance. *Epilepsia* 29:624–629.

Gallassi, R., P. Pazzaglia, S. Lorusso, A. Morreale. 1986b. Neuropsychological findings in epileptic amnesic attacks. *Eur Neurol* 25:299–303.

Garnett, M. R., A. M. Blamire, R. G. Corkill, et al. 2000a. Early proton magnetic resonance spectroscopy in normal appearing brain correlates with outcome in patients following traumatic brain injury. *Brain* 123:2046–2054.

Garnett, M. R., A. M. Blamire, B. Rajagopalan, et al. 2000b. Evidence for cellular damage in normal appearing white matter correlates with injury severity in patients following traumatic brain injury: A magnetic resonance spectroscopy study. *Brain* 123:1403–1409.

Garrard, P., J. R. Hodges. 2000. Semantic dementia: Clinical, radiological and pathological perspectives. *J Neurol* 247(6):409–422.

Garrard, P., R. Perry, J. R. Hodges. 1997. Disorders of semantic memory. *J Neurol Neurosurg Psychiatry* 62:431–435.

Gast, U., F. Rodewald, N. Viola, H. Emrich. 2001. Prevalence of dissociative disorders among psychiatric inpatients in a German University Clinic. *J Nerv Ment Dis* 189:249–257.

Ge, Y., R. I. Grossman, J. S. Babb, et al. 2002a. Age-related total grey matter and white matter changes in normal adult brain. Part I: Volumetric MR imaging analysis. *Am J Neuroradiol* 23:1327–1333.

Ge, Y., R. I. Grossman, J. S. Babb, et al. 2002b. Age-related total grey matter and white matter changes in normal adult brain. Part II: Quantitative magnetization transfer ratio histogram analysis. *Am J Neuroradiol* 23:1334–1341.

Geerlings, M. I., C. Jonker, L. M. Bouter, et al. 1999. Association between memory complaints and incident Alzheimer's disease in elderly people with normal baseline cognition. *Am J Psychiatry* 156:531–537.

Gennarelli, T. A., L. E. Thibault, J. H. Adams, et al. 1982. Diffuse axonal injury and traumatic coma in the primate. *Ann Neurol* 12:564–574.

Ghika-Schmid, F., J. Bogousslavsky. 2000. The acute behavioral syndrome of anterior thalamic infarction: A prospective study of 12 cases. *Ann Neurol* 48:220–227.

Ghika-Schmid, F., B. Nater. 2003. Anomia for people's names, a restricted form of transient epileptic amnesia. *Eur J Neurol* 10:651–654.

Ghoneim M. M., S. P. Mewaldt. 1977. Studies on human memory: The interactions of diazepam, scopolamine, and physostigmine. *Psychopharmacology (Berlin)* 52(1):1–6.

Ghoneim M. M., S. P. Mewaldt. 1990. Benzodiazepines and human memory: A review. *Anesthesiology* 72(5):926–38.

Giang, D. W., D. K. Kido. 1989. Transient global amnesia associated with cerebral angiography performed with use of Iopamidol. *Radiology* 172:195–196.

Giannakopoulos, P., P. R. Hof, C. Bouras. 1995. Dementia lacking distinctive histopathology: Clinicopathological evaluation of 32 cases. *Acta Neuropathol (Berlin)* 89(4):346–355.

Gianutsos, R., J. Gianutsos. 1979. Rehabilitating the verbal brecall of brain damaged patients by mnemonic training: An experimental demonstration using single-case methodology. *J Clin Neuropsychol* 1:117–135.

Gibb, W. R., P. J. Luthert, C. D. Marsden. 1989. Corticobasal degeneration. *Brain* 112(Pt 5):1171–1192.

Giladi, N., H. Shabtai, B. Gurevich, M. et al. 2003. Rivastigmine (Exelon) for dementia in patients with Parkinson's disease. *Acta Neurol Scand* 108(5):368–373.

Gilbert, G. J. 1978. Transient global amnesia: Manifestation of medial temporal lobe epilepsy. *Clin Electroencephalogr* 9:147–152.

Gilbert, P. E., P. J. Barr, C. Murphy. 2004. Differences in olfactory and visual memory in patients with pathologically confirmed Alzheimer's disease and the Lewy body variant of Alzheimer's disease. *J Int Neuropsychol Soc* 10:835–842.

Giroud, M., O. Guard, R. Dumas. 1987. Transient global amnesia associated with hydrocephalus. *J Neurol* 235:118–119.

Glisky, E. L., S. R. Rubin, P. S. Davidson. 2001. Source memory in older adults: An encoding or retrieval problem? *J Exp Psychol Learn Mem Cogn* 27:1131–1146.

Glisky, E. L., L. Ryan, S. Reminger, et al. 2004. A case of psychogenic fugue: I understand, aber ich verstehe nichts. *Neuropsychologia* 42:1132–1147.

Glisky, E. L., D. L. Schacter. 1986. Remediation of organic memory disorders: Current status and future prospects. *J Head Trauma Rehabil* 1:54–63.

Glisky, E. L., D. L. Schacter. 1988. Long-term retention of computer learning by patients with memory disorders. *Neuropsychologia* 26:173–178.

Glisky, E. L., D. L. Schacter. 1989. Extending the limits of complex learning in organic amnesia: Computer training in a vocational domain. *Neuropsychologia* 27:107–120.

Glisky, E. L., D. L. Schacter, E. Tulving. 1986a. Computer learning by memory-impaired patients: Acquisition and retention of complex knowledge. *Neuropsychologia* 24:313–328.

Glisky, E. L., D. L. Schacter, E. Tulving. 1986b. Learning and retention of computer-related vocabulary in amnesic patients: Method of vanishing cues. *J Clin Exp Neuropsychol* 8:292–312.

Goethals, M., P. Santens. 2001. Posterior cortical atrophy. Two case reports and a review of the literature. *Clin Neurol Neurosurg* 103:115–119.

Golbe, L. I., P. H. Davis, B. S. Schoenberg, R. C. Duvoisin. 1988. Prevalence and natural history of progressive supranuclear palsy. *Neurology* 38(7):1031–1034.

Goldberg, E., S. P. Antin, R. M. Bilder, Jr., et al. 1981. Retrograde amnesia: Possible role of mesencephalic reticular activation in long-term memory. *Science* 213:1392–1394.

Goldenberg, G. 1995. Transient global amnesia. In: *Handbook of Memory Disorders*, A. D. Baddeley, B. A. Wilson, F. N. Watts, eds. West Sussex, England, John Wiley & Sons Ltd., pp. 109–133.

Goldenberg, G., W. Oder, J. Spatt, I. Podreka. 1992. Cerebral correlates of disturbed executive function and memory in survivors of severe closed head injury: A SPECT study. *J Neurol Neurosurg Psychiatry* 55:362–368.

Goldenberg, G., I. Podreka, N. Pfaffelmeyer, et al. 1997. Thalamic ischemia in transient global amnesia: A SPECT study. *Neurology* 41:1748–1752.

Goldman-Rakic P. S., S. A. Castner, T. H. Svensson et al. 2004. Targeting the dopamine D1 receptor in schizophrenia: insights for cognitive dysfunction. *Psychopharmacology (Berlin)* 174(1):3–16.

Goldstein, J. 1985. The wandering Jew and the problem of psychiatric anti-semitism in fin-de-siecle France. *J Contemp Hist* 20:521–532.

Golomb, J., A. Kluger, M. J. de Leon, et al. 1994. Hippocampal formation size in normal human aging: A correlate of delayed secondary memory performance. *Learn Mem* 1(1):45–54.

Gómez-Isla, T., R. Hollister, H. West, et al. 1997. Neuronal loss correlates with but exceeds neurofibrillary tangles in Alzheimer's disease. *Ann Neurol* 41:17–24.

Gómez-Isla, T., J. L. Price, D. W. McKeel, Jr., et al. 1996. Profound loss of layer II entorhinal cortex neurons occurs in very mild Alzheimer's disease. *J Neurosci* 16(14):4491–500.

Gonos, E. S. 2000. Genetics of aging: Lessons from centenarians. *Exp Gerontol* 35:15–21.

Good, C. D., I. S. Johnsrude, J. Ashburner, et al. 2001. A voxel-based morphometric study of aging in 465 normal adult human brains. *NeuroImage* 14:21–36.

Goodglass, H., E. Kaplan. 1983. *Boston Diagnostic Aphasia Examination*. Philadelphia, Lea & Febiger.

Goodwin D. W. 1995. Alcohol amnesia. *Addiction* 90(3):315–317.

Gould, E., P. Tanapat, B. S. McEwen, et al. 1998. Proliferation of granule cell precursors in the dentate gyrus of adult monkeys is diminished by stress. *Proc Natl Acad Sci U S A* 95(6):3168–3171.

Graff-Radford, N. R., D. Tranel, G. W. Van Hoesen, J. P. Brandt. 1990. Diencephalic amnesia. *Brain* 113:1–25.

Graham, K. S., J. T. Becker, J. R. Hodges. 1997. On the relationship between knowledge and memory for pictures: Evidence from the study of patients with semantic dementia and Alzheimer's disease. *J Int Neuropsychol Soc* 3:534–544.

Graham, K. S., J. R. Hodges. 1997. Differentiating the roles of the hippocampal complex and the neocortex in long-term memory storage: Evidence from the study of semantic dementia and Alzheimer's disease. *Neuropsychology* 11:77–89.

Graham, K. S., J. S. Simons, K. H. Pratt, et al. 2000. Insights from semantic dementia on the relationship between episodic and semantic memory. *Neuropsychologia* 38:313–324.

Graham, N. L., T. Bak, K. Patterson, J. R. Hodges. 2003. Language function and dysfunction in corticobasal degeneration. *Neurology* 61:493–499.

Graham, N. L., T. Emery, J. R. Hodges. 2004. Distinctive cognitive profiles in Alzheimer's disease and subcortical vascular dementia. *J Neurol Neurosurg Psychiatry* 75:61–71.

Graham, N. L., K. Patterson, J. R. Hodges. 2000. The impact of semantic memory impairment on spelling: Evidence from semantic dementia. *Neuropsychologia* 38: 143–163.

Grant, I. 1987. Alcohol and the brain: Neuropsychological correlates. *J Consult Clin Psychol* 55:310–324.

Green, R. C., L. A. Cupples, A. Kurz, et al. 2003. Depression as a risk factor for Alzheimer disease: The MIRAGE Study. *Arch Neurol* 60:753–759.

Greenblatt, M. 1977. Efficacy of ECT in affective and schizophrenic illness. *Am J Psychiatry* 134:1001–1005.

Greene, H. H., D. R. Bennett. 1974. Transient global amnesia with a previously unreported EEG abnormality. *Electroencephalogr Clin Neuropsychol* 36:409–413.

Gregory, C. A., J. Serra-Mestres, J. R. Hodges. 1999. Early diagnosis of the frontal variant of frontotemporal dementia: How sensitive are standard neuroimaging and neuropsychologic tests? *Neuropsychiatry Neuropsychol Behav Neurol* 12(2):128–135.

Grober E., Buschke H. 1987. Genuine memory deficits in dementia. *Dev Neuropsychol* 3:13–36.

Groenndijk, I., O. van der Hart. 1995. Treatment of DID and DDNOS patients in regional institute for ambulatory mental health in the Netherlands: A survey. *Dissociation* 8:73.

Groot, Y. C. T., B. A. Wilson, J. Evans, P. Watson. 2002. Prospective memory functioning in people with and without brain injury. *J Int Neuropsychol Soc* 8:645–654.

Grossi, D., L. Trojano, A. Grasso, A. Orsini. 1988. Selective "semantic amnesia" after closed-head injury. A case report. *Cortex* 24:457–464.

Grundman, M., R. C. Petersen, S. H. Ferris, et al. 2004. Mild cognitive impairment can be distinguished from Alzheimer disease and normal aging for clinical trials. *Arch Neurol* 61(1):59–66.

Gudjonsson, G. H., N. K. Clark. 1986. Suggestibility in police interrogation: a social psychological model. *Soc Behav* 1:83–104.

Guidotti, M., N. Anzalone, A. Morabito, G. Landi. 1989. A case-control study of transient global amnesia. *J Neurol Neurosurg Psychiatry* 52:320–323.

Guillery-Girard, B., B. Desgranges, C. Urban, et al. 2004. The dynamic time course of memory recovery in transient global amnesia. *J Neurol Neurosurg Psychiatry* 75: 1532–1540.

Gunstad, J., J. A. Suhr. 2002. Perception of illness: Nonspecificity of postconcussion syndrome symptom expectation. *J Int Neuropsychol Soc* 8:37–47.

Gurdjian, E. S., J. E. Webster. 1958. *Head Injuries: Mechanisms, Diagnosis and Management.* Boston, Little, Brown, and Company.

Gurvits T. V., M. E. Shenton, H. Hokama, et al. 1996. Magnetic resonance imaging study of hippocampal volume in chronic, combat-related posttraumatic stress disorder. *Biol Psychiatry* 40(11):1091–1099.

Haaland, K. Y., D. L. Harrington, S. O'Brien, N. Hermanowicz. 1997. Cognitive-motor learning in Parkinson's disease. *Neuropsychology* 11:180–186.

Haaland, K. Y., L. Price, A. LaRue. 2003. What does the WMS-III tell us about memory changes with normal aging? *J Int Neuropsychol Soc* 9:89–96.

Haas, D. C. 1983. Transient global amnesia after cerebral angiography. *Arch Neurol* 40(4):258–259.

Haas, D. C., G. S. Ross. 1986. Transient global amnesia triggered by mild head trauma. *Brain* 109:251–257.

Hachinski, V. C., J. V. Bowler. 1993. Vascular dementia. *Neurology* 43:2159–2160.

Hackert, V. H., T. den Heijer, M. Oudkerk, et. al. 2002. Hippocampal head size associated with verbal memory performance in non-demented elderly. *Neuroimage* 17:1365–1372.

Hacking, I. 1996. Les Alienes voyageurs: How fugue became a medical entity. *Hist Psychiatry* 7:425–449.

Halgren, E., C. L. Wilson, J. M. Stapleton. 1985. Human medial temporal lobe stimuli disrupts both formation and retrieval of human memories. *Brain Cogn* 4:287–295.

Hamann, S., E. S. Monarch, F. C. Goldstein. 2002. Impaired fear conditioning in Alzheimer's disease. *Neuropsychologia* 40:1187–1195.

Hamilton, J. M., D. P. Salmon, D. Galasko, et al. 2004. A comparison of episode memory deficits in neuropathologically-confirmed dementia with Lewy bodies and Alzheimer's disease. *J Int Neuropsychol Soc* 10:689–697.

Hanks, R., N. Temkin, J. Machamer, S. Dikmen. 1999. Emotional and behavioral adjustment after traumatic brain injury. *Arch Phys Med Rehabil* 80:991–999.

Hanninen, T., K. Koivisto, K. J. Reinikainen, et al. 1996. Prevalence of aging-associated cognitive decline in an elderly population. *Age Ageing* 25:201–205.

Harding, A., G. Halliday, D. Caine, J. Kril. 2000. Degeneration of anterior thalamic nuclei differentiates alcoholics with amnesia. *Brain* 123:141–154.

Harding, A. J., A. Wong, M. Svoboda, et al. 1997. Chronic alcohol consumption does not cause hippocampal neuron loss in humans. *Hippocampus* 7(1):78–87.

Harris, J. 1980. Memory aids people use: Two interview studies. *Mem Cogn* 8:31–38.

Hart, J. Jr., B. Gordon. 1992. Neural subsystems for object knowledge. *Nature* 359(6390):60–64.

Hart, R. P., J. A. Kwentus, R. M. Hamer, et al. 1987. Rate of forgetting in dementia and depression. *J Consult Clin Psychol* 55:101–105.

Hartley, T. C., K. M. Heilman, F. Garcia-Bengochea. 1974. A case of transient global amnesia due to a pituitary tumor. *Neurology* 24:998–1000.

Hashimoto, R., Y. Tanaka, I. Nakano. 2000. Amnesic confabulatory syndrome after focal basal forebrain damage. *Neurology* 54:978–980.

Hasselmo, M. E. 1999. Neuromodulation: acetylcholine and memory consolidation. *Trends Cogn Sci* Sep;3(9):351–359.

Hasse-Sander, I., H. Muller, W. Schuring, et al. 1988. Auswirkungen der Eletrokrampftherapie auf die kognitiven Funktionen bei therapieresistenten Depressionen. *Nervenarzt* 69:609–616.

Hauge, T. 1954. Catheter vertebral angiography. *Acta Radiologica Suppl* 109:1–219.

Hauser, W. A., J. F. Annegers, L. T. Kurland. 1993. Incidence of epilepsy and unprovoked seizures in Rochester, Minnesota: 1935–1984. *Epilepsia* 34:453–468.

Hauw, J. J., S. E. Daniel, D. Dickson, et al. 1994. Preliminary NINDS neuropathologic criteria for Steele-Richardson-Olszewski syndrome (progressive supranuclear palsy). *Neurology* 44(11):2015–2019.

Hazlett, E. A., M. S. Buchsbaum, R. C. Mohs, et al. 1998. Age-related shift in brain region activity during successful memory performance. *Neurobiol Aging* 19:437–445.

Head, D., R. L. Buckner, J. S. Shimony, et al. 2004. Differential vulnerability of anterior white matter in non-demented aging with minimal acceleration in dementia of the Alzheimer type: Evidence from diffusion tensor imaging. *Cereb Cortex* 14:410–423.

Head, D., N. Raz, F. Gunning-Dixon, et al. 2002. Age-related differences in the course of cognitive skill acquisition: The role of regional cortical shrinkage and cognitive resources. *Psychol Aging* 17:72–84.

Heaton, R. K., M. J. Taylor, J. J. Manly. 2003. Demographic effects and use of demographically corrected norms with the WAIS-III and WMS-III. In: *Clinical Interpretation of the WAIS-III and WMS-III*, D. Tulsky, D. Saklofske, R. K. Heaton, G. Chelune, R. Ivnik, R. A. Bornstein, A. Prifitera, M. Ledbetter, eds. San Diego, Academic Press, 2003.

Hebb, D. O. 1949. *The Organization of Behavior*. New York, Wiley.

Heikman, P., R. Salmelin, J. P. Makela, et al. 2001. Relationship between frontal 3–7H$_2$ MEG activity and the efficacy of ECT in major depression. *J ECT* 17:136–140.

Heilman, K. M., R. Scholes, R. T. Watson. 1976. Defects of immediate memory in Broca's and conduction aphasia. *Brain Lang* 3:201–208.

Helmstaedter, C., T. Grunwald, K. Lehnertz, et al. 1997. Differential involvement of left temporolateral and temporomesial structures in verbal declarative learning and memory: Evidence from temporal lobe epilepsy. *Brain Cogn* 35:110–131.

Heon, M., J. Reiher, D. Dilenge, J. Lamarche. 1972. Ictus amnesique et hématome intraventriculaire. *Neurochirurgie (Paris)* 18:503–510.

Herman, J. P., W. E. Cullinan. 1997. Neurocircuitry of stress: central control of the hypothalamo-pituitary-adrenocortical axis. *Trends Neurosci* 20(2):78–84.

Hermann, B. P., M. Seidenberg, A. Wyler, et al. 1996. The effect of human hippocampal resection on the serial position curve. *Cortex* 32:323–334.

Hermann, B. P., A. R. Wyler, G. Somes, et al. 1992. Pathological status of the medial temporal lobe predicts memory outcome from left anterior lobectomy. *Neurosurgery* 31:652–657.

Herr Dritschel, B., L. Kogan, A. Burton, et al. 1998. Everyday planning difficulties following traumatic brain injury: A role for autobiographical memory. *Brain Inj* 12:875–886.

Hester, R. L., G. J. Kinsella, B. Ong. 2004. Effect of age on forward and backward span tasks. *J Int Neuropsychol Soc* 10:475–481.

Heutink, P., M. Stevens, P. Rizzu, et al. 1997. Hereditary frontotemporal dementia is linked to chromosome 17q21–q22: A genetic and clinicopathological study of three Dutch families. *Ann Neurol* 41(2):150–159.

Hibbard, M. R., S. Uysal, K. Kepler, et al. 1998. Axis I psychopathology in individuals with TBI. *J Head Trauma Rehabil* 13:24–39.

Higginson, C. I., D. S. King, D. Levine, et al. 2003. The relationship between executive function and verbal memory in Parkinson's disease. *Brain Cogn* 52:343–352.

Hildebrandt, H., S. Muller, B. Bussmann-Mork, et al. 2001. Are some memory deficits unique to lesions of the mammillary bodies? *J Clin Exp Neuropsychol* 23: 490–501.

Hinge, H. H., T. S. Jensen, M. Kjaer, et al. 1986. The prognosis of transient global amnesia: results of a multicenter study. *Arch Neurol* 43:673–676.

Hinrichs, J. V., M. M. Ghoneim, S. P. Mewaldt. 1984. Diazepam and memory: retrograde facilitation produced by interference reduction. *Psychopharmacology (Berlin)* 84(2):158–162.

Ho, A. K., B. J. Sahakian, R. G. Brown, et al. 2003. Profile of cognitive progression in early Huntington's disease. *Neurology* 61:1702–1706.

Hodges, J. R. 1991. *Transient amnesia: Clinical and neuropsychological aspects.* London, WB Saunders Company.

Hodges, J. R. 1994. Semantic memory and central executive function during transient global amnesia. *J Neurol Neurosurg Psychiatry* 57:605–608.

Hodges, J. R., K. S. Graham. 1998. A reversal of the temporal gradient for famous person knowledge in semantic dementia: Implications for the neural organization of long-term memory. *Neuropsychologia* 36:803–825.

Hodges, J. R., K. S. Graham. 2001. Episodic memory: Insights from semantic dementia. *Philos Trans R Soc Lond B Biol Sci* 356:1423–1434.

Hodges, J. R., N. Graham, K. Patterson. 1995. Charting the progression in semantic dementia: Implications for the organisation of semantic memory. *Memory* 3:463–495.

Hodges, J. R., R. A. McCarthy. 1993. Autobiographical amnesia resulting from bilateral paramedian thalamic infarction. A case study in cognitive neurobiology. *Brain* 116:921–940.

Hodges, J. R., S. M. Oxbury. 1990. Persistent memory impairment following transient global amnesia. *J Clin Exp Neuropsychol* 12:904–920.

Hodges, J. R., K. Patterson. 1995. Is semantic memory consistently impaired early in the course of Alzheimer's Disease? Neuroanatomical and diagnostic implications. *Neuropsychologia* 33:441–459.

Hodges, J. R., K. Patterson. 1996. Nonfluent progressive aphasia and semantic dementia: A comparative neuropsychological study. *J Int Neuropsychol Soc* 2:511–524.

Hodges, J. R., K. Patterson, L. K. Tyler. 1994. Loss of semantic memory: Implications for the modularity of mind. *Cogn Neuropsychol* 11:505–542.

Hodges, J. R., K. Patterson, S. Oxbury, E. Funnell. 1992. Semantic dementia: Progressive fluent aphasia with temporal lobe atrophy. *Brain* 115:1783–1806.

Hodges, J. R., C. D. Ward. 1989. Observations during transient global amnesia: A behavioral and neuropsychological study of five cases. *Brain* 112:595–620.

Hodges, J. R., C. P. Warlow. 1990a. Syndromes of transient amnesia: Towards classification. A study of 153 cases. *J Neurol Neurosurg Psychiatry* 53:834–843.

Hodges, J. R., C. P. Warlow. 1990b. The aetiology of transient global amnesia. A case-control study of 114 cases with prospective follow-up. *Brain* 113:639–657.

Hof, P. R., C. Bouras, D. P. Perl, J. H. Morrison. 1994. Quantitative neuropathologic analysis of Pick's disease cases: Cortical distribution of Pick bodies and coexistence with Alzheimer's disease. *Acta Neuropathol (Berlin)* 87(2):115–124.

Hof, P. R., B. A. Vogt, C. Bouras, J. H. Morrison. 1997. Atypical form of Alzheimer's disease with prominent posterior cortical atrophy: A review of lesion distribution and circuit disconnection in cortical visual pathways. *Vision Res* 37:3609–3625.

Hofman, P. A. M., S. Z. Stapert, J. P. G. van Kroonenburgh, et al. 2001. MR imaging, single-photon emission TC, and neurocognitive performance after mild traumatic brain injury. *Am J Neuroradiol* 22:441–449.

Holbourn, A. H. S. 1943. Mechanics of head injuries. *Lancet* 2:411–438.

Hollander, E., J. Fairbanks, C. Decaria, M. R. Liebowitz. 1989. Pharmacologic dissection of panic and depersonalization. *Am J Psychiatry* 146:402.

Hooten, W. M., C. G. Lyketsos. 1996. Frontotemporal dementia: a clinicopathological review of four postmortem studies. *J Neuropsychiatry Clin Neurosci* 8(1):10–19.

Horen, S.A., P. P. Leichner, J. S. Lawson. 1995. Prevalence of dissociative symptoms and disorders in a adult psychiatric inpatient population in Canada. *Can J Psychiatry* 40:185–191.

Horimoto, Y., M. Matsumoto, H. Nakazawa, et al. 2003. Cognitive conditions of pathologically confirmed dementia with Lewy bodies and Parkinson's disease with dementia. *J Neurol Sci* 216:105–108.

Houlden, H., M. Baker, H. R. Morris, et al. 2001. Corticobasal degeneration and progressive supranuclear palsy share a common tau haplotype. *Neurology* 56(12): 1702–1706.

Howard, D., K. Patterson. 1992. *The Pyramids and Palm Trees Test.* Bury St Edmunds, Thames Valley Test Company.

Howard, J. H., Jr., D. V. Howard, N. A. Dennis, et al. 2004. Implicit spatial contextual learning in healthy aging. *Neuropsychology* 18:124–134.

Huppert, F. A., T. Johnson, J. Nickson. 2000. High prevalence of prospective memory impairment in the elderly and in early-stage dementia: Findings form a population-based study. *Appl Cogn Psychol* 14:S63–S82.

Huppert, F. A., M. Piercy. 1979. Normal and abnormal forgetting in organic amnesia: Effect of locus of lesion. *Cortex* 15:385–390.

Huttenlocher, P. R. 1990. Morphometric study of human cerebral cortex development. *Neuropsychologia* 28:517–527.

Ibáñez, V., P. Pietrini, G. E. Alexander, et al. 1998. Regional glucose metabolic abnormalities are not the result of atrophy in Alzheimer's disease. *Neurology* 50:1585–1593.

Ibáñez, V., P. Pietrini, M. L. Furey, et al. 2004. Resting state brain glucose metabolism is not reduced in normotensive healthy men during aging, after correction for brain atrophy. *Brain Res Bull* 63:147–154.

Ikeda, M., K. Hokoishi, N. Maki, et al. 2001. Increased prevalence of vascular dementia in Japan: A community-based epidemiological study. *Neurology* 57(5):839–844.

Ito, M. 1986. Long-term depression as a memory process in the cerebellum. *Neurosci Res* 3:531–539.

Jack, C. R. Jr., R. C. Petersen, Y. Xu, et al. 1998. Rate of medial temporal lobe atrophy in typical aging and Alzheimer's disease. *Neurology* 51:993–999.

Jackson, B. 1978. The effects of unilateral and bilateral ECT on verbal and visual spatial memory. *J Clin Psychol* 34:4–13.

Jacobs, D. M., M. Sano, G. Dooneief, et al. 1995. Neuropsychological detection and characterization of preclinical Alzheimer's disease. *Neurology* 45:957–962.

Jacobsen, T. 1995. Case study: Is selective mutism a manifestation of dissociative identity disorder? *J Am Acad Child Adoles Psychiatry* 34:863–866.

Jacome, D. E. 1989. EEG features in transient global amnesia. *Clin Electroencephalogr* 20:183–192.

Jacome, D. E., G. F. Yanez. 1988. Transient global amnesia and left frontal hemorrhage. *Postgrad Med J* 64:137–139.

Jambaque, I., G. Dellatois, O. Dulac, et al. 1993. Verbal and visual memory impairment in children with epilepsy. *Neuropsychologia* 31:1321–1337.

James, W. 1890. *Principles of Psychology*. New York, Holt.

Janet, P. 1889. *L'automatisme psychologique*. Paris, Alcan.

Janet, P. 1907. *The Major Symptoms of Hysteria*. New York, MacMillan.

Jauhar, P., D. Montaldi. 2000. Wernicke-Korsakoff syndrome and the use of brain imaging. *Alcohol Alcohol Suppl* 35(Suppl 1):21–23.

Jellinger, K. A. 1994. Quantitative neuropathologic analysis of Pick's disease cases. *Acta Neuropathol (Berlin)* 87(2):223–224.

Jellinger, K., P. Riederer, M. Tomonaga. 1980. Progressive supranuclear palsy: Clinico-pathological and biochemical studies. *J Neural Transm Suppl* 16:111–128.

Jennett, B., J. Snoek, M. R. Bond, N. Brooks. 1981. Disability after severe head injury: Observations on the use of the Glasgow Outcome Scale. *J Neurol Neurosurg Psychiatry* 44:285–293.

Jernigan, T., L. Archibald, S. L. Fennema-Notestine, et al. 2001. Effects of age on tissues and regions of the cerebrum and cerebellum. *Neurobiol Aging* 22:581–594.

Joels, M., E. R. de Kloet. 1989. Effects of glucocorticoids and norepinephrine on the excitability in the hippocampus. *Science* 245(4925):1502–1505.

Johnson, M. D., G. A. Ojemann. 2000. The role of the human thalamus in language and memory: Evidence from electrophysiological studies. *Brain Cogn* Mar;42(2):218–230.

Jones-Gotman, M., M. L. Smith, R. J. Zatorre. 1993. Neuropsychological testing for localizing and lateralizing the epileptogenic region. In: *Surgical Treatment of the Epilepsies*, Second ed., J. Engel, Jr., ed. New York, Raven Press, Ltd., pp. 245–261.

Jorge, R. E., R. G. Robinson, S. E. Starkstein, et al. 1993. Secondary mania following traumatic brain injury. *Am J Psychiatry* 150:916–921.

Jorm, A. F. 2000. Is depression a risk factor for dementia or cognitive decline? A review. *Gerontology* 46:219–227.

Joseph, R. 1999. The neurology of traumatic "dissociative" amnesia: Commentary and literature review. *Child Abuse Negl* 23:715–727.

Jost, B. C., G. T. Grossberg. 1995. The natural history of Alzheimer's disease: A brain bank study. *J Am Geriatr Soc* 43(11):1248–1255.

Kaasinen, V., J. O. Rinne. 2002. Functional imaging studies of dopamine system and cognition in normal aging and Parkinson's disease. *Neurosci Biobehav Rev* 26:785–793.

Kaasinen, V., H. Vilkman, J. Hietala, et al. 2000. Age-related dopamine D2/D3 receptor loss in extrastriatal regions of the human brain. *Neurobiol Aging* 21:683–688.

Kandel, E. R. 2001. The molecular biology of memory storage: A dialogue between genes and synapses. *Science* 294:1030–1038.

Kant, R., J. D. Duffy, A. Pivovarnik. 1998. Prevalence of apathy following head injury. *Brain Inj* 12:87–92.

Kanzer, M. 1939. Amnesia: A statistical study. *Am J Psychiatry* 96:711–716.

Kaplan, E. F., D. Fein, R. Morris, D. C. Delis. 1991. *Manual for the WAIS-R as a Neuropsychological Instrument (WAIS-R-NI)*. New York, The Psychological Corporation.

Kaplan, E. F., H. Goodglass, S. Weintraub. 1983. *The Boston Naming Test*, 2nd ed. Philadelphia, Lea & Febiger.

Kapur, N. 1989. Focal retrograde amnesia: A long term clinical and neuropsychological follow up. *Cortex* 25:387–402.

Kapur, N. 1993. Transient epileptic amnesia—a clinical update and reformulation. *J Neurol Neurosurg Psychiatry* 56:1184–1190.

Kapur, N., P. Abbott, D. Footitt, J. Millar. 1996. Long-term perceptual priming in transient global amnesia. *Brain Cogn* 31:63–74.

Kapur, N., D. Ellison, A. J. Parkin, et al. 1994. Bilateral temporal lobe pathology with sparing of medial temporal lobe structures: Lesion profile and pattern of memory disorder. *Neuropsychologia* 32:23–38.

Kapur, N., P. Thompson, L. D. Kartsounis, P. Abbott. 1999. Retrograde amnesia: Clinical and methodological caveats. *Neuropsychologia* 37:27–30.

Karli, D. C., D. T. Burke, H. Y. Kim, et al. 1999. Effects of dopaminergic combination therapy for frontal lobe dysfunction in traumatic brain injury rehabilitation. *Brain Inj* 13:63–68.

Kase, C. S. 1991. Epidemiology of multi-infarct dementia. *Alzheimer Dis Assoc Disord* 5(2):71–76.

Kase, C. S., P. A. Wolf, E. H. Chodosh, et al. 1989. Prevalence of silent stroke in patients presenting with initial stroke: The Framingham Study. *Stroke* 20(7):850–852.

Kaszniak, A. W., P. D. Nussbaum, M. R. Berren, J. Santiago. 1988. Amnesia as a consequence of male rape: A case report. *J Abnorm Psychol* 97(1):100–104.

Katzen, H. L., B. E. Levin, M. L. Llabre. 1998. Age of disease onset influences cognition in Parkinson's disease. *J Int Neuropsychol Soc* 4(3):285–290.

Katzman, R., J. E. Jackson. 1991. Alzheimer disease: Basic and clinical advances. *J Am Geriatr Soc* 39(5):516–525.

Keck Seeley, S. M., S. L. Perosa, L. M. Perosa. 2004. A validation study of the Adolescent Dissociative Experiences Scale. *Child Abuse Negl* 28:755–769.

Kertesz, A., W. Davidson, H. Fox. 1997. Frontal behavior inventory: Diagnostic criteria for frontal lobe dementia. *Can J Neurol Sci* 24:29–36.

Kertesz, A., L. Hudson, I. R. Mackenzie, D. G. Munoz. 1994. The pathology and nosology of primary progressive aphasia. *Neurology* 44(11):2065–2072.

Kertesz, A., P. Martinez-Lage, W. Davidson, D. G. Munoz. 2000. The corticobasal degeneration syndrome overlaps progressive aphasia and frontotemporal dementia. *Neurology* 55:1368–1375.

Kertesz, A., D. Munoz. 1998. Pick's disease, frontotemporal dementia, and Pick complex: emerging concepts. *Arch Neurol* 55(3):302–304.

Kessing, L. V., F. M. Nilsson. 2003. Increased risk of developing dementia in patients with major affective disorders compared to patients with other medical illnesses. *J Affect Disord* 73:261–269.

Kihlstrom, J. F. 1994. Hypnosis, delayed recall and the principles of memory. *Int J Clin Exp Hypn* 42:337–345.

Kihlstrom, J. F. 1998. Exhumed memory. In: *Truth in Memory*, S. J. Lynn, K. M. McConkey, eds. New York, Guilford, pp. 3–31.

Kihlstrom, J. F., E. Eich. 1994. Altering states of consciousness. In: *Learning, Remembering, and Believing: Enhancing Performance*, D. Druckman, R. A. Bjork, eds. Washington, D.C., National Academy Press, pp. 207–248.

Kihlstrom, J. F., D. L. Schacter. 2000. Functional amnesia. In: *Handbook of Neuropsychology*, 2nd ed., Vol. 2, F. Boller, J. Grafman, eds. Amsterdam, Elsevier, pp. 409–427.

Kihlstrom, J. F., D. L. Schacter. 1995. Functional Disorders of Autobiographical memory. In: *Handbook of Memory Disorders*, A. B. Baddeley, B. A. Wilson, F. N. Watts, eds. Chichester, John Wiley & Sons, pp. 337–367.

Kilpatrick, L., L. Cahill. 2003. Amygdala modulation of parahippocampal and frontal regions during emotionally influenced memory storage. *Neuroimage* 20:2091–2099.

Kim, J. J., M. S. Fanselow. 1992. Modality-specific retrograde amnesia of fear. *Science* 256:675–677.

King, N. S. 2003. Post-concussion syndrome: Clarity amid the controversy? *Br J Psychol* 183:276–278.

Kinsella, G., D. Murtagh, A. Landry, et al. 1996. Everyday memory following traumatic brain injury. *Brain Inj* 10:499–495.

Kirkwood, S. C., E. Siemers, J. C. Stout, et al. 1999. Longitudinal cognitive and motor changes among presymptomatic Huntington disease gene carriers. *Arch Neurol* 56:563–568.

Kluft, R. P. 1991a. Hospital treatment of multiple personality disorder: An overview. *Psychiatr Clin North Am* 14:695–719.

Kluft, R. P. 1991b. Multiple Personality. In: *American Psychiatric Press Review of Psychiatry*, Vol. 10, A. Tasman, S. M. Goldfinger, eds. Washington, D.C., American Psychiatric Press, pp. 161–188.

Knight, R. T. 1984. Decreased response to novel stimuli after prefrontal lesions in man. *Electroencephalogr Clin Neurophysiol* 59:9–20.

Knopman, D., L. L. Boland, T. Mosley, et al. 2001. Cardiovascular risk factors and cognitive decline in middle-aged adults. *Neurology* 56:42–48.

Knopman, D. S., A. R. Mastri, W. H. Frey, et al. 1990. Dementia lacking distinctive histologic features: A common non-Alzheimer degenerative dementia. *Neurology* 40(2):251–256.

Knopman, D. S., J. E. Parisi, B. F. Boeve, et al. 2003. Vascular dementia in a population-based autopsy study. *Arch Neurol* 60(4):569–575.

Knott, R., K. Patterson, J. R. Hodges. 1997. Lexical and semantic binding effects in short-term memory: Evidence from semantic dementia. *Cogn Neuropsychol* 14:1165–1216.

Knowlton, B. J., J. A. Mangels, L. R. Squire. 1996a. A neostriatal habit learning system in humans. *Science* 273:1399–1402.

Knowlton, B. J., L. R. Squire, M. A. Gluck. 1994. Probabilistic classification learning in amnesia. *Learn Mem* 1:106–120.

Knowlton, B. J., L. R. Squire, J. S. Paulsen, et al. 1996b. Dissociations within nondeclarative memory in Huntington's disease. *Neuropsychology* 10:538–548.

Koenen, K. C., K. L. Driver, M. Oscar-Berman, et al. 2001. Measures of prefrontal system dysfunction in posttraumatic stress disorder. *Brain Cogn* 45(1):64–78.

Koenig, O., C. Thomas-Antérion, B. Laurent. 1999. Procedural learning in Parkinson's disease: Intact and impaired cognitive components. *Neuropsychologia* 37:1103–1109.

Kojima, S., P. S. Goldman-Rakic. 1982. Delay-related activity of prefrontal neurons in rhesus monkeys performing delayed response. *Brain Res* 248:43–49.

Kolakowsky-Hayner, S. A., E. V. III Courley, J. S. Kreutzer, et al. 1999. Pre-injury substance abuse among persons with brain injury and persons with spinal cord injury. *Brain Inj* 13:571–581.

Kompoliti, K., C. G. Goetz, I. Litvan, et al. 1998. Pharmacological therapy in progressive supranuclear palsy. *Arch Neurol* 55(8):1099–1102.

Kopelman, M. D. 1993. The neuropsychology of remote memory. In: *Handbook of Neuropsychology*, Vol. 8, F. Boller, J. Grafman, eds. Amsterdam, Elsevier, pp. 215–238.

Kopelman, M. D. 1995a. Assessment of psychogenic amnesia. In: *Handbook of Memory Disorders*, 1st ed., A. D. Baddeley, B. A. Wilson, F. N. Watts, eds. Chichester, John Wiley & Sons, 427–448.

Kopelman, M. D. 1995b. The Korsakoff syndrome. *Br J Psychiatry* 166(2):154–173.

Kopelman, M. D. 2000. Focal retrograde amnesia and the attribution of causality: An exceptionally critical review. *Cogn Neuropsychol* 17:585–621.

Kopelman, M. D. 2002a. Disorders of memory. *Brain* 125:2152–2190.

Kopelman, M. D. Psychogenic amnesia. In: *Handbook of Memory Disorders*, 2nd ed., A. D. Baddeley, M. D. Kopelman, B. A. Wilson, eds. Chichester, John Wiley & Sons, pp. 451–471.

Kopelman, M. D., H. Christensen, A. Puffett, N. Stanhope. 1994a. The great escape: A neuropsychological study of psychogenic amnesia. *Neuropsychologia* 32:75–91.

Kopelman, M. D., C. P. Panayiotopoulos, P. Lewis. 1994b. Transient epileptic amnesia differentiated from psychogenic "fugue": Neuropsychological, EEG, and PET findings. *J Neurol Neurosurg Psychiatry* 57:1002–1004.

Kopelman, M. D., B. A. Wilson, A. D. Baddeley. 1989. The autobiographical memory interview: A new assessment of autobiographical and personal semantic memory in amnesic patients. *J Clin Exp Neuropsychol* 11:724–744.

Kopelman, M. D., B. A. Wilson, A. D. Baddeley. 1990. *The Autobiographical Memory Interview*. Bury St Edmunds, Thames Valley Test Company.

Koponen, S., T. Taiminen, R. Portin, et al. 2002. Axis I and II psychiatric disorders after traumatic brain injury: A 30-year follow-up study. *Am J Psychiatry* 159:1315–1321.

Koski, K. J., R. J. Marttila. 1990. Transient global amnesia: Incidence in an urban population. *Acta Neurol Scand* 81:358–360.

Kral, V. A. Senescent memory decline and senile amnestic syndrome. 1958. *Am J Psychiatry* 115:361–362.

Kraus, J. F., M. A. Black, N. Hessol, et al. 1984. The incidence of acute brain injury and serious impairment in a defined population. *Am J Epidemiol* 119:186–120.

Kraus, J. F., D. Fife, C. Conroy. 1987. Pediatric brain injuries: The nature, clinical course, and early outcomes in a defined United States' population. *Pediatrics* 80:501–507.

Kraus, J. F., H. Morgenstern, D. Fife, et al. 1989. Blood alcohol tests, prevalence of involvement, and outcomes following brain injury. *Am J Public Health* 79:294–229.

Krill, J. J., G. M. Halliday, M. D. Svoboda, H. Cartwright. 1997. The cerebral cortex is damaged in chronic alcoholics. *Neurosci* 79:993–998.

Kritchevsky, N., J. Chang, L. R. Squire. 2004. Functional amnesia: Clinical description and neuropsychological profile of 10 cases. *Learn Mem* 11:213–226.

Kritchevsky, M., L. R. Squire. 1989. Transient global amnesia: evidence for extensive, temporally graded retrograde amnesia. *Neurology* 39:213–218.

Kritchevsky M., L. R. Squire, J. A. Zouzounis. 1988. Transient global amnesia: Characterization of anterograde and retrograde amnesia. *Neurology* 38:213–219.

Kritchevsky, N., J. Zouzounis, L. Squire. 1997. Transient global amnesia and functional retrograde amnesia: Contrasting examples of episodic memory loss. *Philos Trans R Soc Lond B* 352:1747–1754.

Kroessler, D., B. S. Fogel. 1993. Electroconvulsive therapy for major depression in the oldest old. *Am J Geriatr Psychiatry* 1:30–37.

Kulisevsky, J. 2000. Role of dopamine in learning and memory: implications for the treatment of cognitive dysfunction in patients with Parkinson's disease. *Drugs Aging* 16(5):365–379.

Kushner M. J., W. A. Hauser. 1985. Transient global amnesia: a case-control study. *Ann Neurol* 18:684–691.

Laiacona, M., R. Barbarotto, R. Capitani. 1993. Perceptual and associative knowledge in category specific impairment of semantic memory: A study of two cases. *Cortex* 29:727–740.

Laiacona, M., E. Capitani, R. Barbarotto. 1997. Semantic category dissociations: A longitudinal study of two cases. *Cortex* 33:441–461.

Lamar, M., C. C. Price, K. L. Davis, et al. 2002. Capacity to maintain mental set in dementia. *Neuropsychologia* 40:435–445.

Lamb, S. M. 1999. Pathways of the brain: The neurocognitive basis of language. Amsterdam, John Benjamins.

Landi, G., M. C. Guisti, M. Guidotti. 1982. Transient global amnesia due to left temporal hemorrhage. *J Neurol Neurosurg Psychiatry* 45:1062–1063.

Langlois, J., K. Gotsch. 2001. *Traumatic Brain Injury in the United States: Assessing Outcomes in Children.* Atlanta, Ga., National Center for Injury Prevention and Control, Centers for Disease Control and Prevention (CDC).

Larson, E. B., M. F. Shadlen, L. Wang, et al. 2004. Survival after initial diagnosis of Alzheimer disease. *Ann Intern Med* 140(7):501–509.

Larsson, M., H. Semb, B. Winblad, et al. 1999. Odor identification in normal aging and early Alzheimer's disease: Effects of retrieval support. *Neuropsychology* 13:47–53.

Lashley, K. 1950. In search of the engram. *Symp Soc Exp Biol* 4:454–482.

Latz, T.T., S. I. Kramer, D. L. Hughes. 1995. Multiple personality disorder among female inpatients in a state hospital. *Am J Psychiatry* 152:1343–1348.

Lauria, G., M. Gentile, G. Fassetta, et al. 1997. Incidence of transient global amnesia in the Belluno province, Italy: 1985 through 1995. Results of a community-based study. *Acta Neurol Scand* 95(5):303–310.

Lauritzen, M., T. Skyhoj Olsen, N. A. Lassen, O. B. Paulson. 1983a. Changes in regional cerebral blood flow during the course of classic migraine attacks. *Ann Neurol* 13:633–641.

Lauritzen, M., T. Skyhoj Olsen, N. A. Lassen, O. B. Paulson. 1983b. Regulation of regional cerebral blood flow during and between migraine attacks. *Ann Neurol* 14:569–572.

Lauro-Grotto, R., C. Piccini, T. Shallice. 1997. Modality-specific operations in semantic dementia. *Cortex* 33:593–622.

Lazzara, M. M., A. P. Yonelinas, B. A. Ober. 2001. Conceptual implicit memory performance in Alzheimer's disease. *Neuropsychology* 15:483–491.

Lebert, F., F. Pasquier, L. Souliez, H. Petit. 1998. Frontotemporal behavioral scale. *Alzheimer Dis Assoc Disord* 12:335–339.

Lee, B. I., B. C. Lee, Y. M. Hwang, et al. 1992. Prolonged ictal amnesia with transient focal abnormalities on magnetic resonance imaging. *Epilepsia* 33:1042–1046.

Lee, H. B., C. G. Lyketsos. 2003. Depression in Alzheimer's disease: heterogeneity and related issues. *Biol Psychiatry* 54:353–362.

Lee, S. S., K. Wild, C. Hollnagel, J. Grafman. 1999. Selective visual attention in patients with frontal lobe lesions or Parkinson's disease. *Neuropsychologia* 37:595–604.

Lemiere, J., M. Decruyenaere, G. Evers-Kiebooms, et al. 2002. Longitudinal study evaluating neuropsychological changes in so-called asymptomatic carriers of the Huntington's disease mutation after 1 year. *Acta Neurol Scand* 106:131–141.

Lendt, M., C. Helmstaedter, C. E. Elger. 1999. Pre- and postoperative neuropsychological profiles in children and adolescents with temporal lobe epilepsy. *Epilepsia* 40:1543–1550.

León-Carrión, J. 1997. *Neuropsychological Rehabilitation, Fundamentals, Directions and Innovations.* Delray Beach, Fla., St. Lucie Press.

León-Carrión, J. 2005. Rehabilitation of cognitive disorders after acquired brain injury: The Combined Method (TCM). In: *Brain Injury Treatment: Theories and Practices,* J. León-Carrión, G. A. Zitney, K. von Wild, eds. London, Psychology Press (in press).

León-Carrión, J., J. M. Dominguez-Roldan, F. Murillo-Cabezas, et al. 2000. The role of citicholine in neuropsychological training after traumatic brain injury. *Neurorehabilitation* 14:33–40.

Leplow, B., C. Dierks. 1997. Diagnostik des Altgedächtnisses mit derendgültigen Lang- und Kurzform des "Kieler Altgedächtistests." *Diagnostica* 43:193–209.

Leplow, B., C. H. Dierks, M. Lehnung et al. 1997. Remote memory in patients with acute brain injuries. *Neuropsychologia* 35:881–892.

Leritz, E., J. Brandt, M. Minor. 2002. Neuropsychological functioning and its relationship to antiphospholipid antibodies in patients with systemic lupus erythematosus. *J Clin Exp Neuropsychol* 24:527–533.

Levin, H. S. 1989. Memory deficit after closed head injury. In: *Handbook of Neuropsychology,* Vol. 3, F. Boller, J. Grafman, eds. Elsevier, Amsterdam, 1989, pp. 183–207.

Levin, H. S., A. L. Benton, R. G. Grossman. 1982. *Neurobehavioral Consequences of Closed Head Injury.* New York, Oxford University Press.

Levin, H. S., W. M. High, C. A. Meyers, et al. 1985. Impairment of retrograde memory after closed head injury. *J Neurol Neurosurg Psychiatry* 48:556–563.

Levin, H. S., C. A. Meyers, R. G. Grossman, M. Sarwar. 1981. Ventricular enlargement after closed head injury. *Arch Neurol* 38:623–629.

Levin, H. S., V. M. O'Donnell, R. G. Grossman. 1979. The Galveston Orientation and Amnesia Test. *J Nerv Ment Dis* 167:67–684.

Levin, H. S., D. Williams, M. J. Crofford, et al. 1988. Relationship of depth of brain lesions to consciousness and outcome after closed head injury. *J Neurosurg* 69:861–866.

Levin, H., D. H. Williams, H. M. Eisenberg, et al. 1992. Serial MRI and neurobehavioural findings after mild to moderate head injury. *J Neurol Neurosurg Psychiatry* 55:255–262.

Levine, B., S. E. Black, R. Cabeza, et al. 1998. Episodic memory and the self in a case of isolated retrograde amnesia. *Brain* 121:1951–1973.

Levine, B., E. Svoboda, J. F. Hay, et al. 2002. Aging and autobiographical memory: Dissociating episodic from semantic retrieval. *Psychol Aging* 17:677–689.

Lewis, D. O., C. A. Yeager. 1996. Dissociative identity disorder/multiple personality disorder. In: *Child and Adolescent Psychiatry: A Comprehensive Textbook,* 2nd ed., M. Lewis, ed. Baltimore, Lippincott Williams & Wilkins, pp. 702–716.

Lewis, P., N. F. Kopelman. 1998. Forgetting rates in neuropsychiatric disorders. *J Neurol Neurosurg Psychiatry* 65:890–898.

Lewis, P. R., C. C. D. Shute. 1967. The cholinergic limbic system: Projections of the hippocampal formation, medial cortex, nuclei of the ascending cholinergic reticular system, and the subfornical organ and supra-optic crest. *Brain* 90:521–540.

Lezak, M. D. 1983. *Neuropsychological Assessment,* 2nd ed. New York, Oxford University Press.

Lezak, M. D. 1995. *Neuropsychological Assessment.* Oxford, Oxford University Press.

Li, Y., J. S. Meyer, J. Thornby. 2001. Depressive symptoms among cognitively normal versus cognitively impaired elderly subjects. *Int J Geriatr Psychiatry* 16:455–461.

Li, S. C., F. Schmiedek. 2002. Age is not necessarily aging: Another step towards understanding the "clocks" that time aging. *Gerontology* 48:5–12.

Lim, A., D. Tsuang, W. Kukull, et al. 1999. Clinico-neuropathological correlation of Alzheimer's disease in a community-based case series. *J Am Geriatr Soc* 47(5):564–569.

Lindqvist, G., G. Norlen. 1966. Korsakoff's syndrome after operation on ruptured aneurysm of the anterior communicating artery. *Acta Psychiatr Scand* 42:24–34.

Lindsay, J., D. Laurin, R. Verreault, et al. 2002. Risk factors for Alzheimer's disease: A prospective analysis from the Canadian Study of Health and Aging. *Am J Epidemiol* 156(5):445–453.

Linn, R. T., P. A. Wolf, D. L. Bachman, et al. 1995. The "preclinical phase" of probable Alzheimer's Disease. *Arch Neurol* 52:485–490.

Lisak, R. P., R. A. Zimmerman. 1977. Transient global amnesia due to a dominant hemisphere tumor. *Arch Neurol* 34:317–318.

Lisanby, S. H., J. H. Maddox, J. Prudic, et al. 2000. The effects of electroconvulsive therapy on memory of autobiographical and public events. *Arch Gen Psychiatry* 57:581–590.

Lishman, W. A. 1988. Physiogenesis and psychogenesis in the "post-concussional syndrome." *Br J Psychol* 153:460–469.

Litvan, I. 2001. Therapy and management of frontal lobe dementia patients. *Neurology* 56(11 Suppl 4):S41–5.

Litvan, I., Y. Agid, J. Jankovic, et al. 1996. Accuracy of clinical criteria for the diagnosis of progressive supranuclear palsy. *Neurology* 46:922–930.

Litvan, I., A. Sirigu, J. Toothman, J. Grafman. 1995. What can preservation of autobiographic memory after muscarinic blockade tell us about the scopolamine model of dementia? *Neurology* 45(2):387–389.

Locascio, J. J., J. H. Crowdon, S. Corkin. 1995. Cognitive test performance in detecting staging, and tracking Alzheimer's disease. *Arch Neurol* 52:1987–1099.

Loewenstein, R. J. 1991. Rational psychopharmacology in the treatment of multiple personality disorder. *Psychiatr Clin North Am* 14:721–740.

Loewenstein, R. J., D. R. Ross. 1992. Multiple personality and psychoanalysis: An introduction. *Psychoanalytic Inquiry* 12:3–48.

Lopez, O. L., W. J. Jagust, S. T. DeKosky, et al. 2003a. Prevalence and classification of mild cognitive impairment in the Cardiovascular Health Study Cognition Study: Part 1. *Arch Neurol* 60: 1385–1389.

Lopez, O. L., L. H. Kuller, A. Fitzpatrick, et al. 2003b. Evaluation of dementia in the cardiovascular health cognition study. *Neuroepidemiology* 22:1–12.

Loring, D. W., G. P. Lee, K. J. Meador, et al. 1991. Hippocampal contribution to verbal recent memory following dominant hemisphere temporal lobectomy. *J Clin Exp Neuropsychol* 13:575–586.

Lou, H. O. C. 1968. Repeated episodes of transient global amnesia. *Acta Neurol Scand* 44:612–617.

Lowy, M. T., L. Gault, B. K. Yamamoto. 1993. Adrenalectomy attenuates stress-induced elevations in extracellular glutamate concentrations in the hippocampus. *J Neurochem* 61:1957–1960.

Luciana, M., E. D. Burgund, M. Berman, K. L. Hanson. 2001. Effects of tryptophan loading on verbal, spatial and affective working memory functions in healthy adults. *J Psychopharmacol* 15(4):219–230.

Ludwig, A. M., J. M. Brandsma, C. B. Wilbur, et al. 1972. The objective study of a multiple personality. *Arch Gen Psychiatry* 26:298–310.

Luis, C. A., D. A. Loewenstein, A. Acevedo, et al. 2003. Mild cognitive impairment: Directions for future research. *Neurology* 61:438–444.

Lupien, S. J., M. Lepage. 2001. Stress, memory, and the hippocampus: Can't live with it, can't live without it. *Behav Brain Res* 127(1–2):137–158.

Lyketsos, C. G., J. Olin. 2002. Depression in Alzheimer's disease: Overview and treatment. *Biol Psychiatry* 52:243–252.

Lyketsos, C. G., M. Steinberg, J. Tschantz, et al. 2000. Mental and behavioral disturbances in dementia: Findings from the Cache County Study on Memory in Aging. *Am J Psychiatry* 157:708–714.

Lyketsos, C. G., O. Lopez, B. Jones, et al. 2002. Prevalence of neuropsychiatric symptoms in dementia and mild cognitive impairment: Results from the Cardiovascular Health Study. *JAMA* 288:1475–1483.

Mabbott, D. J., M. L. Smith. 2003. Memory in children with temporal or extra temporal excisions. *Neuropsychologia* 41:995–1007.

Magarinos, A. M., B. S. McEwen, G. Flugge, E. Fuchs. 1996. Chronic psychosocial stress causes apical dendritic atrophy of hippocampal CA3 pyramidal neurons in subordinate tree shrews. *J Neurosci* 16:3534–3540.

Maher, E. R., A. J. Lees. 1986. The clinical features and natural history of the Steele-Richardson-Olszewski syndrome (progressive supranuclear palsy). *Neurology* 36(7):1005–1008.

Maheu, F. S., R. Joober, S. Beaulieu, S. J. Lupien. 2004. Differential effects of adrenergic and corticosteroid hormonal systems on human short- and long-term declarative memory for emotionally arousing material. *Behav Neurosci* 118(2):420–428.

Mair, W. G. P., E. K. Warrington, L. Weiskrantz. 1979. Memory disorder in Korsakoff's psychosis: A neuropathological and neuropsychological investigation of two cases. *Brain* 102:749–783.

Maki, P. M., D. S. Knopman. 1996. Limitations of the distinction between conceptual and perceptual implicit memory: A study of Alzheimer's disease. *Neuropsychology* 10:464–474.

Malamut, B. L., N. Graff-Radford, J. Chawluk, et al. 1992. Memory in a case of bilateral thalamic infarction. *Neurology* 42:163–169.

Manes, F., J. R. Hodges, K. S. Graham, A. Zeman. 2001. Focal autobiographical amnesia in association with transient epileptic amnesia. *Brain* 124:4999–4509.

Mangels, J. A., F. I. M. Craik, B. Levine, et al. 2002. Effects of divided attention on episodic memory in chronic traumatic brain injury: A function of severity and strategy. *Neuropsychologia* 40:2369–2385.

Mann, D. M., P. W. South. 1993. The topographic distribution of brain atrophy in frontal lobe dementia. *Acta Neuropathol (Berlin)* 85(3):334–340.

Manns, J. R., R. O. Hopkins, J. M. Reed, et al. 2003. Recognition memory and the human hippocampus. *Neuron* 37(1):171–180.

Manns, J. R., R. O. Hopkins, L. R. Squire. 2003. Semantic memory and the human hippocampus. *Neuron* 38(1):127–133.

Marcantonio, E. R., S. E. Simon, M. A. Bergmann, et al. 2003. Delirium symptoms in post-acute care are prevalent, persistent, and associated with poor functional recovery. *J Am Geriatr Soc* 51:4–9.

Marder, K., M. X. Tang, L. Cote, et al. 1995. The frequency and associated risk factors for dementia in patients with Parkinson's disease. *Arch Neurol* 52(7):695–701.

Markowitsch, H. J. 1992. The neuropsychology of hanging: An historical perspective. *J Neurol Neurosurg Psychiatry* 55(6):507.

Markowitsch, H. J. 1995a. Anatomical basis of memory disorders. In: *The Cognitive Neurosciences*, M. S. Gazzaniga, ed. Cambridge, Mass., MIT Press, pp. 665–679.

Markowitsch, H. J. 1995b. Which brain regions are critically involved in the retrieval of old episodic memory? [Review]. *Brain Res Rev* 21:117–127.

Markowitsch, H. J. 1996. Organic and psychogenic retrograde amnesia: Two sides of the same coin? *Neurocase* 2:357–371.

Markowitsch, H. J. 1998. Cognitive neuroscience of memory. *Neurocase* 4:429–435.

Markowitsch, H. J. 1999a. Functional neuroimaging correlates of functional amnesia. *Memory* 7:561–583.

Markowitsch, H. J. 1999b. Neuroimaging and mechanisms of brain function in psychiatric disorders. *Curr Opin Psychiatry* 12:331–337.

Markowitsch, H. J. 2000. Functional amnesia: The mnestic block syndrome. *Revue de Neuropsychologie* 10:175–198.

Markowitsch, H. J. 2002. Functional retrograde amnesia-mnestic block syndrome. *Cortex* 38:651–654.

Markowitsch, H. J. 2003. Psychogenic amnesia. *Neuroimage* 20(Suppl 1):S132–S138.

Markowitsch, H. J., P. Calabrese, M. Wurker, et al. 1994. The amygdala's contribution to memory—a study on two patients with Urbach-Wiethe disease. *Neuroreport* 5:1349–1352.

Markowitsch, H. J., P. Calabrese, H. Neufeld, et al. 1999. Retrograde amnesia for world knowledge and preserved memory for autobiographic events. A case report. *Cortex* 35:243–252.

Markowitsch, H. J., P. Calabrese, J. Liess, et al. 1993a. Retrograde amnesia after traumatic injury of the fronto-temporal cortex. *J Neurol Neurosurg Psychiatry* 56:988–992.

Markowitsch, H. J., D. Emmans, E. Irle, et al. 1985. Cortical and subcortical afferent connections of the primate's temporal pole: A study of rhesus monkeys, squirrel monkeys, and marmosets. *J Comp Neurol* 242(3):425–458.

Markowitsch, H. J., G. R. Fink, A. Thöne, et al. 1997. A PET study of persistent psychogenic amnesia covering the whole life span. *Cogn Neuropsychiat* 2:135–158.

Markowitsch, H. J., J. Kessler, M. Streicher. 1985. Consequences of serial cortical, hippocampal, and thalamic lesions and of different lengths of overtraining on the acquisition and retention of learning tasks. *Behav Neurosci* 99:233–256.

Markowitsch, H. J., D. Y. von Cramon, E. Hofmann, et al. 1990. Verbal memory deterioration after unilateral infarct of the internal capsule in an adolescent. *Cortex* 26, 597–609.

Markowitsch, H. J., D. Y. von Cramon, U. Schuri. 1993b. Mnestic performance profile of a bilateral diencephalic infarct patient with preserved intelligence and severe amnestic disturbances. *J Clin Exp Neuropsychol* 15:627–652.

Markowitsch, H. J., G. Weber-Luxemburger, K. Ewald, et al. 1997b. Patients with heart attacks are not valid models for medial temporal lobe amnesia. A neuropsychological and FDG-PET study with consequences for memory research. *Eur J Neurology* 4:178–184.

Marr, D. 1971. Simple memory: A theory for archicortex. *Philos Trans R Soc Lond B Biol Sci* 1262(841):23–81.

Marti, M. J., E. Tolosa, J. 2003. Campdelacreu. Clinical overview of the synucleinopathies. *Mov Disord* 18(Suppl 6):S21–27.

Martin, N., E. M. Saffran, G. S. Dell. 1996. Recovery in deep dysphasia: Evidence for a relation between auditory - verbal STM capacity and lexical errors in repetition. *Brain Lang* 52(1):83–113.

Martin, R. C., D. W. Loring, K. J. Meador, et al. 1991. Impaired long-term retention despite normal verbal learning in patients with temporal lobe dysfunction. *Neuropsychology* 5:3–12.

Martone, M., N. Butters, D. Trauner. 1986. Some analyses of forgetting pictorial material in amnesic and demented patients. *J Clin Exp Neuropsychol* 8:161–178.

Masur, D. M., M. Sliwinski, R. B. Lipton, et al. 1994. Neuropsychological prediction of dementia and the absence of dementia in healthy elderly persons. *Neurology* 44:1427–1432.

Mateer, C. A., M. M. Sohlberg, J. Crinean. 1987. Focus on clinical research: Perceptions of memory function in individuals with closed-head injury. *J Head Trauma Rehabil* 2:74–84.

Mathew, N. T., F. Hrastnik, J.S. Meyer. 1976. Regional cerebral blood flow in the diagnosis of vascular headache. *Headache* 15:252–260.

Matias-Guiu, J., R. Colomer, A. Segura, A. Codina. 1986. Cranial CT Scan in transient global amnesia. *Acta Neurol Scand* 73:298–301.

Mattay, V. S., J. H. Callicott, A. Bertolino, et al. 2000. Effects of dextroamphetamine on cognitive performance and cortical activation. *Neuroimage* 12:268–275.

Mattioli, F., F. Grassi, D. Perani, et al. 1996. Persistent post-traumatic retrograde amnesia: A neuropsychological and (18)FDG PET study. *Cortex* 32:121–129.

Mattis, S. 1988. *Dementia Rating Scale (DRS)*. Odessa, Fla., Psychological Assessment Resources.

Mavaddat, N., P. J. Kirkpatrick, R. D. Rogers, B. J. Sahakian. 2000. Deficits in decision-making in patients with aneurysms of the anterior communicating artery. *Brain* 123(10):2109–2117.

Mayes, A. R., I. Daum, H. J. Markowisch, B. Sauter. 1997. The relationship between retrograde and anterograde amnesia in patients with typical global amnesia. *Cortex* 33(2):197–217.

Mayes, A. R., J. S. Holdstock, C. L. Isaac, et al. 2002. Relative sparing of item recognition memory in a patient with adult-onset damage limited to the hippocampus. *Hippocampus* 12:325–340.

Mayes, A. R., P. R. Meudell, D. Mann, A. Pickering. 1988. Location of lesions in Korsakoff's syndrome: Neuropsychological and neuropathological data on two patients. *Cortex* 24:367–388.

Mayes, A. R., N. Roberts. 2001. Theories of episodic memory. *Philos Trans R Soc Lond B Sci* 356:1395–1408.

Mayeux, R., J. Denaro, N. Hemenegildo, et al. 1992. A population-based investigation of Parkinson's disease with and without dementia. Relationship to age and gender. *Arch Neurol* 49:492–497.

Mayou, R., J. Black, B. Bryant. 2000. Unconsciousness, amnesia and psychiatric symptoms following road traffic accident injury. *Br J Psychiatry* 177:540–545.

Mazzucchi, A., G. Moretti, P. Caffarra, M. Parma. 1980. Neuropsychological functions in the follow-up of transient global amnesia. *Brain* 103:161–178.

McAllister, T. W., R. B. Ferell. 2002. Evaluation and treatment of psychosis after traumatic brain injury. *NeuroRehabilitation* 17:357–368.

McAndrews, M. P., B. Milner. 1991. The frontal cortex and memory for temporal order. *Neuropsychologia* 29:849–859.

McCarthy, R. A., E. K. Warrington. 1994. Disorders of semantic memory. *Philos Trans R Soc Lond B Biol Sci* 346(1315):89–96.

McCarthy, R., E. K. Warrington. 1986. Phonological reading: Phenomena and paradoxes. *Cortex* 22:359–380.

McClelland, J. L., B. L. McNaughton, R. C. O'Reilly. 1995. Why are there complementary learning systems in the hippocampus and neocortex: Insights from the successes and failures of connectionist models of learning and memory. *Psychol Rev* 102:419–437.

McCusker, J., M. Cole, N. Dendukuri, et al. 2003. The course of delirium in older medical inpatients: A prospective study. *J Gen Intern Med* 18:696–704.

McEwen, B. S. 1999. Stress and hippocampal plasticity. *Ann Rev Neurosci* 22:105–122.

McEwen, B. S., R. M. Sapolsky. 1995. Stress and Cognitive function. *Curr Opin Neurobiol* 5(2):205–216.

McFadden, I. J., V. F. Woitalla. 1993. Differing reports of pain perception by different personalities in a patient with chronic pain and multiple personality disorder. *Pain* 55:379–382.

McGaugh, J. L. 2004. The amygdala modulates the consolidation of memories of emotionally arousing experiences. *Ann Rev Neurosci* 27:1–28.

McGaugh, J. L., L. Cahill, B. Roozendaal. 1996. Involvement of the amygdala in memory storage: interaction with other brain systems. *Proc Natl Aca Sci U S A* 93: 13508–13514.

McKee, R. D., L. R. Squire. 1992. Both hippocampal and diencephalic amnesia result in normal forgetting for complex visual material. *J Clin Exp Neuropsychol* 14:103.

McKeith, I. G., C. G. Ballard, R. H. Perry, et al. 2000. Prospective validation of consensus criteria for the diagnosis of dementia with Lewy bodies. *Neurology* 54(5):1050–1058.

McKeith, I., J. Mintzer, D. Aarsland, et al. 2004. Dementia with Lewy bodies. *Lancet Neurol* 3:19–28.

McKhann, G., D. Drachman, M. Folstein, et al. 1984. Clinical diagnosis of Alzheimer's disease: report of the NINCDS-ADRDA Work Group under the auspices of Department of Health and Human Services Task Force on Alzheimer's Disease. *Neurology* 34(7):939–944.

McKittrick, C. R., B. S. McEwen. 1996. Regulation of seritonergic function in the CNS by steroid hormones and stress. In: *CNS Neurotransmitters and Neuromodulators: Neuroactive Steroids*, T. W. Stone, ed. Boca Raton, Fla., CRC Press, pp. 37–76.

McMillan, T. J., G. E. Powell, I. Janota, C. E. Polkey. 1987. Relationships between neuropathology and cognitive functioning in temporal lobectomy patients. *J Neurol Neurosurg Psychiatry* 50:167–176.

Meador, K. J., R. J. Adams, H. F. Flanigan. 1985. Transient global amnesia and meningioma. *Neurology* 35:769–771.

Meiran, N., M. Jelicic. 1995. Implicit memory in Alzheimer's disease: A meta-analysis. *Neuropsychology* 9:291–303.

Meletti, S., F. Benuzzi, P. Nichelli, C. A. Tassinaria. 2003. Damage to the right hippocampal-amygdala formation during early infancy and recognition of fearful faces: Neuropsychological and fMRI evidence in subjects with temporal lobe epilepsy. *Ann N Y Acad Sci* 1000:385–388.

Melo, T. P. 1994. Are brief or recurrent transient global amnesias of epileptic origin? *J Neurol Neurosurg Psychiatry* 57:622–625.

Melo, T. P., J. M. Ferro, H. Ferro. 1992. Transient global amnesia: A case control study. *Brain* 115:261–270.

Meltzer, C. C., M. N. Cantwell, P. J. Greer, et al. 2000. Does cerebral blood flow decline in healthy aging? A PET study with partial-volume correction. *J Nucl Med* 41:1842–1848.

Meltzer, C. C., J. K. Zubieta, J. Brandt, et al. 1996. Regional hypometabolism in Alzheimer's disease as measured by positron emission tomography after correction for effects of partial volume. *Neurology* 47:461–465.

Mendes, M. H. 2002. Transient epileptic amnesia – an under diagnosed phenomenon? Three more cases. *Seizure* 11:238–242.

Mendez, M. F., J. L. Cummings. 2003. Alzheimer's disease. In: *Dementia: A Clinical Approach*, 3rd ed. Philadelphia, Butterworth-Heinemann.

Merleau-Ponty, M. 1945. Phenomenologie de la Perception. Paris, Librairie Gallimond.

Merskey, H., J. M. Woodforde. 1972. Psychiatric sequelae of minor head injury. *Brain* 92:521–528.

Messer, W. S., Jr. 2002. Cholinergic agonists and the treatment of Alzheimer's disease. *Curr Top Med Chem* 2:53–58.

Mesulam, M. M. 2000. *Principles of Behavioral and Cognitive Neurology*. New York, Oxford University Press.

Mesulam , M. M., M. Grossman, A. Hillis, et al. 2003. The core and halo of primary progressive aphasia and semantic dementia. *Ann Neurol* 54(Suppl 5):S11–S14.

Mesulam, M. M., E. J. Mufson, E. J. Levey, B. H. Wainer. 1983. Cholinergic innervation of the cortex by the basal forebrain: cytochemistry and cortical connections of the septal area, diagonal band nuclei, nucleus basalis (substantia innominata) and hypothalamus in the rhesus monkey. *J Comp Neurol* 214:170–197.

Meudell, P. R., A. R. Mayes, A. Ostergaard, A. Pickering. 1985. Recency and frequency judgements in alcoholic amnesics and normal people with poor memory. *Cortex* 21:487–511.

Meyer, J. S., K. L. McClintic, R. L. Rogers, et al. 1988. Aetiological considerations and risk factors for multi-infarct dementia. *J Neurol Neurosurg Psychiatry* 51(12): 1489–1497.

Meyer, J. S., G. Rauch, R. A. Rauch, A. Haque. 2000. Risk factors for cerebral hypoperfusion, mild cognitive impairment, and dementia. *Neurobiol Aging* 21:161–169.

Meyers, J., K. Meyers. 1995. *The Meyers Scoring System for the Rey Complex Figure and the Recognition Trial*. Odessa, Fla., Psychological Assessment Resources.

Micelli, G., C. Silveri, U. Noncentinii, A. Caramazza. 1988. Patterns of dissociation in comprehension and production of nouns and verbs. *Aphasiology* 2:351–358.

Micelli, G., C. Silveri, G. Villa, A. Caramazza. 1984. On the basis for the agrammatic's difficulty in producing main verbs. *Cortex* 20:207–220.

Miller, B. L., J. Diehl, M.Freedman, et al. 2003. International approaches to frontotemporal dementia diagnosis: From social cognition to neuropsychology. *Ann Neurol* 54(Suppl 5):S7–S10.

Miller, E. 1979. The long-term consequences of head injury: A discussion of the evidence with special reference to the preparation of legal reports. *Br J Soc Clin Psychol* 18:87–98.

Miller, E. K., J. D. Cohen. 2001. An integrative theory of prefrontal cortex function. *Ann Rev Neurosci* 24:167–202.

Miller, G. A. 1956. The magical number seven, plus or minus two: Some limits in our capacity for processing information. *Psycholog Rev* 63:81–97.

Miller, J. W., R. C. Petersen, E. J. Metter, et al. 1987a. Transient global amnesia: Clinical characteristics and prognosis. *Neurology* 37:733–737.

Miller, J. W., T. Yanagihara, R. C. Petersen, D. W. Klass. 1987b. Transient global amnesia and epilepsy: Electroencephalographic distinction. *Arch Neurol* 44: 629–633.

Miller, L. A., D. Caine, A. Harding, et al. 2001. Right medial thalamic lesion causes isolated retrograde amnesia. *Neuropsychologia* 39:1037–1046.

Miller, P., D. Bramble, N. Buxton. 1997. Case study: Ganser syndrome in children and adolescents. *J Am Acad Child Adolesc Psychiatry* 36(1):112–115.

Miller, S. D., P. J. Triggiano. 1992. The psychophysiological investigation of multiple personality disorder: Review and update. *Am J Clin Hypn* 35:47–61.

Milner, B., S. Corkin, H. L. Teuber. 1968. Further analysis of the hippocampal amnesic syndrome-14-year follow-up study of HM. *Neuropsychologia* 6:215–234.

Modestin, J., G. Ebner, M. Junghan, T. Erni. 1996. Dissociative experiences and dissociative disorders in acute psychiatric inpatients. *Comp Psychiatry* 37:74–84.

Monastero, R., P. Bettini, E. Del Zotto, et al. 2001. Prevalence and pattern of cognitive impairment in systemic lupus erythematosus patients with and without overt neuropsychiatric manifestations. *J Neurolog Sci* 184:33–39.

Morrell, F. 1980. Memory loss as a Todd's paralysis. *Epilepsia* 21:185.

Morris, J. C. 1993. The Clinical Dementia Rating (CDR): Current version and scoring rules. *Neurology* 43:2412–2414.

Morris, J. C., M. Storandt, J. P. Miller, et al. 2001. Mild cognitive impairment represents early-stage Alzheimer disease. *Arch Neurol* 58:397–405.

Morris, M. K., D. Bowers, A. Chatterjee, K. M. Heilman. 1992. Amnesia following a discrete basal forebrain lesion. *Brain* 115(6):1827–1847.

Morrison, J. H., P. R. Hof. 1997. Life and death of neurons in the aging brain. *Science* 278:412–419.

Moscovitch, M. 1982. Multiple dissociations of function in amnesia. In: *Human Memory and Amnesia*, L. S. Cermak, ed. Hillsdale, N.J., Lawrence Erlbaum, pp. 337–370.

Moscovitch, M. 1995. Recovered consciousness: A hypothesis concerning modularity and episodic memory. *J Clin Exp Neuropsychol* 17: 276–290.

Moscovitch, M., E. Vriezen, Y. Goshen-Gottstein. 1993. Implicit tests of memory in patients with focal lesions or degenerative brain disorders. In: *Handbook of Neuropsychology*, Vol. 8, F. Boller, J. Grafman, eds. Amsterdam, Elsevier Science Publishers, pp. 133–173.

Moulin, C. J., N. James, J. E. Freeman, R. W. Jones. 2004. Deficient acquisition and consolidation: Intertrial free recall performance in Alzheimer's disease and mild cognitive impairment. *J Clin Exp Neuropsychol* 26:1–10.

Mueller, E. A., M. M. Moore, D. C. Kerr, et al. 1998. Brain volume preserved in healthy elderly through the eleventh decade. *Neurology* 51:1555–1562.

Muller, G. E., A. Pilzecker. 1900. Experimentelle Beitrage zur Lehre vom Gedachtnis. *Z Psychol Erganzungsband* 1:1–300.

Mumenthaler, M., T. Treig. 1984. Amnestic episodes. Analysis of 111 personal cases. *Schweiz Med Wochenschr* 114(34):1163–1170.

Mummery, C. J., K. Patterson, C. J. Price, et al. 2000. A voxel based morphomentry study of semantic dementia: The relation of temporal lobe atrophy to cognitive deficit. *Ann Neurol* 47:36–45.

Mungas, D., W. J. Jagust, B. R. Reed, et al. 2001. MRI predictors of cognition in subcortical ischemic vascular disease and Alzheimer's disease. *Neurology* 57(12): 2229–2235.

Murphy, C. 1999. Loss of olfactory function in dementing disease. *Physiol Behav* 66:177–182.

Murphy, C., A. W. Bacon, M. W. Bondi, D. P. Salmon. 1998. Apolipoprotein E status is associated with odor identification deficits in nondemented older persons. *Ann N Y Acad Sci* 855:744–750.

Murphy, D. G., C. DeCarli, A. R. McIntosh, et al. 1996. Sex differences in human brain morphometry and metabolism: An *in vivo* quantitative magnetic resonance imaging and positron emission tomography study on the effect of aging. *Arch Gen Psychiatry* 53:585–594.

Murphy, D. G. M., C. DeCarli, M. B. Schapiro, et al. 1992. Age-related differences in volumes of subcortical nuclei, brain matter, and cerebrospinal fluid in healthy men as measured with magnetic resonance imaging. *Arch Neurol* 49:839–845.

Murre, J. M. 1997. Implicit and explicit memory in amnesia: Some explanations and predictions by the TraceLink model. *Memory* 5:213–232.

Nadel, L., M. Moscovitch. 1997. Memory consolidation, retrograde amnesia and the hippocampal complex. *Curr Opin Neurobiol* 2:217–227.

Nath, U., Y. Ben-Shlomo, R. G. Thomson, et al. 2001. The prevalence of progressive supranuclear palsy (Steele-Richardson-Olszewski syndrome) in the UK. *Brain* 124(Pt 7):1438–1449.

Nath, U., Y. Ben-Shlomo, R. G. Thomson, et al. 2003. Clinical features and natural history of progressive supranuclear palsy: A clinical cohort study. *Neurology* 60:910–916.

National Institutes of Health. 1985. *Electroconvulsive therapy: Consensus statement online*. Available at http://consensus.nih.gov/cons/051-statement.htm.

Naveh-Benjamin, M. 2000. Adult age differences in memory performance: Tests of an associative deficit hypothesis. *J Exp Psychol Learn Mem and Cogn* 26: 1170–1187.

Neary, D., J. S. Snowden, L. Gustafson, et al. 1998. Frontotemporal lobar degeneration: A consensus on clinical diagnostic criteria. *Neurology* 51:1546–1554.

Neary, D., J. S. Snowden, D. M. Mann, et al. 1990. Frontal lobe dementia and motor neuron disease. *J Neurol Neurosurg Psychiatry* 53(1):23–32.

Nebes, R. D. 1989. Semantic memory in Alzheimer's disease. *Psychol Bull* 106:377–394.

Nelson, H. E. 1982. *The National Adult Reading Test*. Windsor: NFER-Nelson.

Nemiah, J. C. 1989. Dissociative disorders (hysterical neurosis, dissociative type). In: *Comprehensive Textbook of Psychiatry*, 5th ed., H. Caplan, B. Saddock, eds. Baltimore, Lippincott Williams & Wilkins, pp. 1028–1044.

Newman, A. B., A. M. Arnold, B. L. Naydeck, et al. 2003. "Successful aging": Effect of subclinical cardiovascular disease. *Arch Internal Med* 163:2315–2322.

Newton, M., S. Berkovic, M. Austin, et al. 1992. Postictal switch in blood flow distribution and temporal lobe seizures. *J Neurol Neurosurg Psychiatry* 55:891–894.

Ng, C., I. Schweitzer, P. Alexopoulos, et al. 2000. Efficacy and cognitive effects of right unilateral electroconvulsive therapy. *J ECT* 16:370–379.

Nielson, J. M. 1946. *Agnosia, Apraxia, Aphasia: Their Value in Cerebral Localization*, 2nd ed. New York, Hoeber.

Nissen, M. J., P. T. Bullemer. 1987. Attentional requirements for learning: Evidence from performance measures. *Cogn Psychol* 19:1–31.

Nissley, H. M., M. Schmitter-Edgecombe. 2002. Perceptually based implicit learning in severe closed-head injury patients. *Neuropsychology* 16:111–122.

Nobler, M. S., M. A. Oquendo, L. S. Kegeles, et al. 2001. Decreased regional brain metabolism after ECT. *Am J Psychiatry* 158:305–308.

Nobler, M. S., H. A. Sackeim, J. Prohovnik, et al. 1994. Regional cerebral blood flow in mood disorders, III. Treatment and clinical response. *Arch Gen Psychiatry* 51:884–897.

Nordin, S., C. Murphy. 1996. Impaired sensory and cognitive olfactory function in questionable Alzheimer's disease. *Neuropsychology* 10:113–119.

Norman, K., D. L. Schacter. 1997. False recognition in younger and older adults: Exploring the characteristics of illusory memories. *Mem Cogn* 25:838–848.

Norris, J. W., V. C. Hachinski, P. W. Cooper. 1975. Changes in cerebral blood flow during a migraine attack. *Br Med J* 20:676–684.

Noyes, R. Jr., S. Kuperman, S. B. Olson. 1987. Desipramine: A possible treatment for depersonalization disorders. *Can J Psychiatry* 32:782–784.

O'Brien, J. T., T. Erkinjuntti, B. Reisberg, et al. 2003. Vascular cognitive impairment. *Lancet Neurol* 2:89–98.

Oberauer, K. 2001. Removing irrelevant information from working memory: A cognitive aging study with the modified Sternberg task. *J Exp Psychology: Learn Mem Cogn* 27:948–957.

O'Connor, M. G., M. Verfaellie, L. S. Cermak. 1995. The clinical differentiation of amnesic subtypes. In: *Handbook of Memory Disorders*, A. Baddeley, B. Wilson, F. Watts eds. Sussex, England, John Wiley & Sons, pp. 53–80.

O'Hanlon, J. F., H. W. Robbe, A. Vermeeren, et al. 1998. Venlafaxine's effects on healthy volunteers' driving, psychomotor, and vigilance performance during 15-day fixed and incremental dosing regimens. *J Clin Psychopharmacol* 18(3):212–221.

Ohara, K., N. Kondo. 1998. Changes of monoamines in post-mortem brains from patients with diffuse Lewy body disease. *Prog Neuropsychopharmacol Biol Psychiatry* 22(2):311–317.

Olesen, J., M. B. Jorgensen. 1986. Leào's spreading depression in the hippocampus explains transient global amnesia. *Acta Neurol Scand* 73:219–220.

Olson, I. R., J. X. Zhang, K. J. Mitchell, et al. 2004. Preserved spatial memory over brief intervals in older adults. *Psychol Aging* 19:310–317.

Ommaya, A. K. 1984. Biomechanics of head injury: Experimental aspects. In: *Biomechanics of Trauma*, A. Naham, ed. New York, Appleton-Century.

Ommaya, A. K., T. A. Gennarelli. 1974. Cerebral concussion and traumatic unconsciousness: Correlation of experimental and clinical observations on blunt head injuries. *Brain* 97:633–654.

Ostbye, T., G. Hill, R. Steenhuis. 1999. Mortality in elderly Canadians with and without dementia: a 5-year follow-up. *Neurology* 53(3):521–526.

Ott, A., M. M. Breteler, F. van Harskamp, et al. 1995. Prevalence of Alzheimer's disease and vascular dementia: Association with education. The Rotterdam study. *BMJ* 310(6985):970–973.

Owen, A. M., J. Doyon, A. Dagher, et al. 1998. Abnormal basal ganglia outflow in Parkinson's disease identified with PET. Implications for higher cortical functions. *Brain* 121(Pt 5):949–965.

Owen, A. M., B. J. Sahakian, J. Semple, et al. 1995. Visuo-spatial short-term recognition memory and learning after temporal lobe excisions, frontal lobe excisions or amygdalo-hippocampectomy in man. *Neuropsychologia* 33:1–24.

Oxbury, J. M., S. M. Oxbury. 1989. Neuropsychology, memory, and hippocampal pathology. In: *The Bridge between Neurology and Psychiatry*, E. H. Reynolds, M. R. Trimble, eds. Edinburgh, Churchill Livingstone, pp. 135–151.

Pakkenberg, B., H. J. G. Gundersen. 1997. Neocortical neuron number in humans: Effect of sex and age. *J Comp Neurol* 384:312–320.

Palmer, K., L. Backman, B. Winblad, L. Fratiglioni. 2003. Detection of Alzheimer's disease and dementia in the preclinical phase: Population based cohort study. *Br Med J* 326:245.

Palmese, C. A., S. A. Raskin. 2000. The rehabilitation of attention in individuals with mild traumatic brain injury, using the APT-II programme. *Brain Inj* 14:535–548.

Palmini, A. L., P. Gloor, M. Jones-Gotman. 1992. Pure amnestic seizures in temporal lobe epilepsy. Definition, clinical symptomatology and functional anatomical considerations. *Brain* 115:749–769.

Pantel, J., B. Kratz, M. Essig, J. Schroder. 2003. Parahippocampal volume deficits in subjects with aging-associated cognitive decline. *Am J Psychiatry* 160:379–382.

Papez, J. W. 1937. A proposed mechanism of emotion. *Arch Neurol Psychiatry* 38:725–743.

Paradiso, S., B. P. Hermann, R. G. Robinson. 1995. The hetergeneity of temporal lobe epilepsy: Neurology, Neuropsychology, and Psychiatry. *J Nervous Mental Dis* 183:538–547.

Parfitt D. N., G. M. C. Gall. 1944. Psychogenic amnesia: The refusal to remember. *J Mental Sci* 90:511–519.

Park, D. C., G. Lautenschlager, T. Hedden, et al. 2002. Models of visuospatial and verbal memory across the adult life span. *Psychol Aging* 17:299–320.

Park, S. B., J. T. Coull, R. H. McShane, et al. 1994. Tryptophan depletion in normal volunteers produces selective impairments in learning and memory. *Neuropharmacology* 33(3–4):575–588.

Parker, E. S., R. L. Alkana, I. M. Birnbaum, et al. 1974. Alcohol and the disruption of cognitive processes. *Arch Gen Psychiatry* 31(6):824–828.

Parker, E. S., I. M. Birnbaum, H. Weingartner, et al. 1980. Retrograde enhancement of human memory with alcohol. *Psychopharmacology (Berlin)* 69(2):219–222.

Parsa, M. A., E. Szigethy, J. M. Voci, H. Y. Meltzer. 1997. Risperidone in treatment of choreoathetosis of Huntington's disease. *J Clin Psychopharmacol* 17(2):134–135.

Parsons, O. A., N. Butters, P. E. Nathan, eds. 1987. Neuropsychology of alcoholism: Implications for diagnosis and treatment. New York, Guilford Press.

Pasquier, F., T. Fukui, M. Sarazin, et al. 2003. Laboratory investigations and treatment in frontotemporal dementia. *Ann Neurol* 54(Suppl 5:S32–35.

Pasquier, F., F. Lebert, I. Lavenu, H. Petit. 1998. Clinical diagnosis of frontotemporal dementia. *Rev Neurol (Paris)* 154(3):217–223.

Patterson, A., O. L. Zangwill. 1944. Recovery of spatial disorientation in the post-traumatic confusional state. *Brain* 67:465.

Patterson, K., J. R. Hodges. 1992. Deterioration of word meaning: Implications for reading. *Neuropsychologia* 30(12):1025–1040.

Patterson, K., J. R. Hodges. 1995. Disorders of semantic memory. In: *Handbook of Memory Disorders*, A. D. Baddeley, B. A. Wilson, F. N. Watts, eds. New York, John Wiley, pp. 167–186.

Patterson, K., J. R. Hodges. 2000. Semantic dementia: One window on the structure and organization of semantic memory. In: *Handbook of Neuropsychology*, 2nd ed., Vol. 2, F. Boller, J. Grafman, eds. Amsterdam, Elsevier, pp. 313–333.

Patterson, K., N. Graham, J. R. Hodges. 1994. The impact of semantic memory loss on phonological representations. *J Cogn Neurosci* 6:57–69.

Paulsen, J. S., H. Zhao, J. C. Stout, et al. 2001. Clinical markers of early disease in persons near onset of Huntington's disease. *Neurology* 57:658–662.

Pearman, A., M. Storandt. 2004. Predictors of subjective memory in older adults. *J Gerontol Ser B Psychol Sci Soc Sci* 59:4–6.

Penfield, W., G. Mathieson. 1974. Mamory autopsy findings and comments on the role of hippocampus in experiential recall. *Arch Neurol* 31:145–154.

Pennanen, C., M. Kivipelto, S. Tuomainen, et al. 2004. Hippocampus and entorhinal cortex in mild cognitive impairment and early AD. *Neurobiol Aging* 25:303–310.

Perls, T. 2004. Centenarians who avoid dementia. *Trends Neurosci* 27:633–636.

Perry, R. J., J. R. Hodges. 1999. Attention and executive deficits in Alzheimer's disease. A critical review. *Brain* 122:384–404.

Perry, R. J., P. Watson, J. R. Hodges. 2000. The nature and staging of attention dysfunction in early (minimal and mild) Alzheimer's disease: Relationship to episodic and semantic memory impairment. *Neuropsychologia* 38:252–271.

Petersen, R. C. 1995. Normal aging, mild cognitive impairment, and early Alzheimer's disease. *The Neurologist* 1:326–344.

Petersen, R. C., R. Doody, A. Kurz. 2001. Current concepts in mild cognitive impairment. *Arch Neurol* 58:1985–1992.

Petersen, R. C., C. R. Jr. Jack, Y. C. Xu, et al. 2000. Memory and MRI-based hippocampal volumes in aging and AD. *Neurology* 54:581–587.

Petersen, R. C., G. E. Smith, S. C. Waring, et al. 1997. Aging, memory, and mild cognitive impairment. *Int Psychogeriatrics* 9:65–69.

Petersen, R. C., G. E. Smith, S. C. Waring, et al. 1999. Mild cognitive impairment: clinical characterization and outcome. *Arch Neurol* 56:303–308.

Petersen, R. C., J. C. Stevens, M. Ganguli, et al. 2001. Practice parameter: Early detection of dementia: Mild cognitive impairment (an evidence-based review). *Neurology* 56:1133–1142.

Peterson, J. B., J. Rothfleisch, P. D. Zelazo, R. O. Pihl. 1990. Acute alcohol intoxication and cognitive functioning. *J Stud Alcohol* 51:114–121.

Petrides, M. 1996a. Lateral frontal cortical contribution to memory. *Sem Neurosci* 8:57–63.

Petrides, M. 1996b. Specialized systems for the processing of mnemonic information within the primate frontal cortex. *Philos Trans R Soc Lond B Biol Sci* 351(1346):1455–1461.

Petrides, M. 2000. Impairments in working memory after frontal cortical excisions. *Adv Neurol* 84:111–118.

Petrides, M. 2002. The mid-ventrolateral prefrontal cortex and active mnemonic retrieval. *Neurobiol Learning Memory* 78:528–538.

Petrides, M., B. Milner. 1982. Deficits on subject-ordered tasks after frontal and temporal lobe excisions in man. *Neuropsychologia* 3:249–262.

Pexman, J. H. W., R. K. Coates. 1983. Amnesia after femorocerebral angiography. *Am J Neuroradiol* 4:979–983.

Phillips, S., V. Sangalang, G. Sterns. 1987. Basal forebrain infarction: A clinicopathologic correlation. *Arch Neurol* 44:1134–1138.

Pickering-Brown, S., M. Baker, S. H. Yen, et al. 2000. Pick's disease is associated with mutations in the tau gene. *Ann Neurol* 48(6):859–67.

Pietrini, V., P. Nertempi, A. Vaglia, et al. 1988. Recovery from herpes simplex encephalitis: Selective impairment of specific semantic categories with neuroradiological correlation. *J Neurol Neurosurg Psychiatry* 51:1284–1293.

Pike, B. R., X. Zhao, J. K. Newcomb, et al. 2000. Stretch injury causes calpain and caspase-3 activation and necrotic and apoptotic cell death in septo-hippocampal cell cultures. *J Neurotrauma* 17:283–298.

Pillon, B., B. Deweer, A. Michon. 1994. Are explicit memory disorders of progressive supranuclear palsy related to damage to striatofrontal circuits? Comparison with Alzheimer's, Parkinson's, and Huntington's diseases. *Neurology* 44:1264–1270.

Pillon, B., J. Blin, M. Vidailhet, et al. 1995. The neuropsychological pattern of corticobasal degeneration: Comparison with progressive supranuclear palsy and Alzheimer's disease. *Neurology* 45:1477–1483.

Piper, A. 1993. Truth serum and recovered memories of sexual abuse: A review of the evidence. *J Psychiatry Law* 21:447–471.

Pisvejc, J., V. Hyrman, J. Sikora, et al. 1998. A comparison of brief and ultrabrief pulse stimuli in unilateral ECT. *J ECT* 14:68–75.

Plato. (ca. 350 BC). "Philebus." Translated by B. Jowett. Available at http://clasics.mit.edu/Plato/philebus.html.

Plato. (ca. 360 BC). "Theaitetus." Translated by B. Jowett. Available at http://classics.mit.edu/Plato/theatu.html.

Pohjasvaara, T., R. Mantyla, O. Salonen, et al. 2000. How complex interactions of ischemic brain infarcts, white matter lesions, and atrophy relate to poststroke dementia. *Arch Neurol* 57(9):1295–1300.

Pommer B, P. Pilz, G. Harrer. 1983. Transient global amnesia as a manifestation of Epstein-Barr Virus encephalitis. *J Neurol* 229:125–127.

Popescu, A., C. F. Lippa. 2004. Parkinsonian syndromes: Parkinson's disease dementia, dementia with Lewy bodies and progressive supranuclear palsy. *Clin Neurosci Res* 3:461–468.

Porter, S., K. A. Kelly, C. J. Grame. 1993. Family treatment of spouses and children of patients with multiple personality disorder. *Bull Menninger Clinic* 57:371–379.

Poser, C. M., D. K. Ziegler. 1960. Temporary amnesia as a manifestation of cerebrovascular insufficiency. *Trans Am Neurol Assoc* 85:221–223.

Postle, B. R., J. Jonides, E. E. Smith, et al. 1997. Spatial, but not object, delayed response is impaired in early Parkinson's disease. *Neuropsychology* 11:171–179.

Powell, J., J. Davidoff. 1995. Selective impairments of object knowledge in a case of acquired cortical blindness. *Memory* 3(3–4):435–461.

Pribram, K. H. 1971. *Languages of the Brain: Experimental Paradoxes and Principles in Neuropsychology.* Englewood Cliffs, N.J., Prentice-Hall.

Pritchard, P. B., V. L. Holmstrom, J. C. Roitzsch, B. S. Giacinto. 1985. Epileptic amnesic attacks: Benefit from antiepileptic drugs. *Neurology* 35:1188–1189.

Prudic, J., S. Peyser, H. A. Sackeim. 2000. Subjective memory complaints: A review of patient self-assessment of memory after electroconvulsive therapy. *J ECT* 16:121–132.

Pruessner, J. C., D. L. Collins, M. Pruessner, A. C. Evans. 2001. Age and gender predict volume decline in the anterior and posterior hippocampus in early adulthood. *J Neurosci* 21:194–200.

Putnam, F. W. 1991. Dissociative phenomena. In: *American Psychiatric Press Review of Psychiatry*, Vol. 10, A. Tasman, S. M. Goldfinger, eds. Washington, D.C., American Psychiatric Press, pp. 145–160.

Putnam, F. W., R. J. Loewenstein. 1993. Treatment of multiple personality disorder: A survey of current practices. *Am J Psychiatry* 150:1048–1052.

Putnam, F. W., R. J. Loewenstein. 2000. Dissociative identity disorder. In: *Comprehensive Textbook of Psychiatry*, 7th ed., B. J. Saddock, V. A. Sadock, eds. Baltimore, Lippincott Williams & Wilkins, pp. 1552–1564.

Putnam, F. W., K. Helmers, P. K. Trickett. 1993. Development, reliability, and validity of a child dissociation scale. *Child Abuse and Neglect* 17:731–741.

Quinette P., B. Guillery, B. Desgranges, et al. 2003. Working memory and executive functions in transient global amnesia. *Brain* 126:1917–1934.

Rabinowicz, A. L., S. E. Starkstein, R. C. Leiguarda, A. E. Coleman. 2000. Transient epileptic amnesia in dementia: A treatable unrecognized cause of episodic amnestic wandering. *Alzheimer Dis Assoc Disord* 14:214–243.

Rahkonen, T., U. Eloniemi-Sulkava, S. Rissanen, et al. 2003. Dementia with Lewy bodies according to the consensus criteria in a general population aged 75 years or older. *J Neurol Neurosurg Psychiatry* 74(6):720–724.

Rajkowska, G., J. J. Miguel-Hidalgo, J. Wei, et al. 1999. Morphometric evidence for neuronal and glial prefrontal cell pathology in major depression. *Biol Psychiatry* 45(9):1085–1098.

Rami-Gonzalez, L., M. Salamero, T. Boget, et al. 2003. Pattern of cognitive dysfunction in depressed patients during maintenance electroconvulsive therapy. *Psychol Med* 33:345–350.

Randt, C. T., E. R. Brown. 1983. *Randt Memory Test*. Bayport, N.Y., Life Science Associates.

Rapp, P. R., D. G. Amaral. 1992. Individual differences in the cognitive and neurobiological consequences of normal aging. *Trends Neurosci* 15:340–345.

Rascovsky, K., D. P. Salmon, G. J. Ho, et al. 2002. Cognitive profiles differ in autopsy-confirmed frontotemporal dementia and AD. *Neurology* 58:1801–1808.

Raskin, S. A., M. M. Sohlberg. 1996. The efficacy of prospective memory training in two adults with brain injury. *J Head Trauma Rehabil* 11:32–51.

Ratnavalli, E., C. Brayne, K. Dawson, J. R. Hodges. 2002. The prevalence of frontotemporal dementia. *Neurology* 58(11):1615–1621.

Raven, J. C. 1958. *Guide to the Standard Progressive Matrices*. London, H. K. Lewis.

Raven, J. C. 1996. *Progressive Matrices: A Perceptual Form of Intelligence*. London, H.K. Lewis.

Raymond, F. 1895. Les Délires ambulatoires ou les fugues. *Gazette des hôpitaux* 752–762, 787–793.

Raz, N., F. M. Gunning, D. Head, et al. 1997. Selective aging of the human cerebral cortex observed in vivo: Differential vulnerability of the prefrontal gray matter. *Cereb Cortex* 7:268–282.

Raz, N., F. M. Gunning-Dixon, D. Head, et al. 1998. Neuroanatomical correlates of cognitive aging. Evidence from structural magnetic resonance imaging. *Neuropsychology* 12:95–114.

Raz, N., F. M. Gunning-Dixon, D. Head, et al. 2001. Age and sex differences in the cerebellum and the ventral pons: A prospective MR study of healthy adults. *Am J Neuroradiol* 22:1161–1167.

Reading, P. J., A. K. Luce, I. G. McKeith. 2001. Rivastigmine in the treatment of parkinsonian psychosis and cognitive impairment: Preliminary findings from an open trial. *Mov Disord* 16(6):1171–1174.

Rebeiz, J. J., E. H. Kolodny, E. P. Richardson, Jr. 1968. Corticodentatonigral degeneration with neuronal achromasia. *Arch Neurol* 18(1):20–33.

Reed, B. R., K. A. Paller, D. Mungas. 1998. Impaired acquisition and rapid forgetting of patterned visual stimuli in Alzheimer's disease. *J Clin Exp Neuropsychol* 20:738–749.

Reed, L. J., D. Lasserson, P. Marsden, et al. 2003. FDG-PET findings in the Wernicke-Korsakoff syndrome. *Cortex* 39(4–5):1027–1045.

Regard, M., T. Landis. 1984. Transient global amnesia: Neuropsychological dysfunction during attack and recovery in two "pure" cases. *J Neurol Neurosurg Psychiatry* 47:668–672.

Reisberg, B., R. Doody, A. Stoffler. 2003. Memantine in moderate-to-severe Alzheimer's disease. *N Engl J Med* 348(14): 1333–1341.

Reisberg, B., S. H. Ferris, M. J. de Leon, T. Crook. 1982. The Global Deterioration Scale for assessment of primary degenerative dementia. *Am J Psychiatry* 139:1136–1139.

Rempel-Clower, N. L., S. M. Zola, L. R. Squire, D. G. Amaral. 1996. Three cases of enduring memory impairment after bilateral damage limited to the hippocampal formation. *J Neurosci* 16(16):5233–5255.

Resnick, S. M., A. F. Goldszal, C. Davatzikos, et al. 2000. One-year age changes in MRI brain volumes in older adults. *Cereb Cortex* 10:464–472.

Resnick, S. M., D. L. Pham, M. A. Kraut, et al. 2003. Longitudinal magnetic resonance imaging studies of older adults: A shrinking brain. *J Neurosci* 15:3295–3301.

Reul, J. M., E. R. de Kloet. 1985. Two receptor systems for corticosterone in rat brain: Microdistribution and differential occupation. *Endocrinology* 117(6):2505–2511.

Ribot, T. A. 1882. *Diseases of memory, Les Maladies de la Mémoire*. Paris, Bailliere.

Richter-Levin, G. 2004. The amygdala, the hippocampus, and emotional modulation of memory. *Neuroscientist* 10(1):31–39.

Ridley, R. M., H. F. Baker, D. A. Mills, et al. 2004. Topographical memory impairments after unilateral lesions of the anterior thalamus and contralateral inferotemporal cortex. *Neuropsychologia* 42(9):1178–1191.

Riedel, W. J., T. Klaassen, N. E. Deutz, et al. 1999. Tryptophan depletion in normal volunteers produces selective impairment in memory consolidation. *Psychopharmacology (Berlin)* 141(4):362–369.

Riedel, W. J., T. Klaassen, J. A. Schmitt. 2002. Tryptophan, mood, and cognitive function. *Brain Behav Immun* 16(5):581–589.

Robbins, T. W. 1997. Arousal systems and attentional processes. *Biol Psychol* 45(1–3):57–71.

Rocca, W. A., A. Hofman, C. Brayne, et al. 1991. The prevalence of vascular dementia in Europe: facts and fragments from 1980–1990 studies. EURODEM-Prevalence Research Group. *Ann Neurol* 30(6):817–824.

Rogers, S. L., M. R. Farlow, R. S. Doody, et al. 1998. A 24-week, double-blind, placebo-controlled trial of donepezil in patients with Alzheimer's disease. Donepezil Study Group. *Neurology* 50(1):136–145.

Rogers, J. L., R. P. Kesner. 2003. Cholinergic modulation of the hippocampus during encoding and retrieval. *Neurobiol Learn Mem* 80(3):332–342.

Roman, G. C., T. Erkinjuntti, A. Wallin, et al. 2002. Subcortical ischaemic vascular dementia. *Lancet Neurol* 1(7):426–436.

Rosas, H. D., A. K. Liu, S. Hersch, et al. 2002. Regional and progressive thinning of the cortical ribbon in Huntington's disease. *Neurology* 58:695–701.

Rose, D., T. Wykes, M. Leese, et al. 2003. Patients' perspectives on electroconvulsive therapy: A systematic review. *BMJ* 326:1–5.

Rosen, A. C., M. W. Prull, R. O'Hara, et al. 2002a. Variable effects of aging on frontal lobe contributions to memory. *Neuroreport* 13:2425–2428.

Rosen, H. J., M. L. Gorno-Tempini, W. P. Goldman, et al. 2002b. Patterns of brain atrophy in frontotemporal dementia and semantic dementia. *Neurology* 58:198–208.

Rosen, H. J., K. M. Hartikainen, W. Jagust, et al. 2002c. Utility of clinical criteria in differentiating frontotemporal lobar degeneration (FTLD) from AD. *Neurology* 58:1608–1615.

Rosen, W. G., R. C. Mohs, K. L. Davis. 1984. A new rating scale for Alzheimer's disease. *Am J Psychiatry* 141:1356–1364.

Rosenberg, G. A. 1979. Transient global amnesia with a dissecting aortic aneurysm. *Arch Neurol* 36:255.

Rosenberg, J., H. M. Pettinati. 1984. Differential memory complaints after bilateral and unilateral ECT. *Am J Psychiatry* 141:1071–1074.

Ross, C. A. 1990. *Multiple Personality Disorder: Diagnosis, Clinical Features and Treatment*. New York, Wiley.

Ross, C. A., S. Heber, G. Anderson, et al. 1989a. Differentiating multiple personality disorder and complex partial seizures. *Gen Hosp Psychiatry* 11:54–58.

Ross, C. A., G. R. Norton, K. Wozney. 1989b. Multiple personality disorder: An analysis of 236 cases. *Can J Psychiatry* 34:413–418.

Ross, R. T. 1983. Transient tumor attacks. *Arch Neurol* 40:633–636.

Ross, S. J., N. Graham, L. Stuart-Green, et al. 1996. Progressive biparietal atrophy: An atypical presentation of Alzheimer's disease. *J Neurol Neurosurg Psychiatry* 61:388–395.

Rousseaux, M., A. Delafosse, M. Cabaret, et al. 1984. Amnesic retrograde post-traumatique. *Cortex* 20:575–583.

Rowan, A. J., L. M. Protass. 1979. Transient global amnesia: Clinical and electroencephalographic findings in 10 cases. *Neurology* 29:869–872.

Royall, D. R. 2000. Executive cognitive impairment: A novel perspective on dementia. *Neuroepidemiology* 19(6):293–299.

Ruff, R. M., J. A. Crouch, A. I. Troster, et al. 1994. Selected cases of poor outcome following a minor brain trauma: Comparing neuropsychological and positron emission tomography assessment. *Brain Inj* 8:297–308.

Rusinek, H., S. De Santi, D. Frid, et al. 2003. Regional brain atrophy rate predicts future cognitive decline: 6-year longitudinal MR imaging study of normal aging. *Radiology* 229:691–696.

Russell, W. R. 1932. Cerebral involvement in head injury. *Brain* 35:549–603.

Russell, W. R. 1935. Amnesia following head injuries. *Lancet* ii:762–763.

Russell, W. R., P. W. Nathan. 1946. Traumatic amnesia. *Brain* 69: 280–300.

Rutten, B. P. F., H. Korr, H. W. M. Steinbusch, C. Schmitz. 2003. The aging brain: Less neurons could be better. *Mech Aging Dev* 124:349–355.

Ryabinin, A. E. 1998. Role of hippocampus in alcohol-induced memory impairment: Implications from behavioral and immediate early gene studies. *Psychopharmacology (Berlin)* 139(1–2):34–43.

Ryan, T. V., S. W. Sautter, C. F. Capps, et al. 1992. Utilizing neuropsychological measures to predict vocational outcome in head trauma population. *Brain Inj* 6:175–182.

Ryback, R. S. 1971. The continuum and specificity of the effects of alcohol on memory. *Q J Stud Alcohol* 32:995–1016.

Rybarczyk, B. D., R. P. Hart, S. W. Harkins. 1987. Age and forgetting rate with pictorial stimuli. *Psychol Aging* 2:404–406.

Sackeim, H. A., P. Decina, I. Prohovnik, et al. 1986. Dosage seizure threshold and the antidepressant efficacy of electroconvulsive therapy. *Ann N Y Acad Sci* 462: 398–410.

Sackeim, H. A., J. Freeman, M. McElhiney, et al. 1992. Effects of major depression on estimates of intelligence. *J Clin Exp Neuropsychol* 14:268–288.

Sackeim, H. A., J. Prudic, D. P. Devanand, et al. 1993. Effects of stimulus intensity and electrode placement on the efficacy and cognitive effects of electroconvulsive therapy. *N Engl J Med* 328:839–846.

Sackeim, H. A., J. Prudic, D. P. Devanand, et al. 2000. A prospective, randomized, double-blind comparison of bilateral and right unilateral electroconvulsive therapy at different stimulus intensities. *Arch Gen Psychiatry* 57:425–434.

Sacks, O. 1970. *The Man Who Mistook His Wife for a Hat*. New York, Harper and Row.

Sajatovic, M., P. Verbanac, L. F. Ramirez, H. Y. Meltzer. 1991. Clozapine treatment of psychiatric symptoms resistant to neuroleptic treatment in patients with Huntington's chorea. *Neurology* 41(1):156.

Salat, D. H., R. L. Buckner, A. Z. Snyder, et al. 2004. Thinning of the cerebral cortex in aging. *Cereb Cortex* 14:721–730.

Saling, M. M., S. F. Berkovic, M. F. O'Shea, et al. 1993. Lateralization of verbal memory and unilateral hippocampal sclerosis: Evidence of task specific effects. *J Clin Exp Neuropsychol* 15:608–618.

Salthouse, T. A. 2000. Aging and measures of processing speed. *Bio Psychol* 54:35–54.

Samuel, W., M. Caligiuri, D. Galasko, et al. 2000. Better cognitive and psychopathologic response to donepezil in patients prospectively diagnosed as dementia with Lewy bodies: A preliminary study. *Int J Geriatr Psychiatry* 15(9):794–802.

Sanders, H. I., E. K. Warrington. 1971. Memory for remote events in amnesic patients. *Brain* 94:661–668.

Sandyk, R. 1984. Transient global amnesia: A presentation of subarachnoid hemorrhage. *Neurology* 231:283–284.

Santacruz, P., B. Uttl, I. Litvan, J. Grafman. 1998. Progressive supranuclear palsy: A survey of the disease course. *Neurology* 50:1637–1647.

Sapolsky, R. M. 1996. Why stress is bad for your brain. *Science* 273:1705–1711.

Sapolsky, R. M., L. C. Krey, B. S. McEwen. 1986. The neuroendocrinology of stress and aging: The glucocorticoid cascade hypothesis. *Endocr Rev* 7(3):284–301.

Sargent, W., E. Slater. 1940–1941. Amnesic syndrome in war. *Pro R Soc Med* 34:757–764.

Sarter, M. H. J. Markowitsch. 1985. The amygdala's role in human mnemonic processing. *Cortex* 21:7–24.

Sartori, G., R. Job, M. Miozzo, S. et al. 1993. Category-specific form-knowledge deficit in a patient with herpes simplex virus encephalitis. *J Clin Exp Neuropsychol* 15:280–299.

Sawaguchi, T., P. S. Goldman-Rakic. 1994. The role of D1-dopamine receptor in working memory: Local injections of dopamine antagonists into the prefrontal cortex of rhesus monkeys performing an oculomotor delayed-response task. *J Neurophysiol* 71:515–528.

Sawchyn, J., M. Brulot, E. Strauss. 2000. Note on the use of the postconcussion syndrome checklist. *Arch Clin Neuropsychol* 15:1–8.

Saxe, G. N., B. A. van der Kolk, R. Berkowitz, et al. 1993. Dissociative disorders in psychiatric inpatients. *Am J Psychiatry* 150:1037–1042.

Sbordone, R. J., J.C. Litter. 1995. Mild traumatic brain injury does not produce posttraumatic stress disorder. *Brain Inj* 9:405–412.

Scahill, R. I., C. Frost, R. Jenkins, et al. 2003. A longitudinal study of brain volume changes in normal aging using serial registered magnetic resonance imaging. *Arch Neurol* 60:898–994.

Scarpini, E., P. Scheltens, H. Feldman. 2003. Treatment of Alzheimer's disease: Current status and new perspectives. *Lancet Neurol* 2(9):539–547.

Schacter, D.L. 1996. *Searching for memory: The brain, the mind and the past.* New York, Basic Books.

Schacter, D. L., E. L. Glisky. 1986. Memory remediation: Restoration, alleviation, and the acquisition of domain-specific knowledge. In: *Clinical Neuropsychology of Intervention*, B. P. Uzzell, Y. Gorss, eds. Boston, Nijhoff, pp. 257–282.

Schacter, D. L., A. W. Kaszniak, J. F. Kihlstrom, M. Valdiserri. 1991. The relation between source memory and aging. *Psychol Aging* 6:559–568.

Schacter, D. L., W. Koutstaal, K. A. Norman. 1997. False memories and aging. *Trends Cogn Sci* 1:229–236.

Schacter, D. L., D. Osowiecki, A. W. Kaszniak, et al. 1994. Source memory: Extending the boundaries of age-related deficits. *Psychol Aging* 9:81–89.

Schacter, D.L., P. L. Wang, E. Tulving, M. Freedman. 1982. Functional retrograde amnesia: a quantitative case study. *Neuropsychologia* 20:523–532.

Schiavetto, A., S. Kohler, C. L. Grady, et al. 2002. Neural correlates of memory for object identity and object location: Effects of aging. *Neuropsychologia* 40:1428–1442.

Schmand, B., C. Jonker, M. I. Geerlings, J. Lindeboom. 1997. Subjective memory complaints in the elderly: Depressive symptoms and future dementia. *Br J Psychiatry* 171:373–379.

Schmidtke, K., L. Ehmsen. 1998. Transient global amnesia and migraine: A case control study. *Eur Neurol* 40:9–14.

Schmidtke, K., M. Reinhardt, T. Krause. 1998. Cerebral perfusion during transient global amnesia: findings with HMPAO SPECT. *J Nucl Med* 39:155–159.

Schmitt, F. A., D. G. Davis, D. R. Wekstein, et al. 2000. "Preclinical" AD revisited: Neuropathology of cognitively normal older adults. *Neurology* 55:370–376.

Schmitt, J. A., M. J. Kruizinga, W. J. Riedel. 2001. Non-serotonergic pharmacological profiles and associated cognitive effects of serotonin reuptake inhibitors. *J Psychopharmacol* 15:173–179.

Schnider, A., C. Bassetti, A. Schnider, et al. 1995. Very severe amnesia with acute onset after isolated hippocampal damage due to systemic lupus erythematosus. *J Neurol Neurosurg Psychiatry* 59:644–646.

Schnider, A., K. Gutbrod, C. W. Hess, G. Schroth. 1996. Memory without context: Amnesia with confabulations after infarction of the right capsular genu. *J Neurol Neurosurg Psychiatry* 61:186–193.

Schrag, A., Y. Ben-Shlomo, N. P. Quinn. 1999. Prevalence of progressive supranuclear palsy and multiple system atrophy: A cross-sectional study. *Lancet* 354(9192): 1771–1775.

Schwartz, M. L., F. Carruth, M. A. Binns, et al. 1998. The course of post-traumatic amnesia: Three little words. *Can J Neurol Sci* 25:108–116.

Schwarz, M., R. De Bleser, K. Poeck, J. Weis. 1998. A case of primary progressive aphasia: A 14-year follow-up study with neuropathological findings. *Brain* 121: 115–126.

Scovern, A. W., P. R. Kilmann. 1980. Status of electroconvulsive therapy: Review of the outcome literature. *Psychol Bull* 87:260–303.

Scoville, W. B., B. Milner. 1957. Loss of recent memory after bilateral hippocampal lesions. *J Neurochem* 20:11–21.

Seeman, T. E., T. M. Lusignolo, M. Albert, L. Berkman. 2001. Social relationships, social support and patterns of cognitive aging in healthy, high-functioning older adults: MacArthur Studies of Successful Aging. *Health Psychol* 20:243–255.

Seidenberg, M., B. P. Hermann, J. Schoenfeld, et al. 1997. Reorganization of verbal memory function in early onset left temporal lobe epilepsy. *Brain Cogn* 35:132–148.

Selden, N. R., D. R. Gitelman, N. Salamon–Murayama, et al. 1998. Trajectories of cholinergic pathways within the cerebral hemispheres of the human brain. *Brain* 121:2249–2257.

Seltzer, B., P. Zolnouni, M. Nunez, et al. 2004. Efficacy of donepezil in early-stage Alzheimer disease: A randomized placebo-controlled trial. *Arch Neurol* 61:1852–1856.

Serby, M., S. C. Samuels. 2001. Diagnostic criteria for dementia with Lewy bodies recon-sidered. *Am J Geriatr Psychiatry* 9:212–219.

Sheline, Y. I., P. W. Wang, M. H. Gado, et al. 1996. Hippocampal atrophy in recurrent major depression. *Proc Natl Acad Sci U S A* 93:3908–3913.

Sheridan, J., G. W. Humphreys. 1993. A verbal-semantic category-specific recognition impairment. *Cogn Neuropsychol* 10:143–184.

Shimamura, A. P., L. R. Squire. 1987. A neuropsychological study of fact memory and source amnesia. *J Exp Psychol Learn Mem Cog* 13:464–473.

Shimamura, A. P., L. R. Squire. 1991. The relationship between fact and source memory: Findings from amnesic patients and normal subjects. *Psychobiology* 19:1–10.

Shimomura, T., E. Mori, H. Yamashita, et al. 1998. Cognitive loss in dementia with Lewy bodies and Alzheimer disease. *Arch Neurol* 55:1547–1552.

Shulz, R., O. H. Luders, S. Noachtar, et al. 1995. Amnesia of the epileptic aura. *Neurology* 45:231–235.

Shuping, J. R., J. F. Toole, E. Alexander. 1980. Transient global amnesia due to glioma in the dominant hemisphere. *Neurology* 30:88–90.

Shuren, J. E., D. H. Jacobs, K. M. Heilman. 1997. Diencephalic temporal order amne-sia. *J Neurol Neurosurg Psychiatry* 62:163–168.

Shuttleworth, E. C., G. R. Wise. 1973. Transient global amnesia due to arterial embolism. *Arch Neurol* 29:340–342.

Silberman, E. K., F. W. Putnam, H. Weingartner, et al. 1985. Dissociative states in mul-tiple personality disorder: A quantitative study. *Psychiatry Res* 15:253–260.

Silveri, M. C., G. Gainotti. 1988. Interaction between vision and language in category-specific semantic impairment. *Cogn Neuropsychol* 5:677–709.

Simard, S., I. Rouleau, J. Brosseau, et al. 2003. Impact of executive dysfunctions on episodic memory abilities in patients with ruptured aneurysm of the anterior com-municating artery. *Brain Cogn* 53(2):354–358.

Simeon, D., E. Hollander. 2000. Dissociative disorders not otherwise specified. In: *Comprehensive Textbook of Psychiatry*, 7th ed., B.J. Saddock, V.A. Saddock, eds. Baltimore, Lippincott Williams & Wilkins, pp. 1570–1576.

Simpson, G., R. Tate. 2002. Suicidality after traumatic brain injury: Demographic, injury and clinical correlates. *Psychol Med* 32:687–697.

Sirigu, A., J. R. Duhamel, M. Poncet. 1991. The role of sensorimotor experience in object recognition: A case of multimodal agnosia. *Brain* 114:2555–2573.

Sitaram, N., H. Weingartner, J. C. Gillin. 1978. Human serial learning: Enhancement with arecholine and choline impairment with scopolamine. *Science* 201(4352): 274–276.

Sjobeck, M., S. Dahlen, E. Englund. 1999. Neuronal loss in the brainstem and cere-bellum – part of the normal aging process? A morphometric study of the vermis cerebelli and inferior olivary nucleus. *J Gerontol A Biol Sci Med Sci* 54(9): B363–B368.

Skeel, R. L., B. Johnstone, D. T. Yangco Jr., et al. 2000. Neuropsychological deficit pro-files in systemic lupus erythematosus. *Appl Neuropsychol* 7:96–101.

Sliwinski, M. J., S. M. Hofer, C. Hall, et al. 2003. Modeling memory decline in older adults: The importance of preclinical dementia, attrition, and chronological age. *Psychol Aging* 18:658–671.

Small, I. F., J. G. Small, V. Milstein, J. F. Moore. 1972. Neuropsychological observations with psychosis and somatic treatments. *J Nerv Ment Dis* 155:6–13.

Small, S. A. 2001. Age-related memory decline. *Arch Neurol* 58:360–364.

Small, S. A., Y. Stern, M. Tang, R. Mayeaux. 1999. Selective decline in memory function among healthy elderly. *Neurology* 52:1392–1396.

Small, S. A., W. Y. Tsai, R. DeLaPaz, et al. Imaging hippocampal function across the human life span: Is memory decline normal or not? *Ann Neurol* 51:290–295, 2002.

Smith, J. G., J. McDowall. 2004. Impaired higher order implicit sequence learning on the verbal version of the serial reaction time task in patients with Parkinson's disease. *Neuropsychology* 18:679–691.

Smith, M. L., B. Milner. 1989. Right hippocampal impairment in the recall of spatial location: Encoding deficit or rapid forgetting? *Neuropsychologia* 27:71–81.

Smith, M. L., B. Milner. 1981. The role of the right hippocampus in the recall of spatial location. *Neuropsychologia* 19:781–793.

Sno, H.N., D. H. Linszen, F. de Jonghe. 1992. Deja vu experiences and reduplicative paramnesia. *Br J Psychiatry* 161:565–568.

Snodgrass, J. G., M. Vanderwart. 1980. A standardized set of 260 pictures: Norms for name agreement, image agreement, familiarity, and visual complexity. *J Exp Psychol [Hum Learn]* 6(2):174–215.

Snowden, J. S., D. Neary. 2002. Relearning of verbal labels in semantic dementia. *Neuropsychologia* 40:1715–1728.

Snowden, J. S., D. Craufurd, H. Griffith, et al. 2001. Longitudinal evaluation of cognitive disorder in Huntington's disease. *J Int Neuropsychol Soc* 7:33–44.

Snowden, J. S., D. Craufurd, J. Thompson, D. Neary. 2002. Psychomotor, executive, and memory function in preclinical Huntington's disease. *J Clin Exp Neuropsychol* 24:133–145.

Snowden, J. S., H. Griffith, D. Neary. 1994. Semantic dementia: Autobiographical contribution to preservation of meaning. *Cogn Neuropsychol* 11:265–288.

Snowden, J. S., H. L. Griffith, D. Neary. 1996. Semantic-episodic memory interactions in semantic dementia: implications for retrograde memory function. *Cogn Neuropsychol* 13:1101–1137.

Snowden, J. S., D. Neary, D. M. A. Mann. 1996. *Frontotemporal Lobar De-generation: Frontotemporal Dementia, Progressive Aphasia, Semantic Dementia.* 1996, Churchill Livingstone.

Snowden, J. S., J. C. Thompson, D. Neary. 2004. Knowledge of famous faces and names in semantic dementia. *Brain* 127:860–872.

Snowdon, D. A. 2003. Healthy aging and dementia: Findings from the Nun Study. *Ann Intern Med* 139:450–454.

Snowdon, D. A., L. H. Greiner, J. A. Mortimer, et al. 1997. Brain infarction and the clinical expression of Alzheimer disease. The Nun Study. *Jama* 277(10):813–817.

Snowdon, D. A., S. J. Kemper, J. A. Mortimer, et al. 1996. Linguistic ability in early life and cognitive function and Alzheimer's disease in late life. Findings from the Nun Study. *Jama* 275(7):528–532.

Sobin, C., H. A. Sackeim, J. Prudic. 1991. Predictors of retrograde amnesia following ECT. *Am J Psychiatry* 152:995–1001.

Sobin, C., H. A. Sackheim, J. Prudic, D. P. Devanand, et al. 1995. Predictors of retrograde amnesia following ECT. *Am J Psychiatry* 152:995–1001.

Sohlberg, M. M., C. A. Mateer. 1989. Training use of compensatory memory books: A three stage behavioral approach. *J Clin Exp Neuropsychol,* 11:871–891.

Sohlberg, M. M., C. A. Mateer. 2001. *Cognitive Rehabilitation: An Integrative Neuropsychological Approach.* New York, Guilford.

Sohlberg, M. M., C. A. Mateer, S. Geyer. 1985. *Prospective Memory Process Training (PROMPT)*. Wake Forest, N.C., Lash & Associates.

Sohlberg, M. M., B. Todis, A. Glang. 1998. SCEMA: A team-based approach to serving secondary students with executive dysfunction following brain injury. *Aphasiology* 12:1047–1092.

Solbakk, A. K., I. N. Reinvang, C. Nielsen, K. Sundet. 1999. ERP indicators of disturbed attention in mild closed head injury: A frontal lobe syndrome? *Psychophysiology* 36:802–817.

Sosin, D. M., J. E. Sniezek, D. J. Thurman. 1996. Incidence of mild and moderate brain injury in the United States, 1991. *Brain Inj* 10:47–54.

Spanos, N. P., C. A. Burgess, M. F. Burgess, et al. 1999. Creating false memories of infancy with hypnotic and non-hypnotic procedures. *Appl Cogn Psychol* 13(3):201–218.

Spencer, D. W., N. Raz. 1995. Differential effects of aging on memory for content and context: A meta-analysis. *Psychol Aging* 10:527–539.

Sperling, M. R., A. J. Saykin, G. Glosser, et al. 1994. Predictors of outcome after anterior temporal lobectomy: The intracarotid amobarbital test. *Neurology* 44:2325–2330.

Spiers, H. J., E. A. Maguire, N. Burgess. 2001. Hippocampal amnesia. *Neurocase* 7:357–382.

Spreen, O., E. A. Strauss. 1991. *Compendium of Neuropsychological Tests*. New York, Oxford University Press.

Spreen, O., E. Strauss. 1998. *A Compendium of Neuropsychological Tests: Administration, Norms, and Commentary*, 2nd ed. New York, Oxford University Press.

Squire, L. R. 1975. A stable impairment in remote memory following ECT. *Neuropsychologia* 13:51–58.

Squire, L. R. 1981. Two forms of human amnesia: an analysis of forgetting. *J Neurosci* 1:635–640.

Squire, L. R. 1982. Comparison between forms of amnesia: some deficits are unique to Korsakoff's syndrome. *J Exp Psychol Learn Mem Cog* 8:560–571.

Squire, L. R. 1986. Memory functions as affected by electroconvulsive therapy. *Ann N Y Acad Sci* 462:307–314.

Squire, L. R. 1992a. Declarative and nondeclarative memory: Multiple brain systems supporting learning and memory. *J Cogn Neurosci* 4:232–243.

Squire, L. R. 1992b. Memory and the hippocampus: A synthesis from findings with rats, monkeys, and humans. *Psychol Rev* 99:195–231.

Squire, L. R., P. Alvarez. 1995. Retrograde amnesia and memory consolidation: A neurobiological perspective. *Curr Opin Neurobiol* 5:169–177.

Squire, L. R., D. G. Amaral, G. A. Press. 1990. Magnetic resonance imaging of the hippocampal formation and mammillary nuclei distinguish medial temporal lobe and diencephalic amnesia. *J Neurosci* 10:3106–3117.

Squire, L. R., P. M. Chase. 1975. Memory functions six to nine months after electroconvulsive therapy. *Arch Gen Psychiatry* 32:1557–1564.

Squire, L. R., A. Shimamura. 1986. Characterizing amnestic patients for neurobehavioral study. *Behav Neurosci* 100:866–877.

Squire, L. R., P. C. Slater. 1983. Electroconvulsive therapy and complaints of memory dysfunction: A prospective three-year follow-up study. *Br J Psychiatry* 142:1–8.

Squire, L. R., S. M. Zola. 1996. Structure and function of declarative and nondeclarative memory systems. *Proc Natl Acad Sci U S A* 93:13515–13522.

Squire, L. R., S. M. Zola. 1997. Amnesia, memory, and brain systems. *Philos Trans R Soc Lond B* 352:1663–1673.

Squire, L. R., S. Zola-Morgan. 1991. The medial temporal lobe memory system. *Science* 253:1380–1386.

Squire, L. R., F. Haist, A. P. Shimamura. 1989. The neurology of memory: Quantitative assessment of retrograde amnesia in two groups of amnesic patients. *J Neurosci* 9:823–839.

Squire, L. R., B. Knowlton, G. Musen. 1993. The structure and organization of memory. *Annu Rev Psychol* 44:453–495.

Squire, L. R., P. C. Slater, P. L. Miller. 1981. Retrograde amnesia following ECT. *Am J Psychiatry* 152:995–1001.

Squires, E. J., N. M. Hunkin, A. J. Parkin. 1997. Errorless learning of novel associations in amnesia. *Neuropsychologia* 35:1103–1111.

Starkman, M. N., S. S. Gebarski, S. Berent, D. E. Schteingart. 1992. Hippocampal formation volume, memory dysfunction, and cortisol levels in patients with Cushing's syndrome. *Biol Psychiatry* 32:756–765.

Stebbins, G. T., J. D. E. Gabrieli, F. Masciari, et al. 1999. Delayed recognition memory in Parkinson's disease: A role for working memory? *Neuropsychologia* 37:503–510.

Stefanacci, L., E. A. Buffalo, H. Schmolck, L. R. Squire. 2000. Profound amnesia after damage to the medial temporal lobe: A neuroanatomical and neuropsychological profile of patient E. P. *J Neurosci* 20(18):7024–7036.

Steif, B. L., H. A. Sackeim, S. Portney, et al. 1986. Effects of depression and ECT on anterograde memory. *Biol Psychiatry* 21:921–930.

Steinberg, M. 1991. The spectrum of depersonalization: Assessment and treatment. In: *American Psychiatric Press Review of Psychiatry*, Vol. 10, A. Tasman, S.M. Goldfinger, eds. Washington, D.C., American Psychiatric Press, pp. 223–247.

Steinberg, M. 1994. *Structured Clinical Interview for DSM-IV Dissociative Disorders-Revised (SCID-R)*. Washington, D.C., American Psychiatric Press.

Steinberg, M. 2000a. Advances in the clinical assessment of dissociation: the SCID-D-R. *Bull Menninger Clin* 64:146–163.

Steinberg, M. 2000b. Depersonalization Disorder. In: *Comprehensive Textbook of Psychiatry*, 7th ed., Vol. 2, B.J. Saddock, V.A. Saddock eds. Baltimore, Lippincott Williams & Wilkins, pp. 1564–1570.

Steinberg, M. 2000c. Dissociative Amnesia. In: *Comprehensive Textbook of Psychiatry*, 7th ed., B.J. Saddock, V.A. Saddock, eds. Baltimore, Lippincott Williams & Wilkins, pp. 1544–1549.

Steinmetz, E. F., F. Q. Vroom. 1972. Transient global amnesia. *Neurology* 22:1193–1200.

Stern, Y. 2002. What is cognitive reserve? Theory and research application of the reserve concept. *J Int Neuropsychol Soc* 8:448–460.

Stern, Y., X. Liu, M. Albert, et al. 1996. Application of a growth curve approach to modeling the progression of Alzheimer's disease. *J Gerontol A Biol Sci Med Sci* 51(4):M179–184.

Stern, Y., M. X. Tang, J. Denaro, R. Mayeux. 1995. Increased risk of mortality in Alzhemer's disease patients with more advanced educational and occupational attainment. *Ann Neurol* 37:590–595.

Stevens, M., C. M. van Duijn, W. Kamphorst, et al. 1998. Familial aggregation in frontotemporal dementia. *Neurology* 50(6):1541–1545.

Stewart, C., I. Reid. 1993. Electroconvulsive stimulation and synaptic plasticity in the rat. *Brain Res* 620:139–141.

Stewart, C., K. Jeffery, I. Reid. 1994. LTP-like synaptic efficacy changes following electroconvulsive stimulation. *NeuroReport* 5:1041–1044.

Stillhard, G., T. Landis, R. Schiess, et al. 1990. Bitemporal hypoperfusion in transient global amnesia: 99m-Tc-HM-PAO SPECT and neuropsychological findings during and after an attack. *J Neurol Neurosurg Psychiatry* 53:339–342.

Stracciari, A., G. Ciucci, G. Bianchedi, G. G. Rebucci. 1990. Epileptic transient amnesia. *Eur Neurol* 30:176–179.

Stracciari, A., E. Ghidoni, M. Guarino, et al. 1994. Post-traumatic retrograde amnesia with selective impairment of autobiographical memory. *Cortex* 30:459–468.

Stracciari, A., G. G. Rebucci, R. Gallassi. 1987. Transient global amnesia: neuropsychological study of a "pure" case. *J Neurol* 234:126–127.

Strange, B. A., R. Hurlemann, R. J. Dolan. 2003. An emotion-induced retrograde amnesia in humans is amygdala- and b-adrenergic-dependent. *PNSA* 100:13626–13631.

Strich, S. J. 1961. Shearing of nerve fibers as a cause for brain damage due to head injury. *Lancet* 2:443–448.

Stuss, D. T., F. I. M. Craik, L. Sayer, et al. 1996. Comparison of older people and people with frontal lesions: Evidence from word list learning. *Psychol Aging* 11:387–395.

Sullivan, E. V., L. Marsh. 2003. Hippocampal volume deficits in alcoholic Korsakoff's syndrome. *Neurology* 61:1716–1719.

Sullivan, E. V., L. Marsh, D. H. Mathalon, et al. 1995. Age-related decline in MRI volumes of temporal lobe grey matter but not hippocampus. *Neurobiol Aging* 16:591–606.

Sutula, T., J. Koch, G. Golarai, et al. 1996. NMDA receptor dependence of kindling and mossy fiber sprouting: Evidence that the NMDA receptor regulates patterning of hippocampal circuits in the adult brain. *J Neurosci* 16:7398–7406.

Swainson, R., R. D. Rogers, B. J. Sahakian, et al. 2000. Probabilistic learning and reversal deficits in patients with Parkinson's disease or frontal or temporal lobe lesions: Possible adverse effects of dopaminergic medication. *Neuropsychologia* 38:596–612.

Swan, G. E., D. Carmelli. 2002. Impaired olfaction predicts cognitive decline in nondemented older adults. *Neuroepidemiology* 21:58–67.

Swartz, J. R., B. L. Miller, I. M. Lesser, A. L. Darby. 1997. Frontotemporal dementia: Treatment response to serotonin selective reuptake inhibitors. *J Clin Psychiatry* 58(5):212–216.

Symonds, C. P. 1937. Mental disorder following head injury. *Proc R Soc Med* 30:1081–1094.

Symonds, C. P., W. R. Russell. 1943. Accidental head injuries: Prognosis in services patients. *Lancet* 1:7.

Szirmai, I., I. Vastagh, E. Szombathelyi, A. Kamondi. 2002. Strategic infarcts of the thalamus in vascular dementia. *J Neurol Sci* 203–204:91–97.

Tanabe, H., K. Hashikawa, Y. Nakagawa, et al. 1991. Memory loss due to transient hypoperfusion in the medial temporal lobes including hippocampus. *Acta Neurol Scand* 84:22–27.

Tanaka, D., Jr. 1976. Thalamic projections of the dorsomedial prefrontal cortex in the rhesus monkey (Macaca mulatta). *Brain Res* 110:21–38.

Tanaka, Y., Y. Miyazawa, F. Akaoka, T. Yamada. 1997. Amnesia following damage to the mammillary bodies. *Neurology* 48(1):160–165.

Tang-Wai, D. F., D. S. Knopman, Y. E. Geda, et al. 2003a. Comparison of the short test of mental status and the mini-mental state examination in mild cognitive impairment. *Arch Neurol* 60:1777–1781.

Tang-Wai, D. F., K. A. Josephs, B. F. Boeve, et al. 2003b. Pathologically confirmed corti-cobasal degeneration presenting with visuospatial dysfunction. *Neurology* 61:1134–1135.

Tariot, P. N., M. R. Farlow, G. T. Grossberg, et al. 2004. Memantine treatment in patients with moderate to severe Alzheimer disease already receiving donepezil: A random-ized controlled trial. *JAMA* 291(3):317–24.

Tariot, P. N., P. R. Solomon, J. C. Morris,et al. 2000. A 5-month, randomized, placebo-controlled trial of galantamine in AD. The Galantamine USA-10 Study Group. *Neurology* 54(12):2269–2276.

Tarsh, M. J., C. Royston. 1985. A follow-up study of accident neurosis. *Br J Psychiatry* 146:18–25.

Tassinari, C. A., C. Ciarmatori, C. Alesi, et al. 1991. Transient global amnesia as a pos-tictal state from recurrent partial seizures. *Epilepsia* 32:882–885.

Tate, R. L. 1998. It is not only the kind of injury that matters, but the kind of head: The contribution of premorbid psychosocial factors to rehabilitation outcomes after severe traumatic brain injury. *Neuropsychol Rehabil* 8:1–18.

Tate, R. L. 2003. Impact of pre-injury factors on outcome after severe traumatic brain injury: Does post-traumatic personality change represent an exacerbation of person-ality traits? *Neuropsychol Rehabil* 13:43–64.

Tate, D., E. D. Bigler. 2000. Fornix and hippocampal atrophy in traumatic brain injury. *Learn Mem* 7:442–446.

Tate, R. L., G. A. Broe. 1999. Psychosocial adjustment after traumatic brain injury: What are the important variables? *Psychol Med* 29:713–725.

Tatemichi, T. K., D. W. Desmond, R. Mayeux, et al. 1992. Dementia after stroke: Baseline frequency, risks, and clinical features in a hospitalized cohort. *Neurology* 42(6):1185–1193.

Taylor, L. A., J. S. Kreutzer, S. R. Demm, M. A. Meade. 2003. Traumatic brain injury and substance abuse: A review and analysis of the literature. *Neuropsychol Rehabil* 13:165–188.

Taylor, M. A., R. Abrams. 1985. Short-term cognitive effects of unilateral and bilateral ECT. *Br J Psychiatry* 146:308–311.

Teasdale, T. W., A. W. Engberg. 2001. Suicide after traumatic brain injury: A population study. *J Neurol Neurosurg Psychiatry*, 71:436–440.

Teyler, T., J. P. DiScenna. 1985. The role of hippocampus in memory: A hypothesis. *Neurosci Biobehav Rev* 9:377–389.

Tharp, B. R. 1969. The electroencephalogram in transient global amnesia. *Electroencephalogr Clin Neurophysiol* 26:96–99.

Thiel, C. M. 2003. Cholinergic modulation of learning and memory in the human brain as detected with functional neuroimaging. *Neurobiol Learn Mem* 80: 234–244.

Thomas, A. J., R. N. Kalaria, J. T. O'Brien. 2004. Depression and vascular disease: What is the relationship? *J Affect Disord* 79:81–95.

Thomas, L., M. R. Trimble. 1998. Dissociative disorders. In: *Epilepsy: A Comprehensive Textbook*, Vol. 3, J. Engel, Jr., T. A. Pedley, eds. Philadelphia, Lippincott-Raven, pp. 2775–2783.

Thompson, P. J., R. Corcoran. 1992. Every day memory failure in people with epilepsy. *Epilepsia* 33(Suppl 6):S18–S20.

Thurman, D., C. Alverson, K. Dunn, et al. 1999. Traumatic brain injury in the United States: A public health perspective. *J Head Trauma Rehabil* 4:602–615.

Tierney, M. C., J. P. Szalai, W. G. Snow et al. 1996. Predictors of probable Alzheimer's disease in memory-impaired patients: A prospective longitudinal study. *Neurology* 46:661–665.

Timmerman, M. E., W. H. Brouwer. 1999. Slow information processing after very severe closed head injury: Impaired access to declarative knowledge and intact application and acquisition of procedural knowledge. *Neuropsychologia* 37:467–478.

Tiraboschi, P., L. A. Hansen, M. Alford, et al. 2000. Cholinergic dysfunction in diseases with Lewy bodies. *Neurology* 54(2):407–411.

Tisserand, D. J., J. Jolles. 2003. On the involvement of prefrontal networks in cognitive aging. *Cortex* 39:1107–1128.

Tisserand, D. J., M. Van Boxtel, E. Gronenschild, J. Jolles. 2001. Age-related volume reductions of prefrontal regions in healthy individuals are differential. *Brain Cogn* 47:182–185.

Tisserand, D. J., P. J. Visser, M. P. J. Van Boxtel, J. Jolles. 2002a. The relation between global and limbic brain volumes on MRI and cognitive performance in healthy individuals across the age range. *Neurobiol Aging* 21:569–576.

Tisserand, D. J., J. C. Pruessner, E. Sanz Arigita, et al. 2002b. Regional frontal cortical volumes decrease differentially in aging: An MRI study to compare volumetric approaches and voxel-based morphometry. *Neuroimage* 17:657–669.

Tissié, P. 1987. *Les Alienes voyageurs*. Paris: Doin.

Torvik, A. 1987. Topographic distribution and severity of brain lesions in Wernicke's encephalopathy. *Clin Neuropathol* 6:25–29.

Tranel, D. 1991. Dissociated verbal and nonverbal retrieval and learning following left anterior temporal damage. *Brain Cogn* 15:187–200.

Tranel, D., H. Damasio, A. R. Damasio. 1997. A neural basis for the retrieval of conceptual knowledge. *Neuropsychologia* 35:1319–1327.

Treadwell, M., M. McCloskey, B. Gordon, N. J. Cohen. 1992. Landmark life events and the organization of memory: Evidence from functional retrograde amnesia. In: *Handbook of Emotion and Memory: Research and Theory*, S.A. Cristianson, ed. Hillsdale, N.J., Erlbaum, pp. 389–410.

Tröster, A. I., N. Butters, D. P. Salmon, et al. 1993. The diagnostic utility of savings scores: Differentiating Alzheimer's and Huntington's disease with the Logical Memory and Visual Reproduction Tests. *J Clin Exp Neuropsychol* 15:773–788.

Tsuchiya, K., K. Ikeda. 2002. Basal ganglia lesions in 'Pick complex': a topographic neuropathological study of 19 autopsy cases. *Neuropathology* 22(4):323–336.

Tsukiura, T., Y. Otsuka, R. Miura, et al. 2000. Remote memory for items, contents, and contexts: A case study for post-traumatic amnesia. *Brain Cogn* 44:98–112.

Tubi, N., A. Calev, D. Nigal, et al. 1993. Subjective symptoms in depression and during the course of elcetroconvulsive therapy. *Neuropsychiatry Neuropsychol Behav Neurol* 6:187–192.

Tulving, E. 1972. Episodic and semantic memory. In: *Organization of Memory*, E. Tulving, W. Donaldson, eds. New York, Academic Press, pp. 381–403.

Tulving, E., F. I. M. Craik, eds. 2000. The Oxford Handbook of Memory. New York, Oxford University Press.

Tulving, E., H. J. Markowitsch. 1998. Episodic and declarative memory: Role of the hippocampus. *Hippocampus* 8:198–204.

Tulving, E., S. Kapur, F. I. Craik, et al. 1994. Hemispheric encoding/retrieval asymmetry in episodic memory: Positron emission tomography findings. *Proc Natl Acad Sci U S A* 91:2016–2020.

Turek, I. S., T. E. Hanlon. 1977. The effectiveness and safety of electroconvulsive therapy (ECT). *J Nerv Ment Dis* 164:419–431.

Tutkun, H., V. Sar, L. I. Yargic, et al. 1998. Frequency of dissociative disorders among psychiatric inpatients in a Turkish University Clinic. *Am J Psychiatry* 155:800–805.

Tyler, L. K., H. E. Moss, K. Patterson, J. Hodges. 1997. The gradual deterioration of syntax and semantics in a patient with progressive aphasia. *Brain Lang* 56:426–476.

Tzourio, C., C. Dufouil, P. Ducimetiere, A. Alperovitch. 1999. Cognitive decline in individuals with high blood pressure: A longitudinal study in the elderly: EVA Study Group: Epidemiology of Vascular Aging. *Neurology* 53:1948–1952.

Umile, E. M., R. C. Plotki, M. E. Sandel. 1998. Functional assessment of mild traumatic brain injury using SPECT and neuropsychological testing. *Brain Inj* 12:577–594.

Umile, E. M., M. E. Sandel, A. Alavi, et al. 2002. Dynamic imaging in mild traumatic brain injury: Support for the theory of medial temporal vulnerability. *Arch Phys Med Rehabil* 83:1506–1513.

Ungerleider, L. G., S. M. Courtney, J. V. Haxby. 1998. A neural system for human visual working memory. *Proc Natl Acad Sci U S A* 95:883–890.

Unverzagt, F. W., S. L. Hui, M. R. Farlow, et al. 1998. Cognitive decline and education in mild dementia. *Neurology* 50:181–185.

Uylings, H. B. M., J. M. de Brabander. 2002. Neuronal changes in normal aging and Alzheimer's disease. *Brain Cogn* 49:268–276.

Vallar, G., A. M. Di Betta, M. C. Silveri. 1997. The phonological short-term rehearsal system: Patterns of impairment and neural correlates. *Neuropsychologia* 35:795–812.

van der Hart, O., E. Nijenhuis. 2001. Generalized dissociative amnesia: Episodic, semantic and procedural memories lost and found. *Aust N Z J Psychiatry* 35:589–560.

Van der Naalt, J., A. H. Van Zomeren, W. J. Sluiter, J. M. Minderhoud. 1999. One-year outcome in mild to moderate head injury: The predictive value of acute injury characteristics related to complaints and return to work. *J Neurol Neurosurg Psychiatry* 66:207–213.

Van der Werf Y. D., J. Jolles, M. P. Witter, H. B. Uylings. 2003. Contributions of thalamic nuclei to declarative memory functioning. *Cortex* 39(4–5):1047–1062.

Van der Werf, Y. D., D. J. Tisserand, P. J. Visser, et al. 2001. Thalamic volume predicts performance on tests of cognitive speed and decreases in healthy aging: A magnetic resonance imaging-based volumetric analysis. *Brain Res Cogn Brain Res* 11:377–385.

Van der Werf, Y. D., J. G. Weerts, J. Jolles, et al. 1999. Neuropsychological correlates of a right unilateral lacunar thalamic infarction. *J Neurol Neurosurg Psychiatry* 66:36–42.

Van Ijzendoorn, M., C. Schuengel. 1996. The measurement of dissociation in normal and clinical populations: Meta-analytic validation of the Dissociative Experiences Scale (DES). *Clin Psychol Rev* 16:365–382.

Van Petten, C. 2004. Relationship between hippocampal volume and memory ability in healthy individuals across the lifespan: Review and meta-analysis. *Neuropsychologia* 42:1394–1413.

Van Reekum, R., I. Bolago, M. A. Finlayson, et al. 1996. Psychiatric disorders after traumatic brain injury. *Brain Inj* 10:319–327.

van Stegeren A. H., W. Everaerd, L. Cahill, et al. 1998. Memory for emotional events: differential effects of centrally versus peripherally acting beta-blocking agents. *Psychopharmacology (Berlin)* 138:305–310.

Vargha-Khadem, F., D. G. Gadian, M. Mishkin. 2001. Dissociations in cognitive memory: The syndrome of developmental amnesia. *Philos Trans R Soc Lond B* 356:1435–1440.

Vargha-Khadem, F., D. G. Gadian, K. E. Watkins, et al. 1997. Differential effects of early hippocampal pathology on episodic and semantic memory. *Science* 277(5324): 376–380.

Verfaellie, M., P. Koseff, M. P. Alexander. 2000. Acquisition of novel semantic information in amnesia: Effects of lesion location. *Neuropsychologia* 38:484–492.

Vinters, H. V., W. G. Ellis, C. Zarow, et al. 2000. Neuropathologic substrates of ischemic vascular dementia. *J Neuropathol Exp Neurol* 59(11):931–945.

Viskontas, I. V., M. P. McAndrews, M. Moscovitch. 2000. Remote episodic memory deficits in patients with unilateral temporal lobe epilepsy and excisions. *J Neurosci* 20:5853–5857.

Vitiello B., A. Martin, J. Hill, et al. 1997. Cognitive and behavioral effects of cholinergic, dopaminergic, and serotonergic blockade in humans. *Neuropsychopharmacology* 16(1):15–24.

Volkow, N. D., R. C. Gur, G. J. Wang, et al. 1998. Association between decline in brain dopamine activity with age and cognitive and motor impairment in healthy individuals. *Am J Psychiatry* 155:344–349.

Volkow, N. D., J. Logan, J. S. Fowler, et al. 2000. Association between age-related decline in brain dopamine activity and impairment in frontal and cingulated metabolism. *Am J Psychiatry* 157:75–80.

von Cramon, D. Y., N. Hebel, U. Schuri. 1985. A contribution to the anatomical basis of thalamic amnesia. *Brain* 108:993–1008.

von Cramon, D. Y., H. J. Markowitsch, U. Schuri. 1993. The possible contribution of the septal region to memory. *Neuropsychologia* 31:1159–1180.

Vuilleumier, P., P. A. Desplane, F. Regli. 1996. Failure to recall (but not to remember): Pure transient amnesia during non-convulsive status epilepticus. *Neurology* 46:1036–1039.

Wales, L. R., A. A. Nov. 1981. Transient global amnesia: Complication of cerebral angiography. *Am J Neuroradiol* 2:275–277.

Waller, N. G., C. A. Ross. 1997. The prevalence and biometric structure of pathological dissociation in the general population: Taxometric and behavior genetic findings. *J Abnorm Psychol* 106:499–510.

Wallesch, C. W., H. H. Kornhuber, R. J. Brummer, et al. 1983. Lesions of the basal ganglia, thalamus, and deep white matter: Differential effects on language functions. *Brain Lang* 20:286–304.

Warrington, E. K. 1975. The selective impairment of semantic memory. *Q J Exp Psychol* 27:635–657.

Warrington, E. K. 1996. Studies of retrograde memory: A long-term review. *Proc Nat Acad Sci U S A* 93:13523–13526.

Warrington, E. K., R. A. McCarthy. 1987. Categories of knowledge. Further fractionations and an attempted integration. *Brain* 110:1273–1296.

Warrington, E. K., R. A. McCarthy. 1988. The fractionation of retrograde amnesia. *Brain Cogn* 7:184–200.

Warrington, E. K., T. Shallice. 1984. Category specific semantic impairments. *Brain* 107:829–854.

Warrington, E. K., L. Weiskrantz. 1970. Amnesic syndrome: Consolidation or retrieval? *Nature* 228:628–630.

Watkins, L. H. A., R. D. Rogers, A. D. Lawrence, et al. 2000. Impaired planning but intact decision making in early Huntington's disease: implications for specific fronto-striatal pathology. *Neuropsychologia* 38:1112–1125.

Watt, S., A. Shores, S. Kinoshita. 1999. Effects of reducing attentional resources on implicit and explicit memory after severe traumatic brain injury. *Neuropsychology* 13:338–349.

Wechsler, D. 1945. A standardized memory scale for clinical use. *J Psychol* 19:87–95.

Wechsler, D. 1974. *Wechsler Intelligence Scale for Children-Revised.* New York, The Psychological Corporation, New York.

Wechsler, D. 1981. *Wechsler Adult Intelligence Scale-Revised.* New York, The Psychological Corporation, New York.

Wechsler, D. 1987. *Wechsler Memory Scale–Revised.* San Antonio, Tex., Harcourt Brace Jovanovich.

Wechsler, D. 1997. *Wechsler Adult Intelligence Scale* – Third edition. New York, The Psychological Corporation.

Wechsler, D. 2002. *Wechsler Memory Scale,* Third Edition. The Psychological Corporation.

Weeks, D., C. P. L. Freeman, R. E. Kendell. 1980. ECT III: Enduring cognitive deficits. *B J Psychiatry* 137:26–37.

Wegesin, D. J., D. Friedman, N. Varughese, Y. Stern. 2002. Age-related changes in source memory retrieval: An ERP replication and extension. *Brain Res Cogn Brain Res* 13:323–338.

Wegesin, D. J., D. M. Jacobs, N. R. Zubin, et al. 2000. Source memory and encoding strategy in normal aging. *J Clin Exp Neuropsychol* 22:455–464.

Weiner, R. D. 1984. Does electroconvulsive therapy cause brain damage? *Behav Brain Sci* 7:1–53.

Weiner, R. D., H. J. Rogers, J. R. Davidson, L. R. Squire. 1986. Effects of stimulus parameters on cognitive side-effects. *Ann N Y Acad Sci* 462:315–325.

Weinstein, E. A., O. G. Lyerly. 1968. Confabulation following brain injury. *Arch Gen Psychiatry* 18:343–354.

Weintraub, S., D. H. Powell, D. K. Whitla. 1994. Successful cognitive aging: Individual differences among physicians on a computerized test of mental state. *J Geriatr Psychiatry (Neurol)* 28:15–34.

West, R., F. I. M. Craik. 1999. Age-related decline in prospective memory: The roles of cue accessibility and cue sensitivity. *Psychol Aging* 14:264–272.

West, R., R. W. Herndon, E. Covell. 2003. Neural correlates of age-related declines in the formation and realization of delayed intentions. *Psychol Aging* 18:461–473.

Westmacott, R., M. Moscovitch. 2001. Names and words without meaning: Incidental postmorbid semantic learning in a person with extensive bilateral medial temporal damage. *Neuropsychology* 15(4):586–596.

Whishart, D. L. 1971. Complications of cerebral angiography as compared to non-vertebral cerebral angiography in 447 studies. *Am J Roentgenol* 113:527–537.

Whitehouse, P. J., D. L. Price, A. W. Clark. et al. 1981. Alzheimer disease: Evidence for selective loss of cholinergic neurons in the nucleus basalis. *Ann Neurol* 10:122–126.

Whitehouse, P., D. L. Price, R. G. Struble, et al. 1982. Alzheimer's disease and senile dementia: Loss of neurons in the basal forebrain. *Science* 215:1237–1239.

Whitty, C. W., O. L. Zangwill. 1977a. *Amnesia: Clinical, Psychological and Medicolegal Aspects.* London, Butterworth.

Whitty, C. W. M., O. L. Zangwill. 1977b. Transient global amnesia. In: C. W. M. Whitty, O. L. Zangwill, eds. *Amnesia,* 2nd ed. London, Butterworth.

Willams, J. D., M. G. Klug. 1996. Aging and cognition: Methodological differences in outcome. *Exp Aging Res* 22:219–244.

Wills, P., L. Clare, A. Shiel, B. A. Wilson. 2000. Assessing subtle memory impairment in the everyday performance of brain injured people: Exploring the potential of the Extended Rivermead Behavioral Memory Test. *Brain Inj* 14:693–704.

Wilson, B. A. 1986. *Rehabilitation of Memory*. New York, Guilford Press.

Wilson, B. A. 1991. Long-term prognosis of patients with severe memory disorders. *Neuropsychol Rehabil* 1:117–134.

Wilson, B. A. 1994a. The extended Rivermead Behavioral Memory Test: A measure of everyday memory performance in normal adults. *Memory* 2:149–166.

Wilson, B. A. 1994b. Reactivation of hippocampal ensemble memories during sleep. *Science* 265:676–679.

Wilson, B. A. 1998. Recovery of cognitive functions following nonprogressive brain injury. *Curr Opin Neurobiol* 8(2):281–287.

Wilson, B., A. Baddeley. 1988. Semantic, episodic, and autobiographical memory in a postmeningitic amnesic patient. *Brain and Cognition* 8:31–46.

Wilson, B., J. Cockburn, A. Baddeley, R. Hiorns. 1989. The development and validation of a test battery for detecting and monitoring everyday memory problems. *J Clin Exp Neuropsychol* 11:855–870, 1989.

Wilson B. A., H. C. Emslie, K. Quirk, J. J. Evans. 2001. Reducing everyday memory and planning problems by means of a paging system: A randomised control crossover study. *J Neurol Neurosurg Psychiatry* 70(4):477–482.

Wilson B. A., J. J. Evans, H. Emslie, V. Malinek. 1997. Evaluation of NeuroPage: A new memory aid. *J Neurol Neurosurg Psychiatry* 63(1):113–115.

Wilson, G., C. Rupp, W. W. Wilson. 1950. Amnesia. *Am J Psychiatry* 106:481–485.

Wiltgen, B. J., R. A. M. Brown, L. E. Talton, A. J. Silva. 2004. New circuits for old memories: The role of the neocortex in consolidation. *Neuron* 44:101–108.

Winocur, G., M. Moscovitch, D. T. Stuss. 1996. Explicit and implicit memory in the elderly: Evidence for double dissociation involving medial temporal- and frontal-lobe functions. *Neuropsychology* 10:57–65.

Winocur, G., S. Oxbury, R. Roberts, et al. 1984. Amnesia in a patient with bilateral lesions to the thalamus. *Neuropsychologia* 22:123–143.

Wolfson, C., D. B. Wolfson, M. Asgharian, et al. 2001. A reevaluation of the duration of survival after the onset of dementia. *N Engl J Med* 344(15):1111–1116.

Woodruff-Pak, D. S., M. S. Jaeger. 1998. Predictors of eyeblink classical conditioning over the adult age span. *Psychol Aging* 13:193–205.

Woodruff-Pak, D. S., R. F. Thompson. 1988. Classical conditioning of the eyeblink response in the delay paradigm in adults aged 18–83 years. *Psychol Aging* 3:219–229.

World Health Organization. 1992. *The ICD-10 Classification of Mental and Behavioral Disorders: Clinical Descriptions and Diagnostic Guidelines*. Geneva, World Health Organization.

Yasuno, F., T. Nishikawa, Y. Nakagawa, et al. 2000. Functional anatomical study of psychogenic amnesia. *Psychiatry Res Neuroimaging* 99:43–57.

Yerkes R. M., J. D. Dodson. 1908. The relation of strength of stimulus to rapidity of habit-formation. *J Comp Neurol Psychol* 18:459–482.

Ylikoski, R., O. Salonen, R. Mantyla, et al. 2000. Hippocampal and temporal lobe atrophy and age-related decline in memory. *Acta Neurol Scand* 101:273–278.

Young, A. W., J. P. Aggleton, D. J. Hellawell, et al. 1995. Face processing impairments after amygdalotomy. *Brain* 118:15–24.

Yuspeh, R. L., R. D. Vanderploeg, T. A. Crowell, M. Mullen. 2002. Differences in exec-utive functioning between Alzheimer's disease and subcortical ischemic vascular dementia. *J Clin Exp Neuropsychol* 24:745–754.

Zachrisson, O. C. G., J. Balldin, R. Ekman, et al. 2000. No evident neuronal damage after electroconvulsive therapy. *Psychiatry Res* 96:157–165.

Zeman, A. Z. J., S. J. Boniface, J. R. Hodges. 1998. Transient epileptic amnesia: A descrip-tion of the clinical and neuropsychological features in 10 cases and a review of the literature. *J Neurol Neurosurg Psychiatry* 64:435–443.

Zhang, Y., B. Herman. 2002. Aging and apoptosis. *Mech Ageing Dev* 123:245–260.

Zimprich, D., M. Martin, M. Kliegel. 2003. Subjective cognitive complaints, memory performance, and depressive affect in old age: A change-oriented approach. *Int J Aging Hum Dev* 57:339–366.

Zola-Morgan, S. M., L. R. Squire. 1990. The primate hippocampal formation: Evidence for a time-limited role in memory storage. *Science* 250:288–290.

Zola-Morgan, S.M., L. R. Squire. 1993. Neuroanatomy of memory. *Annu Rev Neurosci* 16:547–563.

Zola-Morgan, S., L. R. Squire, D. G. Amaral. 1986. Human amnesia and the medial tem-poral region: Enduring memory impairment following a bilateral lesion limited to field CA1 of the hippocampus. *J Neurosci* 6:2950–2967.

Zorzon, M., L. Antonutti, G. Mase, et al. 1995. Transient global amnesia and transient ischemic attack. Natural history, vascular risk factors, and associated conditions. *Stroke* 26:1536–1542.

Zubal, I., M. Spanaki, J. MacMullan, et al. 1999. Influence of technetium-99m-hexamthylpropylene amine oxime injection time on single-photon emission tomog-raphy perfusion changes in epilepsy. *Eur J Nucl Med* 26:12–17.

Index